Contents

Introduction

Welcome to Volume 7, which starts as Tony Blair makes way for Gordon Brown, and ends as Gordon makes way for David Cameron, bringing to an end thirteen years of uninterrupted, if not always smooth, Labour government.

When Volume 1 was published, covering the build-up to the first of New Labour's three election victories in 1997, at book signings I had a nice upbeat message to write, instead of the usual bland 'best wishes'. Namely, 'This one has a happy ending… enjoy.' Six volumes later, this one has a sad ending. Sad, that is, if like me you prefer Labour governments led by Tony Blair and Gordon Brown to Tory governments led by David Cameron and Theresa May. Sad if, also like me, a part of you wonders if you could have done more to help prevent the Tories getting back into government. Sad, definitely, when you look at the state of our politics today, in 2018, look at the state of our political leadership, on both sides of the Commons, and wonder how we got from where we were to where we are.

That 'we' is we as in Britain, a country as divided and troubled as I can remember us, and seemingly heading out of the European Union, one of Tony Blair's strategic objectives having been to cement the UK as a central player inside the EU. It is also we as in Labour, the Blairite version having deliberately taken the party closer to the political centre, and won those three elections in doing so, while the current leader Jeremy Corbyn is going as far as he possibly can in the opposite direction. It is we as in the world, too: back at the end of Volume 1, as we – Britain – and we – Labour – seemed to be fairly united in welcoming the change heralded by TB's election, did anyone imagine the world would be where it is today? With Donald Trump in the White House cosying up to Vladimir Putin in the Kremlin while turning nasty against those thought to be America's traditional allies; the perils of climate change all too evident; our two main parties convulsed, by Brexit and antisemitism on the left, Brexit and Islamophobia on the right; the extreme right seemingly emboldened by Trump and Brexit; the technological revolution we all found so exciting now seeming much more threatening in what feel to many like dark and dangerous times?

This, however, is a diary recording past events, not an analysis of current ones. It is interesting, nonetheless, to reflect that in a period covering 2007–10, not that long ago in the scheme of things, Theresa May's name comes up just once in 741 pages, as a panellist on BBC *Question Time* – they must have given Nigel Farage the night off. Jeremy Corbyn is not mentioned at all, and if at any time during those years I had ever made the suggestion that he would within five years of the sad ending to this book be leader of the party, then there might have been even more entries than there already are for my wise and calming psychiatrist, David Sturgeon, who has listened to my agonising more than most. Trump doesn't figure either. Now, is there a single day when anyone interested in world affairs does not mention his name? I even dream about the guy, and it's not nice. How distant seems the mood engendered halfway through this volume by Barack Obama becoming President.

So the world has changed, and continues to change fast. Of those questions I ask above, though, it is the more personal one that keeps gnawing away: could I have done more? Gordon Brown certainly thought so. I had forgotten just how relentless he was in trying to get me to return full-time to help him. All sorts of roles and positions, up to and including a place in his Cabinet, were suggested as a way of getting me to commit beyond the half-in, half-out position of unofficial advisor. I did go back, almost full-time, for the last few months, but never in quite the way he was asking.

Whenever I am in the dentist's chair, and the drill is going, I have a little mantra running around my head – 'pain has no memory, pain has no memory'. It is perhaps on that same basis that I realised that, until transcribing and later editing this volume, I really had blanked out my own endless agonising and Gordon's relentless efforts to get me to do for him what he imagined I had done for TB.

Both my psychiatrist and my partner, Fiona, who has endured my mental tortures more than anyone, felt to some extent Gordon was playing to my 'demon', a desire to be needed, to be noticed, to be central, to be seen as having powers and talents that others don't, to be told, as both TB and GB said at times, 'I cannot do this without you.' There might be something in that. But also, if you are British, and Labour, it is not easy saying no to a Labour Prime Minister. Nor was it any easier, in those last days after the election, telling him it was time to go. But what is clearer to me than ever, having now relived the seven volumes, from John Smith's death in 1994 to Gordon's defeat in 2010, is that I have always felt a real sense of duty to help any Labour leader to defeat any Tory. But that sense of service is often in conflict with the sense of self, and whereas with TB I perhaps overdid the service and neglected the self, and family, by 2007 I am less willing to have my whole life taken over again. Perhaps I end up, whatever kind words GB said to me in our last conversation in Downing Street, before he walked out with his wife and sons, satisfying nobody. So yes, I think I could have done more. It may have made no difference. I don't know. What you don't know, you can agonise about, and I do. I did the same when Ed Miliband became leader – yes, there will be a Volume 8 – and while I may not appreciate the reasons, or appreciate the direction in which he has led the party, it is a matter of some relief that Jeremy Corbyn has never asked for my help.

There is a line on page 268 when Margaret McDonagh, former party general secretary, and one of many people in these pages I quote at various points as having given up on the idea that Gordon could lead us to victory, told me I had to get over my 'Catholic guilt' about Gordon and stop propping him up. As it happens, unlike her and TB, whose conversion is recorded on page 92, I am not a Catholic. But I did, and I do, feel a certain guilt about the agonising and the stopping short of what he wanted. I did my bit. I helped with strategy and speeches; I played David Cameron to GB's Gordon in hours of preparation for the first ever TV debates; I was pretty much full-time in the campaign itself, and was there at the very end, through the five days of uncertainty that followed the election, listening in when GB told Nick Clegg he could keep the Queen waiting no longer and he intended to resign, rather than carrying on pretending that it might be possible to lead some kind of coalition or minority government. A sad ending indeed. There was a particularly poignant moment, in what was once my office but which Gordon had turned into his, when GB was on the phone to TB, shortly before leaving to see the Queen, and Peter Mandelson and I were there in the room, overhearing what was, compared with many we had witnessed, a comradely and compassionate conversation. The four of us had been through a lot together, good and bad.

That call underlined that this was not just sad, but in some ways the culmination of a tragedy. The seeds of that tragedy, not least the Shakespearean elements of the relationship between the two most important UK political figures of the late twentieth and early twenty-first centuries, and their inability to work together as we all knew they could and should, are clear across all volumes, this one included. Tony felt GB's distancing from New Labour on becoming Prime Minister was a mistake, and he viewed a new top rate of tax in the same vein; I certainly argued that Gordon sought too hard to define himself against Tony, rather than against Cameron, and that he and the two leaders since, Miliband and Corbyn, did not do enough to cement and secure our record as a positive, and indeed played into much of the Tory narrative against New Labour. This volume sees the first seeds of the next Labour Shakespearean drama growing, that of the Miliband brothers. And might it be, seeing where the Labour Party is now, that a sea change was already under way that Tony and I were too slow to recognise and, frankly, still find difficult to understand?

In its own way, preventing David Cameron from securing an overall majority was a triumph of sorts. There are moments in the pages ahead when virtually everyone in the inner and outer circles, GB included, though he perhaps not as forcibly as others, make clear their view that we are fighting a losing battle, one which will end with Cameron in No. 10. That Cameron required the support of Clegg's Liberal Democrats to get there was surely in no small measure down to Gordon's resilience and huge residual strengths as a political fighter. He was at his best towards the end of the campaign, strangely after what had been without doubt its worst moment, certainly one of the few that broke through to the public, namely his suggestion that Mrs Gillian Duffy, a voter concerned about immigration, was a bigot. I don't think I have ever seen a politician as cut up about a mistake as I saw Gordon a few hours later. He was, as I wrote that evening, like a wounded animal.

That incident, just days ahead of the election, seemed to bring together so many of his vulnerabilities. A mistrust of the media, and a clumsiness dealing with it – he thought, in the sanctuary of his car, that his microphone was off, but learned once more that if they could screw him over, they would; his occasional unease with members of the public, especially when he sensed they were taking the agenda to a place he would rather it didn't go; his tendency to cast around for blame, whether Mrs Duffy for having her views, or his team for letting her near him; his inability to match the easy charm that both Blair and Cameron were able to muster when in tight corners. And then all of it climaxing in that sad, sad shot of an exhausted-looking Gordon in a radio studio putting his head in his hands as his 'bigot' outburst was played back to him by broadcaster Jeremy Vine.

Partly because of my endless agonising – I apologise in advance for just how often I was torturing myself and others about whether and how to go back – and also because of the negativity and occasional depression through which I am seeing much of the world at this time, this volume risks being unfair to Gordon. If his mood was often dark, mine was often darker. I record many negative thoughts about him, and the impact he is having on the new post-Downing Street life I am trying to build, writing novels, doing more in sport, work projects overseas, repairing damaged relations at home, campaigning to change attitudes on mental health, struggling far too often with my own mental health, including not just the all too familiar depressions but weird new forms of anxiety too, including one which struck live on TV. Nor was my mood helped when, into all this, Gordon threw a full public inquiry into the Iraq War. I also record many negative views of others, TB, Peter M, Philip Gould among them, who sometimes stated their view that GB just could not do the job. Yet we all believed in him enough to want to help, even if we were constantly on the lookout to see whether Alan Johnson or David Miliband might try to take over, and even if Peter was the only one to go back fully (and he did it well).

But the title of this volume is *From Crash to Defeat*, and while Gordon would be the first to accept that as leader of the campaign he takes his share of responsibility for the defeat, he played a hugely impressive role in the global handling of the crash. The Tories did a pretty good job, without as much justification as they claimed, in pinning the blame for the crash on the Labour government. Fine, that's politics, and they were legitimately trying to replace that government. But given the risks facing the global economy, and the eye-watering sums of money required to stabilise the situation at home and around the world, they must surely acknowledge the leadership role Gordon played. When there were big issues at stake, he could rise to the moment. He did so when it really mattered.

I record on page 611 my mother's view that Gordon would have been 'a great Prime Minister in the radio age'. She meant it as a compliment. She loved his rich, Scottish voice. She felt he believed in the right things and was trying to do the right things himself. But he found modernity, and especially the modern media and what modern politics was becoming, hard. So when our politics was being defined by the scandal of MPs' expenses, Gordon, who I never once saw as being motivated by money or material things, was in a constant rage – at the mistakes of MPs, but also perhaps at his own in how he sought to handle the fallout. Similarly, the problem with the on/off election, or of the role of Damian McBride smearing Tory opponents, was made much worse by the hesitant handling. There was nothing wrong in considering a snap election. There was something very wrong about letting the debate run in public, then pretending you had never given it a moment's thought.

My former boss Richard Stott, who edited *The Blair Years* and who sadly died shortly before the book was published, and my agent Ed Victor, who died last year, were two of the small number of people who, long before Gordon was leader, had read everything from my diaries up to 2003. Given what they knew from their reading, neither could understand how I was willing to help him at all, let alone devote another large chunk of my life to his election campaign. Partly that is a political tribalism which they did not share. But also it is because though I had had experience of the weaknesses, I knew there were many strengths, and that Gordon was a big part of the successes we had had, whatever the failures with which we ended. Thirteen years is the longest period of uninterrupted government the Labour Party has ever had. That too is a success story, sad ending or not. Also, it is a true, rather shocking statistic that Eton, the school which educated David Cameron, and helped develop the confidence that made him think defeat in a referendum on Europe would never happen, has produced more Prime Ministers than the Labour Party. Three times as many. Nineteen Old Etonian Prime Ministers. Six Labour. Ramsay MacDonald, Clement Attlee, Harold Wilson, Jim Callaghan, Tony Blair, Gordon Brown. That's it.

I have been lucky to have known four of them, and worked for two of them. And whatever faults they had, whatever mistakes they made, I remain utterly convinced that the governments they led were better for the country than the two Prime Ministers who have followed them, and many of the fifty-one who preceded them.

So I want to close this introduction by thanking TB and GB for the opportunity to serve them while they gave often superb service to the country. The sadness at its ending does not negate the many advances the country made under their leadership.

I have mentioned Ed Victor and Richard Stott, whose role in helping me navigate my way through these diaries was enormous. So too Philip Gould and Mark Bennett, also alas no longer with us. I would like to thank Bill Hagerty, who took over as editor when Richard died, shortly before *The Blair Years* was published. So this is the seventh volume Bill has edited and I am hugely appreciative of his commitment and expertise. At Biteback I would like to thank Iain Dale, Olivia Beattie, James Stephens, Isabelle Ralphs, Ashley Biles and Namkwan Cho.

Most of all I want to thank Fiona and our children, Rory, Calum and Grace. I often look through these diaries and wonder how Fiona has put up with me for so long. Looking back on our thirty-eight years together, and loving her more than ever, I am just enormously grateful that she has.

Who's Who

May 2007–June 2010

Tony Blair	Prime Minister 1997–2007 (TB)
Gordon Brown	Chancellor of the Exchequer 1997–2007, Prime Minister 2007–10 (GB)
John Prescott	Deputy Prime Minister 1997–2007, First Secretary of State 2001–07 (JP)
Alastair Campbell	Journalist, author, political aide, former Downing Street director of communications and strategy (AC)
David Miliband	Foreign Secretary 2007–10 (DM, David M)
Ed Balls	Children, Schools and Families Secretary 2007–10 (EB)
Ed Miliband	Minister for the Cabinet Office 2007–08, Energy and Climate Change Secretary 2008–10
Alistair Darling	Chancellor of the Exchequer 2007–10
Douglas Alexander	International Development Secretary 2007–10
James Purnell	Culture, Media and Sport Secretary 2007–08, Work and Pensions Secretary 2008–09
Lord (Charlie) Falconer	Constitutional Affairs Secretary 2003–07, Lord Chancellor 2007, Justice Secretary 2007 (CF)
Jack Straw	Justice Secretary, Lord Chancellor 2007–10
Peter Mandelson	European Commissioner for Trade 2004–08, President of the Board of Trade 2008–10, Business Secretary 2008–10, Lord President of the Council and First Secretary of State 2009–10 (Peter M)
Tessa Jowell	Minister for the Olympics 2005–10, Minister for the Cabinet Office and Minister for London 2009–10

(Lord) Andrew Adonis	Education Secretary 2005–08, Transport Secretary 2008–10 (AA)
Harriet Harman	Leader of the House of Commons 2007–10, Minister for Women and Equality 2007–10
Geoff Hoon	Chief Whip, Parliamentary Secretary to the Treasury 2007–08, Transport Secretary 2008–10
Alan Johnson	Health Secretary 2007–09, Home Secretary 2009–10
Andy Burnham	Chief Secretary to the Treasury 2007–08, Culture, Media and Sport Secretary 2008–09, Health Secretary 2009–10
Alan Milburn	Former Cabinet minister
David Blunkett	Former Cabinet minister (DB)
Stephen Byers	Former Cabinet minister
David Cameron	Leader of the Opposition 2005–10 (DC)
George Osborne	Shadow Chancellor of the Exchequer 2005–10
Nick Clegg	Leader of the Liberal Democrats 2007–15
Boris Johnson	Former Tory shadow minister, Mayor of London from May 2008
(Lord) Philip Gould	Political pollster and strategist (PG, Philip)
Gail Rebuck	Wife of Philip, publisher
Fiona Millar	AC's partner (Fiona, FM)
Donald Campbell	AC's brother
Richard Caborn	Former Minister for Sport, ambassador for Britain's possible 2018 football World Cup bid
David Mills	Lawyer, husband of Tessa Jowell
(Lord) Neil Kinnock	Leader of the Labour Party 1983–92, peerage 2009 (NK)
(Baroness) Glenys Kinnock	Wife of Neil Kinnock, Minister for Europe 2009, Minister for Africa and the UN 2009–10, peerage 2009
Rachel Kinnock	Daughter of Neil and Glenys, Downing Street events organiser
David Muir	GB's director of political strategy
Cherie Blair	Wife of TB (CB)
Sarah Brown	Wife of GB
Lady (Margaret) Thatcher	Former Prime Minister
Sir Alex Ferguson	Friend of AC, manager of Manchester United (AF)
(Lord) Sebastian Coe	President of 2012 Olympics organising committee and former athlete

Brendan Foster	Businessman and commentator, former athlete
Godric Smith	Formerly Tony Blair's communications director
Anji Hunter	Formerly Tony Blair's director of government relations
David Sturgeon	AC's psychiatrist (DS)
Cathy Gilman	Director then CEO Leukaemia and Lymphoma Research
Ed Victor	AC's literary agent
Adam Boulton	Sky News political editor
Nick Robinson	BBC News political editor
Andrew Marr	BBC political show host, former political editor
Sir David Frost	Broadcaster, TV host
Rupert Murdoch	Chairman, News Corporation (RM)
James Murdoch	Chairman and CEO News Corp, Europe and Asia
Rebekah Wade (later Rebekah Brooks)	CEO News International
Piers Morgan	Broadcaster and columnist
Bill Clinton	42nd President of the United States (BC)
George W. Bush	43rd President of the United States (GWB)
Barack Obama	44th President of the United States
Nicolas Sarkozy	President of France 2007–12
Angela Merkel	Chancellor of Germany 2005–
Silvio Berlusconi	Prime Minister of Italy 2008–11
Betty Campbell	Mother of AC
Rory, Calum and Grace Campbell	Children of AC and FM
Audrey Millar	Mother of Fiona

The Diaries

Thursday 28 June 2007

So GB was in. I watched the reshuffle unfold from an exercise bike in the gym. When David Miliband was announced as Foreign Secretary, I sent him a text to say how much our lives had now diverged. He texted back 'Couldn't have done it without you,' which was nice if almost certainly not true. James Purnell, Ed Balls and Ed Miliband [all junior ministers] were all in too, so it had the look and the feel of a young team. Tessa [Jowell, Culture, Media and Sport Secretary] called early, wanting advice, having been offered the Olympics job, outside but attending Cabinet. She was a bit thrown by it but it was probably for the best. Things seemed to be going OK. It was remarkable how quickly it became normal to hear them talking of GB as PM. We would definitely get a bounce too, but whether it was sustained would depend on the decisions and the style.

I had lunch with Rory [AC's son], really nice chat. He felt maybe I should go and work with TB on the Middle East stuff. I don't think so. I was feeling a bit low and flat, and not really part of it. I was wondering again whether I should maybe have taken a different course and gone for a seat in Parliament. It was amazing to see DM there, plus the others from the time I ordered them around as spads [special advisors], all now in the Cabinet. I was also getting more and more worried about the book, that it would piss on GB's parade. I worried it was going to be bad with [Lord] Neil [Kinnock, former Labour leader] too. I was fearing the worst on many fronts, definitely going into one of my catastrophising dips. Everyone else was saying don't worry too much. TB did a clip from Myrobella [TB's house in Sedgefield] and he was looking a bit edgy, the eyes all nervy, body language not good. This must be very weird for him, and when he called after doing it, he said it had been. He was saying he was sure it was the right thing, but with a tinny voice that suggested he didn't really believe it. The reshuffle was OK on the New Labour front, not least David M, but the big message was change change change, and I worried GB would go for defining himself against TB rather than David Cameron.

Friday 29 June

The reshuffle seemed to go down OK, and today the focus was GB's first Cabinet meeting, nothing briefed in advance, and afterwards lines out on policy focus, also a message on the constitution and trust. Again, the trust thing suggested he was going to define vis-à-vis TB. There were two car bombs in London [both disabled pre-detonation], which had the makings of a major baptism for GB and Jacqui Smith [new Home Secretary]. Calum and I set off for Wimbledon, watched Serena Williams, then Roger Federer beating Marat Safin. I bumped into John Jackson [ex-*Mirror* colleague] who said he felt Richard [Stott, AC's former editor at the *Mirror*, and editor of *The Blair Years*, suffering from cancer] had been sent home to die. I just hoped the book was out before he went. Charlie Sale [*Daily Mail* journalist] came over for a chat while I was having a cup of tea with Mark Covell [ex-Labour press officer] and I made clear I just do not talk to the *Mail*. He seemed genuinely shocked. I was revamping the website and getting a few sports interviews lined up for content – spoke to [Irish rugby players] Ronan O'Gara, Denis Hickie, Shane Horgan.

Saturday 30 June

Alex [Ferguson, Manchester United manager] called, said Gabriel Heinze [footballer] wanted to go to Liverpool and he was not going to let it happen. He thought TB's last PMQs had been terrific, felt of all the people in his lifetime, he had always done it the best. He asked if I thought now he had finally got the job that GB would grow into it. Hard to tell. Hope so. I was going through the book to pick out extracts for the promotion on the web. I called Nick Soames [Tory MP] who asked 'Is this all going in your diary?' He said he was really looking forward to it and agreed to do a web interview. He said he thought [former private secretary to Winston Churchill] Jock Colville's diary at No. 10 was the best book on politics ever written and he expected mine would be in that vein. 'I hope it will be serious, and I hope you won't drop me in it by printing all the things I have said about my party!' I told him a couple of the funnies, for example him saying that us banning hunting was on a par with the Tories passing a law to ban 'Burnley fucking Football Club' and also when he was asking TB, when Carole Caplin [former style advisor to Cherie Blair] was in the news, 'What is a style guru, and should I have one?'

He said 'AC' [Tory MP and diarist Alan Clark, deceased] would have loved it. He said Alan felt I was one of the few people who really understood him. 'You saw that beneath all the philandering and the love of "the game", there was someone quite serious about politics and its role in our lives.' He said re the media 'You are a prophet in your own land … you created this fucking beast, but you have seen the damage it is doing before others have. The trouble is they will now use you forever as an excuse for their excesses.' He said he would love a world in which he had nothing to do with them – 'Superficial, in the main stupid, no positive contribution to the world.' He said he had nothing to do with them, ever. He liked being a constituency MP, plus doing other stuff outside. He felt TB had been terrific but never really fulfilled all his potential. 'He reminds me of a racehorse who couldn't always do it fully. But Gordon is not in the same league. He has spent years stopping change and now he says he is an agent of change. It is ridiculous, the public won't buy it.'

He wanted us to have lunch in a very public place 'to set cats among pigeons'. He didn't rate our outsiders. GB had talked of building a 'government of all the talents' (goats) but NS was unimpressed – 'Putting doctors in government, it's like the chef coming out to the restaurant. I want them back in the kitchen. I want doctors in the operating theatre. Alan West [Minister for Security and Counter-Terrorism] will be a problem for you, and Digby Jones [ex-CBI director-general, now Trade and Investment Minister] is just all talk and attention seeking. He will rue that one.' He didn't rate GB, felt he was too set in his ways and would not be able to handle the extra pressures. He was positively raving about Cameron. 'Though I may be a deeply unmodern person, I totally support his modernisation of the party, and I think he has the temperament for this.'

David M asked if I fancied going round to see him in the evening, with a few friends. There was an immediate sign of the league he was now in, the two cops with machine guns outside the house. He was late because he had gone to a COBRA [government crisis centre, Cabinet Office Briefing Room A] on a terrorist car-ramming attack at Glasgow airport [one perpetrator killed; five other people injured]. When he came back he said he would have learned as much watching Sky News. Nice enough mood, and both DM and Louise were clearly happy with his lot. Louise was not quite clear, and a bit nervous, how much their lives were going to change. He was pretty sure Ed Balls would be Chancellor before long, which is why he felt he didn't get it. He felt too that some of the new appointments were a bit odd, including [Lord] Mark Malloch Brown [former UN deputy secretary, now Secretary of State for Africa, Asia and the UN], who PG had taken to calling the minister for anti-Americanism. DM felt we were doing the right things and also was trying to work out if he could simply say he didn't intend to talk about the decision on Iraq but focus on the future, and resolve the issue rather than keep going over the past. I doubted he would be able to. They were both quizzing me lots on the book and I was conscious of how much I was rehearsing answers for interviews, even when talking to friends.

Sunday 1 July

PG [Philip Gould, political consultant, polling advisor] called after speaking to TB who had said he wanted to see us to discuss the possibility of working together on some kind of project on governance, giving advice and support to reform-minded governments. PG was in a bit of a rage about the way GB was projecting himself. He felt that a big part of the GB strategy was constant differentiation, a kind of anti-TB platform, portraying, sometimes subtly, sometimes less so, TB's characteristics as negatives, and promising to be different. He felt it would make it hard for us to work with him going forward. He felt, as I did, that GB's best approach was continuity and change, and the continuity meant defending both TB and the record. But the desire among GB's people was just to focus on the change, so that meant saying no spin, as a way of saying TB was all spin, no sleaze ditto, and also that played into the Tory and media narrative on TB, rather than one which helped us. They were trying to say we were all spin and they were all substance. Ridiculous.

PG was worried it was all going to go belly up after the honeymoon and he really didn't like all the antidote to Blair stuff. I spoke to [Lord] Charlie [Falconer, former Lord Chancellor] who said he felt really flat. He said GB had been very nice to him and had also made clear he might come back but now he felt very out of it. He didn't know what he intended to do now. Maybe business, but actually politics was what he was now really into. We agreed to meet for lunch on Tuesday. Both of us felt that GB was doing OK but he said on his handling of the bomb that TB would have done it much better. Later TB called on his mobile which gave us both a laugh, given he never had one before. He said he was adapting fine. He felt the Commons farewell was good, GB had done OK on the handover, and he now just had to move on as best he could. He was determined not to second guess GB, or get into running criticism, and he said he thought it was possible now he was off the scene, GB's strengths rather than his flaws would come to the fore. The test would come when things got a bit rough.

I asked how he felt about the PG point, that GB was differentiating against him rather than against the Tories. He felt it was a mistake, but didn't intend to say so. He was glad to be getting straight into the Middle East job [special envoy for UN, USA, EU and Russia], and moving into the new house. He asked where we were on the book and the TV series. I said 'Trying to keep it calm.' He said he would do likewise but GB people might be different. We would have to wait and see. I suspected GB would – certainly should – have bigger fish to fry. I was dreading it more every day. He said will we be OK with other world leaders? I said I hope so. He was keen for us to meet soon but sounded pretty chipper. Switch [No. 10 switchboard] were a bit miserable when I spoke to them, said it was 'all terrible'. I called Margaret Beckett [former Foreign Secretary] who said she was 'fine'. She had fought to keep the job. He offered her a climate change panel job but she said no – and intended to take her time before deciding what to do next. She said she felt hurt because she had had a really tough year and it really did rankle a bit.

Monday 2 July

Lesley White round to do an interview for the *Sunday Times*, pushing on the usual stuff. In the afternoon Caroline Gascoigne [Random House] came round to go through extracts we intended to use for promotion. She had the book [*The Blair Years*]. After all the fussing and fretting, there it was, finally. It looked OK, but it felt weird seeing it there. After she left, I drove over to Kingston to take the first copy to Richard [Stott]. He was upstairs in bed, and he looked painfully thin, really ill, weak, his voice struggling. His handshake was firm though and he had a huge smile on his face as he took the book and stroked it. Penny [Stott, wife] had said that he had definitely been hanging on for this moment. 'Quite a journey,' he said, and he meant both the story in the book, but also the story of the book. 'Looks great,' he said. 'Nice feel to it.' Penny was amazing, really loving and caring, but it was pretty obvious he was not long for this world. I wondered on leaving whether it would be the last time I saw him. Hoped not.

JP [John Prescott, TB's Deputy Prime Minister] called as I was on the way home. He said he felt good being out. He was 'Out and proud.' He said Harriet [Harman] or Tessa Jowell would be getting his office. On the book, I talked him through my thinking and he said if things got tricky for me, he was happy to go out and defend me, and defend the right to tell it like it was. GB was really pushing on the anti-spin thing.

Tuesday 3 July

Charlie came round for a bit of TLC and therapy. He had his dog with him, and he, his dog [Alfie], Molly [AC's family dog] and I went out for a walk. Heaven knows what we looked like, the two of us with our near identical Cavalier King Charles spaniels. When we got back, he flicked through the book and kept saying 'My God.' Then 'How on earth did you find the time to write all this?' Then dipping into this page, that page, reading it out loud, and saying 'Oh my God' again. 'This is history,' he said. 'It will be part of history.' He felt TB had done well, and he was proud to have been a part of it. He was pretty down about not having stayed as a minister. GB had offered him a [parliamentary] commission on carers, but then he learned he had said the same to Hilary Armstrong, Charles Clarke and John Reid [former ministers]! He had said 'I don't want to sack you, but I need the space.' Charlie asked 'What about defence?' but then said himself that it was not ideal to do that from the Lords, with two wars on. He was such a nice bloke and this was the first time I had seen him a bit fretful. As ever we went over key relationships etc. He felt TB had got out of it in good shape psychologically but he was worried about CB [Cherie Blair]. He felt she had taken a lot. TB had always managed to stay a bit aloof from the day to day and though he loved the kids she took a lot of the pressure.

He was also very clear that he needed a job of some sort but I talked him through the various stages of my changing attitudes and said 'Don't rush.' For example, see going for a walk as something worth doing. Don't define everything via work. He felt the problem with the book was the efforts people would make to play it into the narrative that TB was all spin, GB now substance. But in truth the book didn't really do that. GB, I hoped, would not want a big thing because he knows there is so much more. We went up to Kenwood [English Heritage house and grounds] and he was very reflective, as was I. He said he felt it was the most amazing period of his life and TB had transformed politics and the country and he had been a part of that. Also felt that he was right to ask to stay but understood why he had to go. Politics was now his main thing, and he can't go back to the Bar because of the rules on former Lord Chancellors. He will get snapped up for all sorts of things though, I am sure. He texted me later to say 'Thanks for teaching me that going for a walk is a good thing.'

TB called later. He was learning to text. His first one to me just said 'This.' Then the next one said 'Is amazing', and the third 'You can send words and everything'. He wanted to see me and PG later in the week to discuss an idea he had. On the book, like Charlie he felt the thing to watch was people using it as us spin v GB substance. I guess they would. Need to be careful. He said GB had called him this morning and had said to TB 'How much you're missed.' TB said 'It's me you're talking to, Gordon.' He said he was actually so pleased to be out. He felt that GB would do fine short-term but then it could so easily go wrong. All this stuff today on the constitution and changes to the working of government just didn't add up.* It gets you back a few of the liberals but they flake off at the next thing. But he said we must support and not be churlish. We have delivered a strong New Labour position and if he decided to build on it in his own way, he will do fine. If he decides to dismantle it, he won't.

He said when we meet on Friday we should go on for several hours. 'Yes,' I said 'because we have nothing else to do... Also, you should get a

* Gordon Brown had announced proposals for 'a new constitutional settlement that entrusts more power to Parliament and the British people'.

spaniel and we can have a New Labour in exile dog-walking club. Then we should sit on sofas to show sofa government in exile.' Good laugh. He said 'When I heard all that shit [about GB ending so-called sofa government] today I was so glad I was out of it.' He was really sounding chirpy, feeling good about doing new things in the future and so on, and was positively childlike in his enthusiasm for the joy of texting. He was just glad to be out and was settling into his new life fine. He said he had texted Liz Lloyd, Kate Garvey [both in TB's No. 10 team], and David Miliband who he felt was going to be in his element. Out to [AC's daughter] Grace's school play. She was terrific, really strong presence.

Wednesday 4 July

Long session with DS [David Sturgeon, psychiatrist] going over my angst about the book but he was really good, saying I had been through the worst, much worse than this, I would get through it and what mattered was what I thought and felt. Everyone else was looking at it from their own perspective, but I had thought through mine and it would be fine. I had sent a copy of the book to Lindsay [Nicholson, editorial director, *Good Housekeeping* magazine and widow of AC's best friend, John Merritt] and went to see her for a cup of tea. She felt it was amazing, very human, would do really well, but also that it showed TB as a very poor manager. 'You really shouldn't ever see your boss in underwear, in my humble opinion!' She also had the feeling that TB didn't really always understand what his key people did, or were meant to do. The interest in the book was really picking up now. Off to golf, dealing with Catherine Mayer on the way, as she was finalising a piece for *Time* magazine and needed a few bits and bobs. Charlotte Bush [Random House] said they had had more bids than for Bill Clinton's.

To Les Ambassadeurs [casino/restaurant] to meet Alex F. Mark Lucas [filmmaker] was in to film a piece of the two of us chatting which we were using for my new website. We had to redo it when Alex told the story of the Champions League final win in Barcelona, and said Cathy [wife] had told him 'Alastair wants to give you a knighthood.' But he was great on Tony and what I did for him and good on the stuff about him advising me on diet, exercise, mental strength. Up to the book launch, [artist] Harold Riley's book of paintings from the night in Barcelona. Lovely guy. Alex made a good speech. Mick Hucknall [singer, friend] on good from. Then as we went through for dinner, who should be sitting there in the corner, watching a documentary about Cherie on TV, but Carole Caplin. She was with Bill Kenwright [theatre producer] and we both did a little 'Ooh' as we saw each other. I said this is clearly one of those moments that is meant to be. I had been thinking about her when doing the book, and wondering whether in fact I had been too harsh on her. I didn't do God, but maybe I was being put in her path so I could tell her that, and tell her that maybe I had.

She said she never really felt I understood where she was coming from but she understood me. She felt TB had come out of his years as PM fine psychologically, but like Charlie she worried for CB. She felt in some ways politics was harder for the people close to the politicians than for the politicians themselves. Also, that politics was so intense people lost what they were about and why they were doing it. She knew Peter Foster [conman, former boyfriend] was a disaster and it was her fault that she had brought him into the TB / CB circle. But she had never intended any harm to anyone. I found myself warming to her and remembering the first time I met her, at the old [Blair] house in Islington, just before our first party conference. I told her I had found her very attractive but that she worried me from the off. There was a big irony here, I said, namely the worry I had had that she would do a tell-all book, and here I was, about to do the exact same thing. I also said she should know TB always defended her whenever I tried to get her out of the system. He liked her and felt I had always been over the top. He was sure she would never harm them. There must have been some hand of fate at work to put us together at this time. The chances of me ever being in a casino were so slim, yet there I was and there she was. It strengthened me in the view, as discussed with David S earlier, that I had to put reconciliation at the heart of my overall strategy, for the book and for myself.

Thursday 5 July

I called Carole to tell her I had seen her in a different light. She said the same. She said she was sure that had we met in different circumstances we would have liked each other, but there was something about politics, and the situation of the times, that tortured all those relationships. She said she really liked Fiona [Millar, AC's partner], really rated her and felt she had been in the wrong job [advisor to CB], should have done something much more substantial because she had such good judgement. And she would really like to keep in touch etc. To Wimbledon with PG and Carolyn Dailey [businesswoman]. Alan Milburn [former Cabinet minister] there and I picked his brains on the diaries, having told him how I was planning to handle them. He was full of good advice. He was sure GB wouldn't go for me, and would know I had watered them down for him. He saw GB last week and said he found it scary. He felt he was not stable. He said he had told Alan [Johnson], Charles [Clarke] and Charlie

[Falconer, all former Cabinet ministers], all three of them, that they would be back in the Cabinet within a year. 'He was just lying.' At PMQs yesterday people had been desperate to support him and cheer but they didn't. He just wasn't there with the force he needed to carry them all. Jamie Rubin [former US Assistant Secretary of State under President Clinton] was reading the book, and said he loved it, found it really as authentic an account as he had ever read.

Friday 6 July

Tired and stressed. Meeting with Charlotte Bush and Susan Sandon at Random House. Susan said some pretty amazing attempts were being made to get the book. Fake internet accounts, people posing as [chair of Random House, wife of Philip Gould] Gail's PA etc. The book was now 4th on Amazon interest levels, with only Harry Potter above me. The website we had created was doing brilliantly, with Alex up today. Mark Lucas had done a terrific job. Martin Sheehan [No. 10 press office] was on saying the neuralgia levels were rising at No. 10 about it. Also, Carol Linforth [Labour Party official] called to say there were the first signs of agitation that the book would coincide with the party fundraiser Dick Caborn [former Sports Minister] and I were fronting at Wembley on Thursday. Dick said they could fuck off, the thing would not be happening without us, and we would do it together. We were up to 500 or 600 people now. Martin said they were getting a bit paranoid and I suggested they just get the book and calm down. I had a couple of long chats with Sue Gray [Cabinet Office official who had overseen the government vetting of the book] and eventually it was agreed we would get one book to Gus [O'Donnell, Cabinet Secretary], two more to her, which Martin and Mike Ellam [GB press officer] could read in her room. She was packaging stuff to send to ministers, making sure they knew about the bits relevant to them. She had been terrific. I then spent an hour or so just signing books. I texted Peter [Mandelson, EU Commissioner for Trade and Industry, former Labour Cabinet minister] to ask if he wanted one. 'Yes, then I won't have to pay for it. I disapprove of the whole thing.' I did one for JP, Alex, Tom Bostock [GP].

I took a cab to 8 Mount Row, [public relations executive] Matthew Freud's bolthole, down a little alley. TB bounded in, in jeans and T-shirt and trainers. I gave him the book, having dedicated it as follows – 'You know more than anyone the ups and downs I have had since you asked me to work for you. But going through my diaries and writing this book has shown me more clearly than ever how privileged I was to work alongside one of the most remarkable political leaders of this or any other time. I am sure that history will judge you well. Whatever the hoo-ha and ballyhoo the book generates I see it as a tribute to you, your leadership, your optimism and resilience and to the steady transformation of our politics and our country. I am proud of the part I played in helping you but the credit is yours and millions of people are in your debt for what you have done. New Labour New Britain. In friendship.'

He read it slowly, said thanks and then we discussed handling. He had re-read some of the US bits and said he felt Iraq and Bush were the tricky bits, if it suddenly went big over there. He said I should say I specifically asked him about other leaders and what was appropriate so yes, some stuff had been removed. He felt I should be clear about it. He felt the two main risks were of some great diplomatic row, or people thinking that I was doing it for wrong reasons. That was why in the end I had been right not to do serialisation. What you want to avoid is 'storyfication', he said. 'You want people to take it in the round. There will only be a GB problem if he goes against it and creates mayhem around it. They would be crazy to do it, but they don't think like us.' He was very down on him, felt he was already beginning to exude his real character. He had weak and wrong people around him who gave bad advice. He had told him the constitutional stuff was not in the end what would reconnect where he needed to reconnect. He said we all had to hope he could get it together but he didn't hold his breath. His luck was that DC was not cutting it but he still might.

Charlie had mentioned our meeting and he thought it hilarious me telling Charlie dog walking was now important. On his own role, he was focused on three areas. The first was the MEPP [Middle East Peace Process] envoy role, which was tricky, but he would give it a go. He said JoP [Jonathan Powell, TB's chief of staff] had gone to see Peter Ricketts at the FCO [Foreign and Commonwealth Office] about getting government funding to pay for his staff doing his MEPP role, and Peter saying they could fund only one, then adding that he had cleared it with Ed Balls, of all people. TB had to get David M to sort. The second area was his interfaith agenda, and he was interesting on his chat with the Pope who knew they had to connect faith to reason to ward off attacks, saying it is all superstition and tradition. He said he was convinced this was the idea for our times, allying faith to reason. He felt it as clearly as he had felt New Labour, he said. He had bumped into Philip Green [businessman] who had been hilarious about it, how TB was getting out of danger and difficulty in one area and going straight back into both in another.

Then his third area was the idea of a strategic consultancy. He said the McKinseys and Price Waterhouses [both business consultancies] of this world were all very clever but they had never been on our side of the table. There was big money to be made from speeches, but even more – and with more impact – from advising from the perspective of having been there in government and done it. It was pretty well recognised around the world that we had achieved a lot of reform, and there were plenty of lessons for others in there. He said some people were offering silly money for all kinds of things. I said he should be careful, and it needed to be clear that he was making big money not just to fund a lifestyle or be part of the super-rich, but to fund the public service side of things he was doing for free, like MEPP, interfaith etc. He wanted me, PG and others from the core team to get involved with it. He was using Clinton's lawyer to do his book deal. He was on good form and great on the big picture of how he could use what he is and the global brand he had become to take forward all three things.

Re me he was full of good advice, saying just keep saying whatever the media frenzy the book provokes, you get an authentic account of what it is like, and we achieved a great deal. 'Don't be defensive about what we did' – as if. He felt the problem with GB's stuff recently was that he was effectively saying 'Game, set and match to the media' because he appeared to be buying their analysis of New Labour, not ours. I asked about Cherie, and asked if he could ensure she did not have a go at me at Jonathan and Sarah's wedding [Powell and journalist Helm], as the last couple of times we had seen her it had been a bit embarrassing. He said when I last saw her she was under huge stress. He said that while he just about accepted his time had been up, she felt what had happened was abominable, the way GB had forced him out, and she was angry. Also, she knew I had put together the plan that led to the denouement. But she was not a bad person, far from it. He said, yet again, I had always got Carole C wrong, and he was glad I had met her and made it up with her. 'She is a good person.'

He felt re GB that the dourness would hurt him. 'It is like looking at history.' Bostock had said something similar to me earlier, that seeing and listening to GB 'It felt a little bit like I was back in the '50s.' TB said people say it is about a lack of charisma but it is something else, they sense character weakness. He said what was clearer and clearer in the past few weeks and months was actually GB lacked settled convictions. I told him JP's line that the entire operation had run on guilt – TB's guilt re stiffing GB, now GB's guilt at forcing him out. TB felt it was a big mistake to reappoint the people involved in the coup. Also I had not realised how involved he seemed to think Geoff Hoon [former Minister for Europe] had been in doing him in. TB said he was so glad to be out of it, but I was not so sure he really meant it. I shared a car home with PG who was being an amazing support at the moment. He was giving me good advice today, especially on the need to make my interviews reconciliatory, including with the media.

Martin Sheehan came round. He said it was all a bit weird in there.

Damian McBride [special advisor to GB] was very strange. The GB people were all pretty rude. He was slightly worried they would fuck me now they had got the book but I felt they had to have it. He and Mike Ellam [director of communications] had read it together, but it was like being with a sphinx. He gave nothing away 'but I didn't have to scrape him off the walls'. MS thought it was an amazing read. We went round to Charlie and [wife] Marianna's for dinner. What a star, really helpful going over tough questions on the book. TB and CB had been round last night. He said Cherie had been as over the top as ever they had heard her re Gordon. TB a bit less so. Really nice evening. His style was just what I needed in advance of all the media I was going to be doing. He was absolutely brilliant at firing questions and forcing you to take them on with a proper argument. He felt I was too defensive about the changes we made and I must not let them say I regretted it all.

Saturday 7 July

Beautiful sunny day, and the build-up to the book was growing. I needed to fill time in a nice way, so took PG and the boys to the Tour de France, which was in London. Dick Caborn had sorted them tickets via Transport for London. He also said if GB's people tried to block me doing the auction at the Wembley event, he would just get me up there. Sheehan and Mike Ellam were in 70 Whitehall reading the rest of the book, MS texting me every now and then re bits he particularly liked, or to say 'No major explosions so far.' Then GB did a bit of a silly clip with Kay Burley [Sky News], saying that he wouldn't read it and he was not sure why I had done the book. The *Sunday Mirror* were doing a story on how Fiona and I came close to splitting; *The Observer* were going on [producer of TV adaptation of AC's diaries] Stuart Prebble's quotes about the impact David Kelly's death had on me, and there was something fairly substantial in all of the Sundays. Good mood out and about at the cycling, though the prologue is not nearly exciting as the big stages we'd been to in France.

I was amazed how much Ken Livingstone [Mayor of London] seemed to be getting away with, loads of posters and other propaganda around the place, lots of hospitality. There were a fair few councillors there and the feeling seemed to be that Boris Johnson [shadow Education Minister] was going to run against him. Lesley White's piece in the *Sunday Times* came out fine, plus a front-page story that TB nearly quit pre-Iraq. The *Today* programme interview was going to be quite a big thing, and Charlie came round to go over it all with me, firing tough questions. He loves this stuff. He felt [John] Humphrys [presenter] would want to go on what did I do wrong that made GB feel the need to make the changes he was making, for example reversing the Order in Council.* Also, they would want to re-run all the arguments about [Lord Brian] Hutton [chair of inquiry into the death of scientist and former UN weapons inspector David Kelly]. I re-read Hutton's conclusions. It was unbelievable that those people still claimed to defend [former *Today* programme reporter Andrew] Gilligan's story as accurate. Even if it turned out there were no WMD, the story was wrong, he said. That had to be something I got over.

Sunday 8 July

Out early with Rory and out to do [Andrew] Marr [BBC TV]. The papers came out fine and the interview felt OK. I never felt Marr was really listening to answers though, so it felt a bit disjointed. He didn't ask me about the story that had been running as a news story and so they asked me to stay on and do a clip with Andrew Neil [broadcaster] and Sheila Hancock [actress, fellow Marr guest] on the sofa at the end. Sheila told me afterwards she felt I should do something in my own right, not just for others. She said she felt a greater integrity coming from me than most people in politics, but I was always seen as someone else's person. Text from Godric [Smith, former AC deputy] 'Interview the stuff of legend.' The extracts went up on the website and immediately got picked up all over the place. I met up with Philip and Gail, and Charlie, and we set off for the wedding. Charlie and Philip just never stopped talking politics, but it was a good way to prepare for the interviews to come, with Charlie continuing to fire in tough questions as though he was Humphrys or [Jeremy] Paxman [abrasive interviewer for BBC TV's *Newsnight*]. I wasn't too worried about the content, but the tone. The main point from both was that I had to show I had moved on in some way and had also accepted I had made mistakes. PG felt the David Sturgeon connection was an important part of it, but I don't think I should get that out there. The toughest part with Humphrys would be not losing my rag.

CF also felt there should be something out there about warning GB about the kind of thing that remains unpublished. It was a lovely, sunny day and the wedding was a nice do, though I was pissed off that Fiona wouldn't go. As Jamie Rubin said, it seemed a bit small minded. But she was finding it hard at the moment, and just wanted separation from the whole TB thing for now. It wasn't exactly on message for the theme of reconciliation I was trying to get going around the book. The wedding was at [advertising executive brother of Jonathan] Chris Powell's house

* On his first day in office, Brown rescinded the order that had given Blair advisors AC and Jonathan Powell authority over civil servants.

in the country, the place that became known as the hunting lodge when JP was excluded from a strategy meeting there in the opposition days. Everyone seemed to think the Marr interview went OK. [Lord] Bruce [Grocott, House of Lords Labour chief whip] was at me again to get a seat. Pat [McFadden, Employment Minister] said things were a bit weird in Parliament and GB's lot not really operating. He felt there was a great irony developing, that they having spent so long, so volubly, claiming that we did not have a clear political strategy, they didn't appear to have one themselves. Peter M seemed very edgy.

Godric S and Julia [wife] were both saying the important thing was for me just to stay calm however much interviewers tried to provoke me. TB said much the same thing. He was also asking me to check out JoP's kids' names and give him some lines for his speech. 'This is where the book can come in handy,' I said, and had a flick through for some JoP stories. The 'Five Bellies' nickname during the Good Friday Agreement talks when he was putting on weight. The time he totally lost his temper when the Unionists were being rude to TB. Not knowing who Noel Gallagher [rock star] was. The fact that he was so not a comms guy but came up with 'Education, education, education.' I was avoiding Cherie – Sally [Morgan, former director of government relations] and she had a bit of a to-do – but otherwise it was really nice to see people. Ruth Turner [TB advisor being investigated in so-called cash for honours inquiry] was looking great and maybe feeling it was coming to its end. JoP had a little dig at John Yates [Metropolitan Police assistant commissioner, head of inquiry] in his speech. Jamie Rubin said he was loving the book.

[Sir] John Scarlett [chief of Secret Intelligence Service] and his wife were there, John saying he disapproved of the book but felt it was a terrific read. Jeremy Heywood [head of domestic policy, Cabinet Office; former principal private secretary to TB] was asking if I would go back in, maybe as Sports Minister. There was a lot of talk among the civil servants about how odd some of GB's people were. Gus [O'Donnell] said he was going to pick his moment to say Damian [McBride] was a problem. He was also saying GB was trying too hard to be different, both to TB and to what he had been at the Treasury. Ed Balls and Douglas [Alexander, International Development Minister] were still in his ear the whole time. He said he would try to calm them all over the book. He was raving – positively – about SG [Sue Gray]. Sarah [Helm, bride] made a very funny little speech about there being 'three people in this relationship'.* JoP having to take

* Diana, Princess of Wales, famously used the phrase 'There were three of us in this marriage' in a 1995 interview in which she discussed estranged husband Prince Charles's relationship with Camilla Parker Bowles.

calls in secret. Working late. Weekends abroad. She was funny too on trying to get JoP to join on anti-war marches, and get him to help with Stop the War banners. JoP good, had a couple of digs though at GB and the cops. There was a very anti-GB feel around the place. TB took the piss out of JoP quite well but then did a big thing on how we could not have done Northern Ireland without him.

There were quite a few journos there because of Sarah but in the main I avoided. It took us ages to get home because of a three-hour traffic jam which meant more and more intense grilling from CF but we got there in the end. Peter M called to ask how Richard [Stott] was and we ended up having a long and rather sad conversation. He said he hadn't felt great at the wedding not because people weren't nice but when he came home now he felt he was not part of it. He felt there was a big difference between us – I didn't really want the establishment, but they wanted me; he didn't mind it so much, and yet sometimes felt rejected. He blamed TB, said he gave him no recognition or acknowledgement. He had never got over the second resignation [in 2001, as Secretary of State for Northern Ireland]. Politics here was his life and it was over. This was so second best. There were so many sad people not getting over things – Fiona re TB–CB, BBC re Hutton, GB's people now running against TB strategically. All so sad really. Carole was right about the way relationships got fractured and tortured. I said we had to sit down and work out a strategy for him that got him back connected. I called PG, said Peter seemed really low, explained why, and he said he needed to re-engage with people from his earlier political life, like our kids.

Monday 9 July

The broadcasts were going big on the diaries and *Today* were giving my interview with Humphrys the big build-up. The papers were full of it. *The Independent* on doubts about war. *The Sun* on TB and God, the *Mail* and *The Guardian* faking a sort of serial. Overall good though, definitely good for the book. Rory came with me to the BBC. He was a very calming presence. We just had a laugh and talked about sport. Humphrys came into the green room. I sensed he had reached the same conclusion – that there was little point turning it into a scrap, that it had to be a serious interview. Rory helped disarm him and then I gave him a book inscribed 'Let bygones be bygones'. It was definitely being seen as something of a moment in the Beeb. I had never seen so many suits through the other side of the studio wall, and they all looked like they were at a funeral. It was a good serious interview though, not without tension, but I hit the tone I wanted and made the points I wanted. At various points I could see Jim Naughtie [co-presenter] nodding at my analysis out of the corner of my eye.

I then noticed on the clock that 8.30 had come and gone, and we went on for some time after. The suits were telling him just to let it run, so we went through news and sport, which he said they hardly ever did. He was still pushing all the Hutton stuff, but unconvincingly, and there was nothing on the substance that worried me. Rory did a little thumbs-up as I came out, and the general reaction coming in was good. [Lord] Seb Coe [former athlete and Tory MP, chairman London Olympics] said I had made him late for work because he sat in his car waiting for it to finish. News 24 which was fine and flirty with Kate Silverton [BBC TV presenter], who was pressing re Diana. I did some clips, then off to sign books at Random House and review strategy. I did ITV live at lunchtime then a few pre-records, including Gary Gibbon [*Channel 4 News*] who had read the whole thing and had some tricky questions, notably GB said three days after I briefed him on [Bernie] Ecclestone [chief executive of Formula 1, £1 million donor to Labour in 1997] that he didn't know about the donation. Could be a problem. Off to Sky with an Iraqi driver who was a terrible driver but who said TB had to do the war because he had the brains and the US had the power!

Book was now top of Amazon and Random House said the second print run had started because they were running out already. I did a good fifteen minutes with Julie Etchingham at Sky, and found myself laying into the media culture harder. Sheehan called me re [BBC political editor] Nick Robinson's blog saying he wasn't that interested in the book, followed by a PS saying having seen it he hoped people didn't think he was in a sulk! To Random House, more books to sign, a few phone calls to check where we were, emails with David Manning [UK Ambassador to the US] re a DC trip. TB called, said his feedback had been good and he was totally fine about it. He was glad that there had not been that much take-up of big and bad stuff on Bush. He said he felt great and was so happy not to be there. GB was now saying he would use scheduled flights for summits rather than charters. So not important. He really felt a light had gone out there. But he said we had to be supportive while moving on. He felt post the book I should try to move on too. Good laugh and as ever his advice on the strategy for the book and the interviews had been good.

I met up with Fiona and we set off for the Palace for [private secretary to the Queen] Robin Janvrin's farewell. I met JoP on the way in and as we arrived the speeches were on. The Queen was there, had her granite look on for most of the time, her lips pouted forward rather sternly. It was a classic establishment crowd, all white, lots of permed hair, upmarket blue rinses, pinkie rings galore on the men. Jonathan turned to me and said 'You do realise we have failed in our mission.' I chatted with Robin and told him Peter Riddell [*The Times*] had said my account of the week of Diana's death really debunked the *Queen* film. Robin said he had been sent that bit and he felt it was good and would recalibrate things. Nice man. John Sawers [diplomat] there. He was off to the UN [as UK's permanent representative to the UN]. Lots of people were saying well done re Humphrys. Lots of 'man of the moment' comments and Calum had said when he was at the gym there had barely been a moment when I was not on one of the screens, and at some points I was on three of them. Met a Burnley fan who works for the Duke of Kent! Tessa and [Lord] Andrew Adonis [Secretary of State for Education] were the only ministers I saw. The Bottomleys [Baroness Virginia and Tory MP husband Peter] and Fiona had an interesting chat with [David] Willetts [shadow minister] and his fascinating-looking wife [Sarah]. I was chatting to Ailsa Macintyre [Queen's press secretary] who was very flirtatious and admitted she had had me as a screensaver in government.

GB came with Sarah [wife] and as he was talking to JoP – a rare event – I went over and said 'Are you OK with me and this book?' Yes, fine, he said, though he didn't look it. Mind you, he would have hated the event, for sure. Earlier Neil K had sent me a text saying GB totally disapproved but… 'Don't give a bugger, your interviews are good.' GB then mingled and when he left we had a longer chat at the top of the stairs. He said he was trying to get better focus. I said I felt he was doing fine but it was all feeling a bit distant from people. He was tired looking but perfectly friendly. He said once the hoo-ha subsided we should meet to discuss things. I said I was happy to help, short of doing a full-time job. I told him about the plans for the Wembley Stadium fundraiser and he asked me to help draft some words. I felt that generally he was a bit down. He really needed to get some lift. Fiona felt Sarah was a bit colder than usual.

Tuesday 10 July

The papers went huge on the book, and there was a hilarious conjunction of some of them running thousands of words while saying there was nothing worth reading. Good interview with Julian Worricker on radio, more human than the others and I was getting onto the defence of politics better. I did a pretty strong HARDtalk [BBC News] interview with Stephen Sackur which was a lot of the usual stuff but I felt there was a strong argument about the nature of the media and the nature of politics. I was starting to get what BC [Bill Clinton] called cellular tiredness. Fiona was working on a piece for *Grazia* magazine about living with me but she was not happy with it because they were pushing too hard on stuff.

Gail called and said the books were flying off the shelves. She said it looked like exceeding wildest expectations. They were reprinting immediately. Mike White [*Guardian*] came into Random House and I did a good hour-long Q&A which was fine. I put up a blog about Nick Robinson which was a pretty heavy whack at him but so what. I did *Richard & Judy* [Madeley and Finnigan, husband and wife TV presenters] in the afternoon, which was terrific. I liked them, and for all that it was a bit soft soap, they were good interviewers. They said it was not fashionable to say you liked TB but they did and always would. On the book they were brilliant on it, really singing praises the whole time. Dick Caborn came round for dinner to go over what we had for the Thursday auction. It had all been coming together fine and looking good. Carol Linforth [Labour head of campaigns] said it was the first fundraiser they had actually enjoyed putting together.

Wednesday 11 July

Tired. About a week now without proper sleep. I was running on empty a bit whilst still planning the fundraiser and doing more book stuff. I pottered a.m. before Catherine McLeod [political editor] came round to do an interview for *The Herald*. Loved the book, she said. Sales still surging, and there had been a lot of coverage abroad. I touched on the Clinton–Gore issue with her and said that defending the Blair legacy is part of securing the Brown future.* I was worried he was doing too much to set himself against Tony. We spoke for an hour or so then watched PMQs. GB was a lot better and I was relieved the book was not mentioned. I had a long chat with JP who was keen to come with me to Ireland for the launch there, not least to talk about him doing a book. Into town for Frank Millar [*Irish Times*] which was fine – I liked talking re Ireland, then to *Newsnight*. Kirsty Wark [presenter] had clearly read it closely, said she loved it, was quoting bits verbatim and she said she also sensed a mutual respect with GB. It was one of the best interviews yet because she got into the mix of political and personal. The feedback was really strong now. Press still kicking away in parts but not that effectively. I had been into Victoria St [Labour HQ] for final planning of the Wembley do. Signing books in there. The combination of the welcome there and not being mentioned in PMQs made me feel a lot happier. There was a drinks do at Random House, then out to the Dorchester for a dinner thrown by Susan Sandon. Fiona, Calum, Grace and I, and about ten of the team. I said something nice about everyone there, ending with the kids and it felt like a nice evening, though it was

* The relationship between President Clinton and his Vice-President, Al Gore, soured after the Clinton–Monica Lewinsky sex scandal and Gore subsequently blamed Clinton for his narrow defeat in the 2000 presidential election.

really sad that Richard wasn't there. Ditto Ed Victor [AC's literary agent] and Sue Gray who were both ill.

Thursday 12 July

Up early, cellular tired, and off to SW1 to do Andrew Denton, so-called Aussie Michael Parkinson [talk show host]. Down the line with a bit of echo but I felt on form and could sense he thought it good telly. I was really pro-Paul Keating, warm enough re John Howard [former Australian Prime Ministers], honest re Rupert Murdoch [media mogul]. These interviews were a lot easier with the book out there now. Neither yesterday nor today did I really feel anyone landing a glove. Then to Western House for a round of BBC regional station interviews, including Wales, Scotland – all about media – and GMR [Greater Manchester Radio] where I was asked if I had sex with Princess Diana, and when I said I hadn't, whether I had wanted to, or then whether I had thought about it. I said I was happily unmarried. The interviewer said she was happily married but if Daniel Craig came in and offered himself… Then Simon Mayo where again I felt on form and it felt like a good old-fashioned interview, in which he asked a question, listened to the answer, then asked another question based on it. I knew he was a God man and we did a bit of religion in politics.

Home to change and then off to Wembley. Had been plugging lots re event. Got there with Rory. Great venue and party had done it up well. Rehearse with Clive Tyldesley [sports commentator] and with June Sarpong [TV presenter]. Dick and I were finalising the auction order. We ended up raising sixty grand for a copy of the book, which we said would be the only one ever to have the collection of signatures – GB, TB, JP, AC, AF. Joe Hemani [businessman] went for it, much to his wife's annoyance, and later told me he would have gone to 100k! We had some great items and by the end of it, with Andy Hodgson [TV auctioneer] and I splitting the auction, we had raised over two hundred grand. Good evening all round. First I was in the party room doing books, then to the reception. Gareth Jenkins, Martyn Williams and Shane Williams from Welsh rugby. Introduced them to GB and TB. Ditto Steve Cotterill [Burnley FC manager] who didn't look out of place. Alex F and Big Sam [Allardyce, Newcastle United manager], Martin O'Neill [Aston Villa manager], Dickie Bird [cricket umpire], Steve Cram and Brendan Foster [former athletes, now commentators], Niall Quinn [former footballer], Jade Johnson [athlete]. I stripped down to a Burnley shirt and got Steve Cotterill up for a natter.

GB was funny on the book – he asked me how much he would have to pay to buy out Volume 2. I said I was really pleased where and how it had landed. I was also saying I was glad to help him more, short of a job.

I had given him a note on tone, words and anecdotes for today. Alex was on great form and I think people were really impressed with his Q&A with Clive on the need to practise and also have coaching seen as a profession, coaches respected at every level, how winning and winners should be celebrated. TB seemed very relaxed, joking about having a mobile phone, having to stop at traffic lights and so on. GB said he had had 'my first row with the Chancellor'. Mick Hucknall and Robin Gibb [entertainers] both did some of their best songs. Denise Lewis [Olympic gold medallist] came up to me and said she was close to going up and stopping them talking about me up there, because there was so much wind-up going on. She said had always liked me from afar. I said ditto.

As an event it was terrific, and people leaving were buzzing with it. Could not have gone much better. I heard a couple of business guys on the escalator ahead of me as we headed out – I suspect they were Tories – saying 'No way in the world are we going to beat that lot any time soon.' I had a good chat with Alex. Both he and Mark [Ferguson, son] felt the book had landed perfectly. TB and GB both spoke well tonight, though Gordon did not look at ease with himself.

Friday 13 July

Loads of good feedback from last night and loads of demands for pictures. A combination of the work on the book and the dinner had really done me in, but I had another stack of interviews to do. One of the radio ones led with 'Unless you have been on Mars you will know AC has a book out.' It really had been saturation across print and broadcast. I did a very funny Danny Baker [BBC Radio 2] interview. He is hysterically funny, that guy. The coverage out of last night was good though there was a bit too much of GB=sport, TB=luvvie. Sue Nye [GB diary secretary] insisted Damian McBride had not briefed that out, but there is no doubt they were on a Clinton–Gore kick – distancing from TB to get definition. I said I felt there were people round him who were pushing anti-TB as a way of differentiation and it was really stupid. I sent GB a note to that effect. He called later and said thanks for yesterday, then that he would learn from mistakes and experience, and he was hopeful I would be able to do more for him. He felt we had moved sport our way last night.

I said he sounded tired, and he said he was. He was down to do the Labour Party Policy Forum tomorrow. He said he felt he had learned a lot already. He remembered I used to say the scale of decisions and the volume would take him aback, and it did. It was a nice enough chat and I could tell he was wanting me to do more. He said he had also called TB. TB said to me later he assumed the call was to try to distance himself from the briefing on the luvvies v sport line. My *Newsnight* interview was followed by reactions from Mike White, Michael Portillo [former Tory Cabinet minister turned broadcaster], both quite positive, Gilligan and John Harris [political journalist]. Fiona seemed to appreciate the way I talked her up.

Saturday 14 July

I had mentioned to GB I felt he had real issues with body language that I noticed in his Wembley speech, and he asked me to elaborate. I sent him a note, and later discussed it with him, said he spoke well, especially when he was funny and self-deprecating and also when he got passionate towards the end. But when people talk about the 'charisma' issue, I think they mean something else. I think it is about confidence. People sometimes sense a lack of confidence when of course what they want to feel in a leader is certainty and strength, albeit an intelligent and sensitive certainty and strength. I said I thought a lot of this could be fixed by body language. For example, he often holds the thumb of one hand very tightly in his other hand, which is a closed and nervous reaction to what is going on around him. I noticed in the speech that on several occasions when the audience laughed, he put his left hand to his right cheek, and kept it there for a few seconds. It signalled that he was not engaging in their amusement of what he said.

I said Clinton was the best at use of hands. Fingers open and relaxed, hand movement linked to the rhythm of the sentence, often facing palms to the audience rather than in on himself, using to pause. He was also very good at looking smart even with one hand in his pocket, if speaking without notes, because the other hand was speaking and his tone was relaxed to match the look. The confidence issue was also there when he was being dragged around getting introduced to people. Again, he often had one hand in the other. He should be more tactile, not just handshake but hand on arm, or shoulder. But always as the main man.

There was one other point I gave him. I had given him a story, and he had used it, about the time AF and Bobby Charlton – who had 105 caps for England – were introduced at a dinner as having '106 international caps between them'. It always got a good laugh when I used it, and GB got a laugh with it too, but he also embellished it by saying he was the one who had introduced them. I said that even when speaking at a jokey dinner he should make sure the anecdotes are accurate. Remember the damage done to TB about the claim that he had seen Jackie Milburn [iconic 1950s Newcastle United footballer] (he never actually said it)? I thought he was taking a risk. Once the honeymoon with the media is over, it is the kind of thing a paper could take up – bounce Bobby C with a question re whether GB ever introduced him etc. To be avoided, sometimes it is the light-hearted stuff that opens the door to the problem. We also had a chat re interviews, and I said he needs to change the body language but also the tone and richness of the narrative. He was interviewed about sport today and it would have been a good time to weave in stories and personalities from last night, not least to show confidence on funding and membership and the like.

I said all that charisma means is does the viewer or listener find this person attractive (even if they don't like or agree with them) and interesting? I know it is a pain, but it needs real strategic thought as to how that is communicated, and once you've decided how to fix it, the doing is the easier bit. He said he would take it on board. I said if this is too personal, no problem, but it seems to me there are a few fairly easy things to be done which will build confidence, which helps to emanate confidence to others which in turn helps breed self-confidence too. He said no, no, I want to hear this, I need to hear this, I know there are things I need to do.

I took Grace out to the stables and went for an OK run while she was with Stella [pony], then a good old natter with George and Catherine [McLeod, journalist] who loved Thursday night, as did the boys. On the book, [*Times* writer, former Tory MP] Matthew Parris's review in *The Times* was far more positive than it might have been and even David Hare [playwright] in *The Guardian* was not terrible. Even the harshest were saying it was at least interesting. Several themes coming through – honest, flawed, boastful, also the idea of a lot of men falling in and out. Back with Grace then round to the Milibands to head for [Alan] Milburn wedding party. David M had been at the National Policy Forum which he said was a democratic fraud. Ditto Pat [McFadden] later, who was now chairing it and said GB basically wanted him to shut it down. David was doing the Marr show tomorrow and we talked a bit about that, how to get over a message. I felt it was in the area of strength and confidence to do good in the world. Douglas Alexander had made a bit of an arse with a foreign policy speech in the US re 'Build not destroy' which was taken as a hit at the Yanks. Also Mark Malloch Brown was having a go.

Emyr Jones Parry [former diplomat] had a pop at me on the betrayal of conversations. Otherwise it was amazing how quiet the book fallout had been, touch wood. Into the HoC [House of Commons] with DM and family. He now had Special Branch guys in tow of course. The Milburn do was a nice event out on the terrace. I briefly saw Peter M who was OK if not warm. I had a good chat with [former Transport Minister Stephen] Byers who said he was going to support GB but couldn't stop hating him. Charles Clarke said everyone was saying I had pulled it off. The feedback on the book was almost all positive. The message that I had been determined not to damage the party definitely got through. Charles was not yet sure what to do with his future. Fifty-five. Like Steve [Byers] he felt he probably had to get behind GB but really thought him terrible and felt we were probably heading for a total disaster. I liked Ruth, Alan M's wife, who was a psychiatrist currently doing a lot on dementia. John Reid was definitely going to be Celtic chairman and would be in his element – as was David. He seemed more substantial as a figure already. I sensed he was worried about Malloch Brown though. I said he must not resile from past policy.

Sunday 15 July

I didn't see all the reviews, but Charlotte sent me a message to say most were fine. I got a cab to the London bikeathon and someone had left the *Mail on Sunday*. Three pages from Carole Caplin which was again not as bad as it might have been. A lot of the coverage seemed to be based on lots of people basically psychoanalysing me and the me–TB relationship. Craig Brown [critic] wrote a very positive review in the *MoS*. So all panning out OK. The bikeathon went fine. I went for the 26-mile version and 'won' it. After I got home, TB called, back from Sun Valley where he said all the US movers and shakers had been. Now off to the Middle East and was really up for it. Said he was amazed how little he missed the job. GB had called him again, and he realised it was because I had said I was pissed off at the way they briefed the fundraiser. He also had a go at asking TB to press me to work with him. I had a kip then headed out to City airport for the flight to Dublin. Dublin airport was buzzing with East European weekend trippers. Got a car to the Merrion and bed.

Monday 16 July

I slept well for the first time in ages. Bruce called. He said my sleepless nights were in vain as it all went fine. I said sleepless nights were the reason why it landed well. I had a stack of interviews, pretty much all day, well into double figures, running around with Paul Allen [Dublin PR]. I always used to rage at TB for getting tired doing interviews but I got it now. It was tiring, though all the questions were coming in the same areas really. NI, Iraq, what I cut and so on. GB was meeting Bertie [Ahern, Taoiseach of Ireland] in the North pre the British–Irish Council but heading down for my launch event at the Merrion. Donncha O'Callaghan [rugby player] was sending me hilarious texts through the day. 'I've seen your book … it's shite … you can't even colour in the pictures …' Albert Reynolds [former Irish Taoiseach] was there, and we had a nice chat, the Attorney General [Paul Gallagher], a few ministers, UK Ambassador

David Reddaway, good turnout from politics and media. Bertie's speech was really nice, very warm and personal. Said I had been a big part of the GFA [Good Friday Agreement] success, that I always found the words to capture the moment, always captured the mood, and was really important to keeping TB going and persevering when it got rough. I was equally nice and warm about him.

Bertie and I had a little chat about GB. He seemed a bit underwhelmed; said 'He is sure different to Tony… I'm sure he'll get there when he works it all out.' On his own [June] election, he said it had been touch and go but they just hit the constituencies one by one and won them round. He had had a whack at their media but it was still nothing like as bad as ours. He also said he understood why I had edited the diaries as I had, but 'You MUST put the whole thing out there one day, you owe it to history. It is an amazing thing to have done and you have to do the whole thing regardless of who might be embarrassed, and why.' Paddy Teahon [former advisor to Ahern] was now in property. I used the line he had once used in the talks, duly recorded, that 'logic has no place in the peace process'. There was a really nice mood and atmosphere all day. The Irish media are so much straighter and people-friendly. Out later with Charlotte Bush and Susan Sandon from Random House, Paul and a friend of Paul's who covers tribunals and I was grilling to get the line right for *Questions and Answers* [Irish TV], the last programme I was doing tonight. Off to the programme, John Bowman in the chair. All fine. Bed by 12. Good day in terms of message and activity.

Tuesday 17 July

Out for a little run, breakfast and then the drive to Belfast. Good straight coverage for the launch with Bertie. Mutual Admiration Society, said *Irish Times*. But good solid coverage. Did Radio Foyle on the way and on arrival *Belfast Telegraph* and *Irish News*. Able to push the line that the place was totally transformed. Hard not to notice the lack of watchtowers on the way up. Tourists. New buildings. Sunshine. Lot of interest in what I thought of the main characters in the peace process. I did the interviews at the Europa [hotel], and the whole place just felt better, more prosperous, safer. Then to UTV, pre-record, and airport. I bumped into Jonathan Philips, permanent secretary at NIO [Northern Ireland Office]. He said nobody had predicted the appointment of Shaun Woodward [GB's NI secretary]. That he was loving it. GB moving Cabinet to Tuesday had made things very different for departments. He felt GB did OK in the reshuffle, though it was still not clear who was in charge of NI in No. 10.

Nigel Dodds [Unionist MP] came along and we were chatting to him,

him joking about Ian Paisley [First Minister] yesterday at what sounded like a fairly surreal event – GB, Alex Salmond [First Minister of Scotland], Paisley and Martin McGuinness [Deputy First Minister], a Welsh Nat standing in for Rhodri Morgan [First Minister of Wales] who was ill. Dodds said that 'the Isle of Man guy was the only normal one there'. Owen Paterson [shadow Northern Ireland Secretary] was next to us on the plane. Full of enthusiasm for the place and the job. He struck me as very old school, and I wasn't sure he had the personality for the nuances there. He and Dodds were both reading the book. Boris Johnson running for London Mayor was the big story and he felt he would give Ken Livingstone a run for his money. I felt he was a disaster waiting to happen for them. Slept on the plane and on landing got the news that the book had gone straight to the top of the hardback bestseller list. 23,900 in three days. The book in second place sold just over 8,000 – a Gordon Ramsay [celebrity chef]. Gail was pleased but she said shops galore just didn't have enough stock. Hopeless industry.

Wednesday 18 July

Early session with DS. He felt the launch had gone fine, but it was important to work out what next now. He felt the book itself showed up real complications in my personality, a never-ending fight between duty and self, between political and personal. To Hatchards, where I signed 1,200 books including a few hundred who queued for signature. Charlotte Bush whizzed them through but there were one or two angry anti-war, all men, one who looked like he might get violent, and I just sat there and took it as a security guy moved in. Another who seemed friendly enough and then said 'Can you sign it David Kelly RIP, sorry,' and I just scribbled best wishes and handed it to him. Generally the mood friendly though. Loads and loads of snappers. To the office to do a couple of German interviews. *FAZ Sunday* and then *Tagesspiegel*. Liked the second not the first. *Leicester Mercury*. Another Aussie radio interview with a Scots guy. Message from Denise Lewis re how much she had enjoyed last week.

Thursday 19 July

Tom Baldwin [*The Times*] sent me an email saying GB was expected in Washington on the same days that I was due. I spoke to David Manning who was over here for meetings. He said he hadn't bothered me with all the various toings and froings on the GB visit because they just couldn't decide. He said the FCO were pleased with DM. Energetic, intellectual, interested and they sensed direction. So fine. German TV then radio. Dutch

TV. Same areas. Iraq, Diana, AC–TB relationship. Nothing really surprising. Then Canadian TV. Again fine and a nice bunch. Home for a kip. Swim.

Out with Audrey [Fiona's mother] to the Institute of Education for the Foyles [bookshop] event. 900 people. Francine Stock [novelist] chairing. Signing loads of books before and after. Big queues. Good event. She chaired well and although one or two were aggressive at the end, it was a pretty warm audience. Good response when I had a dig at Nick Robinson and co. for thinking their pontificating was more important than their reporting. I generally felt the pro-politics position went fine. News breaking that there would be no prosecutions in the cash for honours inquiry. I wanted to get out and say what an outrage the whole thing had been but TB was clear we had to be laid-back, express relief it was all over but say the police had a duty to investigate. What a lot of nonsense. Massive damage had been done by cops on ego trip. The idea they had to investigate a politically motivated charge by an opposition party was ludicrous. Sent a message to Ruth Turner and Michael Levy, both very relieved, but also shared my anger it had gone as far as it did.

Friday 20 July

Out early for an hour-long Aussie radio interview. Alex F was in South Korea, sent me a message to say how much he was enjoying the book, said he found some of it 'breathtaking', and even though he had some idea how much we got published, it was a big surprise to see just how much. Quiet day, just picking up on admin.

Sunday 22 July

Loads of good sport. Test. Open golf. Tour de France in the Pyrenees. Sarah Helm in *The Observer* comparing the police in cash for honours to the Gestapo. Main news floods across central England. Pretty horrific. Fiona rightly sensing I was going into a dip post the hit of the launch going well. Thinking about whether to do more diaries or maybe Ed's idea of a book on winning.

Monday 23 July

Went to see Richard at home to give him the US book. He was a lot worse even than last time. Wondered if it would be last time I saw him. Penny helped him to a chair and he looked at the book a lot, but his hands were shaking and he found it hard to turn pages. It was amazing to think this was the same bundle of laughter and energy. Penny was extraordinary with him but when I left she was a bit weepy. She helped me take all his manuscripts to the car which was a way of acknowledging he would never work on it again. It is just so heartbreaking, she said, and her eyes filled up. So did mine as I drove home. I listened to GB's press conference post his floods visit. He was a bit wooden and stuttery and overdid his 'My thoughts are with the flood victims' and when they tried to get him into the light and shade stuff e.g. whether he was enjoying the job and so on, he was too formulaic. Also things were really hotting up a bit for Cameron. I liked the fact that one of the themes getting traction out of the book was that the Tories underestimated how hard we had to work to win. Both Trevor Kavanagh [*The Sun*] and Theo Bertram [advisor] at No. 10 sent me Ben Brogan's [*Daily Mail*] blog on the same theme which I used for a thing I was doing on 'Five questions for DC' – namely is it true half of your shadow Cabinet have other jobs? Finalising US schedule.

Tuesday 24 July

I bumped into Michael Palin [actor, comedian] in the street then again at Markos' [hairdresser]. Nice chat with him re diaries and publicity tours. He said Monty Python was even more popular in the States than here. OK write-ups for GB's first press conference without being great. Book No. 1 again in UK and also in Ireland. Plus Arabic rights the first foreign rights to be sold. So all fine. Out to JP's flat at Admiralty Arch for a dinner for all the people who had helped him with speeches down the years. Lots of people including Joe Irvin, Phil Hope, Bradders [David Bradshaw], Mike Craven, Paul Hackett, Jonathan Prescott [son], Rodney Bickerstaffe [former trade union leader] recovered from head-on crash, Paul Clark [MP], Ian McKenzie, Rosie [Winterton, MP, former head of office], Joan [Hammell, chief of staff]. JP doing the cooking and creating the usual chaos and mayhem. Good atmosphere. He made a little speech thanking everyone, also saying how much we owed TB, how well things seemed to be going and then we all had to collect little pottery medals and a certificate.

Good speeches. Funny stories e.g. from Rosie who told of the time at a JP PMQs meeting when it became clear he thought Paris Hilton [American media personality] was the hotel. Bradders on how we always liked having JP around because he used the jokes TB refused to. Rodney saying they were not just the Blair years but the Prescott years and I built on that, with the line that they were an amazing double act. Also how he had so often been such a good friend to me. He had been really OTT re me saying nobody had done more for the party, and also how he could always rely on sound judgement re media and politics and we could always talk to each other straight. He went a bit off message later by going on about

GB and the hunting lodge (which he called south of France rather than Southampton) and he told the whole story of how Rosie heard about the meeting, how JP then called me and others before eventually having a very difficult conversation with TB. He was living it with the same anger and energy as when it happened. Everyone said how much they owed JP and enjoyed working with him. Toasted Kyoto with some Japanese drink. JP tended to direct his comments at me the whole time and saved my speech to last. I did a run-through his entry in the diary index and also told a few stories about his support. The boys [Prescott sons, Jonathan and David] took me through to the bedroom to ask for advice about the book he was planning. I said it wasn't sensible. I was worried – as was Joan – that it was all about the money, which would backfire. They were planning to use Hunter Davies [journalist and author] as ghost-writer. Rosie was on great form, very funny on how she got the transport job. She told JP and then Straw she really wanted out of health after four years and Hoon called and asked 'What about transport?' She was with JP who did a thumbs-up. Next, a call from GB who asked 'What sector?' 'Buses,' she said. 'And so I became minister of buses.' JP asked if it was really GB who blocked him from meetings like Southampton. Yes. It was easy to forget sometimes how much they once loathed each other. Really nice evening. Lots of people very supportive about the book and how I had managed to do it without inflicting damage. Bradders was off to work for Tim [Allan, former Blair advisor] at Portland [strategy consultancy] in September, as head of writing.

Wednesday 25 July

Tour de France crumbling amid drug sackings and resignations. David S. He was pushing me to go on a solo retreat in a remote isolated place where I literally cut myself off from other people and outside influences, no TV, no radio, no phone, just take enough food for a month, and see how I fared. It sounded like my idea of hell, but he was adamant we had made progress but I really needed to work on who and what I really was and he felt it was best done through reflection alone. I was saying what happened if the demon was essential to who and what one was. Take it out and then what. He said it was not going to be ripped out, just acknowledged and confronted. It felt like quite a scary thing to do but I couldn't explain why. Into town for a meeting in [Baroness, former party general secretary] Margaret McDonagh's office with her, Dick [Caborn], Carol [Linforth] and team to debrief on the Wembley fundraiser. We raised over 800k with profit at over half a million once we got all the money in. To Labour HQ to do book signings. Good mood. To Commons for a reception for the fundraiser. JP came for a bit. Champagne. Me joking re them not yet knowing what we were planning next. Sleeper to Glasgow.

Thursday 26 July

I slept not badly though I tended to wake up whenever the train stopped. Cab up to the BBC new offices, for *Good Morning Scotland* [radio news programme]. I met up with the RH [Random House] rep, Alan Wilson, and started long day trekking round fifteen bookshops. Some were well organised, some were useless but all seemed to think it was worth doing. All, including in some pretty tough areas, said it was going well. One woman at the Fort [shopping centre, outskirts of Glasgow] said half the people who go into the shop want to be Jordan [pseudonym of glamour model Katie Price]. 'The rest buy true crime and you're there with true crime and Jordan right now.' It was mainly in the stores' No. 1 slot, sometimes 2 behind *Harry Potter* if they mixed fiction and non-fiction. I did a phone-in in Edinburgh and they had arranged for Carole Caplin to be the first caller, nice chat. PG called, said Iraq was the only issue in US politics at the moment and we had to think through how I dealt with it. Got an earlier train than planned. I did an interview with *Scotsman* journalist who got off at Dunbar. Then the fucking train broke down. Off at York, checked into the Hilton, out for a run, stopping only to hear an incredible ABBA tribute band in a pub en route. Went to check if they were miming they were so good.

Friday 27 July

Out for a run, then met up with the rep and round to shops in York and Leeds with a few interviews on the way. The rep got a fair insight into why the media drove me crazy. BBC York was a nice guy but spraying round all manner of stuff just not rooted in fact. A dozy girl from York news who asked seriously stupid questions like what's in it that has been published before. One bloke whacking me a bit but generally OK and all the shops, without exception, said it was doing really well. *Calendar* at YTV and had to do two interviews for the two halves of the region. First was fine, the second I lost it a bit with a wannabe big willie guy who was trying to make out I had taken Iraq out of the book. Out for dinner with PG, Gail, Lindsay and Mark [Johansen, Lindsay's husband], her chemo now over.

Saturday 28 July

Fox TV interview at the Marriott Swiss Cottage. All fine. No real problems and the interviewer was very pro the book, said go heavy on the anecdotes when you get to the US. Swim then later to the Emirates [Arsenal football stadium] with Calum and Terry Tavner [family friend]. Collection of different mainly French people in the EMI box [for pre-season friendly tournament]. Inter v Valencia [0–2] really dull. Less so Arsenal v Paris Saint-Germain, 2–1. Chatted with David Miliband by phone re US visit. Just like GB, he was going to be in US when I was there. DM said they were stressing it was the most important bilateral relationship, also on Iraq that we would stay the course and build on the fact three of our four zones had moved to Iraqi control with the UK in watch-over role. DM was still worrying about how to answer the question 'So what has really changed?' Was it all as before?

I felt for the moment the change was in the context and the challenges. GB generally was doing fine. He was still defining himself too much as not TB but his handling of stuff so far was good. There was lots of talk of a GB bounce and a possible early poll. I was not so sure. But DC was not in good shape. He was getting whacked for going to Rwanda when Witney [Oxfordshire, DC's constituency] was flooded. But it was more that he just wasn't leading them anywhere. There was more pick-up among the commentators on the theme that my book showed how hard you had to work to win, and the Tories just didn't get it. I got a nice call from Joe Hemani, who had read his £60k copy twice already. He said you guys have changed this country for good. Piers Morgan [broadcaster, former *Daily Mirror* editor] called, he said he really liked it, and 'if only you'd listened to me on Iraq you would have gone down as a genius'. The US coverage was picking up ahead of the trip there. *LA Times* said scholars will scour it for years as it was 'history in the raw'. Out for Calum's birthday dinner. Can't believe he is eighteen.

Sunday 29 July

Did Calum's presents then out on the bike with Rory. *The Observer* had a little piece on how my enemies had failed to fuck me over and the strategy had worked and the book was doing really well. Car to LHR. American Airlines. The publisher had asked me to sign stock in the airport shops, but I could find hardly any. A few buried away in Borders. It really was a crazy industry. They endlessly called me to tell me how well it was going, yet they could never seem to get stock where they needed it. The flight was enlivened when my neighbour suddenly noticed I had blood dripping from my lip, and I then realised the nut bowl was chipped and there were bits of porcelain amid the nuts. I told the staff and so sparked quite the most ridiculous over-the-top service. I even had the pilot come out to apologise. It was only later when I got to NY that someone suggested they would have been worried I was going to sue. It had never even crossed my mind. Off to the Essex House hotel, and met up with PG who felt Iraq was going to be the real hot button but it was good GB was here, as I would have that as the main backdrop for the interviews.

Monday 30 July

Slept not too bad. Out at 6 and ran for an hour round Central Park. Really hot and muggy but OK. I got back to a message from Alastair McQueen [former *Mirror* colleague] that Richard [Stott] had died. I called Penny's mobile, which was answered by Christopher [son] and then spoke to her. She was upset I heard on the grapevine and not from her but it wasn't a problem for me. Also she sounded like when she said it was a release she meant it. She was not crying, just said it had become harder and harder to sustain the idea that it was a life. She said he had so enjoyed doing the book, and it had kept him going, and he was thrilled it had gone so well. Calls and emails started and I agreed to do a piece for the *Mirror*. I worked on it, a bit rushed but OK. I had a little cry before leaving the hotel but having seen him as he was the last time I shared Penny's view that it was a release. Syd [Young, former *Mirror* colleague] was upset when I spoke to him. Fiona thought the obit was brilliant. I worried it was too much about me and the book.

Sheila O'Shea was looking after me from Knopf [US publisher], really nice, very smart, plugged in. She had lined up a pretty back-to-back schedule, and kept warning me 'So and so will be quite tough' or 'Expect a curve ball from her/him' but their media is much softer than ours. Did a mix of press, TV radio, online, also a session with Knopf editorial people. An hour-long Californian radio interview. Really hot and humid but we were just in and out of cars and buildings. There was a fair bit of interest in GB but he was not yet on the radar in the way TB had been. I was also being asked a lot about [Rupert] Murdoch who was trying to take over Dow Jones and their *Wall Street Journal*. I did a piece on it, then a couple of phone interviews on Richard, including with Sky, Jeremy Thompson. I watched most of GB's press conference with Bush, which was fine. The body language not too bad. He had prepared remarks of some length and they were fine. Serious, substantial, a long list of issues and concerns. He did enough to allay any worries that were around that Malloch Brown was trying to shift the basic favourable pitch on the US.

GB hit the special relationship buttons fine, but also in tone and content was sufficiently not TB for that to run a bit too. Bush was fine though why did he give Nick Robinson the cheap thrill of saying 'You still hanging around?' and then making a joke about his bald patch and the sun?

In terms of questions I was getting re GB, I formulated the line that his strength was strength, that there would be differences and similarities with TB but he knew how much the US mattered. The Yanks were picking up on the notion GB was doing better than expected more generally, as ours had. I started to make the comparison with Hillary [Clinton, former First Lady], that as a prism changes so a new person can emerge. Our politics was defined by TB–GB. With TB gone GB was stronger and TB would not interfere or backseat drive. So GB was both strong and liberated. Likewise HC had stopped being an appendage to BC and established herself in her own right as a serious, significant player. As Tom Baldwin put it, they were two people trapped in unhappy marriages with more charismatic partners, who were now liberated to do their own thing.

Back to the hotel to do *Women's Wear Daily*, a journalist called Rosemary, who was a bit odd but Sheila was convinced she would do a good piece. Then *The NewsHour with Jim Lehrer* with Jim Steinberg [former Clinton advisor], now dean of Lyndon B. Johnson School of Current Affairs in Austin, Texas. It was odd to hear him being called Dean Steinberg. He said he had seen the book, he had gone to the index, looked himself up and he was pleased it showed him trying to protect the interests of his leader against the spin demands of a foreign power. He was on good form and gave a very intelligent analysis of the US–UK relationship and politics more generally. *NewsHour* asked later if I would become a regular contributor. On to *The Daily Show* with Jon Stewart. The entrance was down an odd little side street. He came back before the show. He was much smaller than I expected, and much more serious. He was fascinated, as many were, by the TB–Bush relationship. They just couldn't understand how TB got on with him, given they seemed so different in so many ways.

Stewart was very sharp but not mean-spirited and it was an OK interview. I raised a few laughs if not as loud as his – his audience adore him and he is seriously funny – but he did at least say it was a 'good and interesting book', as they pretty much all did, and there was only one dig on Iraq. Sheila was pleased with it. We met up with Ed Victor at La Guardia and flew to DC chatting about possible future books. Landed and off to the Embassy. Alan West was in town. He was loving his job and loving presenting himself as one of the people who was inside GB's mind. He loved Digby Jones being around because he was taking all the flak about the outside appointments! David Manning was enjoying his time here, and said GB had been fine today. We watched the Jon Stewart interview together and he thought it was fine, as did I. Nice chat about TB, both of us feeling he needed to be careful how he handled himself in the next stages, and also that it was important he didn't stop engaging on the foreign policy side especially, as there were so many others willing to portray him negatively now he was gone.

Tuesday 31 July

Breakfast with David Manning. He was not sure what he would do in the future. He was probably going to go private sector rather than academia, but he wanted to stay somehow engaged in foreign policy work. I mentioned some of the TB projects being planned, some of which he would be perfect in. He said he had had a breakfast for David Miliband yesterday with four pundits who were all saying GB had not put a foot wrong. He said he had seen me on Lehrer and GB really had cause to be grateful for the way I supported him. David of course knew a lot of the bad stuff, and we chatted over that, whether GB really had the psychology for what lay ahead, whether he would be liberated enough now to rise above it and lose some of the stuff that stopped him from being as good as he could be. We reminisced a bit on the Iraq build-up. He said he was constantly telling a disbelieving media there that the Crawford [President Bush's ranch] meeting was not all about Iraq. It was MEPP and Colin Powell [former US Secretary of State] feeling he was being hung out to dry. Also that he agreed with me Bush was understanding of the difficulties TB faced and the sacrifices made. Not so [Dick] Cheney [Vice-President] and [Donald] Rumsfeld [Defense Secretary] who really did not give a damn. David thin and wan and serious as ever but such a lovely man.

Out for another media round, again several slightly odd. The guy from Politico [political journalism company] had a really intense stare. Then a very long radio interview with a similarly intense guy. The questions were much the same, though much more polite than ours. The woman at Reuters TV had an odd head-rocking movement, and a cameraman from NI with grey hair, earrings and a Harley Davidson owners' jacket. Back to the Embassy, where David was putting on a lunch for me. Good crowd – Melanne Verveer [Hillary advisor], Tucker Eskew [Bush advisor], PJ Crowley [Homeland Security consultant, former USAF officer], Ken Bacon [former Bill Clinton spokesman], Sidney Blumenthal [former Bush advisor], Gordon Johndroe [former Bush assistant], Mike McCurry [former White House press secretary] wearing a Campbell tartan tie, Tom Baldwin. David gave me a handwritten note from Bush, thanking me for the book, saying he missed our chats, had enjoyed writing chapters of history together, valued friendship with TB. 'Not many people get those,' said David, though I think the Clinton people felt we got way too close. Sidney had the book. Ken Bacon had already read it. Tucker was reading it, so there was a lot of interest. Not sure how it would go.

It was lovely to see Melanne who had moved other stuff to be there. She was so nice and warm. She felt Hillary was doing fine. She really liked my GB analogy. After the small talk and the reminiscing we sat down to lunch. After first course I spoke a little about the people round the table. I said David was a great friend and support and embodied the best of public service. I said we got close to Mike and Melanne because we went through a lot together in the early days, when TB was a new PM and Bill going through really troubled times. PJ and Ken in Kosovo – did my usual spiel re how we changed things for the military. Gordon (now National Security Council spokesman) and Tucker post-September 11, Baldwin proof that not all journos were bad. Sidney – I said I really hoped we had a second President Clinton. Then on the book and how I did it. Amazed I found time. Said it was all about showing politics as humans. Good Q&A re our politics and why GB was doing better. Did my prism changes and how HC was like GB. Serious, substantial, less charismatic than Bill as GB was with TB but it fitted where we were now. Need to write a piece on this. Melanne enjoying my analysis that GB and HC both benefiting from a different prism created by TB gone and her having her own profile. Serious substantial people. Felt on form and they were listening.

Off to C-Span, one-hour interview. I was flagging, but Ed came in to say it was No. 1 again. Three weeks in a row. Flew back to New York and over dinner Ed and I had another chat about future books. Maybe just work on the full four volumes we were intending to do some time in the future, probably when out of power. He was gagging for me to do the book Alex F and I had talked about on the differences and similarities in sport and politics re winning. Ed felt I was unemployable, in that there was no job out there that would give me the same satisfaction. He felt I was too big to take on the kind of job others who had been in positions like mine might do, added to which he didn't imagine – rightly – I would want to sit around on company boards. I still felt I would end up doing something with GB. Having read the full versions, he couldn't believe I was even thinking of it.

Wednesday 1 August

I was developing the line that GB and Hillary would represent a kind of post-charismatic leadership based on serious earnest politics; that they emerged from the shadows of more modern leaders. I was starting to work it into a possible article. Sheila was also pressing me to do something on Murdoch for the *New York Times* as a way of getting the book plugged in a different context. Sheila was really very sharp and also acutely political. I wondered if she shouldn't go into a political job. She meanwhile was urging me to get involved in the Hillary campaign, and if not to stand for Parliament myself. I was pushing a harder pro-HC line now and musing on what Mike [McCurry] said, namely that there was nobody listening to Bush any more. To Leonard Lopate [talk radio show host] who I don't think had read the book but it was an OK interview. They had a really different style these US guys. More mellow. All asking the same questions especially totally not getting the TB–Bush relationship.

The main interview of the day was going to be Charlie Rose in the Bloomberg building. I watched him doing Rudy Giuliani [TV talk show host, former Mayor of New York City] which ran on long and Giuliani's people were getting really agitato. I liked Rose. A big guy with big bags under his eyes. He had clearly read the book, went on about how much he liked it and did a good interview. A lot of the usual questions but also lots of his own and though it was an hour long, it whizzed by. Quite a few people saying 'Saw you on *The Daily Show*.' Out for dinner with Jamie Rubin. He was moving back here. Jamie on good form. Clearly hoping to get involved in the HC campaign. He said Mark Penn was by far the main guy in the campaign, that they didn't really have people like me on the road with her. Sheila was convinced that I should come out there and consult – advise politicians how to do strategy and comms. She said they were hopeless at it. Nice evening. Argued about Murdoch in advance of the CNN interview I was doing tomorrow.

Thursday 2 August

I went to the hotel gym and banged out a piece for *The Times* on the exercise bike, partly based on the notes and discussions of yesterday. I was warming to this theme of GB and HC similarities, but also directly answering the question that was being most raised here, namely how on earth did TB, who got on so well with President Clinton, also get on so well with President Bush?

People easily 'get' the Blair–Clinton relationship. They were both modernising charismatic leaders of parties that had to be brought closer to the mainstream. They were both great communicators. They were both also policy wonks who loved nothing more than complicated policy decisions which they could then connect to people's lives. They were in many ways political soulmates. The Blair–Bush relationship takes longer to explain. Part of it is about the reality and pragmatism of modern statesmanship. It was their JOB to get on. The US–UK relationship is a real one with important economic, diplomatic and cultural ramifications.

Then beyond pragmatism there is personality and the truth is that TB and GWB really did get on. Also, as I said on several of the shows I had done, GWB is not the moron of the caricature. It is also the case that the forging of relationships tends to be faster and deeper amid times of challenge and for both, the decision to go to war in Iraq was difficult and defining.

On GB, Tucker Eskew had made an interesting point – that while people who really follow the UK know all about the TB–GB stuff, for most Americans, including in politics, Thatcher and TB are the only figures they know, so GB starts with the advantage of being known mainly as TB's chosen successor. Added to which, he and others in the Bush circle were saying, GB had done fine. In both his press conference with Bush and even more in his speech to the United Nations, he played to his strengths, coming over as a serious, substantial figure focused on the big challenges facing the world and determined to use his power to meet them in partnership with other leaders.

The papers back home seemed to have a lot of commentary that GB has started surprisingly well as Prime Minister. I am surprised at the surprise. The Tories and the press have been so mesmerised by the TB–GB prism, they underestimated the extent to which life would change when TB moved on; especially as TB will definitively not be a Margaret Thatcher-style backseat driver. So despite it all, the smooth and orderly transition happened, and GB has been able to represent both continuity and change, a good strategic position to be in. Also, Gordon doesn't have a Gordon to worry about. GB without TB is in a strong position provided he is competent. That's what people seem to want from him. That is where the comparisons with Hillary come in too. She still might fall, but she is looking strong, serious, competent, despite not having the same charisma or likeability – with the public at least – as Bill. What with [Angela] Merkel [Chancellor of Germany] around as well, maybe we are entering the era of post-charismatic politics. I was developing a line that maybe the next really special relationship in the special relationship will be Gordon Brown and Hillary Clinton. It was partly to help me position my handling of GB in the book. But it might be true.

I did Boston radio down the line with a guy called Stu Taylor who was spectacularly pro-TB. Did the BBC obit programme on Richard down the line and then another NPR show, *The World*, which was as smug and pompous as it sounds. I was chatting to Sheila re a Fox guy in London who was asking about maybe doing a one-hour documentary. To CNN and a couple of really good radio interviews where the interviewers were amazingly positive before I did the CNN Murdoch interview with London which I then used as I started to draft a piece for the *NYT* on him.

Lunch with Sheila and Sonny Mehta [editor-in-chief, Knopf]. Nice chat and they seemed pleased I had gone out though like me Sonny had wanted to do a specific US version of the book. I finished the Murdoch piece in the car to the airport, echoing the howls of anguish now [over the acquisition of the *Wall Street Journal*] with the time he took over *The Times*. Trouble was he did tend to get his way. Talked about the different responses to the pace of change, the fact papers are players not just spectators; talked over our relationship with him. Would we have lost the election if *The Sun* had stayed with the Tories? I don't think so. Would *The Sun* have lost readers if it had stayed with the Tories? Probably not. Would it have lost credibility? Yes. Also on the subtle and not so subtle ways he interferes.

Friday 3 August

Slept fine on the flight home and was reasonably unexhausted. Home then a fairly quiet day except had to go to King's Cross for an event to promote the Loch Ness duathlon. The UK papers were doing a big number on GB getting a bomber jacket from Bush and all a bit piss-takey. Popped in to see Jeremy Heywood, who was about to go on holiday. He said things looked better than they were, that there was a lot of paddling beneath the water and for all that GB briefed he was following systems, he wasn't really. On the contrary it was all a bit seat of pants. Also he had most ministers' mobiles plugged into his own phone and regularly called them. Jeremy said sometimes the centre learned what No. 10 was doing from private office of other ministers. Douglas [Alexander] and the two Eds [Balls and Miliband] had a meeting with GB at 10 most mornings which according to Jeremy was a glorified diary meeting. He felt August would be a nightmare because GB would be looking for things to do all the time. He had called him today with a list of stuff he wanted put to all party processes which sounded to me like a means of avoiding decisions. JH felt the book came out fine and GB seemed to appreciate that I had managed to avoid it damaging him. He said GB had not really changed much. Still micromanaging, and too much wishful thinking.

Saturday 4 August

Felt a bit for GB, trying to get a break, and a foot-and-mouth outbreak [in Normandy, Surrey] seemed to be growing as a problem. Massive on the news. GB broke into his holiday yesterday to chair a COBRA meeting. I got a few media bids to talk about how we had handled FMD [foot-and-mouth disease] in 2001. It had definitely been one of the worst. Off fairly early with Audrey and Rory for the [London charity] triathlon. Really hot again, and I never got going. Did four interviews including one on Radio London where the interviewer, Jo Good, was absolutely raving about the book. Home late and a bit tired.

Sunday 5 August

Fiona, Calum and Grace off at 6.45 for France. I was staying back to go to Richard's funeral. Nice event as these things go. Bill Hagerty [former Mirror Group colleague] did the main eulogy and spoke well, got something of Richard. Bill was the obvious choice to do the diaries going forward I think. I was doing a UK version of the *NYT* Murdoch piece. *The Observer* ran a piece I had done on the GB/Hillary comparison which I sent to Melanne Verveer who was happy with it. Nick Soames called. He said he loved the diaries and felt the book should be required reading for all Tories because it showed how hard we had to work. Also he had been reading Tom Bower [unauthorised biographer] on GB. 'What is it with that man? Why does he spend so much time and energy destroying his own side? Why didn't Tony fire him?' Out with Audrey to see Seth Lakeman [musician son of *Mirror* colleague Geoff Lakeman, for whom AC and Fiona used to babysit when trainee journalists]. Great to see him and to see he had made it as a musician. He had quite a following and was very, very powerful as a performer. Audrey loved it, and we went back and had a drink with him after. Nice kid.

GB had asked me to put down some thoughts re conference, and in particular his speech. I said it has to be a different sort of conference speech. And a different sort of GB speech. The upside of the series of events he has had to deal with is that people have seen he is competent, able, PM material. The downside is that they have sucked the air free of space for him to have communicated a sustained strategic message about change, particularly in the area of real people's real lives. There was some of this at the start but it was either stylistic – methods of working, holidays etc. – or it was one-off policy-focused. Or, it was simply the fact that he was the new PM. But change is not about distance from the past. It is about showing the strength to shape a new and better future.

I was conscious he can sometimes take badly, and get very downcast at, negative feedback. So I said despite all that, what people have seen they have liked, and conference has to embed that sense. Also, you need to use it to answer the question, which otherwise would have been answered in a leadership contest, 'Why Gordon, why now?' So that is all about embedding the sense of normality in the fact he is PM; reminding people why he became leader and of the qualities he has shown since; showing why we remain in the ascendant, because we had the courage to change, to face hard choices in making change and as a result change the landscape and have others now dancing around our flagpole as once we had to dance round theirs; define change as a concept relating to the future not the past; and above all to set out the challenges the party, the country and the world face in the next phase of history. I said it was important he thinks in these big thematic terms. It can't be a 'bit of this bit of that' kind of speech.

I said I felt there had been too much distancing from TB. GB is too much part of the TB government to be able to do anything other than superficial distancing. Indeed, I said he should make a tribute to TB, as personal as TB's was to him last year. But the big themes should be focused around new challenges. It is not enough to say here I am, new leader. It is the new challenges that are important and he has to show why his values and experience make him the right man to meet them. I went back over conference speeches from '94 and '97, and what was interesting was how many of the big challenges had been met. Winning power. The economy. Poverty pay. Jobs. Welfare reform. Underinvestment in public services. Constitutional paralysis. Northern Ireland. Britain sidelined in Europe. Progress on all fronts. But the challenges of today are different, bigger, more complex, often more global in nature.

So globalisation is the backdrop. It can either overwhelm us or be the basis of the next steps of our strengthening as a country and as an economy. We have to make sure we seize the opportunities rather than be overwhelmed by the threats of globalisation. People need to hear what he really thinks of what is happening in the world economy. What are we meant to think of China and India? Global warming-climate change. Ten years ago it was a fad. Now it is the single most pressing challenge the world faces. Again, what does he really think needs to be done? What new alliances to meet the new challenge? Demographics and pensions. The stats are mind-blowing. The impact for policymakers immense. What are the choices we face? Energy policy, global terrorism, global poverty, cynicism in and about public life. I said the old challenges allow you to do values, delivery, tough choices, achievement.

The new challenges allow you to do vision, reach, depth, experience, insight and understanding. And amid it all Britain like all countries is wrestling with the question of what we mean by national identity and what it means to be British in this world of change. So show empathy – a real sense you get the concerns people have – and also an understanding that you're not a top-down leader who thinks you can solve all the problems of the world, but someone who wants to do this as leader of a team working in partnership with every part of our national life. He had used a phrase in the UN speech about 'coalition of conscience', which I liked. I wondered about 'coalition of aspiration' as a way of signalling fresh ambition for people and communities as part of Britain getting on, being stronger, fairer, more prosperous, more powerful. I also threw in my usual plea for a commitment to education about politics and democracy in schools, starting young, and compulsory voting. I sensed it would fall on the same deaf ears TB had always had on that one.

Summer break

Amused by the very clever piece of spin by Travelodge which said my and Piers Morgan's books were the two most left in rooms! Once I flew down to Marseille and joined the others in France, I had my usual holiday crash, and it was a bad one. We had too many visitors, I think, and I was just not getting the chance to switch off. The best day was cycling up Mont Ventoux on hire bikes with Rory. He did 1:38, I did 2:30. I did bits and bobs on the book, for example had to go to Avignon for a day to do some US media. GB called for a chat re his speech and asked if I would think about different ways of expressing the themes we had talked about. TB was in Barbados, then Europe. I called at one point, CB answered but said nothing other than a loud sigh. I said 'Is he there?' No. 'Can you ask him to call?' I might. Then the phone went dead. I then texted to say I had tried to call and 'Cherie said she might pass on.' Back came the message 'This is Cherie you creep. Put that in your diary tonight along with whatever sexist comment you want to add about me.' Wow.

Fiona had said she thought Cherie would be really pissed off at the book, but this suggested something else. I replied 'Charmed I'm sure, will pass on regards to Fiona as I'm sure you would want me to.' Back within a few seconds. 'It would be nice to see HER.' Really strong stuff. There was a lot of good feedback on the book, still doing well in the UK but sales in the States poor. GB was doing OKish but once Cameron went on crime and immigration he blipped up a fair bit. The GB operation all felt a bit fragile. PG was having a fair bit to do with the GB team and said it was all pretty joyless. Bob Shrum [US strategist] over here as a kind of éminence grise and PG wasn't convinced he was good for GB, who needed to be challenged more.

Lots of the kids' friends, plus the Bridges [London neighbours], and Maud and Oscar [Millar, Fiona's niece and nephew] and I probably got a bit grumpy at times. Also the Milibands visited and Fiona and the boys felt there had been a change in David, that he was less relaxed, also very dismissive of e.g. GB and TB. Also he said straight out he couldn't understand why the book was doing so well. PG felt it was just me finding it hard that David and I had crossed on the political ladder somewhat.

Off to Scotland with Rory for the Loch Ness duathlon, one of the ideas that had come out of the brainstorm with the First Group [British transport]. It was great being with him and we had a good time though he didn't rate the organisation of it. Absolutely stunning scenery, as beautiful as anywhere in the world and I had one of my near God moments coming up over a hill and looking down on to the loch. It was a nice event though one of my team came off the bike and was hospitalised. I raised 5k for LRF [Leukaemia Relief Foundation] playing the pipes. I did a bit of telly. Sonia O'Sullivan failed to catch me with a twenty-minute start on a 12k race. Nice to see Liz McColgan [Scottish athlete].

I was drifting badly though, and the scale of the crash in France had worried me. I had a long session with DS. He said it sounded dangerously close to my demon taking over, and somehow I needed to learn to park it in a corner. I had not been drinking yet I was putting on weight and generally feeling lethargic and demotivated.

I saw Bill Hagerty to ask him to edit the full volumes and he was up for it. I was also, somewhat to my surprise, asked to do the eulogy at [former *Mirror* colleague] Christine Garbutt's funeral. We were friends, but I was not her closest friend. I seemed to be spending too much time at funerals of old colleagues.

Wednesday 12 September

Great trip to Paris with Calum to see France v Scotland. Calum had been on pretty good form though I sensed a bit worried about leaving for Manchester [University], but we had a brilliant time, helped by the fact that Scotland won 1–0. Amazing support out there, and the atmosphere was really something special. We had cocked up the Eurostar booking but Kate Garvey [PR executive] put me in touch with Greg Nugent [Eurostar marketing] who sorted. We arrived and went to Le Meridien to see Alex McLeish [Scotland manager] and get tickets. Really nice guy. It was funny how he still referred to Alex [Ferguson] as 'the gaffer'. The chat reminded me a bit of those I'd had often enough with AF before matches, when they have nothing to do and are just wanting time to go by. A good luck letter arrived from Alex Salmond as we sat waiting for coffee. 'Not so sure about him,' AMcL said. Really nice time, lovely dinner in a typical French restaurant, bed. Good trip.

Thursday 13 September

Did a French interview re the book before we headed to the Gare du Nord, the place heaving with Scotland fans. I had been for a run and done something to my heel so saw Mel Cash [physio] when I got back.

Friday 14 September

To Christine Garbutt's funeral before taking Calum off to Manchester. I sensed he was worried, and our anxieties weren't helping. There was a nice turnout for the funeral. Her son Mark and I did the tributes, both very jolly in different ways. There was a good *Mirror* turnout – Syd Young, Alan Shillum, Tom Hendry, Brendan Monks, Bill Kennedy, Bill Hagerty, Phil Mellor, Garth Gibbs with dyed blond hair and a deep tan, Martin Philips, Pauline McLeod, Pat Smylie, Christian and Sharon Gysin. I couldn't stay too long because we had to set off for Manchester. Fiona and I were staying at the Lowry and the contrast with the horrible little prison cell of a room they had sorted for Calum was a bit stark. He seemed pretty down and Fiona was upset the whole time, constantly crying and making it worse for him I think. She and I ended up having a stupid row which didn't help either.

Saturday 15 September

Calum and I were going to Burnley v Blackpool [2–2] so there was a tearful farewell with Fiona before we set off. I was supposed to be getting a helicopter to the Great Scot Awards dinner in Glasgow but the weather made it impossible. I was pissed off but then heard Colin McRae [rally driver] and his son, and two others were killed in a helicopter crash in Lanarkshire. Grim. Beautiful scenery up through the Lakes. Arrived about an hour after the dinner had started but it was running so late it didn't really matter. Mum and Donald [AC's brother] were already there with Cathy Gilman [CEO Leukaemia Research Foundation] etc. Liz McColgan was unaware that she was going to be picking up an award for the work she did for the charity. Alex [Ferguson] was there to accept a Hall of Fame award and during the dinner we chatted a bit about football, mainly family. Alex [McLeish] there, still totally buzzing re Paris. Liz McColgan made a brilliant impromptu speech. She said whatever she had achieved in sport was irrelevant. She wanted to be remembered for helping find a cure for leukaemia. She said there was too much materialism, people worrying about their next house, car, or holiday and not the things that really mattered. She got a fantastic response and Alex said later that he didn't know her but she epitomised the best of Scotland for him.

Donald played [bagpipes] when the 'Scot of the Year' award went to those who dealt with the Glasgow bomb. I chatted to Douglas [Alexander] and his wife [Jacqui]. DA said Philip should be assured of a big role. I said he is totally two-minded about it. He says he wants to give it all up but agitates with them for action. She said 'The trouble is you are all addicts.' Fiona had said the same on holiday. I said I was trying to give it up, I really was. 'And not succeeding?' she said. We chatted about the impossibility of normal life. He said his dad had read my book and was relieved to see it wasn't just them who has their family life ruined every weekend. I also had a very interesting chat with John Brown [GB's brother]. He said he had loved the book 'but you really must do the whole thing so everyone – including Gordon – could see the full truth of how bad he was to TB'. I said there was quite a lot that was not so good for GB. He said it has to be put out there. 'These are big people and these have been important times but there is a full story to be told, from all sides, and your perspective was one of the most important.' I was quite shocked by the vehemence. I didn't sense he was coming at it from a 'anti-GB' position per se, just that he felt it had to be done.

Alex Salmond, striding around in his tartan trews, came over and we had to stop the conversation. I was really quite shocked by it. Salmond was loving the whole thing, clearly loving his position and status and generally being a big thing. His speech later was a little too self-serving but funny. In common with everyone he was making much of McLeish's success. He said as a Hearts fan he was proud there were six Hearts players at Hampden. The problem was they all played for Lithuania. Pretty witty. Mum loved the whole evening, seeing all the different people. I took her over to see Alex and she said she couldn't believe, having read the diaries, how often we spoke. She then told him she didn't like it when he chewed gum!

Sunday 16 September

I was doing the Glasgow to Edinburgh bike ride for LRF, and woke to quite the most horrendous rain, and it was rain which was there for the duration. I was due to do the official start with Nicola Sturgeon [Scottish National Party Health Minister]. Everyone had told me she was the rising star, but I found her a little cold. I sensed she didn't particularly want to be doing this with me. Or maybe, like me, she just wanted to get it over with because of the rain. She had only signed up to do the start and a short ride, whereas I, alas, had agreed to do the whole 55 miles. I was riding with Darren [Cathy's husband] who was a real trouper, kept my spirits up, but God it was the wettest rain I had ever known. Despite that I actually led the ride for a bit until we got into hillier parts and I struggled. There was a hilarious moment going through Queensferry when I was saying to Darren 'GB lives up there, maybe we should pop in for a coffee,' at which point the bike slid under me, and I went flying. A valve had shattered and I needed a new tyre. The charity had sorted me a shower in a house near the finish and it was the best shower I have ever had in my life. Off to the airport and flew home reading the Yasmina Reza [playwright and novelist] book [*L'Aube le soir ou la nuit*] on Nicolas Sarkozy [President of France]. Out for dinner with PG, Gail and Grace [Gould daughter] and round the same old block.

Monday 17 September

Le Monde ran the interview I did and it was really quite bizarre. It sort of got the sense of what I said but with all manner of made-up quotes. I had a couple of speech meetings including with a private equity team, but there was something really not good about them. Daniel Moore from CSA [speaking agency] said something interesting. He said I really arouse strong opinions. 'Some clients just rail at the idea of you if we suggest you. Others go wild for it.'

Tuesday 18 September

Calum and Georgia [Gould] to Euston. He was down again, sighing a lot, not eating, saying he couldn't face it really. But he went and so fine so far. Fiona was upset again but less so than before and was finally getting message we couldn't just run with moods. Though she did perhaps understandably say they had to put up with all my emotions so why not for others. The cab driver who took me to King's Cross was a Kosovan who said he was grateful for what we did there. He used to love reading my briefings and hearing my words. 'I do not believe the war would have been won without you.' I felt both moved and chuffed as he talked about the kind of things his family and friends now did, and the way the country was changing. I said it's a shame the UK public didn't appreciate it more. He said 'That war was being lost and my people would have been butchered. Blair persuaded others but what you did was to transform how what was happening was shown to the world. I loved it when I heard you were at NATO. Jamie Shea [NATO spokesperson] was a good man but he was overwhelmed. You supported him and you organised everyone and it helped turn the war. I am sure of it.' He got quite emotional, told the story of his past, how he came here fourteen years ago, had been jailed for protesting. Now had two kids here, liked it here, was staying. 'My country owes you a lot, never forget it,' he said.

To the first-class lounge where a very funny receptionist said 'My, my, you have put on weight.' I said to her colleagues she had abused me and called me fat. Good laugh. Train to York working on a crisis management speech. There was a really obese guy over the way just sniffing endlessly. To Harrogate. Ernst and Young [professional services firm]. I did a book signing, crisis management speech and OK Q&A, my best by far defending myself re David Kelly.

Wednesday 19 September

To the City for a pre-brief on Berwin [Leighton Paisner, law firm] speech plus sign 400 books for the event. It was annoying that these special sales didn't count on the figures. I was sorting final points for a piece I was doing on Walter Veltroni [Italian writer and politician] for *La Repubblica*.

I got a call from Seb Coe, who said he was due to do the Timber Trade Awards tomorrow but had got word there was an IOC [International Olympic Committee] inspection, he would have to pull out, and could I do it? We had a good laugh about widget of the year and the like, but I rejigged a few things to be able to do it. Then a call out of the blue from Maggie [wife] and then Alistair Darling [Chancellor of the Exchequer] wanting help with his conference speech.

Thursday 20 September

The TTF Awards were quite a good laugh in the end. I started by saying I used to fantasise about standing in for Seb Coe, but it didn't look like this. They were a good crowd. I had a meeting to go over with Stuart Prebble some TV ideas. *Le Monde* interview had had a fair bit of play in France and AFP [news agency] were saying it underlined how the French left needed the kind of approach we had delivered.

Saturday 22 September

I did a note for AD on the train to Bristol City v BFC. It was not dissimilar to the note I had done for GB but focused more on the economy alone. I pointed out it would be strategically stupid to airbrush TB. GB was defining himself too much against TB. The Tories and most of the press would want to rubbish our record. But if we did it too, the public would hear only the negative. Also what was the big point he was trying to make? It wasn't clear. He seemed happy enough with what I was saying. We met up with Syd Young who was really good with Calum. Lunch at Brown's then to the match. It was a reverse of last week. One up, two one down late, then equaliser in injury time. Excellent.

Monday 24 September

Early train down to Bournemouth. I bumped into Bruce [Grocott] at the station which was a bonus and travelled down with him. He was nice as ever and really felt the book had gone as well as it could. I was met by Carol [Linforth] to go through to the Marriott and then down to watch GB. I did a bit of media beforehand and the mood was OK, but I didn't really feel part of it in the way I used to. There was a little flare-up with Ian Austin [Labour MP] who said he wasn't speaking to me because of something in the book. I said maybe I should tell the whole truth about them. 'You didn't tell the truth,' he said. 'About what?' But he walked off. Fuck knows what he was on about. Stan Greenberg and Deborah Mattinson [pollsters] nearby. I didn't think the speech was that good. It lacked big message and felt very Bob Shrum-ish. Fiona texted to say he was better when shafting TB. Rory left halfway through. GB was OK on micro stuff and more personal maybe than usual but it wasn't great. Stan said at the end 'I didn't know he had it in him.' 'What is IT?' I said which was about the only disloyal remark I made.

I did a bit of media and was very supportive but it lacked something and there wasn't the buzz outside that used to follow TB's. Spending a lot of time with PG and Georgia and also worrying re Calum who was still not settling. Up to my room to work a bit then dinner with PG and Georgia, joined by Neil, Glenys and Rachel [Kinnocks] who was basically doing GB's diary. To Young Labour reception. I spoke and did my usual spiel re how important they were, and then Dawn Butler [MP] who was excellent. Dennis Skinner [MP] and his US partner Lois there and had a good old natter. I told the story of when he was asked to criticise us for saying we were the party of the centre – and he said he was just relieved we were not the party of the right. Lois said I should go and work for Hillary. Ed Miliband arrived late and I thought was pretty poor. Not terribly inspiring, flat, clichéd.

Mirror party. Long chat with *Mirror* lot then JP who was on pretty good form, Margaret B who was telling me the story of her sacking and how GB hadn't been terribly nice. I had her in hysterics about Charlie's story of his demise and the offer of a Carers' Commission [government advisory body] which he discovered GB had offered to several others. I had a longish chat with Sarah B after GB arrived and she was very nice. Also pretty chilled. She said life was OK, the week was going fine and they enjoyed doing the rounds. She was very calm I thought. Could definitely be an asset. Sue Nye was being friendly and asking what I thought about election timing. The media obsession was the idea of an early election and the top people didn't seem to be knocking it down. I felt they had to be very careful. Either go for it or don't, but it was silly to let this idea build that they were unless they had already decided it. And it was clear they hadn't.

Neil thought the whole thing was a very bad idea. I could see why they were thinking of it, but I felt it played against who and what he is and what his strengths are. Jon Mendelsohn [party organiser] was saying the money was coming in now. But there was a real danger that after the initial excitement people would say 'Why? What is the point?' and the idea of saying to the public he would follow the Tory conference and then study the polls was ludicrous. As with their distancing from TB, they were confusing strategy with tactics and making a real arse of it. Either do it, or don't do it, but don't for God's sake say it is dependent on the Tories screwing up their conference.

Tuesday 25 September

I had breakfast with Andy Burnham [Chief Secretary to the Treasury]. He seemed to be loving the job though basically he said he spent most of his time just telling people they couldn't have money. I was wandering around with PG and Georgia and getting lots of nice welcome and feedback on the book. There were big queues for the signings and sales were still good. I missed DM's speech which seemed to go OK. I watched it later though and I felt it had been OK without being brilliant. PG was in a bit of turmoil about how deeply to get involved with GB, but he was keener than I was. I was feeling more not less resistant to getting involved. And I didn't want the media interaction at all. I did a session at the De Vere [hotel chain] suite which was sold out with people on stairs and at the back. Nice mood, nothing too tricky. Martin Kettle and Mike White [*Guardian* journalists], who was chairing it, both did positive online pieces on it. I used the line 'We don't do anti-God' in answer to a question on faith in politics.* There were loads of people queueing to buy.

I got the train back with PG. Tony Benn [former Labour Cabinet minister] was on the train with Emily [granddaughter], just selected for a safeish Tory seat aged seventeen. Benn felt GB's speech was brilliant and he should go for it. He also said that I had a duty to publish all my diaries. PG and I were both feeling we had not really been part of the week. But he was also trying to push me back in, said he wasn't keen on the idea of doing stuff there alone. But agreed any kind of interaction with the GB people was a bit tricky. They only engaged on their terms. Down to 15 stone.

Thursday 27 September

Two speeches, first at Berkeley Hotel to corporate comms people, straight in and out, Q&A easy, home. Later a dinner, quite a few bores but I sat next to Bob Brannan, chairman of Dundee FC. Really nice guy. Dundee one of only eight cities which have had two teams who have reached European Cup semis. Dundee! Vienna! Milan, London, Glasgow, Belgrade, Madrid, Bucharest. Business guys seemed to think election good idea and that GB was doing fine.

Friday 28 September

DS. Mainly chatting re Calum and also my feelings of being of but not in the Labour conference. PM train to Leeds, opposite ghastly looking trout with the *Mail*. I was working on the South Africa speech but definitely

* AC had famously intervened in an interview being given by Tony Blair by declaring, 'We don't do God.'

moving towards needing proper project. Ilkley Literature Festival was a lot bigger than I thought. Three weeks' worth of stuff and I was opening. I had a shower in typically dingy backstage toilet. Baroness Betty Lockwood [Labour activist] chairing. In her eighties and at first I was worried would go on too long but it was fine. Audience good. Lively and friendly. Did the rapid-fire thing at the end and it went well. Ditto signing and sales. Independent bookseller saying flew off shelves at first and now slowing down but he reckoned would rise again for Christmas.

Saturday 29 September

Rory wanted tickets for Birmingham v United. I called Alex and ended up having a long chat about his future. I sounded him out on Ed's idea of a book re winning by the two of us, looking at winning in sport and politics. He was fairly warm. He said he had been discussing long-term plans with Jason [son, agent] and a book was one of the options. He said what he liked about the idea was that it gave him another edge to the profile, and could set him up as business and management guru. He said he had no idea when he was going to retire. He had a great deal with United. One-year contract, could give year's notice and get year's money when he left. Some days – like when the kids lost to Coventry [2–0 in Carling Cup tie] – he wondered why he bothered. Other days he still loved it and couldn't imagine jacking it in. He said he felt really badly let down v Coventry because there was just no fight at all. Jonny Evans the worst.

Gym, tiny pool, then set off for Burnley v Palace. Met Chris Buckland [political journalist friend] and Calum for a cup of tea. The match was poor. I managed to avoid Simon Jordan [Palace chairman, controversial for hiring and firing managers] who looked even worse and more ghastly than the image. There was some guy called Chico Slimani performing at half-time. I had no idea who he was and it turned out he had been a runner-up in *The X Factor*. He went down OK but the fans started up with 'Time to go' chant after a while. Palace got soft set-piece goal. We equalised in much the same way. Could have won but 1–1 in the end. Off with Calum on the bus to Manchester.

Sunday 30 September

A text from Tony to call him. Did so and for the first time in a while we had a long chat. He said he was enjoying himself – provided he was out of the country and didn't have to watch 'all the bollocks' unfold. He was more hopeful the MEPP job might lead somewhere, and was enjoying going at it from a different perspective. He was also gearing up for a bigger and bigger operation, with up to forty staff. He was still keen on governance idea, with the focus very much on Africa. He had some irons in fire but had to draw them out. He felt PG and I could be involved, also that we should help GB if asked. But he was pretty scathing about the whole thing. He'd seen Clinton in NY last week who was down on Shrum. TB felt it was a classic Gore and John Kerry [2004 Democrat presidential candidate] campaign, trying to focus on the character of the leaders. But it was always fraught and the worry about GB was the dark side of the character being exposed. He had no doubt at all they were running a differentiation strategy vis-à-vis TB, which would only succeed in the short term. Long term it had to be about something more and deeper. And people were going to start to ask 'Why are we having this election? What is the big change and the big choice that requires a poll so soon after the last one?'

It was clear Shrum only did one kind of strategy and this was it. It was only working at the moment because the media seemed so desperate to buy it. But where was the challenge to the party and the country? He felt they would definitely go for an early election. Bob and DA etc. would be pressing him hard to go for it. He said he would be perfectly happy to be kept right out of it. It was clearly a bit galling to have been effectively airbrushed out of things at conference but he understood why. What he couldn't see was an alternative strategy from GB. We chatted a bit about the kids, football, Alex, but I felt in a way both of us were going through the motions rather. Neither of us mentioned CB and the rather unpleasant exchanges we had had.

I had lunch with Calum, left for the station and home. The train was heaving. Two guys got on opposite me. One Albanian, the other Kosovan, both settled here. The Albanian knew who I was and couldn't believe the Kosovan didn't. They were very funny. The Kosovan was manager of a Pizza Express in Hulme in Cheshire. He was full of stories of footballers going there. Nicolas Anelka [former Manchester City player] a real gent. [Ruud van] Nistlerooy [former Man Utd player] very open. Roy Keane [former Man Utd player] very closed and not a big tipper. He once complained his food tasted funny. 'Why you not laughing then?' Hard to imagine all these top footballers wandering into Pizza Express but he seemed genuine enough. They were both on second-class tickets but had not found a seat. The guard announced it was OK for people in standard class to go there. We were joined by a real geek and they pretended the Kosovan was a famous film star. They were also showing us pictures of his girlfriend she was sending via phone. The Albanian reminded me a bit of Rory. Big smile and sense of mischief and knowing his own space. Home. The limp was worse. The heel really sore, so fixed to see Mel Cash again. We went out for dinner but Fiona and Grace had to get back early to watch *The O.C.*, some fucking American serial they were both obsessed with.

Monday 1 October

To the Marriott Swiss Cottage to do Greek TV. Yet another foreign station asking about New Labour and why we kept winning when other left-of-centre parties, like the Greek socialists in their recent election, kept losing. It reinforced my view that GB was playing a dangerous game in the distancing strategy and almost buying into the notion we hadn't done that much. The interviewer was a nice young guy who was planning a big number on that theme – why New Labour was not seen at home as the success it was viewed as abroad. Home to do a Radio 4 interview with Kim Fletcher for a series on the so-called death of newspapers. I found him a bit old fogeyish and the interview a bit superficial. I left for the airport and off to Cape Town. Heathrow was not nearly as bad as people were saying especially considering how massive the flow of people going through.

Tuesday 2 October

Piers came on asking if I would do a *GQ* interview with him. No harm, I thought, and agreed. I didn't have much on until the conference tomorrow so, unusually, did a bit of tourism. Down to the Waterfront, did Robben Island. Also a huge session in the gym.

Wednesday 3 October

I watched some guy saying he was in the alarm clock business and when the mobile came out he assumed like everyone it would be good for business. He said it had wiped him out. He realised the writing was on the wall when he was stopped at airport security once and the security people were going through his bags, saw his alarm clock and said 'Wow, not seen one of those in ages.' The alarm on the mobile had destroyed his market. But now he had gone into vintage alarm clocks and was doing OK. The speech went fine, a quick lunch and then off to the airport. It was a long way to go for a speech but, as Fiona said, the money was good. I read Ruth First's book, *117 Days*, on her incarceration under the Ninety-Day Detention Law. Emphasised the incredible change that is South Africa, as did a documentary on apartheid I watched. Got home and watched a recording of Cameron's speech to his conference.

Friday 5 October

To the Marriott for two hours with David Aaronovitch [*Times* journalist] for his TB TV series. OK I think. He told me Sally [Morgan, political advisor] had basically said I lost the plot towards the end and TB didn't know how to reign me in. I left for TB's new house in Connaught Square to meet TB with PG. Nice enough place, loads of work going on all over the house. TB not in a good mood because of the nonsense of GB's positioning and his handling of the election issue. He said he was probably going to have to call one but it had been woefully handled. I did a note for GB saying I thought given the way it had developed it was becoming a seriously bad idea to have an election in these circumstances. The worst thing had been effectively to tell the country it would all depend on polls. PG said he had been to a few meetings with e.g. DA, Spencer Livermore [strategy advisor], Peter Watt [general secretary, Labour Party] and basically the general feeling was that things would get worse not better. Also, there was not the bank of new policy we might think. Everyone had thought for so long that GB was holding back on policy because of big things he wanted to do when he finally landed the job, but it just wasn't there. I said it was like WMD. We all convinced ourselves. 'Sore point,' said TB.

PG said there was no doubt there was a differentiation strategy. But worse than that, it was all very personal re TB. He said he heard again the view that TB was the problem, we were in a terrible position because of TB. They didn't really want to take on the reform agenda because it was TB's, added to which they didn't think it was delivering. TB said the Tories would not have to do much to get into a very strong position. What we had managed to do was keep them out by getting the country to think they were not an alternative government compared to what they had. If GB is not careful, Cameron will look like he is a reasonable alternative. He said they were worried GB was being rumbled and so would want to go for it now. Leaders attracted their own kind and this was a weird introspective self-obsessed bunch, who were also tactical obsessives. He went off on one. He was worried about Balls's judgement. Douglas is weak in the face of GB and would be thinking he would be being lined up for blame. GB is weaker than he lets on. Shrum has a terrible record and doesn't really understand our politics.

TB said 'I kept my side of the bargain, left when I did, helped him take over in a strong position, and we had a policy agenda ready to take forward. He didn't want it but what have we had – a bit of mini crisis management and the rest all tactical and trying to present him as a strong character. But if you go around accepting we were all spin, sleaze and no delivery, you do the Tories' and the media's game for them. It is not just that it is insulting, it is also pathetic, and strategically inept.' He said when he was out of the country it didn't bother him, but he couldn't stand being here and watching this horror unfold. PG said why not call him. He said what's the point? – they're so paranoid they'd think I'm offering fake advice to make them do the right thing, because they think we operate like them. It really couldn't be much worse. He said we had to be careful of schadenfreude. I said in the end it is better for him that GB does well. He said it is all about egoism. He wants to show he can win elections the same as I did. It is not the country's interests first, not even the party's, it's his. As for the policy agenda – they have given up on anti-social behaviour and crime. Jack Straw's have-a-go hero stuff was ludicrous.*

Re MEPP job, he felt there was some hope. He said he was having his eyes opened about the Israelis and how they whacked the Palestinians on stuff that had nothing to do with security. Working well with Condi Rice [US Secretary of State]. He said he was getting loads of money in for his foundation and Ruth Turner was working well. He was working up a project on climate change that seemed to have fired him up. The issue is part technical, part political and the important thing is how you get China and America to agree something as a plan forward. He was in good form re himself, though neither of us mentioned CB. He said he was being offered millions for various business and speaking projects, and was going to take in the money to set up the foundation and run the governance side. PG and I both said he needed to be careful because Labour leaders out of office always get judged more harshly than the Tories. He needed to develop the concept of 'post-politics public life', but make clear the money he made was about delivering a different kind of public service in new ways.

Generally he seemed OK though was too thin again and a bit yellow. He was travelling non-stop. He said he had a number of countries he was talking to about advice on governance and they were always keen to know if I would be involved and advise on comms and strategy. He asked if I might get involved in Kazakhstan. Later I sent a pretty tough note to GB re the election handling and general positioning.

Home then off to Cheltenham to speak at the festival. Staying at the Hotel du Vin which was pretty funky. I had dinner with Susan Sandon, Richard and Charlotte Bush. They were pretty happy with the book. My event was at the racecourse, 2k-seater Centaur venue. Francine Stock was chairing/interviewing. Liked her, and the Q&A was fine though a bit predictable, dowdy and slow. I preferred the tougher questions or the funnier ones to the easy hits. The on/off election scene a disaster now. The polls all narrowed and GB was going to look either daft and opportunistic doing it, or weak and incompetent not doing it now. In the end only he

* In a clear break with Blair's law and order thinking, Children and Families Secretary Ed Balls made a speech in which he said the Blair initiative of anti-social behaviour orders (ASBOs) should 'be put behind us', while Straw criticised the effectiveness of laws on protection for 'have-a-go heroes'.

could decide but he had got himself into a right mess. I had started out totally against, had moved a bit but the 'let's see what the polls say after the Tories' conference' was the worst of all places.

I sent him a note, saying that it felt in a very bad place to me. Elections are big moments in the national life and there always has to be a good reason for them. Usually that is decided by the parliamentary timetable. For a snap election there has to be a fundamental choice that cannot otherwise be met. I don't believe the public understand what it is. Therefore they won't understand why we are having one. But the big problem was the briefing in the build-up. The sense of him poring over polls before a decision, and the unfortunate publicity arising in some quarters from the visit to British forces in Iraq, which looked exploitative and opportunistic, reinforces the sense this is putting party before national interest. I also thought it was unwise, if it was done, to respond to poll shifts by saying it was about inheritance tax.

I said that on the question 'Why are we having the election?', 'Because we think we can win' is the worst possible answer. So before going ahead two questions have to have very clear answers. Why are we having an election now (and the answers have to be about policy). And can we deliver a bigger majority? The second is important because if he has an election and the result is roughly the same, or a smaller majority, people really will wonder why they were put through it. It will really weaken him as PM on return, especially taking into account the big drop in seats already.

The question of the policy choice is central here. The problem with conference is that people didn't get a sense of the big forward policy agenda that would fill a manifesto and give the country a big choice to make. I said that unless it is being held very tightly 'this seems to me your central problem'. It is one thing to go to a 'normal time' election relatively policy light, or steady as she goes. You can't do it in a snap election. And the polls did not exactly indicate a big swing in his favour was coming. I was partly doing my 'think in ink' thing and settled on the fact that he would take a big hit for not doing it, but it must be the point at which they regroup, focus on policy and the long term and a different strategic framework to the one that seems to have been in operation in the past couple of weeks.

> The reason I have been uncomfortable re this early election is because of this – if your strength is strength, substance and the long term, this cuts right across it. It looks tactical and selfish, not strategic and thought through. And without the policy dividing lines strong and in the right place, there is a risk the campaign dynamic runs away from you. There are two other points I want to make. I felt at conference that there was a sense that we were accepting the last ten years had not been successful.

This is a big mistake. Go around the world, and parties left and right look to us as a success story, politically, economically, socially. The party needs us to defend the record better. So does the public. We need to show more fight on this. This is vital if we are properly to exploit the superb strategic position you have the capacity to exploit – as being continuity and change. And the change needs to be more than about character.

I felt the conference speech focused insufficiently on policy and big challenges facing the world and was too much about the character question. It felt Clinton–Gore and I really believe that approach of differentiation vis-à-vis the predecessor was a mistake for Gore and would be for you. You have character as a strength, record and substance. That is all part of continuity. The change has to come in the way you frame challenges and the way you provide policy responses. That, not polls, has to be dominant in all the debates.

If you go ahead, there has to be a really strong explanation. And it has to be rooted in policy. But all things considered, the way this thing has developed, I think you will be better off taking the hit, cutting down any chatter about it, not playing the blame game, simply saying that while some may want an election, the government has a forward programme, intends to keep taking it forward, and will prepare in a more considered long-term way the policy challenges for the next election further down the track. I know these are difficult decisions that in the end can only be made by one person, and that conflicting advice is not always welcome. But I really do feel this is in the wrong place, and an election is a dangerous place to be without all the questions clearly answered.

Sunday 7 October

GB was on Marr. Car crash. He basically said he had never been thinking about having an election. It was not convincing on any level because it was so far from what people knew to be true. This is where he just lacked that bit of finesse. It would be far better to say something closer to truth – I have thought about it, I was being pressed in some quarters, there are certain temptations, but I have decided not to. He could also have said that he should have avoided the speculation, but in any event this is now the focus and on we go. TB called and said the whole thing was a disaster now, and they would be scrabbling around on the blame game. He said there has to be a gripping of his operation and there has to be an explanation to the party what really went wrong and how we can still rebuild if we learn the lessons. He said he was intending to write a note to GB and he wanted to run it by me. His first point was that there had been a truly lamentable confusion of tactics and strategy. Tactically, it was thought clever to define by reference to TB, no more spin, no more sleaze, we will be honest, frugal (subtext: they weren't).

This was all about style, but strategically the consequence was to diss our own record, and instead of saying we are building on the achievements, confronting the new challenges, we joined in the attack on our own ten years. He was banging the same drum I had been banging with GB, that unless we correct this it could be a fatal mistake. Secondly, because they are disowning us as a government, they have junked the TB policy agenda but had nothing to put in its place. All of that has helped nobody but our opponents. He said the media were going on about how well the Tories did at their conference, but the real problem was the hubris and vacuity of our own. This then meant that the Tories didn't have to be great to be considered good. And by having at least something to say on policy they appeared substantial and able to represent the future. He said we somehow had to persuade GB to go back and recalibrate the strategy, based on a defence of our own record and a policy agenda that forces the Tories to choose – exactly what the policy review was supposed to achieve.

He said GB's own briefing operation had helped the Tories get even more from [shadow Chancellor George] Osborne's inheritance tax move than they would have got anyway.* Cameron was actually in a bit of trouble before TB left, but that was because he was being forced to choose on New Labour policy and found as a result that he couldn't differentiate properly. He felt GB trying to give a different message was also a mistake. He never needed to worry about distancing on Iraq – it was never going to be seen as his issue; but on domestic policy he really needed to be seen as continuing New Labour not ditching it. By trying to be change, he played exactly the game the media wanted, but it is not the game that gives us the only chance of a fourth term. Meanwhile Douglas told PG that there was a big discussion going on about me, with GB keen to get me more involved, possibly centrally, and Balls arguing against. I had a real sense of foreboding about the strategic picture and how bad it could get quite quickly. Both the Tories and the media were piling in pretty hard.

Monday 8 October

First thing I recorded a whole stack of Middle East interviews pre the trip to Dubai. Then out for a bike ride, and I missed GB's press conference where he seemingly got a bit of a mauling. Then his Iraq statement where he announced a reduction of British troops and got hit hard there

* At his party conference, Osborne had announced that a Tory government would raise the inheritance tax threshold from £300,000 to £1 million, at a cost of £3.1 billion.

too. It was obvious he needed a lot of help. I was not feeling like giving it but part of me was. I could sense for the first time he could actually lose an overall majority to the Tories. Classic confusion of tactics and strategy almost from the word go. I had lunch with Tim Hincks [Endemol media company] who had the idea of a programme in which I try to galvanise dads and sons in a tough school and get them to develop proper relationships. More interesting than most. Spoke to Calum about it. He was still not enjoying Manchester.

Tuesday 9 October

Alex called from France where he was having a few days off during the international break. He had finished my book and said if it didn't win Book of the Year, there was no justice. I said there was no way that was going to happen, partly because it was me, partly because it was not the whole story, and I had admitted as much. He said the last sections on Iraq and my departure were riveting. 'Even though I knew what happened already, it was like reading a thriller.' He shared my alarm about the recent GB kerfuffle, said it had come over as very amateurish and cack-handed. I found myself being more open about my criticisms though still not publicly. It was not possible to defend recent events and retain credibility though. PG said again Balls was the one keeping everyone else out.

Trying to pin down Bill Hagerty as diaries editor. Then to speak at a lunch for US correspondents in London. I found myself being fairly frank on strategy and tactics being confused in last few days. Then to see Nick Goddard, orthopaedic surgeon, who diagnosed an inflamed tendon on the Achilles, which would need ultrasound and rest. From there to Merchant Taylors' for Brewin Dolphin event. 500, mainly men, mainly Tory I would say, but did usual speech and good Q&A and felt pretty well. Again did why GB should not have let the election chat get out of hand. PG called, said GB's lot were still struggling to work it out. He said he had been shocked last week by how little there was there, how they felt it was all going to go to shit, how they blamed each other the whole time etc.

Wednesday 10 October

Darling and GB were getting hit pretty hard re stealing Tory ideas on inheritance and aviation tax.* My complaint was that it was going to give

* In his pre-Budget Report, Darling announced plans to double the inheritance tax threshold for couples to £600,000 and to make airlines rather than passengers responsible for green taxes. The Tories claimed both policies were stolen from their party conference.

DC and Osborne credibility they didn't deserve. GB was on a really bad roll – election on/off, hammered over dithering and trust, mistake to do it on Marr not all round, press conference not honest, Iraq statement not clear, CSR [Comprehensive Spending Review] not great and today PMQs a real monstering. I saw David S who felt I was doing OK and it was fine not to be rushing into things. I was in a very privileged position then and now, and there was no need to apologise for that or feel guilty about not wanting to do more. I had arranged to meet Piers at the Honest Sausage café in Regent's Park – he liked that idea – but he couldn't find it so we went to the café in the inner circle instead. He said he wanted to say we were at the Honest Sausage even if we weren't. Lots of his questions were about lying, and of course he wanted a ding-dong about Iraq. We had a good natter though and even though he was so self-obsessed, it was hard not to like him. He managed to stay positive whatever was happening around him.

I worked on a piece on the arrogance of the All Blacks for the *Sunday Times*, then to the Ian Botham knighthood investiture party at Lord's [cricket ground]. He and Kath [wife] in good form. Good turnout. Mike Brearley, Graeme Fowler, Mike Gatting, Brian Close, Freddie Flintoff [cricketers]. Nice do, a few little speeches. Really nice time. Left for Cardiff, another ludicrously lucrative speaking gig. I wish I could persuade myself it was work. David Miliband called as I was getting driven home. I said if GB didn't learn the right lessons, Cameron was in. He said the press conference, the CSR and PMQs suggested they were not learning the right lessons at all.

Thursday 11 October

The GB situation was not good, and there was not much sign he was getting out of it. Cameron was on a roll. Charlotte [Random House] called to say the *Standard* were doing a piece saying I was badly depressed. Hard to deny it. Quiet day, long bike ride, then to ultrasound scan of Achilles. The doctor also did Arsenal players and was going on about how badly some of them treated their wives. He said the Achilles tissue was degenerating and I was definitely not to run till it was sorted. He felt physio ought to do it but it might need surgery. I didn't like the sound of that.

Friday 12 October

Out first thing to do an interview for a documentary on Seth Lakeman. Seth had asked if I would do it, which was fine, though the interviewer was treating me as though I was an expert on folk. Then to WC1 for a photoshoot with David Bailey [celebrity photographer] for *GQ*. The studio was unchanged since last time, and so was he. Three male assistants. Wife there, tall and striking, pictures of her breasts on the wall and in a little book of ideas. He said he had worn women out. He said to his assistant, who had a Jesus beard, 'What are the five words I always say to women – what do you mean no?' The bloke from *GQ* arrived. Very *GQ*. Tight jeans and pointed shoes, tall and dark. When he said the pictures were to illustrate an interview with Piers Morgan, Bailey (as they all called him) asked 'Who the fuck is Piers Morgan?' I think he's a chef, said Mrs B. I texted the exchange to Piers. When the phone pinged with a text a few minutes later, I said 'I bet that's Piers and I bet it says "Who is David Bailey?"' Spot on.

Bailey was a jumble of opinions, most of them a bit ill-formed and incoherent and like a lot of media people driven as much by how people treated him as what they actually did. Likes Boris [Johnson], hates Ken [Livingstone]. Doesn't know how Tony can sleep at night because he lied about Iraq. 'No, he didn't.' 'Yes, he fucking did and you know he did.' 'No, I don't.' [Tony] Benn a good bloke but you wouldn't want him running anything. Had [Lord] Norman Foster [architect] yesterday who said he was in a bit of a rush because he had to see the Queen. Told the story of bumping into King Abdullah of Jordan and not realising he was the King. Liked Keith Richards [Rolling Stones musician]. Referred to Diana as 'the blonde chick'. He said people never understood what other people did. I didn't understand what he did, he didn't understand what I did. He was very tactile and funny. It was all a lot easier than last time when I was with Joe Haines for a *Times* piece on protégés, and Bailey kept asking if we were gay. All over in just over an hour.

TB texted and I said it was a total mess. He said all recoverable with the right strategy. I texted Neil to say if GB didn't learn the right lessons Cameron was in. 'What are they?' he asked. I said it has to be continuity plus change. If it is just change he gains nothing from the record. He has to defend the record and position himself against Cameron not TB. He has to realise Balls has poor strategic judgement and Shrum doesn't understand Britain. Neil added he has to trust own instinct, not the advice of people who have only known success. Chat with Charlie F who said 'You sound angry.' I was angry at the self-inflicted nature of it all.

Saturday 13 October

Bike a.m. Big day of spectator sport. Scotland v Ukraine. England v Estonia [football]. Leeds v St Helens grand final. England v Sri Lanka ODI then England v France Rugby World Cup semi. England win over France impressive. I texted some of the Lions guys and got some nice replies.

Sunday 14 October

I was really missing running though enjoying getting out on the bike more. The GB situation was not really improving. I was not sure he or they had it. Cameron is tougher than they imagine. TB texted to say let's have a chat. I said I found it all very depressing and all so avoidable. Predictable too, he said. Recoverable if they adopt the right strategy but don't hold your breath. Some of the Sundays had stories about TB being disappointed with GB so far and he put out a statement denying. The trouble was that people would know he would be disappointed so it wasn't the hardest story to write. TB even wondered if the GB lot had been behind it, based on the note he sent him, because it allowed them to go into victim mode. Tessa's 60th at the Wards' in Gray's Inn. David [Mills, husband] seemed a bit out of sorts.

Monday 15 October

Chat with TB. He said he would be willing to help but they want to do it on their own. GB's problem is personal – he wants not only to show he can do it without us, he wants to establish that he not I should have been leader in '94. It is tragic. And of course he has bad advice from Balls and Shrum going in his ears 24/7. They basically live with him. Shrum's name came up the other day at a meeting and Henry Kissinger [former US Secretary of State] said the guy is all tactics and no strategy. TB felt GB was being rumbled by the public. It was one of the myths we created that GB was the ideas man and the strategist, he was the front man and I did the media. Truth be told he was good when he was given the strategy but he had to be directed. And now he was on his own, he didn't really have the vision. Charlie F had fucked up a bit with an article on *Times* online which was taken as a whack at GB. TB said we are all best saying nothing, certainly nothing that can be taken as unsupportive. It is in our interests he succeeds and at some point he is going to realise he needs to change tack. He said he was only really OK when he was out of the country because it made him so frustrated to see them fucking up.

Into BBC for a pre-record of Steve Wright [afternoon presenter]. It was OK, and I like Steve a lot, but I could feel myself slightly going through the motions with these book interviews. He said he became fed up with TB towards the end. He tried to get me to join the Blairites going publicly for GB but failed. Home then out later to White City for *The One Show* with Adrian Chiles and very nice Northern Irish girl called Christine Bleakley. They wanted me to play the pipes, so I warmed them up beforehand, then when we went on, they had weighing scales, weighing my book alongside the complete works of Shakespeare, Thatcher's and then Adrian's book.

Ming [Menzies] Campbell [Liberal Democrats leader] resigned just before we went on air – the Lib Dems were going nowhere just now – so I did a short reaction on that. He was basically forced out though he seemingly felt it was media obsession with his age that became the deciding factor.

Tuesday 16 October

Out first thing to Liverpool St then Colchester for a book signing at TBS Random House warehouse. About 2,000 books, real military operation. They had Nigella [Lawson, celebrity chef and author] yesterday. Interesting mix of people. I was reading [former Burnley player] Martin Dobson's novel about two kids who get to Wembley. The design was a bit of a car crash and the writing was clichéd but I promised to read it and I did and I was sure I could get a piece on it with him somewhere. I was getting very down at the thought of Calum being miserable.

Wednesday 17 October

DS – mainly talking re Calum and whether he was trying to make us make the decision for him that he should leave. To Random House to sign some books. Briefly saw Susan S who was buzzing at one of their books [*The Gathering* by Anne Enright] winning the Booker Prize last night. Then to Sky, signing loads of stuff on the way. Nice crowd at the Book Show. Sophie Dahl [model and author] said her mum [writer Tessa Dahl] remembered sitting next to me at a Chequers dinner to raise money for the Roald Dahl Museum. Liked her, chatted re her – 5 ft 11 – going out with Jamie Cullum [jazz singer] who can't be much more than 5 ft 5. Also re how she had too much to drink last night. She had chosen *Tender Is the Night* [F. Scott Fitzgerald] as her book she wished she had written. I chose *Team of Rivals* re Lincoln. Nice little programme, one of Prebble's. Fiona had bad conjunctivitis, was really miserable with it.

Thursday 18 October

Train to Manchester, for a speech to Modus, [Burnley director] Brendan Flood's firm. Good laugh on the way because a woman down the carriage was reading something called 'Modus Daily', a paper with me on the front. She was clearly going to my event at Modus as the paper was like an invite. I texted Brendan and asked who she might be. Describe her. 'Early forties, slim, brown hair, no wedding ring.' Jill Hagland he said. I asked for her mobile number. She had the *Mail* so I texted her a message to say reading the *Mail* was bad for her health. She looked really startled.

I then sent another one saying did she want a lift and when she started to look around she saw me, a bit shell-shocked. She couldn't believe I knew her name, had her number, knew where she was going. Explained in car.

Nice enough do, and quite lively Q&A though they had a crap set of pipes for me to try and I could barely get a note out of them. Signed a few books. Collected Calum then Ellen Flood [wife of Brendan] then off to the YPO [Young Professionals, meet-up group] dinner. Good bunch. I did get a bit ratty with a couple at the end, told one bloke he sounded like a *Mail* editorial. Nice chat with Brendan who struck me as genuinely committed to BFC. He said at his first board meeting they had talked about slashing the wages bill and he said he would not have anything to do with mediocrity so put in more of his cash.

Friday 19 October

Breakfast with Brendan, then a car to Piccadilly to meet Martin Dobson to interview him for his book. He still walked elegantly. We sat up on the balcony café, nice Croatian snapper from an agency in Birmingham doing the pictures. Dobbo a lovely guy, happy with his lot, good on old players, not bitter at all about the wealth of the new players, very positive about the book experience. I wrote the piece on the train. Home for a bit before Fiona and Grace set off for the US to see Suzanne [Gibbons-Neff, friend of Fiona]. To RUSI in Whitehall for filming for a Michael Cockerell documentary with Tim Bell and Tim Razzall [Tory and Lib Dem strategists]. We watched fifteen or so clips of Cameron and then talked about them. My main point was that he was technically good at presentation but there was no policy. Tim Bell said they wouldn't do policy. And why should they, especially now it was clear Labour would steal them? I quite enjoyed it as an exercise. Audrey was looking after me in F's absence. She was reading a big review of Robert Harris's book *The Ghost* in *New Statesman* and particularly enjoyed a reference from a piece by Harris making him and me sound chummy on the '97 campaign bus, and my diary saying he was the last thing we needed on the bus recording every spit and fart.

Saturday 20 October

Set off for Barnsley v Burnley. Huge build-up to Rugby World Cup final on the radio. Took bike with me and had an hour or so round Barnsley then met Calum. Fiona called. Leo Blair and Jackie [nanny] were on the plane out. TB–CB in NY at Waldorf Astoria. Calum seemed happier. Burnley were terrific in the first half but only one up and we got pulled back.

Sunday 21 October

Long bike ride. Text from TB about the *Mail on Sunday* stuff from Anthony Seldon's book which was being spun as Blairites rocking the GB boat. [Lord] Roy Hattersley [Labour peer] on Marr was reviewing the papers and pushing it that way. TB said it showed again how they seem to enjoy the victim mode. Took Audrey for dinner at Philip and Gail's. PG very down on GB. Peter M texted him to say he was having a party next weekend. No chance of me being invited because Reinaldo [PM's partner] thought I defenestrated PM. Had a discussion about who were the biggest human brands of all time. Agreed on Jesus and Mohammed but then it all got a bit tricky. Philip and Georgia didn't want to accept Hitler was a brand because nobody bought into it. I said Shakespeare had to be in there. Gandhi. Ali? Luther King. Mao. Marx. So it went on. PG googled them all to see how many mentions as if that was the judgement. George Bush highest of current people.

Monday 22 October

Woke up after long and vivid dream in which GB and I were having a really heated exchange. TB there, Fiona, Philip and Gail. GB was asking why I was intending to do more books. I said why did he worry about things that would not happen while he was PM. Why didn't he get himself a proper strategy? I said he asked all these questions because he imagined we operated like he did, selfish, always undermining, no team spirit. If only he learned the real lessons of the TB era he would not be in such a mess. Got really heavy at points, both ways.

The Lib Dem leadership was getting a fair bit of play but largely on the theme of there being no difference between [Chris] Huhne and [Nick] Clegg [candidates]. Huhne so unutterably dull. Clegg seemed Tory-lite but probably going to win. GB seemed to have managed to quieten things down after the EU summit in Lisbon but the issue was still not going away. [Anthony] Seldon's book* rumbling at low level. Heaven knows why people co-operated with him. All the usual anonymous stuff but of course grains of truth in there. Focus building on Balls. I didn't much fancy his chances of surviving really intense pressure. Out for an hour on the bike and then a chocolate binge. Felt bad afterwards but real gorge. To Oxford for Rory's birthday. Grace and Georgia on good form. Browns restaurant. Nice time.

* *Blair's Britain, 1997–2007*

Tuesday 23 October

Out to Stuart Prebble's office for a meeting with BBC. He and I had a pre-meeting to go through a few ideas, including on sport, the theme of winning etc. Extraordinary beginning to the meeting, the two BBC guys bemoaning life there, the way it was led, programming, response to technological change and so on, but like it was the only discussion on earth. They asked my view – I said the BBC had lost its way, didn't have a defined mission or purpose and had become bloated, introverted and arrogant. The discussion underlined that. We kicked around the idea of me doing some kind of programme or series in which I examine the big public issues. The woman said I was one of the few people in politics that young people thought reasonably cool. 'My son would talk to you, but wouldn't talk to most politicians.' We groped our way towards the idea of me having a team of young people and trying to galvanise, lead and educate them to make a difference in small limited ways, changing the law, getting someone to do something. Good meeting though I found these telly people so self-obsessed and obsessed with their own world.

Home and out for a long bike ride. News from the heel scan was an inflamed tendon. Rest and physio required but hopefully cycling OK, though it was starting to get really cold. Audrey was out at a No. 11 reception for Vital Voices [women's political participation organisation] and came back nicely merry before making me dinner and regaling me with stories of who was there – Magi Cleaver [No. 10 press officer] saying everything went downhill after I left.

Wednesday 24 October

Session with DS. He was very keen on getting me to a croft and total isolation. Also chatted about the circumstances in which I was tempted to drink. Out on the bike, hills, then to Gay Hussar to meet Joe Haines and Jill Palmer [former *Daily Mirror* colleagues]. Joe had lost a couple of top teeth and had a few more mottled marks on his face but was on good form. Jill also looking good having lost a lot of weight. Ed Owen [Labour advisor] arrived to get some books signed. Jill had one. Then John [Wrobel] from the restaurant had one, then his waitress went off and bought one. Told Susan Sandon I should just live in restaurants. Joe and Jill both very down on GB. Joe had always been dubious but felt he lacked courage. He said if I was in a trench I would rather be with Blair than Brown. Jill said he just lacked the personality you needed. When Sarah [Brown] helped get Jill's daughter work experience at the Treasury, she bumped into GB, asked him a question for her dissertation and he talked to her like a weight machine. Nice enough time. Stayed till gone three.

Bumped into the Miami Dolphins coaches (in town for the first ever NFL match, at Wembley at the weekend) as I was contacting art colleges about getting a sculpture of the kids for F's birthday. Met Nancy [Dell'Olio, ex-partner of former England manager Sven-Göran Eriksson] at 6 at Home House [private members' club]. She had been doing a photo shoot all day. Looking good. Flirty as ever, said she had never really found a man in England worth having an affair with. 'You and Tony seemed taken.' She and Sven had basically split up but he was holding on. She said she didn't mind as much as people might think to Sven's sex-with-others thing but it had become a bit embarrassing. Hard to understand her at times. She was another one very down on GB. The general line – that he was doing OK, better than expected – had gone right back. Walked to Claridge's to meet Stuart Le Gassick [businessman]. We went to Brian Turner's restaurant at the Millennium Hotel. Young woman with enormous breasts at next table. She went out for a fag. When she came back he said they say smoking's bad for your chest. Not done you any harm. Stuart was just back from Dubai having got 20 billion for an infrastructure investment in India. Clearly major league now. I was resisting getting involved or taking money. Nice enough evening though.

Thursday 25 October

My Google news alert had a good one, a book review from Seattle-based TheStranger.com. 'This book will get you laid' was the headline. Very funny and by and large favourable review. Waited a.m. for F and G to get back from the airport. Clearly had a great time. I took Grace out to the stables and went out on the bike from there. The political news was dominated by another GB chattering-class speech on bill of rights, democracy etc., all well and good but unlikely to set the heart skipping on the estates. Worse though, he had appointed Paul Dacre [editor, *Daily Mail*] to be part of a review of the thirty-year rules [legal arrangements re availability to the public of official records]. Both TB and I thought it was a joke when we first heard it. Philip said it was beyond parody. Bradders, who had been helping a bit on PMQs, said there is no tent big enough for us and Dacre. Hilary Coffman [former press advisor in AC team] – 'Words fail me.' And so on. I thought about sending a message to the effect that it was shame Harold Shipman was dead as he could do a review of the GMC. I had yet another dream in which I was hiding as GB, Clinton and Gore were in a field or a garden looking for me. Mark Lucas popped round to deliver some DVDs, and chat about things. The non-election week was a nightmare, he said. He said at least you lot tended to know what you wanted. He was working on a broadcast for the Queen's Speech and had basically been told to do what he wanted.

JP called for a natter. He was progressing on the book with Hunter Davies who had done twenty chapters. He also had some speeches lined up. Said he was pretty happy with his lot. Appalled at the events of recent weeks. He had bumped into Balls and DA in the lobby last week and said are you two going to cock it up again? They produced a poll saying they had gone up two points. He said forget polls and start governing. Nice chat, asking for help on his speech. Out later to Ernst and Young dinner at Royal Horticultural Society. All accountants at a conference today. Pretty dull bunch but I splattered a guy at the end who asked a clever-clever question about when the book would be remaindered. Susan called and later TB texted re him doing book deal with RH and Knopf. I said she had to make sure mine remained No. 1 priority. TB said he couldn't believe the Dacre move. It is not the disloyalty but the stupidity. GB has basically inhaled the critique that we are all spin, sleaze and no delivery and so weakens himself.

Friday 26 October

Out early to the airport. Terminal 2 pretty chaotic but how on earth they manage that steady flow of anxious, agitated, selfish humanity is beyond me. All stressing about the same things. First experience of Emirates. Pretty good. Watched the film about Graeme Obree [bipolar cyclist], *The Flying Scotsman*, which I don't think played up his mental issues enough but it was OK. The cycling parts really quite moving and needless to say I cried when he won the world champs. Stupidly I'd come without my case studies for the conference and Fiona had to sort by email. Working on my presentation for Dubai. Going to be literally all day, 9 to 5, blathering away. Arrived, met by Jennie Bishop from II RME [Middle East management company] who were doing the conference. Nice enough though I never naturally warmed to expats in places like this. Staying at Mina a Salam, part of the huge Jumeirah Beach complex. Someone had said Dubai hit you a bit like Las Vegas and I saw what they meant. Sea nice, great gym but too many *Mail*-reading type Brits around. Didn't venture out of the complex, went for a longish run on the beach and then the gym and worked on the speech while channel hopping.

Saturday 27 October

Out for an on-the-record breakfast with a group of English-language journalists from the region. Some of the Arabs invited never turned up. Jennie said it was par for the course. Quite an interesting bunch. Usual questions – media, GB, TB in Middle East role, Iraq. There had definitely been a shift in opinion re GB though. One of them said they had been surprised he started well and not surprised at all it was going a bit wrong. *Gulf News* guy a very posh Brit who was formerly editor. They were interesting on the way Dubai was developing. There was fairly strict media control, mostly self-censorship. Criticism of the leaders totally off limits but TV and the internet was beginning to change things a little. Remarkable the extent to which they felt things worked. No crime worth the name. Big issue was the treatment of migrant workers and it was a real issue they would have to address. Quite a good session though it was odd the extent to which they talked to me as though I was still fully engaged. Conference team all in cheap grey suits and red tops. Pretty professional though. Had no doubts tomorrow would work. Had felt a mild pang of guilt at earning 25k for a day's talk but then saw they were charging delegates $1,600 a head to hear it, with a free book thrown in.

Back to the hotel and time to kill. Exercise, a bit of wandering, emailing and waiting for John Watts to arrive. Also trying to find a bar that would be showing Burnley v Southampton. Interesting collection of people in the hotel. A mix of aspirant Brits, mainly obese, nouveau riche Russians, a few Germans and French. The souk was like any other shopping set-up. Felt about as genuinely Arabian as Brent Cross. Nice to see John Watts [former advisor to TB] who was working for Brown Loyd James [PR company] in Doha. Glad to be out of No. 10. Said he was there during the crazy week and it was beyond crazy. Not working that hard but enjoying it for a year or two. Good people-watching as we sat at a Persian restaurant, part of the complex, and watched all the obvious Brits and Russians go by. Great picture to be had of an Arab in full gear sitting at the bar knocking back a pint of lager. Went on the hunt for BFC on TV and eventually found it at Dhow and Anchor bar in Jumeirah Beach hotel. Poor game and we lost 3–2. Only saw second half.

Sunday 28 October

Breakfast in hotel, most of the tourists thankfully not up. To the conference centre where delegates were gathering and it all seemed pretty well organised. Mix of Anglo Saxon and regional, from most countries in the region. They did my CD then I spoke for maybe ninety minutes, very big picture and basics. Q&A pretty straightforward. Frank Kane [ex-*Observer*] asked whether Kamal Ahmed [*Observer*] helped re the second Iraq dossier. Used it to deny and also talk about media self-obsession. Did a coffee break, signed a few books. Split them into eight groups and set them a strategic challenge based round objective, strategy and tactics mantra. Anti-global warming, pro, pro-TB as MEPP rep, anti, Dubai, mend Bush image in Middle East, etc. They did pretty well, particularly when led by Brits.

Couple of PalmPilot quiz surveys e.g. re who best communicator – it went Bill C, TB, Nelson Mandela then [Vladimir] Putin [President of Russia] and Bush with nul points. Also how many crises we had, which they did pretty well. Mind you, one of the earlier ones was a choice, including John and Mohammed, of most popular first name in the world and 4 per cent said Alastair. Lunch with a group of them outside and then to pm session on crisis management. Did my spiel, Q&A and felt on form and the evaluation feedback was really strong. More books selling through the day. Then a head-hunter, Omar Kahn, asked for help in finding 'an AC figure' for the government there. Package $1 million tax-free. He didn't ask directly whether I would do it but I sensed it was what he was getting at. The girl from Jumeirah and a woman from Bahrain said it was their best day of education on comms ever. Good atmosphere at the end. Went for a swim. Legs exhausted after being on feet all day.

Dinner at a Moroccan restaurant in the souk. Colleen Harris [ex Prince Charles advisor] setting up her own business, Dignity, advising companies on equality and diversity etc. Told Colleen the background to the royal bits of the book, and how they had raised no objections of the version they saw, and she said 'They're scared of you.' She felt they would have imagined all the terrible things I could have said and so were relieved but also would have worried about trying to get me to change anything and have a great row about it. Nice enough evening though I was glad to get to bed. I really wished I could count this all as work. It was well paid and maybe today I did manage to teach a few people a few things but I still can't see it as work. It is earning not work. Good row with Colleen re the PCC [Press Complaints Commission], how useless it was, and how [Sir Christopher] Meyer [chairman] was compromised by his serialisation deal (for his memoirs) with the Mail Group.

Monday 29 October

Out to the airport. Jim Davidson [comedian], who was resident in Dubai, had a word in the lounge. Davidson so right-wing but said when he went to entertain the troops in Basra some of the locals thought he was TB. On the plane I watched *Amazing Grace*, the story of Wilberforce's anti-slave trade campaign and again had a sense that I was wasting some of the best years of my life just swanning around playing at different bits and pieces. Starting to think about the [late (Lord) Hugh] Cudlipp [former Mirror Group chairman] lecture but I was wanting to move away from the whole media scene. My piece on Martin Dobson appeared and got a good reaction. He said his phone didn't stop ringing. I got a stack of messages, mainly people either remembering him as a player or saying how inspired they were to see him saying he had no regrets or resentment at today's players. Fiona out for dinner at Carole Caplin's with Carole and Lyndsey, CB's sister. David Miliband called having gone to the US and now had adopted the second child, Jacob. It was all made part of the story about the Saudi King visit to London, people claiming it was a bit of a diplomatic incident that he wasn't there. All just an excuse to get the personal story into the political mix.

Tuesday 30 October

Ed [Victor] called to say he felt either late November or early January I should commit to and do another book deal. Did a list of the options – winning book with Alex. Guide to crisis management. Depression. Maybe make five days in David S's so-called croft the subject of a book. Novel, either the psychiatrist story or maybe the croft. Fiona thought winning or guide to the media, strategy, crisis management. Dealing with emails and the odd bit of work but it was all pretty drifty.

Wednesday 31 October

David S. Like a couple of old friends talking in a pub. I said I wondered about doing the croft as a book, writing the whole time I was there. He said that would keep the demons at bay rather than confront them. The demons – and angels – were in there. We didn't know what they were. The purpose of total isolation was to bring them out. He said I was in the position where habit and public interest had forced me to construct a shield of armour. It was necessary to keep people out. But maybe it stopped good things from coming in. Interesting thought. Went to Battersea with Calum to let Kirsty Tinkler [sculptor] take a look at him. I had had this idea of a three-faced sculpture – with all three kids' faces on it – for Fiona's birthday present. Thirty-six-year-old Aussie, very nice and seemed to know what she was doing. She measured Calum's features and took a few snaps. They were in makeshift studios while the usual place over the road was refurbished but it was a nice enough atmosphere. Quite a few odd looks from the people in there.

Got a phone call from Joe Hemani [vice-president, Chelsea FC] who said he really liked my piece on Martin Dobson and had today ordered 100 books. He intended to keep one and give ninety-nine to Burnley to sell in the club shop. He said he didn't have a regular charity so he gave out money on impulse and this seemed a good cause because he was such a good player. Nice chat. Met Martin Sheehan and Emily Hands [No. 10 press officer] for tea at St Ermin's Hotel. Things seemed pretty grim in

No. 10. They said it was absolutely day to day. A week was about as far forward as anyone ever thought. Even GB's Praetorian Guard rolled their eyes at some of his characteristics. Emily said she had been reading all my stuff from years ago, memos etc., and it was of a different quality to the work these guys did. Nobody had a grip at all. She felt the problem was his personality and the fact he surrounded himself with like-minded people. Sounded pretty crap all round. To Labour HQ meeting to get involved in planning for another sports fundraiser. Starting to head for a major plunge. Also starting to think seriously re novel idea. Helle [Danish politician, wife of Neil Kinnock's son, Stephen] called, halfway through the campaign in Denmark. She sounded pretty chirpy. She wanted TB and me to put a few nice words on her blog site.

Thursday 1 November

Bit of work then to St Bride's for [*Mirror* photographer] Alisdair Macdonald's memorial service. It was a nice do and captured a lot of what he was about. I did a short preamble to the reading of the Wordsworth poem 'Composed upon Westminster Bridge'. Three parts – *Mirror, Today* [newspaper] and his later career when he seemed to spend most of his time doorstepping Downing Street. Good do afterwards as well. Nice to see all the old *Mirror* snappers. Lovely messages from his widow and daughter Helen afterwards. Train to Norwich with a bit of work then met by Charles and Carol Clarke. Charles [former Home Secretary] even bigger than ever. Even more pessimistic than I was about the political scene. He felt it was fairly clear what GB needed to do to get a strategy together but he didn't believe he could do it. Felt that he had been sussed out. His view was that he was never a strategist. He joked that he assumed it had been part of our strategy for making TB look good to get GB to follow him. He wanted advice on whether to accept an unpaid position dealing with deportation of foreign prisoners.* But he felt the whole thing felt really flaky.

All he heard from inside the government machine was bad. He didn't think DM was making any impact. He felt Jacqui Smith was OK. But by and large it was a bad scene and that was because GB didn't have a clue what he wanted to do with the job. Carol was even more scathing. Felt TB had been terrific and the party was now making a hash of things. Charles said he hadn't spoken to Neil K for ages. Felt he and Glenys had both

* In April 2006 it became known that 1,023 foreign prisoners had been freed without being considered for deportation. Clarke offered to resign as Home Secretary as criticism of him mounted, but following Labour's poor performance in the May local elections he was removed in a Cabinet reshuffle.

been too pro-GB in the build-up to the transition. Also that when CC had been speaking out a bit, GB had used Neil in a very heavy-handed way to rein him in. We set off for the event and first of all a mini tour of the city centre which was impressive. The party event at the meeting rooms was small and select, 35 quid a head plus book signing. First of its kind as a way of raising funds just for his seat. Nice crowd including [Lord] Alan Howarth and [Baroness] Patricia Hollis who was very down on our chances. Alan felt, genuinely, that I had been too soft in what I said about the media. Maybe had a point. Generally good questions but definitely a shift in mood on GB. Over to the Marble Halls for the RBS [Royal Bank of Scotland] event. Felt on form both in opening and Q&A. Some days did better than others but even on good days I couldn't really say it was work.

Saturday 3 November

A second rest day. Heel hurting again after physio yesterday. Donald was down for the London Piping tournament. Calum went with them while Rory and I set off for the Emirates for Arsenal v Man U [2–2]. Long chat on arrival with Mary Parkinson, [former Tory Cabinet minister] Cecil's daughter. She said he and her mum recently celebrated their golden wedding. She had not touched drugs for sixteen years and was now teaching yoga. A massive United fan, season ticket holder. Lots of 'Burnley not playing here' comments from fans, especially Arsenal. Good match but Alex would be livid at losing the lead so late. Off to Kensington for the piping, Donald and his pal Davie saying I should take up competitive piping again. Round to see the Milibands and the new baby. Briefly chatted about politics, DM saying it was bad in there, that nobody had a real sense of what the GB strategy was. He said it felt like a hung parliament. I said unless he got a grip it could go the whole way. The Tories don't need that much.

Monday 5 November

I had been mulling over the idea of a novel about a psychiatrist and his patients and out on the bike, going past a funeral at Golders Green Crematorium, I got the inspiration I needed. I had no idea whose it was but imagined it was a shrink and his family were taken aback by all the people there they had never met, his patients down the years. It was enough to get me going. I got into it pretty quickly and even as I started the plot started to evolve in ways I hadn't planned, for example make him (the psychiatrist) one of the key depressives. I probably managed to get 10,000 words done and started to sketch out a handful of different characters.

Tuesday 6 November

Queen's Speech day and I felt totally divorced from it. Off early and met Greg Nugent [Eurostar] for a coffee. Today was also the day the Queen was officially opening St Pancras. The build-up had been terrific though he said the egos and politics attached to the whole thing were pretty grim. But he struck me as a good bloke doing a good job. I was working on the novel any spare moment I could find, so the train journey to Brussels was productive. I was wondering whether I could call it 'Psychological Flaws'. Felt it was coming on OK, though very different to how I had mapped it out when the idea was percolating. Off to Brussels, bumped into Ian Hargreaves [former editor, *New Statesman*] both ends of the journey. Now at Ofcom. Chatted re BBC. Arrogance now really hurting them. No sense of what they were for. Met John Grant, now out of FCO and working for Aussie mining company. He had just had lunch with Kim Darroch [senior civil servant] and said they were full of stories re GB's people just looking frazzled, frenetic and out of their depth. Grace was on a real kick about wanting to go to school in the US. Calum was at Burnley v Hull. Lost 1–0 in last minute and he said it was the worst game he had ever seen.

Thursday 8 November

Out early for Will Greenwood [former rugby player] testimonial event at the IMAX, mainly business and PR professionals. Well organised, did my usual spiel and then was on pretty good form for the Q&A. Good range. Mentioned in passing Steve Cotterill was the longest serving manager in the Championship (around the time he was being shown the door). Did a bit of a double act with a very ebullient Greenwood who was really nice about me and my contribution on the 2005 British Lions tour in his opening remarks. He said the players had all sorts of expectations but what they got was someone who was totally open and honest and was able to engage them in argument in a way they had never imagined possible. Good event though. I was surprised going around today how many men, including older ones, were not wearing poppies.

I went for a pee as I left, and the organisers told me there was a radio crew outside wanting to talk to me. I smelled a rat as soon as I saw them. They claimed to be from something called Residence Radio. Ignored them, into the car and then they had loudhailer out and camera, the guy shouting I was a war criminal and would be tried at The Hague. Driver slow to get off and they walked round to block his path. Couple of sallow-looking ill-shaven tossers. Bawled away for two or three minutes then pulled to one side. Train up, and I got a text from Andy Hodgson [Burnley fan] saying Steve Cotterill was out, was I going for the job? I thought it was a joke but checked with Cathy Pickup [club secretary] who said yes it was true – mutual consent! – and then Brendan Flood who said it was a tough decision but time for a change. Alex spoke to Steve later and said he felt sorry for him, that he had done a good job and was never fully appreciated. I got a few calls on it but it was all a bit of a mystery. He had not done that badly but he would take it really badly I guess.

I arrived at [Manchester] Piccadilly and bumped into David Cameron as I was waiting in the taxi queue. He came over and we shook hands and had a little chat, mainly about TB's Middle East job and should he get a briefing before going to Israel? Introduced me to his team travelling with him, all women, three of them, all quite attractive in a Sloaney kind of way. It was all fairly light-hearted stuff. He said he felt a lot more confident taking on GB than he did TB at PMQs. Picked up Calum, then to the Hilton before going for a walk and lunch. Bloke came up alongside me in his car and said he wanted to shake my hand. He said I had done more than anyone for Labour and he was really grateful. He was black, as so many of the people who seemed to warm to me – another later wanted his picture taken – were.

The dinner was bearable. Manchester Chartered Accountants. The head guy from London was not as boring as the suits usually are. I was sitting next to a guy from BNFL [British Nuclear Fuels] who was probing away re me and TB and at the end said he thought we should give ourselves very high marks for what we had achieved and also that I was a very solid bloke. He felt TB had done a good job and was an honest leader who had strong beliefs but he questioned his judgement of people sometimes – he named JP, MB and Reid. He was a big fan of Charles Clarke. I texted CC to say he thought he should be back in the Cabinet. CC texted to say he was clearly a man of judgement. Speech was the usual spiel, then Q&A where I got pretty rough with one bloke going on about spin and who wouldn't let go of the mike. Suggested he go to bed and hold on to something else.

Friday 9 November

Swim then breakfast with Cam, then off to Carrington [Manchester United training ground]. Half-hour drive, set way back, through two sets of barriers. Met Alex on his way to the press conference, first all of them then the Sundays. Pretty tame lot. He said he'd decided two years ago just to have a laugh at their expense and not worry. Lots of people talking about Steve. Over to first team training. I had a chat with Micky Phelan [coach] about Burnley. Both he and Alex were thinking Steve should have stayed. The players were playing head tennis and generally having a laugh until Wayne Rooney caught his foot in the base of the net, went over and it was obvious straight away it was serious. He was surrounded by the other players, then

AF and Micky went over before he was taken off on a stretcher. We went to the dressing room where he was being strapped up, and then the doctor took Alex to one side and said it was probably ankle ligaments. Rooney looked absolutely gutted, just threw his head back and sighed.

They seemed a good bunch in training, all seeming to enjoy it, loads and loads of energy. Other foreigners maybe. Alex took us for a little tour, really proud of it. So different to Gawthorpe Hall [Burnley training ground]. Massive kit room and laundry. An eye specialist who was working on speeding up the reactions of players. An underwater treadmill for rehab. We bumped into some of the young kids from Norway and Italy, for example, who seemed a bit mesmerised when seeing Alex. Edwin van der Saar and a 52-year-old fitness coach were doing hundreds of sit-ups in the gym. Into Alex's office for a chat and a cup of tea. His desk was a lot less tidy than the last time we were there. He said he was exhausted, doing too much. He had been in London last night for a Shine [sporting charity] dinner. GB and Sarah were there. Alex said he was so tired he kept calling Sarah 'Fiona'. He said Gavyn Davies was there, didn't say a word, probably because he knew Alex was close to me. The 'Book of Regrets' we had both contributed to was on his desk – mine re not reading enough at university, his 'None really apart sometimes losing his temper and also picking the wrong team.'

Saturday 10 November

Took Grace to the stables, then back to head for the new St Pancras station, looking absolutely stunning, and head for Leicester v Burnley. I was really motoring on the novel, whacking out a thousand words here and there on the BlackBerry. Loud-mouthed West Ham fans on the way to Derby were a bit of a pain but good quick journey. The match was OK. Played with real fight. Andy Hodgson was really badgering me to have a go for the manager's job. He said they could surround me with good coaches. It was only when I learned he was also calling Barry Kilby [chairman] and Dave Edmundson [CEO] that I realised he was serious. A Burnley fan, a soldier, sat opposite me on the way back and I got no work done. He was a nice enough bloke but it can be annoying when people think they own the space around you. We had Penny Stott and the Jacksons [journalist friends] round for dinner. Penny was looking very thin and clearly struggling a bit but enjoyed it I think. Jacko totally unchanged. Ditto Barbara.

Monday 12 November

Work then out for a jolly lunch with David Frost [television host] at Mossiman's. Winston Churchill [former Tory MP, grandson of the former Prime

Minister] was in there with [Lady] Mary Soames [youngest daughter of former PM Winston Churchill]. He was involved in marketing Winston cigars and came over with a box for David. Mary told me she was a great fan of my book. I said I was a great fan of her son Nick. We had a bit of a natter, and she said something Alan Clark used to say, that the 'upper clarse' were all rather obsessed with me. David was pretty down on GB. He felt we were the stars of our generation and this was now the afters. Home for more work on novel. I told Ed Victor who said he was shocked and pleased in equal measure but then said he shouldn't be shocked because I was always surprising. He suggested I mention it to nobody. Also that I should include a politician in the list of character-patients. He loved the idea of the title, Psychological Flaws, but I felt it was fine as a working title, but not the actual thing. Not sure I could do it. I watched GB's Mansion House speech. It was OK without being great, and his rather odd hand mannerisms were really becoming noticeable.

Tuesday 13 November

Breakfast with Nick Keller [sports entrepreneur] at Kalendar. He was raving, and said others were, at my presentation at the IMAX. He wanted me to let them market me more strategically. He was also trying to get me involved in a big way in a Beyond Sport Awards plan that he was pitching to the Qataris who were pouring squillions into sport. Back to write, and I was really feeling the novel might be the main project for a bit. I was enjoying it and felt I was doing OK. Someone had said to me, re myself, that they sensed I had 'been through a storm and not a blade of grass had moved', which I worked in. There was definitely lots of my own breakdown emerging in here. I was over 30k words now and reckoned the final thing would be 90–100k.

Wednesday 14 November

Great bike ride. Back to work on the novel. Bill Hagerty finally signed up so hopefully we could get going on the 'whole story' volume edit. Out for a Hilton Hotel black-tie job where Lindsay [Nicholson] was getting the Mark Boxer Award [for outstanding service to the magazine industry]. Junked my planned jokey speech to make it a bit heavier about John [Merritt], death and leukaemia etc. I met the editor of *Heat* and told him I really hoped the celebrity bubble would burst. I felt they and reality TV were partners in a very damaging trend. He said 'We are giving people what they want to see.' I said people would have watched the Jews being sent to the gas chambers if they'd had the chance. He said 'This is a better option. See us as an alternative to public executions.' Lindsay had no idea she was getting the award and was totally overwhelmed. She got a nice reception though the whole thing reminded me a bit of Fleet St circa '70s and '80s. One of the winners was barely able to walk. Again, I was a bit shocked how many people were saying GB had no chance.

Thursday 15 November

Out at a dinner, a bank thing, pretty dull, but I was troubled by one guy who said GB just looked so old and tired and Cameron looked fresh and 'would not need to do much to knock him over'. I was hearing it too often just now.

Friday 16 November

JP called. He'd had TB at a dinner in Hull and was buzzing with it. Said he was really warm and generous about his role and they had a great night. He was really down on GB and his whole operation. He felt they were not defending the record at all and also that in talking of only change not continuity they were setting themselves up for failure. Balls a menace. He said he may understand economics but he has no judgement at all. Calum and I went down to Oxford to collect Rory and watch his football match. Lost 4–2. Drove back working on the novel. Totally motoring.

Saturday 17 November

Up early with Calum and off to Luton for the flight to Glasgow. I was working on the book every spare moment. To town for lunch, walkabout and did a couple of book signings. Donald came for us and back to flat then to game. He seemed a lot better. Match [Scotland v Italy] amazing and Scots should have won. One–nil down first minute. Better team most of game. Equalise then dire free-kick decision at end, lost 2–1. But great atmosphere. Also saw Jack McConnell [former First Minister of Scotland] and John Brown who were both very down about the political scene. GB and Salmond in royal box. Salmond rocking, GB looking dire. Donald collected us and out for dinner.

Sunday 18 November

Out to the airport and fly down. The whole family at home for dinner which was great. I miss the boys a hell of a lot when they're not home but Calum seemed to be settling in better.

Tuesday 20 November

I was so into the book now. I was waking and almost straight away grabbing the BlackBerry and either straight to writing or planning out the next steps. It was taking me in all sorts of directions I never expected, both plot and also the kind of things in the past I drew on, and in which context. Maggie Darling, who had called me at the weekend to say would I talk to Alistair about Northern Rock, which we had discussed ahead of his statement yesterday, was now calling to tell me he had another disaster looming and would I call again?* It turned out all details of all child benefit recipients had gone missing in two CDs handled by Customs. This would connect too. They were having a run of bad luck, for sure, but the slip began with the on/off election. I popped round to see Michael Palin to plan publicity for the Leukaemia Research event next week. Good job I did because his emails to me had been going to spam, and he had thought as I had not been replying that maybe it was off. Such a lovely bloke and OK about doing some publicity on Monday to flog tickets.

Wednesday 21 November

David S. I told him about the book and went over some of the characters and he pressed a bit on where I felt they were coming from. He seemed a bit gobsmacked I had done so much and was interested in some of the themes. When I said my fictional shrink was a depressive he asked straight out 'Do you think I am?' I said I couldn't imagine how you stayed totally on top of all your patients without being affected. He had some good insights, for example that disaster survivors often find God. I said I would make a contribution to his department at UCL [University College London] if he would read it for me when I finished it and point out anything that was just wrong. But also I felt he might have things he could add to it as well.

Tessa called. She said there were no words to describe how disastrous things were. Also that they were lying when No. 10 said Cabinet had discussed the Customs disaster and the missing details of all child benefit claimants.† She said it was like slow death. She felt I really needed to go to see GB and tell him what I thought, but honestly, I was not sure he would be able to change. If he had followed the strategic course we talked

* Northern Rock had been the first British bank in 150 years to suffer a bank run when in September it was forced to apply for emergency lending from the Bank of England after its borrowing costs soared in the summer credit crunch. Darling came under pressure to clarify how long taxpayers' money would be used to prop up the bank.

† Two computer discs owned by HM Revenue and Customs and containing child benefit data had gone missing. Shadow Chancellor George Osborne described it as 'a catastrophic mistake' and 'the final blow' for government plans for a national ID database.

about he would not be in this mess. People accept things like Northern Rock and Customs happen. The question is how you look when you are dealing with them, that you seem in control and on top but also not too fazed and always with an eye on core strategy. Their strategy was not right. England 2, Croatia 3 and Steve Maclaren [manager] for the chop. Dire performance. At Burnley it was looking like Owen Coyle [manager of St Johnstone].

Thursday 22 November

Worked on the book, then out on the bike to see Kirsty Tinkler who was working on the statue of the kids. Looking good. Did Robert Elms Radio London re Palin event. Lots on that but also beginning to get 'What should GB be doing?' and the tone of the questions meant it was almost a given that he wasn't doing well. Out to Reading to present the Thames Valley Business Awards. OK enough event. John Madejski [Reading FC owner] there. I had always liked him whenever I came across him, even if he was a Tory, and we had a good chat about politics and football. Another one unpersuaded by GB in the way he had been by TB. He was determined to get out of football. He said the money now was utterly crazy and getting worse. But he would only sell to a billionaire. I felt on form when speaking and was weaving in words given to me by the people on my table. I did a basic defence of politics, and though one of the award winners had a bit of a pop, I hit back and I sensed the centre of gravity was with me not him. Then at the end a woman in a bright red dress basically came over and propositioned me, said she had a room upstairs and if I wanted to join her I was welcome. I got in the car and wrote a version of it into the novel. I was up to 70k words now.

Friday 23 November

Out to do a BMI [British Midland Airways] thing with Phil Gayle [broadcaster]. Home then a long, slow drive to Manchester. Used the gym at the Lowry, then Calum came round and we set off to the fundraiser for Arlene McCarthy [Labour Member of European Parliament]. I felt on top form. Good speech. Found the right balance between continuity and change. Trying to explain the blip etc. Lots of people saying come back including Graham Stringer [Labour MP] who was clearly moving effortlessly from undermining one leader to another. Calum really enjoyed it though. Quite a few saying I should run for office and that fifty was not too late. The novel was definitely my main thing at the moment though, and I didn't feel the desire to be doing this kind of thing all the time.

Saturday 24 November

Gym, then Louisa Cheetham [former British Lions media officer] came round for coffee, and we had a good natter re Lions. She was moving up north to live with Gary O'Driscoll [former Lions doctor]. Off to Burnley. Owen Coyle's first game. 0–0 but we played well.

Sunday 25 November

The papers full of stuff re God from the David Aaronovitch programme on TB, TB saying he didn't go on about it in case people thought he was a nutter. Book sales up again pre-Xmas. The papers full of government being incompetent and lots of fire trained on Darling. I felt Balls was a real problem. Madejski last night telling me he had done a whole speech to Thames Valley calling it Thamesgate. I was really thinking I should have gone for a seat at some point. A bad funding story in *Mail on Sunday*, businessman donating anonymously through third parties. GB in Uganda looking a bit lost. Long bike ride at the stables then home to write more, now up to 80k words.

Darling called. He sounded end of tether-ish. He agreed the real problems started at the on/off election. He felt the PBR [pre-Budget Report] had gone badly because it was designed for an event that never happened. He hadn't really wanted to do inheritance tax but GB was pushing it. He sounded to me like he might throw in the towel. E.g. said he was not getting up to Scotland enough, he had always been clear there was life outside and he was not seeing enough of it. The truth was he didn't have the money GB had had as Chancellor for largesse. Too many chickens were coming home to roost, he said. Five defence chiefs were out attacking GB in particular. It all looked a bit orchestrated and political but it was not good. All I could say to him was they had to show more fight and get back on a bigger and clearer message.

Monday 26 November

The big story outside the government stuff was Nick Griffin [chairman, British National Party] and David Irving [author, Holocaust denier] at the Oxford Union.* But then later Peter Watt [Labour general secretary] resigned over the secret donations story. GB was obviously in one of his panics and felt someone had to fall for it. I did a bit of work on the novel,

* Demonstrators protesting at Griffin and Irving's presence at a debate on free speech staged a sit-down protest. After order was restored, the pair spoke in separate rooms as the debate continued.

then out with Michael Palin, who had given us an hour to do media to promote the event. We had a quick lunch en route and we ranged over John Cleese [Palin's fellow Monty Python comedian] and how brilliant/difficult he could be, my stalkers, TB–GB (on which the mood was bad). We were meant to do fifteen minutes for LBC but ended up doing forty-five, including lots of questions about homoeroticism and a ménage à trois. God knows how we got on to that. Seemingly I set off the fire alarm as I left. Then off to Random House to discuss production of the full volumes of the diaries. OK meeting, and I felt Bill H would be good. Ran home. I was absolutely motoring on the novel now. I was also really happy with the mix of characters, and the fact I was waking up in the middle of the night in recent days and having ideas while I dreamed and then just pouring it out.

Tuesday 27 November

I worked on the book then out for lunch at the National Portrait Gallery with Denis Hickie and Shane Horgan [Irish rugby players]. I wore my Lions tracksuit for a laugh. Both on great form. I hadn't realised Denis had retired. Both really bright on the political front as ever. They had a real understanding of what was going on, and felt GB was starting to reap what he had sewn on several fronts. He was getting a dire press all round just now. Chickens roosting. Off to Watford v Burnley, won 2–1 and played really good attacking football. Fantastic night. I was getting loads of media bids on the 'What should GB do?' theme. Deal with it and get focused on policy and dividing lines. The Tories were looking smug and cocky and they will become vulnerable again. But it won't happen by chance. *The Guardian* were asking me to go to LA to interview CJ from *The West Wing* [actress Allison Janney]. They couldn't believe I had never watched it. It was a long way to go to interview someone I have never seen.

Wednesday 28 November

The funding stuff was still raging. I did a bit of last-minute media to flog the last tickets for the Michael Palin audience, which had sold out by the end of the day. I was trying to finish a very rough draft of the novel to get it to Ed Victor and David Sturgeon ASAP. I had done 98,000 words in under a month but I knew it was going to need a lot of work, particularly on the structure. But it was OK as a first draft. I finally told Fiona and the kids what I had been doing and they seemed genuinely impressed. I was helping Rory with his essay on New Labour before heading out to the Criterion Theatre for the Palin event. My intro was not great, don't know why, I just wasn't on form, though I did OK auctioning my and Palin's diaries for 8k.

Michael switched effortlessly from comic to serious and back again. Some really funny moments. My favourite when Alan Yentob [BBC arts presenter] waltzed off, and Michael said 'I knew he would get bored at some point.' Great sketch of the Monty Python lot in drag taking the piss out of Palin's travel programmes. The audience loved it. Genuinely nice and genuinely funny man. Then to the Wolseley [restaurant] and nice enough time. Alan pretty down on GB. He said the funding story felt like it was engulfing them. He felt that it was not the issues so much as the fact that it exposed GB more and more and people were really unsure. It all felt pretty grim. I felt it was more that he had so put the focus on change from TB – no-spin no-sleaze all delivery – that the slightest thing will be used against him now. Combination of Northern Rock, Customs CDs and now the Abrahams situation were all building pretty badly.*

Thursday 29 November

I saw DS, and gave him the manuscript. He, like Fiona and Ed, was pretty amazed I had done it. Good session and I felt fairly up I had done the first draft. Re him I said I would be amazed if he wasn't affected by all the angst and grief he had to deal with. Bit of exercise. JP called, said he was thinking about getting involved, stepping in with GB. He couldn't believe how badly things were being handled. He was even thinking about standing for deputy leader and doing a gen sec type role now that Peter Watt was gone. He was adamant that the real problem was the change change change message which meant GB was virtually running against our record and our past. Also he did not have strong people around him. He was keen to come to Fiona's birthday do in Paris.

DM called while I was watching Spurs UEFA Cup match against Aalborg BK. Louise was in the States getting her violin repaired so the kids were with him. He asked for my analysis, which I gave him. I said that if GB didn't show some strategy and some fight, he was done for. David felt that things had got much, much worse but he still sounded a bit detached from it all. I asked if he ever raised this stuff with him. He said the walls had gone up a bit. Did I think it was terminal? I didn't but they were going to have to show some signs that they got it. I said he should be out emphasising it was always tough under TB, but what was

* As the party funding row escalated, Gordon Brown announced an internal inquiry, to be chaired by former bishop Lord (Richard) Harries, into the circumstances that allowed businessman Peter Abrahams to keep donations worth £650,000 secret.

required was dealing with the issues but also getting that sense of strategy going. He felt GB didn't know how to change tack, didn't have a different mode, and was locked into the notion that all his problems were someone else's fault.

Friday 30 November

Up early and off to Paris on the Eurostar. St Pancras was looking fantastic. Beautiful ceiling, nice statues around the place, and everything running smoothly. Paris grey but fine. We went out to the restaurant we were going to rent for Fiona's 50th. Pretty funky with sexually explicit paintings all over the walls. The owner said they would be replaced by the time we came back. Met Emilie and Philippe [Senes, French friends], to their nice flat nearby and then out to a little café-type restaurant. Heaving. Fair few Brits around. Wandered around a bit then train home. Really tired but nice day, and the thing would work.

Saturday 1 December

Off with the boys to see Kirsty Tinkler at RCA studios. The three-headed statue was looking good. The boys were good with her. Grace being a bit precious about going to sit. Off with Calum to Charlton v Burnley. Terrific match and we were playing really well. Won 3–1. Great turnout and atmosphere. PG called and said that Peter Watt was in a bad way. I called him. He was scathing re GB. They just panicked, he said.* They didn't deal with it. He said he felt shafted but it's what he expected. He refused to resign so he had got a pay-off and legal costs but he was going to defend himself. GB, Harriet, Dromey (yet again claiming he was in the dark) all pathetic. *The Blair Years* named as Political Book of the Year in the *Mail* of all places.

Sunday 2 December

Out to the stables with Grace and took the bike out for a long ride in the pouring rain. Back for lunch and a chat with Catherine who was starting as a spad with AD tomorrow. He was keen to meet me. She said he had had the scales well and truly fall from his eyes. She was asking how I thought she should go about things. Nobody from No. 10 had been in touch. Her

* Having resigned as party general secretary, Watt revealed that he knew David Abrahams had donated £600,000 to Labour through third parties in apparent breach of electoral law but had not appreciated that he had not complied with reporting requirements.

sense was that nobody tried to co-ordinate or really instil strategy. The things she was suggesting were minimums but the impression was of no real strategy at all. Alistair was going to need a lot of support, because his natural tendency would be to get very down at the way GB operated. She was going to have to bolster him but also just keep plugging away at the No. 10 operation. Out to Jamie Rubin/Christiane Amanpour [wife, CNN correspondent] farewell dinner before they headed back to the US. JoP and Sarah the only people there we really knew well. The rest were all mainly his hunting-shooting friends. Jemima Khan [journalist and campaigner] was unbelievably flirtatious. I sat between [writer and critic] A. A. Gill's partner Nicola and someone called Bella who said Jamie had told her she had to flirt with me because I could be difficult and anti-social. A few little speeches and I said if Jamie had set out seven years ago and said this would be his social set when he left, I doubted it. In his speech he said women had taught him how to flirt and men had taught him how to shoot lots of birds.

Christiane and Jamie both nice yet clearly loved the social side of high-end London life in a way we didn't. All on about skiing and schools and shooting. They were both really special people though. I had a bit of a natter with Jeremy Clarkson [*Top Gear* presenter, journalist], who was in major wind-up mode. I said I was convinced that if the Tories were in power when he became a name he would have been a raving leftie. Nightmare scenario from the third-round FA Cup draw. As it was going to clash with Fiona's birthday party in Paris, I was hoping for a non-event. But we got Arsenal at home. It was going to be a nightmare unless it was the late Sunday game on TV. Ed came back with his judgement on the novel. He said he really liked it. He felt the story was good and the characters were strong. But he felt I needed to strip all the stories out and mesh them better. 'It could be absolutely terrific. I certainly won't have any problem getting it published. I assume you want to give Gail first choice?' Indeed. I was pleased at his reaction and had also been moving to the view that I couldn't leave it open-ended.

Monday 3 December

Kate Phillips [BBC producer] came round to tell me of the Speak Up for Britain idea, which she wanted me to front. Nice woman and it seemed better than most telly ideas. No news on when the Arsenal match will be. Tim Hames in *The Times* had a good piece using my diaries to point out that TB had it very tough just after the honeymoon so people should calm down a bit about GB. The polls were still pretty bad though, but worse, where was the sense of a strategy? Nick Keller [Benchmark Sport] was pressing me to get signed up with his outfit.

Tuesday 4 December

Working on *TBY* paperback intro and also restructuring novel. I was a bit stuck on both, but broke it late pm, found a whole new surge of stuff for the novel after going out for a run.

Thursday 6 December

No. 10 called, asked if I was around and could I see GB tomorrow. I can't say I felt a great leap of the heart.

Friday 7 December

In to see GB. Through 70 Whitehall, met by the duty clerk and off through to No. 10. The place felt a lot flatter. There seemed to be hardly anyone around. Up to the study, now called the Thatcher Room according to the papers. Classic GB. Thinking he could buy a bit of favour with a certain constituency by what ultimately was little more than a gesture. I sat there, thinking how I used to be here every morning for the main meeting kicking off every day, and how important it was to what I did. I now felt totally divorced from it. Well, not totally, but I was barely in and wanting to get out as soon as I could. It just didn't feel where I wanted or needed to be. He came in, looking tired and grey. His blind eye was barely open, he had a little patch of facial hair below his chin, and he was jowly and looked as exhausted as I had seen him. As usual he started with a sporting reference. 'You not running?' I said my heel was injured and I was seeing a running specialist osteopath. He asked me if I thought Alex would be up for managing the UK Olympics football team. I felt not. He felt he would. He asked if I would work on him. But there was a chance there would be no Scots involved as players because the SFA were being difficult.

I had been expecting a chat on general strategy but he got straight to the issue of funding. He said he was going to bring in a bill and just get big changes through. Though he was raging at the double standards in the way we got treated on funding compared with the Tories, he felt the Tories were really vulnerable. [Conservative Party deputy chairman Michael] Ashcroft's money was pouring in and it was still not clear if he was here or Belize. He felt there was a whole load of stuff going on in Belize that needed to be exposed. Would I head up a team to take it on, and really make it into a big issue? I didn't mention that I had already heard he had asked Charlie Whelan [GB spokesman] to do the same. I said I would help, but without looking or sounding too enthusiastic about it. Then we shifted to general stuff. He said he was finding it harder than he expected. The last few weeks had been tough but he felt we had made the right decisions. I was a bit alarmed by how he seemed to think News International had screwed his conference, rather than all the election talk, but he was adamant. On the on/off election he defended it as all being a bit overdone. On the lost discs he reckoned they were probably still in the building. Party funding: 'I don't want to blame but…'

I went back to my main point that he needed to do continuity as well as change and do it so people noticed. He scribbled it. His writing still as mad and messy as ever. I said I totally disapproved of his relationship with Dacre. He said he didn't have one! Ludicrous. We went round the blocks a bit but it was all a bit depressing. He said he would send me the stuff on funding but really felt the Tories were vulnerable. Defended his inner team but also said he would need to get more in, including from different places. Asked if I knew any, said if I had people I wanted on the inside, with me working on the outside, that could work. It was an OK meeting but I didn't feel lifted. I remembered what Alex said re TB, that you always feel better leaving the room. I didn't feel that today, I felt GB was burdened and I felt burdened by his wanting to share them, because I knew we were likely to reach different conclusions. Added to which, though he defended his team, there were some of them I just couldn't work with productively.

Off to Le Flâneur [deli restaurant] for a French interview, then picked up Mum and Kate [Naish, niece], then later to [businessman, former Labour advisor] Mike Craven's for a reunion of TB's 1994 team. TB already there. Peter M, PG, Geoff Norris [advisor], JoP, Anji [Hunter, advisor], PH, Kate G, Sarah Hunter Allan [policy advisor], Tim, etc. no James Pat or DM. All nice enough. Lots of down-on-GB stuff. TB said fox hunting ban and FoI [Freedom of Information Act] were his biggest regrets. He looked in good shape. No thinner. Tanned. Smart casual. PM said his biggest regret was that I had defenestrated him.

Sunday 9 December

To stables with Mum, Kate, Grace and Sissy [Bridge, neighbour]. AD and Maggie there. AD out helping George [Mackie, farmer] get trees. Good chat when he came back. It was clear the scales had well and truly fallen. He felt GB needed to calm down, get less involved in everything and be more strategic. He was up too late pre-PMQs and exhausted. The Tories were very confident but he believed we could get them on policy. He was very down on Balls who he felt was all the time trying to stop GB widening his circle. I gave him my usual spiel, said it all flowed from GB thinking he should have been there before, he couldn't bring himself to define the earlier era properly so we lost the gains of a broadly good record. And the change wasn't clear, so if he wouldn't do continuity, and there was a lack of clarity to change, he was in a strategic no man's land. He felt if the New Year didn't show an improvement, things were tricky. Out for dinner with the Goulds. Gail said do not get involved with GB. Go and read your own paperback intro about getting a life back, she said. 'Do you really want to lose it all over again?' Fiona said 'He won't be able to resist it.'

Monday 10 December

Working on the novel all day, before taking Mum and Kate to *The Sound of Music*. GB package on funding arrived with a scrawled, totally illegible letter.

Tuesday 11 December

I was driving up to Burnley v QPR when the writer's block that had been stopping me doing the novel's key scene when Sturrock [fictional psychiatrist] cracked up seemed to lift. I pulled in at Watford Gap and just banged out 3,000 words on the BlackBerry. Top stuff. Was in tears at one point. Then Calum called, and I was running late. Terrible match [lost 2–0], comic second goal. Over to Manchester, stayed at the Renaissance.

Wednesday 12 December

I was in bed when David S called and asked where I was. I had mixed up my dates. He was OK about it but it was not good to forget like that. He had finished reading the book draft and agreed with Ed that the shrink must die. I was really motoring on the rewrite. Much better than the first draft but will still need lots of work.

Thursday 13 December

Lunch with Syd Young, Geoff Lakeman, Christian Gysin, David Leigh [friends]. To JLA [speakers' agency] to sign a load of books they were giving out as Christmas presents. To Hampstead for the Waterstones 'festive authors' session. Lots of local authors. All a bit odd. The big draw was Japanese-born Booker Prize-winner Kazuo Ishiguro. Met Kate Garvey to go to Matthew Freud's party, which seems to get bigger every year. MF told me he was seeing GB and felt he was in bad place. Rebekah [Wade, editor, *The Sun*] – 'Everyone is moving over to David.' John Reid fairly discreet. Carine [Reid's wife] less so, felt GB was a disaster before and thinks it even more now. Ken Livingstone telling me how he was he totally on my side re Gilligan and had told him so. Jamie Rubin there, Jessie [Mills, daughter of

Tessa Jowell and David Mills], Emma Freud [broadcaster]. Nice chat with Gordon Ramsay and his wife re Soccer Aid [charity event] – we both talked about it loads – and running. Cameron came over to JR and me and said 'Ah the A team the B team won't use.' Osborne said he read I was being drafted back. 'You must so want that given how much help GB gave you to make your life easier.' He said he loved my book, 'mainly for reading where it was obvious where you had made the cuts to protect Gordon'.

Cameron was joking about our meeting at Manchester station cab rank. I told him the reaction of the guy behind me in the queue who, after they had left, said he had to admire a man who could travel with such attractive women. He was much more relaxed than last year, which suggested he was more confident, and both he and Osborne were talking fairly dismissively of GB. I told them I seemed to be following in [former Tory leader William] Hague's footsteps everywhere I went, doing loads of speeches at events where 'we had William Hague last year … he was very funny'. TB arrived as I was talking to Andy Coulson [Tories' communications director] who said he couldn't believe how I got away with the editing of the book. He said he saw one interview where I said it was a historical document alongside another saying I had kept out stuff damaging to GB. 'Can't be both.' 'But the other stuff will follow.' 'This is the one that counts though.' TB just back from Bethlehem, said we needed to talk but we didn't talk properly there. Nice enough do. Home half eleven. Big news was GB missing the EU Reform Treaty signing in Lisbon.

Friday 14 December

GB getting hammered over his non-presence for the treaty signing. Tessa called to say she felt ashamed to be British. She had to decide whether it was worth carrying on like this. The simple truth was he did not have the psychology for it. He looked terrible. The civil service were leaking all over the place. And the worst thing was he didn't have a clue what he wanted to do. Set off with Rory at lunchtime and it took us almost five hours to get to Manchester. Fabio Capello [Italian football manager] getting the England job was wall-to-wall on the news. I was staying at the Lowry, went out for a really nice evening with Rory and Calum, though the whole place was heaving with Christmas revellers aka people pissed all over the place. Slept badly.

Saturday 15 December

Gym then to Calum's to pack his stuff into car. Usual joke re me getting through four years at Cambridge with one bag. Lunch with Paul Fletcher [former Burnley player turned businessman] in the boardroom. The match was really frustrating. Penalty turned down first minute. One up. Then they score two. Equalise. Two sendings off. Ref dire. Everyone cross at the end. Drive over to Liverpool. *Match of the Day*. Amazing array of accents of people going to the match Liverpool v United tomorrow. From all over the world.

Sunday 16 December

I went out for a run in the freezing cold. I liked the Liverpool cathedrals, and the City centre generally was so much better than it used to be, and the whole City of Culture [prize awarded to Liverpool for 2008] thing would be great for the place. When we were having breakfast, Rory spotted a running foot headline on Sky – Labour slump to lowest level in polls in fifteen years. It was all beginning to develop the smell of death. Sad but maybe it was becoming inevitable. Out to the ground and park up. Freezing cold. Rory and Calum had tickets for the away end, I was in the box. I joined Martin Ferguson [AF's brother] in the directors' lounge. It was a poor game [0–1], but United scored a good goal and Alex was happy enough. I met the very nice American guy running Liverpool's year of culture programme, who invited me to the Paul McCartney events.

Monday 17 December

Set off first thing for Eurostar. Paris not as cold as London and with the wintry sun it was really beautiful. I was staying in the former Nazi Abwehr [intelligence service] HQ, Hotel Lutetia. There was a nice little café nearby with a stunningly beautiful black waitress. I went out looking for restaurants for the Friday of Fiona's 50th weekend. Hung around most of day then out late for TF3 TV *Ce soir (ou jamais!)*. Nice guy presenting it who said it was the one programme on TV where you could 'finir la phrase'. The other guests were Pierre Moscovici [French National Assembly member], Yves Jégo [French centre-right politician] and a spokesman for Sarkozy. Also an odd-looking philosopher named [Bernard] Siegler whose basic pitch was that politics had destroyed democracy because we treated people as consumers. Five minutes with me at the top then a long discussion. It flowed OK and my French held up fine. We talked about the focus on Sarko and Carla Bruni,* which I felt was fine but I didn't really believe the

* Twice-married Sarkozy, divorced from his second wife shortly after being elected President in May, had met Italian-born singer Bruni at a dinner party and entered into a relationship with her, causing much media speculation.

French when they said they didn't care about private lives of politicians. It was just that it was not a main reason for voting one way or the other. But they wouldn't like it if Sarko's private life became a soap. French media was jam-packed with Sarko / Bruni and their seemingly orchestrated coming out together at Disneyland.

Moscovici was clearly a big fan of what we had done and was pushing his agreement with the basic New Labour position as recipe for socialist party. The philosopher was very, very French, talked a fair bit of nonsense and at times I found it hard not to laugh. Jego clever if a bit obdurate and too keen to go party political with Pierre. Nice chat with Moscovici on the way out. He said everyone he talked to in London seemed to think GB was done for. It was certainly beginning to feel like that. He could recover if he learned but it was not going to be easy. He asked if I would go back. I said I didn't have the will for it really. I had got a life back. He said '*Tu sembles très content. Vaut mieux pas le risquer.*' Inadvertently discovered TB was also in Paris, for an MEPP meeting, which was briefly mentioned on the news.

Tuesday 18 December

Michael Williams [foreign policy special advisor] was on my train back to London, having been at the same meeting as TB yesterday, a MEPP meeting re cash for Palestine. I asked him to join me and we had a good chat. He seemed to think GB had both structural problems and character problems. No. 10, he said, was dysfunctional compared with our time. Nobody knew who to reach to get a decision. When Jonathan and I had been there, everyone knew how to reach a decision. At conference he was asked to line up Middle East people and did but then couldn't get a decision on whether GB wanted them there.

On his own appointment as MEPP rep it was all very vague. First he was No. 10 but then GB said he was cutting back on spads so he had to be FCO-based. He said senior diplomats were really getting agitated at how indecisive No. 10 was, and lack of clarity in policy and decision-making. He said at least with me people knew there was someone trying to co-ordinate. On the press side there is Damian McBride, on strategy there is nobody. He asked if I would go back. I said not full-time and I didn't rate his inner circle. He felt also Mark Malloch Brown was a disaster waiting to happen. Miliband had asked him straight out if he was a problem. 'I had to say yes.' I said I felt all GB's problems stemmed from him doing everything through the 'not TB' prism. In No. 10, he had thrown the baby out with the bathwater and so had no strategy worth the name.

Wednesday 19 December

Phil Townsend [communications director] called, a story had broken about an alleged rape at Manchester United players' Christmas party. I felt they needed a pretty tough line out there about the responsibility on players but Alex felt they should try to keep their heads down on it. The detail sounded really sordid but his big thing was not making it go even bigger and badder as a story in the run-up to Christmas. Maybe he would get away with it.

Thursday 20 December

I had done a note for Phil and Alex called to go over stuff on the Jonny Evans arrest and the wider issues for the club. I said I felt he needed controlled anger and strategic grip. It was running big and bad for the reputation of the club, reputation of the players, individual and collective, at a time people are willing to believe the worst of Premiership footballers as overpaid, out of touch with reality and lacking in any sense of responsibility. Also his reputation was being tested here too, in particular relating to discipline and grip. I felt he needed a very careful and strategic response which requires buy-in from management, senior players trusted by management to deliver a message, and supporters. Evans was at risk of being shredded by the briefing going on, and though the public are not that sympathetic, they would be ready to believe there will have been a set-up of some sort.* Also worth pointing out that the law regarding anonymity appears to have broken down and now protects only the alleged victim, not the alleged rapist.

I said his first comments would be important and he could either hide behind process and say nothing or show the club takes it seriously, and is dealing properly with the fallout; underline AF's reputation as someone of deep-rooted values; make clear his view that whatever the facts of the case, he believes his players have responsibilities to behave properly at all times; state publicly that there will be no such event next year – he said Rio Ferdinand had been the main fixer / organiser – and that he has communicated this to those who organised it. Equally make clear his determination that this should not affect how the club performs in a busy Christmas period. He said he would mull, then came back and said he really felt the public would think it was a set-up and there was no point him stirring things up. So he intended to say he was saying nothing and he would just deal with it internally. I watched Michael Cockerell's programme on Cameron, in which Tim Bell, [Lord] Tim Razzall [Lib Dem politician] and I discussed various clips. It seemed to work OK, but I was

* Subsequently it was reported that Evans would not be charged with any offence.

annoyed my main point about Cameron not doing policy decisions was cut out of every answer.

Saturday 22 December

Bike then out to Ipswich for the Burnley game. On the drive I started to get calls about TB's conversion to Catholicism. I did a few interviews when we got there, including one at half-time, saying it was not really a surprise. Usual stuff about 'We don't do God'. It was interesting how he was still capable of being the main event. John Spicer was sent off at Ipswich but we hung on for a nil–nil draw. Long drive to Tessa and David's. Tessa constantly wanting to talk re politics and I didn't. GB stories were now getting out there more about how he panicked, treated people badly etc. David's Italian case was being extended so he was pretty down about that.*

Sunday 23 December

Two hours on bike. Loads of football. Liked Dawn Airey who came with her partner and child. David's old aunt was very funny and not PC on the idea of lesbians having kids. I had a terrible back pain by the time we got home. Too long on the bike in the cold.

Monday 24 December

My back was dire. Ron Marx [physio / osteopath] came round and by and large sorted it. I was starting to work properly on the Cudlipp lecture, Hugh's widow [Lady] Jodi having asked me to do it. I said yes, but I was really fed up thinking and talking about the media and politics. The diaries were still getting a bit of play in the end-of-year reviews but the real sellers were the popular populist telly people, like Richard Hammond and Jeremy Clarkson [*Top Gear* presenters]. Russell Brand [comedian] was the biggest seller over the Xmas run-up. I was starting to develop a theme though that the Queen was the only figure bucking the trend in popularity / respect and she never spoke to the media.

Tuesday 25 December

Ed V called. He was reading the new draft of the novel, said he liked it a lot more than the earlier one. The day went fine though my back was in agony.

* Lawyer husband of Tessa Jowell had been accused in Italy of money-laundering and tax fraud when acting for Prime Minister Berlusconi in the early 1990s.

Thursday 27 December

Benazir Bhutto [former Pakistan Prime Minister] assassinated. Shocking yet unsurprising at the same time. Watched rolling news and it was dire, breathless, repetitive, cliché-ridden.

Saturday 29 December

Long chat with Alex. He was in the hotel pre the West Ham game. He said he couldn't sleep, and sounded nervous about the game. He was going to be confined to the stands because of his whack at Mark Clattenberg [referee] and he said it was the most satisfying two-match ban yet.* We had a long, rambling chat over loads of stuff – Catholicism, Islam, South Africa, the rape story. He sounded like he just wanted to talk and kill time. He was adamant he was right to shut down the Evans story as he had. He was probably the only person in football who could do that.

Sunday 30 December

Out to the stables. Brian Wilson [Labour MP] there with his family. He said what was happening with GB was totally predictable. The only solution was for him to go before an election. He said JR was really getting into being Celtic chairman. He turned up in a tracksuit at one point. My back was still not great and later Len Findlater [osteo] came to see me and absolutely battered me, but it felt better afterwards. I was thinking of switching to cycling. Benazir was a total news sponge and Pakistan on the edge.

Monday 31 December

I had breakfast with Nick Keller. He had suggested twenty days' commitment to Beyond Sport [celebrating the use of sport to address social issues]. I wanted to cut down. He said I had done a great job rebuilding my own profile post-2003 and going back to GB would undo it all. He also felt it would feed into the idea that GB was done for. Across Christmas on the usual circuit the mood on GB had been good. Alex felt the Tories were back in if there was an election tomorrow. I had lunch with Ed Victor, who liked the novel now and wanted to present it to Gail

* Annoyed with the performance of the referee in a match at Bolton in November, Ferguson made his feelings known and was charged by the FA with 'using abusive and insulting words towards an official'. Bolton won 1–0. Ferguson was given a two-match touchline ban and fined £10,000.

and Susan next week. He felt they would be gobsmacked at how good it was, and also that the theme and characters were so deep. He disagreed with Fiona's analysis that it was all about sex, and he felt that was just her worrying people would read into it things about us. I told him the story of the novel Fiona accidentally deleted on the old Amstrad back in the '80s. Now it was his turn to be gobsmacked. But I felt sure some of the elements had survived in my head and they had gone into this. He said he had no doubt he would get a publisher for it without trying too hard. He also liked the idea of me doing a TV film alongside it, that was factual on mental illness.

Later I went out to Dalston to collect the three-headed statue I'd got made of the kids' heads for Fiona for Christmas. Looked really good and strong. Kirsty was really happy I liked it. To Lindsay's then the Blundells [friends] then up Kite Hill for midnight. I had put on six pounds over Christmas.

Wednesday 2 January 2008

Fiona's birthday, and the statue went down really well. Out in the evening to see *Mamma Mia!* I enjoyed it but felt I was coming up to a dip.

Thursday 3 January

Bit more Cudlipp lecture work. Geoffrey Goodman [former *Mirror* colleague] loved it. I was starting to write a strategy note about the novel. To Essex to get a bike for Rory. Very excited about it. The kids were really good at the moment though Grace getting more and more teenagey.

Friday 4 January

A big bad plunge definitely coming on. Not helped by the fact that there were so many arrangements attached to Fiona's fiftieth in Paris. Grace set off with the Bridges. We set off lunchtime for Eurostar and the arrangements were definitely beginning to stress me a bit. Loads of people at the station, and I was getting very irritable. At the Gare du Nord Fiona asked if I was OK. I clearly wasn't. She asked if the demons were coming out. Probably. I did a radio show down the line with Owen Coyle ahead of our Cup game with Arsenal. He was very articulate and smooth. We had dinner at La Maison Blanche after drinks at the Kennedys' [friends] hotel. It was a nice enough place. PG and David Mills were arguing mainly about the war. I was dipping badly, and didn't engage, and slipped out to make a call to David S.

Saturday 5 January

I felt bad anyway, and even worse knowing it would spoil things for Fiona. Had a heart-to-heart with F first thing. I said a while back she said she was sure I would do something to ruin it, but this was not deliberate. There is literally nothing I can do to stop it. It is just a horrible, horrible feeling inside and I can't stop it. She knew she shouldn't have said it, and said so. Just get through the day as best you can. Nice enough little hotel and bar next door. Lots of seeing people arriving and it was all a bit much. I needed to get away for a bit and stayed in the hotel p.m. and just tried to sleep it off. But I couldn't sleep. PG and Georgia went back to London for the Chelsea QPR game. I managed to get myself in slightly better shape for the do itself. The place worked out really well. Mum and Liz [AC's sister] and her kids were loving it. Mick Hucknall serenading Fiona. JP and Pauline [wife] on form. The neighbours loving it. The speeches went fine and there was a lot of warmth there for Fiona.

Sunday 6 January

Calum and I out on the RER [rail system] to the airport, and off to Manchester. Cab to Turf Moor. [Arsène] Wenger [Arsenal manager] came up to the boardroom before the match. We had a little chat, mainly about the sheer volume of games around Christmas, and a little bit on the political scene. The game was OK. Kyle Lafferty hit bar before they scored. We had far more chances and played better football but it was not to be [Arsenal 2, Burnley 0].

Monday 7 January

The kitchen was being ripped out, which wasn't helping my head. Drove out to Chigwell to get Rory's bike, then we had a decent ride around Regent's Park and Kenwood. GB appointed Stephen Carter [former CEO, Ofcom] as a special advisor which was being portrayed as him trying to get serious. Ed saw Gail and Susan about the novel. I had called it 'Psychological Flaws' on the cover, but had already decided that was not right, for all sorts of reasons, including my and the book's positioning. Ed said both were totally gobsmacked. Gail said that very few things surprised her, but this really did. I was working on Cudlipp speech and sending it around to various people for comments.

Wednesday 9 January

Long session with David S. He really liked the revised book, but on the down side felt it showed there was still too much going on in my head, and he had been worried about the plunge in Paris. He was still pressing me to go off on my own somewhere and really drill down deep. To the Honest Sausage to see PG. Hillary Clinton took New Hampshire [Democratic primary for presidential candidate] which was seen as an amazing comeback after losing Iowa. Another French telly offer on the back of the last trip, but it sounded a bit wanky. Random House came back with an OK offer on the novel. Gail felt it would need a fair bit of work with an experienced fiction editor. Deal seemed OK, obviously way, way less than the diaries. I wasn't that bothered about the money on this one, though Ed said for a first novel it was good. I was meanwhile close to persuading Eurostar to get behind a new and different sort of charity triathlon – namely swim in Brussels, bike in Paris, run and prize-giving in London, with Eurostar doing the journeys in between.

Thursday 10 January

Out on the bike when Gail called re the book. She said it was remarkable, but – and then there were lots of buts – this is a world you don't know, fiction so different blah blah, and it was all a bit annoying. She said there was an editor called Rebecca Carter she felt would be good. Susan much more positive. She felt parts of it were brilliant and could be really improved with tweaking. Gail said she wanted to protect me reputationally, not least re the diaries, and that meant ensuring it was a good novel per se that would get good reviews. She felt I had to take more advice than I was used to. Susan called half a dozen times and was really full of it, had read it closely and was buzzing re which bits she liked, which characters she liked. I felt she had a better take on the novel itself than Gail. Also her finance director had read it and said she had to take half an hour to cry her eyes out at the end. I worked on Cudlipp and on the paperback intro on the train to Manchester. Cudlipp was coming on, but I had to be careful not to refight too many old battles, or to do too much of 'wouldn't have happened in my day'.

Car to Old Trafford, where I was doing an event for CIVICA [outsourcing services company], mainly local government bods. Alex came up for the speech. He was looking really tired. They wanted a general spiel re strategy, which was fine and then in the Q&A lots of obvious stuff, GB, Hillary etc. I left with Alex who was saying Spurs were wanting £38 million for [Dimitar] Berbatov [Bulgarian footballer]. Home for dinner. The boys were out and I had a heart-to-heart with Grace who was really upset. At one point she said she was scared of my moods and depression, and she didn't know what to do when I was really low. We talked for ages and she felt better after I think. Molly was troubled by the work going on in the kitchen, and barking all night. Tessa called after the final judging on the Channel 4 Political Book of the Year. She said it was down to me v Tony Benn in the end, and I won, just. She said it was touch and go because there was a sentimental feel for Benn and Tony Howard [journalist] had been very pompous and sniffy about it. But it was fine. She felt I should be very gracious about the whole thing. Pretty bad coverage for TB joining JP Morgan [American investment bank] as a consultant. There was loads building up about him being in it for the money. PG and I both worried about it.

Friday 11 January

There was a big piece in the *Camden New Journal*, following on the *Mail* and *The Independent*, on Fiona's bash in Paris. Harmless enough but irritating. Gail called and we cleared the air after yesterday. She didn't mean to sound negative, just wanted to make sure I understood what I was getting into. She felt Ed had maybe indicated too much it was a done deal, which pissed him off, given he hadn't. He was pushing hard for a decent deal and when at one point he said he would show it around, things got a bit tense and scratchy, Susan even saying to Ed she would cancel lunch on Monday. Ed called at one point, said 'You and I are not the most popular boys in Vauxhall Bridge Road.' Gail and I had good chat but when Ed said he would take it elsewhere to see how much it could get, she and Susan both went spare. Fiona felt it was really not worth falling out over, but I felt there was a lot of being taken for granted going on; an assumption I would only deal with RH, an assumption I would do tons of media, an assumption I would go with whatever editing process they wanted. I told Charlie Falconer I had written it, and he was the latest to be gobsmacked. He loved the story, was really keen to read ASAP, but hated the idea of 'Psychological Flaws' as the title. He said the whole point of the book would be to take me to a different place, a mental health voice not a political voice, fiction not non-fiction, and PF would just get me mixed up in the politics of it. Totally right. Ed and I had already moved to that and I was doing a self-brainstorm on possible ideas. 'All in the Mind' was the simplest, maybe too obvious, but that might be a good thing.

Saturday 12 January

Out on the bike and then off with a subdued Calum with the car full of his bags for university. I finally got hold of Derry [Irvine, former Lord Chancellor] to invite him to Richard's memorial. Richard had always said Derry had been brilliant when he was taking on Reg Maudling [former Tory Chancellor who sued the *Mirror* over its allegations of corruption but died before the case came to court]. Derry concurred. 'He thought I was a genius!' He had read the diaries, and said he had one criticism. 'As it was a diary, there was no way of going back and saying you were wrong!' He felt the GB scene was not great, and getting worse, but he felt whereas TB had shown his ability to be decisive on difficult personnel issues – i.e. his sacking of him – he clearly found GB a harder thorn to wrestle with. It was a nice enough chat and he said he wanted an invite to the Cudlipp lecture.

Margaret McDonagh called. She was helping Peter Hain [Work and Pensions Secretary] who had got into something of a mess on the funding of his deputy leadership campaign, and she wanted me to have a word with him. I said I had read Steve Morgan [political consultant] and John Underwood [political advisor] were advising him, and I would not be happy if it got out I advised him. She said he was on his own at the moment and would just appreciate a chat because when the shit flies like this people walk away and he just needed a bit of support. PH and I had a few chats. He sounded pretty edgy about it. He went through the facts and though it was difficult he seemed on top of the detail finally and provided GB was supportive, and provided there wasn't a raft of new stuff to emerge in the Sundays, he should be OK. But Peter Watt having been thrown overboard, GB had made a real rod for his back. He had frankly been too keen to try to set himself out as Mr Clean on funding, when the reality was all fundraising could be made to look bad, and it had to be done.

Peter sounded pretty down. He needed to say something definitive today. I said you need to have a couple of big-picture messages. How you wanted to be deputy leader, thought you could do it, but it needs a professional campaign. How politics and democracy need funding, and we take it for granted at our peril. How you wish political debate was not all about this. He was fine with it all, knocked out a draft which I played with and sent it back. But then he called later and said it took No. 10 four hours to clear it. He said in my day it was possible to do things quickly and clearly. They just faffed all day and so it looked worse than it was, especially as the news outlets were trailing all day that he was going to be setting out his version. I advised him not to wear weekend clothes as pictures will be used out of context. He said he was grateful. Added that the current No. 10 operation was 'piss-poor'. Over to Burnley, good game, beat Plymouth one–nil. Over to Manchester. Unpacked Calum's gear, out for dinner, good chat.

Sunday 13 January

The novel stuff was getting very messy, and Philip sent me a note, saying he was worried about it. He felt I should try to make it work with RH come what may, and thought Ed was playing too hardball with Susan. It was all getting a bit out of hand. Ed and Susan at a stand-off position. PG and Gail were also worried it would come out that he and I shared a shrink!

Monday 14 January

Charlie was motoring through the book, loving it and also having some good thoughts. He also had good ideas on the Cudlipp draft, particularly on how politics was now mirroring some of the worst parts of the media. My throat and chest were playing up and I was worried I wouldn't have my voice for Wednesday, so I went to see Tom Bostock, in the usual rage about the NHS, government, said they hated single GPs and they were determined to get rid of him. He felt he was going to lose. I said I would help him out in any way. To the Tate to meet Susan for lunch. She felt Ed's dramatic moment – threatening to go elsewhere unless the money was upped – had backfired. She felt it would be a disaster if we went elsewhere. She said what they were offering was obviously way down on the diaries but this was a first novel, a different world, and although they knew I could generate publicity for it, that was not going to translate in the same way.

She went through some of the numbers for other writers and this was way ahead. She felt maybe we needed to meet in the middle. She later went back to Ed with an offer of £75k with a more demanding bonus scheme. Ed felt for a first novel it was not bad. I was not that bothered, just keen to get it sorted and then get on with working with a proper fiction editor to hone and improve. Charlie sent through a quite extraordinary note on it, signed Leo Tolstoy. Felt it was as good as anything he had read, particularly on depression. He was such a brilliant and attentive reader, and he restored my confidence that Ed was right to fight hard for it, and also that I would be able to use it to do a lot of good campaigning on depression and broader issues. Really cheered me up after all the angst with and between Ed, Gail and Susan.

Tuesday 15 January

I had written the tribute for Richard's memorial tomorrow but I was really worried about my voice, which was weakening and sore. Another day without training. Annoying. Grace was also not great and was off school. Out for dinner at Charlie and Marianna's. Charlie on good form, funny and sharp as ever. He was absolutely raving about the novel, by contrast with Fiona who still hadn't read it and when she mentioned it was more in the Gail camp than Charlie was. He couldn't understand Gail's position. He felt it needed just to be seized and it would really fly with support but we had got off on the wrong foot. He said don't let them change much, he felt it never dragged or jangled, and he really couldn't put it down once he got into it. Ed was still haggling with Susan. Charlie had turned down a big job with an American law firm. He was getting plenty of work offers but nothing yet that really gripped him. He was much more restricted as ex-Lord Chancellor than most former ministers. Marianna was the main breadwinner.

We were all a bit concerned at the way TB was being defined through the prism of money. We had both emphasised to him that he had to keep communicating as a politician, and have a rationale for the money that was about building a different form of public service which he had to fund himself. I think TB was too chilled in thinking people would see that anyway. Charlie felt it was close to a tipping point, also that the correct decision not to risk being seen as a back-seat driver for Gordon exacerbated the damage to TB from GB's differentiation strategy on spin, sleaze, policy positioning etc.

Wednesday 16 January

I stayed home, working upstairs but totally resting the voice, then off to St Clement Danes with Fiona for Richard's memorial. I took a diazepam on the way and even now, at the end of the day, can't remember as much as I ought to. There was a great turnout though and it was nice to see both Derry and Peter M there, in among loads of the old *Mirror* crowd, and a good smattering from elsewhere. I think it was the first time I had been inside the church, which they had managed to get on account of Penny's dad's military service. Really beautiful and the choir was just as good as [journalists' church, Fleet Street] St Brides'. Perhaps they were the same people. Hannah [daughter] did a nice first address and just about held it together when she got to talking about Phoebe [grand-daughter]. Penny did a reading and when she got through it fine, I knew I would have to as well, though I was feeling really on edge. Tina Weaver [*Sunday Mirror* editor] was very funny and her speech had a similar balance to mine – half funny anecdotes and lines, half what a great journalist and a great guy.

I was up after Nicola McAuliffe [actress friend of the Stotts] sang 'Swing Low Sweet Chariot', which again had a nice calming effect. I got through fine, the only choke when I caught sight of Fiona as I was talking about the last time I saw him. The two really big laughs were when I said the transformation of the Stab [old *Mirror* pub, the White Hart, nicknamed the Stab in the Back] into a pizza parlour was a rare blot on the otherwise unblemished modernisation of Britain under New Labour, and also the line re Peter M's column at *The People* being written by more people than read it. The structure was all the big breaks he gave me, first shifts on a national, first job, move to Parliament, support when I cracked up, another chance, support when I moved to work for TB, support throughout and then completing the circle as editor of the diaries. It definitely worked and I felt relieved when it was over.

Dozens and dozens of people mingling outside and a really nice mood. Then to the old City Golf Club, now the wine something or other, and it really was a bit like old Fleet Street though with less boozery. Some real old faces, just about everyone really. Drivers, photo assistants, secretaries, copytakers. The old sports desk secretary saying how proud she was of me and how she loved TB and what we did. It was a really nice do, and Penny seemed fine, though it was so strange to think he was gone. There were too many people from our early days in journalism already gone. I headed home via France 24 [French TV] bureau in Camden where I was doing a discussion with Manuel Valls [socialist party politician] on socialism. The peg was TB speaking at Sarkozy's UMP conference, which I was not sure was such a good idea and had said so to TB. He liked Sarko, fair enough, but given there was a battle going on in the PS [socialist party], and some wanted to push them to a more New Labour position, it wasn't exactly helpful to them. I am not sure it was too helpful to TB either. They played the clip of him saying what he would be in French politics. He joked he would be President then said no, he would be with the sensible socialists. Valls seemed fine with it. Again my French held up fine. My main point was that French socialists were having the same arguments, being promoted in many cases by the same faces, as when I lived there thirty years ago, and they had to face change. TB was clearly seen as the role model for winning from the left with arguments of the right, and I knew from my discussions with Valls when he worked for [Lionel] Jospin [French Prime Minister] that his instincts lay in that direction. But the old-fashioned elements in the PS were perhaps harder to take on than we had found in Labour, and so he was maybe more left-leaning in his comments than actually he was.

Thursday 17 January

Saw David S first thing. He felt the rows with Gail on the novel would not be good for me, especially given Philip had become involved. He was pressing me on why I thought I wrote it in the first place, and the various layers of rationale. It was hard to answer that. The idea literally popped into my head when I saw a funeral at Golders Green when out on the bike, and I wondered who all the mourners were, then carried on cycling and I just started out with this idea that it was a psychiatrist's funeral and then I started mapping out all the people who would be there – family at front, colleagues behind, then dozens and dozens of people he had helped. So maybe it was all inspired by lots of my sessions with David. He felt the depression and the psychosis explanations in there were fairly obvious, a way of me making sense of it all. I felt it was more the desire to give a creative expression to something that had been pretty dire. It was all very interesting in a way but I couldn't always know where this stuff came from and why.

Most of the characters were not in the original plan. Sturrock's death was not in the original plan, and if anything it was David S who had pushed me to that ending. 'So what does that say about you, that the shrink wanted to kill off the shrink? Maybe you need to go and find your soul on a desert island.' He laughed. We did have a good time chatting when I was in OK mood. He asked if I felt in any way that I was cleansing myself in writing it. He suggested maybe Psychologically Floored would be a better title. Calum felt his exam went OK. Ed and Susan still haggling bad-temperedly. Ed had not realised they felt world rights and serial would be included in the deal. I said basically get on and do it but it was a bad taste in mouth situation. A plane crash landing at LHR was a news wipeout. GB was caught up in the delay en route to China.

Friday 18 January

Out to do telly for Cathy Gilman on a Leukaemia Research project focused on identical twins which suggested the leukaemic cells were in the womb and also that treatment should be less violent in future. I got a nice email from Rebecca Carter, Gail's chosen editor, who said she thought the novel was 'wonderful' which meant we ought to be OK on the editing front. Liz [sister] finished it and said she was in floods of tears. She felt that it was very, very dark, and would make people worry about me! But she liked it and thought it would go well.

Saturday 19 January

A week without exercise. Feeling below par still and cough nagging away. Left fairly early for Coventry to meet Calum. GB on his trip to China and India. Plane stuck at LHR after crash landing still dominating the news. We won 2–1 at Coventry. Bumped into Fletch [Paul Fletcher] in the car park and had a chat about [former Burnley player] Andy Gray's departure. Player power. He was away for roughly double the money and the club felt they couldn't hold him once it was clear he so wanted to get away. Fletch taking the piss as ever, saying what's it like being wealthy with no obvious idea of what to do? Good game but I was feeling shit, both physically and the startings of a bit of a mental collapse too. I could sense a major dip ahead.

Monday 21 January

Went to see Bostock first thing. Keep going on antibiotics, he said, but I didn't feel much better. I felt weak whenever I stood up suddenly. Earache too. GB seemed to be doing OK in India – needless to say his talk of UN reform, and the idea of India on the Security Council, was going down well there. There was mayhem in the markets though with big talk about recession. Alistair Darling's Northern Rock [nationalisation] plan was getting a bit of a hammering.

Tuesday 22 January

I met Rebecca Carter at 10. Liked her. We agreed the structural problem related to the way the days mingled with each other, and also whether a suicide came on us too suddenly. I felt she got the book in the main. I wasn't sure whether the changes would be easily made but I was willing to give it a go. We chatted over it for a couple of hours. She said some of her book fixing went on for years. Effectively we had till May. She thought it was three-quarters there. I did a bit of thinking re restructuring. I was slipping down a few notches after another row with Fiona, and then with Grace who was telling us all sorts of stories about where she had been. Big tax bill to pay. I was supposed to meet TB but it turned out he was ill as well. The papers were full of Jeremy Paxman complaining M&S underwear does not provide 'adequate support'!

Wednesday 23 January

Mum was reading the book and though she had some concerns about it, she said once she got to the end 'greetin'' [crying] she had a better idea and appreciation. Saw DS and explained I had felt low all week. Again he was pressing me on whether there were feelings in my childhood like this, and like some of those in the novel. But if there were I couldn't remember them. It was all a bit meandering and I was not sure where it was all going. Stuart Prebble came round for a meeting and we went over a few ideas but was mainly focused on whether there might be spin-offs for TV from the book. He took away to read. Also had an idea for a series called *Driven* about what makes people driven.

Into town for lunch with Sally Morgan and PG at the Italian restaurant

I last went to with Nancy D. It was booked in Lord Gould's name which gave me a good piss-taking theme. Sally was late because of the police march against a staged pay rise which along with turmoil in the markets, Northern Rock and the general malaise feeling was creating a pretty bad mood around the place. Nice talking to Sally. We all felt TB was in some ways in a very good position but had to be careful about being seen as driven by money. There needs to be a charity element to what he is doing as well as the high politics. Sal was asked by GB to go into the government but resisting. None of us felt the enthusiasm though PG felt we had to do what we could. Tessa called. She had the norovirus so wouldn't be doing the awards tonight. I was down to win the Political Book of the Year and she was due to present the award. Out with Fiona and Gail and off to Channel 4. Gail seemed to be over our recent difficulties. PG had said they were genuinely taken aback that I had let Ed take the lead. He felt I was always best to represent myself, but I was happy for Ed to do it all.

Tony Benn was arriving as we did. 'You're bound to win,' he said 'but you must publish the whole thing as promised. And keep a diary for ever!' He was raving about what Melissa [Benn, daughter] said about Fiona's party in Paris. Next up Stephen Pound [Labour MP] who shouted out on entry 'Must be awful for you having to mix with all these B-listers?' I didn't feel great being there in that political/media mix and wished I wasn't doing the Cudlipp lecture or the select committee next week. I chatted with Anthony Seldon who said it was right I won and if I hadn't it would have been purely for political reasons. George Osborne, who won 'Opposition Politician of the Year', was saying (as he did last time I saw him) that he loved reading my diaries to spot where GB disappeared when the going got tough, and guessing where I had edited him out to protect him. He had a real glint in his eye, and a ruthless streak in him, I think. 'He must have made your life hell. But don't worry. We're killing him.' F, G and I were seated next to Peter Capaldi [actor] and Armando Iannucci [screenwriter, producer]. They were both perfectly nice and friendly, though Iannucci definitely seemed to have a genuinely well-developed cynicism about politics. Peter looked very different to his Malcolm Tucker [director of communications character allegedly based on AC] look because he was growing his hair to play Charles I. They were also working on a feature film based on *The Thick of It*, in which they went to the States. 'I'm sure we'll come out of that very well… Is there a war?' 'Might be.' They were there to win the Politics in the Media award. Interesting, not just from that but also from a lot of the jokes and the banter through the awards, that TB and co. were still the main focus. Capaldi said when I went and then TB they worried the programme would become almost redundant but nothing had really replaced us on the satire front. Similarly, when Hague won 'Politician's Politician' his best story was about TB. Brilliant delivery, as ever. When I went up to get the award and speak I didn't really get the balance right between grace and playing to the caricature. The film of the judging session was pretty negative, a Welsh Nat using the line about my book being the one most left in Travelodges. Amazing I won, really.

Geoffrey Robinson [Labour MP] said in his speech [presenting the award] it was accurate re my role in his downfall from his all too short ministerial career. I did a line thanking Benn for his advice – 'Listen to the lawyers' – but then had a dig at Clare Short [former Labour Cabinet minister], defended politics and politicians, and said I was glad Hague had not won elections and hoped Osborne didn't. I ended with a dig at Norman Baker, who was nominated for his David Kelly book [*The Strange Death of David Kelly*] – on which Charlie lacerated him in the little judging film, saying he might have done better in the science fiction awards. Someone who said they had worked with Baker said to me as we were leaving said I was very rude and needed to see a shrink. I said I already did and I would pass on his views. We got away pretty quickly. I hadn't handled the whole thing terribly well. I said to Fiona on the way home I felt ill at ease about the whole thing, hated that whole politico-media mix when everyone was pretending to get on, and it probably made me revert to type. Only chatting with Capaldi and Iannucci had made it bearable really. They were very likeable and funny.

Thursday 24 January

I had missed the news yesterday, but the Information Commissioner had ruled John Williams's [FCO] draft dossier had to be released. So WMD would be back on the political agenda. I was becoming more and more conflicted about Iraq. I was still feeling it was the right thing to do but the planning was so clearly wanting, there was too much bloodshed still, and too many of our own people were dead and injured. I still liked to think for millions of Iraqis life without Saddam was better, but it was not wholly clear. Calls for an inquiry were back on the agenda too.

A Danish magazine photographer was over doing pictures for the profile done by Helle's biographer. He had interviewed me about her for the book but then decided to turn it into a piece on me. I had been in email exchange with the snapper, called Sacha, and imagined a tall Danish blonde. Sacha turned out to be a man with a beard but a nice enough guy. PG and Georgia called round and we set off with Calum and Sacha for LSE. I was doing a talk for Philip's postgrad course on campaigns. He was on good form. Twenty-plus students, mainly overseas, and he did a presentation on theoretical strategy which was pretty good and larded with praise for me as the best ever which was nice for Calum to hear even if I was not sure it was true. They did some war room [strategy] exercises, as the campaign teams for Barack Obama, Hillary, Boris [Johnson] and Ken [Livingstone]. They were all very down on Ken. They felt he had no message and was slowly being taken out by the [Lynton] Crosby [Tories' election strategist] campaign through the right-wing media. There was a bad moment when PG was playing some clips of a TB speech and when there was a cutaway to GB, they laughed. Afterwards I asked some of them why, and they said he just looked so angry and bitter and they could tell he hated Tony!

I did half an hour off the cuff on strategy which seemed to be OK though I didn't leave long enough for questions. Off to lunch after more pictures with the students and I started getting calls to do stuff on Peter Hain resigning. The Electoral Commission had referred the case to the police so he decided to resign to clear his name. Nice to be with Calum and Georgia. I sensed the friendship of our kids and Philip and Gail's would endure long after we were gone. Liz called, worried about Donald and Graeme [brothers], Donald because he was going through one of his silent phases, Graeme because he was losing weight. She felt a lot of our issues stemmed from the different impacts we all felt when Donald was first diagnosed [with schizophrenia]. I went for a walk with Fiona and said I needed to decide re whether to get a job or not. The novel had filled a hole for a while but now less so, especially as it was becoming part of a bigger process now, and I could see there would be another wave of media promotion to do.

Friday 25 January

Two annoying diary items. A Capaldi quote in the *Times* diary saying I asked him to interview me as Malcolm to promote the book. And in *The Guardian* something about my Cudlipp lecture on Monday and so-called efforts made to keep war protesters out. Basically designed to get a few there I imagine. Not working much.

Saturday 26 January

To Kent for Joe Haines's 80th. I'm always struck in Kent by how fabulous some of the countryside is, yet it rarely springs to mind, compared with Scotland and the North, whenever thinking of great scenery. Joe had taken over a pub restaurant. Mainly friends from down there. But Gloria [Sharp, Haines's former PA], Penny [Stott] and Jill [Palmer] were there. It was a nice enough do, though I didn't sense Joe was enjoying it that much. I caught the news before *Match of the Day*, and post-Hain any funding stuff was going to fly, but it was ludicrous that the Beeb led on a *Sunday Mirror* page lead about Alan Johnson [Health Secretary] and a £3k donation not being declared.

Monday 28 January

TB texted. 'When good time to call?' We had not spoken for a while, and he was in good form. He wanted me to get involved in some of the Africa work. I said I thought he had to watch it a bit re the money he was making, or at least get explanation out there as to why he was making all this money. He said another contract was being announced today, Zurich. He had a lot of people to employ for the organisation he was building up, and the Foundation was going to be big. I said he needed to have an argument out there about post-power politics, that leaders were becoming leaders younger and so leaving younger and they still had a lot to give but they needed to fund their own operations. He sort of got it, but I felt he couldn't see why he needed to keep justifying everything he did. It was more, I felt, that unless there was a narrative about why he made the money, his enemies would define their own and it would all be about him getting rich, nothing to do with any good he could do.

On MEPP he felt he could see how to sort it and he could make a difference, but the US had to let him do the politics, but they don't really want to let go of it all. Condi got it but the others didn't really. He felt GB was slightly retracing his earlier steps, realised it was not great if people felt he was less New Labour, anti-reform etc., but people sussed it. They were wondering why did he take a different turn before and why was he turning back now? There was a lack of sincerity or authenticity there and people sensed it. He felt GB didn't know in himself what he wanted to do. TB was serious about going for the top EU job [President] but he felt the Germans didn't really want him, added to which Iraq and the Euro were both quite difficult issues held against him. But he felt he should see if it might happen. I told him I'd written a novel, and while he was surprised, he clearly felt that I should do something much bigger and more committed on the politics and policy front, but I was fine at the moment.

We chatted for an hour or so, very much like old times in some ways but we were now leading very different lives. He was all over the place – Middle East, China, speeches in the US, which he admitted were a bit soul destroying, Davos, Paris to see Sarko again tomorrow. I said have you actually ever sat down and really tried to reflect on how you got to where you are right now, and where you want to go? I sensed he never stayed still, and although he was doing lots of interesting stuff, seeing interesting people, still plugged in to a lot of the key issues, I sensed there was something missing, and he wasn't happy. He said he had not quite realised what he was letting himself in for when he did the UMP conference. But once he was there he was in for a penny, in for a pound in his approach as ever. Sarko was appreciative but it went down badly with the PS. We talked about what the kids were up to and so on, all very chatty. He wanted to meet up soon on Africa.

To Premier League HQ to see Dave Edmundson [ex-Burnley CEO] re his new Football League Trust job [CEO]. Nice guy and totally impassioned about his work, hoping I would want to get involved. I said I would put in a word with Andy Burnham [Secretary of State] who had just moved to DCMS [Department for Culture, Media and Sport]. Home and then out to London College of Communications with Fiona and Audrey to give the Cudlipp lecture. Lots of old friendly faces – Tony Miles, Geoffrey Goodman, Jill Palmer, Bill and Liz Hagerty, Roy Greenslade. Packed house with overflow and not a protester in sight. I'd done a fair bit of work on it, tried not just to make it an anti-press rant and felt I had one or two useful things to say about the way the media culture was changing. I sensed it went down well despite a bad sound system and a popping mike, but I felt they were pretty engaged. Jodi Cudlipp said publicly it was the best yet. Good Q&A, nice event. *The Guardian* said they were running extracts. I did a few snaps and chats with students, mingled, getting a lot of good feedback. Out for dinner at the Baltic with a group of the students including a young reporter from *The Independent* who won the Cudlipp bursary. He was with his girlfriend from *The Guardian* and it was nice to see them so clearly idealistic about what journalism could do. Jodi was really effusive. I regaled her with a few Maxwell stories.

Tuesday 29 January

Only *The Guardian* and *The Indy* did much with the speech. There were lots of positive responses on text and email and TB said he felt it would be like his feral beast speech, a slow burner that would be talked about for a while. But it was pretty clear the media did not really want the debate about their standards. I heard the *FT* were planning to do piece on the lack of reporting of it, along those lines. I was trying to wire some money to Graeme [brother] in Poland. I was on the phone to Western Union when PG called. I answered it, just saying 'Can I call you back?' 'OK,' he said, 'it's quite urgent.' When I called back, he just said straight out, 'I've been told I've got cancer.' Fuck. He said he had been having trouble swallowing for some weeks, had first been told he had an infection but further tests had shown a malignant tumour in the gullet. It sounded grim as hell but he was being amazingly Philipish about it all. He said it wasn't a great cancer to get but he totally bought into this idea that you have to stay positive, and the people around you have to stay positive too. We talked about the girls, Georgia knew but they were going down to see Grace in Oxford this evening and tell her. I just said we would do whatever, but what a fucking blow.

I told Fiona and our kids, who were really shaken. Fiona said it was impossible to imagine life without Philip around all the time. I talked to Georgia who was up doing some research in Manchester and later got Calum to go to see her. She was totally knocked sideways. I went to see Philip before he set off for Oxford and he was being very upbeat. But it did not sound great to me, and I sensed a real worry in his eyes, for all the positive upbeat talk. He had to have days of tests now to see if it had spread. F and I were out for dinner with Brendan [Foster]. Nice evening but I couldn't stop thinking about Philip, and how hard he would find it to tell Grace without everyone freaking out. I don't know why, given so many people survived cancer these days, but I feared the worst. Brendan was very down on GB. He felt the Tories' tails were up and he was not sure how they get pulled back in.

Wednesday 30 January

Breakfast with Liz Murdoch [daughter of Rupert] at the Berkeley. She was full-on charming, and keen for me to do pretty much anything. I had no idea that her TV company [Shine] was quite so big already. She said presence plus charisma plus a way with words plus caring about big issues plus having good ideas was a winning formula and she hoped I would do some kind of format thing with her. I told her I had a bit of a love/hate thing with telly, and was being inundated periodically with really shit ideas. I said though that I was keen to do stuff on mental health, told her about the novel and her eyes lit up. She said she would love to read it, so I agreed to send it to her. I sensed she and Matthew [Freud, husband] were getting on OK, but that there were a few tensions between him and the rest of the Murdoch clan. I suspect she was veering a bit off-centre, and a bit closer to my side of the argument about the media. She wasn't exactly effusive about them all. She felt her dad was still going strong, and had a lot left in him. Her enthusiasm for the novel, and the story as I told it, told me that regardless of whether she did anything with it, I would have no trouble doing some decent mental health stuff on the back of it.

I walked to the Commons, for yet another select committee appearance, and went through to the committee corridor. It was so different to previous committee appearances. No crowds to get through. Only a handful of media. A few Tory MPs came by for a chat including Nick Winterton who said the whole place just wasn't relevant like it used to be. Chris

Meyer was giving evidence and they asked if I wanted to go in to hear him. I said no. I could hear him through the door anyway, droning on in his pompous manner, and he warned I would probably have a pop at the PCC which indeed I did. I had a real whack at the *Mail*, said Dacre was evil, defended our overall strategy and said that the media had changed so much it was no longer really about ownership but standards and speed. They tried to get me going a bit on the Beeb but I was pretty gentle. It had been useful to do the Cudlipp lecture and get the arguments clear in my head. I hadn't particularly enjoyed going back there. I had lunch with Bruce Grocott who said he was feeling liberated.

Thursday 31 January

Danny Finkelstein [*Times* comment editor] called asking if I would do a piece on Britney Spears [American singer] for *The Times*. He said he had asked for 50k to ask and 100k if I said yes. But I agreed to do it for nothing and felt, as she was rushed to hospital once more, that it was worth asking the question if there was any room for humanity left in journalism. She had reached that near-Diana level of fame that meant she was no longer really viewed as a human being, but the sight of a great convoy chasing her on her way to hospital was sick. I knocked it out quickly and Danny came back and said they loved it. But James Harding [editor] wanted me to take out the reference to Dacre specifically as the one I most loathed. He thought just say the *Mail*. I felt it was cowardly and didn't really buy his line that he intended to go for him one day but wanted to pick his moment. Then Tina Weaver called asking if I could do a *Sunday Mirror* guest column. I did a lead on the US elections, a whack at Nick Robinson's endless processology and opining. A piece on Fiona and sport. Vote Ken v Boris.

Then out for two hours on the bike before going to see PG again. He was not hiding it from anyone and was really jokey about it but deep down he must be really worried. The stuff I had read on the internet was grim. 'Oh, I've read far worse,' he said. Basically a good result meant he might have a few years. JP sent me through a draft of his book. I read it with a mix of amusement and alarm. It was fine, and in parts a good read, but I felt he was playing too much to the media caricature, and so it was a lot less serious a book than he could have written.

Friday 1 February

The Britney piece really connected, and I got a stack of calls from TV, radio and other media here and in the States. I did Radio 5 prior to them doing a phone-in on it. Interesting too that there was quite a positive response on Times Online and when people did the usual kneejerk critical, quite a few were defending me. I had another look through JP's book, and decided to send him a note, basically saying it was a bit demeaning of him, and potentially damaging for others. I knew how sensitive he could be, didn't particularly want to say it was badly written, so said it was an interesting, racy, pacy read, will get a lot of attention, should sell outside the obvious political circles, with some genuinely groundbreaking stories in there, personal and political. BUT – big but – that it didn't do justice to him, his role, or the depth and breadth of his character.

The fundamental problem was that it reads too much like an extended interview written up by a ghostwriter, not sufficiently like a considered self-analysis and account of a fascinating life and career. The anecdotes and the views roll along nicely, but I was left wanting more passages where you then reflect, and give today's perspective on yesterday's events. I urged him to sit down on his own, go through it and add in a sense of genuine reflection. It had the potential to damage GB now, and TB's record of back then, and I was sure some of the attacks on colleagues and others, and some of the observations about them, would be counterproductive, a risk exacerbated by the fact of serialisation. He'd asked me what stories I thought a paper would take from it, and I said one would be TB–GB and the 'threat to resign', which I feel is overwritten and doesn't give a broad enough feel for all the things going on at that time. Him saying CB–Sarah [Brown] relations were not good would also be seen as a big story, alongside CB 'hating' GB and wishing him ill. The bulimia story would go very big, and it was fascinating to read.* But again it was not written in a serious enough style.

I said I was worried it would even leave him open to ridicule when he would be doing something really important in saying all this. He needed more on the nature of the illness, properly researched or a commitment to get involved in a charity or campaign about it. Then there was the whole story of his affair with his secretary [Tracey Temple]. We spoke a couple of times during the day, and I said it was quite negative about a lot of people, and not that positive about many. It needs to have bigger and more policy-based analysis of how we did what we did – why TB was right for the time; why GB was so brilliant as Chancellor; why Labour values are still relevant for today; how other characters in the government helped to deliver real change. Otherwise there is a risk it is just seen for all the whacks at Harriet, Neil, the policy wonks he dismisses as Mekons [comic-book villain], dour GB, TB not liking the party and being more SDP-type, his obsession with the 'Beautiful People', saying focus groups

* JP confessed that he had suffered from the eating disorder for two decades.

were the same as reading tea leaves, all feuds and spats and fights, being excluded from events. And why say all MPs are the same when they're not? It gives it away that a ghostwriter had done it.

I also suggested he should call the Labour people by their first names – Tony, Gordon, Neil. It seems pretty harsh when it's Blair, Brown, Kinnock. There was also way too much about the stuff that plays into a sense of JP's insecurity – 'Do you really want the [Matthew] Parrises and [*Guardian* writer Simon] Hoggarts to know how much they get to you?' – and too much about what will be seen as perks/trappings – Jags, Dorneywood, croquet, security etc. It plays into the idea it is all about the chips on shoulders. I said it reads as though having a nice car or being able to play croquet without the press bothering you is as important as policy stuff that really matters. There was also a proper fact-check needed, far too much 'I can't really remember the detail but…' Twice, I said, you have me on the wrong paper at the wrong time. It doesn't matter in the scheme of things, but it tells me there has been no real fact-checking.

Then there are big facts that are wrong – e.g. it says Clare Short resigned before Robin Cook – not so. Or the chronology of the TB/GB discussions after [former Labour leader] John Smith's death. Also, he effectively confirms a Granita [restaurant venue of TB–GB meeting to discuss leadership in 1994] deal, whilst admitting he can't know for sure what was said between them, which will not be good for GB/TB. It also says TB regularly broke his word, which either needs to be properly substantiated or not used. He uses the word 'con' at one point. Heavy. Saying to TB 'You know fuck all about Ernie Bevin [legendary Labour wartime and post-war minister]' – really? I couldn't tell if he was taking it in or being pissed off I was saying all this. I sent him through name misspellings and told him he has Robert Armstrong as Cabinet Secretary when it was Robin Butler. But the main thing is that there is not enough in there about policy and politics. Even Iraq – he basically just says 'It's a disaster,' Bush is a 'gangster movie star', and moves on.

It says to me there has not been enough actual research – of speeches inside and outside the House; really important policy debates the detail of which he has maybe forgotten. There is not enough of that, and too much of the stuff that focuses on personality, which is particularly important in that he castigates the press, yet lets a journalist write a book like this which will be serialised in a newspaper. And while accepting it was a bit rich coming from me, I said there was too much swearing. I said I had no memory of the incident he describes of him swearing in a Cabinet meeting. 'Well pissed off' – too colloquial. TB 'buggering off to Australia'. Another part – 'I dunno why.' I said it is a book, not a conversation, and wouldn't do him any good if it is written so colloquially. And saying he had no idea what the price of a Tube journey was a bit daft given he was in charge of transport. He said he would have another look, but I suspected it was well down the track.

To a Random House meeting on both diaries and the novel. All seemed fine about both. I was still worrying about the title of the novel. I had put 'Psychological Flaws' on the manuscript cover, but more to grab attention than as a planned title. But some liked it and some – Fiona, Gail for example – hated it. The art department had done a really nice selection of possible covers, and it felt real seeing it like that. We were aiming for paperback of the diaries in May and the novel in November. Gail was holding up pretty well. She and I drove back to their house in Regent's Park and later Fiona joined us. I agreed to stand in for Philip for his LSE course on strategy and campaigns, which I think was hanging over him a bit. TB saw him earlier and PG was full of it, how nice he was, what a great man, great politician, so much superior to the rest. TB had said PG was the one whose spirit always kept us up when the going got tough. Lots of people were calling him and worrying now. Fiona said she was shocked at how weak he looked, and how hard he was trying to pretend he was OK. I didn't want to stay too long because I had a bad cold and was worried about infections.

Saturday 2 February

Rebecca Carter sent through a much more detailed analysis of the novel than I expected, almost all of which I agreed with. Her concerns that the narrative pace needed to vary more. She said she felt it needed a fair bit of restructuring, which looked a bit alarming, but her analysis note led me to believe she knew what she was doing. She said a novelist–editor relationship was not always easy, but she hoped I would trust her. I sensed that I would. I liked her and could see she was clever. Off to West Brom, meeting Calum there. My cold was worse, it was freezing and I felt ill, but I didn't want to miss it. Huge Burnley turnout, the club having provided free coach travel. Good atmosphere. I bumped into John Motson [BBC commentator] in the car park who had just had a car prang, so he spent forever telling me about that before picking my brains on the team. He was such an enthusiast, and such a pro. We went one up and the place went mental. Pegged back, then 2–1 down, then Brian Jensen [Burnley goalkeeper] saved a penalty but we couldn't nick a late goal. Drove back and was feeling pretty ropy.

Sunday 3 February

Seb Coe came on asking for a copy of the Cudlipp lecture as had among others Jonathan [Powell] and Bob Geldof. JoP was hating his [Morgan

Stanley] bank job. He said he really wasn't interested. He clearly wanted to be back with TB chasing the Europe job which he seemed to think might be possible. David M called to talk about PG, as were lots of others, but we turned to the political scene. He said it was truly dire. No strategy or leadership. No co-ordination. No sense of the purpose of them being in government. He also said the top four jobs now were shadowed by people who in their own way looked just as good or just as big as our team. I felt tired and depressed even thinking about it. God knows what it was like being there. I said I saw no real fight or spirit and no strategic narrative. He says the trouble is GB doesn't really know what he wants to do.

Monday 4 February

A meeting on the full volumes of diaries. Still working on novel title. Bruce pretty opposed to 'Psychological Flaws'. Cudlipp lecture still getting a bit of comment and quite a lot of ongoing TV bids from abroad. Bruce said he thought it was superb but said 'Now old lad you have to come up with some answers.' Seb and Geldof nice about it.

Tuesday 5 February

I was working on a BBC NE film on the Eastwood family from Middlesbrough, who effectively started Leukaemia Research by selling the toys of their child, Susan, when she died, and sending the money to Great Ormond Street. I started with Cathy who interviewed really well. Then to GOS with a press officer, Jo. I went to Fox ward where Ellie [Merritt, daughter of Lindsay and John] had been when she died but also the Elephant day room where we used to visit her. God that was an awful time. I interviewed Nick Goulden who was registrar when Ellie there. He also treated Sissy and Victoria Bridge [Sissy's mother] went all misty-eyed when I said I had met him. Headed to King's Cross and did a piece to camera on the train to Newcastle. I was talking to a Paris agent about the title of the novel in French. Translation was under way. I felt dreadful and after arrival at the Copthorne just went to bed after a session in the sauna. God knows how long I've been feeling under the weather. Quite a while.

Wednesday 6 February

Gym, breakfast and off to Middlesbrough with the crew. Still feeling rough. To a pretty tough estate to record a 'This is the house where it all began' piece to camera. Neighbours a bit hacked off, several worrying it was something to do with the DSS [Social Security]. Dogs, litter, young couples pushing prams. All a bit *Shameless*. Then to a beautiful hilltop for a classic 'This is Teesside' shot and a trailer. To Banksfield primary to see ten-year-old survivor Rachael and her mum. Kids great. Another tough area but good teachers and obvious improvements. Sure Start [government childcare and early education initiative] down the road. Fantastic sports facilities. Computers all over the shop.

Super Tuesday [numerous US presidential candidate primaries] results showing Hillary and Obama neck and neck, [Senator] John McCain the clear runaway for the Republicans. To Knayton to see Sylvia Gaunt, Susan Eastwood's sister. Nice village, nice tidy house. Loads of books on Diana and she mentioned several times me sending her a copy of my book, which I did when I got home. She was nice, though I sensed a bit peeved that the charity didn't do more to recognise the story. Made the 3.30 train and got home to watch England v Switzerland [2–1].

Thursday 7 February

Dentist then off to Oxford to collect Rory who wanted to come back with his bike. Did a bit of work, pottering in the main, then out to Cirque du Soleil. Incredible acts of physical endeavour. Enjoyed it more than I thought I would.

Friday 8 February

David S. He seemed a bit low himself, which is exactly what PG had said about the last time he saw him. Long bike ride, lunch with the boys – both back from university despite being in term – then to see PG who seemed OK but maybe a little more subdued. I was agonising about 'Psychological Flaws'. I can't seem to find a better alternative, but there is a nagging doubt, and the fact it keeps nagging means there is no doubt at all.

Saturday 9 February

Chest infection, antibiotics. Sheila O'Shea [US publisher] was in town and came up for a cup of tea. I told her about the novel, told her what it was about, then the working title which she loved. Then I told her about the baggage re GB, and she changed her mind.* She said it would take me back to my past and this had to be about a new future and a radical

* After a briefing from AC in 1997, *Observer* journalist Andrew Rawnsley used the phrase 'psychological flaws' about GB. AC denied using those exact words but admitted he had been 'pretty heavy' in talking about GB.

departure. She was right. Others had said it but somehow she crystallised it better. She was really nice as ever, yet again urging me to get a seat and go for the top job.

Sunday 10 February

Rory really not well. Out on the bike for two hours, then watched Man U losing [2–1] at home to City in the Munich air crash anniversary game.* Spoke to Alex later who said they just froze amid the emotion of it all. He felt it was the scarves all held aloft that got to them. To Neil's to see them plus Helle and the kids. Steve [Kinnock] out seeing someone re a job. Helle still seemed OK re the future and fairly confident but it was tough. Neil thought I should do a book on opposition. Told them re the novel. Had a discussion about whether we were all mad.

Monday 11 February

Finally decided on the title that 'Psychological Flaws' was wrong on so many levels. Sheila O'Shea was the clincher. I had a meeting with TB, to introduce him to Nick Keller and try to get him involved in Beyond Sport. Sport as social good was a strong theme for him if he wanted to get into it. He was in a pro tem office in St James's Square while waiting for his own office to be set up. It was very much set up like his private office, and some of the same people from No. 10 added to that impression. Jo Gibbons – pregnant. Catherine Rimmer, Ruth Turner, Victoria Gould and Katie Kay. Gavin Mackay. Matthew Doyle [all members of TB's Downing Street private office staff]. Some of the cops were the same, though there were a couple I didn't know. Nick did his presentation which went fine, basically the same pitch he had made to me, and both Ruth and Jo were pushing for it. TB was asking a few questions but clearly was fairly keen. He kept saying he was working harder than ever which seemed a bit odd.

After Nick went out we had a little chat. He was seeing GB tonight. He intended to tell him the situation was recoverable but it had to be based on something real. He was doing lots of New Labour stuff now but it left serious people wondering why the distancing had happened in the first place. Re Balls, he said he was a lethal combination of very bright, able to take decisions – more than GB in some ways – but lacking in political judgement at times. For the rest, there was nothing much coming through.

* On 6 February 1958, twenty-three men died when the aircraft carrying the Manchester United team, staff and football reporters crashed on take-off in bad weather at Munich-Riem airport.

He said again he would like me to do something on Africa and governance with him. I said I needed to be clearer about what exactly he felt I could achieve that he wouldn't get from someone else. I didn't just want to be advising dictators how to be a bit less dictatorial. He said that I had a reputation with a lot of leaders and sometimes I could say things he couldn't. People knew I was direct, and clear thinking, and these people needed help.

He agreed I should be moving away from comms in so far as it related to media management, but not when it came to advising on developing and implementing strategy. So few people got it at all. He seemed pretty good and fit and enjoying himself. I said if it was true he was working harder than when PM, he needed his head looking at. He needed to chill a bit. But he said he was determined he was going to build something big and enduring, and the Africa and Middle East stuff in particular really mattered. My sense was he was having big doubts re GB again but he said he intended to be very frank with him. Again, I said. I showed him the artwork of the novel cover, with the 'Psychological Flaws' title. He laughed, then said 'You can't do that.' I kidded him on for a while that I would.

Tuesday 12 February

To Kensington Hilton for Labour fundraiser planning meeting. Then to QPR v Burnley. I met up with Cathy Pickup and crew and had a quick drink in the Trophy Room before heading round to the away end, where a bunch of anti-war protesters were handing out leaflets about me and Leukaemia Research, saying my role in the war and the use of depleted uranium meant I caused it. I thought they were flogging fanzines, but as I got closer, I heard one of them shout out 'Here he is,' then a few shouting 'War criminal.' I'd had no warning they were there and one or two got pretty unpleasant as I arrived but the Burnley fans turned on them pretty loudly and I just carried on in. Then during the second half they invaded the pitch and ran towards the away end with banners saying 'Campbell causes leukaemia' etc.

The Burnley fans were good, first just shouting at them to get off the pitch, then chanting 'Who are you, who are you?' and 'You sad bastards,' then around me 'There's only one Ali Campbell.' The cops and the stewards got them off fairly quickly. I spoke to Owen Coyle [Burnley manager] later and he said Steve Davis [assistant] thought it was a protest about Campbell's soup. On the field, it was a fantastic game. We went two down. Then Andy Cole got a hat-trick plus one from Ade Akinbiyi made it a great turnaround and massive celebrations at the end with Cole parading round with the ball. Calum was on the phone the whole time wishing he was there. I went back with Georgia [Gould, a QPR season ticket holder] who was mortified about the protests, apologising and saying they were not QPR fans. She was clearly really worried re PG whose chemo started today.

Wednesday 13 February

Heavy lifting on the novel edit. I was rewriting new sections to take in some of Rebecca's ideas. Rory was better but still not 100 per cent. Out in the evening for another LRF fundraiser. Need to wind back a bit maybe.

Thursday 14 February

I was doing the first of my standing in for PG in his political strategy course at LSE. I got the Tube in with my briefcase feeling very lecturer-ish. A couple who had been at the QPR match were asking me about the protest and if it happened a lot. I said it was the first time anything like that had happened at football. 'Must be very weird,' the woman said. 'It's like they were acting as though the war was your decision.' I quite enjoyed the LSE session though I couldn't see myself in that role long-term. A lovely Greek girl came up and said hello, said I had inspired her to do politics and she wanted to be a strategist when she left. Andrew Cooper [Tory strategist] was helping with his own presentation. I did my main strategy spiel and talked about how we used polling, quantitative and qualitative. Andrew seemed to think we were in trouble but also that the Tories should be doing better. The students were bright, quite challenging, and clearly liked PG a lot.

Back to do more work on the edit, then in with Fiona to Sarah's No. 10 reception, for the Piggy Bank Kids [disadvantaged children's charity]. Nice enough time. Lots of people being friendly. Nice chat with Seb and David Davies re sporting stuff. Seb such a good guy, and smart. Piers was there, usual mix of tension and bonhomie. Dacre. His relationship with GB really was nauseating. I talked mainly to David Frost, who was on fine form. Alistair Darling asked us up to the flat, and he was really not in good shape. All the problems came pouring out and little sign of solutions. He said he had thought the other day about packing it in. He felt GB was almost certainly depressed. He found it harder and harder to have what you would call a normal conversation with him. Gordon veered between rage and sulking silence. Neither exactly made for effective co-operation between 10 and 11. And of course GB having operated in No. 11 the way he had with TB, he assumed AD was likely to be doing the same.

He felt they had been operating OK, and doing better in terms of policy, around Christmas and the New Year but things had gone backwards again. He looked low and sounded low, and I felt the fight was going out of him, that he could not really see how he could take the GB modus operandi much longer. He was very down on Balls, also on Douglas A, who he felt was also working against him. He was definitely wondering, probably most of every day, if he had had enough. I asked where our Tory attack was. He agreed there was none. All a bit depressing. He felt if GB hit real trouble several would turn. A couple of his and Maggie's friends were there, and even with them he seemed very down about things. He really looked weighed down. I told him I was less motivated to help GB when I saw him cuddling up to Dacre again, as earlier tonight.

Friday 15 February

To Western House [BBC radio] to record the voiceover for my LRF film. Also doing *Mirror* piece on the same. Up to Wales, straight (packed) train to Flint. Met by [Labour MP] David Hanson's wife Margaret, and to the hotel. Lots of old people staying there. Dinner for around seventy, and did usual pitch and a short Q&A. Decided to stay up for the United v Arsenal game tomorrow. I sorted tickets with Alex and told Calum while Fiona sorted a hotel. The party event went fine, good solid people, but I sensed some concern re the Welsh nationalists, and also that GB was beginning to be much more of a negative than when he started.

Saturday 16 February

Over to Manchester first thing with David and his young son. Lovely bloke. He was enjoying his job as Prisons Minister, but it was tough. He was fascinated by and fascinating about prisons. He reckoned the worst was Acklington in the north-east where they had lost control and they had a no-go zone where there was violence and drugging etc. He shared a lot of the usual worries re GB, and also felt TB had to watch himself in terms of how his reputation developed. Up to Old Trafford to collect tickets, then to the Midland Hotel for lunch before heading up to the match. United [4–0] rout. Nice time with Calum.

Sunday 17 February

On the train back, I was sitting next to two women arguing passionately about whether *Strictly Come Dancing* or *Dancing on Ice* is better. I thought they would come to blows. I asked them if they ever got as worked up about anything to do with politics. They looked at me like I was mad, then went back to it. PG round with Gail later. He was handling things really well, but I sensed Gail was low. The big news was Northern Rock to be nationalised, and Alistair D was getting it big time in the neck again.

Monday 18 February

Golf at Swinley with David Mills, Harry [Portsmouth manager] and Jamie Redknapp. Portsmouth had won again in the FA Cup, in the last minute yesterday, and the draw for the sixth round was happening as we went round. Harry kept saying 'If we avoid Man U, we can win the whole thing this year.' He was on the phone to Peter Storey [club secretary] when the draw was happening. We all stopped and he was passing on the details. 'Pompey at home,' he said. Big thumbs-up. 'Please not Man U.' Then, when he chucked his club about as far as he had been hitting the ball, we realised it was Man U. 'Fuck, fuck, fuck.' He couldn't get it out of his head after that.* Nice guy, good stories. I was playing as well as I had played in years. We were four up at one point but we blew it and ended all square.

Tuesday 19 February

Claire Round [Random House] round to film for their marketing sales conference. Work then ran to King's Cross and back to get train tickets for Retford next week. I was finding more and more that I needed some purpose other than just the run to get out and should do a longish one. Into Random House to meet Charlotte Bush and Fiona McMorrough, a freelance who was going to help with the launch and PR strategy. I liked her. Irish and smart. Then to the InterContinental hotel for a paid speaking gig. Quite a good bunch. Standard speech plus a few off-the-cuff bits, then short Q&A. Good laugh with a woman whose husband reads the *Mail*, and she hates him for it. Another anti-war demo turned up, and they advised I go out via the basement.

Thursday 21 February

Saw David S. Actually I'd been OK on the head front for a fair while now. Maybe the novel had helped. He certainly seemed to think I had put a lot of myself in there. He seemed pretty unfazed by the idea that he was in there too. My second session at the LSE standing in for PG, and I roped in Margaret McDonagh as the guest speaker. She was really good, well prepared, very tough, and with a lot of detail. They were taking so

* Portsmouth subsequently beat Manchester United 1–0 and went on to win the Cup, beating Cardiff 1–0.

many notes, realising this was such a good practical demonstration of how politics and political machinery worked. I think we dovetailed OK. It was ludicrous she was not still running the party machine, or at least centrally involved. She said she had an idea that we should identify thirty or so future candidates, get them elected and then put our feet up. In the US, the momentum really was with Obama now but the LSE team felt he was coming under more scrutiny and not coming out great. They were enjoying the practical brainstorms we did on the various campaigns. I was back running, very slow but at least I was doing it. Did an hour, running various errands.

Friday 22 February

To BBC TV Centre to do a bit of radio and telly on the film I had made about the Eastwood family. Good spread in the *Mirror* today. Did Radio Tees, then Radio Lancs on something else, and then BBC World. Eve Pollard [journalist] was in reviewing the papers and as always it was so nice to chat with her. A real glass-half-full person. Fiona McM put out the announcement about the novel at 11 and seemed to get good initial response. Also *Newsnight* wanted to do a number. Though we had agreed low key best, decided it was too good to miss as it basically said this mattered, so after toing and froing we went for it. Gavin Esler was doing the interview, all fine. There was a bit of a silly pre-package but quite good fun. The guy from Waterstones saying I might not be popular with everyone but people were fascinated. Edwina [Currie, author, former Tory MP] saying I should have done political thriller and me saying no. Good positioning overall. I stayed to see the papers. *The Guardian* did it on the front, with a little spoof extract, and bits and bobs elsewhere.

Saturday 23 February

I was working on planning for the Sports Awards while watching loads of football. Birmingham v Arsenal [2–2] including [Arsenal player] Eduardo's horrific injury followed by mega sanctimoniousness from the Sky commentary team and OTT reaction from Wenger. Then Man U winning 5–1 at Newcastle. All the kids were home. I love it when all three are here.

Sunday 24 February

Rebecca was starting to put through chapter-by-chapter line edit of the novel. Mainly OK stuff really. Happy enough with most of it. I did a one-and-a-half-hour run. Chelsea losing to Spurs [2–1] in Carling Cup final.

Monday 25 February

I'd not seen Mum for a few weeks, so I took the mid-morning train and met her in Retford. Still looking good for eighty-plus and is totally compos mentis. Driving along and chatting away. She was still a bit troubled by the book I think but she had read it again and said second time around she got better what it was about and why I might have written it. We had a really nice day and I remembered John Madejski saying how important it was to spend time with your parents before they died. Our kids were doing fine, though Grace was not working hard enough and Rory had got into a really bad fight with some rugger bugger who had called me a war criminal. Rory put the guy in hospital. Fiona was worried because of his temper, but he was clearly very proud he had stuck up for me. Georgia said the other guy was a renowned twat.

Tuesday 26 February

All day on the Sports Industry Awards panel. Bloomberg building, which had a weird and rather cultist feel to it. It was the place we had come for the TB–GB big economic launch during the last election. We were today down in an auditorium where around a dozen of us spent a few hours going through a dozen or so categories. Quite a few marketing whizz-kids there. Just two women. No non-whites. Jon Holmes, [broadcaster and former footballer] Gary Lineker's agent, who won his fight to get Setanta Sports [TV channel] as Business Achievement of the Year. Quite enjoyed it. Headed home for a while, then out to Shepherds to meet Fiona and DB. They had been doing one of those Carole Stone [networker, media consultant] debates v [Lord] Norman Tebbit [former Tory minister] and Chris Woodhead [former Chief Inspector of Schools] among others. David had had to leave for a vote and they lost the debate ['All schools, state as well as private, should be allowed to select their own pupils'] vote, which they would have done anyway because the whole thing is right-wing dominated. They were bound to be the kind of people packing out the private schools.

David seemed OK if a bit subdued. Still obsessed about people sneezing without a hanky. Two people at nearby tables sneezed within seconds of each other and he said very loudly 'No hanky, no tissue, I can always tell.' He said he was making plenty of money and also had a relationship with a GP up north, but clearly missed being in government. GB had given him a couple of things to do but they were just to keep him in rather than out. They didn't add up to much. He felt the scene was pretty poor, and that the lack of direction and strategy was clear. Nice enough to see him but I really didn't like being in that Westminster world any more. TB definitely did the right thing getting out immediately. Felt sorry for the ones who had been up there and now struggling with being around all the time but unfulfilled. Calum was texting all night from the Burnley win over Coventry [2–0].

Wednesday 27 February

Picking up on the line edit again. I was quite keen to get the whole thing over and done with. It felt a long time till November. I suggested that we bring it forward but Gail was adamant they needed time to do selling in, whatever that is. Rebecca was querying what 'winky wanky' meant. I gave her a number of possibilities including Japanese translation of 'All in the Mind', and ailment confirming masturbation makes you go blind. She went for that one. Enjoying working with her, but it was too slow at the moment.

Thursday 28 February

To the LSE, via Costa Coffee, to meet Alan Milburn. On good form, both joking about the ludicrous nature of our post-frontline lives and some of the things we did. He was heading off afterwards to meet a hedge fund boss. He said he mixed making money with trying to make political arguments but felt GB was not really listening too much to anything outside his little circle. The students were pretty good with him. He overdid his role in the Oz election a bit. We were mainly talking about relationships and structures and also media management. All good stuff I think. I walked to Swiss Cottage to do a French TV interview at the Marriott for a documentary on Sarkozy's comms. All the usual stuff. Carol Linforth called. She sounded like if something else came up, she would take it. I said I would always give her a reference. She said the atmosphere was terrible. I said I felt totally demotivated re the sports fundraiser, plus GB–Dacre and especially with what the *Standard* were doing to Ken [Livingstone, re. forthcoming London mayoral election], which was appalling. I kind of felt in last-straw territory. Also whatever else, we were seen as winners and I didn't want to be part of the losing.

Friday 29 February

I was finding running difficult again so did a long walk. Went to do a Dutch TV interview re my Cudlipp speech and all the issues. Title of the show 'The Lie Rules', apparently something Queen Beatrix said under her breath about the media. Felt it was OK. Then to Eurostar for a meeting on the three-city triathlon plan which everyone seemed to be up for now.

Saturday 1 March

At the No. 10 do recently, AD had asked if I could meet him somewhere away from Westminster to go over the Budget. Grace was going to the stables in Essex so we met for breakfast at Catherine Macleod's. He was still pretty down, both looking and sounding as though all the cares in the world were upon him. I emphasised the need to lift his mind out of the defensive posture. Things were not as bad with the public as they were with the media. He seemed to buy it rationally but was very down, not of course helped by the fact GB was too, and showing little sign of lifting himself. Added to which he clearly felt Balls was undermining him through the media. Balls was now seemingly convinced he was leadership material. We did a line by line on his Budget speech and I wondered whether he was even committing some kind of offence showing it to me, but he trusted me not to say anything to anyone.

He had worked on it a bit but it still read too much like a civil service brief. It needed more economic context. He should also make a virtue of not trying to hide the fact we were heading for a more difficult period. Must have been there a couple of hours and I think he found it helpful. I was just trying to give him some very basic advice but he was taking it all down and wanted to discuss again. The general structure was OK, content a bit civil servicese, better green section than envisaged. My main point was to root it in the overall strategy of the last decade, with sights on the future. And no pretence. GB did well so many days on the day of the Budget itself but then suffered from the unravelling which followed. Calum at BFC draw v Watford, 2–2.

Sunday 2 March

Dick Caborn called and I had the same discussion as I had had with Carol. Totally unenthused and uninspired. If I did the sports dinner it was for him really. Mother's Day. Russian elections farce with Putin shepherding in [Dmitri] Medvedev [as President] and his 'massive win'. Interesting piece on the white working class in *Observer*. This was clearly picking up as a cultural and political theme, the idea they were a forgotten group. We had not handled this well, especially given how much in policy terms we actually had aimed at helping them. I said to GB last time I saw him, as I had said to TB, that we never warned of a downside to globalisation, just gave the sense it was all win–win.

Monday 3 March

Did a piece on spin for *La Repubblica*, then a Q&A for a student doing her dissertation on press secretaries. Out on the bike then to see PG and Tessa re the

London campaign. I had made clear to Tessa I wasn't really up for getting too involved. Said what I thought re big picture and also getting some fight back in Ken's campaign. As with AD she took it all down but I didn't think I was contributing much really. I was reading McCain's [Vietnam] war years autobiography. Amazing stuff. Resilience was clearly not going to be a problem.

Tuesday 4 March

Line edit a.m., then out for lunch with Natascha [McElhone, actress] at Soho House. She hadn't known about the novel but loved the idea and when I sent her a few chapters later, she said she loved it. She was so beautiful and clever and I loved the way she sought to stay low-profile. Got picked up later to head to Random House sales conference. British Aerospace dinner. [Air Chief Marshal Sir] John Day, ex-deputy CDS [Chief of Defence Staff] under [Field Marshal Lord] Charles Guthrie in the Kosovo campaign, was there so I chatted to him a fair while. He said they loved working with TB and me, and JoP, but the word was that GB relations were not good. He said when he used to stand in for Guthrie he felt everyone was friendly and polite apart from GB who was rude as hell. Top table quite a good bunch. Good event and Q&A good. Chatted to head of defence intelligence, Joe French, plus their political guy who was quite bright. Main boss Mike Turner was not there because he was watching United beat Lyon. I managed to avoid knowing the score [1–0]. Natascha sent a message saying she was loving the novel.

Wednesday 5 March

I was out on the bike and did a detour to sign a book for Michael Beloff [lawyer]. Had a little chat, but I was always struck by how sorry I felt for people who went to an office every day. Yet I missed having a big team and I was getting a bit irritated at there being no real separation between home and work. Would be on the phone and the neighbours ring the doorbell, or Fiona shouts up and asks me to do something. Conference call with a guy called Ninian Wilson [operation director] re Royal Mail speech in Belfast next week. Sounded up my street. Main theme change. He said it was a nightmare organisation to get to face up to change. Mark came round and we started transcribing outstanding '04 diary stuff. Also Bill came round to go over what he had done on '94. Good stuff.

Thursday 6 March

DS. Explained low-level depression that had been chugging on. Cab to Kingsway Costa Coffee to meet Lynton Crosby before going over the road to see the students. He went to the wrong café so not much time for intros etc. He was nicer and warmer than I had been led to expect and I sensed we shared a lot of views about campaigns. He had a dry sense of humour and a nice manner. He felt Boris was a lot better than we thought, insisted there was more to him than the comedian, and Ken was a bit clapped out. He said he only did Tories '05 election because Michael Howard was a personal friend, but he never felt that we felt threatened. He felt that TB did the right thing in going while still at the top, but that GB would struggle to win an election. The students seemed to be getting a lot from the course, that was for sure.

Worked on the book, then to Institute of Engineers for KPMG dinner. Virtually all white all male. Good enough event, Q&A OK and the dinner not so bad. Nice Scottish guy to my left who was clearly one of us and was pushing back at some of the usual facile arguments of his colleagues, e.g. not any difference between the parties. 18k for a talk and then having the same old same old chats at dinner. I wish I could persuade myself it was work.

Friday 7 March

I was working on the line edit a.m., then to Galvin [restaurant] for lunch with Ed Victor. Interesting and fun as always. Really pleased I had done a novel, and having read it again he was keen to explore film options. He had also got Linda [his PA] to retrieve the original 1994 diary from the bank, and as I suspected, there was a whole load of new material from the death of John Smith and the point at which the *Blair Years* extracts began. I took it home and flicked through it all, part of me dreading the fact that I would have to be back on transcribing duty, which had been a bore a lot of the time, part of me fascinated to relive it all. I had forgotten just how integrated I was into TB even before I started officially working for him.

Alex called re [son, manager of Peterborough United] Darren's court case with his ex-wife. I said my instinct was that he should simply let the court case proceed, endure what will be a difficult day, some bad publicity for a day or two, and then try to put it behind him. That should be his public and private posture. I said it would be better if Darren via himself or a lawyer made a statement in court that would speak for itself and be seen as his last word on the subject – admission of guilt, acceptance that there can be no excuse for violence against a woman, acceptance that we all have to be responsible for our own actions, and the choices we make in life, and it is a matter of great sadness that the marriage ended badly. So plead guilty, apologise, accept the punishment of the court, then move on.* I sent AF a

* Darren Ferguson was charged with common assault on his estranged wife. He subsequently pleaded guilty and was fined £1,500.

note about how Darren should conduct himself on the day. At the end of the case, as leaving, make a short statement summarising the above. Alongside it a statement from Peterboro saying he is a good manager and this does not affect his situation in any way at all. Focus now on promotion.

Saturday 8 March

A rare unpleasant foray into the real-world stuff that so dements Fiona. I got a call from the bank asking if I was in the Philippines. No. My card had been used four times there overnight, three small sums, one largish. But I had it with me. It had been skimmed. Dementing. Call centres. People working from forms and talking like robots. Eventually I lost it, called someone high up and ranted, and it worked, in that they said a new card would be delivered Tuesday, and to leave it with them. Over to Stoke for the match. Met up with Bruce [Grocott] and we headed for lunch with Peter Coates [Stoke chairman]. He was still a big Labour supporter but he felt the government was all at sea. He rated GB as Chancellor but worried he didn't have TB's breadth. There was nothing to give him hope it was turning around, and he could see the Tories getting back in. Bruce was so glad to be out of it too, though he still helped out with PMQs, and went regularly to the Lords. He had another go at persuading me to go in. Both he and Peter also said if I wouldn't do the Lords – and both Fiona and I had decided 100 per cent it was never going to happen, for either of us – I should get a seat.

Peter reckoned if we lost, we would need big people to rebuild and I had to be part of that. He said no serious person actually believed the image the press had created for me. Very few politicians have charisma or guts, and I had both, he said, and I should not let them go to waste. We had an interesting chat on football finances. The numbers were getting ridiculous. So the TV money was vast but the demands of players and agents were sucking most of it out of the game. Even bog-average squad players were on way into five figures. Bruce felt the Premier League was built on sand and it would collapse. I doubt it. I also wondered whether there was any limit to the money, given the brand was growing so fast globally. All the power lay with the Premier League and the clubs. Good match, early lead and then we blew it with a last-minute penalty that should have never been. Fergie was going mad at the ref after going out to Pompey [Portsmouth] in the Cup in the morning match.

Sunday 9 March

Out for a run with Jon Sopel [BBC presenter]. GB media operation malfunctioning, he said. Slow and too prone to favouritism. Charlie Falconer came round, then Tessa. Charlie was so supportive on the novel. He read it so well and had come round for the latest version. He sent me a note later to say it felt stronger though he couldn't see where it changed, which suggested Rebecca had done a good job in the changes she had suggested. Charlie had some good small-point ideas too and Rebecca didn't seem to mind. Top bloke. Like me, he was still wanting to find a purpose, I think. We agreed to have lunch Wednesday. Tessa called to say she wanted to see our new kitchen but it was really to pick my brains on London. Ken was doing a bit better but there was no real sense of the campaign still. I said a big part of me felt she didn't need to be doing the London campaign, and especially not for Ken. I was probably reflecting my own feelings about things though. I told her I had lost my passion for the government. I would help of course but I was not sure what I could do. That being said, AD was grateful I know for positioning advice on Budget. But I didn't really want to do too much.

Monday 10 March

A dreadful call from Gazza [former footballer Paul Gascoigne]. I had texted him when he was sectioned, just to say if he wanted to have a chat etc., and I assumed he had not had his phone with him.* But now he was out, staying at his uncle Paul's, and he came on with a real rambling kind of call, words slurred, which could have been tranquilisers I guess, but equally it could have been drink. I asked if he was drinking and he said not much, which was never a good sign. He said he had been stitched up by Jimmy Five Bellies [Jimmy Gardner, childhood friend], but I couldn't understand how. It was one of those calls where I was trying to ask rational questions but he would just fly off in another direction. He was going on about how all he had been thinking about when he was locked up was wanting to play football with me and the kids in the garden at No. 10. He was describing goals he was making and scoring, and how the Pope and the President would be watching from inside a meeting with Tony. All really sad. I just said I was glad he was out, but he really needed to look after himself. His uncle came on and said he was doing fine, better than he had been, but in the background he was shouting out all sorts of rubbish. It was so hard to know what to do.

* Suffering from mental illness and alcoholism, Gascoigne had been sectioned under the Mental Health Act following an incident at a Newcastle hotel that was said to have had guests feeling threatened.

Tuesday 11 March

Work a.m., out for a run then lunch at Galvin with Katie Phillips and Kieron Collins [producers], who were really pushing on the Speak Up for Britain pitch, an idea for BBC on kids doing public speaking / politics. Part of me was keen, the part that felt it might show politics in a different light, and engage kids; part of me not, the part that felt when all was said and done it was another reality TV idea. Ed felt I should devise my own TV idea that came out of me and what really motivated me. Fiona felt it was too much an elimination contest and risked being exploitative. Met Carol Linforth at the Labour Party for a fundraising meeting. Usual crew – her and Kamlesh [Karia, Labour official] (now working as a volunteer), Dick Caborn, John Reid and Margaret McD. None of us were as enthusiastic as last year. All feeling we would be dumped on if it went wrong, which was not a good sign of the way people felt about the party culture right now. And why the fuck did we need to be the people doing this anyway? Dick did his usual rah-rah enthusiastic bit and by the end of it we all agreed, with varying degrees of enthusiasm, we would give it a go. Finalised the back cover of *The Blair Years*.

Wednesday 12 March

Lunch with Charlie F, mainly talking about the novel and my own madness in the '80s. He was a brilliant inquisitor, endlessly fascinated in the detail. Charles Kennedy [former Liberal Democrats leader] was in there, which was a happy coincidence as I was planning to invite him over to Conaglen [Scotland] when we are there. I heard the first bit of the Budget before the lunch. AD was attacked as dull and ignoring the reality, but he did pretty well considering. To the Lords with Charlie. Bumped into Norman Tebbit. Good old chat and he seemed really pleased to see me. Charlie said it was like watching two old pros relive their best fights. I said less of the old, he is almost thirty years older. NT said he felt the government lacked coherence and cut through and also he felt we were continuing to take a wrong turn on Europe. Chatted a bit about the way the campaign world was changing, and he said he felt GB didn't have the agility to deal with it.

He asked if I ever thought of coming in here. I said I couldn't imagine it. It is a beautiful place, and there are lots of interesting people in there, but ultimately it all feels a bit sad and second string. Also, though Tebbit wasn't the pompous sort, a lot of them were. Meeting with Andy Burnham with Dave Edmundson. Andy seems so young. He needs to get himself some decent suits. But I think his heart is in the right place on sport and he and Dave could clearly get something out of each other's agenda. To the Galaxy Book Awards shortlisting event. A bit grisly. Lots of photographs but I refused to do one with a piece of chocolate in my mouth. Francesca Simon, who wrote the *Horrid Henry* books, was horrified that Katie Price [aka glamour model Jordan] was on the kids' books list. These things were all too aimed at the celeb market. To the Young Vic for *Mules*, a play directed by [Labour MP] Margaret Hodge's daughter Amy. Really strong. To Livebait for dinner. Margaret was a tremendous gossip, and full of the usual fulminations re GB, but I was conscious of not engaging much on the political scene.

Thursday 13 March

To Costa Coffee to meet Charlie and PG before we did our final session of the LSE course. Charlie, top man, had agreed to do the judging of the final groups' presentations. PG wanted to be there for the last one. He seemed OK. Chemo was kicking in but he looked reasonably fine and his morale was good. He was a terrible flirt with some of the women in the group. Charlie, even in this setting, was waxing lyrical re my novel, and afterwards a couple of the students wanted to talk about it. One said she had been having chronic anxiety, the other had a mother who was often suicidal. The session was excellent. They had done some pretty good work on the various major campaigns going on, in the US and here, though in the Q&A Charlie picked them apart a fair bit.

The Democrat team had the hardest job because they were presenting two campaigns for the price of one, both Hillary and Obama. Also the divisions between Hillary and Obama were being played out clearly among the students. The Republicans were the hardest edged. Ken's team did OK and I thought Boris's team was probably the weakest, too focused on the need to play down the candidate. But Charlie thought they were the best, PG and I felt the Republicans won it, so we gave it as a tie. Nice atmosphere as we left, signing books and T-shirts and so forth and some wanting further help with their dissertations. I could sense some of them – and indeed Philip as well – wondering if it would be the last time they saw him. They were really effusive.

Car to City airport, flight to Belfast. I bought Bill Bryson's book on Shakespeare [*Shakespeare: The World as a Stage*]. There were 4,000 books / serious studies written on him every year. Nice little book, did not try to repeat all the others, instead a snapshot but with some interesting life and times stuff. Landed, got to SAS Radisson and then briefed myself on the issues. Scale of change in NI breathtaking. Did a long run down by the riverside which was a nice way of seeing a lot of the change. BBC *Let's Talk* programme – OK but the old arguments kept rearing their heads and the divisions were still pretty clear, especially between Jeffrey Donaldson [Democratic Unionist Party] and the guy from the Ulster Unionist Party, despite both being Chelsea fans. I did not feel on top form. The audience was a bit leaden but the team said afterwards they were better than usual. Interesting guy in the front row who had golf club sweater, slightly Patrician look, seemed classic Unionist type but when he spoke he was major league Sinn Féin. One or two Trots in there. Owen Paterson, Tory NI shadow, who seemed pleasant enough but I'm not sure he really got the scene.

Friday 14 March

Out for a run. Catherine McLeod [now a Treasury advisor] called for a chat on the Budget aftermath. I felt AD did OK but he was getting hit on being dull and also revised growth figures, and the sense there was not really a long-term plan. She was full of how awful the civil servants had been, constantly pushing back on his stuff, and not wanting to support in the way they should. He would change the speech, and they would change back and eventually he gave up on the morning. Alistair called too, to say thanks for help. He felt he had just about got away with it. He made a very interesting observation about something GB said when he called him the day after the main event. He asked him 'Has anything unravelled yet?', which must be the result of his own experience of all those great write-ups he used to get for his Budgets, followed by a sense of unravelling. Alistair said no, he took the hits on the day. Talking to AD, I always got the sense of them feeling a bit ground down and beleaguered.

I watched the Champions League draw then in for the Royal Mail speech at the Hilton. Middle management. Very white, lots of ex-army, but usual mix of jokes, strategy – drawing a fair bit on change in NI – and an OK Q&A. Felt it went well, and the feedback was pretty good. Straight to the airport afterwards and off to Manchester to see Calum's flat. I liked it a lot. Dinner with Fiona and Calum then she headed off back while we were at the Midland [hotel]. Stephen Carter [No. 10 chief of staff] had arranged a meeting with all the spads. I got a text from Carol saying he had said he was not me and did not want to be, to which she and others were saying that is the problem. The whole operation was feeling weak at the moment. Morale was low. The news was dominated by the suicide of Manchester chief constable Mike Todd, and stories of his affairs were coming out, including with Angie Robinson, chief executive of the chamber of commerce.* I reminded Alex they were at the dinner I did that he came to and we sat with them. He was still pissed off about the defeat to Pompey, and the ref.

* An inquest found that Todd had died of exposure on Mount Snowdon when the state of his mind was affected by alcohol, sleeping pills and confusion over turmoil in his private life. A police investigation discovered he had liaisons with thirty-eight women during his six years as head of the force.

Saturday 15 March

Gym in hotel then over to Burnley. Visited Towneley Hall [museum and art gallery]. People really nice there. There was an exhibition going on and the organisers asked me in and I ended up buying three exhibits. Poor game [v Wolves] and we were 3 down when we left early [result 1–3]. I got a letter from Alan Rusbridger [editor, *The Guardian*] about the Hugo Young [late political columnist] papers. *The Guardian* were planning to publish lots of his notes and records of chats with people. All the references to me seemed fine apart from two, and I worked on a note on the train back explaining why I didn't want them included as written – one because it was political, namely I had been talking about how I thought Ken was a dreadful mayor, which was not exactly helpful right now; and one because it did not represent what I thought – namely he said I had said Becks [David Beckham] was an idiot.

Monday 17 March

To Paris for a telly thing. Picked up Ian McEwan's *Amsterdam* on the way. Enjoyed it. Really wanting to get on and finish the novel edit and also get on with publication. Paris sunny. So clean as well. Every time I go I am more struck by the difference with London. I was tired though and feeling a bit under the weather.

Tuesday 18 March

I called Alex about who we should get to present the lifetime achievement award to Bobby Charlton [former Man Utd and England star player] at the Sport Industry Awards. He spoke to Norma [wife] who thought Roger Hunt or Nobby Stiles [former England colleagues] but neither was available. Out with Fiona and Grace for a screening of *Love in the Time of Cholera*. Pretty good but I did not really enjoy these events out among the London chatterati. Margaret and Henry Hodge were there and she nabbed me for a fundraising dinner. Henry looked better than I thought he would after hearing how ill he had been. PG told me Spencer Livermore was leaving. He had really had it with GB and the whole set-up.

Thursday 20 March to Thursday 27 March

Holiday in Ardgour, Argyll. Fiona set off crack of dawn with car, dog and bags. We set off with the Bridges for a late p.m. flight, then got a car up to the house. I was trying not to get down but I was not enjoying the hassle and crowd and knew I was dipping. The first couple of days I was very down and the whole week really I was on a pretty negative kick. Could not get motivated for much. One day totally down. Fiona saying she didn't understand it given how much we had going for us but that was the point really. It just is and maybe it will never get better. The scenery was fabulous, better than anything anywhere, but even that couldn't seem to lift me. Rory and I got road bikes from Oban and were out – including the long route round to Fort William a couple of times – every day. Goulds up for the weekend, PG back from a flying visit to the States to check out the 'best in the world' hospital. I felt he might be better just sticking with things here. I can't imagine the travel helps.

Mark, Lindsay and Hope were up and all was OK but the week did not hang together as say last year and a lot of that down to my mood I guess. Charles and Sarah Kennedy [wife] came round for dinner one night. I had bumped into him with Charlie Falconer at Quirinale [Westminster restaurant] and asked him up. He lived in Fort William and of course knew the area inside out, but was very funny when I asked how often he had been up Ben Nevis. 'I've never been to the bottom never mind the top … not many voters up there.' He was driving and so didn't drink, but he was looking a bit nervy. He sneaked out for a fag a couple of times and on one occasion I went for a little walk round the garden, and he said he was interested in how I managed to go from heavy drinking to zero. He said he was not sure if he had a problem but he knew he drank too much at times. I said if he felt it damaged his work, his health or his relationships, he had a problem.

He looked pensive and said he would like to talk about it more when we were back in London. Sarah was very nice, really chatty with everyone. PG and I had running gag of Charles really being Labour. He said he was a Highland Liberal, but accepted if he lived in London or Glasgow, he might have been. He felt Wendy Alexander [leader of Scottish Labour Party] had had it. He also felt we had underestimated Salmond. He was going to stand again at the next election. He loved the area and he liked being the MP there, and he could still have a national voice too. He was very nice about Nick Clegg [Lib Dem leader]. Clearly not keen on Ming but not OTT. Fiona and Calum took the car back while the rest of us flew.

Friday 28 March

Got the final chapters from Rebecca and worked on that most of the day. I felt we were finally getting there. Still feeling a bit low the whole time. I did a half-decent run just to get in some kind of shape pre-Sunday's event, but I was definitely slowing down.

Sunday 30 March

Out early with Calum, out to Richmond for the Human Race run. I chose to do the 8-miler and was through six in roughly the time I took to do eight last time. Very slow, feeling heavy. Good Leukaemia Research turnout. Home, bath. Out to PG's party. TB was in the States, GB in Scotland, and both spoke to him but couldn't come. Philip said GB sounded really down. Good turnout. Gail a bit stressed out. Neil and Glenys in good form. I agreed to go to Cardiff v Barnsley Cup semi. Grace was asking who my five best friends were. Tricky question. PG definitely, Charlie, Tony maybe but it was not so easy when he was such a big deal, Alex maybe but ditto, Syd and Geoff from the *Mirror* days, though I didn't see them so much. I was also maybe a bit wary having lost close friends, especially John [Merritt]. Carmen Callil [writer and publisher] told me I was to blame for a lot of things that were wrong in the world, because I was the power TB drew on. [Lord] John Browne [former BP CEO], with his new partner, said he had felt like he was stripped of his insides when the media went for him.* I said I was surprised at how much he worried about the media. He said it took him a long time not to care. Also that most boards and business people are far too focused on press.

He said neither TB nor I were suited to business, because we had minds much more suited to politics. Anji and Liz were there, also JoP. I had read his book over the break and it was excellent. He seemed pleased with the reaction it had, good media and reviews. He said his 'We should talk to Al Qaeda' suggestion was a 'Talking point à la AC ... I felt I learned at your feet!' We were first in last out. PG's speech focused on the huge support and how he appreciated it and then love for Gail and the kids. Georgia and Grace seemed to be enjoying it. Susan Sandon there and we had a good chat re the novel. I was singing Rebecca's praises. PG felt the party was worth it, though he was shattered at the end.

Monday 31 March

Slept badly. Don't know why, maybe because of Philip. Out to meet Frederique Andreani [*Le Point* magazine] at St Ermin's for her piece on life post-TB. Liked her. Then to do a speech for a PG party at Victoria Street, being organised by Marianna. All about friendship and teamwork and dedication, and how he would fight his way through this. They showed a video of our greatest hits, with some old campaign footage. Rather

* Injunctions by Browne preventing publication of allegations about his private life and sexuality eventually failed. Browne, a gay man, commented, 'I have always regarded my sexuality as a personal matter, to be kept private.'

subdued mood. Gail, the girls and Rory there. Lots of the staff plus Tessa, Pat, Douglas, a few others. GB came with his entourage and was nice enough. Sarah too. GB mingled, then spoke, very nice about Philip and what he has done and also his courage in facing up to illness. Cake. Then PG said how much he loved the party and the winning mentality. I spoke. I did a fairly long speech, mixing piss-taking with serious stuff re his role and the need to fight harder but the mood was not good in the party right now. PG was very nice re me, said if there was anyone you wanted around when things got really tough, it was me. And he thanked me for helping his family.

Later heard the PLP [Parliamentary Labour Party meeting] was awful, that they had heckled GB and catcalled etc. Needless to say, the ones prominent in going for TB who had backed GB were first in the queue. Boris beating Ken in the polls. Sarah stayed for my speech and we had a little chat afterwards. Left for Covent Garden and the brainstorm with Mike Lee [Vero Communications] about Beyond Sport. It was OK, but I can't get enthusiastic for this stuff at the moment. I found myself thinking of meetings I used to chair re big issues, big events and this just did not get the juices flowing. But what would? Of recent stuff only the book had really. And even that faded at times. Home to three batches of notes for Rebecca. Good chat with her as we neared the end. She finally told me she had also edited JoP. She said she hid it from me because she didn't want me to know how knackered she was.

Tuesday 1 April

Into Victoria Street for the second day running for a sports fundraiser meeting. Kamlesh Karia (still not being paid), Carol, Dick C, Margaret McD, a guy from KPMG and Jon Mendelsohn [Labour organiser]. JM clear they really wanted it to happen. Margaret very strong re how the culture – and I said it had got worse since GB – was to drop people in it if things went wrong, and she did not believe we should have to take responsibility for this. She would work hard if it happened but the experience of the last one was not good. She was equally heavy about how the silly new laws were not properly understood by staff which meant people got into difficulty. I said the blame culture was dreadful, also was pitching to come at it via auction first, that maybe that was a better way to look at it. But in the end we agreed to go on the basis of getting an auction catalogue out early, then go for table sales once we have good stuff already in. Earlier I called Joe Hemani to ask what I should be looking for re auctioning a walk-on part in the novel. He reckoned minimum fifty grand. Lovely bloke, nice chat.

Joy Johnson [journalist and Labour activist] was in the building and asked me to speak to the Ken [mayoral election] team. I did so. John Ross looked exhausted. Hilary Perrin pretty sound, kept asking the right questions – e.g. what is simple message to put through to those who are just not engaged? Simon Fletcher OK but they all seemed a bit shot to pieces. They also gave different reasons why things had slipped, and different remedies. I said Ken had to rediscover his mojo and get back to his old style. They had to use the fact it was close to show there was fight in him and show it mattered. Stage 1 – why the job matters. Stage 2 – why Ken is right. Stage 3 – why Boris would be a disaster. They had to get sharper attack and defence strategic lines. Ross kept going on about environment. He said Ken had been complacent and they had lost ground. I said the media had whacked him systematically and they had allowed Boris too much space to reposition. I told them some of the stuff the students had said – what is the strategy? What is their best attack line? What is the forward offer? That was a problem, they said, they did not really have one. All a bit depressing.

I said the idea of Boris as mayor is a joke and Ken had to fight harder to stop it. But I worried. They were too vague and their stuff did not hang together. Tessa called later to say it had gone down really well, and they had loved it and would I do it again? She said when I walked into party HQ I could not imagine the positive effect it has. It is rock star stuff, she said. I said I would but only if they acted on what I said. Margaret McD was telling me how ghastly the PLP had been, a total disaster, MPs heckling at GB and he was basically saying give me ideas. Tessa said Stephen Carter was doing a good job but was getting hammered by the old guard. GB had been poor at Cabinet, ponderous and clunky. She said there were plenty of them running a mile from London. She felt London was still winnable, but it was going to be tough. GB press conference came and went without much to report. The big news was Zimbabwe, election results moving towards [President Robert] Mugabe's departure.

Wednesday 2 April

Rebecca delivered the final edit so it was annoying I was going to be out all day and wouldn't be able to work on it for a while. Then to LRF for the staff strategy meeting. A Nigerian taxi driver drove me in. Father of four. Degree in petrochemicals. He gave up a middle management job to be home more to help kids with education. Very bright guy. Said 'You won't win the next election because people don't like Brown. Blair made people feel good. Brown makes people feel bad.' It was a pretty dire analysis. He was adamant – he would vote Labour because he always would but floaters would not. He said GB had a total lack of charisma. 'These jobs can only be done by strong, popular characters now. You should get a seat and go for it,' he said. I did sometimes wonder if I should not have got a seat when DM did. I said I worried it was too late now. Nonsense, he said. Never too late. I saw Cathy Gilman before the meeting, where she did a very nice intro about me always being there for her, and always up for doing whatever they asked for, before I spoke for a bit and then showed the Eastwood family film, and short Q&A.

Calls started coming through about Bertie Ahern announcing he was standing down as PM and FF [Fianna Fáil] leader in May. I did a couple of interviews before heading to Paddington for train to Oxford, where Tony Benn and I were doing a talk together about diaries. I was on the phone to Ed Victor when I spotted Tony and Melissa through the window of a restaurant. I joined them for lunch and we had a good natter. Melissa was very keen to know my view on her novel and say she was keen to read mine. *The Guardian* had asked her to review it but she felt best not to review friends. Tony and I agreed we did not want a big argument on politics but to talk about diaries. Razor-sharp memory. Had a contraption on his back, like a rucksack but he said he could turn it into a seat. Keen to know any background re Bertie and Mugabe who looked like he might be going at last. Lots of talk re books and general stuff. He was eighty-three tomorrow yet apart from the slow walk totally sharp. A few surprised glances as we walked down to Christchurch.

Jean Seaton [academic] chairing the event, of that upper-middle-class academic type a bit too wrapped in their own world. We did the *Oxford Mail*, then photos and then to the marquee. The event was fine, though Jean burbled on too much. Benn was very funny and eccentric. Hilarious on his own archive. 'I was checking today how many times I had mentioned the IMF [International Monetary Fund] in my diary.' 'Why?' I said. He had a bit of a teary eye talking about Caroline [late wife]. We had remarkably similar views on the media. He was a bit like TB said of Mandela – becoming so revered he could say any old nonsense. Q&A fine. A few good laughs. Nice reception afterwards. Signing books together. [*Private Eye* co-founder] Richard Ingrams's partner Debbie came up and said she loved me, which maybe explained why he hated me. Roger Bannister was there too and had a chat re China [Beijing Olympics] and whether the boycott mood would grow. Tibet protests were definitely growing and the torch relay was getting a lot of attention.*

Train back with Emma Mitchell from Random House. From Burnley. Flirty and a very good laugh. Collected from station by *Newsnight* and

* Pro-Tibet demonstrators disrupted the Olympic flame ceremony in protest at Chinese human rights violations.

went to TV centre to record a tribute to Bertie. Nice chat with Paxman in his little office. He reckoned one of the *Newsnight* team had tipped off the press about the underpants exchange with M&S. Then to Luciano's restaurant to meet Moir Lockhead [First Group] and Rosie Winterton. They seemed to hit it off and we had a chat on the general scene. She said the mood was bad. I said GB had focused on change but not been clear what it was. It looked like a lurch to old Labour and when he realised that was going down badly he lurched back and people wondered what he was really all about. And needless to say all the 'Blair out, Brown in' people were now front of queue in saying he was not doing well enough. Add in the public feuding of his old and new guard and it was a bad scene. Moir said there was a feeling they had had an instinctively pro-business government and now they were less sure. But there was not any general view that the Tories had the answer. I felt it was recoverable but only if they showed a bit of fight and leadership which at the moment was not there.

Thursday 3 April

DS. Fiona came too. Dreadful. My low-level depression plus her honest assessment of how hard it was to live with it, and it was all a bit dire. Maybe I had underestimated how bad I had been in Scotland. Then all day on the final edit. Glad it was coming to an end. Rebecca had definitely made a difference. Felt good with it. Left for JoP's book launch at the Irish Embassy. He had done well on his media stuff. Good turnout. Chatted to Tom Kelly [former No. 10 spokesman] re his new job at BAA [British Airports Authority]. Gus – said my usual get a grip. He said they did have a grip, but there was none on the political side. Sue Gray there. John Reid pretty open about the need for leadership change – in front of Phil Stephens [*Financial Times*]. [Lord] David Trimble [former First Minister of Northern Ireland] cold. Not sure what his problem was. Lots of the NIO [Northern Ireland Office] guys there.

Good speech by the Ambassador and by JoP, quite serious, making the point that it was not inevitable we got an agreement [over devolution of police and justice powers in NI]. Nice do though. Lots of the No. 10 old guard. General feeling that we were fucked. The IRA linkman to HMG was there and took me aside to say he liked my style because there was so much bullshit and I cut through it so keep going. TB not there because he was doing his Faith Foundation speech at Westminster Cathedral. Dealt with 'We don't do God' and made his big point that we had to face up to the importance of faith. Also how power was shifting eastwards.

Friday 4 April

I did a last skim-read through the novel and then sent to Gail, Susan etc. Then to see TB is his new office [of Tony Blair Faith Foundation], 9 Grosvenor Square, right on the corner. Nice place and he was clearly happy there. Same photos in the office as in his den at No. 10, Mandela, the kids. A few books. Smartish furniture. Stacks of the old No. 10 team in there, Vic Gould, Katie Kay, Parna Taylor, Ruth Turner, Gavin Mackay. William Chapman there for the religious. TB was seeing JoP and some rich dude as I arrived. Seemed pretty chipper. On the political scene, he said he was not at all surprised. 'I could have predicted it in almost every detail and in many ways did. I tried to tell all of you that it was inevitable because in the end he [GB] is not a leader. It is not in the DNA.' So why did you go along with it? 'Because it was unstoppable in a way.' Now he felt the younger ones had to start focusing on the future. DM. James Purnell. Etc.

In government the party and the unions did not matter so much. In opposition the unions can get back controlling your policy-making. He could see us being out for another generation unless we faced up to the changes needed now. He had told DM he had to start articulating a forward policy agenda for the future and do it now. He said he had given advice to GB but the problem was he lacked his own conviction. He didn't know what he was about. So he did all the change stuff, then realised he needed reform and then it was grasping at anything. It was pretty galling, he said, that GB had fought so hard to block him on academies or public service reform and now was singing their praises. But take academies.* Everyone knew GB and Balls were opposed. They see them now saying they support them. But they lose the real academy people because they know it is not sincere and they lose the left who thought there would be change. He is in a kind of strategic no man's land. But where Balls and e.g. Jon Cruddas [MP] have a point is that if GB retreats from the 'GB is change' message, and does Blairism, what is the distinctive edge? He looked at some of the stuff GB was doing – nuclear, academies, public service reform, and though it may be right, it lacked any sense of conviction or bigger picture.

He felt there was not a hope in hell of the country electing him as PM. 'They just don't like him and they think he and his people are odd.' On his own set-up, he said he was busier than ever because he was doing so much travelling. Next few days several countries doing speeches to earn money to help set up the organisation. Had his Middle East envoy strand, climate change, consultancy, setting up governance project, speeches, book

* Controversially, Blair's government had elevated some schools to academy status, funded directly by the Department for Education and independent of local authority control.

(on which he was behind schedule). He wanted me to get involved in one of his governance projects in Africa. He felt I could probably do with one more strand that really gave me a public policy contribution to make. He said it had really freaked him out when I said I fell off the wagon. Ben WP [Wegg-Prosser, TB's former director of strategic communications] in there too, on a short break from Moscow. He had just seen David Muir [director of political strategy], one of GB's new people, who wanted to see me. Ben said it was a lot worse than people thought. GB was treating people terribly. Morale was dreadful. TB said he was not making speeches about the past, despite the pressures. He was much more interested in still making a contribution to current debate especially on the new and big issues. Not entirely sure what he wanted me to do but he was probably right that I was missing a big policy component to what I was doing.

Saturday 5 April

Out to Liverpool St and off to Norwich. Lunch with Delia [Smith, TV chef] and Michael [Wynn-Jones, husband, majority shareholders in Norwich FC]. Delia another voice saying she thought we could lose the election even though the Tories were useless. Charles Clarke popped in as did Phil Webster [political editor, *The Times*]. Phil said No. 10 was in a weird kind of meltdown. No grip at all. Charles telling Delia she did a great job with her latest book and all the attacks were from food snobs. Match poor and we lost 2–0. Afterwards agreed to meet again and she wanted a proper chat on football. Still low. Had new pills.

Sunday 6 April

OK run, 7 miles. Off to Wembley with Neil K for the Cardiff–Barnsley [FA Cup] semi-final [1–0]. Neil said he could not believe how lacking in conviction and indecisive GB appeared to be. Felt things were dreadful. Also that he was letting the party slide away. Strategy had to be aimed at the party. If not – big trouble. He and I seemed to share a lot of analysis and problem. Hard to see how he was going to get out of it. I said how do you think he is feeling? He said he will be in that state of panic he had, knowing it is going wrong but not sure how to rescue it. He needed a clearer long-term strategy. It did not need to be articulated but implemented.

Good mood going in. Alarmed how many people inside were saying the same thing. At our table a former Welsh rugby player and a Cardiff director saying GB was not a leader, just could not follow TB. Even the mayor of Barnsley said he wanted TB and me back 'because we are losing the plot.' Saw David Triesman [FA chief executive] who was in pig heaven in his new job, though he knew it was a tough organisation. Neil was like the coach during the match, constantly pointing to players, telling them what to do. 'They can't hear you,' I said. 'Oh, they can… they can.' There was a nasty incident on the way out. Some guy turned on Neil for being a rugby man. Pissed, and really offensive. It quickly escalated into nose to nose. I felt, as did Neil, a real desire to twat the guy but I called over a cop who sorted it.

Monday 7 April

Feeling very down. This has been going on and off for weeks now. It is a big setback, having thought the gaps between the downs were growing. Third day of anti-depressants and I felt my voice weakening. Quiet day. To Shell for a meeting to discuss their idea that I might do speaking or strategic advice for them. Up to a meeting room in the rather old-fashioned building opposite Waterloo. The head of global comms seemed rather keener on what I was saying that the fat Tory guy who had worked at Central Office. Usual spiel. Interesting how defensive they were in general as a company but they were trying to change it. Olympic torch procession yesterday getting massive coverage. Now in Paris. Sense of Ken's campaign turning a little bit. Calum back to Manchester. Going to miss him a lot.

Tuesday 8 April

Pills kicking in quite a lot and slept pm. Out on bike. DS. Pretty grim but had to get up for tomorrow, when Fiona and I were going to Perugia where I was due to speak at a journalism festival.

Wednesday 9 April

Tied up a few loose ends then off to Heathrow. I had been trying to get a switch to another airport but in fact Terminal 5 was fabulous. Train good. New terminal building beautiful. Lots of polite assistance. Queues not bad. I banged off a letter to *The Times* about it while waiting to board. I was determined to get on with Fiona and we were at least having a few laughs. Two-hour drive other end through fabulous scenery to Perugia and hilltop five-star Hotel Brufani. Dinner and bed.

Thursday 10 April

Nice run. Lots of hills. We wandered around a.m. Museum. Shops. Lunch with Carl Bernstein [US journalist, Watergate investigator] and the Italians on the panel. Out to the debate centre. Slightly chaotic. Other panellists a guy from Umbria introducing, well-known Italian journalist chairing it, Carl B. And a guy called Marcello Foa, who had written a book on spin and was full of the usual conspiracy theory bullshit. Carl Bernstein and I were in broad agreement re the state of the media and the need to put things in a proper context. I liked him a lot. Not at all up himself considering what a media legend he is. Very interesting chats re Hillary [Clinton]. Fiona and I had diametrically opposed reactions to his book [*A Woman in Charge*]. I felt it had been OK for her (as did he) but F did not. He said the two things that really struck him after doing it were 1) that she lived in fear of failure and shame and humiliation and 2) that she had a difficult relationship with the truth. Bill was livid with him for constantly saying that. He said he had started out not unsympathetic to her but felt she had fought a nasty [presidential candidacy] campaign. She and Bill treated Obama like he was the vast right-wing conspiracy. Felt it was all helping McCain now.

Very bright guy. Unassuming and modest in his own way. He agreed with my assertion that the long-term impact of the 'gate' part of Watergate had been damaging as everything had to become a '-gate.' He also took on Marcello who, when he had asked why Carl's was the only story in so many years to topple a President, said it was because the spin doctors now controlled everything. Carl said it was not their job to topple governments but to try to publish the nearest attainable thing to the truth. He was also interesting on how Watergate was not a single story but a whole series of stories with cumulative effect. He was big on how lazy so many journalists were now, and how editors lacked patience. And in agreement on how the context for journalism had changed without people really analysing the change. We both piled into Marcello towards the end. Good response generally though. Out for dinner with Carl and his very tall wife Christine. Earlier he had been asking us re [Baroness] Margaret Jay [Labour peer] and what she was up to.* Very nice Italian restaurant. He was quizzing about Iraq in the main. He was convinced GWB had deliberately lied. He had been strong on that earlier and also wondering if TB had been spun by the US. I did my usual line. The more I met Americans the more struck I was that they were prepared to give TB a lot of the benefit of the doubt, but not the US. Plenty more talk re Bill etc. Also he was big on the former Pope, felt after his book [*His Holiness: John Paul II and the History of Our Time*] he was one of the great figures of the last century, that his support for Solidarity [banned Polish labour movement] was vital to the collapse

* During a previous marriage, Bernstein had an extramarital relationship with Jay, then wife of Peter Jay, UK Ambassador to the United States.

of Communism. Agreed to try to get him more speeches in the UK. I said it must be extraordinary to have your whole life, whatever else he did, defined by one word: Watergate. He seemed very relaxed and at ease though. He said he guessed I was similarly defined via TB and also spin doctor. He is always introduced as Watergate, I am always introduced as TB's spin doctor. The Italian media seemed fascinated by the whole spin thing and yet they had a far more obvious problem – media ownership in [Forza Italia leader] Silvio Berlusconi's hands – that they seemed not to worry about. Not much sign of an election going on, but the general view was Silvio would win.

Friday 11 April

Out for a run, then we had breakfast with Roy Greenslade [media journalist] and Noreen [Taylor, journalist wife]. Pre-meeting then to the theatre for the main interview there. Beautiful theatre. Good event. Loads of young people. Mainly an interview from the stage, usual stuff but I felt I was more relaxed than in the UK. Could be more analytical in a way. Roy quoted a piece from Times Online, someone called Susannah Herbert that at the Oxford Festival said last week I was a study in paranoia and the white coats should have taken me away. A bit harsh. As yesterday, things started late and it was all a bit chaotic. Stunning little venue and interesting that a town like this has a festival like this, and at a fair old cost. Left 12.45, I was working a bit – or certainly thinking – about a new novel on the psychological impact of fame. Out running, I had been thinking if I did the fame novel the main character would be called Maya Lowe, and immediately I saw a shop called Maya, so decided to go for it.

Saturday 12 April

I was keen to try a first-person narrative novel and was starting to flesh out a few thoughts. Definitely on the theme of fame and celebrity and whether it is possible to get off the fame train. As with *All in the Mind*, I was going to see if I could start with themes and characters first and then do the plot as it came.

Sunday 13 April

I sat down at the computer and just started out. Then later working on the BlackBerry. It was definitely going to come this one. Rory off to the Bahamas, playing poker. Cycled to Liz Murdoch's to drop off *All in the Mind*, which she wanted to read.

Monday 14 April

Out to Chiswick. Long session with Bill Hagerty a.m. to go through diaries '95. All fine. Bill really enjoying it. Motoring on the new novel. Characters good I think. Later I went with Fiona to see *No Country for Old Men*. Brilliant, and Javier Bardem superbly scary. Zimbabwe election still dragging on with government refusing to announce results and [Thabo] Mbeki [President of South Africa] a disgrace in not pushing.

Tuesday 15 April

Went to meet PG at Honest Sausage. He was looking fine but seemed more worried. Walked to Regent's Park gardens. And then we had a really nice chat at the tennis club café about where the kids were in their lives. He seemed pretty confident about what he was facing. It was also a beautiful spring day, and he said since he was diagnosed he had started to enjoy things more, like the fact we could just sit outside here and watch birds fly around.

Wednesday 16 April

Mark Bennett [AC's assistant] at home most of the day going through the diaries. Later in for a meeting at Random House. They didn't think I should do much media-wise but I was getting loads of bids because of the political scene generally, and also because it was Depression Awareness Week coming up. Ed said he was also getting a lot of translation interest in the London book fair. Talked to Prebble about a possible film to go with the novel. I had a few fairly spiky exchanges with Susan and Charlotte who were not keen on me taking up any of the offers to do stuff on depression yet. I told them at times I felt like granny being asked to suck eggs. They had very fixed ideas and underestimated how to use the layers of coverage to grow rather than diminish interest.

Thursday 17 April

Out to Excel for a human resources conference. Interviewed by Francine Stock and then pretty good Q&A. Book signing afterwards, including someone who said her husband was a Serbian minister. Samaritans [emotional support charity] director was also there to ask me to do stuff with them. Good event then off to City airport for delayed flight to Dublin. As with *All in the Mind* I was now whacking stuff out on the BlackBerry the whole time for the new novel and felt it was good stuff. Bought some books then lunch and plane finally took off an hour late. I sat next to a young guy who had done the marathon at the weekend. He said things really were as bad as people were saying. He was also about the tenth person this week who was telling me that GB was unelectable. Also noticed one or two people saying he kept popping up talking about things that had nothing to do with him. Today for example telling US television that he loved American TV.

Media making a big thing of the fact the Pope [Benedict] was there in the States overshadowing GB's visit. I made the point that if it had been during the honeymoon period people would have said how clever he was to see Bush when nobody would notice. Met by Paul Allen and we went for dinner at a nice modern restaurant in Howth. Good natter about everything. He felt there was more stuff to come out against Bertie but he had calmed it by announcing he was going.* Bed late. Reading. Dealing with the *IoS* about a piece on depression.

Friday 18 April

Writing a speech for the travel trade event I was doing at the Crowne Plaza. All made up of business-class flight bookers. Introduced, and later interviewed, by Miriam O'Callaghan [Irish broadcaster] who was lovely. I did about fifty minutes without notes and really felt on form. Great response. The big message about toughing out a clear strategy was so clearly what GB had to do. He was having a better day today. He was seeing the main players in the US, and then a big speech. Looking more the part. But he was still lacking big message on the big issues. I was fixing to see David Muir, his new strategy guy.

Saturday 19 April

Really motoring on the fame novel. Twenty thousand words in under a week. Long bike ride. Out for dinner with PG and Gail. St Albans in Regent street. Jeremy King [restaurateur] told me he had seen a travel piece by [singer] Lily Allen's dad Keith [actor] saying he saw me as his ideal travelling companion to find out what I was really like. Nice enough evening though I was still feeling low, and feeling worse for feeling like that given what PG was facing. He was pretty philosophical about things. I sensed though that the dinner was part of a round of goodbyes without saying goodbye. He reeled off all the people he had been seeing and wanted to

* Ahern announced his intention of resigning as Taoiseach following an investigation by the Mahon Tribunal and allegations that he had received payments from developers, which although not corrupt were not satisfactorily explained by him.

see. We shared a cab back and he just got out of the cab and went into the house. I said it was just his way. Fiona thought he was avoiding emotional farewells. Earlier Philip was saying Ken [Livingstone] could recover fine but GB was looking dead. Ed Balls was convinced he could be next leader and he was looking round the Cabinet table and could see nobody he did not think he could push over. I had been working on a piece for the *Mirror* on Boris [Johnson] and Ken and even after very limited research I was left with the view that he should never have been in the race at all. The whole party just lacked confidence at the moment.

Sunday 20 April

Awake from two to five and then what seemed like hours of dreadful dreams. In Russia I think. The boys with me. Big hotel and at one point Grace and Sissy told me Fiona was on the roof. Went to find her but there was no way of getting to the roof. Then lots of efforts to get to different places and the landscape kept changing. Go through one room and when I came back the room had gone. Caught up in the middle of big fights between rival hooligans. Then Calum lying in bed and he was still dressed so I helped him undress and then tried to sleep on a chair next to him. Then back out somewhere under attack from soldiers. Pretty heavy stuff. Woke up tired.

Tony called. In town for a day before back off to the States tomorrow again. He said he had sent a note to Ken saying he needed to get up more on the future. Also the fact that he was a big figure, one of the top mayors in the world. We agreed that Ken had taken too closely to heart the press stuff and he was looking a bit old and stale. He had also sent a note to GB saying inter alia that he should get out and fight for Ken, no matter all the grief he had given us in the past. He felt if we won that one it would help change the mood. But on the general scene he was pretty gloomy. He said no matter what Gordon had tried to do to him he was not deserving of the ridiculous press he was getting. As ever, they couldn't resist going over the top and GB was target No. 1 just now. The problem was that he had come in and the whole strategy was based on differentiation vis-à-vis us. The press led him down a cul de sac and then when he realised he was on the wrong track and losing serious opinion he switched back to something akin to New Labour but by then the damage was done. Also he was not sure why he had gone back to the fight over forty-two days' terror detention without charge.*

* The Cabinet was split on the need for the proposed new law, but GB was determined to force the increase from twenty-eight days through the Commons.

As for scrapping the ten pence tax rate he remembered Gordon arguing for it and he asked if he was sure. By then TB was on the way out and had too many other fronts he was fighting on. It was not a good move because too many people were losing financially. The problem is that he was totally unsure and confidence had seeped out of the party. He said these MPs causing him grief were just spineless and knicker-wetting all over the place. But they needed leadership and an operation. He said he had big characters around him who people respected. Not just me but lots of us. They knew we had a professional outfit. This lot are amateurville. He was worried about JP's book. I said we had to hope all the focus went as per the *Sunday Times* today, namely bulimia. I told him about some of the difficult stuff re him and GB. He said it was true that he had said he would go pre the last election. But then it was perfectly obvious GB was stopping the reforms and he was going to have to stay. The party was being led backwards. The Tories were poor but they did not need to do much. He said he was amazed how often he was asked about me in the States. Also did I want to get involved in the Middle East and TB Associates.

Monday 21 April

I did a phoner with the *Lincolnshire Echo* pre-Lincoln Book Festival. Stuart Prebble round. Kicking about ideas for films to go with *All in the Mind*. Eventually I had the idea of maybe doing one about my breakdown. He adapted to be more general – Cracking Up – talk to different people who had cracked under different illnesses etc. Coincidentally an independent asking if I would front a documentary on schizophrenia. Talked to Donald who felt it would be a good and useful thing to do and he would be happy to do it. Mum not keen because she worried about him being out there with his head above the parapet. SP put together a proposal which we were going to work up. Alex called. He was clearing through old messages and had seen an old one from me about whether he or Lynne knew a good cleaner. He did. I said I honestly thought he had better things to do than worry about my cleaner. He was livid after the Blackburn game and in particular the penalties he thought they should have had. Still sounding confident and felt there would be goals in Barcelona on Wednesday. The 10p tax rebellion was picking up and GB was taking a pretty big hammering.

Tuesday 22 April

Bike ride, then working on Maya novel, and thinking maybe Maya should be the title. I decided to set part of it in New York so I could have a work excuse to go and see PG when he was getting treatment there. To a lunch organised by Fred Michel [networker, lobbyist] at a posh Knightsbridge restaurant. It was a dining group made up of the French (who gave me a bottle of wine which we later learned was valued in the hundreds), German, Dutch and Danish first secretaries [diplomats]. Bright bunch, each very much of their own country. All felt GB was not cutting it. Two felt he would recover and win. One went for a hung parliament. One said Cameron would win. They bought into my arguments about GB playing an anti-TB strategy and not focusing enough on the long term. The French guy was interesting about the Sarkozy visit to London, said it was all a bit high-wire and last-minute. They were all amazed at the media love-in for Carla which had some impact over there in terms of recalibrating for Sarko.

The Dane said Helle was having a tougher time and losing support to the party to the left of her. Fred said afterwards they all said they could not understand why GB did not come and get me back. I said it would be hard to say no but I was hoping in many ways he didn't ask. I was still just about able to talk about GB without being critical or disloyal, but it was difficult. He just wasn't cutting it. The faults we had hoped would be buried by the strengths were now becoming clearer. The MPs were feeling their weight. The majority had never known what it was like to be in opposition, losing elections. David Muir had been texting to fix a meeting but he kept cancelling because e.g. GB going on a visit or the 10p 'crisis'. Not a good sign if they couldn't keep to meetings.

Wednesday 23 April

Eurostar. Met Greg [Nugent] for a chat. Triathlon plans coming on. He was thinking of moving on because he felt the company was too complacent. Typing the whole way. Really motoring. Panic at Brussels when I left my phone in a cab. Unbelievably, stupidly, I didn't think to call it. I stopped a cab and the driver said call your own number. After two times he answered and then brought it back. To the Sofitel for a meeting on Shell. Late lunch at a fascinating Portuguese restaurant full of Africans and a succession of guys coming in off the street trying to sell CDs, porn movies, sunglasses, toys. The 10p tax issue was rampant. Neil called and said it was a disaster zone. GB had made a mistake and he would do better to admit it and fix it quickly. The tax cut had been unnecessary and a gimmick to fox the Tories. We lost the credit for it and now had all this backlash from core people. He sounded more disillusioned than I had known him to be.

Back in time for Barca v Man U. Alex had said yesterday when we spoke there would be goals, but it was an odd game, all Barca really, though Ronaldo missed a penalty. David Muir was chopping and changing about meeting and Tessa, in one of her 'What to do about Ken?' calls, said Stephen Carter was so exhausted he looked like the walking dead. GB clearly worked people into the ground but without inspiring them as TB had.

Thursday 24 April

Guardian had a big page 1 piece saying TB and I were Ken's secret weapon, advising on his campaign. Although it was fairly accurate apart from the headline, and quoted me accurately, it was not terribly helpful if you ask me. Also it was bad for GB because it looked like TB was still the one they looked to for winning strategies. Tessa said serious opinion formers were saying 10p tax issue was the end for him e.g. James Harding [editor, *The Times*], 'Once you've delegated your tax policy to disgruntled backbenchers you've had it.' Not a happy scene. The great strategist – part of the myth we had conspired in developing in part to keep him vaguely sweet – was unravelling.

Out at lunchtime to speak to a Treasury staff away day at the Royal Opera House. It was being organised by John Kingman [Treasury official, ex-spokesman] who was very down on GB and the current set-up. He said of course they all knew what he had been like and he had advisors who were able to control the excesses. But they had come to the end of that road for now. He felt he just lacked that ability to connect and relate to people's lives. I spoke without notes, did my usual strategy message, keep on keeping on etc. Also I did a bit of frank assessment of the Treasury's image, said there was a view they never got other people's big picture, and re the civil service that some confused independence and impartiality. For example the opposition to the government comms review at times felt political. Also TB often felt the Home Office in particular had a view that it knew better. I watched the London mayoral debate, which Ken won but not as decisively as he should have done.

Friday 25 April

Bike, work, then train to Keighley via Leeds. Writing a speech for tonight and working on the novel. Two nice Welsh guys on the train. Both basically Labour. Both echoing what I was hearing everywhere just now – GB is not going to win. They got him. Felt he had spent ten years scheming and when he got it he didn't know what he wanted to do. They thought TB was a legend, made them proud to be British. Met by John Dennis [sports organiser] and off to Stanbury. Had a run around Howarth. Staying at the Old Silent Inn. Dinner about celebrating sport in the area. Good turnout. Good sports show. Speech went OK without being electric. Gerry Sutcliffe and Ann Cryer [Labour MPs] both bemoaning GB's lack of grip and leadership. Jane Cryer [daughter] – really nice and very attractive – said TB should never have gone and soon everyone will want him back. GB just does not have it. Awards for young athletes. Karate and bike exhibitions. Got a lift with parents of one of the fourteen-year-old winners. Gerry and Ann both said I had to go back, that everyone was saying it. I just didn't feel like it.

Saturday 26 April

Drive to Manchester to see Fiona and Calum at the flat, then off to Burnley. To Turf Moor. I was doing a charity cheque presentation which involved cycling round the pitch to do the draw. Nice reception, then back up for the match [v Cardiff City], 3–3 draw Willie Irvine, Mick Docherty and Jim Thomson [former Burnley players] doing tours for fans. To business centre for bike set-up. Round the pitch and do the draw. Got good reception. Back for the match 3–3. Great goals but the first half felt very end of season. I drove back with Neil K, who was really down on GB. We had an interesting chat about himself. He said he blamed himself for '92 defeat. He felt he could have conducted himself better personally, e.g. losing temper in public, but also he should have fought harder to win the argument for the shadow Budget to be later rather than earlier, so they had time to explain. John Smith was adamant, however. He came back to the theme two or three times as we drove down. He was clearly still sore about it. 'I try not to think about it too often, but it's always there.'

He was more down on GB than ever, said he felt that he could never have imagined he would cave in like he has. I said TB pretty much predicted it. But what to do? He felt there was no way he would go and no way there would be a challenge. But he could see the Tories making it back. Also he agreed there just wasn't enough fight in the bellies of some of the main people. GB had tried too hard to make it a one-man show and now was paying the price. He felt he had a few months to sort things but it had better be done quickly. He was running out of time. I was hearing it from everyone at the moment. Every day people were saying they just couldn't vote for him. I got back to calls about Michael Levy's book [*A Question of Honour*] being serialised in the *Mail on Sunday*. Main lines – including from the interview – seemed to be that TB told him GB couldn't win, and Levy warned TB about his massages with Carole [Caplin].

Sunday 27 April

Went to the cinema to see *Happy Go Lucky* with Fiona and Gail. Fiona and I were on no-speaking, mutual deep freeze, after some pretty harsh stuff being said. Both saying the other was selfish and self-indulgent blah di blah. I was talking to Donald about maybe making the TV programme on schizophrenia. He was keen, Mum not. Long bike ride. First puncture in ages. I got the final, final version of *All in the Mind* from Rebecca and went through it pretty quickly. Back to her and now ready for proofreading and copy-editing. Almost done.

Monday 28 April

Bike, another puncture. More deep freeze with Fiona. Nick Ferrari [LBC]. Train to Manchester. Out with Calum for dinner.

Tuesday 29 April

Run by canal. All day then at BBC in Oxford Rd doing regional interviews to promote the *Blair Years* paperback. Nice feel to how TB and I were seen. Bad for GB. Waterstones. Levy doing a signing next week. They felt I should do more media for the paperback. Doing lots of novel and diary. Sue Nye called asking me to see GB. PG called, OKish, but nervous about the op on Thursday. JP called at one point, said he wanted to see me before his book [*Prezza: My Story*] came out, to discuss positioning. He was really worried about GB and as things stood he was not sure he could be terribly supportive. He had spoken to him a couple of times and said for God's sake talk about the record, but of course GB wanted to give the impression it all started with him. I was so convinced now the continuity plus change strategy could have worked, but maybe it was too late. JP said GB called him when the bulimia story came out and said 'Sorry to hear about your illness.' JP told him it was all over, and he was fine, but he was really worried about the political situation. He wanted my advice on how to pitch it, and I said the best way is to send it as a message to Labour MPs – we won, but we could lose if we lose focus, discipline and strategic direction. It was the message I was putting out.

He felt MPs were losing the will to live. At the PLP he held back a little, said we had to unite, but there was a message for GB too – the PLP just do not feel involved. He also felt the public were beginning to see the differences, TB could empathise and explain, GB said he was listening but he wasn't. He said it would be disastrous if there was another leadership situation but it was not good. I said GB needed to peer into his soul and if he thought he could not win, he had to follow the logic of what we were saying – he can't win, so why not go? But he said there was no chance of him doing that. Tessa called too, and said the worst thing was the gutlessness of people. Apart from her, Hutton, Straw, Jacqui Smith and one or two others, nobody would go up. Ed Miliband, meant to be in charge of co-ordinating the government response, had said he would be in Doncaster at the weekend and not available. She said that things were slipping because the anti-government stuff was also beginning to hit Ken.

She filled me in on the saga of Charlie's pension as Lord Chancellor, which GB was trying to block. GB having said to Charlie he wanted to do it and the others were blocking it, Charlie now had the correspondence which showed that not to be true. She also told me of a fundraiser where they had been auctioning dinner with the PM and as the bidding went up quite high, the auctioneer said 'I should make clear this is GB not TB we are talking about.' Standard round of interviews – York, Hull, Hereford, Stoke, Leicester etc. then finally GMR live, when they replayed the last time I did it, when I was asked if I slept with Diana. I admitted that a lot of the stuff I did these days was just to pass time, and that was true in a way. Interviews were fine though and the tone OK.

Off to the Man U v Barcelona game with David Frost and Stuart Le Gassick [businessman]. Fantastic atmosphere at the end. Great goal by Scholes. Messi was breathtaking but United held on [1–0]. Up to Alex's little office afterwards for a drink and something to eat. He was claiming he wasn't nervous at the end. Lots of the old United guys there. Fair amount of booze flowing. Fabio Capello popped in. [Sir] Richard Greenbury [businessman, AF friend] really loathed GB. He said he did not deserve power. Nor did Balls etc. because they plotted and schemed against a real leader.

Wednesday 30 April

10.15 train back with Rory, and David Davies, talking of the absurdity of Sven [-Göran Eriksson] being for the chop at Manchester City. Tosser on the train saying he was going back to vote for anyone but Ken and Labour. Tessa felt things turning back a bit but still tricky. Sol Campbell [former footballer] and Sky Andrew [football agent] came round. Sol wanted to use his Stratford connections – born there – to get involved in the Olympics. He believed in discipline, hard work etc. and he wanted to get in there and work in the schools. I gave him advice on how to position and we agreed maybe get it sorted and then announce something at the Wembley fundraiser. Good chat re some soccer stuff. Quite a deep character I think. Arrived with a big black hood, obviously not wanting to be seen. He said he might do business but mainly wants to help kids learn proper values through sport and discipline. Tessa came round. She said GB had made it clear he was going to ask me to go back. She felt don't do it. I could feel the old duty v self-interest conflict stirring again. Certainly not dancing for joy.

Thursday 1 May

PG op. Train to Bristol. Syd [Young] picked me up at Bath. Lunch at Loch Fyne. He was totally opposed to me going back. He said GB was going to lose and unless I was convinced I could stop that 'just don't do it'. He was really clear about it, passionate, angry I was even thinking about it. Syd said GB just didn't cut it and everyone was saying it. Later at the business dinner I was speaking at people were nice about TB and me, terrible about GB. Did an off the top of the head leadership and strategy speech and it went well. There was a good speech by a former drug addict explaining how the Prince's Trust saved her after three years in jail. Good reception for speech. The guy hosting the night said I was a brand and a strong one and whatever happened I had that and it explained why there was still such interest in me. All ran late. Bed by 12. I watched the [local] elections coverage and clearly it was not going to be good. Tessa doing a brave face job. [George] Osborne looking pretty smug.

Friday 2 May

Tessa called. Boris v Ken was close but the Tories were saying they'd got it. She felt re GB that there was a hideous inevitability. At a profound level the public had decided they'd had enough of us. They gave us a good go and TB being replaced was a way of seeing whether GB could do better but he had been far, far worse and psychologically he was incapable of pulling it round. She said Gus, Jeremy and others were saying he should pull me back in but even if I made a difference, and galvanised people, would he really be able to do what was needed? She said I would not be able to tolerate the Ballses and the Ian Austins and Tom Watsons and so forth. GB would never see the damage these malign relationships and this negative politics did.

She said it was humbling yesterday to see queues of black people voting for Ken. But other forces were working against us. Cameron was not doing much but in a way he didn't need to. She really felt I shouldn't go back. I said the whole story could have been different if GB had worked properly with TB. She said when the full story is told it will be clear that GB blocked and obstructed at every turn. She did not think the party would turn on him i.e. go for a contest. It would only happen if he realised he was losing confidence and decided to go, but he would not do that. And who was there? David Miliband? Maybe. But not overwhelmingly clear. Breakfast at the hotel and then off to the train. The election results generally were far worse than had been predicted, and pretty humiliating for GB. All day waiting for the London mayoral result and when it came it was a pretty clear win for Boris.

I called Alex re GB and whether to work for him. 'Off your head. Don't go near it. You've got reputation and prestige because of all the things you've done and you could lose it. If you thought you could turn it all around, fine, but can you, can you really change what is happening? He is set in his ways and you don't have that same relationship you had with Tony, who would always listen. I really would worry – for your reputation, and also your "marriage". Look back at the stick you got, and the pressure you were under, and that was when you were winning. It'll all be back and not in a winning environment. You'll go fucking crazy.' He was pretty chirpy on the football front. West Ham tomorrow. Trying to get Rory a ticket for Moscow [Champions League final]. Lunch at Camden Brasserie with Rebecca. Told her the Maya plot. Liked it but not sure whether she could edit another one. I also told her about GB wanting me back and she felt it would be great, and I should do it. Ditto Rory who said I had to help if I could. Good news from PG on the operation, said it went well.

Saturday 3 May

Dire chat with Fiona, who couldn't believe I was even thinking of going back. TB called re GB and what he wanted me to do. JP was on as well. Bit like the old days. JP's main point was that he had his book out the week after next and he would be doing a lot of media and needed to decide what to say about the GB situation. He was clearly thinking, as were others, about whether there was an alternative. He wanted to see him get a fair chance and it was not a good idea to have a second change. But there was no doubt he'd made mistakes and needed to learn from them. He was too keen to portray his period as leader as a new era, the Brown era, nothing to do with TB, and so there was nobody fighting or campaigning on the record. He said he was going to ask for a meeting with GB and make a few points and also offer to help out. I told him he had asked to see me and we should keep in touch. He felt GB's closest allies were lacking in guts and loyalty. Apparently Ed Balls was saying he had only seen GB three times in two months. Douglas Alexander and Ed Miliband were fairly quiet too.

TB called again. He had sent a note to GB and was also speaking to him. GB had asked whether he thought I would do strategic comms for him. He said it was a bit of a problem if he thought that was the over-riding problem. It was a real strategy problem rather than comms alone. TB had predicted bad council results but even he was surprised at the scale. He felt GB was not sure how to react, or what he really wanted to do. TB felt I could help, as he could too, but that I would hate it if I went back in. I would not tolerate the culture he had encouraged – Balls, briefings against people and so on. He still wanted me involved in the MEPP stuff. GB's problems, apart from the personality stuff, were all in the differentiation strategy he pursued on becoming leader. I still felt he could say it – that TB was right for then, had an amazing record, but now there were new challenges for the future needing a new approach.

Sunday 4 May

Rory and I were picked up and taken to Crawley to join the Burnley fans cycling to Selhurst Park for the Palace match. Nice day and good fun. Left early when we were trailing 3–0 [result 5–0] because the rest of the cyclists wanted to head off to Burnley and my bike was in the van. Home but the mood with Fiona was awful.

Monday 5 May

Bank Holiday. DM called. He was at Chevening. I could hear the birds in the background. He asked if I was offside. I said not. He said Louise had had a couple of texts from Fiona which sounded like we were. I said no but I was watching the implosion with horror. He felt GB did get what was wrong but he was not sure what to do about it. We agreed on much of the analysis. GB had gone for a message of change and it meant there had been no defence of the record. He had also made it all about him at the expense of the team. There had been a deliberate strategy to diminish people. He thought he was doing OK on the foreign stuff and hoping to get more involved in the domestic situation. He felt the results were a kick in the teeth and actually deserved. 'We have been crap. We're not doing the basics required of leadership – clarity, signs of progress, team, motivation, confidence.' There has been a lack of confidence emanating from GB. He felt the Cabinet didn't really know what to do by way of support. Many of them had disappeared because they hadn't been part of the build-up. David reckoned there was not an appetite to throw him overboard. Equally there was no doubt that if things did not improve it was not guaranteed. But how?

I said the only way was to have a PM alongside an incoming leader, and at some stage we make it clear that is the situation. He said I was the only person apart from him who had thought of that. He said nobody was saying that yet but it could happen. I told him I was seeing GB tomorrow. He said he had always thought it would not be good for the government if I went back, because of all the baggage, but things were so bad maybe it was the right thing. JP called. He had seen GB yesterday and told him he had to do more to defend the record, and also have a clearer sense of what they're about. He felt he was in better form than he expected. He knew he had to sort the 10p tax situation or else it would bite him again. He also needed to be more focused and less all over the shop. And he needed to get more people out looking like they were a team.

I rewrote the ending to new novel, then watched Newcastle v Chelsea [0–2]. Premiership going to the wire. Alex called. He said, re GB asking me to go back, Jock Stein once counselled him against taking on too much too soon by saying 'Everyone thinks they can be John Wayne but there is only one John Wayne. The rest of us have to put left leg forward then right and just try to move in the right direction.' He said GB will be trying to make you feel like John Wayne riding in to rescue him. But there is only one John Wayne.

Tuesday 6 May

Beautiful sunny day. Out on the bike for over an hour round the park trying to think through what to say to GB. Into Millbank to do *The Politics Show*. I put up an OK fight for party and government but off-air Andrew Neil said 'It is going to be a horrible slow death, like Major's.' Trevor Kavanagh was on, saying GB had six months, and that there was endless plotting going on. I did my continuity and change line plus the party as a whole needing to fight harder. Back for lunch with Calum. Both he and Rory thought I should help GB up to and including full-time. Rory's view was that if we lost by a narrow margin I would never forgive myself. Calum that I needed something full-on again, and this was the right thing to do. Stuart Prebble came round to talk about the 'Cracking Up' film. I told him about my dilemma. He felt I was GB's only hope but could see why I was loath to do it. He felt just start a day a week and see if there was a modus operandi that could work. I said the problem was I knew if I started on that basis, I would get sucked in.

I set off and arrived at the Cabinet Office at 5.25 and was met by Peter Howes, the duty clerk. I said do you remember the last time we met like this – at Marseille airport when he flew out with my diary after Hutton asked for it. He said his friends didn't believe it was him in the book! Up to the study. Sue Nye came in for a chat, then GB. Really hot in there. He had the sun on his face but kept his jacket on. Small talk on football. He asked how Alex was. I said fine. Didn't say what his advice was re this. He asked if I thought he should go to Moscow for the Champions League final? I felt yes. He felt there could be trouble between the United and Chelsea fans and it would be difficult. He then launched into his 'big idea' as it were. He said he was sure he had the right ideas for the future. Scope and scale of change defined the world. Countries which adapt are the ones that will succeed and it is all about talent and potential. Britain better placed than anyone. It was a classic opportunity message but at least he came alive with it.

He knew the election results were bad but he felt they were recoverable because the Tories had no real vision for the future. As he rattled out facts and figures and ideas I was left thinking why none of this was coming over. Then he said 'I think I have the right ideas and a coherent set of ideas, but why can't I fucking communicate it?' The media was drowning him out. He didn't want to be day-to-day but that was what they forced you to do. Crises or trivial rubbish. I said crises had to be dealt with, trivial rubbish should be ignored. He acknowledged he had been too accommodating of the press. He had made a mistake in thinking communications didn't matter. He had made a mistake in allowing the general election speculation to go on. 'I know I have made mistakes. I also know there are things I've done I'm not proud of (relations with TB, I think he meant) but I think I am the right man to take the country forward. If I thought the younger ones were ready I would walk away and live with the fact my place in history was zero, beyond what I did as Chancellor. But I don't think they are.'

He said it was a communications issue and he needed help. He said he needed a genius who could do what I did with TB and have everything filtering through a message framework that got through to the public. I knew where it was heading. I said I had been fearful he was going to ask me to come back to No. 10 and I was ready to take out a revolver and shoot myself if he did. He looked desperate. 'That's exactly what I'm asking.' When I said the media would see it as weakening of him, he said it was time for him to stop caring what they thought. He slipped in the occasional slagging off of the *Mail* which was probably just for my benefit. He looked tired but had a bit more fight in him than I had anticipated. I was a bit alarmed the extent to which he seemed to think I was the answer to his problems. 'I can win an election. But I know I can't win it without you.' There was no acknowledgement of the downside for me, just a straight appeal to duty, and fear that we were going down. 'We have always done best when we have worked together. I need that genius you showed for Tony.'

He said he was speaking to TB regularly. 'The only one I can't make progress with is Mandelson.' He felt a bit bereft of big-hitters, that the younger ones had not really broken through yet. He really laid on the pressure – I had helped build it up and couldn't let the Tories knock it over. They had no ideas for the future. I said I could help him put his ideas into a strategic plan. But I was not sure coming back was the right thing. We had almost an hour but Sue Nye was pressing him to leave for an event at the Dorchester. She had said to me earlier 'Nobody ever told us it would be as bad as this!' One of the No. 10 people had told me even she never told him what he didn't want to hear. He spent hours doing emails and being in a rage.

He wanted me to read a couple of speeches, including one for Friday. I gave him advice on PMQs. There would be more focus and interest than usual at the next one. He had to turn it on Cameron, say that he had better enjoy it while he can because there would come a time where the scrutiny falls on him and it would even up. He said 'Do you think I can just say what I plan regardless?' Of course. Likewise I said his next speeches will be watched more closely and he had to make them work. Then he asked if I could help write them. We didn't go into the team, but I sensed he had lost confidence in them a bit. He was going back to New Labour but as TB said the question now was authenticity. Was it real?

I had mentioned Greg Nugent and he was asking about him as we walked to the car. He tapped me on the arm and said 'I'll call you tonight. I really need your help.' He called again a couple of times and said the same stuff, progressive politics, how we can win these arguments, then picking my brains on PMQs again. I was slightly losing the will to live already. Pat McFadden called. I filled him in. He said he was torn – it was what party staff, spads and most MPs wanted to see. But he felt it would be dreadful for me. He would love it for himself but hate it for me. He said the mood in there was terrible at the moment. In Wolverhampton he was the only one of the three MPs with a Labour win in their seats based on last week's results.

DM called. Similar, though he was more focused on his own position. He wanted to know if GB had a plan, whether he had a sense of the team he needed to build. He was clear though that there was no mileage in a challenge or even an agreed handover. He had to show he had the fight and go for it and they had to support him. But he said that Balls etc. were never happier than when they had an enemy on their own side and were busily trying to do him in. I went to bed and called Neil. A bit of advice, I said. What's the problem? I told him, as neutrally as I could, what GB was asking me to do. He was very clear in his analysis. The need is obvious, he said. Everyone he met was saying why can't he find an AC or ask AC himself? He said he had not encouraged anyone down that route because he didn't think it was fair.

He was surprised GB had asked me outright. He said he felt the advantages were all his, the disadvantages mine. He was sure I could make a difference. BUT – would I have real sway? It would only work if there were no ifs and buts, what I said went and that meant GB taking orders on strategy too. Would I be able to deal with all the people already there and round him? They were not my friends and they would not mind if

I took hits. In fact, they would welcome it. He said the media would go mental. 'They are after GB's blood at the moment but it would be even worse, much worse this time. Don't underestimate it. And even though you're used to it, it would be like first time all over again.' He went over the pros and cons again. The pros are that the party would like it and it would send a message that 'stern professionalism' would be back. 'The antis are all for you.' He also said that the repercussions of defeat would go deep and long and they would damage the reputation I had. He said if I was his son, he would advise me strongly against.

Rory was the only one really saying go for it. He said he felt sorry for GB. Also I would not be able to live with myself if he lost by a tiny margin. If people thought I could make the difference I should do it. Calum much the same but he said he and Rory were younger and I couldn't ignore the judgement of people like Alex and Neil. PG sent a message about his pathology test results. Good news. He was happy about that. I said bad news here – he wants me to work for him! He said only do it if you really want to. He may not be the future. Fiona was pretty much saying I had to decide, and she wasn't going to sway me either way. I was heavily swayed by Neil. He was clearly saying he thought I could make a difference but would go crazy with the situation there. He said he would support me if I went in. But he felt it was a call way above the call of duty. And as Fiona said, I liked TB and working with him but still hated it a lot of the time. This would be harder. Went to bed. Barely slept. Could be a 'Where there is doubt there is no doubt moment.' I had a lot of doubt.

Wednesday 7 May

TB texted first thing to say call before 8.30. I filled him in though as he was on the carphone in Israel all a bit coded. I explained what had happened. He said 'He's not asking you to go back in there is he?' I said he seems to be. He felt that was a really tough call. He agreed with Neil it would be huge with the media and they would make it weakening for him. He said GB had come back to New Labour as the basic position but had to show it was authentic. He could get these arguments at an analytical level but did he get them intuitively? He was not so sure. He was coming after me though because he now realised they had been feeding him the wrong strategy. He felt I should play it slow, say I would help put the strategy together but not go in there full-time as I would hate it.

We had a good laugh – I said now go and bring peace after your massage, tennis and breakfast. He said sadly only one of those has happened. He called four or five times as the line kept going and ended up saying 'Good luck!' He was as ever giving good advice though – play it long, be supportive, don't get too drawn in yet and end with real clarity on the situation I was expected to deal with. Out at half seven to do *BBC Breakfast*. Marilyn, who used to make me up when I reviewed the papers in the early '90s, was still in makeup. Louie was still the driver. He reminded me he was driving me in 1994 when I got the call that John Smith had died. Off then to do fifteen BBC regional interviews re the diary. Same old stuff really. Several asked if I would work for GB. Otherwise running round the usual blocks.

Thursday 8 May

Liz Murdoch and Eric Fellner [producer] both said *All in the Mind* was a hard filmic concept because so much is internalised. BBC said yes to the *Cracking Up* documentary. DS first thing. He was pretty clear going back to No. 10 was not a great option. Partly because it was going back. But also he said he sensed GB was desperate and looking to me to lay golden eggs that I may not be able to lay in a new and changed environment. He said it was the usual clash between duty and self-interest but that he felt I had to do what was right for me. If I feared it was the wrong thing for me, my health and family, don't do it. I said there was a divide in the family. The boys said do it, Fiona said she was neutral but was in reality opposed, Grace didn't want me to do it. I also felt that GB underestimated how much of what we did was down to the whole team, not just me, and I would not have those people there.

In for the Wembley fundraising dinner meeting at Victoria St. On table sales they were quite confident but I was not so sure. Also I gave them the bad news Alex would not be there, as he had a ceremony at Liverpool Cathedral on the same day. We would have to build up the Sol Campbell element. Ran there and back in amazing heat. Lost five pounds in water. Paul Goodman round to do *House* [Commons] magazine interview. Mainly re LRF work but also some politics. It was getting harder to hold a line about how we were doing. Also he too asked direct 'If GB asked you to work for him, would you do it?' And I had to obfuscate, say it was not my place to say what he needed. But at some point this might become an issue I guess. Out later to the Association of Investment Companies black-tie dinner at Dorchester. Pretty right-wing bunch. Chairwoman Carol Ferguson a right-wing Scot with a sparky manner and deeply irritating views. Change of mood was very noticeable. When I mentioned Boris he got a cheer. I got heckled when doing a big defence of our overall strategy, just one drunk but it was annoying and it made me cut things down a bit. But I would say the momentum was definitely swinging back to the Tories.

Friday 9 May

All day on and off working on a note to GB. I had decided I could not go back in the way he wanted me to. It was beyond me to make the difference he thought I could. But I made clear he should do a better job of defending the record and that meant at some point saying TB had been the right man for the job as a way in to a proper defence of the record. I didn't think he would get heard about the future, or get a hearing from the people we were losing, until he had done that. He called but I missed the call then sent the note via Sue Nye. Later we managed to speak, but he was on his way to a meeting so it was fairly brief, but he could tell I was not keen.

In the note, I said I had been thinking deeply about our conversation, but I felt I had to get my thoughts down on paper, partly to help my own thinking, but also so he was in no doubt where I was coming from. I said the political mood has changed substantially and we were facing a difficult period ahead. There was no great positive appetite for the Tories, in the way there was for us in '94–'97, but they are definitely being listened to in a way they were rarely listened to when TB was leader. Their tails are up. I also told him I had been shocked at the scale of negativity towards the government I was coming across anecdotally, whether at football matches or at business dinners, or just randomly going about. Much of it is unfair, but it is there, real and growing. He had to focus on devising clear objectives and strategy to meet them, and only then thinking through the tactical considerations about how to do so. At the moment it all seemed too tactical.

At first, there was a huge emphasis on change, but because of the obvious significance of his role in the past, at times the resonance was difficult, or there was insufficient sense of substance to what the change was. This allowed the media, in the honeymoon period, to say it was about style, and the differentiation was vis-à-vis TB not Cameron, which became a problem, not least in relation to defence of record. GB's focus on 'No spin, no sleaze, massive challenges ahead' played into our opponents' attempts negatively to define the record, and also meant professional communications and fundraising became more difficult at a time the Tories were improving on both fronts. Then the on/off election gave the media a new prism for a while, which the Tories exploited well and have continued to do, creating a mood that the momentum is with them. That has to be stalled quickly, or it will become self-fulfilling. Also, on policy, there has been a message of change followed by a sense of continuity but because the two had not been successfully run together, the impression was of a shift of gear, first forward, then back, so now there are doubts about authenticity.

Amid all this, there has been too much focus on day-to-day tactical considerations, and a sense that two extremes of a coalition – in newspaper terms the *Mail* and *The Guardian* – can be kept happy with very different priorities and messages. That was possible – just – as Chancellor, not as PM. I said he needed, fast, to get an agreed set of objectives, strategies and messages that resonate and connect across the board, whether they are short-term popular or not.

- On objectives, the political focus has to be in renewing and strengthening Labour – organisation, finances, policy, centre of gravity – to get in proper shape for the next election. Rebuilding the party.
- On style, the objective must be to re-establish as a given the competence and stability GB built his reputation on when Chancellor.
- On policy, the aim must be to agree the small number of genuinely major priorities – economy No. 1 – and focus relentlessly upon them. It's showing the government has a coherent and workable plan to ensure the public properly understand economic events, and more importantly that Britain emerges well from a global downturn, with opportunities and living standards improving.

If you do the above three well we will be in a much better position. I said he should then agree which are the other major issues to focus on, and recommended, to play to his strengths, these should relate to further modernisation in public services. Poverty. Social mobility. Pensions. Energy policy. Climate change. Modern challenges requiring modern responses. And all dependent on values of interdependence closer to a Labour view of the world than a Tory view. I suggested that all the rest, all his attempts at the touchy-feely stuff, he should just leave to one side. 'It is not what you are there for.'

Re. strategy – each policy area requires its own, but as an umbrella approach, the best framework for the current mood and situation is in the area of facing up to the difficult choices now to prepare Britain properly for the future in a world defined by the pace of change. Your strength, which is being undermined by drip-drip media and political effect, is the sense of long-termism, keeping going, wrestling with the big challenges. That has to be regained quickly. Big speeches with genuinely illuminating insights and ideas for the future are one important plank. Parliament is another. It is key to the steady exposure of a forward-looking modernising agenda, and just as important the exposure of vacuity and inconsistency at the heart of Tory policy.

I sketched out a framing narrative for the strategy on these lines. 'Time for a change can be a powerful political impulse. The question is change to what? In a world defined by the pace of change, governments face a number of important choices about the future. How our economy performs, how our society and public services develop, what role we play in the world, will be decided by those choices. The political choice for Britain is Labour or Tory. Between now and the election GB will lead the government and party in setting out what those choices are, leading to a manifesto programme for the future, based on a record we are proud of, but always looking to the challenges of the future.'

I said the record was going by default. Because of the earlier focus on change not continuity, insufficient defence of the record in a way that connects, and inadvertent playing into the media and Tory agenda that nothing much happened in the last two terms, has been hugely damaging. It has to be recovered as part of the everyday dialogue about politics. There needs to be a much more rigorous approach to this. It is not about reciting lists of achievement. It is about defining change for the better in every part of our national life, explaining how difficult much of it was, how the Tories resisted it and why, how it is now taken for granted. We remind to reassure of our values and competence going forward. I said the success of the past is the key to persuasion about ideas for the future. And again the focus should be economic, social, public services, role in the world. I said the key to opening a new appreciation of the record was for GB at some point, in a very personal and high-profile way, to say something like this… I knew he wouldn't like it, but said it was a necessary precondition of being listened to.

'I did think I could have been leader in '94. But TB was the right man at the right time. I am very proud of what we achieved together, him as leader and PM, me as shadow chancellor and chancellor, with our colleagues in Parliament and beyond. I think history will see the last decade and more as a period of great reform and progress. The record is a good one and we can be very proud of it – agreed set of key facts needed here. But now we are in an era even more defined by change and interdependence than ever before. New challenges. A new leader and a new team to meet them. Our values unchanged but the times in which we apply them very different. Politics is in some ways more complex and our task is to set out the choices facing the country, and face up to the difficult decisions we need to make now.'

I could tell from talking to Sue and others that they worried this was just about me trying to get a stronger defence for TB and the record, but that was because they saw everything through the GB prism. I said to him in terms that for every person he might be winning over because he was not TB, I sensed he was losing more for the same reason, and he had to re-find the continuity message before they heard him on change. He said to me earlier that his big passion is the unlocking of potential, which is fine, and can take him into work, education, welfare, public services, social mobility, race, rights etc. It allows him to make big points about big areas but in ways that translate to choices we have to make. Each area requires real clarity and focus, but related to that overarching message about talent and potential, but I said I found some of the recent speeches on it over-complicated, lacking in clarity. These speeches do not need to be 'every nut and bolt' policy prescriptions. They need to be setting out key challenges and choices, with genuine talking points for the future.

I tried to be as forward-looking and optimistic as I could, while also being frank and honest. When he called and we talked it over, he said he got it, he understood it, and he was sure he could do all of that. I said are you really up for the proper defence of the past, and the focus on continuity as well as change. He said that is what he was trying to do, 'but what your note says to me is I need your help.' He was on to the John Wayne bit, said he had good people, he was sure I could get on with them, but 'I can't do this without you'. I said I didn't think it would be right for either of us if I went back to No. 10, or to anything approaching my old role. In the current climate in particular, it could be a very weakening move for you. I said I also had other commitments now, workwise but also to the family, which made any major public role difficult for me. But I said I was willing to help devise the plan that could maximise the chance of all of the above happening.

I could tell he was disappointed, and he had another go at saying he really needed me heart and soul. I said for now, let's proceed like this. I had spoken to Greg Nugent and he would be up for coming in, and I would be able to work through him from a half-in, half-out position. He said he would like to meet him. I also said that I wanted my note to stay private between me and him. I said I was alarmed by how much the internal divisions spilled out, and the briefings and counter briefings simply have to stop; too many of your own people seem to act as commentators as well as players. Once you get any agreed strategic framework, everybody has to go for it. He said he was sure if I went back, I would be able to get them in line. I said I was not so sure about that, given the track record of some of them. Fiona asked how I 'felt' about the thought of going back at all. I said I felt a mix of dread and duty, which was not a great combination.

Saturday 10 May

Cherie's book [*Speaking for Myself*] was brought out early. TB had clearly got hold of the topline spin, the main media focus being the line that TB was advising GB on how to win the election. But otherwise she was definitely straying into too-much-detail territory e.g. that she had forgotten her 'contraceptive equipment' when Leo [Blairs' youngest child] was conceived at Balmoral. I texted TB – 'A royal baby!' Fiona thought she had brought the book forward either to cause more grief for GB at a time he was vulnerable, or because she or the publishers were worried that GB would not be there later in the year and it would be worth a lot less. Also Michael Levy was about to do the media rounds on his, and there was the build-up to JP's book as well.

Gail called from the States and things were definitely moving in the right direction re PG. He was in pretty good form when I spoke to him, said he felt OK considering how big the operation had been, also felt sure the hospital was the right place to be, though he said it was more brutal, less TLC, than he had expected. Gail was gently quizzing me about the second novel, though I already knew from Ed her view that it was mad to do another one before the first was done with. Apparently when Rebecca had fed back I had done another one already, they were in a bit of a tizz. He felt that they were a bit staid and unimaginative, and could not work out how to deal with me.

Sunday 11 May

Up early and off to the Woking bikeathon. Seemed quite fitting to be there doing a cancer fundraiser, given it was PG's birthplace. Fabulous hot day, perfect for the ride. I was feeling on form, did the hills well, stayed with the lead pack most of the way, and eventually came second after a game of cat and mouse with three teenagers. I probably overdid it because I was knackered by the time I got home and settled down to watch the climax of the Premiership. United winning at Wigan, Chelsea drawing at home to Bolton. All over. The papers were pretty grim for GB.

Monday 12 May

Bill Hagerty round. Making good progress. The publishers were asking whether we might have to change schedules as there was such a bad mood around GB. Maybe he was done for. I was struck by how virtually everywhere I went there were people really negative about him. The Tories had their tails up and we had to hope they got cocky and genuinely believed they did not have to bring forward policy. Sorting tickets for Moscow and Manchester. The Cherie stuff was picking up and there was a real mood developing that she, Levy and JP had really done damage with their books. It was politically bad because it looked like it was all we cared about, the tittle tattle and the settling of scores.

Tuesday 13 May

The serialisation of CB's stuff in *The Times* was pretty dire. A lot of it was focused on me and her rowing about Carole Caplin. Also, some of them were picking up on the idea that TB and I had virtually been using CB's miscarriage to deflect from bad [Iraq] war coverage, which was ridiculous. It was all a bit crazy, but also it was not just unpleasant about me but she seemed mildly obsessed. Anji called. I said I was surprised how much she seemed to hate me. She said she totally hates you and me. She hates anyone who she felt stopped her doing what she wanted. Anji was quoted as saying to CB 'You don't understand politics.' Just as ludicrous the claim that I said to André [Suard, Cherie's stylist] 'You're only a fucking hairdresser.' Just no way I would say that, and no way André would have said I did. And the exchanges over Carole, whilst yes, we had exchanged harsh words at times, she had a stack of actual quotes and full conversations that just didn't reflect reality. It was pretty extraordinary stuff. I texted TB to say I hoped the ghostwriter went back to Mills and Boon. He said when he had gone through it he had only really been watching out for GB problems and had removed them. He had assumed that there would be others watching for other problems.

Fiona said it sounded like he was a little bit – or even a lot – in denial about it, she had insisted on doing this kind of book, and was portraying herself as a victim. She wasn't coming over well, though, and was being hammered by most of the press. I was so glad I had not serialised *The Blair Years* and also that I had been clear about not wanting to do damage to GB or anyone else. I had a few bids to respond to CB but decided against, and instead went out on the bike. A part of me was angry that she had gone for me the way she had, but I also felt sorry for her, and felt she had been hard done by in a lot of ways. The press definitely treated her differently to the way they had treated Norma Major [former PM's wife], and it was too easy to say she had not helped herself. I think it was part of the general bias against us. So yes, maybe she played into their hands sometimes, but so what?

But even after all the ups and downs we had had, I was quite taken aback that she had committed all this to print in a way that it was very hard to see anything other than real animus. She also seemed to separate me out from Fiona. I think deep down she must know she didn't treat Fiona well, but she persuaded herself it was my fault, and there was even a sense that she and Fiona had a shared solidarity in having me in their lives! Fiona was pretty livid about it too. She was also sympathetic though, felt Cherie had never really had a fair crack of the whip from the media, and also that internally she was seen as a problem, not the asset she could be.

I worked on the leadership speech I was writing for the Henley management college. Headed down there at half four. Met by the as ever friendly and spikey John Madejski with his lady friend. Impressive set-up. Nice buildings, good feel to the place. There were around eighty or so business people, plus others from academia and other walks of life. Good mood around the place. I did a basic spiel on principles and different styles of leadership, but even as I had been sketching out the arguments, for example the focus on leadership style, the importance of clear strategy, the need to engender teamship and loyalty at all levels, boldness, making the weather, turning setback to opportunity, I felt – and could sense the audience feeling – that TB had it in ways that GB didn't. I also noticed one or two of the business people saying they 'felt sorry' for GB, which reminded me of the time Dennis Skinner said once you have sympathy in politics, you might as well go home.

Good lively discussion at the dinner, and a good mood at the book signing. But I felt once more that there was a real problem with GB's leadership at the moment. It was interesting how these moods took hold at different times in different ways. I had sent Philip my note to GB and he said he both agreed with it and also stressed that if I was going to be involved in any way at all, it had to be on the basis of talking very honestly and straightforwardly. Catherine McLeod [AD's advisor] was staying over, and we were up till gone 1 a.m. talking over some of the reasons why everything was so dreadful. She said lesser men than AD would have gone by now given the way GB and co. treated him. Also, she could not understand how we had allowed the TB–GB thing to get so bad, but it was very hard to see what we could have done differently. She felt that things people had always suspected about GB, and which the media had known but conspired in keeping low-profile, were becoming apparent and doing lasting damage.

Wednesday 14 May

The CB stuff was getting worse and worse. Really dire, and she was starting to take a hit. TB had said he had only watched out for GB-damaging stuff, but he cannot have read all this. Fiona said there was a pattern: he indulged her and let her do things she shouldn't and then got furious with her when she did. Matthew Doyle confirmed that Hilary Coffman had worked with her on it but apart from the GB bits, TB had not really engaged. Some of the chatterati were starting to say she appeared to have a bit of an obsession with me. I was somewhere or other among all the extracts, and all the bits that were getting the media attention. We listened with Catherine McL to Alistair D on the radio, defending yesterday's move to deal with the 10p tax row.* He did OK though there were too

* Darling announced that following the scrapping of the 10p tax rate he would help low-paid workers by raising their personal tax allowance by £600.

many ums and ahs and too much sense in the coverage that it was all a bit of pre-Crewe by-election bribery. It really annoyed me the extent to which there was so little fight on that kind of thing. The Tories were getting away with too much.

Marianna [Falconer] came round with a book to sign. She said it was getting worse every day in the party, and lots of people were looking to get out. 'Even your B team is better than their A team,' she said. I had sorted tickets for the Europa Cup final, Rangers v Zenit St Petersburg, and headed off to Manchester, met up with Calum. There were Rangers fans absolutely everywhere. Most of them were nice enough. Only one saying 'What are you doing here?' And one guy having a gentle pop re NI, saying we had given too much to the IRA. Pre-match I met up with David Triesman and chatted re football – he was loving the job, though realised more than ever how hard the FA was to change – then politics, where he shared the general mood and analysis. He was pretty down, as we all were, and annoyed because he didn't feel Cameron was up to that much but we were making him look good.

Alex and Jake [grandson] arrived and we had a drink with them and crowd. I upbraided Alex gently for being warm and welcoming with [Alex] Salmond, given I knew what he thought of him. The match was a bit dour after all the hype, and despite having so many more in the ground, Rangers fans were virtually outsung by the Russians. They never really looked like scoring, and in the end losing two–nil probably flattered them a bit. Then as we were having a drink with AF at the end, news started to come in of some pretty bad trouble in the city centre after a screen where the match was being shown failed. Sad. It's all people would hear about. Glasgow council leader was there and came over and asked me to go back to help GB. He said we were losing the plot all over the place. I sent a text to Sue Nye saying I thought he did better at PMQs, and also that the draft Queen's Speech outline was OK, but I didn't get a reply. I wondered if he was smarting a bit from the note, and also the directness with which I said I couldn't face going back full-time.

Thursday 15 May

The media was wall-to-wall Rangers tearing up Manchester. The CB book stuff was now into caricature territory, it was almost funny. Up at 6 and off to Surrey for a charity golf thing, Jamie Redknapp and I having been auctioned off as a golf pair. Did a few calls en route. E.g. NK who was seeing GB. There was some sense of things coming back a bit but only because people felt it was all getting OTT re GB. But Crewe was virtually a goner, people seemed to think. Got there at 10. Jamie was such a good bloke to do it for LRF. The match was OK. I hit a few decent shots but my shoulder was a real problem, and we lost on the extra hole. Nice lunch in the restaurant, signing a few things, nice day, raised a few grand. Left at 10 for *Newsnight*, where I was up defending GB. I felt reasonably confident in what I was saying, but the vibe back – Paxman, then Andrew Rawnsley [*Observer* columnist] and Sheila Gunn [former John Major advisor] – was all pretty negative, though Andrew did say he felt he had two years.

Thea Rogers from *Newsnight* showed me a text from a colleague saying 'Great get' re me on there. I said she should call her book that. She texted afterwards to say I was indeed a great get, and asked why GB didn't ask me to go back! I felt depressed at the way the political scene was just crumbling and there was so little sign of real fight. GB did loads yesterday but it had not really broken through and the follow-through was very old-style media stuff. Maybe it was just all up. I probably felt it worse though because he had explicitly asked me to go back and I couldn't face it.

Friday 16 May

DS. Mainly talking re CB, and how I felt about it. He seemed surprised that I wasn't angrier, and still tried to defend where she was coming from. He said he had heard her on *Woman's Hour* [BBC radio] and thought she came over as avaricious, and a bit selfish. I said I think it was just that she was confused about her role, and having clearly so wanted TB to become leader and then PM, her own role within all that was very limited. The thing was still running, and in today's stuff she was pretty vile about Derry Irvine, on how much he drank, and also sexism. Charlie called. He and Marianna thought the whole thing was dreadful for her, and for TB, but also for all of us because it seemed to confirm some of the bad things people thought of us. Greg Nugent came round with a book for me to sign. I explained I had mentioned him to GB but he had not got back to me since a brief chat on the day I sent my note. I suspected he was angry because I had not jumped at the chance of going back. Greg had a good sense of what needed to be done, and I felt he would be able to navigate the GB people quite well, and I would be able to work through him if GB took to him.

I had a long chat with Jeremy Heywood. He said the last few days had been better but there were still real problems. He had realised GB was intellectually capable of realising he had to change the way he worked but practically he seemed to be incapable of doing so. Stephen Carter had made a difference on the practical organisational side but he had no politics. His side had started the briefing war but then McBride, Austin, Balls had hit back and he was bruised. He could not understand why GB was so wedded to McBride but the reality was that he was, just as he had been with Whelan. He was also talking about taking on Kevin Maguire [*Daily Mirror* political journalist]. Paul Sinclair [Scottish journalist] was also a possibility.

I explained about Greg, how I felt he had a lot of talent, and also had the right personality to be able to navigate. Jeremy said the problem was GB had set his mind on me going back and helping him and he was rejecting anything else as second, third best. He said he had been going on about it for ages, and it had been quite a big thing for him to come straight out and ask me, and even though he knew I was likely to have doubts, it was a bit of a blow when I was so clear about what they were. I asked if he thought I should do it. He said he would like me to, but in all honesty he felt I would hate it because of all the infighting and GB's style, but 'even half of you would be better than what they have'. Also there were a lot of layers of people doing different things and not pulling together. Ed had a decline from Knopf on *All in the Mind* which was surprising considering Sheila O'Shea's reaction, but he was sure he would find another US publisher.

Saturday 17 May

Half decent run, a bit of work and then watched the Cup final [Portsmouth 1, Cardiff City 0]. I had to leave before the end to head for Lincoln. GB called saying he wanted to take forward the discussions on my note 'for which I'm grateful'. I think I had been hoping he would leave me alone for longer, because he did not like some of the things I had said in the note. But he was keen for me to get more involved. He said that what people were not yet fully across was the extent of economic difficulty. We were beyond the credit crunch. It was also oil and food prices. He sounded like Crewe was a goner, despite the massive influx of ministers over the weekend. The campaign – portraying the candidate [Edward Timpson] as a Tory toff – had been hopeless, totally lacking in grown-up politics. The extent of the problem was clear from Frank Dobson [former Health Secretary] on *Newsnight* the other night, defending the class attacks and saying he did not have to defend TB – hopeless. GB was on his way out but he wanted to fix a time for tomorrow. I said I was wondering whether he felt I had been too frank in my note. He said he agreed with it, but needed help in how to make it happen.

I had another long chat with Charlie F who said CB's friends were really at a loss to know what to do or say about the book. He said Derry felt totally betrayed. It was one thing to lose your job as Lord Chancellor for what he could rationalise as political reasons. It was another to have this personal attack stuff. Charlie said Marianna was in a real rage about it. Fiona's view was CB had several sides to her personality and was able to put them in different compartments at different times. Mum, wife, lawyer, fervent Catholic, socialist, activist, celebrity and so forth. What was clear from the book was that she hadn't really worked out how she wanted to project herself, it was more that she just wanted to make a splash, be noticed, be taken seriously politically. But because the media inevitably focused on the more sensationalist bits, and because there was no real framing of the book, it had come out really badly for her. I sensed TB would be pissed off but it was too late, having let her go too far. Charlie said Derry was angry with him because he had bothered to look out for bad stuff about GB, but nobody else. He said it left people feeling he didn't really care about anyone's reputation but his own.

I arrived at the Drill Hall at Lincoln. Full house, nice atmosphere, mainly Q&A. Only one angry question on Iraq, and a couple on spin and politicisation but I was on form and the questions were generally fair. Two asking me to go back. A few anti-media. One asked why TB did not give CB the same advice he had given me about the need to avoid 'storification' by not serialising and so not conceding to others how the book was projected. Quite, TB said when I told him. A couple asked why I had never stood for Parliament. I probably should have done. Audrey was convinced I was the only one with the attributes to stop Cameron who was currently getting away with murder.

Sunday 18 May

GB called as I was driving south. Another exposition on the economy. He was also protesting that he tried to defend the record all the time, but nobody listened. I said it needed something dramatic as per my note for it to break through. He said he knew my thing was 'continuity plus change' but he felt that with the Tories playing on 'Time for a change' it was important that he had emphasised change. He did not seem to agree with my main point but was trying to say he did. We agreed there was a capacity problem re the younger ministers who had not grown into it at all, which was a problem. 'A lot of the focus is on me though,' he said. I said he needed a team to bolster him, even one that was publicly identified as such a group. Crewe was difficult. He said 10p would not have hurt so much had it not been for the economic change. Now the party was behaving as though it was all about low-income families and he knew we had to keep the focus on middle income.

He quizzed me about Greg and wanted to see him today. I tracked him down and arranged for them to meet at 4. Greg really keen though I warned him of the scale of the difficulties he was heading into. TB called as I got home. Re CB and the book, he said 'There is nothing to say. It is bad and just has to settle now and go away.' He said he had not got on top of it sufficiently. He had focused on GB stuff to the exclusion of other issues he should have addressed. He accepted it had been damaging, not least with people who thought they were still her friends. I had been surprised by the extent to which she didn't like me. There was something close to hatred there, CF felt. TB did not want to go into it. He said we just have to let it blow over. On the GB situation he said he was not showing strength and leadership. It was day-to-day tactical. Serious people probably gave him one last go but the press were now in kill mode. He felt that if Crewe was a disaster and things did not improve quickly there would be a move internally.

He was still hoping I got involved in the Middle East stuff. I said he had to watch the money stuff, and do a better job of explaining how the money he made was being used to fund all these other things he was doing. The idea of CB doing a sensationalist book for good money had damaged on that front too. I know, he said. I sensed he and CB had had some pretty harsh words. She was getting a bad press but probably didn't see it. He was much more down on GB than before. He said it was possible to give him a plan or argument but he always mangled it and made it too complicated.

Greg called after seeing GB. He said he had really enjoyed it and felt GB listened and was also more aware of the problems than he had expected. Greg had emphasised the importance of role clarity. Also that there needed to be a core vote strategy, a plan to show he was a leader, policies to break open the Tories, and proper structures. GB asked him to see Stephen Carter tomorrow. Perhaps work alongside David Muir. He said GB was obsessed with the idea of how to get me more involved. He had said without me and PG any campaigning lacked potency. Greg was even keener on getting involved having met him, which was good. Part of our problem was that we had the same people saying the same things, and working in the same way as they had been doing for ages. A bit of new blood could go a long way, and I felt Greg understood both strategy and also the way the media landscape was shifting.

Monday 19 May

Out first thing to Stamford Bridge for the Cystic Fibrosis Trust v MPs football match. Usual crowd plus for us Gus Poyet [Uruguayan former player], who was as fit as ever. Neville Southall [former Welsh international goalkeeper] in goal, huge but still had it, Warren Barton, later Luther Blissett [former players]. Darren Campbell [former athlete] up front missing sitters galore. DJ Spoony [disc jockey] man of the match. We won 7–1 and I played OK. Nice little do afterwards. Lunch with Rory and Zoe [Richardson, girlfriend] in St John's Wood, then home to finish a read-through on the novel. Charlie F and Blunkett around for dinner. DB looked a lot better, had lost weight, had a bit of colour in his face. Very down politically. He said he would only go back as Chancellor and GB was never going to offer that. He felt Charles Clarke was convinced he was the next leader. Charlie said Milburn was playing a longer game. DM, Balls and Purnell probably all thought they were up to it but none of us agreed really. Balls was widely viewed as a problem. David left for a vote and CF opened up re Cherie. He made a joke about throwing a party for all the people who were upset with her. She had called him the other day to ask him to defend her against the judge who was saying she should quit the law. He had not said what he thought, and she was probably fairly oblivious. He felt TB had let it go and would now be angry. Charlie felt her hatred for me and Anji was all about the fact that she felt we took him away from her and we all had a great life together. He was about to start with a US law firm and make some decent money. He said GB was being terrible re his pension, that he was claiming it was others who were stopping it when the papers showed definitively that it was him. 'I just wish he could be honest.' The general feeling was that GB could not change his ways and that he was probably done for. Agreement too that the Crewe by-election was a disaster.

Tuesday 20 May

About to go out on bike when I realised I was supposed to be meeting David Frost for breakfast, to help him prepare his interview with Alex post the Champions League final. I called him and he came round to the house and hopefully I was able to help him a bit with some pointers. Greg saw Stephen Carter and found him a lot less open and welcoming than GB but he felt it was moving in that direction. Cherie's book went in at No. 1 but only just over 3k sales, compared with the 20k in my first week for the hardback. Rory home before heading off to Moscow for the Champions League final.

Wednesday 21 May

The Cherie stuff was ticking over and she was getting a pretty big hammering for it, some of it unfair, some not. Charlie F had escaped the wrath pretty much. His take was that she saw Anji and me as the two who took TB away from her and she worried he seemed happier with us than her.

So maybe a read across to Fiona and her antipathy to TB, as seen by DS. Rory set off for Moscow early and I was so pissed off at not being able to go, all the more so for the nature of the event I was doing. A smallish dinner for about thirty clients of Tower Brook, financial investment firm. I tried to get the timetable rearranged so that I could at least watch the match but the Tory-supporting host Ramez [Sousou] went on for ages, with a pretty gloomy assessment of the world economy, whose grimness was so severe he described it as 'great for us' – the business guys – because there will be plenty of companies to buy. I did an OK job, mainly on leadership plus current issues, shortish Q&A and then watched second half.

Calum had texted me re Ronaldo's goal but Frank Lampard equalised on half-time. Rory texted that United should have had it dead and buried. Chelsea better team second half. I left the Lanesborough for home as the ninety minutes ended and was there for the last twenty minutes of extra time and then, with Rory on the phone, penalties. John Terry's miss let United back in, then Edwin van der Saar saved from Nicolas Anelka and it was over. Rory wild on the phone. Alex was looking as happy as could be. Then news of absolute tragedy – Natascha's husband Martin [Kelly, surgeon] dropping dead of a heart attack as he arrived home. She was filming in the States. I spoke to Roy [Greenslade, Natascha's stepfather] to see if there was anything we could do. Beyond belief.

Thursday 22 May

I had a meeting with Stuart Prebble and Judith Dawson on the film. Later Annie Robinson [broadcaster, friend] agreed to be part of it. Rory got home around 2, tired but happy and we watched extra time and penalties again. The *Mirror* asked for a piece on Alex, which I did, and another for *La Repubblica* who wanted to run it on the front for Friday. The Crewe by-election was clearly going badly. I did not stay up for the result, but the inquest was starting already. The class campaign had backfired. It just showed such a lack of imagination. Cameron was looking like the man with momentum and GB was looking ground down.

Neil called to say he was due to see him next week and what did I think? I took him my note of a couple of weeks ago. Yet already it seemed outdated given the scale of the problem. Neil seemed at a loss too to know what to advise him. He felt everything he did at the moment just went wrong and it was not easy to see the way out. We agreed on a lot of the weaknesses – no attack, young guns not firing, lack of big players around the place. But the real issue was GB's inability to give a sense of where he was going. The proofs of my novel arrived so I worked through those. I also sent a letter to *The Times* rebutting the notion I called André 'only a fucking hairdresser'.

Friday 23 May

Crewe – 7k majority overturned with a 17.6 per cent swing, Tories in with 8k majority.* Dreadful though I guess the way things had felt in recent weeks, it could have been worse. But there was little sense of where the fightback was going to come from. Ed Miliband called. He asked what I thought. I gave him my basic analysis which was that previous strategic errors had built up and the existence of a less benign economic scene had brought them more harshly into play. There had to be more contextualising and explanation. Better defence of the record. More attack on the Tories. More argument. Jack Straw was clearly diddling a bit, which suggested they were starting to think it might be all over for GB. Ed was mainly in listening mode, didn't have much to say by way of solution, but he knew things were bad, could not go on as they were. Alan Milburn called. He said the Cabinet was key to this now. He said every one of them basically said there was no way GB could win, but the one person they didn't say it to was him. They were going to have to find some guts from somewhere.

He felt the current situation was untenable but there was a risk we just limped on. He said none of the candidates was perfect but anything had to be better than this. PG felt GB had been given a go and found wanting and there was little point pretending any more. Greg had seen GB several days ago now and had seen several in-betweens from Carter down but he said he had the growing sense it was going nowhere. It was not clear what they were trying to do, he said. And although GB had signalled he wanted Greg to be hired, he felt all the others felt threatened and were suspicious. He said 'with most job interviews you end with the boss after seeing the others. With GB, it seems like you start with the boss who says he wants you, then you get worn down by the others.' Certainly not the best way to go about building a team. Greg still keen but felt there was too much opposition and GB didn't just say what he wanted and get it. He felt he was still hoping I would overcome my resistance and just do it.

Saturday 24 May

More CB stuff going into the weekend. TB maybe over optimistic in thinking it would blow over quickly. Long bike ride. JP called. He was doing Marr tomorrow on his book and wanted to be supportive of GB without being silly about it given the current mood. We talked over ways of expressing it, the need to focus on what he did as Chancellor, also the strength and the breadth of his intellect. But the backdrop was now Crewe, and also

* The by-election was called upon the death of sitting Labour MP Gwyneth Dunwoody. Her daughter, Welsh Assembly member Tamsin Dunwoody, was selected as the Labour candidate.

all the chatter about GB not being up to it. JP clearly felt Straw was up to no good, but said there was no way he would be leader. He felt Balls was diddling as well. He felt GB was probably still the best we had, but he had to do better than this.

Sunday 25 May

Out on the bike for 2:45 with Rory over to Richmond Park. Loads and loads of cyclists out. Felt OK but Rory was so much faster, he kept having to hang back. Tessa called to say happy birthday and then to say it was getting close to the time when a delegation would have to go and tell GB they had lost confidence in him. But she said if it went to a contest we could not rule out Balls winning. I doubted that. David M called. I found him a bit more reticent these days, in that he seemed to be calling to find out not just what I thought but more what I knew about what others were up to, and especially what was going on in GB's mind. He asked lots of questions but said little himself. I said he and others had some real decisions to make. He was emphasising the new Labour message and was clearly sensitive to the DC post-Crewe line that it was the death of New Labour. He kept asking me what GB was saying, and whether I was helping him. I said while he was leader, I would help, but not in the way GB wanted.

If there was a change, then it seemed to me he – DM – was the best placed, but he needed to be very careful how that came about. But the reality was most members of the Cabinet and most MPs seemed to think GB could not win. If we were the Tories, we know what they would do if that was so clear. The thing was every now and then GB could show how good he was, but of late it had all been pretty lacklustre. Chickens were coming home to roost, said DM. He said he had loads to keep him busy on the foreign policy front, but he could not emphasise enough how bad the atmosphere was politically. I said that the only hope was a GB departure coinciding with a leadership campaign as the springboard to a general election. Out with the family to Camden Brasserie for dinner. The boss was back from his break in Uruguay. He said to me as we left 'They need you back but you must not go. Politics takes too much of you. You're better off where you are now.'

Monday 26 May

Bank holiday and my first decent long run for ages, in pouring rain. In the evening I watched the whole of the 1967 Celtic Inter Milan game in Lisbon. Absolutely incredible match. Amazing performance by Celtic. So deserved to win [2–1].

Tuesday 27 May

Alex called first thing and we had our first proper chat since the CL Final. He said he was having trouble sleeping. He had had no more than three hours any night. It was just taking a long time to come down to earth. He really believed when Terry was going up to take the penalty that it was all over. But maybe sometimes fate does intervene. He felt they should have had it all wrapped up by half-time. He also felt he got most of his decisions right. Leaving out Park Ji-sung was tough, maybe the toughest selection decision he had ever made. His whole family seemed to be over from Korea, and the conversation telling him he was not playing was really, really tough. He had been working his balls off and doing OK but he had not been giving him that something a bit special, a goal or an assist. By the way, he said, 'Anderson won it for us ... his penalty and then whacking the ball in again and getting the fans going, we were not going to miss after that.'

He felt he got the subbing OK. [Paul] Scholes was playing with a broken nose and not breathing too well and maybe he should have taken him off earlier but he was not sure [Ryan] Giggs could last a half plus extra time. So he did fine on all that. He was telling me all this in the context of GB having called him to congratulate him and then said he would appreciate getting his advice some time. Alex said he was happy for me to say to him that he would think about it. What he felt was that GB needed to address the personality issue by saying yes, I am a dour Scot because that is my background, but here is what I believe. He agreed with my take about GB needing to say TB was the right man. And also that because in a way he had encouraged disloyalty against TB so he should not be surprised to be on the receiving end now. What you sow, you reap.

He said he felt Balls came over as a real problem, that he did not have the kind of dynamism and honesty in his relationship with GB that I had with TB. I told him what GB had said about not wanting to admit bad appointments. He said that is worrying. If he has made bad appointments he has to fix them. Look at all the changes made under TB. Mandelson out twice yet he would still have worked for TB. If Balls was given the boot, he would be trouble straight away. But on staff it was worrying if he could not make decisions. When Ruud van Nistelrooy was scoring forty goals for him, yet a problem in the dressing room, he got rid of him. He had to for the bigger picture. And that was fine. He worried that GB lacked those basic leadership skills. He sounded on good form but tired. Re Avram Grant [Chelsea manager] he felt if they had won he might have survived but the problem was he had lost control.* The players had more power

* Grant's contract was terminated at season's end.

with the owner – John Terry, Frank Lampard and Didier Drogba were running the show. He was lucky to have the backing he had at United. He wondered whether he had the last generation of decent management at a big club, who let the manager more or less manage. Mark round to transcribe [diaries] earlier. Covering the period in 2004 when TB was close to going – and talking about how he intended to spend the rest of his life doing faith matters. This as he was about to launch the Faith Foundation in New York.

Wednesday 28 May

Out early for the Eurostar to Paris. Greg called, said he sensed yet more stalling on getting the job at No. 10 sorted. I was met at Gare du Nord and off to Ivry-sur-Seine for an interview on the diaries. I was also going through the proof of the novel, and confident it would get translated into French when I met the publishers. It was interesting the extent to which the mood was very down on Sarkozy. My theory doing interviews and stuff, including with the Beeb, was that he was doing what he said he would, and changing the style as he said he would, and what was the problem with that? Yet what seemed to come back was the feeling he was a bit vulgar, not like a President, maybe too close to the people.

I got to the Residence and had a chat with Peter Westmacott [UK Ambassador]. He felt Sarko was a bit on the vulgar front too. There were a lot of odd stories about his behaviour e.g. womanising, though maybe it had changed post Carla. He was also still far too active, getting involved in too many issues not important enough for him. And times were tough for so many people. Some raised the first few days of the presidency – partying, saying he needed a holiday – and felt he had not really recovered from that. Peter liked him on one level and said it was great for us that he had put the word through the system that the Chirac anti-Britain mood was over. He loved TB and tried hard to get on with GB and there was lots we could do together. He was scathing re the No. 10 scene. He said Tom Fletcher [GB's private secretary] in particular tried hard to get some order into things but Simon McDonald was too distant in the Cabinet Office, Jon Cunliffe was doing Europe, but two other big areas as well and they were all working for someone who bounced far too much from issue to issue.

It was not easy to get decisions. Strategy was not clear. He felt EU defence was a good issue for him to move on, that we had France and US in a better position than ever, but GB was worried re the sceptic press, and did not want to push it. He said TB had said he would press him and he was sure he was, but it was not clear where GB was. We were speaking in my room, one I had stayed in before, with a view out on the courtyard. Peter very suave, very friendly, but it was clear to me he felt the Tories were on their way and would be in power before too long. He said that worried the French even more because they sensed, especially via William Hague [shadow Foreign Secretary], that they would be more sceptic. But he said the GB scene was widely seen as disastrous.

He picked my brains a bit on where key people and the party generally were. I still sensed no appetite for a leadership election, but things could not go on like this much longer without something giving. His American wife Susie popped in and we had a little chat about the States. She was a big Hillary supporter and was worried the Republican machine would marmalise Obama. They were hosting a do for the UK Paris community. Peter said he had upset some by scrapping the Queen's birthday bash and this was the sop. I did the main BBC interview re Sarko on the top floor with their now solo Paris correspondent who filled me in a little more on the problems he was facing. I said if I were advising Sarko, I would only worry if he was being deflected by the polls from doing what he said he would. He had to keep going, the same as GB did.

It was a good enough event, hosted by WH Smith [booksellers]. I spoke for ten, fifteen minutes and then did half-hour Q&A which could have gone on for hours. Good questions. Quite a few political students and academics. Signing afterwards during which a woman about my age, quite attractive, said 'You once rescued me.' It was the Danish journalist I helped out at a Tory Party conference when I was on the *Mirror*. She now lived in Paris, was married to a UK diplomat, had four kids. She reminded me of the postcard she sent me after the conference – 'You know everything about British politics and nothing about Scandinavian women.' In other words she was surprised we didn't get off with each other. She said she was upset that it appeared in Peter Oborne's book and a profile by Andy McSmith when I left. Nice enough woman, quite intense. Also a couple of women from the Embassy who said they were unashamed groupies. A few Qs re CB book which I think I dealt with fine, played for laughs.

Thursday 29 May

Frances, the Embassy press officer, came up for a chat, asking me how to do strategy basically. Nice woman and I sensed she had a good feel for it. Peter joined us after his breakfast and we had another run round the block on GB and he was even less guarded in his criticisms today. He basically said we all had a fair idea it would be as bad as this. That is probably true. He asked if I thought it was recoverable and I felt it was, but he was going to have to get a move on and improve things quickly. It was a common theme from people that the operation was not what it was.

Neil called as I headed to the train. He agreed with my GB note. He also felt he needed to be told he had to relax a little and stop being something he wasn't. He said he got hurt when the Tories used to say re policy changes that they were pleased he had gone over to their view, but... In other words play on insincerity and he felt we should do that with the Tories. But if anything it was GB's authenticity being called into question. Neil was due to see him next week and wanted to be constructive but also say the truth. He worried nobody would be doing so inside the operation. He was still of the view I should not go back. 12.13 train, into town then worked with Mark on diaries. Calum back for a couple of days in between exams. Seemed to think he had done well. I was tired after too much rushing around sweating in unexpected heat yesterday and not enough sleep. But Paris had gone pretty well.

Friday 30 May

Out to the stables with Grace. Took the bike and as I finished GB called. We got cut off and took an age to get reconnected. He wanted to discuss how to take forward our earlier discussions. Stephen Carter was seeing Greg shortly. SC felt director of comms at the party was the best place for him. I said are you sure that's not just him not wanting someone around who might challenge him. GB said he would prefer him in No. 10. In which case make it happen. We talked a bit about that, then football, my cycling and various injuries, before we got back to politics and government. He said the problem was the media trivialisation of politics so that it was not possible to get a proper debate about serious issues. I said it was true they were a pain in the ass but it was still possible. He was the PM. He was able to command attention. He could define major issues and set them out.

He was then back on the chat up. He said I was 'uniquely placed and capable' to make that argument. He wanted to see me again to discuss these issues. I said I was supposed to be seeing Ed Miliband at home at 3. By the time we had finished the call I was meeting GB at 3 and seeing Ed beforehand. I felt a real sense of dread. I really did not want to be doing this. But it was hard to refuse point blank to help when he was so insistent and when it was clear the Tories were on the march. Ed came round and we had forty minutes or so. I gave him my analysis and said much the same as I had said in my note to GB, with maybe a bit on top. He said it was important I didn't go OTT with GB as he was pretty fragile. I said there was no point sugar-coating or pussyfooting. If he didn't change, he was done for. He felt there really wasn't any desire for a contest or a change of leadership but he accepted things were not good.

The media was a real problem. I said the media would be less of a problem if GB had a proper strategy and a proper operation. Lack of capacity at the centre was a problem. He agreed the younger ones had not come through, there was little Tory attack and too much division. He was not of the view Carter was making much of a difference. I often felt with Ed that he was good at problems but weak on solutions or giving any sense of ownership of the plan to get out of things. I was also struck every time I saw ministers the extent to which they identified their reality through various arms of the media. Ed was the same. I asked how DM was. He said enjoying being Foreign Secretary but not enjoying the general situation. He wasn't speaking terribly warmly about him. I think he worried DM might be plotting to make a move.

I got a cab into Whitehall, through the link door with a new Geordie duty clerk then up to the study. Stephen Carter and Greg were already in there. It was the first time I had met Carter. He seemed quite tense, very angular, a bit android. He did not immediately come over as very sympatico. We did a bit of small talk then I gave him a rundown of GB's call this morning and my view he was worrying too much about the media and not enough about the medium and long term. He said it was a message he gave him every day. Greg told me later his body language had changed markedly when I went in, like it really wasn't comfortable and he looked really nervous. GB came in. Again, more small talk. SC then trying a bit too hard to set out his analysis of where they were and why. Honeymoon, overstated positive position, on/off election the key to the switch to negative. GB said it would have happened anyway.

Railing at the media, especially Nick Robinson who, he said, had no interest in or knowledge of policy and did everything through personality. SC talked too much about polling and positioning and was definitely too keen on the 'problem is' formulation. He also said at one point, 'When I was a normal person before I came to this job…' I said you are still a normal person. He said thanks for that. 'Living an abnormal life.' He went off with Greg and left GB with me. Champions League talk. I used it as a bridge to say what Alex had said about the need for him not to deny the charges against him – like dour Scot – but if there was something in them, to explain them. I said he should take all the criticisms from focus groups and try to give them a proper context that allowed him to speak to what he is and what he is trying to do.

He said he believed he really understood the world of change and also how to get Britain in shape to meet the challenges. He went through the new industries and the share of the economy they were taking. How, for example, an iPod saw a small share of the profits go to China where it was built and most to the UK people who developed it. A million cars being built for a grand a pop in India. He was really passionate about it and I said he needed to find ways that he could get that kind of passion and his understanding of the issues out there. He said he had been to speak at a Google event and someone from Warner had suggested they do an Al Gore-type film, like the one Gore did on climate change [*An Inconvenient Truth*], on the kind of things he was saying, how the economy was changing fast and how the challenges of change could be met. I said grab his arm off.

I reminded him of the big *Newsnight* series TB did when we were going through a really tough patch. He said maybe not Paxman but an hour with Robinson. I said 'What, the one you just said was a trivialising jerk?' Think outside the box. Do four press conferences in a week, say you are going to bore them to submission on the world economy. Day one, explain oil. Day two, food. Day three, other issues. Day four, your prescription. Maybe do that bit in Parliament. Make it heavy, serious, use it to explain. 'Can I get off with that?' he said. Definitely. It is about doing it with force and vigour. Real energy and breakthrough.

Then he said again, as he had last time, that he could not do it without me. 'I am at the end of my tether and I would give anything to get you involved.' He looked pretty desperate. I wanted, there and then, to say I did not want to get too involved. Instead I said did you read my note properly? I was happy to help but I did not want to come back in anything like a full-time position. He said what about if I speak to you every morning? When do you get up? I said a lot later than I used to. 'Seven, half seven, is half seven too early?' I said he also needed to understand I did not read the papers or follow the broadcasts and I did not intend to. He said he would not expect me to but he wanted to be able to call on my instincts. I was being sucked in. It was very hard to say I would not help, even harder to be totally frank about what I thought – about past, present and future.

PG's view was that he had had it and the best thing for the party was that he made way for someone else. He had had his chance and it had failed. He still had the advantage of a Tory Party not that good but on that too PG felt that DC was better than we thought. GB was due to get into black tie and head off to Windsor Castle for a BOA event and Carter was coming in trying to wind up the meeting. He walked me out. As we went down the stairs he said he was grateful for all my help. I felt I was not doing much. But I worried I was being drawn in further than I wanted. He was just desperate and believed I could somehow lay a golden egg in there. GB talked a little about the US as I left. He felt Obama was really warm and clever, HC in trouble, McCain was the most frail. So his money was on Obama. He thanked me again and I went off for a cup of tea with Martin Sheehan [No. 10 press office] and Paul Brown [government planner]. Both said things were getting worse not better and I would be mad even to think about it. I got the sense they felt Carter was weaker. He was definitely manoeuvring to get Greg to the party.

Home, feeling a bit down about it all. Out to La Casalinga with F and Calum. Lucio [restaurateur] saying GB had had it. Time for a change was on the march. Nice chat with Rebecca Carter. I was asking her to edit on freelance basis Novel 2. Charlie had done really good notes on it and I felt it needed her at this stage. She very kindly said she would read as a favour but could not take on as a proper job. She agreed it was frustrating they could not see the value of going for two at once.

Saturday 31 May

Could not sleep, really bad dreams when I did. I was up and out on the bike by six. PG was home overnight so Calum and I went to see him. He was looking pretty good. Full of NY and the whole experience. He felt he was in the hands of real pros, but bedside manner not their big thing. Re GB he felt we had to decide what really was the best thing. Gail felt I owed it to history to tell him to go, and simply refuse to help him. We had all conspired in getting him there and what was going to be clear was that we did not think he was going to be capable. Great to see PG, even though he was looking weak he was still with us and seemed reasonably confident he was going to see it through.

To Tessa's. Both Matthew and Jessie were there and Rory and Zoe came up too. Jessie played us her music online which was really good. Tessa was thinking about when to get out. The family clearly wanted her out, but she seemed to be in turmoil about it. I felt she should announce after Beijing that she was not going to stand again, be active in finding her successor, sort herself something related to sport and the Olympics. GB called, left a long message, basically saying he was wanting to send me a paper, would I read and comment? I did not return the call. I felt bad, but I was losing the will on this. [Lord] Ted Short [former Labour deputy leader] called to thank me for the book I had sent him, said he really enjoyed it. He said he always wanted to thank me for everything I did for the party. He said 'You must be very depressed at what is happening and how your success is all being undone, so fast, and so unnecessarily.' I said you have seen similar in the past. He said 'Nothing so fast as this, nothing so self-inflicted.'

I took Audrey into Stratford-upon-Avon. Every time I go there I'm struck by the sheer volume of visitors, there purely because of the lasting genius of one man. I spent a bit of time googling all the different words and phrases he had invented, and through the day started counting how often they came up in conversation. David [Mills] was on good form though the gypsy encampment at the bottom of the hill had cost him dear in terms of trying to sell. He bought a house down in the village before the sale on his own fell through. David had decided to let the house out to a holiday company. GB called again. His big thing at the moment was Charlie, Charles Clarke and [Lord] Peter Goldsmith [former Attorney General], who all backed plans for ninety-day detention under TB, now rebelling against 42. It was not easy to take his lectures on loyalty though even if, as he said, Charlie was doing it as a way of signalling he would cause trouble if he could not sort his pension, on which, again, GB claimed his hands were tied.

He told me yesterday he had foregone his additional PM pension 'though you get fuck-all credit for it'. That's why these gestures ultimately don't mean much, I said. I said I thought CB first turned against me when I persuaded TB to give up the MPs' pay rise in opposition. I remember Derek Scott [former TB economic advisor] arguing it was a foolish and futile gesture. He was probably right, but it had been effective politics at the time. He asked what I thought of Cherie's book, and I told him. GB said he thought he was her no. 1 enemy but I seemed to be a rival. He said Stephen Carter had said it all added to fin de siècle feeling, which may be true. The weather was fabulous and we ate outside, David the usual mix of serious and funny, very clever. Basically of the view we were fucked under GB and possibly fucked anyway. He felt DC was no TB but that he did have the extra something leaders need.

Sunday 1 June

Out for a run with Grace, then chatted with David over breakfast about whether and how much to help GB. He felt it would be dreadful for me, I would get tarnished and if it got out it would not help GB, as it would be tantamount to an admission he could not do the job. Tessa seemed quite down about her own position. She said Alan Milburn was always phoning and obviously wanted people to suggest to him he should go for it. The feeling re Straw was unprintable. 'Vicar of Bray' said David. 'Always looking after No. 1' said Tessa.

We drove back and when I got home GB called again. I said – for the nth time – that he had to get a proper explanation out there about the economy. Maybe do in stages – fuel, food, family finances. I remember TB saying even if you gave him help he somehow mangled the idea, mashed it into something it wasn't. He was doing that with this, not seeing its simplicity and focusing too much on the vehicle rather than the product or message. He was trying his hand at small talk and then came to the purpose of the call – he was trying to get me to agree to a regular morning call. 'When can I call tomorrow?' We agreed any time after 7. I said I was not going to read the papers and I was not going to be responsible for follow-through for anything we discuss. He said fine, he will get others to do that, but I knew what he was doing, just pulling me in bit by bit.

When I had discussed it with David S last time, he said he felt the addict in me wanted to be drawn in, but it didn't really feel like that. He felt it would probably be better for my own mind if I just said No, and held firm on that, but I found that so hard to do. It was duty v self again. But DS thought it was more complicated, and Fiona agreed, that I couldn't let go of being able to make a difference in these campaigns, and feeling that I could and so should. I just lacked the enthusiasm I knew was needed. There may come a point where I just say bollocks to it. It was a totally unsatisfactory means of running the operation, for sure. There was also still no clarity re what they wanted Greg to do. They were so confused about things. I sensed GB was disappointed with his appointments but could not admit it, not to me anyway, perhaps not to himself. But I said if Greg did not get clarity pretty soon, I would advise him he should not go. I said to GB he just had to decide who he wanted and how. He laughed, said well you know who I want and you know how, but you won't do it. Fair point.

Monday 2 June

First of the morning calls. I had not slept well. Lots of bad dreams. I had read a weird book by Philip Roth last night, *The Dying Animal*. Somehow the title – though not the highly sexual content of the book – got mixed up with GB. Dying animal. In one of the dreams, he was like a big beast being shot down. He had his white shirt hanging out, he had bloodstains and inkstains all over them, he was holding his guts, which were spilling out, and he was saying 'I refuse to die, I refuse to die, you have to help me keep going.' It was horrible, woke me up and I sat up and wrote it all down, to share with David S next time I saw him. GB called around half past seven. I'd been up since before half five doing a rewrite on Novel 2, based partly on the excellent analysis Charlie sent through yesterday.

I was in full flow when GB called. He was at his desk and was banging at his computer as I spoke. It really was an odd way to work. He needed systems but bypassed them and I feared these morning calls would be another plank to that. I was saying the same thing as I had for days. Explain what is happening. It does not have to be about new policy. Just explain. Part of the job is to explain the context, be open and frank about what can and cannot be done. He would straight away go to process. A speech or a press conference? A visit? A document? He was firing all over the place.

Then I would talk and I could hear him banging away. And a short while later a note would come through, in his big capital letters, saying what I had said. It was pretty hopeless though I would try to help if I could. But I could imagine what followed. Banging out a note. Telling his officials what he wanted. Then mangling it.

He said he had the Japanese PM in pre-G8 today. 'Shall we start it there?' Then 'No because all they'll be interested in is 42 days,' and then into another run round the block on that – Charlie, Goldsmith, Charles – but where was the counterattack argument I said? Then off on another tangent, why didn't *The Times* splash on his article? Then back to his favourite facts and figures on food and fuel and finances. He could sometimes explain it well. At other times not at all. He at least was saying he was beyond caring about the criticism which even if not true was a better mindset to get into. I filled in Fiona who said she felt sorry for him. He was obviously finding it really hard, and didn't feel he had the support he needed. Through the day a bombardment of emails from him. I had a nice lunch with Eve Pollard at the Camden Brasserie. Lots of 'those were the days' re the *Mirror* times. She was also of the view GB may have had it but said there was not much warmth for DC. She had been with Sue Nye and Gavyn Davies in France at the weekend and sensed Sue was down on Carter though discreet.

We had a good chat about novel writing, a mutual lament on the state of the media, then I ran home, so slow as to be embarrassing. My knees were hurting a lot. My shoulder was bad. I felt fucking old. Getting past it. I worked on the book then went out for dinner with Grace. She was giving me a hard time at the moment because of my moods and being too hard on Fiona, and generally not being nice enough. But we still managed to have a good laugh. Mum called, upset because of some story in the *Yorkshire Post* about Lydstep [the house in Oakworth where AC had lived as a young child] being sold, and the estate agents using the fact I 'grew up' there as a selling point. She said it wasn't even true, as we only lived there a few years before we moved to Keighley. I admitted I had no actual memory of Lydstep, except through photos. 'Exactly,' she said. I couldn't quite understand why it upset her, but it really did.

I had a funny text exchange with Peter M. I asked him for his analysis on a post card. 'Manageable but not salvageable under GB. And difficult under any of the alternatives. Et tu?' I said I agreed and thought the alternatives had weaknesses. He felt DM was the only one, possibly Milburn. 'I assume you are speaking to David. He needs to be more leaderish to move the market.' I said I felt they were all a bit all over the place. 'GB lacks strong advice around him so he has lost confidence.' Send for Mandy, I said. Or Alastair, he replied.

Tuesday 3 June

Not feeling great. Throat, knee, shoulder in agony. Another GB first-thing call. Ranting about the 42-day rebels. Ranting about Nick Robinson only being interested in process. Then me trying yet again to say he needed to provide a series of explanatory events. Him saying he would get something over to me. Tap tap tap on computer. One of the kids trying to get his attention. Sarah in the background. It felt chaotic. I spoke to PG who felt what GB said yesterday on 42 days was fine but he looked dreadful. Tie not done up properly. 'Like a few inches out.' PG, both for the same reasons as me, plus the added ones to do with his illness, was also not keen to get too involved. I spent the train journey to Newcastle working on the novel.

Brendan [Foster] met me at the station. Lunch at Jesmond Dene House [hotel]. He was totally down on GB. The chorus that he was unelectable was growing all the time. A couple on the train had said the same. The woman said she was feeling sorry for him, but she still wouldn't vote for him. Brendan said everyone was seeing how good TB had been. Also that there were too many mistakes of the past coming back to haunt GB. I asked him what he thought about me getting more involved and he said don't go near it. He's lost. That's it. He felt DM might have it, thought he was bright and more human, would certainly give us a better chance. Cameron was superficial but people felt he had something. He said it was incredibly depressing yet in a way predictable. Bumped into Chris Ward [ex-*Express* editor], now working for the World Wildlife Fund and living in Scotland. We chatted a bit about the *Mirror* days, him being one of the people who interviewed me and Fiona for the MGN [Mirror Group Newspapers] training scheme.

Out to Muckle's law firm at 6, for a book signing and speech. It was a good event, and an excellent Q&A. But the mood on GB, even among Labour supporters, dreadful. One guy was saying he was really moved by stuff I did on depression, and also he said he hoped I was able to ignore all the hate because with TB I had helped make the world a better place. Warm applause. There was a real pro-TB mood there. They had moved to new premises near St James's Park, and the event was to celebrate that. They had rebranded their whole image. I met the ad man who did it and it revolved around bright colours which reminded me of the '97 election pledges. The Q&A went on for seventy-five minutes and they were still asking for more so it seemed to go well. I got back to the hotel and caught the end of Frostie's interview with AF. It was OK without being great. Alex was not really giving much.

Wednesday 4 June

I had another night of really bad dreams, the usual stuff about not being able to reach where I was trying to get to. In one of them the kids were on the far side of a river, and there was a bridge leaving my side, but as I walked on to it, it started to give way and then when it collapsed into the water, I started to swim but realised there was a current pushing me back. Calum had been reading *All in the Mind*, and the new novel, and said he was enjoying working out which bits were really about me! He said he found the depression stuff really interesting, and a bit scary.

Jon Holmes [Gary Lineker's agent] called. He sounded like he was trying to mix being friendly and being menacing. He asked if I was still in touch with 'the beknighted one'. I said do you mean Fergie? I do. Yes, I said, I was. He asked if I had seen his interview with Frost? I said not all of it. 'Did you see the bit where he mentioned Gary?' No. He said they had been advised by 'm' learned friends' that it had been 'libellous or slanderous', because, contrary to what AF said, neither Lineker nor he on his behalf had ever taken action to keep bad stories out of the press. He said there was a problem in that this had set the papers off trying to find out what these stories were and this was causing difficulties. He said yesterday he had advised Lineker to do nothing but today it was clear this was going to rumble on into the weekend and that might cause him to change his advice. I asked if he felt it might get to lawyers. I said if so it was not appropriate for him to use me as a conduit and if it reached that stage he would have to deal with it formally. He said he did not at this stage want it to get into the hands of lawyers. 'Gary will take my advice. I can start down that route. Or I can not start down that route. That is why I am calling you.'

I asked what Lineker wanted to come of it. He said he wants these stories to stop. And he wants to be sure Alex accepts there's nothing to them. He said he thought the best thing would be for the two of them (AF and GL) to sit down and talk it over. He said his opinion was AF did himself no favours not talking to the BBC.* I said I felt they were flogging a dead horse if this was about trying to get a rapprochement with the BBC. He said he thought AF also did himself no favours doing a big sit down with Frost. I didn't engage. I said I would speak to AF to make sure he was aware of what he said, but repeated that if we were talking legal action, then it was not my place. He then said Lineker had always had a high opinion of AF and when he tried to sign him he had written to him to thank him for his interest.

I subsequently spoke to AF in France this afternoon. He said I should tell Holmes to get in touch with Les Delgarno [AF's lawyer]. He had no

* Ferguson had fallen out with the BBC over a 2004 documentary examining business dealings between him and his football agent son, Jason. Sir Alex Ferguson subsequently refused to speak with any BBC journalists.

interest in talking to him and agreed with me it was inappropriate for Holmes to try to use me as a conduit. I did a note for Les. Alex didn't sound too troubled, said he didn't much give a damn, and was perfectly up for another fight with them. But Les Delgarno felt he should move towards rapprochement with the Beeb. He felt the ongoing row was a bit childish and not good for Alex, most people had forgotten what the row was about in the first place. We talked over it at length and he felt he would have to say something like public figures like them do try to protect their image and the privacy of their family.

Alex was pretty gung-ho but Les was not keen on going down another legal route. We had a laugh about the recent FA hearing. Les had told Alex he didn't have a leg to stand on and yet he won it. The train was delayed so I was late for the fundraising meeting at party HQ and eventually missed it. Got home to upload the end of Novel 2 and work on that. Still not perfect but much better. I did long conference call with Ontario Liberals ahead of my speech to their conference next week. I was virtually doing it as a day trip but hopefully I would get other stuff done too.

Thursday 5 June

Bike. Katherine Fry [copy editor] round first thing to do a line edit on *All in the Mind*. Katherine had done a good job spotting a few inconsistencies, easily fixed. We were done by 12. I headed into town, for a meeting of the elections planning team. Neil was in seeing GB but we missed each other. I texted Neil to say a mood was forming, it was getting much worse and if GB did not change mode, message and team soon he was dead. I said even small decisions were not being made. 'As I feared' he said. We spoke later and he said he had found GB quite troubled, and not clear about the way forward. Rachel [Kinnock, head of political events, PM's office] called to invite me to a surprise party on Monday to celebrate twenty-five years of GB as MP. She sounded OK. But there was a feeling of fatalism around.

Calum said he had noticed how often Tories were appearing on telly without any Labour challenge. Too many Tory ideas were just being met with 'We're already doing it.' And GB was still not talking properly about the economy. TB was doing GMTV ahead of a select committee on MEPP. He just reminded everyone how good he was, at the policy and the comms. Too many people saying they felt sorry for GB. I was seeing Liz Murdoch later. She arrived a bit late having 'been on the phone to Dad about Barack Obama'. She was really enthusiastic about him. Also Rupert M had seen him yesterday and was impressed. He had also 'got an assurance' he would not appoint Hillary Clinton as No. 2. She had done a 'phone fundraiser' for him which was the biggest single fundraiser at which he did not physically appear. She had the same story as did so many others right now re GB. No leadership. Nothing happening in the Cabinet, party a vacuum. She felt it was sad for the country and the party. 'You guys have every right to be furious.' I was probably way too indiscreet about helping GB.

Comic moment in the day when Tessa called to say Sol Campbell had cancelled his meeting with her 'because his Bentley broke down on the way'. I was stopped several times in the street today by people saying variously they thought GB was a goner, we were a goner, I should go back, so on. I had a long chat with David Frost over the weekend, first about the Alex interview. He said he was pleased, but I could tell it had not gone quite as he hoped. He had been expecting to do it as AF's house, but last minute there was a change of plan and they did it in a hotel, and it was all a bit antiseptic. But he was now obsessed with doing a big one with GB, and he was asking me to help get him to do it. I suggested later to GB that there might be a case for doing a three-hour interview – roughly sectioned as domestic, foreign policy, and personal – which was streamed live, or which could be edited and then uploaded as live.

David had said he thought it would work best around GB's first anniversary as PM, as an event with an audience, to which other media could be invited, but with the output strictly controlled as a website operation, so that the public know that is where it can be seen first. On any commercial opportunities for David, that would presumably come from overseas packaging, but he didn't seem too fussed, he just wanted to do something different that got noticed. He could either do the several hours over one day, or over several days. Whatever, the output could be released in stages and used as an opportunity to set an agenda over a sustained period. Another option was to do as a No. 10 website operation, but with David as interviewer and using very high production values. It would be a big logistical and technical job, and there would be propriety questions – like could he do pro-Labour, anti-Tory stuff on an interview for the No. 10 website. But there was definitely something in this worth thinking through.

GB had to strengthen his comms. One of the problems he rages about is the relentlessly trivialising coverage of politics, of which the BBC is a part. They are obsessed with process not policy. They swim with whatever tides the press mood sets down. I did a note to David Muir, said whatever his strengths or weaknesses this new media world makes it harder for someone like GB who is essentially serious, not good at the fluffy stuff, not interested in the soap opera the media tries to create. It is all getting in the way of a broader message getting through to the public. I told him one idea I was kicking around with GB was a series of long and detailed interviews that would be for and on the Downing St website, linked to wherever is agreed. Partly the thinking was based on the time TB was going through a rough patch, when we went to *Newsnight* and agreed a three-hour stint with Paxman to run over three nights. It showed him engaging in depth and in detail and the ensuing coverage helped change a mood.

When I mentioned this, GB had said he could not repeat the same thing but what about Nick Robinson? I said there was an irony in that Robinson was the one he kept complaining about as the ultimate BBC trivialiser. He snorted his agreement, so the idea was quickly dropped. When I suggested David, he said 'What – on Al Jazeera?' [Frost had presented a regular current affairs show for Al Jazeera English since 2005.] I said no, why not try to come up with something that had not been done before. If we went down the website route, there would have to be careful thought given to how to deal with the efforts the mainstream media will make to do it as a process story, and as it involves the public sector, all manner of questions would and could legitimately asked and both we and Frost would be in their firing line. But I was sure GB had to start upping the game and doing it in different and unexpected ways that got noticed and cut through.

I said to David, imagine for example, on the current economic situation, a series of exchanges in which you did, roughly, fifteen minutes on food, really go in depth into what is happening, and why, and what government can realistically do; fifteen minutes on oil; fifteen minutes on property markets; fifteen minutes on what government can do to help or hinder in all of them. And/or, on the bigger picture; an hour on domestic policy; an hour on foreign policy; an hour on GB the man. Available to all media. When we did the thing with Paxman we had a strong storyline for all three and they generated enormous coverage. Meanwhile, an email from No. 10 came through, clearly written by GB himself, huge caps and the subject line – THIS IS THE TEXT FOR ALISTAIR CMAOPABELL. Clearly when it came to my name the keyboard got a real hammering.

He said it was based on our conversations. Well, up to a point, I suppose it was, but it didn't really amount to a strategy. He said he wanted to launch a new slogan, Keeping the Economy Moving Forward. He wanted to focus on three areas, food, fuel and family finances. He would kick it off with an article, saying this was to be his focus, and that he intended to get the world to take joint action on cutting the cost of food, fuel and money. He would follow up with an interview, then publish a document arguing for more nuclear power stations to cut the cost of fuel. Go big on renewables, say the world needed half a million large wind turbines, insist we have to curb the addiction to oil.

He would then make the need to act on food and fuel the focus of the next European Council and the next G8. Get agreement on a new trade policy, a new energy policy, a new food policy. A lot of it was internationally facing, a new deal with the oil-producing countries, criticising the bans on investment that prevents the development of new suppliers, move to get rid of the restrictions on a free market in oil. That would also mean allowing the Saudis, the US, Japan, to invest more in Europe. Then he would by the weekend after launching all this bring it all together at some kind of globalisation event, call on Europe to face up to big shifts taking place in the world, work for a better deal with the oil producers.

Sometimes when we spoke all I could hear was him bashing on a keyboard. And then I saw the results. E.g. he said GM food was coming back as an issue. I said that and nuclear were good issues for him to take strong clear positions on. He said who could I get to chair something on it!? Robert Winston [scientist]? I said, what about [Baroness] Susan Greenfield [scientist]? When his note came through both were there in it. It was hand to mouth. Also the usual mix of caps and lowercase and words spelled wrong. More spelled wrong than right. His spelling of my name was extraordinary. Weird in fact. He was at least – weeks late – starting to focus on this world economic stuff. But I was not feeling great about any of it.

Also Sarah had texted Fiona asking us to dinner. Needless to say he wanted to set up a big expert committee, this time on GM foods, maybe get Susan Greenfield and Robert Winston to work with the current and former chief scientists. Then in advance of George Bush's visit to the UK, put forward a joint plan to drag the world out of economic downturn. Then day by day up to the European Council stepping out with e.g. Sarkozy, [José Luis] Zapatero [Prime Minister of Spain], setting this new agenda, not least for a new world trade deal. He was certainly firing, but whether it added up to a strategy I wasn't sure.

Friday 6 June

Out for a briefing meeting on an upcoming speech to JP Morgan. Then to Bill's to finish his Volume 1 changes. Stayed for lunch, nice chat and he was loving the work. Train home to meet Fiona McMorrough to work out a plan for the publicity for *All in the Mind*.

Saturday 7 June

No. 10 sent over a copy of a speech GB had drafted on oil, one of the key parts of the note he had sent over on Thursday. It was too complicated, not clear enough and too jargonistic. I did a note on it. I said in the medium term, GB needs to take real ownership of the whole issue of the world economy and the concerns people have. He needs to be seen as the leader with the best understanding, and the greatest commitment to making sense of it and coming up with the ideas to emerge from it well. So he needed to set a bigger context for this speech. About the role of leadership in taking decisions to steer the country in the right direction. But also the importance of explanation of what is happening in a world now defined by the pace of change. I suggested he explicitly state he intended, now and in subsequent speeches and events, to explain the context for that change.

Be clear about what we can and cannot do, what we can and cannot influence. Spell out both challenges and opportunities. Set out the reality of how the modern world works, downsides as well as upsides. Be clear these speeches will be long, detailed, complicated. Urge the media to treat them seriously. Say you are starting with oil, then food, then family finances. I said his draft was too technical and jargonistic. I said he should get a secretary or a messenger to read it, and if there are any parts they don't get, do them again. Also, how can you make a speech like this without addressing the issue of fuel prices at the pumps, either explaining and defending the fuel duty, presumably in the context of overall public finances/investment, or at least indicating that you get the concerns people have?

I was also worried it sounded like only the poor were struggling, whereas life for people on middle incomes was easy. He called, and I said I wasn't persuaded as it stood that he painted a convincing picture about how he will be able to bring down prices. It needed more edge in the passages where he was talking about other countries, particularly the producers. Who are they? Name them in order of oil power? And if he really was to make something global of this, he should maybe announce a visit to the Gulf, purely to explore these issues, also an Anglo-French-German plan to put pressure on the US over energy efficiency. At the moment it all felt like a 'calling on others' agenda, a 'car makers' summit', blah. Even his nuclear power section felt muted, far less strong than the way he had talked about it before.

He needed to challenge those who would just protest without thinking through the consequences. He needed to say the very things they campaign for – security in the world, the sharing of prosperity, the right of people to have food on the table, the sustainability of the planet, are threatened. He needed to make more of interdependence, explain why leaders have to spend so much time dealing with other leaders. I could hear him tapping away in the background. He didn't have much to say. I said it had the makings of something but it was not there. I was working on a *Time* magazine piece on sport for TB, as part of Nick Keller's Beyond Sport launch. Went to see PG later. He was OK, though seemed a bit thinner, and his voice was quite weak. He and Gail both felt I had to get out from under re GB. But it was difficult. He found that too. It was not easy just to turn away and say no when he specifically asked for help. Start of Euro 2008 [football tournament]. The AF–Lineker situation still not resolved and I was talking to Les about that.

Sunday 8 June

Really hot day. Off with Fiona to meet Neil, Glenys, Joe and Grace [Rachel's children] on the Heath. Joe was a real handful, beating me up endlessly. Neil said he felt sad for GB when he saw him last Thursday. GB had even said he wondered if he should not have let the young guns take over straight away. Neil said he must not think like that. But he felt he had lost all confidence and was bereft of people and ideas. Neil had tried to push him in much the same direction as I was – big messages, economy, party, team. But he felt GB was constantly looking for excuses and 'the problem is'. He sensed he had lost faith in his team. Neil and Glenys both felt there was very little chance of getting back from this. Neil felt he was now struggling even at the things he used to be good at. 'It's just sad to watch.' Fiona not well. Hay fever turning into some kind of fever.

Monday 9 June

GB called first thing. Really hot morning. I took the call out in the garden. He said he was intending to do the economic series as soon as the 42-day vote was over. I asked how it was going. Cue the same stuff I heard most days last week. He started to read through the note he had done. He was going to go big on nuclear as per my note of yesterday. Started to rat-a-tat all the stats out to me. Also go country by country on what others were doing. He called three times by 10. Plus at one point he obviously hit his last number dialled button on his phone and I heard a part of their morning meeting. I also noted on the email he sent over there were exchanges on other stuff at the bottom, like the fact DM was hoping to miss the 42-day vote for a Middle East visit. Off with Fiona to do a photocall for a litter blitz on the Heath. Then to a reception in No. 10 to celebrate GB being an MP for twenty-five years. Rachel had asked me to go though I feared it would be all the GB crony mob.

It was out in the garden. Sally and Anji were both there. I chatted to various bods and there seemed less consciousness of how bad things were. Unless they were just keeping a brave face. I had a brief chat with Balls but I always felt he tended to avoid substance with me. He probably knew what I thought. Douglas Alexander was asking me what I did with my time, and when I said tonight's Euro match was the first I had missed since the start of the tournament, he said 'Here we are with the ship of state slowly sinking and you watch football all day.' And night, I said. I was not clear who, apart from Sue Nye and Jeremy Heywood, was even aware I was talking to GB so regularly. Geoff Hoon was all very small talky, mainly football. Ann Cryer [Keighley MP] was trying to get me to do the Keighley [agricultural] Show. Charlie Whelan a bit pissed, faux friendly.

Ian Austin and Tom Watson both came over briefly, and I sensed neither of them knew GB was calling me the whole time. I bumped into Michael Wills [Justice Minister] who had a pained look, perhaps the result of the diaries. Nice chat with Caroline Flint [Housing Minister] and Hazel Blears [Communities and Local Government Secretary] who at least showed a bit of fight. I stayed about an hour but was glad to get away. GB took me aside as I left, said again he thought he had the right arguments and went through them again. He went over some of the things he would be doing in the next weeks. Also that he liked the Frost idea. I walked out with one of the messengers. He said it was like amateurs had taken over from professionals. 'Don't go back,' he said. 'You're flogging a dead horse.' Andy Grice [*Independent* journalist] was chasing me, and I was avoiding him, because he said he had been told GB had asked me back. I didn't want to go back and certainly didn't want a great blah in the press. I jumped in a cab and headed home for Holland v Italy [3–0].

Tuesday 10 June

DS first thing. I went over all the GB stuff, the comings and goings and my desire not to get too drawn in. He was of the view, politically, that it was all pretty bad, that it felt like he was really struggling. It had the makings of a rather dark Wagnerian tragedy. On me, he felt all seemed reasonably OK but he wanted me to stay on the pills for another couple of months just to stabilise the wiring a bit more. Home to do a bit of preparation for the lunch at the QEII Centre, British Property Federation, who wanted me to do London, GB–DC and the US elections. Wrapped it up fine in a bit of humour. Then a short Q&A moderated by Sarah Montague of the *Today* programme who I gave a right old roasting to over her claim that the trust issue was all about us. I whacked her over not wanting to go over the Hutton Inquiry, and the BBC's role in the events that led to David Kelly's death, and got a good round of applause. I felt that though it was not easy to put a great pro-GB argument it was not difficult to do anti-DC and win support for it.

Home, then out on the bike, when Tessa called, sounding very down. She said Pat had told John Hutton [Business and Enterprise Secretary] that

I had said GB had told me he would make way for DM if he thought he was ready. News to me, and one of those rumour/gossipy/he said/she said conversations I was hoping to live without. There was clearly a bit of movement against GB but I was not convinced it would go anywhere.

Wednesday 11 June

Working on the novels. Mark round to do 2004 transcribing, so working on three books at once. Surreal at times. At one point I was transcribing from 2004 re what was happening say in 1996, and at was the same kind of thing as now – TB–GB, DM not sure what next, Tessa, me having trouble with CB. I went into town and popped into Victoria Street. They were having a real struggle to flog tables for 10 July fundraiser. We must get purchase soon or we're dead. Calum was working in there now, clearly popular, but one or two of them said it can't be easy being my son in there. To the QEII to meet Sol Campbell before taking him to meet Tessa. We chatted away while we waited for Sky Andrew. Sol was a nice guy I think, and actually quite an interesting mix of shy and confident. He was asking about politics e.g. what was GB really like? He felt he was too reactive and not setting the agenda enough – and he was interested in Boris. Sky arrived. We went over to the Commons and you could tell there was a buzz going on re the 42 days. Tessa felt we were possibly going to lose.

Good meeting. I was impressed by Tessa's manner, which they liked too. She was emphasising her commitment to the poorest parts of London, to kids, to sport, so pressing all the right buttons, and saying she was really keen to harness the energy and experience of people like Sol. There were a couple of civil servants there who were probably a bit iffy about what we were doing which is why I did not mention the Wembley dinner. But I think Sol was keen and felt Tessa knew what she was doing. I bumped into all manner of old faces as we did the rounds. Nick Soames who was with his brother and did a very funny, very loud, booming 'Ah, the great man has returned … marvellous to see you are here supporting the party in its hour of need.' A few MPs, ex-staff and journos. Also a few researchers appeared out of nowhere as we were leaving via the Central Lobby, with copies of *TBY* to sign.

On the way out I said cheerio to Sol and Sky and then was immediately assailed by a snarling sweating spittling woman with a megaphone and a guy with a camera who were part of the permanent protest over the road. They were yelling and screaming right into my face, war criminal, how dare I walk the streets when I ought to be in The Hague, I started the war, and killed people and I was making money from it all. People were stopping to take photos, I just smiled and got in a cab and headed off. The driver seemed to take my side. Nice chat, mainly politics, lots of football. Jeremy sent me through a draft from GB for a presser tomorrow. They won the 42-day detention vote by nine thanks to the DUP amid lots of – denied – talk on deals that has nothing to do with the issue. But the mood was still febrile and they needed a sense of strategy and purpose.

Thursday 12 June

GB sent through a rewrite which had pretty much taken in what I had suggested. Then he called, the first of several calls. He regularly repeated himself conversation to conversation and I wondered if he was really just looking for reassurance. He was still banging on about 'these bastards in the party' being difficult and disloyal and had Charlie up there as the worst at the moment. He was also telling me any initiative with the Saudis was a risk. I said at the press conference he had to really push back on the questions being about anything other than his subject, the economy, and not be too giving in terms of calling the broadcasters first. But he did and they all went for the 42-day deal stuff. The print guys were better, and he was at least able to get a part of his message up, though I doubted it would carry widely. I went out to do LBC to push the upcoming LRF sports events but also had a run round the block on the current political scene.

David Davis then somewhat took Westminster by storm, announcing he was resigning as shadow Home Secretary and his seat to fight a by-election on 42 days and other civil liberties arguments. I felt it was an opportunity for us – to engage on the argument. But also to highlight Cameron's inability to lead a party capable of making big decisions. It was a huge story, bigger than I expected, partly because it came out of nowhere, and we had to turn it badly for Cameron. But the initial reaction was from Tom Watson and, as I said in a note to Sue Nye, it was utterly limp, no real hard edge. TB called me and said for the first time he wished he was back in there because this was an opportunity, the first chance to turn the weather back in GB's favour. He had tried but failed to reach him and was clearly miffed that GB had called me twice. He said tell him HE not some junior should go up on it and with the confidence of the argument win on civil liberties and show Cameron's Tories were divided and out of touch.

Tim Allan texted to say we should field a military guy or a cop independent of GB to go up and say how much they needed this tougher approach. GB called three times in half an hour but was taking too long to decide. This was one of those situations where speed would show confidence. He was being slow footed. By the time I got to TB's office for the launch of Beyond Sport, GB called again and I put him on to TB who was really trying to push him on it – get out there and say this is the argument the country has to have, to show we are on the side of security against civil liberties. To show they were soft on terror and soft on crime. GB felt it was more about Tory division and it brought back memories as they had one of those pretending to agree but in reality disagreeing conversations. GB also said at one point I [AC] should go out and do media and TB just said wearily 'He is missing the point here.' Also told me he had volunteered me to the President of Sierra Leone to help re their comms.

Down to the Beyond Sport launch which was fine. The Honda sponsor guys really enthusiastic. Ditto [Sir] Keith Mills [entrepreneur]. [Sir] Martin Sorrell [businessman] a bit iffy and spent the whole meeting doing emails. Stephen Rubin [businessman] positive. I tried to get him to buy a table for Wembley but he was another one who did not want to support GB. He felt he was anti-enterprise. Luke Dowdney, son of Mark [former *Mirror* colleague], spoke about a project he was doing in Rio. One of several good speakers, and the buzz to the event felt good. BBC and *Time* magazine were both getting behind it. An impressive guy called David Butler from Honda F1 who had been involved with Laureus [Sport for Good Foundation] but now felt this was better. Seb Coe came later to do media and he and I had a little chat about the Davis situation. He felt he had just flipped. Told me a funny story from Hague who said DD took him for a four-hour walk at the time of the DC leadership contest and how he 'was convinced at the end that I had to vote for the other David'. He felt Davis would give us a breather but also that GB was basically finished. 'There is just too much of the feel of the Major government.'

TB seemed pretty relaxed and the office functioning well. Left for home for a bit then out to the Capital restaurant in Knightsbridge for the Durrants [media monitoring firm] dinner for LRF. Bunch of business guys mainly comms and marketing. Book signing then a fair bit of small talking before doing standard leadership speech over dinner in the context of London, UK and US. Held up a little by seemingly never-ending presentation on burgundy wines. But the event seemed to go fine. Happy enough with it though I found it more tiring these days. Earlier Louise Miliband round to see Fiona with the boys. Chatted a little re the political scene. She felt it was unremittingly grim but had no sense where it was heading to. PG told me he had seen one poll which had 3 per cent saying they thought GB was a good PM. Pretty dire stuff. Today was a good example where Davis gave him an opening but he took too long to react and when he finally had the line it was mangled all over the place. The media and other Tories really got there first.

Friday 13 June

Met Ed Victor for a coffee in Regent's Park. He said he needed to force Gail to read the second novel. They were basically saying I was too productive.

I understood the diaries were the main focus, but we had one novel in the pipeline ready to go so what was wrong with getting ready with another one? Home then out to the airport. Working on the speech for Ottawa. I slept a fair bit on the plane and also read 200 pages or so of an old book on Jacques Brel [Belgian musician], having been asked to make a radio documentary about him by someone who had read of my interest in him. Interesting the extent to which he was really about himself. Not nice to his daughters. Depressive. Self-driven clearly. Wife Miche in Brussels tolerating his relationships in Paris. Interesting read though and should make OK programme.

Seven-hour flight. I had completely forgotten I went to Ottawa before, that we were there at the time of the FMD [foot-and-mouth disease] outbreak. Freezing cold then. I remember Godric and I went out for a run and it was like the inside of your lungs were freezing up. I was met by a nice young guy from the Premier's office, Paul Logolin, and taken to the Westin Hotel. As so often when out of the UK, struck immediately by the clean streets. And people looking more relaxed, less angry. Watched a bit of the Euros, then out for a nice run. Pretty flat. Nice war memorial and some great old buildings. A kind of open-air museum effect too, old photos of moments in Canadian history all over the place.

Out for dinner with some of the Ontario Liberals' key campaign team. Ontario Premier Dalton McGuinty's brother Brendan. A Greek guy with a loud laugh who was an avid follower of the whole UK scene. Classic polling hack. Asking after PG. He said he didn't know him but they knew all about us and everything we did. Dave, organiser guy, Chris comms director, Laura who was logistics. Good bunch, really funny. They reminded me of us a few years ago. United, committed, confident, really on top of their game. We had a discussion of the GB scene and they were clearly of the view it was a total Jean Chrétien–Paul Martin [former Canadian Prime Minister and Finance Minister who had difficult relationship] situation.* They followed it closely and as one of them said 'It feels smelly from here.' I was probably a bit too frank about what our problems were but they seemed a good bunch.

Quite clear we had a big influence on them not just in campaigning but in policy direction too. McGuinty was a big TB follower and fan. He had led them to their first ever consecutive back-to-back victories. Now facing the third term and worrying about complacency and where to get ideas from. The Greek guy said he had met me when we had a state dinner with

* Chrétien and Martin had a disharmonious relationship during much of the former's premiership. Martin succeeded Chrétien after his resignation in 2003, but retained power only as a minority government the following year and then lost the 2006 election.

Chrétien. He had read the book. Told Chrétien he was reading it. 'Am I in it?' Yes. 'Do I come out OK?' Yes. 'Fax me the bits.' So he did. Several had read the book and like a lot of political staffers really identified with some of the ups and downs.

Off to a rally addressed first by another McGuinty brother, David, a federal MP and also the party's environment spokesman, and then Dalton. They were a Catholic family of ten kids. Dalton spoke pretty well if a bit wooden but he certainly got them going. Waving white T-shirts in the air like football scarves. Excellent video which rooted what they did in the changes taking place elsewhere in the world, especially China and India. E.g. comparative birth and growth rates and then what their response should be. Loud cheers when the film mentioned smaller class sizes and higher spending and access rates. Very similar to one of our election broadcasts. Got to bed via watching the Euros in a pub with some of them. In some parts of Canada, they now had more than 50 per cent born outside Canada. Huge crowds were watching in bars as all the different European countries had their own followings.

Saturday 14 June

Got the 2 a.m. ping, woke up and just could not get back to sleep. I waited till just before six and went out for a run along the canal down to the stadium. Really nice route but God have I slowed down. I did maybe an hour, and then had a proper look at the memorial in the centre, and the arrangements of all the provincial and territorial flags. Ontario 13 million people. One riding [electoral district] was the size of France. The same living standards issues we were dealing with. Major domestic powers to the provincial governments. Federal government currently pretty right-wing. Paul came to get me and took me to the venue. Really got the big build-up as the man who made Blair, masterminded victories etc. I adapted my leadership speech to the idea that they were principles for campaigns and it went down as well as anything I had done in ages. Not just the initial response but people for the rest of the day telling me how inspiring it had been, and how they wished I could stay and help them fight. I just wish GB and co. could apply the same.

I weaved in stories and anecdotes with ten principles of campaigning, mainly from pen and ink notes, and it went well. Then to a book signing. They had got just about every book in Canada there and were charging $1,000 a pop. I was there almost an hour and they must have raised well into six figures. Into the lunch where I was seated with Dalton and his wife Terri. Nice lady. Also the French Canadian leader of the federal party [Stéphane Dion] who was a bit odd. More like a priest than a politician. He looked uncomfortable waving at the crowds and so forth. Dalton spoke pretty well. All about the future and what they were planning. Nice about me and what we had done, and how New Labour was an inspiration. We had a good chat over lunch. A real listener. Asking about how I adapted after the pressure and both he and his wife were asking about the novel, and whether family life had changed for the better.

She was a bit like Fiona, had never really wanted him to do the job but was clearly being supportive. His brother David asked my view on something they were planning in the next few days – announcing that they were shifting from income tax to carbon tax, aiming to be revenue neutral. A big risk, he said, especially against a government that is more right-wing and anti-Kyoto than Bush. He was clearly worried but also felt they had to be bold.

Nice event, off to meet his outgoing principal secretary Gerald Butts who was going to run the World Wildlife Fund Canada. He was very down on Canada's self-image, felt they were worse than America for failing to see how they were. For example the total dominance of oil in parts of Canada. 'Environmental obscenity,' he said, but unless someone else from outside said it, nothing happened. He felt the GB scene looked bleak and possibly unrecoverable. He was close to Michael Barber and Matthew Taylor [TB advisors] and echoed the point that they had taken a lot of policy ideas from us. Set off for the airport. Really good trip. Quick, in and out, speech good, book sales good, fundraising good, and able to put experience hopefully to some good use. I slept fine on the way back but was still tired when I got home at half seven-ish.

Sunday 15 June

I had a kip in the garden then a really good bike session round Regent's Park with Rory. It was great having the boys home, especially with the football on. Fabulous tournament so far. Went to see PG. He looked OK but a bit turkey-necked and he was becoming stooped. He and Gail had just seen Peter M. He said PM and I ought to do an event at a theatre, literally just talking about his second resignation.* He said Peter had total recall and though everyone said move on, he was the one who lost his job and he couldn't. I said but what kind of life would he be leading now if he was still there? He really felt both TB and even more so I turned against him and turned a muddle into a disaster for him personally. Perhaps we

* Despite insisting that he had done nothing wrong, in January 2001 Mandelson had resigned as Secretary of State for Northern Ireland following allegations that he had used his position to influence a passport application.

did. PG said it was fascinating hearing him and he really felt we should try to resolve it somehow.

He felt Peter wanted to resolve things with me but found my refusal to take blame for what happened made it hard. I said that was because he didn't want to accept he was fired by TB, not me. But it was a muddle, that is his point, said PG, and if it had been anyone else we would have toughed it out. There might be something in that. He felt GB was dead now. He showed me a note he had done based on polling from Andrew Cooper. His ratings were lower than IDS [Iain Duncan Smith, former Tory leader]. Yet the maths were such that even if we were several per cent behind he could still form a government. So it was there to fight for. He had seen David M who was clearly thinking about the top job, and wanted it, but was not prepared to wield the knife. The logic of the situation meant someone had to but he was sure DM would not.

GB called as we were speaking. A bit of small talk re PG. Then on to David Davis and how he intended to make a big speech on the whole agenda at some point. Also Bush was about to arrive in London and he was hoping to get him to do something on oil and the economic agenda. Police were all over the park and several parts cut off to the public as Bush flew into Wingfield House by helicopter.

Monday 16 June

Got the lunchtime train to Sheffield via St Pancras. Another guy – black like a lot of the people who came up to me like this – came up and said I had to go back, as it was all a bloody disaster and we were heading over a cliff. Reading Brel book on the train. Clearly a total egomaniac and not really moved by his daughters' needs, e.g. not wanting to see them when he was dying. His mistress seemed to have the upper hand a lot of the time but his wife seemed not to mind even if the daughters did. To Radio Sheffield and a half-hour slot with 'Howie' Pressman. He had a very downbeat style. I could not really work out whether he had read the book or not, or was just reading from prepared questions. In any event it was OK. One or two texts in but nothing difficult.

Cab to the university and met Mum, Liz and Kate [Naish, AC's sister and niece] before going to the Broomhill Festival [community celebration] event. It was organised by a guy called Mark Willoughby, the full-time president of the students' union who was extraordinarily bright. He was determined to be a social entrepreneur, had no interest in making money. He wanted to set up his own charity. Broomhill Festival crowd was pretty good as well. They said Broomhill was the Sheffield equivalent of Islington. Did the *Sheffield Star*, quite nervous girl who was asking me what I was going to say and seemed taken aback when I said why not wait till I've said it. Chaired by a friend of John [former UK Ambassador to France] and Penny Holmes, who was now chair of Sheffield leukaemia charity I was raising money for. Did a fifteen-minute opening spiel without notes, and then Q&A. All pretty lively and OK. The Blackwell's people almost sold out, just three books left, so the signing went on till 9ish before I did some photos and off.

Mum enjoyed it, I think, especially as I made a fuss over her, and said, when asked if I would ever think of going back to my old job, that I couldn't really because I had promised her I wouldn't. As at other events recently, the mood was pretty hostile and negative on GB. But again I felt there was an argument there to be made and won – especially against Cameron – but it just was not being made. I got driven back, and listened to Germany beating Austria 1–0 in the Euros. I got the driver's sad life story – he had had two women leave him; the first one left him to look after their kids who then went to her and her new man. And another one had just left recently after twenty years together. We got back just after midnight, and as he had said he was interested in politics, I gave him an audiobook for the drive back. Felt really sorry for him as he drove off.

Tuesday 17 June

Out first thing to JP Morgan and their staff diversity event. Went fine. I felt much more confident just absorbing a brief and then mixing planned remarks with spontaneity, rather than working from a script. They had a link up to their offices in Edinburgh, Bournemouth and Swindon and 'real time' Q&A via email. A fair few questions on mental health, and the rest more general and political. Any time I mentioned the novel now, I felt real interest and engagement. Home to do all-day transcribing with Mark. Steaming through '04. Would soon be up to date. The Euros were providing great games night after night and it was definitely better England weren't there [having failed to qualify].

Wednesday 18 June

Another fabulous day so I managed a longish bike ride round the park. But I was back over 15 stone and had a bit of a mental block re doing my usual drills on Highgate Hill and Swains Lane. Even in the park though I overtook more than I was overtaken. Walter Smith [football manager] came up trumps re helping with the Labour sports dinner. It was also looking good for a group of Wales rugby players to come, but flogging tables was still tough. The party was briefing a couple of papers on the TB tennis match [auction prize] and some of the other prizes. But the sense was of a media bored with anything other than bad stories about a party that had lost its will and its way. GB was having some success in forging on with the EU Treaty despite the Lisbon vote in Ireland but of course all that did in a way was let people say he was out of touch on that too.*

Stuart Prebble and Ed Victor were toing and froing about the *Cracking Up* film. The problem was the BBC having initially seen no problem about the timing of the programme to coincide with the *All in the Mind* book, now they did. All part of the usual telly bollocks. More football. Great having the boys back to watch it. Grace was up and down and with some spectacular tantrums but basically fine, and at times really funny. I was reading Douglas Kennedy's *The Dead Heart* and enjoying it. Every time I read a half-decent novel I felt I was learning something.

It was odd how I had lost a bit of interest in my own for now. It would come back. I definitely needed a sense of team and collegiate activity. I enjoyed writing some of the time, but I would not enjoy doing it all of the time, and I was spending too much time on solo projects at the moment, not enough that involved teams. That being said, I was resisting the party stuff. I did not feel part of the GB team and did not have much of a desire to be so. I got a call out of the blue asking me to play in a match at Stoke on 12 July, when Pelé was coming over to unveil a statue of Gordon Banks [former England goalkeeper]. Definitely up for that. I got Andy Burnham roped in too.

Thursday 19 June

Session with DS. A bit same old same old. The pills had definitely kept me on a more even keel. I said I had been neither up nor down. He said is that good or bad. I said it was neither good nor bad. Or maybe it was both. Good because I was on an even keel, had not plunged down for a while now, bad because of a lack of intensity in how I felt about anything. I just felt flat most of the time. Not suicidal, not even depressed, just a bit numb. He still felt a major project would come along and fill a gap, and in the meantime I was hibernating. He felt the novels had fulfilled me for a while. I said yes, but then the intensity went as quickly as it came. We had messed up the timings today and so were only together for just over half an hour. I didn't really engage. We talked as much about me as him. GB had had it, he felt. Like watching a tragedy.

I got a cab to Margaret McDonagh's office for a meeting on the 10 July

* The first referendum on the Treaty of Lisbon on European reform saw the Irish electorate reject it by 53.4 per cent to 32.9 per cent, a potentially serious setback for Europe.

dinner, meeting with her, Dick Caborn, Carol Linforth and Kamlesh Karia. I arrived a bit early so had a cup of tea on the terrace of a café when Ben Wegg-Prosser [former TB director of strategic communications] walked by. He had seen Peter M and said GB was all over him like a rash, as he was with me. He felt things had maybe gone too far, that DM needed to get out there and people would follow. He felt the Tories were really not up to much but there was no pressure on them at all. He said TB had been in Moscow last week. The meeting was OK but we were still struggling on all fronts apart from turnout and even in that we had a problem because Alex might not make it. We discussed whether we could have Bernie Ecclestone there. Dick knew for example that he wanted his wife to be able to play tennis with TB and would bid for it. But could he come to the dinner? We all felt so but agreed No. 10 would have to say yes or no. I agreed to speak to GB about it later. Dick said if we invited him it would be taken as a signal he was on for a knighthood. He had a point in saying if anyone else had done for a single sport and industry what Bernie had done, they would have got a K, but the donation was totally held against him.

We gave ourselves more lists of people to chase and so on and it was all maybe coming together but I really had my doubts. I went to see PG on the way home. He seemed a bit more down. Sally Morgan was there as well, and later said to me she felt he was actually a bit scared. Rory popped round too. Felt he was OK. Philip was convinced I should go for the mayoral candidacy against Boris and that I could do it. I wasn't, not least because I was on record as saying I didn't feel like a Londoner. PG was looking older, and seemed more frail even than a few days ago. I got a message to call GB from there. He was about to have lunch with Sarko. I said he should ask him if Carla Bruni could sing at the Wembley dinner. 'That bad?' I said it was proving really hard to shift tables and we had to gear up a bit more. He seemed to think it was the economy. I suppose I could have told him the truth, that a lot of people were saying it was all about him.

I had spoken to Joe Hemani, for example, who had been so generous at these events in the past, to ask if he would help flog tables and was met with a half-hour rant. He was not taking the table. He had resigned his party membership. He hated GB and he hated the government. Useless. Useless. Germany 3, Portugal 2. Home to do a bit of work. Called by Burnham's office about a story that Shami Chakrabarti [director, Liberty, human rights organisation] was threatening to sue Andy Burnham over remarks in an interview about her 'heart-melting' late night calls with David Davis. She was saying it was tawdry innuendo. I had heard the rumours but apparently he hadn't. His office put out a line that he regretted any offence etc. as none intended. I said to Jen and later to him that they should not give ground. All he was doing was commenting on the odd political relationship between a traditionally right-wing Tory and the champion of civil liberties. It was odd. Also she was the one who put their late night calls into the public domain. And she was supposed to be a believer in free speech etc. So bollocks to her. He agreed. But I was a bit alarmed the extent to which he seemed to think it was a big thing. 'It's horrible being at the centre of something like this.' I said it's hardly a maelstrom. He said it feels like it.

Friday 20 June

I was hoping to persuade Jeff Weston [football agent] to get me Rio Ferdinand for 10 July. I packed two signed books and headed out by bike to his house in Mill Hill. Missed the turnoff and ended up in Potters Bar, so at least I got a decent cycle out of it. He was recovering from a heart attack. He greeted me in his dressing gown as two Polish cleaners – how can you not support Europe when we get lovely girls like this? he said – were cleaning around us. Chatted in his kitchen. Rio was in Israel. He had been spotted in a club and the press were trying to make something of it.

A pretty sordid description of the way the players operate in some of the Cheshire clubs. 'Minders go ahead, clear out the riff raff and then rooms get set up for them with girls at the back.' Really? Anyway he was pleased enough with the visit but later sent me a message saying Rio was flattered but would be in pre-season training by then so no go. Fiona and I, with Molly, set off for Berwick-upon-Tweed at lunchtime. A simpering-looking man got on opposite us on the train and plonked down his book, John Major on cricket [*More Than a Game*]. Then a ghastly wife came along, bad twitch, spots on her lip, London Scottish rugby T-shirt, and declared herself allergic to dogs. Fiona moved! She should have asked the ghastly cow to move. The ghastly cow's ghastly husband said 'I didn't know you were allergic.' 'I'm not. Just don't like dogs.' Eventually we found another table but then someone got on with a cat – to which Fiona genuinely is allergic. Like a bloody zoo.

Reading *Engleby* by Sebastian Faulks. Really good. A lot of it was set in my time at Cambridge, or thereabouts. He also seemed to share a lot of my views on the press. Had to accept it was a far, far superior piece of work to *Maya*. We arrived to be met by a driver, Steve, with shorts and an earring. He drove way too fast on the little windy roads and I had to ask him to slow down. Lovely scenery. Nice event when we got there. Six thousand visitors to a town of 2,500, Melrose. We were staying in a lovely four-bedroomed house in the shadow of the abbey, looked after by a Heriot-Watt student, Claire. Got our bearings and were then collected by Chris Ward and off for dinner at his house on the other side of Jedburgh. Nice man and his second wife Nonie, a Zimbabwean, was also really good company.

Odd to think if he had made a different decision interviewing us all those years ago, Fiona and I would never have got together. Nonie was a Lib Dem. I reckon he was Labour but he was very anti-GB. He just felt he couldn't do the job. I had to watch how indiscreet I was at times. It was just that my frustrations came out more than they used to – I was happy to help GB if I could but it really annoyed me the way the basics of a political operation had been allowed to weaken, and also the lack of political drive. He was doing things he should not be involved in at all. And he was increasingly asking me to do things a staffer should be taking on – not just speeches but now PMQs lines and trying to fix a candidate for the David Davis by-election, which emerged over the weekend.

Saturday 21 June

Lovely day for most of the day, then torrential rain once my 9 p.m. event came along! But still packed out with waiting list and a fabulous atmosphere. The whole Borders Festival was the brainchild of a journalist/writer/broadcaster/historian Alistair Moffat, and he really had built up something good. They paid next to nothing but looked after people and it had a nice feel. [Dame] Tanni Grey-Thompson [former wheelchair racer, parliamentarian] was speaking, Ming Campbell, Douglas Hurd [former Tory Cabinet minister], Rory Bremner [impressionist] who had married into a toff Borders family. Earlier we went out to see Elizabeth Barr, my oldest cousin, out at Pirntaton.

GB sent through his speech on social mobility and I made a few suggestions. It felt stronger in some places but was weakened by the inordinate length. Parts were repetitive. There were too many moments where it felt as though it was about to end. And it lacked politics. I said he needed to find a way of linking to his own politics now the section on his background and moral purpose. It needed to be punchier, less listy, less repetitive and more rooted in politics. I sent over the wonderful quote from Gareth Edwards [ex-rugby player] in the interview I did for *The Times*, when he named his biggest influence as a PE teacher called Bill Samuel – 'I had a talent and it flowered' – but he said Samuel was the man who made it flower. That notion of everyone having talent and needing teachers to make it flower may have something in it, but GB needs to name one or two teachers too.

I had a terrific run down by the river, then off to the event. The marquee was almost flooded on top, and they had a load of fire hoses in to drain the water off. Moffat did half-hour interview then opened it up to the audience, who were by and large very warm and friendly. Nothing too difficult. The only question I had never been asked before was 'What are David Dimbleby's politics?' Good quickfire session at the end. Fiona thought I spoke too much re TB, not enough re myself. Maybe. Drinks do after the signing. Back to watch highlights of Russia beating Netherlands [3–1].

Sunday 22 June

Out to see Jenny Shields [former political journalist who had moved to Scotland]. Nice kind of life probably. Back to say farewells then a delayed journey home. GB called to say there was a chance a guy called Paul Dadge, who was a survivor in the 7/7 attacks, would stand against David Davis. But he wanted *The Sun* to back him. It felt a bit half-baked. Tony Wright [Labour MP] was talking to him, then talking to Geoff Hoon who was briefing GB. I said don't do anything with it until it is properly pinned down. But he could not resist and called Rebekah Wade who of course got all excited about it. He told her I was dealing with it, and she should speak to me. It was so fucking tactical not strategic. It meant I was having to try to fix something without really being able to pin the detail. Meanwhile beginning to motor on the Labour dinner. Table sales picking up a bit. But apart from Dick, Margaret McD and me, nobody bringing anything to the table. Really beginning to get my goat.

Monday 23 June

Hoon was on several times re Dadge. I kept asking what the details were – when did he have to apply, how, how would he be funded? There was no detail there at all. Waffle. Ditto GB who was just assuming it was being done. He was in Saudi trying to push his ideas on lowering oil prices yesterday. Today he was back on the blower about that but asking where we were on Dadge, then chasing Hoon, then back to me. What the hell did his staff do? He was micromanaging and having said it was happening he was determined to make it so, but it just wasn't pinned down. The Greg Nugent business was typical of the way his operation just meandered along, without decisions. Greg said it had been a real eye-opener. Not good. I had a long chat with Susan Sandon about *Maya*. She liked it but felt it needed a lot of work. We both felt I had learned a lot from working with Rebecca. However, she could not start until the New Year. Ed felt that was probably intended as a brush-off. Maybe. I went to see Tom Bostock about my shoulder which was giving me gyp. He was in the usual rage about the government and NHS reforms but did at least feel I looked a lot better. He felt we were fucked though.

Tuesday 24 June

Out really early and off the first Eurostar with Russell Finch, who was producing my Brel documentary for Radio 4. Nice day in Paris. Out to Olympia, lovely old venue, to interview the old artistic director who was there on the night Brel did his last concert, when he had to be persuaded to come up for an encore because the audience was refusing to leave, and eventually he did, with a fag and a drink and wearing a dressing gown. Then to an accordion store to talk to Jean Corti, who had played with Brel on some of his best recordings, and finally Olivier Todd, one of JB's biographers. Todd was feisty and quite funny but the interview was too much about him not Brel. As a set of interviews they would be good though. Corti was really funny, played Brel tunes the whole time as we talked, quizzing me as to what they were, and I got most of them. I loved his descriptions of the way they worked, Brel would come in with an idea, a theme, maybe a starting line, and then they would almost make it up as they went along. Sometimes he had written the whole song and they would then just adapt the accompaniment as they went. He was always in control, he said, but free-thinking too.

Did a few other meetings, also calls to flog a few more tables for the Labour dinner, getting angrier at inability of ministers to do anything. Dick Caborn had an excellent idea that if MPs found a table buyer half of the money would go direct to their CLP. Not one delivered on it. Meanwhile GB and Hoon were calling me regularly about Dadge, as were *The Sun*. Dominic Mohan [deputy editor] agreed it was best Dadge did it with their support rather than as their candidate. But when finally I spoke to Paul it was clear he had nobody really talking him through what it entailed. It felt half-baked in the extreme. He did not know deadline for entry, rules of candidacy, had no funding plan, no PR worked out, had pretty much nothing sorted. He sounded up for it and capable but I'm not sure he knew what he was letting himself in for.

GB called later and I said to him, having had a long chat with all concerned, the Dadge plan felt a bit half-baked. Nobody seemed to have answers to basic questions: When would he have to announce? What would he have to do to do so? How much should he reckon on a campaign costing? Who would raise the money? What are the legalities? What help could he reasonably expect from other parties? GB seemed to think at the start that him standing as the *Sun* candidate might be the best way forward, but none of us thought that would work. He should be doing this on his own. *The Sun* will offer political support, but it would backfire if it were to become a fully fledged *Sun* stunt. I said it was completely unfair on the guy to expect him to go into this without the above having been thought through, and with expert advice. I was being left to sort it without proper knowledge of the procedures on by-elections and the rules on funding.

We also discussed PMQs, which he was fretting about because of the one-year-on stuff, which was overwhelmingly negative. Again, though, he was thinking tactically when he needed a strategic response. The narrative the media and the Tories want to establish is that the last year was bad for GB and good for Cameron. He has to go with the flow of that a little, and use it as a fulcrum to point to a new narrative for the next year – the year when GB led party and country through tough times, and DC started to fall apart under pressure. Cameron was doing better in the polls than he deserved to, given the paucity of policy decisions. He was good at the glib one-liners and the photos, but on something like terrorism, he can't even win an argument at his own top table. On Europe – he has to cave in to the far right. On tax and spend – he says yes to his tax cutting tendency and he says yes to every spending minister out there appeasing every lobby going.

I said he had to play to his own strengths – economy, taking decisions on the difficult issues – and turn Cameron's strengths into weaknesses. He needed to do to him what we had done to Hague, stopped him being funny by saying that was all he had. He needs to get over the idea there is nothing to DC but the communicator, make him feel the need to do more on policy, and make mistakes. I suggested a line in PMQs that the choice was between a government and a Prime Minister who take the difficult decisions needed to take the country forward, and an opposition leader whose most vigorous internal debate has been about whether to part his hair to the right, the left or straight down the middle.

Wednesday 25 June

I watched the DVD of Brel's last concert. Fabulous stuff. The power and the energy, and the crowd going wild for it. Physically he was not a great specimen, and when he sang there was often an ugliness to his face and its contortions, but my God could he pump passion into a song and into a crowd. GB called about Dadge and I said I thought it was still not properly cooked. Rebekah was chasing, he said. That is why he should never have mentioned it. To be fair GB was decisive enough but it should have been gripped days ago. Greg sent through the job description Stephen Carter had – finally – sent him. It was fine in terms of what the job could be but he had to report to David Muir which I felt would be a problem.

Dick called saying he was going to get a brochure to all the Cabinet with a note from him re the event. We needed to get them engaged and understand they had to get involved in making this a success. Could none of them call in favours that could at least guarantee a good turnout and some decent auction prizes? It seemed not. We worked on a note for GB to send around to them, though I knew he would be reluctant. But if they did not pull their fingers out, this would not be a success and they would set the tone for the fundraising (lack of) up to the election. He and they needed to know just how poor so many ministers and MPs had been. Dick said if GB wouldn't send it, he would, and I said if you are worried about taking flak on it, you should share the load and do it as a joint letter from you, me and Margaret. That would have the added benefit of underlining the point that this has all been done by the old regime.

We worked on a covering note to go with the brochure of auction items already in, and urged them to circulate it to potential bidders. We said that if every minister was able to generate at least one substantial bid for one of the items, we would be in a great starting position for the night. It is surely the case that every member of the government must personally know someone likely to want, and be able to bid substantially for, some of the items we were offering on 10 July.

GB did a bit better at PMQs. I was spending loads of time dealing with Paul Dadge and his on/off by-election plans. It was so annoying that this was only gripped so late. *The Sun* were pushing hard, desperate for him to do it. I was basically advising he did not have the planning or the capacity. Also, I was just feeling I did not want another hand-holding exercise which in any event would be hard to do by phone. By the end of the day he decided not to do it. Out to Lord's for the party to celebrate 100 editions of *The Observer* Sport Monthly. I was hoping to see lots of sports people we might get to the dinner. Dick Caborn was about the only well-known sports person there! Speeches then off with Dick to the Mandela 90th birthday dinner. I went home to watch Germany beat Turkey [3–2]. Dadge and Wembley were taking up too much time. I could feel myself heading for a bit of a plunge.

Thursday 26 June

Saw David S. I was definitely on a bit of a plunge. He felt it was because I was getting more and more drawn in. Also I was sensing Fiona was totally conflicted about it, and so conflicted about me. In to Victoria St. I had a bit of a bust up with Dick because the meeting was so chaotic and we kept going over the same thing again and again. But got a few things sorted. Then Chris Lennie [party official] asked me to pop into a meeting room. He said he was not being disloyal to GB and he would try to make everything work. 'But this is not tenable for much longer. We are lurching day to day. No leadership, all crisis stuff and I cannot see how we get through the next few months like this.' He was not planning to do anything but wanted me to know that was his view. I said we should keep in touch.

Then in came a text from Dadge. He was on his way. He said he had woken up in the middle of the night and felt shit that he had decided not to do it. He now felt he had to do it and he really would not forgive himself if he didn't. *The Sun* were helping him find nominations but when he submitted the names some were not from the seat and so his papers were invalid. He was really frustrated but it was all inevitable because it had gone off so half-cock. Nobody had gripped it, everyone assumed someone else would. Meanwhile the party was running out of cash. I then had a bit of a flare-up with Carol Linforth who asked if we could meet to resolve the issue of those ministers insisting on where they sat at the Wembley dinner. They could get stuffed, given how little they had brought to it.

I jumped in a cab to NW8 to see Mel Smith [comedian] for the Brel programme. He was a massive fan, and had done a show based on Brel songs. He gave me all the research material, tons of it, including some nice pieces of memorabilia. I had driven past his house in Grove End Road loads of times without realising that he lived there. He had three West Indian transvestites staying with them, and we had a little chat with them before we got going. It was a good interview, the right mix of funny and serious and passionate. Nice art. Lovely swimming pool. Liked him. And he definitely loved Brel, that came through. Interesting too that he spoke next to no French but he said when he heard the songs first time around, he always guessed more or less the themes and the feelings.

Out to Barking with Margaret Hodge for her fundraiser. She was convinced GB had to go. She was wondering about trying to get maybe a dozen or so junior ministers to resign. She said hardly anyone felt we could win. She had not spoken to GB as he did not acknowledge her really. He probably thought she was totally offside, but she said it was a common complaint that there was no direction from anywhere. The arts world was moving against us, she felt. She had been at an event where Boris Johnson got a standing ovation before he spoke. There was just a feeling that the mood was moving in their favour.

Good turnout at the meeting, packed out. We had a curry, then I did my speech and Q&A, big-picture stuff, talking up Margaret, and trying out some of the lines we were developing on Cameron. The politics were tough. One woman was going on about 'the coloured people' getting everything, and the whites feeling they were second best. Another guy said I had to go back, and later said it would be on my conscience forever if I didn't. We ran out of books at the sale/signing afterwards. Nice mood, and Margaret was clearly popular and seen as strong, and she was bringing in a fair few new members, but there was real worry there on the immigration front. Home by 11 to watch highlights of Spain v Russia [semi-final, 3–0]. Spain v Germany in the final.

Friday 27 June

I wrote the My Week column for *The Observer*, blatantly plugging the dinner and the Pelé game. Out to Capital Gold to do a pre-record on the LRF bikeathon. Nice bunch and I recruited Kid Jensen [radio DJ] to the dinner. Getting a few more tables coming through. Walter Smith said yes to coming. Alex McLeish maybe. Christ knows how much time and effort I was putting into this at the moment. I hadn't been sleeping well, mainly the dinner and the general GB pressure. I did a short run to Philip's and chatted to him about stuff. He seemed a bit more down. He had overseen two groups which were dreadful for GB. He felt the mood had simply settled on GB. They saw him as tired and lacking in understanding of their lives. Physically, PG was looking worse, and sounded a bit more scared when he talked about the illness.

Saturday 28 June

I was feeling down. Couldn't sleep. Up at half five and out on the bike. I stopped in Camberwell and had an idea for a *Mirror* piece on the Gordon Banks match I'd been asked to play in. It was interesting how often a thought – in this case an intro – came into my head as I was out on the bike, and then the rest followed. I was sitting outside a café and a Somali woman propositioned me. She was wearing a headscarf and long dress. She said could she have a coffee with me. I said no, I don't think so. Then could she give me her number? I said no, I didn't want her number. Then did I want to go to her place? I wasn't sure if she knew who I was or if she was a rather unlikely looking prostitute, or mentally ill, or genuinely on the pull. But at 6.30 a.m.? Again I was struck by how many people were out at that time and how much debris there was on the road after a Friday night out.

Home to a row between Rory and Fiona because he had lost his watch at 3 a.m. somewhere. Out to the cricket, the final one-day international against New Zealand at Lord's. Faffing around with the *Observer* photographer who was doing pictures for the piece I had done. There were too many people around watching and commenting. They were all perfectly friendly but I found it all a bit embarrassing. ECB [England and Wales Cricket Board] with Dick Caborn. Nice bunch. Giles Clarke [businessman, ECB chairman, former England player] and his wife Judy, who used to be with me at the *Sunday Mirror*. Dennis Amiss with lots of reminiscing about

Geoffrey Boycott [former England player] and the famous run out he has never failed to mention since. He said after it [Amiss's refusal of Boycott's call for a second run against New Zealand] Boycott said he was going to run out Amiss and only a warning from Ray Illingworth he would never play for England again if he did kept him in check. [Sir] Michael [TV presenter] and Mary Parkinson were there, Mary saying she was desperate for me to do a chat show so that I not Piers Morgan was seen as 'the new Parky'. She had always thought I should do telly and she wanted me to meet their son Michael, who was also Parky's agent, to go over some ideas.

They both felt the current media set-up was dreadful, and boy did she dislike Piers. Michael felt it would never get better now, that it had been set on a downward spiral that might be halted but he didn't hold out much hope of improvement or a better culture. She said it would only change if people like me went into it and showed it was possible to do serious stuff that was also entertaining. It was a fabulous day, nice people, great weather, nice food. There was a nice American woman called Kay Ord who had never seen a cricket match before and I was teaching her the rules, or trying to. Not easy. When lunch came, I had to go to get some more pictures done for *The Observer*. Then on the way back, I spotted the anti-war protester who had attacked me at the Hatchard's signing, and I could tell he was intent on no good.

He came into my face, said I was a fucking bastard. I walked on, just ignored him, but he came after me, glass in one hand, bottle in another. A guy who saw what was going on, in his thirties maybe, moved in between us, getting his body in the way of the protester without actually touching him, and I walked on. But it seemed to wind him up even more and he pushed past the guy and kicked out at me, missing the first time, but then landing one right on my calf. Another guy got involved now, stepping in and saying to him 'Hey, there is no need for that', and off he went again, bastard, fucking bastard. I managed to make my mind go into slow motion and I just walked away. I was rather pleased with myself. I had not even been tempted to clock him. I must have looked a bit shaken up though because when I got back Mary P asked me if I was OK.

Sunday 29 June

I had a chat on the phone with Gordon Banks to top up the piece for the *Mirror*. Really liked him. David Miliband called. He said he had been in Japan and while there he had felt things were getting better. But now he was back they felt if anything worse. He said the mood at Cabinet was becalmed, all focusing on the business of government, but almost as a way of not facing up to the issue in hand. He felt there was nobody who thought GB could turn it around. I asked where he was on it. He said he would take it, but he would not strike or wound. In a way there had to be a mood that made it happen. I said I didn't think Gordon would be overly affected by mood. The question was whether he had anything to fear from a challenge. David repeated that he would not strike or wound. He asked if I thought we could get to conference and beyond like this? I felt maybe, but no stronger than that. He felt that if GB went people would come to him, but he couldn't be seen to be agitating for that. He also believed there would have to be a contest and that he would win it. He felt GB was stupid not to have had a contest, even if it had been against John McDonnell, to show he was confident in his arguments and he had broad support.*

He was quizzing me on what GB's current mood was. I was a bit down on all of them. PG felt DM was the only option. None were perfect but he was beginning to break through and he was fairly positive on the feedback from the groups he had done last week. We had a lunch at home for Michael Foot [former Labour leader]. Neil and Glenys, the Goodmans [journalist Geoffrey and wife Margit], Ian Aitken [journalist], Bridget Clements [widow of former Labour advisor Dick], George and Catherine McLeod. Michael was looking even more frail. He walked very, very slowly, and the bodily jerks were more violent than ever. The left eye had gone completely. He was still talking away though and was pretty bright. He said he wanted to go to Burnley v Plymouth but Jenny Stringer, his minder-carer, said long journeys were difficult bordering on impossible. Catherine told me that in Aberdeen last week she had been shocked by GB's mood and behaviour. The whole operation was dysfunctional. Geoffrey made a speech saying Michael was the white Mandela which was OTT, as was his statement that we would all vote for him to be leader now. Everyone seemed to think GB had to soldier on but Neil and I seemed to be in agreement it was all a bit hopeless and a lot of it because his characteristics were coming through.

Fiona and I were having dinner with GB and Sarah. I was dreading it, partly because it would be several hours of not getting to the point but also because he would try to reel me further in. And we would not be able to watch the Spain v Germany final properly. We parked in the L-shaped road, up to the flat, saw the kids before they went to bed. GB chatting football. [Baroness] Shriti Vadera [Under-Secretary, International Development] was there. She was clearly a genuine friend and they would need a few of those. Sarah was being very warm and friendly. We were going through a few possibles for buying tables at Wembley, GB doing his usual of making a list, and then repeating himself endlessly. He told a few stories from the recent Mandela events. He felt he was frail and beginning to lose it a

* MP McDonnell had criticised the lack of a challenge to GB's leadership in a *Guardian* article.

little. Oprah Winfrey and Elton John had been bidding beyond £1 million for a letter by Mandela. The whole set-up was a bit odd. The chef from Chequers had cooked and left the food. No table laid. Wine and drinks a bit higgledy-piggledy. We went through and there was a fair bit of small talk before someone mentioned a four-year plan on some policy or other. I said, so how do you intend to ensure you are still here in four years?

He went into his usual thing about the economy, how things were really tough for people, how we had to have a proper explanation and be seen as the people who could steer through and then have the right approach beyond that. He was not terribly inspiring though and a bit whingey about things, always coming back to the media and people who were being disloyal. I said he had to repoliticise his ministers. They were pretty hopeless. He said he had felt he had to get rid of some of the older ones when he took over. The young ones had not been as effective as they might have been. We went over how they might be re-energised and Sarah asked if I would go in and train them. Re the US he felt Obama should win, that McCain lacked energy, but that the right would really gear up against the wife, also that some Obama positions were not thought through. Sarah was clearly very key to a lot that was going on. He snapped at her at one point though, telling her to be quiet. Fiona and I both shocked. I sensed from Sarah's and Shriti's reaction that it happened quite a lot.

GB kept saying that there was no real point going after the Tories or laying out other big arguments 'until we have scored some successes'. I said now was the time to be laying the ground, experimenting, showing a bit of fight, testing out new voices. He needed a team, maybe including ex-ministers, who could start to take on the Tories really aggressively. He said but nobody was listening. I said we had to make them listen. They would listen if we had interesting things to say. He was scribbling away madly. It was a bit of a non-argument and I felt he was both blaming and looking for excuses not to do things that needed to be done. We went over some of the economic stuff too. I told him the full story of the Dadge fiasco and he was angry. Yet he and his people should have gripped it.

We went up to watch the last half-hour of the match. A bit of light relief for a while. He sat cross legged close to the TV. I wondered if his sight was getting worse. Spain were terrific and deserved to win [1–0]. As soon as it finished he sat in one of the chairs, took out his paper again and said he had a proposal for me. Would I oversee a team to prepare a strategy for conference? I asked what was happening with Greg (several weeks on). He said he was fixing it. He was keen. Maybe start him in No. 10 and then move to the party as comms director. But he knew conference was make or break in some ways and he had to get through it strong. He was not giving up on reeling me in. I need your help. I need you around as much as you can be. I said I will help but I do not want to come back in full-time. I don't want all the blah that would go with it. I don't want to stop doing the new things I am doing. He said he was sympathetic to that.

Then he asked if I wanted to go to the Lords as Sports Minister. He said he knew I didn't like the Lords, but this was a proper job, I would do it well, and people would not be able to object because they knew how passionate I was about sport, and with the Olympics on the horizon, its political profile was going to rise. It was weird, as Dick had been saying yesterday I should get into the Lords while I could. I think he might be a bit taken aback that GB was offering me his old job. The sports job was an offer out of the blue. It had a certain appeal but was probably just another way of getting me in and then getting me to run the campaign. Added to which, I really did have an aversion to the Lords, and I would be stuck there long after a ministerial job had come and gone.

I asked him what everyone else did. He continued to defend appointments but Greg and Sue Gray had both said independently the operation was a shambles as nobody was taking decisions and so he was doing too much of the things he should not be doing at all. Fiona felt he was funnier and more human than she had expected, almost but not quite like the old days. But I think we were both glad to get home. She said when GB and I were alone, they had been going over various issues and people and she felt the 'them and us, for us or against us' feeling was really bad, much worse than under TB. There were very few people they spoke warmly of, let alone fondly. The old crew a bit – Balls, Cooper, Ed M – but on all of them they had just not delivered as well as they should have done.

Monday 30 June

Working on the dinner. Researching Brel. Out at lunchtime to LBC's studio to interview his daughter France Brel down the line. I was due to do the Ken Livingstone show and they had agreed to let me do the interview from there even though it was for the Beeb. She was really nice and added great colour and texture to the whole thing. She was not at all what I had expected. I had read so much about how poor he had been as a husband and father but she was determined to be positive about her life and about him as her father. There was some great stuff for the programme and for the piece I was doing on Brel for *The Times*. Then an hour with Ken Livingstone on his new show. It confirmed to me I was right to resist this kind of thing. LBC had been sounding me out for a regular slot and something held me back from going for it. There was something lowering about it. I couldn't put my finger on it, but Ken seemed a little diminished by it. He was also too obsessed with talking about his own demise.

It was all a bit backward-looking, and without a sense of a forward agenda, politically or personally. He was also a big Brel fan so we talked about that too. Few calls, usual mix of pro- and anti- and then off. There was something deeply unsatisfying about virtually all media just now. I said as much to Prebble and Richard Klein of BBC documentaries over dinner. He was quite an odd-seeming bloke for the BBC, wore a crucifix. He was also a Tory. He struck me as being of the BBC culture but thinking that by wearing an earring and saying he did not like the current affairs coverage that he could pretend he was not. Stuart was a cut above these guys in that, for example today on the world economy he could see a bigger picture and understand the world beyond the bubble of UK centric coverage. But the extent to which TV people saw TV as the only universe was extraordinary.

Tuesday 1 July

Worked on the Brel piece for *The Times*. Also shifting tables. Nigel Doughty [Labour supporting businessman, owner Nottingham Forest FC] called after my email and offered 30k for the Fergie lot – a day at the training ground. Good news. Cabinet clearly got the letter I had suggested Dick, Margaret and I send as I started to get calls from Tessa, then Andy Burnham, and later Maggie Darling, saying they had ideas for people to call and things to do. Tessa said we had not been clear what we wanted. But it was the fact that we had not really had people coming towards us. I was picking up more and more negativity re GB but also no real pro-Cameron feel. Jon Mendelsohn [Labour fundraiser] called to say he was really grateful, that we were doing great stuff, but also that the situation was in some ways not as bad as we thought as there were some major donors lined up for long-term stuff. He agreed I should send an email to high-value donors on the auction. Out for a long bike ride in blistering heat with Rory. Great news on *All in the Mind* – sold French translation rights to Albin Michel [publisher]. Really chuffed it would appear in French.

Wednesday 2 July

I had a long chat with Charlie Falconer, trying to get him to take a table. He'd had dinner with [Jonathan] Sumption [government barrister at Hutton Inquiry] last night who had taken issue with Charlie's assessment of him in my diaries, though at least he saw the more I was exposed to him, the more I liked and respected him. And Charlie had been wrong in thinking we would not get on. He said Sumption had said he was struck by how decent and moral I was. He said he had also seen Godric yesterday, 'so I had a whole day of Campbell praise fest'. I was telling him taking a table would be good for his internal PR – showing that the pension row and 42 days was not a sign of being offside generally. Stuart Le Gassick was keen to see me to discuss some project or other – turned out to be a public–private sector plan to implement Lord [Ara] Darzi's NHS proposals [to move care from hospitals to GP-led independent polyclinics].

Stuart sent Brian his driver so we had a 200k Bentley up the street for a while. He took me out to Chiswick and waited while I went through Bill's edits on the early stuff from '94 post John Smith's death, so before the start of *The Blair Years*. Bill said he found the whole thing fascinating. The biggest surprise for me in there was how TB clearly felt Peter was initially operating all out for GB, and now it seemed GB was calling on Peter and me more than perhaps even his own usual advisors, and certainly more than he had done for a long time. I was working a bit on Brel and also Gordon Banks, and trying to get a decent bidder for the piece Antony Gormley [sculptor] had offered for the auction next week. It was becoming a nightmare and despite one or two responses from ministers post our round robin, we were getting next to no feedback, positive or negative, and so having to lift the load ourselves.

Back to Shepherd Market, worked on the Bill stuff while waiting for Stuart, then to a little restaurant where he set out, first alone then with a rather dour ex-Deloitte's guy, Mike Kerr, public sector expert, an NHS plan. It was more interesting than most of the stuff I had seen from them and I promised to pass it on. Avram Grant appeared in a car outside the restaurant terrace. He got out, wandered around, got back in and went. Alex called a few minutes later to confirm he couldn't come to the Labour dinner. Calum said when I transmitted this news the people at Victoria St were totally shocked. Yet I had been telling them for ages. Alex was on good form and confident he could keep Ronaldo. I did the last bits and bobs on the proof as I watched Rafa Nadal hammer Andy Murray [Wimbledon tennis].

Thursday 3 July

David S. Mainly on GB and my confliction re going in there at all. Also Fiona up and down again. Into Labour HQ with Calum. I took a list of donors and arts supporters and did dozens of cold calls. I think I got a bit of traction but it was not easy. Johnny Hornby [businessman] very funny about how he was going to take the table but he was finding it hard to get anyone who wanted to go. Quite funny reaction from some on me saying who I was. A moment when they didn't believe or thought it was a wind-up. It was all about tables and the auction now. Gordon Banks had agreed to come, and that we could do something with him for the auction.

I got a call last night from GB saying could I go in for an early evening meeting tonight. Him, Carter, David Muir and Greg Nugent. In through the L-shaped road. GB held up by a mix of some fucked-up vote on MPs' expenses and meeting Simon Fuller [entrepreneur, TV producer]. I chatted with the other three. Carter seemed a little more on top of things and Muir, despite a rather odd habit of closing his eyes when he spoke, was more impressive than I had been led to believe he would be. He was also more immediately likeable than some of GB's people. I quite liked some of his thoughts. We did a mix of small talk and strategy. Carter said he had been given my book by his wife, and he had just got to the bit where Neil was saying don't do it because it will ruin your life, when GB called. Since when he had had no time to read anything.

GB came in all flustered, raging about the vote – they had whipped on a free vote to keep the pay rise down, but then let go of the whip on the so-called John Lewis list and he was in a rage about it.* He did seem to let the slightest thing provoke these simmering outbursts which just filled the start of the meeting with a whole load of negative energy. We were trying to agree a strategy for conference. He knew there would be a sense of make and break about it. He had to get into a better place by the end of the conference season. Muir was working on fairness and something like fair rules, fair chances, so that they could do some pretty tough stuff on welfare, also on immigration, but hold to fairness. It was fine in so far as it went but I felt they should be playing far closer to where people were – namely economic tough times, and the sense we were in a bit of trouble. We went round in circles. Eventually I suggested 'in a fight for your future' which gave a sense of us accepting we were in a real fight with the Tories but also gave you the difficult policy choices. It lacked values but it might do.

I was also suggesting that GB – by now furiously note-taking – had to say at some point that he got why people had had doubts about him. He had to give a sense of how we had got to this. He was constantly saying it was all about the economy which suggested he didn't want to say it had anything to do with him. Muir was really pushing for fair rules and fair chances but it was not big enough. There had to be more grit in there, policy and politics. Cameron also had to be taken on far better. *The Times* had done an editorial saying it was not enough for GB to coast and there had to be more substance and policy. He volunteered an article which was frankly pathetic. Martin Sheehan had left to work with Tim Allan at Portland, so that created more space maybe for Greg, though he was beginning to wonder what he was heading into. It was not a bad meeting but GB kept allowing his mind to be dragged back to the expenses vote, which ultimately would be forgotten. It

* The list, based on prices at the John Lewis store, from which MPs could claim some expenses and Commons officials could determine whether claims were within reasonable cost.

was like a displacement. He was also still singing this refrain that we could not go for the Tories until there had been a few successes. It was bollocks. Meanwhile Carol was telling me her conference staging budget had been slashed to 125k, which meant a tiny stage and a useless backdrop.

I called PG who said he was feeling a bit down. Peter M thought the fight line was OK provided we were clear who the fight was with and what it was about. I felt GB had to focus relentlessly on big stuff, stop being drawn into piddling stuff in the Nick Robinson-led BBC soap opera. And we had to have proper attack on the Tories. As Greg and I left for a chat on the way out, GB was making more noises about the ministers, including Jacqui Smith and Andy Burnham, who had voted the wrong way. And as we walked down the corridor, we heard a shout and then the sound of his phone thudding against the wall. I was beginning to feel sorry for Carter. Greg started laughing and by the time we were at the car we were close to hysteria. It was all a bit fucking mad.

Friday 4 July

Off with Stuart Le Gassick, his daughter Danielle and Mike Kerr to Sandown Park. A few interesting characters there and I was trying to get bids in for the auction. Had so far got 30k for a session with Fergie, 25k to get a mention in my novel, 15 from Frank Warren [boxing promoter] for a TB tennis match and 10 for the Gormley. But we were still short of where we needed to be, and short on tables too. Nice enough day at the races but it was not really my thing. Sky Andrew fixed Rachel Yankey [footballer] and Hope Powell [England women's team manager] which was good. Joe Calzaghe [boxer] pulled out but Frank had some decent boxers for us. The *Mirror* did fine on the Pelé piece. *The Indy* ran a big piece on GB turning to me and Peter M for advice. It was a fair and accurate enough piece but annoying. Alan Pardew [football manager] also on board for Wembley. I left a message with Ann Keen [GB PPS] saying how useless the MPs had been.

Saturday 5 July

Stewart Wood [GB advisor] sent through a draft of GB's speech for the sports dinner. Made a few suggestions. We were getting there on the choreography but the sooner it was over the better.

Sunday 6 July

Reworked the Brel piece for the *Times* magazine. It helped to shape the radio piece too. Fairly long bike ride and a bit of work before watching the

Nadal–Federer final [Nadal won in five sets]. Superb. Alex called after and said he felt it was about as good as sport and athleticism can ever get. Out for dinner at Strada with Tessa and Jessie Mills. I was going into a bit of a dip though, and Grace was giving me a hard time about my moods. Tessa said the political scene was worse than we thought. She felt it was only because the Tories were so poor that people had not given up on us for good. She felt her people in Dulwich would be willing to give us another four years of government but not of government like this. In other words we had to get a grip and pretty quick too. She felt the Tories were not really breaking through as an alternative but they were looking more competent than we did. Yet she agreed with me that there was nobody really emerging as an alternative to GB. I doubted DM would go for it, he might be expecting it to fall into his lap. Also did he have what you seemed to need these days on the charisma front, or the nous to build the team he needed?

She said Ed Balls was unelectable because of a basic lack of human appeal. James Purnell was not a serious contender, at least certainly not yet. So it may be they had to stick with what they had. Jessie was interested in the novels, and seemed really chuffed when I said her dad had really helped with the first, and that his comments led to some significant changes. I had a long chat with Jeremy Heywood re the scene at No. 10. He was very open about how he did not rate Carter. He said David Muir was pissed off at the lack of clarity about the Greg role, so they had that in common. Greg took them to the limit on spads but GB just would not get rid of people. Peter M had been making the point that he must make people see they had to work in one structure. He had all these different strands of advice operating divorced from each other and it was hopeless. Jeremy wanted me to keep sending in the advice but I said I was not sure how much good it was doing.

Monday 7 July

In with Calum and based myself all day at Victoria St trying to seal a deal on table sales and auction bids. Meeting with Dick, Carol and Kamlesh to take stock. We could get to 500k at a push but it would not be easy. Cut price for those who had already bought. MPs too. Walter Smith pulled out because he had to go to Lithuania. Dick and I spoke to Tony Lloyd [PLP chair] so Dick could do another pitch at the PLP. But it seemingly backfired a bit and he was heckled. I had a long chat with Peter M who had been at Chequers over the weekend. He felt that the central problem was lack of project and lack of clarity about what the government was for, what GB wanted to do. Added to which GB clearly did not seem to trust his own team any more, largely because they had created them as ministers.

He said at least he (PM) had a day job that took him out of Britain but GB clearly believed that I was around the whole time and available to him at all times. He felt that we gave TB strength and he wanted that strength for himself. He felt that the problem was less GB's ability to devise strategy than to see it through, not keep changing tack the whole time. Peter was very funny about the ongoing Sarko row over trade 'I didn't start it, he did' – and on the difficulty people had been having in getting businessmen to the dinner.* He said GB felt that to stop businesses thinking we were anti-business we just had to say we were pro-business. But it didn't quite work like that. To RH to go through all the little changes to *All in the Mind*. Rebecca was sorted for Novel 2 as well but not full-time for a while. Ran home but I was not feeling great and the whole dinner thing, plus GB pressure, was getting on top of me.

Tuesday 8 July

Feeling tired. Up early and off on Eurostar, reading [author and journalist] Sally Brampton's book on depression [*Shoot the Damn Dog*]. Really strong. There was a lot of read-across to my own stuff, but hers was far worse and more sustained. Some of it though was spot on, really caught how it felt. There was also a great line about religion being for people who don't want to go to hell, and spiritualism for people who've already been. Usual loud businessmen on the train out. Nice sunny day. Telly and media. One or two of the bigger names were dropping out of the dinner. Got Peter Reid [football manager] and Viv Anderson [former England player] and thanks to Sky Andrew, more of the women footballers. Back, really tired but I headed to ICA for [broadcaster] June Sarpong's political website launch. The mood on GB still very down.

Wednesday 9 July

Selling flat out. Tables, got a few more individual sales late on. Mark Cavendish [cyclist] won a Tour de France stage and we had a green jersey signed by him and expression of support. Working loads during the day and getting stuff done, but the dinner was all I was really thinking of, plus what to do with GB. His Japan trip had not gone well and he had been panned for talking about the need to save food and poverty on the way out, only to be hit by a row about the scale of the banquet on arrival.

* The French President had blamed Mandelson's handling of a round of trade talks for Ireland's No vote on the Lisbon Treaty. Mandelson disagreed publicly and commented, 'I'm not going to be bullied.'

Nothing was really going right. Also none of the other ministers were cutting through. I had done him a few notes in the past few days, and all it did was lead to more of a demand. When he got back from Japan they were sending me all the drafts and so forth yet when it came to it he phoned himself and did the rat-rat-rat thing, listening to what I was saying and then just typing it really loudly. Yet this was exactly the kind of speech that needed to be natural not over prepared.

At lunchtime, at [auctioneer] Melanie Clore's suggestion, I cycled in pouring rain to [friend of FM] Janice Blackburn's where she was hosting a rich ladies' lunch. They were all paraded up one by one to have me go through the catalogue. One or two were interested in the Gormley and the tennis. Ronnie Newhouse, Mrs Condé Nast [mass media company], wife of Jonathan [Condé Nast chairman], was interested in the boxing gym lot, and offered just under 5k when I explained the rules. But she emailed later to say she had rethought, that actually she 'loathed' GB and his non-dom laws might make them leave the country. Ho hum. Kathy Lette said she would pay 5k to have sex with me. I said I'd already got more for the novel. I liked Ronni D'Ancona the impressionist who had just had a baby. She and Kathy were defending GB strongly. Home to change then out to David Frost's party. Pouring rain so people were crowding in the marquees. I had a chat with Stuart Rose [CEO, Marks & Spencer] who was very funny about the flak he got. He said at the AGM today when someone said he was worse than GB, he went through all the other insults and said he could live with that. Had a chat with John Scarlett but it was always difficult to talk in those circumstances, just little snatches as people wandered in and out of the conversation.

Cameron was there and we had a little chat, mainly small talk about TB and tennis. Nice chat with Annie Robinson. Quite a lot of 'When you going back?', fuelled by Colin Byrne [former Labour official, now businessman] taking a real whack at the GB media operation in PR week, saying some of the things that had happened recently would never have happened had I been there. Andy Coulson [Cameron's communications director] was getting quite a good press at the moment. GB said on one call that Coulson was taking politics to the gutter and getting the press to ignore serious debate. It was beginning to get through though that DC was not doing serious debate. *The Times* and the *FT* both on that theme recently but still the general sense that the government was a shambles and the Tories just had to motor on and it was in the bag. Out to a local curry house in Chelsea with Stuart and Margaret Le Gassick. Stuart was much less loud and showy when wife and Fiona around. Actually quite a serious debate about policy. Loud table alongside. But nice night all round.

Thursday 10 July

Out to do BBC World Service [radio] on strategy and comms for their Insiders Debate, with Lynton Crosby and John Nagenda [political advisor] from Uganda. There was too much on the press as the be all and end all, and we all ganged up a bit on the presenter [Owen Bennett-Jones]. Nagenda was quite funny about the way he used the penal code 'to get journalists to behave'. Crosby and I agreed more than people might expect us to, especially on the need for strategy, and for the need to understand the public was not the same thing as public opinion as expressed by the media. The presenter was a bit irritating because it all came back to media good, spin bad and we had to hit back pretty hard. Off to Vic St. I called Bernie Ecclestone for one last go at getting him to bid for some of the auction lots. He said that he was fed up forking out for every cause and it was a no. He was perfectly friendly but very clear.

Went to see PG on the way home. He had lost more weight and looked a lot more worried. He was off to the Royal Marsden [Hospital] again and was due to have an endoscopy next week. I ran home feeling a bit down, waited for Calum to get home from work and we set off for Wembley. The venue was looking pretty good. Numbers were slightly down on last year but only just and we had a few more bids coming in. GB called and we had a long chat about what he should say. Rat-tat-tat. He needed constant reassurance that the stories he planned to tell would go down well. Constant asking of questions about who was going to be there. I am not sure he was always listening to the answers. I said at one point I was not doing this again because it had been so difficult and the politicians had been useless. He ploughed on. He was overdoing the how grateful he was kind of thing, in between raging about the press coverage of Japan – 'There was no fucking banquet with eleven courses' – and he was peppering the whole conversation with questions about who had been good, who had been useless, who did I think was any good among the ministers.

Bobby George [darts player] was first to arrive. Rachel K making a big fuss of him. We were re-ordering the whole event to the last minute. Margaret doing well generating money and phone bids. Frank Warren was up for doing more. Nigel Doughty told me he would go to 40k for the Fergie lot. So we were in OK shape, it was coming together. There were a few late drop-outs and I got Rory to fill the gaps with mates. Calum was really working hard and had a lovely manner with people. He was greeting the sports stars and several told me how nice he was. Really proud of him, the way he had grown into things these last few weeks.

I was asked to pose for pictures with guests at the trophies – we had the Premiership trophy, the FA Cup and the Carling Cup. It was interesting to see just by how much the Premiership had overtaken the FA Cup in terms of interest. As people came in, pretty good atmosphere. Pete Winkelman [chairman] of MK Dons [football club] was in good form and loving it. Sol Campbell arrived. He was a bit heavy and ponderous and not great with people really, but it was still good to have him there. I avoided Harriet Harman and Jack Dromey as they came in, as I was still simmering at the way he had behaved over the loans and TB.* Gordon Banks arrived just before GB so we sorted pictures of them with the trophies and then alone. I had a long chat with Ed Balls. I said 'When is someone going to get a grip?' He said 'I thought you were. It's what GB says. He says you are going to run the campaign.'

I said I was happy to help but I was not going back, and in the end it was up to the politicians not staff. It was no good blaming Carter and these guys. There was no attack. There was no coherent agenda and strategy. There was no real fight or focus. And it would make no difference who went into No. 10 if that did not change at the ministerial level. GB's line was that he had tried to promote the young guns but none had really risen to it. Balls did what he always used to do when we argued about the TB/GB stuff in the past – listened, nodded, said he agreed with a lot of what I said and could we speak next week? He texted later to say could we meet up to continue the conversation?

Peter Reid was hilarious, especially with the women players. I sorted picture of GB giving a merit award to a very chuffed Audrey. Beverley Knight [singer] gorgeous. Nancy was all over me. It was so hard to understand what she was on about. But she added a bit of glamour and coming up on stage when we did her lot definitely helped drive up the money. It was possible to see as she walked around that men still really went for her. JP with the Hull Kingston Rovers [rugby league club] crowd. The business people were not too bad, but all saying how tough things were. Great to see Stephen Jones and the Welsh rugby guys, and his lovely girlfriend Gwen Rowlands. GB's speech went down well, as did the little film we had made for the evening. Sol was on first. He was OK but there were too many 'kind of, you know' in every sentence. There was a good response though and the interview slot idea was definitely working.

Gordon Banks was excellent, really warm and decent and humble. Fantastic reaction to him. He said he was really chuffed to be sitting on the PM's table. The auction went pretty well. Calum had had the idea of Andy Hodgson [Burnley fan, TV auctioneer] doing it and he was really good at driving up bids. The Gormley piece got 55k from Unite. Fergie

* When, in 2006, there was a party official internal inquiry into millions of pounds of loans allegedly hidden by No. 10, Labour treasurer Dromey had said that Downing Street 'must have known' about them. Dromey also said publicly that he had known nothing about the loans.

40k. Tennis with TB 20k. 25k to be named as a small character in my novel. The old memorabilia stuff did not work terribly well, but the money can't buy stuff did. Got to £383k total for the whole auction which amazingly was more than last year. Perhaps more important was the lift it gave confidence wise. There were loads of messages coming in saying so but as I said to Dick, it was ridiculous that it took the old guard to do it. There had to be more people in there who could inject a bit of energy.

Jon Mendelsohn and [Baroness] Cathy Ashton [Union for Foreign Affairs] were all over me, saying I had singlehandedly rescued it, that people gravitated to me and they wanted to use that for fundraising in the future. Jon sent so many OTT texts that I asked him to stop – hero, talisman, blah di blah. It was good that we had made it work, but part of me worried all it would lead to was more pressure to get involved, more party speaking engagements, more GB on the phone. It was extraordinary the extent to which the politicians now, so many of them, could walk down any street without people knowing who they were. They just did not connect at any level. So we were losing chatterers and working people alike and those in the middle were feeling squeezed.

Stuart Rose had had a similar take economically, people at the top felt the worst of the credit crunch, people at the bottom felt the pinch, people in the middle bought the idea that things were worse and they were all feeling everyone else was better off. The result was that people were not spending. It was a good night all round though. Steve Cotterill [Burnley manager] was really pleased to be asked and said that he felt it showed we could still do stuff well. Nigel Doughty was such a nice guy and determined to play a part to help New Labour become enshrined. Home by half twelve and stayed up for ages chatting to Calum who was going through all the different people and what he thought of them. Ed sold *All in the Mind* to a US publisher.

Friday 11 July

I was pressing RH to change timing of publication of the novel because of the US elections. It seemed to me a no-brainer to bring out a product for which we wanted publicity at a time the whole world would be talking about something else. I fixed the *Sunday Times* for first main interview after the *Guardian Review* ran extracts. Stephen Fry was reading it with the hope he would do something for the front cover. GB called, asked if I would go in and see him. He said again he wanted to put me in as Sports Minister. But I feared it would just be the first step to campaign co-ordinator. I was tired and didn't want to go in. I made excuses through the day as I feared it would be the same conversation about the same problems. The

Greg thing was dragging on, now six weeks or so after we thought it was sorted. Sue Gray called me privately to say did he know what he was walking into? I said he did and Greg was in a way more determined to do it the more dysfunctional it seemed to be.

Sue said Carter had been stalling. His email to Greg today that they needed one more conversation with GB, and they were 'bogged down post Japan' was ridiculous. Rachel K admitted to me last night that it was a horrible place to work because there was so much factionalism. I said to GB he had to sort them out. If people were not up to it, they had to go. If they did not sign up to the basic strategy, they had to go. If they briefed against each other, they had to go. And he had to get in the so-called young guns – DM, the Eds, Burnham, Purnell – and tell them that they needed to start firing. He should tell those who were being talked up as his successors that they should use it to build their profile, that far from being worried about it, he welcomed it because they had to build a sense of a strong team and also take some of the hits and the heat from him.

He had to bring in some of the ex-ministers and give them a public role. He had to get his key team sorted and agreed and if he couldn't the ones who stopped him had to go. He was in major 'the problem is' mode, on virtually every level. And I could sense he was worried at my idea that he encourage the DMs etc. to build their profile. He was already starting to ask if there was any point keeping going on trying to get over a big message about the world economy. I said it was vital he kept going. It was the key to turning a current weakness into a strength. We had to get the choice out there, and it was not him or TB, or him and perfection, but him and DC and who had the strength to steer us through. Another 'the problem is' was the media not pressing the Tories on policy and also the fact that Coulson – 'He should never be there given his standards as a journalist' – was dragging debate down. It was becoming one of his new obsessions.

It was a bad day on the crime front, several stabbings and deaths. Caborn said he was constantly being asked when JP was going in there to confront GB. He felt it would be madness to change leader again but JP was intending to tell him unless he got a grip, things would have to change. JP said to me he could not believe how quickly it had gone the wrong way. He had to get back to some basic politics. In the third GB call he was asking me who I rated and I had to say of the Cabinet, there was hardly anyone who had really impressed me. He said that since being elected as deputy leader Harriet felt she could be more than a voice, she could make decisions on direction etc. Straw was at it, he said. The young guns were not firing. David M and Ed Balls were OK, he said, probably the best of them, but not good at connecting with the public.

He was pro-Tom Watson, said he was good at politics. I said I was not convinced he could do strategy and he didn't have the skills to connect with the public. I sensed he was very wary of Balls all of a sudden. When I said I had talked to him at the dinner – 'Was he there? I didn't see him,' which was a bit odd. I was getting tired of raising the Greg thing with GB and asking him to sort it. If he took so long to sort something like this, what about the bigger decisions that were coming down the track as we got nearer to an election?

Saturday 12 July

Up with the girls – Grace, Ella [Rogero, friend of Grace], Nina and Sissy – and off to St Pancras for the train to Stoke via Derby, for the Gordon Banks–Pelé match. Grace was not feeling great after her Wales school trip. I don't think she is made for mountains and camping. Sissy was intrigued by some guy at the café at the station just staring at me and wanted to go and talk to him and ask him why. We took a cab to the Tollgate Hotel where people were gathering, but it all felt a bit shambolic. Certainly not Soccer Aid level of organisation. Considering they had Pelé coming to manage one of the teams, and be there for the Banks statue unveiling, it was all a bit B and C list. Several of the celebs I had never heard of. They had sold only a few thousand tickets. Player-wise Matt Le Tissier [former England player] was probably the biggest. Mike Pejic [England]. Asa Hartford [Scotland] on the Brazil team which was mainly soap stars. Plus singers from a couple of bands I had never heard of. I suspect Pelé would wonder what on earth he was getting into with this one.

There was a nice enough mood but it did not feel like a major event. There was a shambles with the buses too which meant we ended up sitting waiting for ages and eventually got dropped in the wrong place. We got to the ground, had a very average lunch, then changed and went out to warm up. Then hanging around for ages after hearing Pelé was coming out. The ceremony for unveiling the statue was fine, with [South African Archbishop] Desmond Tutu the star of the show. Banks very humble again. The game itself was a bit of a nightmare. I was playing centre back alongside Ken Monkou [former footballer]. My first real touch was from a Pejic throw, but one of the *Hollyoaks* guys, Kelvin something or other, nipped in, took the ball and Pejic gave a penalty away. One down. Then I gave one away when Kelvin beat me for pace again and I clattered him to the ground. I could hear Grace shouting 'Oh my God, Dad has hit Kelvin!' It should have been a red card but the ref ignored it, other than giving a penalty. We were three down after a few minutes. One of the Brazilians took control and sent me out to the wing.

The squads were too big and we played rolling subs. As I came off

Gordon Banks said 'I thought you were supposed to be fit?' I said I was, just useless. I played better second time on, when I went up front. A Scottish guy behind the bench was obsessively asking me to get Pelé to pose with a shirt for his anti-racism campaign. Managed to get it at half-time and the guy was so excited. What a life for Pelé though. Everyone just wanted a signature and a photo, me included. We lost 5–1. The girls were having a nice enough time, but I felt the whole thing had been very sub-average. To the hotel, more hanging round, then a grisly journey to the dinner with two buses looking for cash points because there was no credit card facility at the marquee in Trentham Gardens where the dinner was to be held. Surreal stop at a Spar shop where a host of actors, singers, footballers were queueing for money. We stayed for the starter and the speeches and Tutu's very funny grace – which he sang – then got driven back. Home half eleven. Not quite Soccer Aid. But Pelé very dignified and patient with so many people. He ran in for the dinner, still looking pretty good.

Sunday 13 July

I was meant to have a chat with TB. It ended up being by text as he was away somewhere. He said 'two questions. Is it retrievable? If not, change?' The second question mark was important. But he was clearly thinking it was not retrievable with GB. Philip was feeling the same. I was seeing more and more signs of someone unable to focus on the things he should be focusing on. It was all too bitty and not gripped. TB felt that things were not getting better and that the team round GB just wasn't strong enough. But fundamentally the problem was at the top. Cab out with Rory to Chelsea for the LRF bikeathon. I did the 52 miles route. Rory took a wrong turn at one point and did an additional 8 miles, but still won. I was tired a bit during, and very tired after. I was bollocked by Rory when I tried to jump the queue for the massage by saying I had to do a load of telly.

I had sent *All in the Mind* to Ian McEwan [novelist], and he sent me a really nice, thoughtful note. He said he read it 'with pleasure and interest', liked the shape – a strong, simple and psychologically sound idea, a number of plausible cases, deftly unfolded, all slowly and believably improving. He thought the press, desperate to get an angle, would read it as an allegory of Blair, or Blairism. He also had some really helpful smaller observations, almost copy-edit points. He also thought I had a tendency to over-explain, over-determine. He said I should insist on a really good copy editor to spot that kind of thing. Overall though, I was chuffed. One, that he had read it. Two, he liked it. Three, he made suggestions that would improve it.

Monday 14 July

Greg was still not sorted and he was beginning to think that it was not worth persevering. He really felt David Muir in particular just did not want him there. To the Savile Club in Brook St for interviews for *Cracking Up*. First Chris [Boffey] who was surprisingly reticent then Syd [Young] who was very funny and light. Both were on the main point that I was obsessive. Chris said he didn't think I was an alcoholic, but an addict. We had a very nice lunch in a little Thai restaurant and chatted away about old times. But first I did a pretty remarkable interview with Pat Hewitt [former Health Secretary]. First re the day I cracked when I was with her. Then she opened up about her own sister's repeated breakdowns. She was almost in tears at a couple of points. She was looking ten years younger out of office. Also much more warm and open.

I told her that Fiona basically thinks she saved my life, when she told the police in Hamilton who I was.* In the afternoon, we went up to the house and Judith [Dawson] interviewed Fiona. I didn't listen in, but Judith said it was impressive and moving. I was working on the Brel radio script. It was amazing how few words a half-hour radio gives you compared with an article. Out to Monday night football. Played not bad. Grace said I had to get myself a proper football coach. She said I was embarrassing at Stoke and was 'a total idiot for pushing over Kelvin' – or was it Calvin?

Tuesday 15 July

GB called first thing. I missed the call and, listening to his message, I felt bad at how relieved I felt. Both PG and Gail felt I should go for the Sports Minister job. But it was not what it seemed, I was sure of that. He just wanted me inside the system in a way that at the moment I was still more or less outside. If he got me into the government, I had no doubt he would ask me to do the campaigns co-ordinator job pretty quickly. Meanwhile, out of left field came a text from Marianna [Trian, Labour official] saying that they were about to announce Derek Draper [former researcher for Peter Mandelson] as overseeing a review of the party's campaigns and structures. GB had mentioned him when we talked about the Davis by-election, but to my mind he was not heavy enough for this and potentially real trouble. Whelan was still on the scene too and possibly involved in this.

Into Random House for a meeting on the diaries. Volume 1 still way too

* During his drinking period, a very drunk AC had been arrested for his own safety and detained in a cell at the police station at Hamilton, south Lanarkshire, where he stripped naked and scratched drawings on a wall. Pat Hewitt, then Neil Kinnock's press secretary, tracked him down and arranged his release, on condition he went to hospital.

long. I also gave them the last changes to the novel including some based on Ian McEwan's note. I really appreciated his note. He did not want to do a cover endorsement though because he said it was a minefield. Ed still fixing the US deal. Small publisher and unlikely to be great money but he felt they would do it well. RH meeting OK. Off to the Savile Club for more *Cracking Up* filming. I interviewed a nice Scottish guy called Mike, gay, depressive, alcoholic who was now dry and sorted and running a rehab centre for others. Also Dr Paul Keedwell, lecturer and author on psychiatry who tried a bit too hard to interview me and let me know how much he had studied me. Went OK though. It was good to be able to work with Judith and crew again and at least I felt I could trust them. I was feeling tired too often at the moment. General ageing, or downswing?

Wednesday 16 July

Rebecca Carter came round for a chat on the second novel. She really liked it, thought it could be great, but felt it needed a lot of work. We agreed I would mull, ponder and rejig. She would see it again in September. Later to Old St area to the offices of Somethin' Else [media company] to record Brel. Came out fine. I noticed though I was becoming more and more irritable in the face of any faffing around re radio and telly. Later I watched the Olympia concert with Calum. He got his results today. 2:1. He had done so well to stick it out, work hard and do well. Redid the Brel piece, and was also reviewing the [Haruki] Murakami book on running [*What I Talk About When I Talk About Running*].

Thursday 17 July

Early flight with Judith and the film crew from City to Glasgow. More and more people were learning about City and it was a bit more crowded than usual but still totally painless compared with the big airports. Flight virtually empty. Met by a 24-seater bus for the five of us and we set off for Dr [Ernest] Bennie's, the psychiatrist who had looked after me in 1986 up in Paisley. He was retired but his wife was a fair few years younger and away at a mental health tribunal in Lochgilphead. He was pretty much as I remembered him. Small, quite earnest, with a bustling walk. He was a total natch for the cameras, much better than I at redoing meetings and pretending we were seeing each other for the first time. We sat down at a dining room table and pretty much got down to it.

He could not remember me specifically and there was no real reason why he should, given the hundreds and hundreds of patients he had seen. But he had clocked the name when I became well known, and had realised.

He was excellent on the general issues and interesting in his view that alcohol caused depression every bit as much as alcohol was a response to depression. He said Ross Hall, the Glasgow hospital where he treated me, no longer took psychiatric patients. He had retired fully and said he felt a bit out of touch. Also that he felt psychiatrists got a bad press because basically people feared them. Some of it was irrational. It was a nice chat, and he seemed pleased that I had remembered him and credited him with being the one who made me realise I had to change my ways.

It was raining as we left and headed for Hamilton civic centre. A very nice woman called Mhairi was looking after us and we quickly found the foyer where I had finally cracked and been arrested. I did a little chat with Judith there. They clearly wanted me to say it was all a bit odd going back but partly because I had been there since anyway, and partly because I had always been open, this part did not feel so weird at all. I was quite pleased to be back and to relive it all, given I was in so much better shape now than I was then. We did lots of faffing around entrance shots and a fairly long interview going over what actually happened, then over to the police station. The cops were a mix of friendly and unco-operative and 'everything has to go through media services'. Judith was hoping for us to be able to film in the cell I had been in but she was pretty clear that we were not getting anywhere with them, and as the guys at the Sherriff's Court were much friendlier, she asked if we could film in one of the cells there and for a fee we could.

It was pretty grisly in there. Beans on the ceiling where prisoners had flung their food. Lots of IRA graffiti. The guys working there very helpful. They said they basically saw the same people again and again. Mainly drink and drugs. Did another very echoey interview in the cells where I said the reason it was not difficult for me was because I decided back there and then that I was at the low point and the only way was up. Off to the hotel near East Kilbride, where a very boozy wedding was going on. GB had been trying to fix a meeting but instead we went for a phone call. He said there were some things he wanted to discuss face to face next week. But meantime could I head up a September to December fightback plan to get a message out above the media.

Friday 18 July

The fourth anniversary of Dad's death. Felt like yesterday. Four years. An Olympiad. A modern parliamentary term. I was glad I was in Scotland. I went for a little run before breakfast. Wet and wheezy. Judith had been hoping to do the interview in the open air but the weather put paid to that, so we had a lot of hanging around, before heading to Hamilton to do an interview in the back of a car going over the paranoia, describing what it was like when every road sign and shop sign said something to you. Then to Ross Hall Hospital. The blue railings were still there at the front and the beautiful garden at the back. We were met by the chief exec who had started as part of the nursing staff. The director of nursing, a woman called Liz, showed me around.

Bits came back. The wooden staircase in the listed part of the building. The gardens looked the same. I described where I thought my room was but then through a process of elimination we worked out it was room 115 of the Argyll Suite. Liz and I had a chat in there, me sitting on the bed, then we did another interview in there. It was almost dark by the time we finished. Of all the places we had been, it was the one that brought it all back most vividly. The room was exactly as I remembered it, except the TV was in a different place, lower than before. We did some farewell shots, then all aboard the bus for the plane home. Judith felt they had got a lot out of it and I had quite enjoyed it in a way.

Saturday 19 July

I was beginning to do the main second draft of the second novel. I was taking on some of Rebecca's ideas. Topped 100k words after a while. Did an OK long run though I was feeling stiff a lot of the time.

Sunday 20 July

The *Sunday Telegraph* had a big piece in the diary about Anji [Hunter] slagging me off for the book. We spoke later and she said she was totally done in. She said she was a bit pissed off that she came over as being less central than me and Jonathan, and she felt the whole thing was a bit macho at times, but she had not slagged me off to the paper. We had a nice chat about things. She felt GB was done for but that we were right to try to help. The Sunday papers not quite as shite as in recent weeks but they were still pretty dire. GB due to be heading off to Iraq.

Monday 21 July

I got a lovely email from Stephen Fry [TV presenter, comedian] saying how much he enjoyed *All in the Mind*, that he found it really moving, and he said he was very happy to give a quote for the cover. Gail and Ed all thought his name as endorsement was about as good as it would get. It was really nice of him, and he got the book totally, and I think shared my view that I could use it for mental health campaign purposes too. Calum and I went in at 4.15 to meet the fundraising dinner team for drinks on the terrace at the Commons. I saw some of the old coppers, including some who had been there when I was a journalist. Though it was nice enough with Dick, Carol L and her team, I didn't particularly enjoy going back. Nice to see Kim Howells [Welsh Labour MP] who was having a chat with two constituents. He said he and Paul Murphy [former Cabinet minister] had been talking at the weekend and said the best thing GB could do was get me back. But he said he fully understood why I might not fancy it. They gave Calum a merit award for his 'weeks of service and putting up with us' which was nice. Brief chat with Des Browne [Secretary of State for Scotland] who was very down about things. He said if I was talking to GB, tell him to get out and lead, get ahead of the government, don't just manage. I headed home via Philip's who was still suffering badly with nausea, and then to the Heath for football. I played badly again but had signed up to the second Soccer Aid so I just needed to get in as much practice as possible.

Tuesday 22 July

The Home Office security team were in sorting alarms and windows. I left for the University Women's Club and a day of filming interviews for the documentary. First Sally Brampton who had a pretty haunted look. She was a wonderful talker, really eloquent about herself, about her depression and the way drink got to her. She was crying when she talked of the moment she first told her husband that she wanted to die. Really bad depression and though she said she was having better days I did not sense that in her eyes and her face. She was very powerful on suicide, and how she totally understood why people did it, and how she faced a constant struggle not to. Then Gerry Cottle [circus proprietor] who had come up from Somerset. Sex and cocaine addiction. He said his addiction now was the circus. He was very funny and lively and had a mischievous look whenever he talked about his time with 'bad girls' as he called them.

He was not convinced he had been a sex addict but he was hooked on cocaine the first time one of his bad girls gave it to him. It was the combination of sex and drugs he then went for the whole time. Rehab failed. Eventually it was when he realised he was letting down the whole family, not just his long-suffering wife, that he knew he had to change. He had left his grandkids at Glastonbury and was off with a hooker and saw the mud on TV and decided to go and get them. He said he had been clean ever since. I went home to work for a bit, a run, then to Bostock's, where we were going to interview him for the film. We had a chat beforehand and he seemed OK, if edgy. But once the cameras started rolling he came out with all sorts of weird and wonderful stuff – Freudian analysis re me, saying my problems came from Dad being of one culture, Mum another, much more strait-laced, also that a part of me probably liked the Scotland breakdown episode because in an odd way it took me closer to where I wanted to go – centre stage in Labour campaigns, and in Scotland.

He said I was a walking one-man Greek tragedy. It was a bit of a nightmare. Then he went off on one about how awful it must have been to run to No. 10 and lose my guts, a reference to the time I first got hit by colitis. Several times I said 'cut' and the film crew were loving it but even though he was good on the Glasgow episode, and how he helped me afterwards, it was all a bit odd. He then went off on a rant about Iraq, and said I had been hallucinating re WMD. And then off on another one about the health reforms. Judith was a bit taken aback by the whole thing. I had been going on about how great he had been for me, and he spent most of the time going for me.

Wednesday 23 July

I was having breakfast with Nick Keller at Kalendar when GB called and left a message which I listened to, and Nick overheard. 'How he sounds is how the country feels,' said Nick. It was true that the gloom was in every syllable. He was so downbeat the whole time. I really did not want to get more involved but it was so hard just to tell him to get lost. Nick was asking me to see Martin Sorrell and get him involved in Beyond Sport. He felt re GB 'Just don't even think about it. I know so many people who will not vote Labour because of him.' I was avoiding calling back but when I was out on the bike he called again and I agreed to go in at 4.15. Mark Lucas came round to look at stuff for the sports website. He felt GB still had it, that he had seen him with people and he was better than his image. But he said dealing with No. 10 was a bit of a nightmare all the time. There was no clarity of structure for decisions or general direction.

Off to Wapping for lunch with Rebekah Wade. Bostock had said yesterday that it had always been obvious to him that being a hack journalist was never going to be enough for my talent or ambition and I felt something of that going back to Wapping. I never much liked the feel of the place and didn't like it now. Rebekah was perfectly nice but it was all different to when I used to speak to her most days. She had been at a board meeting and said as ever she was arguing for more money for *The Sun*. Needless to say we pretty quickly got onto GB–TB–CB etc. She had had a one-on-one lunch with Cherie. 'She was almost civil.' She said my name came up when she told CB Tony was thinking of not serialising his book. 'He's been talking to Alastair again. I will get him to change his mind,' she said. She said she felt Cherie always resented the time Rebekah spent with TB on her own.

On the general scene, she felt GB had made a lot of mistakes. Murdoch liked him personally for the same reasons Dacre did – he worked hard, had morals and convictions. But he was also a bit disappointed. She told me GB had asked RM what he thought he should do to deal with all the negativity and Murdoch had apparently said 'Get Alastair Campbell back at your side.' So he was to blame! She said apparently Bush said the same thing. 'If you have Bush and Murdoch pushing him to get you, hardly surprising he is.' I said kindly tell Rupert to leave me alone. I went through my dilemma with her. She felt it would be good for him and the government, terrible for me. It was nice to see her again and I felt perfectly comfortable putting arguments for us and against the Tories, but no enthusiasm for being back in that world. I had too much going for me in different ways.

It was a blistering hot day. I took a cab towards Whitehall, and got out and walked the last bit and tried to work out what to do with this meeting. Philip was clear – he said I was not doing what I normally did which was to analyse objective and strategy before doing tactics. I was being sucked in against my will. I had to think hard on strategy. If I did I would probably reach the view that he could not win and what I should be doing in those circumstances is help whoever I thought would be better placed. David M was calling from time to time – yesterday for example – and I could not quite read what he was up to, whether he was just trying to find out my take on GB or, as yesterday, to ask for specific help, this time on an article about the Tories. I was met by Karen the duty clerk and taken to wait for GB in the Cabinet Room. I was on the phone to Greg, asking what the state of play was re him but as he rang GB came in. He said let's go out in the garden.

Some Welsh Guardsmen were setting up to play at the staff barbecue. I said I used to do the entertainment for that. 'Bagpipes?' said one of them. We sat in the sunshine. He said he had just seen Gerry Adams [Sinn Féin leader] and Martin McGuinness who were in pressing for him to be harder on the [Ulster] Unionists. The specific issue was fairly arcane but he said they had a point. He said the Tories were about to do a deal for closer ties with the Ulster Unionists even though they only had one MP – Sylvia Hermon – left. He had very quickly got into the TB mode of seeing both sides as being unreasonable. He felt Adams was in his way more statesmanlike. But he felt McGuinness was more interested in making it happen.

We then had a chat about his visit to Iraq. He felt there was real progress there. He said he felt on all the big policy areas he had the right answers – he felt he was the only world leader with a plan to do something to bring down the oil price. He felt on nuclear, housing, first-time buyers, family–work balance, he had the answers. He felt neither the Tories nor any of the young guns – 'They're immature in their response to what's happening. They see me in a bit of trouble and just think of their own position' – had a different solution or a better policy proposal. But he said he had to acknowledge that he was not communicating well and nor was the government as a whole. He felt that if he was doing the policy and I was doing the communication, we could get back on track.

I said what do you analyse as the main comms problem? He said he could not get a big message through. The media were not interested in policy and were determined to keep kicking him till he went. 'But could anyone else do better?' he asked. 'I don't think so.' I said, as I had many times before, there had to be defence of the record, better co-ordination and use of ministers so it did not all fall on him, proper attack and rebuttal, and the development of the forward agenda. Without it they had had it. He was still very blamey. I said at one point I thought Alistair D had done quite well considering and he just raised his eyebrows. He no longer bothered trying to persuade me that Balls was as good as he used to try to tell me. He said he had two specific proposals. He knew my reservations but he really needed me to say yes. One – come back for September to December and oversee a strategic plan to rebuild. Two – go into the House of Lords as Minister for Sport and the Olympics, or any other area I was particularly interested in, but on the understanding I would be there to help with comms and strategy.

He said they had nobody of my ability and experience and I am humble enough to admit I need your help. I avoided giving a direct reply. I said I would need to think and discuss with the family. He pressed me pretty hard, said this was about saving the Labour Party, that whatever had happened in the past was the past and now we had to work together to try to rescue the party and stop the Tories. He really felt we could win but it would require him to have the best people available to him. Sue came to wind up as he was running fifteen minutes late. He said he had to see Prince Charles and then the Queen. He did a fairly passable imitation of Charles asking if we couldn't work better with the Tories to do something for the good of the country. 'Does he want to be head of a government of national unity?' I asked. 'I don't know.' He had another go at asking me to 'really think'. PG was adamant. 'Don't get involved. You'll go crazy.'

Thursday 24 July

I went for a run along the canal, then ran to see PG who was looking weaker. He said he had sorted out his nausea. I noticed him wincing when he swallowed a pill. I suspected it was dawning on him that he would never really be the same again. He was even stronger than yesterday re GB. He said he was destroying the party. Andrew Cooper had polled eight groups recently and said there was real contempt for him. PG said some said they were almost becoming ashamed of Britain because he was Prime Minister. That felt over the top to me, but PG said he was not going to win and he could not recover. That was all there was to it. I should be thinking of how to help the party, not just him. There was a danger I would be used to help keep him afloat, but at even greater cost to the party. I said it is very hard just to tell him I won't help. 'He is a Labour PM directly asking me, pleading, and I can't just tell him to fuck off.' 'Just don't get sucked in any further,' he said. 'He knows you have a big loyal streak and he is playing you.'

I went home to collect Calum, then set off for Mum's. I called TB en route. I filled him in on the state of play. He said he understood how difficult it was for me. Calum was listening intently as the call was on loudspeaker and I noticed him nodding a fair bit. TB's basic view was that what GB was doing was asking me to do things that only he as PM could do. 'However you dress it up, he is hoping you can help him find direction. But that can only come from him. The operation may be useless inside No. 10 and it may be there is no clear strategy but that has to come from him. He has always believed you and Peter did everything. It's his way of thinking he was better than I am. Of course you were important to me, but you were important as someone who helped me deliver on what it was I was trying to do. You cannot get direction from advisors. You have to provide the direction and they have to help you steer. What is blindingly obvious is that he does not have the clear direction.'

He said he sympathised because he felt the same as I did, that we had to help if we could. But he felt I had to be careful not to get 'besmirched' by the whole thing, or for people to think I am doing it for the wrong motives. He felt there might be a way of helping steer events to a proper conclusion – he said he was talking on a mobile and did not want to go into detail. I knew what he meant. That we help engineer a situation where GB can be replaced in some way. But neither of us felt in our hearts he would walk away. Yet TB saw maybe a hint of that. He also felt the others, come September, would realise that something had to give. And then something would give. He felt David M was thinking about it. I said I felt he was thinking about thinking about it. I told him about the Lords offer. He said if I wanted to go in the Lords, there was nothing wrong with that, but even if GB wanted you to do the Olympics, we know he is just trying to get you in to do the campaign. The offer was a ploy to get me in.

Once he got me in he would use me for election planning, strategy development, everything, and I would be totally hitched to his falling star. He felt I should play for time, not commit until it was clear whether anything was going to give. He said GB knew I found it hard not to help. He would also be taking it personally that I was not enthusing to do it as I had with him. I said 'enthusing overstates'. I suspect GB had asked him to have a go at me. I sensed he was giving genuine advice though. He said if I went in, the party would breathe a sigh of relief because they would see a grown-up had gone in there. The Tories and the media would have a field day and would build me up even more. But the worst thing about it is that people would conclude he had given up, that even he felt he could not do the job. It was evidence of how bad things had got that he really seemed to think I could turn it around for him.

We chatted for maybe half an hour and TB concluded by saying 'You must do what you think is right and only you can decide. But I think the costs are high and the benefits low. For the party the benefits are higher, but not if there is another plan that comes along and you are part of the plan that just keeps him going a little longer. You have to think of your own position in all this.' I had told him Alex's earlier view, that I was seen as a winner and I should not put that reputation at risk. He said he was absolutely right. Listen to him. But then by the time I got to Wheatley and was out on a long bike ride in the sun, Alex called from his South Africa tour. I filled him in on where things were. He said he had changed his mind a bit. 'I don't know why but I have a wee instinct you should do it.' I was a little taken aback. I think if he, TB and PG were all saying no, I would go to GB fairly soon and say this far and no further. He said things were desperate and as things stood we were going to lose.

He said if he was managing a game and he was losing it and time was running out, he would throw the goalkeeper up to play alongside the striker. You take risks. He is asking you to charge up and take the risks. He said he obviously didn't rate his own people and he needed you there and maybe he was right that you could turn it around. He said he had been thinking about it and I certainly shouldn't dismiss it. I said in a way it was the last thing I wanted to hear. I didn't believe GB would make all the changes I felt he should. I was not entering my own strategic space. It was like you retiring and then in a couple of years being asked to take on the club after someone else had made a bit of a mess of it. But you had to keep the same staff and players. I see that, he said. But maybe the Lords is the other option and you build from that a new departure whatever happens.

He felt the three factors that I should allow to hold me back were 1) Fiona – if it was going to lead to difficulty there, best avoid it. 2) TB – make sure he is happy with it because even though times have moved on that is an important partnership, and 3) – what else do you have to give up?

Weigh it up and see where it ends. I asked him to mull a bit more. He said he would. He was enjoying the tour. He was still chasing [Dimitar] Berbatov [Tottenham Hotspur] and still trying to hold Ronaldo. His last words were 'Don't forget that even though it was a nightmare from time to time, the best thing you ever did was the job with Tony and you were good at it. It may be different with Gordon but you'll still be good at it and you might enjoy it.' Fiona meanwhile was saying it has to be up to me but she could see no way he could win.

Friday 25 July

Woke up to the news that we had lost Glasgow East by-election (Scottish National Party gain from Labour with a majority of 365). And that was with a good candidate [Margaret Curran]. I went out on the bike to see Robert [Templeton, sick relative] at East Stockwith. I stopped off at a Costa Coffee in the new shopping centre at Gainsborough. All very new and shiny and feeding the country's shopaholicism but all around I sensed political movement. It was an instinct thing as much as anything. But it was strong. I chatted to Mum for a while, tried to allay her worries about the breakdown film but she was clearly not keen at all. In truth Bostock may have been right in the tension theory, between Dad's side as risk takers and Mum very cautious. Needless to say she was totally opposed to me going back in.

I drove back with Calum. GB called a couple of times and I ended by saying I had not had time really to talk to Fiona. I would get back to him. 'Is there anything else you need by way of information?' he asked. I said no. He said it was typical of his luck at the moment that we lost by just over 300 votes. He was convinced it was economic, said again that he did not think anyone else could do better. Dinner with Neil and Glenys at La Casalinga. They were full of stories from Rachel of how dysfunctional and demoralising Downing St was. They both felt I had to steer clear. Neil felt I should try to persuade GB that it would make me such a big story that it would become damaging and weakening for him. I said I had tried that. I said I may just say the family won't let me. He said that will only put him off for ten minutes. I said he is not going to win. They agreed yet did not think any of the others could do better.

It was a nice evening, and I was glad both felt I should resist though I still wished I could find a way of rejecting the offer without it being undermining of GB. I watched *Newsnight* for the first time in a while. Appalled how they were using anonymous ministerial quotes from tomorrow's *Telegraph* re plots v GB. The whole set-up was dire for Gordon though Ed Miliband did an OK job pushing back.

Saturday 26 July to Sunday 3 August

Out early and drove to the airport. Avoided the papers, pretty wall-to-wall grimmery. TB called. He had had a long chat with GB yesterday. He had told him to focus on overall direction, get a strong message and drive it through. And the only way to deal with the media now was to ignore it. The idea that another phone call to any of these people would change anything was absurd. He just had to get tougher and drive on. But TB said the logic of the position was obvious and what was required was to wait and see if anyone had the courage to do anything. He said he was doing nothing to bring it about and he would help with any advice he could, but he worried the country had simply decided. They didn't much care if Cameron was not up to much. They just did not want GB.

He had persuaded himself it was all economic. But in a way he and his people were reaping what they had sewed. People were not daft. They sensed someone's character and they had got him. So it would not make that much difference whether you, me, Peter and Bill Clinton were advising him – he does not have the wherewithal to make it work. He said David was calling him a fair bit and he thought he might be up for something but what had to happen was that people thought hard between now and September. It may be nobody can win but the difference could be between defeat and wipeout. As to how the party would react afterwards, heaven knows. On my situation he said if I were you I would not get drawn in further for the time being. You must not become part of the denouement and there is a risk that would happen, that you go in at a time when it is beyond repair and you get besmirched as well. So buy time, don't commit and see where we are come September.

We had arranged to visit Suzanne and Doug [Khan, friends] out in Maine from Saturday to Thursday and in between times she had been diagnosed with breast cancer so it changed the trip a little. But they were fabulous hosts and we had a great few days. Lots of swimming, running, eating. I mainly read and slept. Absolute charmer of a man on the immigration desk at Boston, called John, so unlike the New York lot. Big fan of TB and of Obama. I gave him a signed book. Brilliantly organised, consumer-focused car hire. En route we bumped into Helena Kennedy and kids. Small world. Huge great car and great to drive. The nearest town to Doug and Suzanne's – Camden – and the Lord Camden Inn, were perfect settings for some of the Novel 2 scenes I had sketched. The house was down a windy track and situated superbly on a lake, with our guesthouse thirty or so yards away. Doug had his own plane, seaplane, speedboat, fishing boat, pedalo, the lot. We went water skiing every day, Grace a total natch, me a complete dolt. Calum and I went fishing. He caught one which got away. I got nothing.

Out for a couple of nice dinners, lobster at home after visit to lobster farm and a real caricature of a cold country fisherman with white beard etc. Very like UK in parts but hotter in summer and the whole place frozen over in winter. We had no mobile access the whole time we were there, which was nicer than I expected it to be, and no BlackBerry either, so just occasional access via laptop. The big thing kicking off at home was David M writing an article in *The Guardian* which unleashed a great hoo-ha about a leadership challenge. This was clearly what TB had been referring to earlier when he said he was not so sure, after I said I doubted David would ever go the whole way. His piece was all about the need for greater focus, attack, defence and clarity about the future, plus humility and as it barely glanced at the existence of GB it was seen as pretty full frontal. Then he had a press conference with the Italian Foreign Minister so got another day's run at it and it rolled on as a new thing for the soap operatics to chew on.

When finally we got back into mobile territory, it was amazing how many messages pinged through, and how few required a response now. The first person to call was GB. I had sent him a message to Southwold via Sue Nye that we were out of contact and I had been glad to be free of the repetitive and depressing calls. I had thought a lot more about his various efforts and offers to get back and it held little attraction. The only thing that had unsettled me in a fairly firm conviction that I would not do it was Alex's change of view, from total opposition – thinking purely of my interests – to pretty solid support – in the interests of the party. GB called on the Thursday afternoon as we were driving towards Boston. I got Fiona to answer and they did a bit of small talk and she said I was driving and would call back. By the time we reached Boston, via Harvard, then a shopping mall where Fiona, Grace and Sissy were consumering with the help of the low dollar, I couldn't face it.

Calum and I went to a café. GB called again. We did lots of small talk about the States and respective places and I was just avoiding the subject really. Re DM, he said he had just been immature and been trapped into fuelling the story the media wanted. He did not think it had been as thought through and deliberate as people were saying. Thought through? Maybe not. But my sense was it was pretty deliberate. Carol Linforth sent me a message that Derek Draper, who had started working for GB, had been saying the DM piece had my fingerprints all over it. PG – still nauseous and now also with bad colitis – viewed the Draper appointment as a step beyond the pale. GB went off on his mantra – how it was all about the economy, food and fuel prices, people feeling under pressure, and he got it and he was sure he had the right policies for the future, but he could not communicate them.

He asked direct if I had given further thought to his proposals. I said I had, and it was difficult. I had been clear I did not want to go back to doing anything like the old job. Of course I wanted to stop the Tories but it was hard to imagine how I could be effective without going back in a very upfront high-profile way. I also said that the family – and not just Fiona – were against it as they feared it would be back to square one. He said we had to find a way of doing it so that did not happen. I said I couldn't see how that was possible. The minute I did it, it was big news and the Tories and the media would have a field day. He said he wasn't bothered, all he cared about was getting an effective operation. I said there was another problem – I did not build his team, did not know some of them, did not rate others. I felt the dithering and fannying around over Greg was a bad sign.

He said if I did it I could have freedom. I said I was not sure the oppositions were surmountable. I would be happier to keep things informal as now. He then tried the guilt trip. He said well we have to stop the Tories and I need you to do that. I need a controlling genius mind to do the big themes and help me communicate. I said it was not the same as before. I had never hidden from him that I did not want to go back as before. That was what he was asking me to do. He sounded down, and pretty desperate. He must have asked half a dozen times in different ways. Calum had been listening to my side of the call and said he felt sorry for him. He said you told him everything apart from the key thing – 'that you really don't want to do it'. I was conscious of the need not to plunge him even lower by being so upfront about that.

I really did not want to do that, but Calum was right. Deep down it was me holding myself back. Fiona had said she thought the whole scene was dreadful and she thought I should stay out of it. I ended the call by saying I had to leave and we left it that I would call him when I got back to London. But the whole prospect really depressed me. I just felt it had gone beyond. Meanwhile DC was continuing to get away with murder. No pressure on policy. Endless wanking off in *The Guardian* and *Observer* about how it was OK to be posh because he looked like something out of a Boden catalogue in his holiday photocall. This guy was sleepwalking to PM without the slightest pressure from us.

The Miliband piece had flared divisions a bit more and then on the Saturday the *Mail on Sunday* alerted Matthew Doyle to the fact they had the memo TB sent to me, Peter M, Sally, PG, probably JoP and maybe Anji and others re GB last year post the on/off election. Someone had clearly been sitting on it ready to push it out. Matthew called Sunday from Beijing to say that they were battening down the hatches but Sue Nye had called him to ask him to ask me to put out a statement to the effect that the note did not reflect his views. Given he wrote it, and I received it, that seemed a bit tricky. It was also indicative of how they tend to respond to these things. I could not see what a statement from me was likely to do.

Mum had an interesting take though – felt there was sympathy for GB and Miliband had overstretched and damaged party and self.

Greg finally decided – after thirteen fucking weeks of fannying around, or more accurately being fannied around – that he could not do the job as envisaged. He would help out unpaid from time to time and see where we got to. GB had asked him to go out to Southwold [Suffolk holiday] and see him but by now he had had enough. Long call from Gazza. Sober. Sounded better. He wanted me to help him make contact with a lawyer again. Determined to sue the people who had been ripping him off. Saying I was 'different class' and how it always helped him to think he knew me and would help him. Often incoherent but better than before. He said he was going to see Sir Bobby [Charlton] and AF in coming days.

Monday 4 August

Up at 6 to see off Fiona, Calum, Grace and Molly, who were driving down to France. Off for a longish run. Bit of work then a long interview with Peter Wilson for *The Australian* magazine. Usual stuff but at least he had done proper research. Long chat with Alex. He felt for me, going back was all downside, though he was not convinced the media would really go for me as before. He said they liked having me there. It was like Beckham. They wanted him to stay around. You left and if you went back they would want you to stay. Also, he felt there was nobody else who could go in and sort things out. When I explained though some of the 'team downsides' he saw it was not so simple. He said only do it if you really think you can make a difference. The truth is GB's personality is a problem and it means building up the others. He felt Miliband had something about him but he was in danger of looking disloyal. He thought there was a danger we were heading for meltdown. Alex said it would not be nearly as much fun as with Tony, and it may be he just cannot be turned around but he did not know of anyone else who would be able to do it and he felt if I thought I could do it I should go for it. Chat re Chris Eagles, who we [Burnley] had signed from United. We got a very good deal – 400k down, 200k for forty games, 300k if we go up, 20 per cent of any sell-on deal. JP called as I was heading to Southampton, to go sailing with one of the top teams, which had been fixed for me by Nick Keller. I was getting a decent fee for it. JP was with Dick. Would I write a statement for the group we were putting together to take a lead in making the case for a fourth term under GB? Go Fourth. Something very basic. Get a grouping together for conference. He said he had seen GB and told him there had to be change and he wanted to be part of it.

Also that he had called David Miliband and asked him what he was up to. He might well be future leader but this was damaging the party. He said the fourth term group could appeal to everyone who wanted Labour not Tory. Needed a short statement. Down to Southampton. Stacks of sailing stuff in the room. Four bags full. I walked to the Red Funnel [ferry terminal] with Georgie Thompson [presenter] of Sky Sports News and James Haskell [England rugby international] and family, Georgie just as cute as on screen but absolutely tiny. Haskell very rugby player and quite a character. The water was a bit choppy going to the Isle of Wight. I could not believe the crowds of people around the streets. Very boozy rugby-type atmosphere. Dinner at the house rented by the Artemis [investment management firm, sponsors] people. Nice enough bunch. Getting a few tips off Simon Clay [yachting manager], my skipper, and [Sir] Robin Knox-Johnston [record-breaking sailor]. Nice enough food and chat. Boat back then fitful sleep.

Tuesday 5 August

Up at 6, breakfast, then off to the Red Funnel again. Wet and windy. Bit of hanging around the other end, meet the other teams, get introduced then off with Simon and media by rib [rigid inflatable boat] to the boat, meet up with the crew, and off we went. Enjoyed it a lot more than I thought I would despite some pretty vile weather. Mainly on the grinder [winch] which was a pretty good workout. Definitely moving to a piece re debunking old prejudices about the sport as a whole. Fairly busy most of the time. There was a half an hour quiet period after we went round the Needles. Salt water taste all the time by the end. Impressed by the team and technology. Bit wobbly at the end. Hung round for a while, interviews and presentations. Nice mood. Great way to start a holiday. Lift to Gatwick with Georgie talking about all her plans for Superchick, her new women's fitness and lifestyle venture. She did a broadcasting degree at Leeds and did her dissertation on the 1997 campaign. She promised to dig it out. I stayed over at the Sofitel at Gatwick, absolutely knackered but having surprised myself by how much I had enjoyed it.

Wednesday 6 August

Up at 4.20 and through to North Terminal. Could not believe how busy it was for that time of morning, and how much shopping was going on. On the 6.05 flight to Marseille, met by car and at Puymeras long before lunch. All pretty relaxing and stayed in all day. Finished the *Sunday Times* piece on the sailing. Out on my bike but it did not really fit the length of my body. Rory's perfect. Did an interview with the *FT* for their Saturday charity column.

Thursday 7 August

Off early to Cavaillon to change the bike. I was getting into a rhythm of bike early, swims, bit of football. TB was in Malaysia having been in Beijing pre the Games. Greg Nugent and his girlfriend Karan up for the day. Nice enough time and she was really lovely. Greg going through in detail the whole GB madness of recent days. He said at one point he called him seventeen times in two days. He was convinced it was all about getting me more involved, not about him. But he felt it was extraordinary that he was asked thirteen weeks ago by GB himself to do a job and it still had not been fixed.

He was now going to go in from time to time, hopefully morning and evening. I felt he was setting himself up for worst of all worlds, but he was keen to get involved at some point in some way, despite his witnessing of the dysfunctional nature of the operation. Karan said she was keen at first but had gone right off it. She ended up thinking GB must be really hopeless if he could not even sort this out. Greg was clear that I would be mad to go back. GB had not called for a few days, and I wondered if he thought I had been involved in the Miliband move. I was pleased not to be getting his calls though every time I picked up a paper and saw the easy ride DC was getting it made my blood boil.

Friday 8 August

The Beijing opening ceremony [Olympic Games] was superb and getting rave reviews. Tessa called a couple of times to say I should be there, and I had to get involved in the London Games. She said it was typical that GB could not see why he should have been there. Bush was having a great time. Ditto Sarko though not staying for long.

Saturday 9 August

Seb's dad died. How sad is that timing, just as the Games begin? They had their ups and downs but it must be one of the most remarkable father–son relationships in sporting history. Dropped him a line before we went out to Nyons for dinner.

Sunday 10 August

Long bike ride, 42k. Loads of hills. Eased off brakes. Big flare-up with Fiona when she had another go about people thinking that nagging negative wife in Novel 1 would be based on her. I said it wasn't so that was that. Off to football with the boys. David Miliband called. First time in a while. He asked whether I was still advising GB. I said less, because he kept trying to tempt me back with different suggestions and I had little appetite. I asked whether his move had been a move, or over interpreted. He said both. It went bigger than he thought but he did think someone had to challenge the dire fatalism there was around at the moment. He was making clear that there was an agenda to be pursued but it took more than was on offer at the moment. He said he felt that if GB stayed in charge, there was a danger of wipeout. It may be that we have had it anyway but I think there has to be change. He asked me what I thought would happen. When I said conference was key, he was clear that something may give before conference. He felt it could not go on much longer like this.

He said it was important I was not in a position where everyone was asking me for advice. I said I felt the only scenario that would not be damaging was one where GB went voluntarily. Do you see any sign of that, he asked? None, I said. He puts his political problems down to the world economy and he puts what you and others are doing down to immaturity. I said I was not even sure he would go if half the Cabinet demanded it. He would promote his second-rate supporters even more. DM said Straw was pivotal. If GB buys him off in some way – maybe Deputy PM, back to FCO – he is pivotal. He has engineered himself very well into a totally pivotal position. Of his own position, he had no real idea of support. He felt he had had to show he could put himself out there and show a bit of guts. The reaction of the GB people had been typical and pathetic. He was speaking as an opponent, no doubt about that. But I still didn't feel he had a clear idea where he was heading. I said he had to go for the Tories more, make clear this was not about personal ambition. Ended fine, but there was definitely a little bit of distance developed there considering he used to be here on holiday. Great show in the *Sunday Times*, paper and online, for the sailing piece.

Monday 11 August to Wednesday 13 August

Holiday settling into good routine. Football when Calum was doing his tennis. Stepping up the bike training. Mainly eating in. Watching loads of the Olympics and a few DVDs and working on next draft of Novel 2 whilst trying to read a few too. The phone stayed fairly quiet. I kept in touch with PG most days who had had another blast of chemo and said it was 'hit by ten trucks time'. But he still sounded chirpy and strong. Very little contact with TB. A bit of traffic re whether he should co-operate with the Hugo Young book, and also on whether I should go to the Ryder Cup in Louisville (Kevin Baker [businessman] had invited me along as guest of one of the sponsors). He and Alex both felt I would take a bit of a hit if I went to the States when GB thought I was going to be helping him. The

Greg situation limped along. As he said, it was gold, silver and bronze in the non-gripping event. GB doing really well in Beijing – two surprise golds for Rebecca Aldington in the swimming, good in rowing and sailing and utter domination in cycling. Christine Ohuruogu awesome in the 400 final. Brendan sent a couple of messages saying I should be there.

GB was not getting into the spirit. Whenever I spoke to him, he sounded so down and defeatist. There was an ad running the whole time on Eurosport for Qatar sporting academy – aspire today, inspire tomorrow. He did neither. He sent me a draft of his conference speech in the second week of the holiday. It was OK without being great. It had some good passages, one or two terrific. It had lots of work to do on it, and some bits that didn't work. It lacked an overall argument but I could see it was work in progress. I did a long note suggesting where I thought it worked and where not, and also saying one or two bigger points – need for a 'My argument is' single page, also the need to defend record better and need to identify Tories in interesting way. He called back the same day, seemed to get most of it but was so defensive and, again, saying his real problem was lack of communications strategy. It was hard not to draw the comparison with these athletes who were so going for it because they believed in themselves. If I had to listen once more to him setting out what he saw as the policy analysis, e.g. for the world economy, or for welfare or housing, and then bleat 'but I cannot communicate this' (unspoken 'but I would be able to if you came back') I would scream.

He did not have the skill set for this, to lift himself and others. One day out in Vaison, I heard a British family discussing him a few tables away and the mum said: 'He just makes me feel depressed.' When I discussed things with Philippe Senes at the village fete in Puymeras, he said 'The guy is a loser.' So I continued to be torn – wanting to help but enjoying the greater freedom I have. Keen for him not to implode but not wanting to devote too much time and energy to it. Thinking I could make a difference but also fearful the country had just decided it was time for a change and he was not a Prime Minister. So Cameron continued to get away with murder. 'Cameron on Cameron', a book of interviews with Dylan Jones of *GQ*, was the latest piece of flimflam getting uncritical coverage. The Tories were also doing better at capitalising on the Olympics – [Boris] Johnson out saying there would be a victory parade, [Lord] Colin Moynihan [former Minister for Sport] saying GB had to make good the pledge for more investment in sport.

Thursday 14 August

Did Mont Ventoux with Rory. We did the Bedoin route this time. Rory on form, beat me by way over an hour. Really tough but made it. Perfect conditions at the top. Thigh pain and horrible sweat rash. Called Roger the ex-Tour de France masseur who lived locally. He said it was noticeable I had put on too much weight.

Friday 15 August

GB asked if I could get Alex to come to conference, maybe with me interviewing on stage. I texted Alex about it and his initial reaction was lukewarm. Fiona and Calum both thought it was asking too much of Alex, also that it was just another little way of drawing me in. The speech was not that bad, but it was obvious he was not that much fresher coming back from his holiday. And every time I spoke to him, he sounded more miserable – weather, press, whatever, world economy. At the weekend I did and watched loads of sport. Another disaster day for Burnley, having lost 4–1 at Sheffield Wednesday last week, now a 3–0 defeat at home to Ipswich and a Red Devil parachutist landed on the roof of the Cricket Field stand [one of six display parachutists delaying kick-off]. Text from Alex worried that we were not getting the credit due re the Olympics. Instead it was coming over as all being down to Major's lottery, Boris for London, Moynihan for the BOA. Coe. Brits third in the medal table after China and the US, which was incredible really, given where we came from. Cycling doing really well.

Tuesday 19 August

Olympics really picking up. [Cyclists] Chris Hoy won a third gold today, Victoria Pendleton gold. Good shots of TB and family at the Velodrome. GB called during the 1,500m final. He asked how the weather was. I said fine. He said 'It's pissing with rain here.' Brief chat about the speech. Another whinge about not being able to communicate. Asked about Alex. I said he was not keen because of fixtures. 'The fact is it's in Manchester though, so it ought to be easy for him. Would it help if I spoke to him?' I doubted it. There was something just wrong about the whole thing. Tories getting away with murder, but we were not fighting hard enough. There was no message about anything. The idea of the Tories getting back was grim, but the sense was, according to the groups, that it was more or less over. Yet what was DC about? PG said people had decided he was probably up to it, and GB almost certainly was not. They didn't like GB. They found him odd. They were not willing to give him the benefit of the doubt any more.

Wednesday 20 August

Tessa called from Beijing. She said it had been hard for the first few days. TB was the political leader everyone wanted to be with. At one point she had had a visit from the Games' organisers putting on pressure because she had said something critical about an arrest that had been made. She had then felt a bit of buggeration, like being made to be late for a couple of events. The UK were doing really well, and there was a great mood about the whole thing, but the sense of power shifting was revealed in the extent to which the media did not want to put any credit the government's way. There seemed to be as much focus on Major for launching the National Lottery as on the fact we had directed so much more money e.g. to cycling, sailing, rowing governing bodies, the ones who were delivering loads of medals. And when TB was at the track finals for Pendleton's gold and Hoy's third, when the cameras cut to him the Eurosport guy said 'and let's not forget John Major'. Colin Moynihan was of course out greasing all over the place, Boris throwing his weight around at the closing ceremony, while Tessa said Seb was just sad at his dad's death. He was also looking to his own future within IAAF [International Association of Athletics Federations] and the IOC.

Tessa sounded pretty depressed. She said she had given seven years of her life to this and to watch it all being handed on a plate to the fucking Tories was more than she could bear. They had not changed at all. You could see that in the Tory boys round Johnson, she said. But what was unforgiveable was that GB had been most responsible for giving it away. One evening in the week before we came home we went for dinner at the Senes and I texted Peter M. After chatting a bit re Propiac, where he had once come with us on holiday when the boys were small, he said George Osborne was at the next table in the taverna in Corfu. I said tell him sometimes things go to those who don't deserve it. He did so and Osborne said simply 'GB.' Nice evening, friends of the Senes, from just outside Paris, real anglophiles. The guy said he thought TB spoke superb French so we joshed around on that. Also that 'George Brown' – he meant Gordon – has so much less charisma than TB.

David Muir was sending me drafts of the GB conference speech and I was feeding back thoughts. It was OK. GB called a couple of times and went over all the arguments again. I was feeling even worse at not helping more, but also more convinced I did not want to be drawn further. In another of her calls, Tessa said when he was at Beijing, GB just lacked electricity. He did not fill the room. Most people managed to look OK in their Team GB gear. He didn't. And the worst thing was that to be part of the government now was to be seen as though you had leprosy. Meanwhile the Tories were just walking in and milking it, having done so little to deserve it.

On the closing day of the Games I cycled to Seguret to meet Fiona who was meeting the Blakes [family friends]. TB texted to say was I free to talk. I had been sending him the odd message saying how awful the scene was, topped by the fact Boris would be centre stage in Beijing for the handover of the Olympic flag. He said it is the price of losing. And he felt we were losing now not just because of the economy but because a totally flawed and confused strategy had been exposed. He said the failure to stand up for the record was criminal. Last week's schools and health results should have been the moment for a major injection of confidence. Instead of which we sat back and took all the negative arguments. Likewise we should have been over the Olympics like a rash. But because GB saw it as TB's thing, and he was more interested in trying to get a World Cup, we had failed there too. There was no fight for a message and there was no message. He felt he had one more shot but was probably fucked. Peter M felt the same, he had texted me last night.

TB said again he wanted me to get involved with him in China. On GB he felt I was right not to get drawn too far in. But I should continue to try to help. On the polls saying it would make no difference if GB went, he said bollocks. Cameron's one fear will be a change. Obama had picked Joe Biden as running mate which was seen as a pretty good choice. TB sounded on good form. He loved the Olympics though in common with Tessa and Nick Keller, he said it was all a bit soulless. London would be better. And the Tories would preside over it. Grim.

The kids had all gone back by the Monday so Fiona and I had a couple of very nice days together. I was starting to write Soccer Aid stuff. Also planning a trip to Australia, with loads more bids coming in. We drove back via Saint Preuve and came across a British military cemetery near our hotel. Beautifully kept and really moving just to walk through it. By the time we finally got back, we had had close on a month's holiday and it really had felt like a break. Apart from a bit of work on the book, GB's speech, final touches to the Brel article and radio programme, and a piece for *Sainsbury's Magazine*, work took second place for most of the time.

Thursday 28 August

Finally home. Fiona had had the builders in again to knock down the middle wall in the sitting room. It looked OK but there was a real male/female divide on this stuff. The boys could not much see the point. Fiona and Grace were waxing lyrical about it. I went to the BBC to record the trail for the Brel programme. Got a full CD for the first time. I just don't understand why Brits don't really go for Brel in the way others do. I spoke to Rebecca and we agreed to wait till end September before I give Novel 2 to her. Good news on the diaries front. It seemed the full Volume 1 was running at around 380k words, not 470 as we thought.

Friday 29 August

Work-wise getting back in slowly. Doing lots of stuff to promote Soccer Aid. Felt very chilled and relaxed post-holiday. Out for dinner with Tessa and Matthew at Strada. Tessa pretty much thinking we'd had it. She said it was noticeable with GB, for example on the flight home from China, how downbeat he seemed. He just lacked the something that leaders had to have. Also at the Games he did not command the space like others did. He felt they obsessed on real micro stuff, like Sarah not being happy that the fireworks at London House [England's Beijing shop window for 2012] went off after Boris not GB, or the way he was obsessing about getting Alex to the conference, something he had mentioned to me three or four times. Tessa was wanting me to compere a session at conference with the bike guys e.g. Hoy and Dave Brailsford [British team performance director]. She said people like [Dame] Kelly Holmes [former Olympic champion athlete] and Hoy, she was sure, were sympatico, but like everyone else they felt the wind was blowing. Also Moynihan was a little twerp using the whole thing politically, Johnson ditto, and Seb was bound to become more Tory as the thing neared. Despite Obama's acceptance of nomination speech, and John McCain appointing Sarah Palin [Governor of Alaska] as running mate, news was leading on a *Guardian* magazine interview with AD in which he allegedly said the economy was going into its worst phase for more than for sixty years.

Saturday 30 August

Off to *Soccer AM* at Sky HQ in Osterley. Good young crowd and it was interesting to watch a successful formula at work. There is always something a bit depressing about the whole factory feel to Sky, but the mood at the programme was good. Young people having a good time and generally up and optimistic about things. Max Rushden was the new presenter, along with Helen Chamberlain who had done it so often she was unbelievably relaxed about the whole thing. Mickey Thomas [former Manchester United player] and two musicians from Feeder [Welsh rock band] the other guests. Good mix. I'd had some 'Burnley twin town Trelleborgs' T-shirts printed [The Norwegian part-timers had famously beaten Blackburn Rovers in a European Cup match] and wore one on the way in, and threw one at the Rovers fans, who were guests for the day. Plenty of plugs for Soccer Aid. Flew along fairly well. I did a crap penalty when we went outside. But Soccer Aid were pleased enough.

Home and out on the bike with Rory. I spoke to Catherine McLeod [AD spad] who said she had had a pretty grim twenty-four hours. Decca Aitkenhead, who had done the interview for *The Guardian*, agreed Alistair had not said all the things they hyped in the front-page story. Yes, he had been downbeat and warned there were troubles ahead, but they had really gone OTT. Catherine said No. 10 had not engaged in trying to agree a strategy to handle the fallout. She got one sarcastic text from Mike Ellam [GB spokesman] asking if this was the headline ['Economy at 60-year low, says Darling. And it will get worse'] they had planned. And McBride sent out a text saying 'Darling disastrous interview in *Guardian*.' So they were expecting more briefing against him and more 'it would not have happened if Balls had been Chancellor'. No teamwork at all. She said she did not know how I did what I did for so long. One day of this kind of fire-fighting had left her exhausted and shredded. George and Robert [Mackie, her husband and son] loved the Trelleborgs joke.

Sunday 31 August

Another long bike ride and feeling fairly fit. Papers the usual mix of shite and trite. It was becoming a total given that Darling said things he didn't. Some good Brel previews in the radio guides, *ST* and *Observer* both positive with the usual snide bits. Another GB draft of his conference speech came through, and I did another note. David Muir also sent through a 33-page document for the commentariat. OK without being brilliant. Some of the papers were saying Carter was getting moved on. GB called a couple of times re conference and asked again whether I could get Alex to go there, and also whether I would do something with Brailsford and Hoy at the Velodrome. He sounded in reasonably good form but it must be a nightmare the way things keep piling up on him. PG's view (just back from Venice and said he felt not bad) was that GB's personality was dragging the government and the country down and he just had to go. *Mail on Sunday* half-page on TB, me, Nick Keller and how TB was trying to muscle in on London 2012. Nick was a bit worried about it but I persuaded him with help of Mike Lee and Ruth Turner it was not worth worrying about.

Monday 1 September

Going through Novel 2 again. Mix of tinkering and a few new good ideas. Thinking about whether to do a Francophone Brel programme. Maybe Belgian telly though apparently they were a nightmare to deal with.

Tuesday 2 September

Out early to do the Wright Stuff on Five. I had said yes thinking it was Steve [BBC radio presenter] not Matthew! Matthew a good guy too though, and smart. Tim Brabants [Olympic medallist] was also a guest. Really nice, very unassuming. Bright. I gave him a bit of advice re public speaking and put him in touch with all my speaking agencies. Did a demolition of the *Guardian* interview with Darling and the way it was spun by them and the rest of the media. Then a discussion on help for homeowners, the Olympics and date rape. Quite a good programme. Plenty of plugging of Soccer Aid. Home in pouring rain, trying to sort loads of tickets for Soccer Aid on Sunday. Then out to Motspur Park, Fulham's training ground. Refurbed changing rooms. Nice kit. Another set of gear. Out for a kickabout with Nicky Byrne [musician].

GB called while I was warming up. Would I do an interview with Dave Brailsford at conference? And would I speak to Alex again? I did speak to Alex, busy after sorting the Berbatov signing from Spurs, and he was not too keen. Manchester and football generally were buzzing with the Abu Dhabi lot buying Manchester City. Alex said he reckoned they had more money even than Abramovich, and they would finally be able to challenge. GB was doing the new housing package today and sounded chirpy.

Soccer Aid felt a bit downscale of last time, not quite the same mix of people, or the same excitement. Lots of the usual pretty TV girls wandering around. Car to the hotel to do a bit of work then later met up with most of the other players. Brian McFadden [Irish singer-songwriter] had put on a bit of weight. He still had unbelievable enthusiasm for the soccer thing, but said he had had to push his way in having been told they were going for new people. Kenny Dalglish [former Scottish international] was our manager, a lot friendlier and funnier than I expected. Making jokes about how I could train at dinner by sitting up straight 'like you do on the subs' bench'. Also telling the players if they needed a press release, ask me to help, and firing out a few headlines. Good mood.

Harry and Jamie Redknapp arrived. Harry was managing England, and probably regretting devoting a whole week to this as everyone absorbed the transfer market news. The Abu Dhabi group buying Man City had been like an electric shock through the game. There was a danger that all our big clubs were going to end up like this, toys of richer countries and individuals.

Bit of a chat about the media over dinner. Kenny definitely came from my side of the school on it, not fond, like a lot of old players and managers especially the ones who turned pundit from being player. Gilles Marini [actor] was so French. Women all over him and he over them. But I liked him. Also gave me his spare tickets so making progress on that front. Brian Lara [cricketer] unbelievably laid-back. He had played football to an OK level in Trinidad. Santiago Cabrera [Chilean-British actor] not bad. Of our pros, only Paulo Di Canio [Italy] was here yet. Luís Figo [Portugal] was coming though, and the England lot were pissed off as he is basically still a player. We had a bit of a kick about but the serious training starts tomorrow. I must admit that given how badly I played at Old Trafford two years ago, I was as surprised as I was thrilled to get the call up again. Into my fifties and still getting this kind of thing. I was definitely going to be the oldest there on the playing side.

Gordon Ramsay was our captain again, and as well as Lara and Nicky Bryne, we had Kenny Logan [rugby player] and actors. On the proper footballer front we had Peter Schmeichel [Denmark], Jaap Stam [Netherlands], Franco Baresi [Italy], Di Canio and, someone not far behind Pelé and Maradona in the legend stakes, Romário of Brazil. Kenny's assistant was Ian Rush [ex-Liverpool], Harry's assistant was Bryan Robson [former England international] and among the players were David Seaman, Alan Shearer, Teddy Sheringham, Les Ferdinand, Graeme Le Saux and Jamie Redknapp [all former England players]. On the celeb front a real varied bunch – Gareth Gates, Craig David [singer], Jamie Theakston [TV presenter] and Danny Jones of McFly among them.

I had a little chat with the Unicef guys who said the first Soccer Aid raised £2.6 million which was spent on specific projects to help Aids victims in South Africa, children without clean water in Nepal, young victims of malnutrition in Sierra Leone as well as supporting disabled children in Georgia and protecting street children in the Philippines.

Wednesday 3 September

All aboard the bus out to training. Dalglish constantly making jokes about me being on the bench. Got to the Fulham training ground and got kitted out. Bad news though. Peter Schmeichel was injured. Brazilian keeper Cláudio Taffarel is on his way. Paulo Di Canio led the warm-up and impressed with his stretches. Still really supple. Ex-Manchester United coach Eric Harrison took us through same basic ball drills and gave us a fabulous soundbite – 'If you're not in possession, think of position.' He was basically a Burnley fan, so lots of chat about past players and coaches. Then Kenny Dalglish oversaw a kind of five-a-side in which there were no goals and Di Canio played for both teams. Then we blasted a few balls at Patrick Kielty [comedian]. Eric said he was surprised at the quality of the non-footballer players. I reckon we have a better squad than last time. Cricketer Brian Lara played with Dwight Yorke [Sunderland] for Trinidad and Tobago boys up to the age of fourteen. [Gilles] Marini [*Sex and the City*] looks pretty sharp, though I wish he could stop being quite so French with all the TV women fawning over him. Total charmer. Westlife's Nicky Byrne had three years with Leeds United as a goalkeeper and looks pretty handy outfield too.

And actor Cabrera [*Heroes*] played semi-pro. So even before Figo gets off the plane, things were looking good and England were looking jumpy.

Mission no. 1 accomplished. Former Blackburnites Dalglish, Alan Shearer and Graeme Le Saux all unwittingly signed my T-shirt commemorating Burnley's twin town as Trelleborgs. I fear however my anti-Blackburn jibes might be jeopardising my chances with 'The Gaffer'. More jokes about me needing to warm up my bench-sitting skills. Boot fitting time. I felt a bit of a monster asking for size 12. Until I heard Gordon Ramsay asking if they had size 15! Funnily enough, they didn't. But they've been ordered. There was a bad story about Gazza in *The Sun*. He was in Portugal and there were 'eye witnesses' who said he was behaving really oddly, and one said they knew he was hallucinating because he said he was talking to me. But he was. He had taken to calling me in the middle of the night and clearly wished he was with us. But he was in a bad way.

We had dinner in the hotel, then to the bar with Brian, Nicky etc. Teddy Sheringham was telling me about his life playing poker – plays all the time, yes, it is addictive, he said, but he loves it. Frank Lampard Sr [former player] came down. Nice guy. Good chat with him. Shearer on what a joke Newcastle [his former club] were at the moment. Ant and Dec [TV entertainers] down earlier. Quickly into the same rhythm as last time – breakfast, dawdle, bus to training, hang around upstairs, warm up, train, in, shower, eat, sign stuff, blog on the bus, back to hotel. Also having a couple of hours' physio on neck and shoulders. The shoulder still really painful.

Thursday 4 September

Wet miserable day but a feeling things coming together more. No injuries. Good mood and morale. Training went well. Charles Clarke had a right old go at GB, saying he should turn it round in two months or go. I did *Newsnight*, and they promised not to film below waist – I was wearing jeans and trainers – but needless to say they did. Main message – defend record, do positive agenda, fight Tories harder.

Friday 5 September

Breakfast, bus, did Heart FM and LBC on the way. Finally made contact with Dave Brailsford and had a really good chat. Not over-political but happy to come to conference and do a Q&A with me, and talk over the way they worked. We had a presentation from the Unicef guys. One great fact in there – it would cost \$3.5 billion to give an education to every child without it, and the world spends \$25 billion on golf. Also two films on abandoned children in Georgia and street kids in the Philippines which were heard in total silence. Then training and though it was my best session yet, I reckon I would be lucky to get in the starting line-up this time. I dispossessed Di Canio at one point, also made a goal with a really sharp pass. Kenny D was away in Alicante for a wedding so Ian Rush and Eric were the main men. I reckoned I would get a half at most, at centre or full back. Slightly dreading it.

Romário had arrived and was amazingly skilful but didn't move much. He was also a bit up himself, not really getting into the spirit much. Taffarel a good guy. Still no sign of Stam, Baresi or Figo and the game was only a couple of days away. Their pros were going to be better organised and Shearer was looking really good. Our celebs probably nicked it. We practised penalties as it might end in a shoot-out. I volunteered to be one of the five. Kielty said let's be clear, if it is 4–4 our last penalty taker is AC! Lara pretty good. Major sleeper on the bus. I did a fair bit of telly and then bus back with Eric, Ian Rush and Brian. Grace, Nina and Ella came down at the hotel. Gilles Marini being charming to them and inviting them to the club everyone was going to later. Rory came down too, and I got a sign of how well plugged in to the poker scene he was when Teddy Sheringham welcomed him like a long-lost friend. 'I didn't know you were Rory Campbell's dad.'

Brian McFadden hilarious going off on a major rant about 'Bob the fucking Builder… He is nothing but a fucking plasticine cunt. May he rot in hell.' I asked Nicky Byrne for an explanation of Brian's rage, now almost a decade old. 'We [Westlife] had seven no. 1 hits in a row,' he said. 'We had several more after Bob the Builder. If it had not been for him we would have had twelve no. 1 hits consecutively, something nobody has ever done.' 'Get over it,' I suggested. 'Would you have got over it if you lost those elections with Tony fucking Blair?' At least Kenny Dalglish was starting to take the piss out of Brian as much as he did of me. 'Brian,' he shouted at one point, 'you are without doubt our best no-touch player.'

'At least I don't need stabilisers on my boots,' said Brian. Fair to say Kenny moves around a little less quickly and less elegantly than he used to. I said to Kenny that as the oldest, wisest member of the squad, I will probably be able to cope with the disappointment of being told he has decided to play Romário up front instead of me. But I'm not sure Brian will. I mean if he is still not over Bob the Builder!

The cameras were everywhere, including as we headed to the showers sometimes. An excuse for most of us to wait rather than have the reality of our ageing bodies exposed. Not so Gilles Marini. He couldn't get out there quickly enough. I suppose if I had a body like that, I might feel disposed towards displaying it all over the place, but it's not exactly great for team morale, especially when some of the female camera operators faint and drop their cameras as he walks by them. They would love to have been there for his descriptions of how to do sex scenes without having sex, or without over-exposing yourself to the dozens of people on the film set. 'Some people prefer to wear a sock,' he said.

Saturday 6 September

Breakfast then more physio, to the gym with Rob to do some exercises for my neck. I was working up the launch piece of the fourth term group for the *New Statesman*, Caborn and JP having seen GB and got his backing for the idea. Dick was in his sports dinner mode and full of fizz about it. I felt slightly underwhelmed and not sure they would get everything in place but decided to go for it. Home to rest and wait for Fiona, Mum, Calum and Audrey to get back from Manchester. Then just letting time pass, wanting tomorrow and the match to come. Watched loads of sport, but it was impossible not to want tomorrow to hurry up.

Sunday 7 September

I left for the hotel and after a quick breakfast went up for more physio on the neck and shoulders. Much more serious mood around the place. A lot of tension. Jaap Stam arrived. Really strong handshake. Still looked fit as a beast. Nice guy too. Figo ditto. Romário and Baresi were the disappointments. Di Canio superb, though the tattoos on his body did have a fascist feel to them. Interesting to watch all these footballers together. Lot of nerves, lots of old stories, lots of logistics – when are we due down here, what do we do with the bags etc? Lunch with Gilles and Mr and Mrs Stam. Talked about Fergie. Jaap said it was an honour in a way to be the one mistake he admitted to, when he said he regretted letting him go. But at the time it was all pretty brutal. He was not at all bitter though. He said Alex was responsible for massive success, and that had been a big part of his life. He asked me to pass on his regards if I was speaking to him.

Lots of hanging around in our suits before we were called down and given the team. Kenny came in with Ian and Eric, holding a little piece of paper, said it had been great working with us, this was the worst part of the week because he could not start everyone. He went through the team, and given I was only ever likely to be on as a full back, I knew after the first few names I was going to be on the bench. So were Brian McFadden and Brian Lara. We were all very disappointed. England guys looking really up for it. Once on the bus I tried to lift myself, did some of the songs Pete Boyle [Manchester United songster] and I had written. Also Kenny Logan said he bet I couldn't get TB on the phone to wish us luck, and I did, put him on loudspeaker, and they were all singing 'We've got Tony Blair on the phone.' We hadn't had as much time with the pros as the England guys had which was probably going to be a problem.

We arrived at Wembley, the crowds on the way in nothing like it had been at Old Trafford. Straight to the pitch. Fabulous stadium which felt even bigger from the pitch than from the stands. Nice enough atmosphere. Into the dressing room, change for the warm up. Starting to rain a fair bit. I'd managed to sort more than thirty tickets in the end, with more late on from Gilles and Nicky Byrne, and I caught sight of everyone sitting up in the posh seats, Mum waving madly. It was good to see Philip there too, though Grace said later he had been quite frail and not really able to get into it. Back in where Kenny and Eric did little pep talk and a bit of tactics. Out for the introductions with Geoff Hurst [former footballer] and Unicef. Felt pissed off then heading to the bench. It was a decent game and we should have walked it. Gordon Ramsay was injured early on, and I thought given I had been left back in a lot of the training Kenny might have put me on but he went for Brian Lara. Half-time came and he told us to stay out and get warmed up properly.

Into the second half. Still no sign. Brian McFadden getting really pissed off, Kenny getting the silent Bob the Builder treatment. It was only when we went 4–3 down that he put on me and Ian Rush. I suppose it was great to get on, especially with the announcement 'No. 11 Romário replaced by No. 14 AC', but I was fucked off just to get a few minutes. Mind you, I got more touches in the few minutes I was on than in the whole forty-five minutes last time. Good one-two with Di Canio. Almost got by Le Saux. Clattered the kid from *Harry Potter* [Tom Felton]. Cross-shot. Almost nicked a header. The boys said later they were convinced I was going to score. But it all flew by too quickly. England winners again, us trailing around waiting for medals. Figo had to leave early, said goodbye to everyone first. Stam a real gent. Really disappointed with Romário. Patrick Kielty said Kenny felt he lost the point of the whole thing. He and Harry Redknapp had a real bust-up when Harry was putting on his weak players and Kenny wasn't. All the usual signing etc. then up to the reception. The kids enjoyed it and were having a great time, ditto their friends so that was fine. Took Calum to meet Kenny. Ditto Mum, who gave him a hard time for keeping me on the bench. Great chat with Stam and Schmeichel. Both talking up TB, saying they felt we had really lost something. Mrs Stam saying most Dutch people would not even know GB was PM. Left at 12 for the hotel with all the boys plus Maud [Millar, Fiona's niece]. It was all a bit flat compared with Manchester. Eventually bed at 2. Boys up till 6.

Monday 8 September

Didn't sleep well. Up at 6.30 and headed home. The usual post-match reliving. Everyone seemed to think I did OK when I came on, but also that Kenny should have given everyone at least twenty minutes. He had claimed last night he didn't realise how far gone the match was, but I didn't believe that. I had not realised how close I had been to scoring opportunities. Got back to a bit of work, planning speeches, Oz schedule and working on the novel. TB called. I told him he had been No. 1 choice for a phone call on the bus. Even among these foreign guys, the message re GB was really negative.

He felt GB's main problem remained strategic – he had not really decided, and therefore was not really clear, whether he was going to pursue New Labour or not. It lacked conviction. But he still felt it was possible to turn it round. The Tories were vulnerable because they had not really thought things through. He said if I was speaking to GB to tell him that he was willing to help with the speech and the positioning. GB's calls had trailed off. Also I was struggling to get a definitive answer on Brailsford and whether they wanted him for the conference. They so obviously lacked proper decision-making structures. TB was also asking me to get involved with the Palestinian Authority FA and advising [Ehud] Barak [Israeli Prime Minister] in Israel.

TB had had his housewarming at the weekend, same day as Liz Murdoch's seemingly very lavish 40th. I had ducked out of both because of the football, but people who went to his said TB looked a bit strained. Tessa said it was an extraordinary house and really a nice do but it all felt odd. She said she was struck at the football how people gravitated to me and were looking to me to do special things. I was beginning to think I should get stuck in to something more significant than what I had been doing of late, but beyond the GB situation I couldn't see what it was. I went to see PG and the boys came round. He said he felt he was rediscovering his wit and his joie de vivre. He felt politically we were fucked and that Cameron, who he saw at the Murdoch do, was developing OK. He felt I had to help GB but not get more sucked in. Greg had been going in and said it was carnage in there, total lack of grip.

Tuesday 9 September

Out early for a speech at Canada House. Steljes Smart technology distributor. The high commissioner to the UK James Wright came along and we had a little chat about my Ottawa visit and the upcoming general election. He was pretty sure [Stephen] Harper [Canadian Conservative leader] would win. I had adapted my leadership speech to their theme of decision-making, and it went down fine. The speech was fine and the Q&A likewise but afterwards, as I was being shown the technology, a guy came up and basically suggested it was time I stopped my bits and pieces existence and took on another big challenge. I had mentioned the challenge of global education. He said with the contacts you have and the skills you have you could lead a campaign to make that happen. You should do something like that, not this kind of thing. I was actually fairly defensive with him, said that I had been doing different things, spending more time with and for family, and nothing had come along to fill the gap. He troubled me though, provoked something that was stirring in me anyway. Perhaps GB's blandishments had stopped me thinking of other ways in which I could make a difference.

Wednesday 10 September

Breakfast with Ed to take stock re future book projects. I took Mum to King's Cross. Back for an interview with an overly earnest guy from *The Bookseller*. He said he liked the book but he was obsessed with what I thought of reviews. John and Gwenda Scarlett came round for dinner. John looking really well. They seemed fascinated by the idea of my novel. Also he was much more supportive of GB than virtually anyone else I had heard, said that he had promised more resources and delivered, took the issues seriously, addressed them seriously, didn't interfere. He seemed a bit taken aback at some of my analysis, e.g. re lack of decision-making, poor team, confusion of strategy and tactics. He had not realised GB had asked me back and seemed pretty stunned by it. He thought it would be hugely enervating, and would send a signal he was serious about tackling his problems. On the other hand, it would send a signal how serious the problems were. I asked him outright if he thought I should. He said it would put me right back in the firing line. But he said if he heard it was happening he would feel pretty excited about it.

He was clearly enjoying the job still. Terrorism top of the priority list. He said they were having to make some pretty tough choices with Iraq, Afghanistan, Middle East, Russia, China. Russia was recreating itself as a different sort of superpower based on interference in areas of influence. China's growth was astonishing and happening without the West really seizing its significance. Terrorism was becoming more and more sophisticated. He felt he had good relations with the Tories and the criticism of him in the past had abated. He clearly felt – and the Service felt – [Sir Richard] Dearlove [former head of MI6] had got too close and too supportive of one PM, TB, and John had operated differently since getting the top job. I mentioned there had been a vague approach from the Georgians and he was totally against me working for them. The Russians may not be saints but the Georgians were pretty tricky on this too.

Thursday 11 September

Car out to City airport and as ever found some good books at the little shop inside departures, including *The Reluctant Fundamentalist*, which I had half read by the time we reached Glasgow. Met by Lindsay McGarvie [political journalist] and we drove out to Ayrshire. Trying still to fix the conference Olympics event with Dave Brailsford. Lindsay had organised a lunch with some business guys, mainly BAE [Systems, defence and aerospace company], at an Indian restaurant near his house. Pretty good crowd. I did the basic leadership speech dressed up as how to lobby government, then Q&A which these days tended to focus on what should GB do to get out of his mess? That was all beginning to pick up with rumours of resignations and plots.

Lots of emails back and forth via David Prescott re the fourth term group. JP had put in a bit of rabble-rousing stuff which I thought weakened it and we sorted that. Also trying to devise a design. Tessa called for a chat on the general scene, which she felt was worsening pretty quickly. Brian Donohoe [Labour MP] was at the lunch, set off with him for Irvine to prepare for tonight's party fundraiser. Brian pretty up about his own situation but felt generally we were close to being fucked. He shared some of his analysis – that there was a lack of politics and strategy. All too bitty. Alex Salmond running rings round them up north, Tories ducking away. Did an OK run before heading to the event. Shifted stacks of books. Donald piping. Aunt Jean [Caldwell, AC mother's sister-in-law] came along.

I was sitting next to Brian Souter [businessman] who was a lot more personable and sharp politically than I expected. Still a Nat, but he clearly liked Brian. Paid 400 quid for me to play the pipes. Some fucker seemed to tape my speech because *The Scotsman* had it in no time, on the line I was saying GB had blown it – which I never said. I did say there had been strategic errors but also that it was recoverable provided we defended the record, promoted policy better and took the fight to the Tories. Good atmosphere though and I felt if only everyone showed a bit more fight and passion, it could be won back.

Friday 12 September

Siobhain McDonagh [Labour MP] was out saying there should be a leadership election. There was some suggestion No. 10 effectively outed her having written a letter to the party NEC. Not clear though if it was the start of a concerted campaign. Another light run a.m. through Irvine then a lift with Brian to Glasgow airport. Finally had a decent chat with Dave Brailsford and agreed an outline for next week. Flight down fine, finished the novel I was reading. Home to change before going out to film at Gospel Oak Primary School. Just pictures, but it took a fair while.

Saturday 13 September

Off to Nottingham for the Forest v Burnley game. TB called. He said if the Siobhain move – followed today by Joan Ryan [Labour MP] – was orchestrated, part of a plan, he was not aware of it. Good game, won 2–1, then drove to Walberswick for [personal friend] Mike Lownes's 50th party. Tired and a bit ratty when I got there, and it was cold, but Grace cheered me up. Ed had called and said he could get me to see Lindi King with her – top drama agent. Quite a few people mentioning the Brel programme, and liking.

Sunday 14 September

Long walk on the beach with Fiona, breakfast. Interesting chat with a liver transplant surgeon. I mentioned the game I'd been asked to play in for George Best Foundation [charity], and he said Best and his doctors had set back transplantation because people felt why give when it was so clear it would be abused? Drove home and later to PG's for a barbecue. Usual chat re TB–GB but more GB than TB. Georgia saying the whole thing was indeed being orchestrated because there was a growing feeling he just could not win. Margaret McD was saying to anyone and everyone he had to go. But there was no way of getting seventy-one MPs to nominate someone else, and there was nobody putting themselves forward, so where did it all go? Peter M called. He said if I was speaking to GB it was important he understood that if it all went tribal, like the dismissal of critics as a Blairite rump, not only was that stupid, it was also making it harder to broaden support for him. He felt GB's speech was bog standard, it would do *a* job but not *the* job. He felt he did not have the strategy and he was reverting to type.

Monday 15 September

Greg Nugent came round with the producer who had helped Shane Meadows make *Somers Town* [award-winning film]. Barnaby Spurrier. Nice guy. Loved the book. Surprised at how sensitive it was, but it was not for Shane, not working-class enough. He felt it might make a mini-series for

TV. Round to Avalon for a meeting to plan the documentary screening at the Royal Society of Medicine. Could get a bit complicated but enough people there who seemed to know what they were doing. Dinner with Melanne Verveer. She was clearly worried McCain was on the march. Obama being drowned out by Palin and her celebrity status. She said she despaired of education that delivered peoples who seemed ready to give power to people like Palin and Cameron. But she was not sure Obama knew how to fight back. Good fun reminiscing but it was so depressing talking about the political scene here. Global news now economic – collapse of Lehman Brothers [US investment bank], unthinkable up till now, and probably just the start.

Tuesday 16 September

Out to do photos for the BBC in Fleet St, for their promotion of the *Cracking Up* film. Didn't like getting picture taken in busy public places like that. Then another interview with Judith, this time at another rented house in Kentish Town, basically trying to make me more introspective. Stuart had mentioned to me that it currently felt like I had it all too sorted. Fiona did a new interview too, Judith obviously trying to push harder on the idea that there was something other than drink that had made me go crazy. I probably opened up about the depressions more than I had ever done.

Wednesday 17 September

Out for breakfast at the Wolseley with Richard Wallace and Conor Hanna [editor and deputy, *Daily Mirror*]. They were keen to be loyal, but also clearly reaching the point where they wondered if the whole thing was going to go down so badly that there had to be a change, and they were going to look at David Miliband. They felt he neutered the appeal of Cameron – young and telegenic and looked like a member of the human race. They felt when they last saw GB that he was dejected and a bit clueless. Also, he had asked them for Kevin Maguire to do his comms, which was another bad sign. They had said no, and agreed it was not a good idea. Lots of pressure on the UK banks now, with HBOS in the firing line and looking to be taken over by Lloyds. I liked Wallace and Conor, even if the paper was pretty downmarket now. They clearly loathed Sly Bailey [Trinity Mirror CEO] and her lack of planning, lack of nous. Cuts the whole time. I met Gary Gibbon [Channel 4 political editor] for lunch. He felt GB was recoverable – just. Said his operation was dire, and he needed just to get out and do the job. David Muir sent over latest GB draft, which had improved in some ways, gone backwards in others. Personal stuff better. Argument weaker.

Thursday 18 September

The *New Statesman* was out and so we were getting bids on Go Fourth. JP and I split them between us. He did *Today*, I did Radio 5 and the regionals. I felt confident in the message – focus on Tories, who were getting away with murder, public unaware, always have to fight – but it was becoming co-opted as a Keep GB group, with a few Old Labour tinges too. The good thing was that at least we were out fighting and whacking the Tories. I got into a *Sun* v *News of the World* tug of war. Both had heard and both wanted a piece saying the same things. *NoW* asked first and I said yes. Rebekah then asked and despite her trying to dick over *NoW* I said no. Worked on the *NoW* piece only to discover later that *The Sun* had simply lifted my words from the radio and turned them into a 'My View' piece. Pissed off. She apologised but it was a bit shabby when they knew I had committed to *NoW*. Later out with Grace to see Lindi King and Olivia Homan [theatrical agents]. Really nice. Grace very nervous at first but quickly into her stride. Home via *Channel 4 News*, and did another OK chat re the need to focus on the Tories, and how we had always defied conventional wisdom. The Go Fourth message had landed fine.

Friday 19 September

NoW really pissed off at *The Sun* but still planning to run the piece. Mark came round and we finally finished transcribing the diaries. Mark said later it was one of the best and most enjoyable things he had ever done, and we should take a photo to record it. Calum now back in Manchester, Rory back from Greece but straight into poker mode, and Grace always out with her friends. Out with Fiona to La Casalinga.

Saturday 20 September

Set off for Manchester with Mark. The financial meltdown was really dominating everything now, even if GB, conference and survivability were leading the bulletins on the way up. I had been planning to go up later, or via Swansea v Burnley, but yesterday PG took a call from GB saying he wanted to present him with a special award at the conference tomorrow. PG was going up with Gail and Georgia, and I felt I ought to be there. Traffic dire but got to Manchester in OK time. To Calum's flat to change then off to the conference. Same old same old. Anti-war march. People thrusting leaflets at you. Well-honed security. Into the zone and then just hard to move without being approached by loads of people. Media, delegates, MPs and ministers, everyone having the same small talk as big talk chats. It would be so much easier not to be there. I felt a little railroaded re the Go Fourth group in that JP and Dick knew I had said no to GB, and going back with him, but was keen to help in some way if I could.

Calum looked great showing people round the stands. He had come on so much and the people at the party exhibitions side of things adored him. PG etc. arrived and had a run-through. I sat in the front row and he went up for a special award after the merit awards. GB made a nice little speech, and PG did a good number on the need to keep on fighting. Standing ovation. Very moving. He was looking better than of late and spoke well. Back to the flat for a meeting with JP, Dick and David Prescott. Taking stock and setting up forward plans. Focus on a big launch but as we discussed I wondered whether we needed a big launch as such, whether not better to go for an event that the press could cover. JP was in pretty lively form. He and I were both of the view it was less about media coverage than getting out and about in the party and also generating outside support too. JP was clearly up for turning it all into a loyalty to GB thing too, which was not necessarily where we needed to be. It was a throwback to the old JP meetings where you had to go round in circles before we sort of got a point.

Calum was making them tea and later said he thought the whole thing was hilarious. JP wisecracking and messing about, Dick full of it, David P trying too hard to be dynamic and fizzing with ideas. He wanted us to do a big thing tomorrow with Glenys handing out stickers to people arriving for conference. All beginning to feel a bit Rolling Rose, JP battlebus [previous Labour campaign features], but at least I suppose we ought to be able to get up anti-Tory messages. Calum and I had dinner with the Goulds. But Catherine McLeod and then AD called and asked if I would help with his speech. My heart sank a little but I said yes. Another spad brought it to the restaurant. It was pretty poor. Why these guys did not work on their speeches properly during the summer was beyond me.

The first half of the speech was an attempted explanation of the international crisis, but it was a bit Janet and John [characters in toddlers' reading books]. Other parts were way too defensive and too much about the Tories. Gail, PG and Georgia all had a quick read and felt it was pretty poor. Philip was clearly moved by the presentation but looked tired now and a bit beat. Georgia far more into the 'Brown must go' camp than I realised. PG felt I had to be careful not to let Go Fourth get used as a 'loyalty to Brown at all costs' group. Felt I should not slag off the rebels and critics as I had. There was a fine line between saying disloyalty helped the Tories and saying people should not be allowed to say what they thought. Back to the flat with Calum and in between watching *Match of the Day* and the Ryder Cup [golf] I tried to have a go at improving AD's speech.

Sunday 21 September

A sure sign of being conflicted both about being at conference, and getting drawn in too deep, namely that I had a bad night with asthma. I went for a run but even though I had now lost well over half a stone, I still couldn't get going properly. Gave up after a while. I had breakfast in a little café where a nurse from the local hospital said she had spotted me and one of her friends thought I was in *Hollyoaks*. I called Catherine and gave her both an overview and also some specific changes I thought AD should make. Big picture. Not defensive. Forward policy. Serious, sober etc. She sounded grateful for some help. She said she had no idea how difficult and gruelling it was all going to be. Over to the conference centre and after doing a bit of media and wandering round the stalls with Calum, I did the Go Fourth photocall on the steps. JP had already done *The Politics Show* and was totally going for the rebels. He talked about Blairites, Brownites and Bitterites. It was exactly where we didn't need to be.

Stephen Byers and one or two others were saying I should take a look at the kind of MP who was getting behind us – the ones mainly who wanted to take the party backwards. It was a lovely day and not least with JP's ranting and raving the mood was good, and a lot of fun. But it didn't feel right. I went along with it but worried it was part of shoring up something unupshorable. I was getting a fair few people – Margaret McD face to face, [Lord] Clive Hollick [Labour peer] by email, Byers, Darren Murphy [TB advisor], saying all it was doing was helping him survive and his survival was a death blow to Labour. Margaret said that 'You and Philip have to get over your Catholic guilt' about GB. She said you owe him nothing. It hurts and nobody likes to hurt him even more but the party is going under if he stays as leader. She said you have a big important voice and you are using it to help him but it harms the party.

When I bumped into Charles Clarke later, he said much the same. He said I know deep down you agree he has to go but you feel you have to be loyal. He said TB, Peter M and I are 'huge totemic figures' in GB's mind. Our support is disproportionately important to him. Equally, he said, it would have a massive impact if we went against him and he felt we should. TB was texting me fairly regularly, asking if I was helping with the speech, and how the mood was. Peter M coming in but only very briefly. I wandered into the conference itself at one point and they appeared to be speaking in Welsh. Back out and eventually managed to get away and watch United at Chelsea [1–1].

Fiona Phillips [TV presenter] was interviewing me for my 'Audience with...' event. She was really nice and so pro-me it was almost embarrassing when she introduced me, going on and on about how special I was and how the party owed me etc. etc. Q&A perfectly friendly. One or two asking why I didn't go back and why I didn't stand for office. Otherwise fairly standard mix. TB called again. He had one or two ideas he wanted to feed in on message re the financial crisis and also how to use the recent trouble as a platform for him to say he is what he is and was not going to try to be something different. I was really enjoying seeing Calum grow in confidence and the ability to hold his own in these circles. We had a nice chat over dinner and then back to the flat.

Monday 22 September

Calum off to conference while I set off for the Velodrome. I stopped at Asda to buy some fruit. A fireman in there. 'Shouldn't you be somewhere else helping your old mates?' Arrived at the Velodrome. The Sky team, led by James Murdoch [BSkyB non-executive chairman], were in for a presentation by Dave Brailsford. About twenty-odd people there from Sky. I had a little chat with James, who was clearly a massive cycling fan and was looking to up Sky's sponsorship, possibly to include a Tour de France team. On GB, he clearly felt he was getting close to last chance saloon. He had too many layers of advice and needed just to decide what he wanted to do with the country and get on and do it. He said he was due to see him later. He felt he cared too much what people said about him. Felt the people gunning for him were pygmies he could knock over. Yet he seemed cowed by them.

The cycling stuff was fabulous. Dave did a little video presentation about the way they had built the team, the successes they had had in the Olympics, and it was totally designed to get the hair standing up on the neck. Totally brilliant. Shane Sutton, his Aussie coach, was taking the piss out of my Wembley performance. 'I thought you were bad two years ago, this was even worse! Let's hope you can cycle better than you can play football.' Chris Boardman [former cyclist, technical director] still looking fit as a fiddle. Jamie Staff (gold medallist) with enormous thighs. How do you get thighs as big as that? I asked him. By living in a gym, he said. Out on to the track after getting fitted up for bikes and shoes. It took me a while to get used to the fixed gear bike without brakes, with the coaches trackside helping us get the hang of it. The steep banks were pretty scary at first but brilliant once you got into it. I was chatting to Dave in between times, getting him fixed for conference. Really nice guy, also very good in talking to these corporates, but clearly with a ruthless streak. The atmosphere was very much of a team that knew what it was doing.

After lunch a presentation from sports psychiatrist Steve Peters, who Dave had described as one of his most important appointments. He gave an analysis of the brain. Men driven by sex and ego. Women neurotic and in need of constant reassurance. We have to accept these realities which go back to the beginnings of time. Primal. Inside us all there is a real self and a chimp who worries us, undermines us, gets us to focus on the wrong things, makes us do and say things we shouldn't. For sports people, it stops you developing and performing well. He was very open talking about Victoria Pendleton and how long it took him to get her to see the need to control her emotions. Interesting team ethos in that they built it between people who would also have to compete against each other. I was hugely impressed by the whole set-up, and could see the Sky guys were too.

Dave said he needed them to go for it bigtime if we were ever going to get a British Tour de France winner. Sadly I had to miss the science presentation because I was off to see Alex and Jason. AD's speech seemed to go OK. He and Catherine both seemed reasonably happy with it anyway. Alex and Jason arrived and we went through to his office for a chat re various things. Hodder had pretty much agreed to a second autobiography focusing on the last ten years. I said he needed to be clear what the book was for. Just a record. Or part of a broader strategic plan to take his life forward in different directions in the future. He said he intended to have some role as a United Ambassador. Also some days a year for Unicef. Business. Travel. Speaking.

I said the book was a strategic building block. And perhaps later we could do a book on sport and business and what they can learn from each other. And in between a book he and I do could do together – in conversation about winning. Take in chats. Bits of research. Pictures. Add politics to the sport, business mix. Could be really successful. It would be good fun doing and would really work. He was on good form generally. Raging about [referee] Mike Riley's seven bookings at Chelsea. Good discussion re how we could build out from a couple of chats to a transcribed book which really made a splash. He was buying into it. I said how did he know when he retired, that he wouldn't want to just have a nice quiet life for a while? No chance, he said.

Told him about the Velodrome and suggested he should take a look. He said his guys had been trying but they'd been stopped by the cycling guys. I filled him in on the psychological side, e.g. Steve Peters saying that all that rugby chest thumping and huddling and pumping up did not really help. Sapped energy. Adrenaline good – a drug that makes you more energetic and aware but when you start it fades. Anxiety bad – instead of focusing on performance, you worry about all the things that might go wrong. Also lack of logic in sport. Why don't footballers hit the ball towards where the keeper can't get it every time? Because too many are thick. We chatted about GB and he felt I should still go back in some capacity. Jason said why would you want all that round your head again?

And why risk a reputation for winning? Alex said, but you might make the difference. I said I could make a difference, but I was not sure if I would make THE difference.

Back into town then over to the Midland for a meeting with Tessa, Carol L, Rachel and Stewart Wood from No. 10, plus Dave B and Tim Brabants [Olympic kayaking medallist]. I was sure they were going to be good. Dave excellent on team building and ethos. Attention to detail. Really liked them both. I had a little chat with Dave afterwards on how the stuff he did could apply to politics. Very difficult to do though. Off to the Olympics reception. Good smattering of medallists. Simon Clegg [BOA] was there. I was chatting to him when he made clear – and apparently it had been in the papers – that he was moving on. He was putting on a brave face but I assumed – rightly, Seb told me later – that he was shafted. Clegg said he was ridiculed when he said we would be fourth in the medals table. The difficult thing now was whether we could stay up there. Russia had done badly and would do better next time. Nice guy, and it was dreadful if he was being pushed out now.

Tim Allan and Godric were both there. Nice chat re old times. I had a chat with Brendan Barber [TUC] who said GB handled the unions really badly. Far worse than we did. That's saying something, I said. He said they just went day to day and he had too many people messing things up for him. Good interviews by Jonathan Edwards [former gold medallist, now TV commentator] and then a terrific little speech from Seb, really pumped up and giving a sense of how great London would be. I arranged to meet Seb for dinner but first went to Radisson to meet Fiona after her fringe meeting. I bumped into GB who asked me to go up to his room later when he got back from the receptions. My heart kind of sank again. It was almost impossible to get away from people endlessly coming up to talk. Got to Don Giovanni and Seb arrived with his assistant Joe, who used to work for Peter M. By now I had the GB speech and was flicking through it. Not bad but still needed more. Seb was on confident form re the Games. He said he could not understand why the government did not make more of the link between our investment and results. He wanted to make sure there was political support across the board, not least because there could be a change of government before the Games, but he really felt that we were missing tricks all round.

Back to the hotel to see GB. Met by David Muir and taken up to fourteenth floor. Kirsty McNeill [advisor] and GB were sitting at a big screen typing. GB read me page upon page and was basically just looking for assurance. Then TB called him and he read chunks to him too. TB gave him some thoughts on how to present the economic stuff. There were a couple of not very good jokes in there and I suggested no jokes at all, make a virtue of it being serious and sober. He had some pretty heavy lines on Cameron at last. I got him to redo the beginning to make it very in your face. And also the ending and a new 'I know who I am' section. Sarah came in a couple of times and tried to get him to bed. He was pretty short with her. He was doing a lot of the typing himself. David kept telling me how much of a help I had been but I can't say I felt it. I was glad to get out – around half one. I chatted with Douglas on the way down. I asked him where it was going to end. He said he genuinely didn't know. PG and Spencer Livermore were both of the view that GB would not stay for an election and that he needed to be given an honourable way out. Yet with a decent speech tomorrow I would say things had strengthened in his favour.

September '08: Using Peters's chimp for new thinking

Tuesday 23 September

Fiona off for a swim early. Another bad asthmatic night. Stuart Holmes, the anti-smoking campaigner I knew from my *Mirror* days when he used to protest outside the *Mirror* building, was on a soapbox as we filed in through security. He spotted me and started off on one – how I used to know him before I was rich and famous. Then a big thing about how he was the greenest man in the country. He had moved on just from smoking. I did a bit of media then hid away in the exhibitions bit and scribbled some thoughts for the Q&A with Tim Brabants and Dave Brailsford. They arrived, then Tessa, and we sat around for a while. Calum is a good judge of people and he really liked them both. We were a bit late because in the previous debate Jack Dromey droned on a lot longer than his allocated time. The session went really well. Dave so clear and eloquent and his stuff on team building was brilliant. If only we could apply some of this in politics. I was focusing on outcomes, sticking together, knowing roles and so forth, all so relevant to recent failings. Several bursts of applause and a really warm standing ovation at the end.

We sat through Andy Burnham's OK speech. Had a good chat with Dave about stuff, then did a load of media, mainly pressing my line about the Tories needing to be under proper scrutiny. Then waited for the GB speech. Sarah walked on to introduce him. Big surprise for the audience, and it worked pretty well. Alex texted me to say he thought it made him look a bit weak. But I felt it was fine. His speech went down pretty well. Some good passages well delivered, others less so. It still lacked a big defining theme but it was OK and most people seemed to think he did better. Georgia had told me I was being seen by the Blairites as seeming to back GB come what may and I recalibrated a little in the interviews, for example talking up DM, not dissing Charles Clarke. Charles said to me

Carol [wife] had seen me whacking him and saying he had become a commentator. I said it was a reference to the government and MPs generally.

GB's pro-NHS stuff and anti-Tory attacks went down best. But it didn't really get people going as TB used to. It was good but could have been better. I did some more telly on the way out then Calum and I went for something to eat. Off to Burnley v Fulham. Listening to the radio coverage of the speech on the way, it seemed to be going down OK. But I was glad to get away. GB called to say thanks for the help and said it had showed him how much he could benefit if I spent more time helping him. Hitting the guilt buttons hard again. Dinner at Turf Moor. There was a smallish crowd but a great atmosphere and we ground out a good win [1–0]. I did a cheque presentation for Leukaemia Presentation at half-time. Home by 1ish.

Wednesday 24 September

Several people had mentioned an Adam Boulton [Sky TV political editor] piece in *G2* on Monday which apparently was an extract from his book [*Tony's Ten Years: Memories of the Blair Administration*]. I hadn't seen, but it seemed to be the usual AC = liar/bully stuff. After only a few days away, and even with the BlackBerry when travelling, there seemed to be a big backlog of emails to deal with. I was trying to operate life according to Steve Peters's chimp – the thing inside telling me to do, say and think things that got in the way of self and true performance. It had made a big impact, and there were several instances where I told myself very forcibly to think a different way, and did so. I also remembered his observation that psychopaths' brains were the same as ours, except that they did not do compassion or guilt.

Ruby Wax [actress and comedian] and her Headroom [BBC mental health campaign] team came round at 2, to do a mental health interview. The usual TV bollocks, for example wanting to do the same interview in three different places. But she was great, really lively and in your face in a good way. Also it was quite helpful in that it helped me get used to some of the questions I would get when I was out talking about the novel and the documentary. Her big thing was that she just couldn't cope with criticism, and she was pressing me on how I managed to deal with all the shit thrown my way. Out to Goldman Sachs for a speech on mental health. Nice enough bunch of people, very welcoming etc. Speech well received, again using some of the content of the documentary and working out how to deal with trickier questions. Bright bunch though it was hard not to sense the notion that they had been knocked sideways by the financial crisis and insight that they were not quite as invincible as they thought.

Thursday 25 September

David S. Both of us felt I was in much better shape and agreed we could cut back on the sessions, maybe see him more when I felt I needed to. We went over all the stuff from the holiday, ups and not many downs, the sense of being conflicted about conference activity, and basically feeling I was better out of it. It was very much the usual conflict between self and duty / service. I told him about Steve Peters's presentation and he certainly bought some of it, especially the part about how we underestimated our own abilities to influence how we feel. I had now lost ten pounds as well and was feeling fitter physically again. The Bush attempts to get 700 billion rescue bailout dominating news around the world.* It was a pretty dire end to his presidency, which was already being judged one of the worst ever. At home yesterday's bizarre – with Damian McBride at the centre of it – Ruth Kelly [Transport Secretary] resignation [prior to GB's impending Cabinet reshuffle] was dominant. Alex called, said 'Is it the beginnings of others?' There was definitely a feeling of ministers thinking it was all up.

To Edinburgh, bathed in warm sunshine and looking fabulous. I needed to buy a practice chanter for my children's charity photocall on Monday. I went to so many junk shops before finding one that was actually playable. They were manned almost exclusively by non-Scots. Eventually I found Bagpipes Galore, where a rather miserable English guy sold me a 35-quid chanter, then I wandered back to the George Hotel. There were some really annoying email exchanges between the BBC and the Royal Society of Medicine about the joint event to launch *Cracking Up*. We were clearly getting into a 'too many cooks' situation and the whole thing was getting way too complicated. I sent a pretty snappy email saying could we just get on and sort what we had already agreed. I sensed the problem was BBC paranoia about me using them to promote the novel.

The dinner speaking event was OK. Merchants Hall a bit stuffy with pictures of the royals all over the walls but an OK bunch of people. Someone called Anne took me round to meet virtually everyone but did it charmingly. Hosted by Aeolus [wind turbine power company] but not just business people. E.g. I was next to the head of Strathclyde Fire Service Brian Sweeney. Nice guy. Friend of John Reid. We both agreed John needed to go for Holyrood. The general view was that Salmond was running rings round us and that Iain Gray [Labour leader] was not the answer. One or two people said to me the problem was that GB disempowered Scottish politicians and yet he was a bit behind the times. He did not realise things had moved on.

* A $700 billion financial package designed to rescue the slumping US economy and stabilise world stock markets.

I did a mix of funny stories and leadership ten points. Went well. One woman came up afterwards and said I was the first political figure she had ever heard who had made her think of voting and getting involved. Questions fine. Mainly current stuff, like the financial crisis or whither GB, but also a few asking me about Lance Armstrong [American former cyclist and AC interviewee, banned for drug offences]. I was due to stay over and get the first flight back but on the news there was a report about a glitch, with air traffic control computers not functioning and planes were being disrupted. Someone suggested getting the sleeper. Good idea. On the train by half eleven, into Euston just after seven, slept OK.

Friday 26 September

I worked on the script for the documentary. I was worried Mum would be upset by it and so I calibrated a little. Out p.m. with Cathy Gilman for a cheque presentation. I was going down with a cold. Home then a bit more work before going out to Café Rouge with Tessa, Jessie and her boyfriend. Tessa just going on about the GB scene far too much. Fiona said to her if she hated him so much she should think about getting out. If not there had to be some sense of a team pulling together. The problem was that she just felt too much all the things he had done in the past, and also the way he treated people even now. He was now in the States, speaking to the UN today then on to see Bush tomorrow. The credit crunch aftermath was now whipping up into a major league crisis and nobody had any real sense as to where and how it would end, though GB did at least look like he was motoring on it. Heady stuff though, not easy.

Saturday 27 September

I set off at 9.05 for Leeds. Leeds to Burnley then met up with Calum in beautiful sunshine. He seemed in pretty good nick though said he felt he might be more suited to work than to studying. He had clearly enjoyed the week at conference again. Good match [Burnley 3, Preston NE 1]. Preston took the lead but Joey Guðjóhnsson scored a brilliant equaliser, then two more. Good buzz round the place at Burnley getting Chelsea away in Carling Cup. I was praying for it to be on the Wednesday not Tuesday as I had a speech on the Tuesday.

Sunday 28 September

Feeling pretty rough. Lying in bed when GB called. I had half assumed he was still in the States. He was straight back with pressure on me to go back. He said thanks for everything you did at conference. I said I wasn't sure I did so much. He said it showed what could be done when a few people capable of strength put over a united and disciplined message. He said the next stages were all about the economy and he was going to need help putting over the messages on a strategic way. Also, he felt I could help him with some of the more 'immature' Blairite young ministers. He felt DM had got himself into a bad position. He had been pushed by Clarke and Alan Milburn into declaring a 'kind of interest in the leadership', but he had not thought it through. There were others, he thought, I could help bring round more. He wanted to see me ASAP to discuss. He said he knew I had reservations but it was time to get the best people together, because we needed some discipline back in the system.

The big news was Bradford and Bingley [bank] being nationalised. AD had also called to say thanks for help at conference. He said the next period was going to be worse than anyone had predicted, and the consequences would be far-reaching and possibly dire. Rebekah asked for a piece on the Tories which I knocked off before the football.

Monday 29 September

Out to the Post Office to collect a package. Turned out to be the printed version of the novel. Good moment. Looked good. Liked the cover. Liked the feel of it. It felt real now, after all the waiting. Out to see Bostock who was in a good mood, has a new girlfriend on the go. Put me on standby antibiotics. Then to Gospel Oak Primary School to record the pieces to camera for the film. Judith was under pressure to make more of the programme a personal journey, which I wasn't too keen on. But we agreed on a few changes. Fiona was up in Birmingham at the Tory conference to do a fringe meeting on education. She said there was definitely something happening to change the Tories. She had a nightmare journey back. Body on the line. I had a bad night. Coughing badly.

Tuesday 30 September

A *GQ* guy came round first thing to do an interview for *All in the Mind*. I liked him. Felt OK re the answers. It was pretty obvious where people were going to come at me from and I just had to get the pitch right. I had been talking to Liz [sister] about how to handle Mum and Donald about the documentary. It wasn't easy. Mum was not keen on me talking about all this anyway, but I was sure it was the right thing, and also I wished I could talk about Donald too. There was a gap there in the story I was telling about why I was doing all this. The truth is Donald's diagnosis had had a massive impact on me at the time. Likewise I think it was the reason I had some of my own issues, and it was definitely the main reason why I felt I should campaign on this. We had decided not to give him the book but after seeing him I got one sent to him. He said he was not sure if he would read it. He found it hard to concentrate for reading.

I walked into town, and the rain got heavier so eventually I hopped on a bus. GB had called asking me to go for lunch. In through 70 Whitehall. I bumped into Geoff Hoon. He felt the leadership issue had faded but would come back at some point. He felt GB was good at this economic crisis stuff and had to show it. Cameron had done an emergency speech in which he said they would support the government in trying to deal with the economic crisis. Hoon felt the Tories' lead was vulnerable, they were not really as strong as they might think. He felt they had not addressed the real questions, and if GB could come through this period well, he still had a chance, but he needed to change his ways of working and build more of a team. Then he laughed, as if to say he doubted he was capable of it.

I was met by Helena Hopkins [duty clerk], one of several while I was there who asked if I was going back. Everyone you spoke to gave the picture of a pretty gloomy and dysfunctional place. She took me up to the Small Dining Room where a cold meats salad and a bowl of fruit were waiting for us. GB came in, threw down his notes and went straight into it. The Irish had announced a move to help Irish banks and customers at the expense of others. He was intending to complain to the ECB [European Central Bank]. It was blatant protectionism. He said he was working on a plan to raise up to £100 billion from other countries, mainly in the Arab world. His goal was to get more capital into the markets without having to use the taxpayer. He swore me to secrecy, said he wanted to get on with it before other countries had the same idea. He drew a little diagram – Qatar, UAE, Saudi, maybe Norway. He was confident he could make it work but it needed to move fast.

Politically he said he felt on strong ground. He felt the Tories were not serious. I told him Phil Webster had called me to say he thought Cameron was impressive this morning, but GB felt he was immature. He had called him last night to discuss the crisis and he sensed with Cameron everything was nakedly political. They were worried that the rampant free marketism they believed in was not working as they believed it should, and so it was easier for them to associate themselves with what he was doing. He repeatedly called Cameron / Osborne, and some of the younger Cabinet ministers, 'immature'.

He went through some of those he believed were out attacking him all the time – Tessa. Hazel Blears. He said Hazel was pretty hopeless in many ways, he hadn't needed to give her a big job but he did. James Purnell – GB said he took a risk on a young gun, gave him a big department. He said he could have given it to someone he was closer to politically. He wanted to broaden the team, show the divisions were behind us. He thought he might be repaid with some kind of loyalty. But no. Caroline Flint. John Hutton. The same. He felt DM was in a different place. He did not believe he was trying to mount a challenge. He was pushed into doing something because CC and AM were making clear they would look to someone else rather than him unless he indicated he was up for it. He was putting down a marker but had no intention at all of mounting a challenge. He had now damaged himself on both sides. He said he was determined to continue to be inclusive and build a team. I said he needed to be open about the importance of the team and build up some of the younger ones, even if it led to him being written up as weakened. It didn't matter what was said so long as the team actually worked better. I said also they had to signal a change in culture with regard to negative briefing.

It pissed me off that I was identified with that style when in fact most of that stuff had come from the GB culture not mine. He said there was wrong on both sides. Maybe, I said, but I had spent most of my time talking people up not down, even when provoked. 'Not always,' he said. 'Anger and frustration,' I said. 'And very rarely.' I said there were journos who used to tell me they were amazed how restrained I had been at times about some of the stuff his lot got up to. And I was clear I was not putting myself back into that mix, and also that there were some people, and some styles, I could not work with. He said I only needed to work with him. Not so, I said. Because the people around him were also important to how he worked. He said he wanted to know whether I could help him. I said I thought I was.

He said why don't you go into the Lords as Sports Minister? I thought I had seen that one off but he asked it as though for the first time. He said you'd be good at it. I said but that's not what I'd be doing. You'd get me there and I'd be full-time on the campaign. For a while he tried to pretend it would just be doing sport, then said 'It would send a very powerful signal, that we were working as a team, it would show the junior Blairites how to be more mature, it would signal to everyone we were serious, it would signal more discipline and control.' He said Labour's problems were competence and unity. For ten years we did not too bad on both. For the last year for various reasons we got hit on competence but we could get that back. The real problem now was unity. He felt if I was back it would help with some of the Blairites. He said 'It would be a big moment and it would upset the Tories to think you were back in a serious way.' I said it was really difficult for me. I had made promises to the family and this would go substantially towards breaking them.

Truth be told I did not have enthusiasm for it. Even though he was on good form today and on top of things, and fairly calm about it all, I did not have any great desire to be back in there. We chatted a bit inconsequentially about other stuff then Tom Fletcher came in to tell him about his next meeting with DM on Europe. GB asked them to leave us another five minutes and he had another go – he was sure he could win, he was sure he had the policy ideas but he needed strategic comms and only I could do it. If I was doing a job I enjoyed and would do well, like sport, the advice job could run alongside. At the moment – and he was right about this – it was neither one thing nor the other. I asked who his key people were but he knew I did not rate many of his people, and he knew also who not to mention. I told him the Greg episode was not good. He had too many layers of people he lost trust in and needed to sort. Instead he let them all run around and do their own thing.

His son Fraser came in and we then went downstairs. DM was there. He seemed a bit surprised to see me and the atmospherics were suddenly very odd. I had been railroaded a bit – by GB into the kind of limited involvement I had, by JP and Dick into the Go Fourth stuff, but deep down I did not have the heart for it. I left for home and texted TB who said if tempted make sure there was a portfolio 'but beware'. Agreed to meet tomorrow. Fiona really not sure. I lost my glasses again, always a bad sign. Out to Berkhamsted for the LRF golf day dinner. All very Home Counties. I did a speech and prize-giving then back for football. Burnley beat Watford [3–2].

Wednesday 1 October

Out to the edit suite to watch a rough cut of the documentary. Pretty strong. Felt quite emotional at parts. I could see why Mum might be upset by it but I felt the topping and tailing of the point about stigma and shame was strong enough. Fiona came over very well. I only had very small points to make about it. Car to Grosvenor Square to see TB. He was looking pretty thin. Odd suede shoes. Smart shirt and trousers. Nice new paintings on the walls. 'You have to admit my offices are quite classy,' he said. I filled him in on yesterday's meeting with GB. He felt he was in a stronger position but once this economic crisis was through, he felt people would go back to the fundamentals and he would not be in a strong position. Cameron was not that good but he was good enough. 'To be Prime Minister?' I asked. 'Yeah, probably.'

Re my own situation, he said he could see real benefits in me going to the Lords and in doing sport, and there were advantages for GB if I was around with him more. He felt there were big downsides for me – the press would be straight back into me. He felt GB became very people-dependent and I would be that person. He did not think I would enjoy working with him and his team. That was definitely true. He felt if I went back to No. 10, I would need certifying. I should certainly not think for a second that he would resent me working for GB. On the contrary he too wanted to help and thought we all should if we could. He had been giving advice to DM if he asked for it but not in a way to damage GB. He had concluded that DM probably didn't have it in him. Of course it didn't help that he had been done in but that was how they operated. He said he could see arguments both ways and in the end only I could decide. He felt all I could do was mitigate the result.

He did not think GB could win now. We might get a smaller majority against DM but he felt maybe it had gone too far. He was really worried if we lost that the party would just slide. GB and co. had somehow managed to make Blairite a swearword. He was in good form and seemed to think he could still make progress in the MEPP if he was allowed to. But even though he was going out there next week, things were pretty much on hold until the US elections. He said he felt he was in a weird position of responsibility without power. He was the only player who had a rounded strategy but he did not have all the levers needed to make it happen, so it was all a bit unsatisfactory. He was still keen for me to get involved, possibly via sport. His team seemed pretty happy with life.

On Adam Boulton's book TB felt that all these 40–50-something media guys could not cope with the fact we were the same age and we had actually done something with our lives. Standing outside No. 10 all day talking – what did it actually amount to? Home to watch Cameron's speech. It was not as good as it should have been. He hit lots of *Daily Mail* buttons but lacked a big argument. No boldness there. Then out to the Marketing Group of Great Britain dinner. It was my quid pro quo for Johnny Hornby's donation to the party for the Wembley dinner. Nice enough crowd and lots of old faces including Howell James (now at Barclays, said he knew nothing about banking so not exactly the best time to start). Lively bunch and I was on OK form. Did the basic leadership speech and felt I was hitting home in saying DC did not do what he needed to today. Good response. Interesting how sometimes it clicked and sometimes it didn't.

Thursday 2 October

GB was really piling on the pressure. Couple of calls, and at the end of the second, when he asked me if I could go in tonight or first thing tomorrow, I said I could, but I was not going to say yes to going into the Lords. 'Under any circumstances?' he asked. I said certainly not at the moment. He said why? I said for the same reasons as before – I had made promises not to go back full-on all the time, also that I had other things on and I was not sure I wanted to give it all up. He said OK, but let's speak again tomorrow. He so clearly was not going to let go. I felt conflicted again. I both did not want to, and did want to, help. But my heart was not in it, that was the truth. I wanted to help but only on my terms. I sent Rory an email setting out the upsides and downsides, partly as a way of thinking things through myself.

The downsides list was longer. Upsides – proper job and status, purpose and mission; could make a difference in sport; could make a difference politically. Downsides – have to give up everything else (books, speeches, business, any outside earnings); press and media back on my case big time; hardly any time at home / no freedom; would probably be caught between trying to do one job well as minister while what GB really wants me for is politics and campaign; no real sense of alliance with the core team; if we lose, my reputation as winner gets tarnished.

Rory said on that list the downsides outweighed the upsides, and that everyone would see through the 'sports job' as a GB ruse. But he felt there were two upsides I was overlooking – it would not be for as long a period of time as the last time he asked me. Also, it may just be I could turn it around, and my reputation would be enhanced.

He felt it all came down to how much the purpose, status and of course making a difference matter to you. He thought they matter a lot more than even I might realise so for that reason he'd lean towards doing it but only if I felt the team was manageable and wouldn't drive me crazy. I spent part of the day going through diaries Vol. 1 unexpurgated to see whether there was a way of doing something while Labour and GB were still in power. There was some pretty bad stuff in there, though maybe not as much as I anticipated. Might be doable, might not. Out later to an investments firm dinner in Hook, Hampshire. Nice enough crowd at my table, but the general audience was a bit grungy and I was not on great form. Definitely one of those nights where I felt I was there for the money and from their perspective a bit of a performing seal.

Friday 3 October

Out walking on the Heath with Fiona and the dog when I started to get calls asking me to do interviews on 'Peter Mandelson's return to government' [with a peerage, as Business Secretary]. It seemed odd that GB had been working on both of us simultaneously without telling me. Again it suggested the difficulty he had in working in a climate of trust. As TB said when I spoke to him later, it made more sense for Peter – unlike me, he was desperate to go to the Lords. He had an economic job now and so they could put it under the economic crisis umbrella. And it got him back to the UK. Peter M had asked for his advice and he had said do it. Re me, he said the only questions were – could I make a contribution, and did I want to do it? I felt the answers were yes, and not really. So I would probably just keep on as I was for the time being, offering a bit of help from the sidelines.

The Peter M news was big, game-changing stuff, but heaven knows what the public would make of it, or what they would have made of it if he had done the two of us together. Part of me felt I should be in there and part of it. Part of me just didn't want to know. The phone going with media the whole time was one of the reasons I didn't want to know. I avoided the news most of the day but the bits I saw were wall-to-wall Peter. Other reshuffle moves – Margaret B back at housing, Damian McBride and Stephen Carter sidelined, new department for Ed Miliband [Energy and Climate Change] – were just side shows. PM definitely the main event and of course he was loving it. Filmed being applauded back into the old DTI [Department of Trade and Industry], which must have been a really precious moment for him given his departure from there. John Woodcock [GB advisor] called and said Tom Watson had sounded him out about whether he would do McBride's job. The problem was that GB was pushing McBride into a backroom [strategic planning], but could not bring himself to get rid of him, go the whole hog. There seemed to be an assumption I would now also go back, but I was not sure at all. I said to TB I would think about it if the operation was changeable and the election was winnable. He said it might he changeable, but he didn't think it was winnable.

PG was in the States for tests. Like me, he knew nothing about Peter's return in advance. He felt it could cut both ways. He felt it made it harder for me to go back. In a way I felt the opposite. There were lots of references in the media to my diaries and their accounts of the GB–PM spats down the years. Going through Volume 1 unexpurgated was also underlining how much time and energy we wasted on it. It had certainly changed the Westminster weather though, but PG felt if both of us had been announced going back today, it would have been pretty neuralgic. He felt that reputational strength was probably best maintained by being on the outside a little. I had established myself as a loyalist, and everyone knew I would help out, but there was a danger the whole thing was just becoming a gigantic soap opera.

TB was also of the view that once the economic crisis calmed a little, people would go back to the things they thought about GB before. I texted DM to ask what he thought of it. He called back later. Something had definitely changed between us. He clearly felt I was a lot closer in than I was, and also, as he said, that I had been central to conference strategy.

I said I had been helping out but in part as a way of giving myself space to refuse other stuff. He felt GB could build a little from where he was. He also said he'd had a bad conference. I asked if GB involved him at all in general strategy. He said he spoke to him only if he had to. On Peter, he felt it was bold and he would add something, provided he kept his nose clean. Lots of the reaction was of that nature – could be a good move, provided he does not fuck it up. Peter's line was 'third time lucky'.

Out for dinner with Fiona and the boys at La Casalinga. Rory was now strongly of the view I should do it. Calum less so. Fiona saying I should do what I felt I should but she was clearly not keen. Lucio [waiter] was interesting – a couple of weeks ago he had been very down on the government. Now he was saying he would rather have serious, experienced GB there than 'Who the hell is he, this Cameron?' Back home to watch the *Cracking Up* film with the boys. They seemed to be OK with it. Cam taking the piss about the bit where I said I was paranoid about colours: red good, blue bad. 'Total propaganda.'

Saturday 4 October

TB called first thing. He felt the media and public would cut Peter M a bit of slack, but he really had to be careful, as the media would love to kill him. On my own position, he did not think it changed it fundamentally. Those two questions – could I make a difference, and did I want to do it? – were the same as before. It was good news in political direction and strategy terms that he had gone for PM, seemingly without even properly consulting Balls. Nick Brown [now chief whip as well as Minister for the North-East] and some of the junior appointments showed that GB in the end could not give up a certain style of politics. He felt the thing was not built on strong foundations. But we should try to help if we can. GB called as he was leaving for the mini summit Sarko had called in Paris. I said where did that come from then? All my idea, he said. He thought it was game-changing. He said he had hoped to get me in too, and he still did.

He said he understood my reluctance. Then another tack – would I come in on Tuesday and Wednesday to help with PMQs? I said this coming week was tricky as I was going to Australia. 'Come in on the way to the airport. We'll get you a car.' There was something a bit desperate about it. Long chat with Alex. He said he was still really torn for me. He felt I could help turn it around. But I would not be with my own people, and I would be giving up a lot of stuff. He felt on the sports job that I would do it well, and enjoy it, but everyone would know that was not the real reason I was there.

Off to Reading v Burnley. Chatted to John Madejski and his daughter over lunch. He felt the Peter thing was OK in itself but the public were probably already well dug in in their views. Said the whole business world was really tough at the moment. Nobody really fully got what was going on. Lost 3–1. Popped back to see them all, then headed home. Media still chasing me to say whether I would go back or not, and what I thought of PM's appointment.

Sunday 5 October

JP called, pissed off at Peter M's appointment and anxious about reports that Shaun Woodward [Northern Ireland Secretary] was getting a bigger role. He said it made him less keen to get stuck in with Go Fourth. He sounded quite down, felt maybe GB had used us a bit. I thought about telling him about GB asking me to go to the Lords but decided against. I was still thinking about it, but more negatively than before.

Monday 6 October

I met PG at the Honest Sausage in Regent's Park. He was just back from the States and was in pretty good form. He felt I was in the right place, that I should not commit further, that I would hate it if I ended up more fully in there. He was OK but tired and knew also that PM – who would be feeling pretty isolated – would want to draw him in more. He felt GB would not be able to win but a hung parliament was possible.

Tuesday 7 October

Out early for the screening of the documentary. I had a feeling it was not going to deliver what we needed and I was right. The Royal Society had focused very much on specialists, and the Beeb's paranoia about being thought to have given me another opportunity to use them to plug a book meant it was not as well media-attended as it should have been. There was something very trad and samey about these royal bodies. We were in a room with old portraits of fairly identical looking men who had been presidents. Presidents got a portrait. Deans got a pencil drawing. The head of psychiatry introduced the film. Nina Bell of BBC Headroom spoke very warmly about me and then came the film. It was strong. Some of the questions afterwards were a bit wacky but the reaction was good and at least it allowed me to get a feel for where questions would come from. I felt totally fine about answering all the questions and not remotely worried. Nobody asked about the stories in the papers today about me going back to some kind of frontline role with GB.

He had called me at 7 a.m. and again while the screening was on, asking me to go in to help with PMQs. I didn't fancy it. I did him a note and told Sue we could speak on the phone later. Partly it was because I was going away and wanted to spend a bit of time with Grace before I left for the airport. But also I felt I was being spun into going more deeply in and I wanted to put down a marker and also give myself more time to think. I still did not have the heart for it. I left for home. PG had come to the screening and thought it was by far the best television thing I had done. He said it was because it was authentic and all that would go if I went back. That was the problem. It did not feel right for me, right now. I knew what needed to be done but rather than seeing that as a challenge it just annoyed me that it was not being done by others. What did they all do? Why was there no real political attack? Why had nobody really emerged?

Alistair D's statement yesterday had been pretty dire and had seen shares dive even more. It showed a complete lack of co-ordination and also lack of understanding of how you needed to use these big moments for change and progress. My note to GB said it was no longer good enough to keep saying 'We will do whatever it takes' without doing something. It was getting close to parody. He needed to set out where we were, how we got here, where we were going and how. And they had to organise PMQs so that the vulnerabilities for Cameron – lightweight, did not make a great speech, does not get the economic stuff – were hit home. I had a chat with Godric on my situation. He said it would be great if I did sport. They would love it. But he realised it would not be the real reason for being there.

I was sitting talking to Grace when Peter M called. It was the first proper chat we had had since his return. He said it had all been pretty sudden. Yes, they had been talking for some time, but he was not angling for it and it was GB who suggested it, quickly. He seemed to know he had also been trying to get me back in via the Lords, but he did not know at the time, any more than I knew GB had been trying to get him. He said he felt a little bewildered. He felt on balance public reaction was OK. All the usual negative stuff was balanced by the sense it gave that GB was serious, determined to build unity, use the best brains and also it would help bury the leadership issue. On me, he felt I should do what I was good at which was give strong and clear strategic advice. He felt they were woefully weak on that front.

I said I did not like the way someone was spinning up that his coming back presaged mine. He said he had been partly responsible because he had said he knew who would run the campaign and it was someone he liked and trusted. Everyone had assumed it was me. I said to him what I had been saying to GB – that I was willing to help but not go back full time. I told him that actually I felt pretty reluctant about the whole thing. On the economy he felt GB was doing OK but nobody really knew where it was going to end and with what damage. He asked whether I thought PG would be able to do more. We agreed that if both of us had gone in together it would have been overwhelmingly about spin. But GB seemed not to mind. He said his one worry was if the press and the *Mail* in particular just kept on and on and on. He wondered about whether to take some kind of action against the *Mail*. Peter said GB had said he would speak to Dacre but he doubted he would. I said the relationship with Dacre was obscene.

I left for the airport and a good-looking Palestinian woman came up to me at the check-in and said she had really enjoyed watching me operate for TB and wishing me luck in the future. I needed it instantly. I had not realised I needed a visa. Thankfully the guy at the check-in knew how to short-circuit the system and I was able to buy one for thirty quid. Could have been really embarrassing. The first leg was to Bangkok and I watched *In Bruges* which was hilarious in parts. A bit daft by the end but good. As I stepped off at Bangkok, where we were stopping for a couple of hours, I was greeted by a TV with GB announcing pretty huge bailout for our banks and urging others to do the same. He seemed to do fine and there was without doubt a major leadership role to be filled here. It was his last chance for reinvention and cut-through. I had a shower in Bangkok, did a bit of work then slept pretty much the whole of the leg to Sydney.

Thursday 9 October

Flying into Sydney has to be one of the great landings. Beautiful beaches. The harbour with the opera house. Vast suburbs then even vaster landmass. Met by John the driver and off to the InterContinental. Alysha Farry from Random House had arranged one radio and one telly later but had left in a few hours to rest. I went for a run through the Botanical Gardens. Lovely sunny day. Had lunch down by the harbour and just watched the world go by for a while. The media was wall-to-wall financial meltdown. Pretty big interest in GB in the Australian media. Concerted interest rate cut [joint action by six major central banks]. Grace sent over her excellent history essay on whether the '20s were a golden era which really cheered me up. I had a swim, managed to stay awake, met Alysha then off to the first interview, 2GB radio. As ever struck by how much more polite non-Brit interviewers are. Then to ABC to prerecord *Nightline*. Fine though stumbled over words a couple of times. It was meant to be the equivalent of *Newsnight* but was really anything but. Nice enough time though.

Dinner at the Exchange Club hosted by Margie Searle at RH. She had read

All in the Mind and felt it would do well. Nice bunch from RH plus a couple of journalists they had invited. It turned into a pretty lively and enjoyable Q&A. It was amazing how closely they all followed UK politics. They were all pretty worried about the economic stuff. A lot of interest in whether I would go back and also if not why not. One guy – Alan Oakley [*Sydney Morning Herald*] – asked direct whether it was because I thought GB could not win. I actually felt this current situation potentially played to all his strengths. But I still did not want to go back in anything like a full-time capacity.

Friday 10 October

Didn't sleep well despite taking one of Fiona's pills. Judith sending me texts expressing her growing anger at the refusal of the Beeb properly to promote the documentary because they were worried about being accused of promoting the novel. I went for a swim. Asthma not great at the moment. Had breakfast then met Alysha and off on the media rounds. Fran Kelly [ABC Radio] really nice and warm. There was something much less cynical than our media. She went through a lot including the novel and the doc. Media-wise it was wall-to-wall financial meltdown. GB was indeed doing OK. The problem was, as Alan Milburn said when I called him, that once the initial crisis was over, there would be economic fallout and also the reasons the public went against him in the first place would still be there. I chatted to PG who felt not to get further drawn in at this stage though he said he was worried about Peter who would be feeling very isolated in there. Fran asked me direct if I was going back and I think I got the right formula – happy to help but don't want a full-time job.

Off to Classic FM for a kind of *Desert Island Discs* [BBC radio programme]. The show had been going for fifteen years five days a week. I insisted on choosing one bagpipe tune and one Brel. Good chat. Alysha delivered me to Scaffidi Hugh Jones for the lunch. PR company, nice bunch. Signed books for everyone. At the lunch I rehearsed the first part of my speech for Monday's conference which was based on something PG had done. Nice woman from the business community who had done a lot of research on business and the Sydney Olympics. Agreed to put her in touch with Seb or Tessa or Godric. Also *Australia Post* boss who was telling me they had sold 25 million stamps brought out specially each time an Aussie won gold. I went out to the airport. TV blaring away re another dire day in markets. I was tired. Even on the half-hour flight to Canberra you got a taste of the vastness. I was met by Helen Liddell [high commissioner] at the plane. Then met by Michael Morgan of the ALP [Australian Labor Party]. Helen couldn't come because it was a party event so off with Michael to a function room at the Old Parliament buildings.

The big news for most of the audience was chief of staff [to Prime Minister Kevin Rudd] David Epstein – who I was due to have dinner with – resigning to be replaced by a 29-year-old, Alister Jordan. Nice enough do, mix of advisors and party business supporters. I did half an hour off the cuff, Q&A and then signed books. Lively enough bunch. Really followed our politics and they were also pressing on whether I really thought GB could win and whether I would go back. Off to Helen's residence. Like a Home Counties golf club. Why were these residences always the same? The royal crest and photos in the hall. Piano covered by more photos. Helen loving the job and really plugged in. Alistair [husband] also really into the whole story. They had been all over the country and were hugely knowledgeable. She clearly felt she had landed upon something she did really well e.g. pushing the Aussie government on climate change, defence and intelligence link-up. She had senior ISC [Intelligence Services Committee] members in town, including Michael Mates and Richard Ottaway [Tory MPs]. They were being put up in a hotel rather than here, in truth because I was there, ostensibly because she said – true – she was meeting the PM's office for dinner. She didn't say I was the cause of the dinner.

Epstein came despite the upheaval. Hard to find out what had really happened. He was an old timer but probably just a victim of the churn that happens. He was really bright and on top of policy detail but I had been hearing a fair bit that Rudd had been good at the symbolic stuff – e.g. the national apology to the Aborigines – but not good at driving forward hard policy graft and important decisions. Too many reviews etc. Helen and I were fairly open in front of Epstein, Ben Hubbard from the DPM's office, his Danish wife, and Michael re GB and the dysfunctional No. 10. They knew it anyway in that they were always having to play catch-up with the one-on-one mobile calls etc. I was fascinated by some of the stuff I was learning re the Aborigine movement and history, the sense of a ticking timebomb and nobody really sure how to deal with it. Sex abuse. Alcohol. Porn. No engagement. White Australia's basic racism and also inability to understand their culture. Hard to get your head round it. They felt descended from the animals and lived a totally different life. Welfare to work impossible because, for example, if a relative died they might have to disappear in the outback for months to find their dreams.

Helen full of stories of her time there and clearly round peg in round hole. She said she mentioned me at every dinner because her son had bought her two steel balls after my comment about her having balls of steel way back. She was on great form and clearly glad to be out of the frontline back home. She said GB had not spoken to her. Even when she was ready to tell him the election result he avoided her. She felt the whole machine was poor now. Clearly thought I was right not to dive back in.

Nice evening and I was enjoying being back in that atmosphere, but perhaps more so because I knew it would not be for long. Ben Hubbard had been at Millbank during the '97 campaign so we relived a bit of that. Nice guy. Very funny about canvassing with Fraser Kemp [MP] up north and nobody being able to understand a word he said. The scale of the place – Helen said she knew an MP with ten thousand voters in a constituency the size of Portugal. Most had pilot licences so they could go round their seats properly. Chat re the impact of minerals boom for China in Western Australia. Helen on how [John] Howard went at her because of her pressure on climate change.

Saturday 11 October

Another bad night's sleep. Nice and rare day of pretty much full on R and R. Out for a run up Red Hill. Kangaroos bopping around. Fabulous birds flying around. Asthma not great and no pace. We walked down with their dog to the brunch restaurants. Good chat on GB and the general scene. Helen felt as I did that once the initial crisis was over, the fundamentals would return. She felt nobody was ready to take over though. She really wanted John Reid to get into Scotland. She was not sure about going to the Lords and doubtful GB would have her. Really nice morning just chilling and chatting. Bought a few presents. Out to a couple of smaller towns. Local paper splash was about a group of dogs barking in unison to church hymns last Sunday. Back via the war memorial and museum which was probably the most impressive and moving memorial I have ever seen. Two long walls with hundreds of thousands of names of dead servicemen and women. If any poppies lay on the floor, you looked for someone of your own name and put the poppy in the wall by the name. Dozens of A. Campbells. Put a few poppies in there, and on an R. Millar [Fiona's father Robert]. The tomb of the unknown soldier surrounded by huge murals in a lovely room at the far end. We then toured the museum and you felt the pride they felt as a nation of their veterans and fallen. It was deep in the psyche especially since Gallipoli.

Back to do a bit of work. James Macintyre [political correspondent] had been driving me mad trying to persuade me to do something for the *New Statesman*. He was virtually in tears begging me. I said no but then worked on a possible piece that he could do. Also working on a piece for the *Times Literary Supplement* re the novel. We chilled out a bit before Tim Clayden and his wife and Peter Elder and his wife came for dinner. I last knew Tim working on Europe for SIS and Peter when working for me in No. 10. Tim was quite large and very jolly and great company. He was also very bright and once we had gone through the usual small talk and badinage we had a fascinating discussion re Al Qaeda. He reckoned the whole focus on getting Osama bin Laden was a waste of time and a distraction. He also thought that the military solution alone was not going to work. He felt it was my kind of expertise needed not just theirs. We needed to build the arguments that would persuade people there to take on the extremist argument. All the bombing did was create more extremists.

We had to take a leaf out of TB's domestic agenda – education, education, education. He felt the US had never got it and he doubted McCain would or that Obama would have it as priority. But it is scary stuff. He had spent a lot of time in Islamabad and clearly did not think the Pakistanis were really helping. A. Q. Khan [Pakistani nuclear physicist] was still there and we had got nowhere nearer seeing him. Yet here was a man who had given the bomb to others. He was a national hero. They were genuinely worried Iran might get it and use it. The Pakistanis had helped the Yanks with a few rendition cases but at heart they were not really motoring for us. We did a run around other areas – Indonesia, broader Muslim community, China and the scale of change and advance, Russia and what a nightmare they were becoming.

When we got on to GB there was a general feeling it had moved away. They were not that impressed about Rudd either. Peter felt he was getting a reputation for indecisiveness and lack of clarity. Really nice evening and again Helen terrific at engaging and putting out some terrific anecdotes from around the place. Tim was a big fan of the diaries and asking lots of question re process and purpose etc. He was wondering if I would get more involved in the kind of thing he was talking about. I had increasingly found myself saying I was enjoying real freedom for the first time and I didn't fancy too many really big projects. I probably should get more into this though. It was a late night but I enjoyed it.

Sunday 12 October

Breakfast with Helen and Alistair. Fairly depressing chat on the Aborigine issues and all the stuff on drink, porn twenty-four hours a day in some places, massive child sex abuse. Howard had tried to sort out with military and cops moving in but it was felt to be for show. She said they had tried Welfare to Work [welfare reform] but they would get a young Aborigine into work and when his first cousin died he would have to walk in the outback for six weeks or even months. There was such a cultural gap. Added to which it was not long since the government had a white Australia policy and open racism was rife. She had totally got into the politics, the history and culture of the place and they would find it hard to re adapt to life in Scotland. She said it may be impossible to face living in a country run by Salmond.

They drove me to the airport. Said farewell then off to Perth. Stunning flight. Part vast green, part vast red. Sitting next to a distance teacher who looked after sixty kids all over the state (which was 'roughly' the size of Europe). He loved his job but clearly it was tough. 'Fuck off white cunt' was a common greeting. Yet some kids were super bright. Interesting guy. He said he was warned many of the kids were abused sexually. Many of the males were driven by drink and porn. Helen had said it was sub third world. He felt the same. I was tired and fell asleep almost till Perth. Met by Tom Mackay and Dominic Patterson who had organised the conference I was speaking at, for the PR institute of Australia. I had the rest of the afternoon off and first went for a run along the South Beach. Blue, blue sea. Warm and sunny. Lots of happy healthy people around. Pretty amazing place. Then out to the dinner at the Maritime Museum for the Fellows of the PRIA. Bit of a dry lot in the main. All fundraising going to LRF. I did a Q&A on stage and then opened it up. Went down well. Odd to think how big we were out here. They still saw us as the best in political comms.

Monday 13 October

Out for another wheezy run. The time difference was now only seven hours so from 4 a.m. I was starting to get loads of messages about *Cracking Up*. Mainly saying brave, honest and would help others. Reviews pretty good considering it was me and most media could not quite bring themselves to go the whole way. I was also getting loads of bids on the back of it, but couldn't do them from here. Lots of good feedback on Fiona's contribution, and also to the fact she had stood by me like she did.

I had breakfast with the organisers and American academic new media expert Jen McLure. I had redone the speech having been here a bit and was now cutting down. Basically the analysis of how comms had changed followed by leadership template. Almost 500 PR people there. Went down really well I felt. I can always tell where there is real engagement and there really was. Warm and positive feedback. Did a Q&A with Jen where I pushed back a bit on her new media stuff as I was not convinced that the order of significance of things – TV and radio, then press then new – had really changed, though it might yet, in fact almost certainly would. Book signing which seemed to go on for ages. Nice crowd. One Swedish woman really coming on strong. Ditto another from South America. And loads asking for pictures and you felt the ones just pulling your body against theirs. I sensed they could be a pretty wild bunch. Kind of relieved to get out. Met up with Justin Langer [Australian Test cricketer] who was doing a session on business using sportsmen. He was a really nice guy. We both did leukaemia stuff. Also re his life in Somerset. His presentation was OK. But he told a story about how he had thought hard about doing a Johnnie Walker whisky ad and he was glad he did it because it made him more famous outside of Oz than cricket did. I said to him afterwards it was not clear how he had resolved ethical questions and I always felt if it was a choice between cash and reputation always go for reputation. He texted me later to say he had thought about it and he agreed. He also asked me to give any thoughts on how he could improve and I did him a note.

I pottered around for a while before the awards dinner. I was rather dreading it but it turned out to be OK. The compere was a tall good-looking presenter from Channel 9 called Dixie [Marshall] with a big smile and big glasses and a hugely flirtatious manner with me. I was sitting with an editor of the Australian magazine and a lovely young reporter, who had been doing a story on Hell's Angels murders – they were still really heavy down here – and she felt she had not done it as well as she could. She reminded me in some of her attitudes of me at the same age, twenty-five. Loads and loads of young PR women wanting pictures and flirting away. Then someone produced a set of bagpipes which I played and they all went pretty wild. I left to go to bed but got waylaid by the Swede and two others for a while. I stayed for a drink and then left after half an hour or so. The reaction had been more celebrity than comms specialist. Tom Mackay said as much. It was frankly a bit weird.

Tuesday 14 October

Down to the beach and a fabulous swim in blue, blue water. A few guys out waiting for surf. It was not hot by their standards but perfect by ours. I had to do another book signing session before getting ready to leave. They had sold all the hardbacks and all but a few paperbacks. I had a bit of time to buy some presents for the kids around town – really busy – before Tom and Dominic took me out to the airport. They were effusive about the way the whole thing had gone and Dominic in particular felt there would be a lot more work there if I wanted it.

I did a bit of work on the plane, next to a guy who was laughing loudly at a comedy compilation. It was so much easier coming back from Perth rather than Sydney. Couple of hours in Singapore then onto a BA flight. I had meantime written up a piece for the *Statesman* and sent it through to James Macintyre on landing. Then into the kind of thing I can't stand dealing with any longer – can we say this, can we say that, what about if… And when we landed in London I discovered they had made up a couple of quotes e.g. 'the New Labour family is coming back together.' Yuk. He was thrilled then apologetic. I had dinner on the plane then, despite no more pills, decided to lie down and try to sleep the whole way. I didn't do too badly. Felt reasonably human as we landed just after 5 a.m.

Wednesday 15 October

I pinged a note to GB, of a possible line of attack on Cameron 'weak on policy, weak on the causes of policy' to help get to a place where it becomes clear GB understands this complex situation and DC does not. He gets policy. DC does not. The obvious resonance to one of TB's most memorable soundbites reminds that soundbites are all DC does. He does not do the policy heavy lifting. I suggested GB had to communicate – show not tell – the economic equivalent of the sort of leadership TB showed post-9/11. It turned out he was at a European summit. He was getting good plaudits for his handling of the crisis and the Tories were looking more vulnerable but there was still the problem of the fundamentals that would return afterwards – the reasons why he got down in the first place and also the loss of jobs and decline in living standards etc. I was glad to be home but it had also been good to be away from the whole political scene. I suspected I would be sucked back in again now.

Thursday 16 October

Slaughter and May law firm crisis management seminar. Fairly stuffy bunch but the event went fine. Did the opening keynote, then a panel trying to make a crisis worse as another panel at the opposite end of the room tried to deal with it. Then two workshops dealing with real scenarios which went well. Robert Peston [business editor] was on the panel and was clearly loving his sudden celebrity as the BBC face of the crisis. Home for lunchtime. Later TB called. He felt glad for GB that he was getting decent plaudits and also that it meant there would be something positive to say when he went. But he felt there would be a return to the fundamentals once the crisis was stabilised. The reasons he went down in the first place would return. And the economic fallout would be real and difficult.

He felt re me that I had been right not to go in the Lords, particularly if GB had been thinking of putting me in at the same time as Peter. PM had been wanting to get into the Lords for some time. He felt I was a much more anti-establishment figure and that would be dissipated if I went to the Lords. He felt I should carry on helping – we all should – but not go in. And he was keen for me to do more with him. He had not seen the film but had had lots of feedback on it and said it sounded pretty amazing. He said if he had known I had been drinking again while working for him he would have been really worried. I went to see PG in Regent's Park. His big thing was that we should all be moving on. He felt the documentary was the best thing I had done because it was so honest and authentic.

Friday 17 October

Still tired and maybe starting on a downward dip. But nice enough day. Walk with Charlie Falconer on the Heath, both with our spaniels getting some very interesting looks. The rebels had defeated the 42-day detention plan. He was pleased about that, also pleased that GB seemed to be handling things well, but like others he was not convinced it would endure. He echoed something TB had said yesterday, namely that the reshuffle had in some ways seen a lot of the bad people he could not do without promoted under cover of Peter's elevation. He felt re me I was probably just about in the right place. Drove down to Oxford for lunch with Rebecca Carter and a chat re *Maya*. She liked it and had some good ideas for improvement. Out for a curry with F and Rory in Hampstead. I was definitely beginning to dip though.

Saturday 18 October

Calum wanted to go out for lunch with Rory and me and said he really thought I should get another big job, that I needed a new challenge and the novels were not enough. Rory was of the same view, thought I should go back full-time with GB. Saw PG, looking a bit tired and stressed. I was well and truly down now.

Sunday 19 October

Really down. Worrying I needed to go back on the pills. I was pottering mainly, trying to do a bit of work after everyone left. Mum said she was worried about me. She felt I had lost too much weight and seemed very fed up. I was very grouchy and feeling a bit drained of energy and hope. Polls narrowing but perhaps not as much as all the punditry pro-GB would have led you to expect. I did a piece for *La Repubblica* on the theme that maybe this time economic woe would not automatically mean political woe.

Monday 20 October

Lesley White round to do a piece for the *Sunday Times*. Although we talked a fair bit about the novel, there was too much GB, TB, PM, Cherie etc. I didn't feel on form and maybe she sensed it. She did say I seemed to be in a good place mentally which is not at all how it felt. I liked her though. Charlie F had said she once said to him she sometimes thought she shouldn't like me and TB but then she met us again and always did. But I did not feel I had worked through what I should be saying about all this. Lunch with Calum on the way to taking him to Euston, then back to read Gillian Slovo's novel, *Black Orchids*. She and I were to do a radio programme together. She had read mine and emailed to say she had been reduced to tears on a train journey from Leeds. She really liked it, found it moving and readable. Ed's main worry was that the market was just not vibrant. Out to a club in West End to do the Leukaemia Research Bike-athon Awards. Gary Lineker had pulled out so it was all a bit last-minute. Bit of schmoozing then home. As I walked through the door, a call from Margaret Hodge. Henry was back in hospital and they were getting conflicting advice re whether or not to have a bone marrow transplant. She was in tears at various points and asked if I knew anyone she could speak to. Put her in touch with Cathy Gilman.

Tuesday 21 October

Out to do a session with a group of South African government and tourism comms people. Nice enough bunch. Did some pretty big-picture stuff then a fairly lively Q&A. The government people wanted me to go there to do more. Home then out to La Casalinga for the 'Lunch with the *FT*' slot for next week with Gideon Rachman [chief foreign affairs commentator]. Nice guy who had read both books closely and I was on better form than with Lesley. Met Stuart Le Gassick and headed to Manchester for the United game against Celtic [3–0]. Someone pranking by sending a succession of Addison Lee cars to home. Really annoying. John Reid [Celtic chairman] furious re two offside goals. Said he had seen my film. Margaret McD and her mum his guests. She felt GB was now staying and we should help. She felt I should do the Olympics.

Wednesday 22 October

Meeting with Kieron Collins at the Beeb about a new programme, *The Speaker*, testing out young kids to do public speaking. Agreed to do one weekend filming for one episode towards the end of the process and maybe get them to go to a top private school and defend state education. They had decided against a single judge after I had decided not to do it and instead had a weekly guide and three judges whittling them down. Sounded better than most such stuff.

Thursday 23 October

Rory had another spill on the bike and sprained his wrist so it was looking like he may have to pull out of Sunday's race. I had a session with DS. Against putting me back on the medication. Feeling really low again.

Went to see PG at the Honest Sausage. He was slightly manic, I was on a major down. He said he had a bad feeling about the Peter M scene. The whole business of what happened when he and [George] Osborne were on some Russian oligarch's yacht was getting massive coverage after Nat Rothschild [financier] wrote to *The Times* having a dig at Osborne.* It was damaging all round and PG felt there was a real worry re Peter. He felt I had done the right thing in not going back. Yet it was becoming a near fact that I had in fact gone back. Despite the tiredness and everything else he had done some groups and a note. He was not persuaded that the handling of the economic crisis was going to turn the situation around for GB. He felt I should work out of Victoria Street on Cameron attack.

Met up with David Mills who was more worried than I have seen him before re the way the Italian trial was going. He felt the judge was determined to stick something on Berlusconi and the only way he could do it, now Berlusconi had changed the law to avoid prosecution while serving, was via David. As ever it was not easy to pin down all the details but he was definitely more alarmed than before. He gave me a lift round to the Hodges'. I took Henry a copy of the book and he seemed really touched by it. I had put Margaret on to Cathy at LRF who had fixed for her to see [specialist] Ken Campbell tomorrow to help them decide what to do about the conflicting advice they were getting on whether he should have a bone marrow transplant. He was not in as bad shape as I expected though he had lost all his hair. Until the split opinion, and apart from the food, he said he had had great care. She was glad to be out of government and pretty sure GB would have sacked her, but she was still minded to fight another term because she wanted to keep on working for Barking.

Friday 24 October

Still feeling down and empty. Not sure if it was major league dip or not, but it definitely had the makings of it. I kept in touch with Margaret Hodge who was seeing Ken Campbell at LRF. She called after spending a couple of hours and said everyone – especially Cathy on the phone and Ken Campbell in person – had been brilliant. She and Amy left feeling so much better and later, after they briefed him, so did Henry. I was pottering around a bit, not really motoring. I was trying to lift myself to go out with Fiona for dinner at the Blackburns' in Notting Hill. Nice Jewish

* Mandelson and Osborne had been entertained at the same time at Corfu on the 'superyacht' of Russian oligarch Oleg Deripaska, during which it was alleged that Mandelson had 'dripped pure poison' about GB. An angry Mandelson insisted the visit was purely social during his summer holiday.

couple there. Did not get their names as we arrived. Fiona knew them. He was supremely wealthy and she was well connected in the arts world. Nice enough evening and I was pulling out of the slough.

Saturday 25 October

The Guardian had the first big review of *All in the Mind,* plus an extract. Massive show but I felt Adam Phillips [psychologist and writer] missed the point. According to DS he was an anti-psychiatrist and was using the review to promote his own agenda. He was perfectly nice about the book but did not really get it and was praising me for stances and techniques I had not adopted. I was pleased with the extract and PG and Gail both liked it. To Charlton Burnley. Michael Grade [executive chairman, ITV] there as ever. Said he loved the Brel programme. Also that the business environment for ITV was dire. Good match. We battered them first half but only scored once. They took the second half so a 1–1 draw fair, I guess.

Afterwards we went down to see Alan Pardew [Charlton manager]. I bumped into several of our players who seemed pretty fed up. Great in a way that we were the more disconsolate team after an away draw. I had a good chat with Owen Coyle and Sandy Stewart [Burnley manager and No. 2]. Both seem really nice guys. Sandy told me he used to be manager to Owen's assistant role at Airdrie. Turned it into a quiz question for Alex who went mad at his inability to get it – name a current manager whose No. 2 used to be his No. 1.

Sunday 26 October

Out to the BBC to do Marr on the novel. Jonathan Dimbleby and Amanda Platell were doing the papers. Amanda was so right-wing in her review. Loads of Peter M but it seemed to me nothing deadly. Felt the interview was OK. He didn't really push too hard re GB and I had a fair bit of time on the book. He did ask direct if GB had asked me to go into the government via the Lords. I stayed for breakfast which – cuts no doubt – was canteen not the boardroom days of Frost. Andy really doing stacks of stuff. Just back from Central America making a programme on Darwin. TB called before heading to China tomorrow. In good form but busy.

Monday 27 October

Really motoring on the book publicity. Christina Patterson from *Independent*. She said she liked the book and was crying at the end. There was clearly going to be lots on the extent to which a novel reveals more than e.g. the diaries. Pre-chats for *The One Show* and *This Morning*. *One Show* researcher said he loved the book. Like Christina had cried. Read it through in two sessions over the weekend. Later did Five News. Nice enough but pretty downmarket. Leading on the row over Jonathan Ross [TV presenter] and Russell Brand broadcasting [on BBC Radio 2] an obscene call they made to Andrew Sachs the actor about his granddaughter. It was becoming one of those media storms. I felt it would blow over but the Beeb were handling it so badly it could go wrong pretty quickly.

Got a bit on the book though not the four minutes promised. I was tracking where it was on Amazon future releases and it was racing up the chart pretty fast. Fiona and Grace were up seeing Calum so Audrey came round to cook dinner. We watched the JP programme on class. Best bit when he engaged with a young so-called chav who was really bright yet did not know who GB was. Lunch with Earl of Onslow. The best thing was the way JP connected with the young girl. They sort of got each other.

Tuesday 28 October

Out to do Steve Wright. OK interview and I was certainly getting the chance to talk properly about the book. And also set out the reality on the idea I was 'back' helping GB. I was comfortable with the line that I was happy to help and in particular go for the Tories, but no full-time job. GB called on his way to Paris to see Sarko. He sounded OK. Said it had been pretty tough. I asked where it would end. Not sure. And where was the Peter M situation leading? He laughed. No idea! Peter had seemingly managed to get the thing shifted on to Osborne but the media was still digging into Peter much more than the Tories. GB was asking me how I felt he should position Cameron tomorrow, and we talked over the note I gave him. But he did not really bite re big attack. He didn't ask me again re going back. I suspect he'd have been briefed about what I had been saying. Out to *The One Show* with Adrian Chiles and Christine Bleakley. Whizzed by. Good fun and again with a bit of space for the book.

Wednesday 29 October

Liam Byrne [Cabinet Office minister] and his spad came round at half eight. I didn't know him that well. He wanted to pick my brains on how to get systems in place and how to use them to devise and drive strategy. He said he was pretty shocked at what he had gone into. No real systems. Too many egos. People of very varying ability worrying all the time re their relationship to GB. GB himself lacking clarity and not always seeing decisions through. I went through what I saw as Cameron's vulnerabilities and the tricks we were missing, and the note I had done for PMQs for GB, as I did later with Peter M. Both agreed that it would wound DC. But deep down I knew GB would not do it. And he didn't.

Thursday 30 October

Out to do *This Morning*. Fern Britton and Philip Schofield were away so I couldn't upbraid her for serialising in the *Mail*. Eamonn Holmes and his new lady love Ruth Langsford were stand-in presenters. Richard Wilson [actor] was also on and when Alex called for a chat I put him on. 'I'm worried about Cristiano's attitude at the moment,' he said. 'You leave the worrying to me,' said Alex. He was raging about the Ross–Brand situation, said it was all about dropped BBC standards. He was sounding pretty upbeat on the football front. Felt Arsenal were fading. Liverpool unlikely to sustain. Chelsea the threat still. The interview went pretty well though heaven knows if it was shifting books.

Round to PG's. He was pretty chipper post his trip to California. He was almost back to his old self and back to his strange ways re me and whether to go back. On the one hand he was saying I did the right thing not going in. On the other he was constantly thinking of ways I could get involved. Peter M, back from Russia, texted to ask where I was. At PG's, I said. Wish I was there, came the reply. Then he called. How was it? I asked. Odd, he said. 'On the one hand I feel I can do things and make a difference. On the other hand it is all a bit dysfunctional.' He said he was still in regular contact with GB but in some ways less than before, and he was definitely not learning the right lessons of the past year. He was clearly now thinking he had been right about himself all along. Yet PM said it was pretty clear the problems were still there. We agreed to meet up soon to discuss it in detail. Every time I got close I wanted to pull back. The book was on Amazon pre-release chart, hovering between 3 and 10. Out to Camden Brasserie with Fiona.

Friday 31 October

Christina Patterson piece ran in *The Independent*. Text from Martin Sheehan [No. 10 head of strategic communications] asking how much I paid her. She obviously liked both me and the book and said so. But also, she basically concluded I should go back into politics. E.g. there are lots of novels. There aren't many ACs. Went to see DS. A lot better than a week ago. On the efforts to get me into politics again – open like the politicians, unintended like the press – he said they were 'reeling in the addict'. Douglas Alexander was on, clearly put up to it by PG, asking for a meeting re what I might do. I set off for Cambridge to meet up with Godric for a bike ride. He was on terrific form. Good chat as we were out, maybe two hours plus, on the bike. Stopped to visit the US military cemetery. He was keen for me to get engaged in the Olympics. Thought I should speak to Seb about the right role. By the time I was home Donald was down for tomorrow's bagpipe tournament.

Saturday 1 November

Calum home for reading week. The *FT* interview came out well. *FT* review good too. Ditto *The Times* alongside my own piece. Out to Kensington for Donald's tournament. He played OK but no prizes.

Sunday 2 November

Crap reviews in the *Sunday Times* and *Telegraph*. Good in the *Mail on Sunday*. Big day of sport. Out on the bike. Rugby league. Watch Lewis Hamilton become world champion seconds after it looked like he had blown it again. The news agenda now all pointing to Tuesday's US election. Looking like wipeout for Obama.

Monday 3 November

Brian [driver] arrived before 8, collected Fiona McM and set off for Somerset. I'd agreed to do the first signing at the Slab House Inn as a thank-you to Stuart [Le Gassick, proprietor] for his 25k cheque to the party which, even though he had not yet paid it, I was confident would come. We arrived at his country pad in a place called Ashwick. Real lord of the manor stuff. Nice house though. His sister there with husband up for the day. They had sold about forty seats for the lunch, which included a copy of the book. Real Tory crowd for the lunch. Did pictures for the locals and SW news, interview for *Daily Press* which made the front, lunch – best lamb ever eaten – then a little speech without notes, then ever friendlier Q&A. Stuart said he had amazing response later and it had confirmed him in his view I should go back to help out GB. He thought DC was really weak and vulnerable.

Tuesday 4 November

Another day another interview. Matthew Wright show. Only he was ill and Lowri Turner [journalist and TV presenter] was standing in. Bit of a waste of time. Too downmarket, not enough discussion of the book and it became a jokey but ultimately silly series of spats about stories of the day. Carole Malone [columnist] also on with real *Daily Mail* agenda bollocks. The editor apologised, felt Lowri went OTT, for example throwing the book on the floor. Then a little reading. To a panel on crisis management which went fine – John Inverdale [sports presenter] interviewing me, [Sir] Paul Condon [Commissioner] of the Met Police, Phil Hall [journalist turned PR] and Paul Charles of Virgin Atlantic. Good enough session. Nick Keller happy with it. Then me interviewing Dave Brailsford. On great form and you could have heard a pin drop. Good response and feedback.

Email from Susan Sandon. Disappointing BookScan figures – in Top 50 but only just, which given the scale of publicity was low. Gail and Susan both felt we were still in OK shape but it was disappointing. Douglas A came round for a chat. He was keen to work out a way that I could get involved at Victoria Street, galvanising the party and maybe heading up some kind of unit on DC. But he was very frank re the weaknesses – no money, paper-thin staffing levels (e.g. three press officers v thirty at CCO). But also the worst thing remained the dysfunctionality at the centre. On balance he felt Peter M was a good thing for the government and it was useful that he had rebuilt a proper relationship and dialogue with GB. Indeed, some of the coverage of their trip [promoting British business] to the Gulf had been all about how the two of them were inseparable. But GB, he said, would not confront the weaknesses in all the relationships. He would not have e.g. Balls and Peter M in the same meeting.

He had Ed chairing meetings that Liam [Byrne] should be doing. Liam not totally sure what he was supposed to be doing. Lots of people brought in as the next new key person and when they didn't work he never got rid or rearranged properly. It sounded more not less dysfunctional than before. Added to which, he said he still had the old machine politicians holding too much sway. Nick Brown. Tom Watson putting in Unite [trade union] people and politics at every level. I said it sounded terrible. He said yes but that's why you should come to the party. I said if No. 10 is not functional then it won't matter where I am. He said what GB had not done was put in place the layer of people – me, JoP, Sally, Anji types – who could take most decisions. They even had situations where they did not have a strapline for events because he was doing that kind of thing. Really sounded hopeless.

He said he owed it to me to try to arrange a situation that was at least bearable if not enjoyable. I said I worried they were all accepting situations that were not acceptable on the basis that they could be even worse. Christ, when you compared the operation with what we had, or what Obama was putting together. He seemed pretty disillusioned on GB. He said that it was alarming how he was not really learning the right lessons from the past year. Instead, because he was in a better place as a result of the financial crisis, he was emanating a sense that nobody should ever have doubted him. I said after the economic storm was over, there would be economic fallout and without proper systems there would be implosion. What he was describing to me had all the ingredients for implosion, that was for sure. He said I was best used at the party and we could make it work. I said what about Harriet? He said GB does not pay her much attention which is creating its own difficulties. He should manage her better. He was doing an audit of the party's capability. I said let me see it and then we can see if there is a way forward. But I felt even less enthusiastic.

Then out later to the US Embassy for the election night party. Giant TVs everywhere but it was impossible to follow what was actually going on and I was quite keen to leave. Chat with Gus O'Donnell who said despite the perceived improvement things were still pretty dire in No. 10. He felt Jeremy was doing well on the civil service front but there was no political clarity or strategy. Lots of different people just clunking around. Good chat with [Sir] Jeremy Greenstock [former diplomat]. He was very nice about the diaries, felt I got most of the main players home and abroad pretty well. Steve and Rachel Kinnock. Mark Thompson [BBC director general] looked a bit whacked out. Odd mix of people though. Glad to get away and follow it properly at home. One or two people had been suggesting Obama was losing Virginia. Turned out to be balls. Obvious by the time we were home that he was heading for a big win. Grace and her friends keen to follow it and seemed genuinely enthused.

Wednesday 5 November

Obama home and dry. Fabulous speech in Chicago. Beautifully written and gracefully delivered. I was trying to work out, amid the incredible outpouring of happiness and emotion around the world, the last truly global galvanising event. Diana's death? No. September 11? But that was fear not hope. NI? For us maybe but not global. Mandela's release? Sport? One country at a time. In its own way this was far bigger and more hopeful than any of those. I was watching the news on and off in between emails etc. and writing stuff for today. Out p.m. to the NHS comms conference. 300 of them. Did a mix of analysis plus advice on strategy then a Q&A panel with Gavin Esler [BBC presenter] in the chair. They seemed pleased enough. Did an Obama transition interview, then home before going out to La Casalinga with Brendan Foster. When F told him GB had offered me the Sports Minister's job, he felt I should take it. He thought I'd be able to make a big difference and do it well and get some politics into it for once. He could not believe how we had allowed the Tories to dominate the Olympics board. F and the kids also thinking I should do a real job now. I was still holding back though. Brendan telling us how jumpy the Beeb were at having TB involved in starting the Great North Run.

Thursday 6 November

Obama appointing Rahm Emanuel as chief of staff. Good move. Sara Latham [Clinton aide] out there. Would love to be there and involved. Our show seemed so threadbare and visionless by comparison. Even yesterday's PMQs, where GB should have been big and above it all, was dire, squabbling over what it meant and trying to claim for us that it was a win for left-of-centre progressive politics, for the Tories that it showed time for a change and OK to be a novice. But it reminded people of just how special Obama was and how ordinary our guys seemed. Out to Hatchards. Five snappers but none of the excitement or the queues of the time I did a signing of *The Blair Years*. The shop guys felt the reviews had been good and there would be a good market for some time and then for the paperback as we had what they called 'selling' reviews. Lunch with Fiona McM next door at Italian restaurant. She said if I wanted to build profile as fiction writer I would have to do the main festivals as well as all the media stuff etc. I guess so. Also she felt I had to have my own website and keep it up there as a big thing driving a rounded image.

Off to Brighton. Xchanging [business services firm]. Nice enough event. Did a new speech, based on the question 'Has there ever been a single event that has so galvanised people in so many countries!' I don't think so. Good crowd. Q&A pretty friendly and as fairly often recently it was easier to make the case GB was doing better and DC worse. I did the usual thing of asking three people at my table to give me a word to weave into the speech. One said scissors, which I got in in a story about the Queen opening something. The second said trousers, which I used in the story about being filmed in the loo in NZ. But the third, from the woman chief executive, was cunnilingus. No easy way to work in so as I got to the end I just started to tell the story of how I always got these words to get in and I was not sure how to get in hers. She looked horrified and begged me not to so I busked my way out of it.

Friday 7 November

Round to Philip's. He seemed in pretty chirpy form. He was now into megadrive re how good my novel was and how it would help people on the mental health front, but he felt I had to get into a major Michael Dobbs-type political thriller next. Peter M, back from his trip to the Gulf with GB, arrived around 9. He had put on a little weight but was looking pretty relaxed. We got over the small talk fairly quickly, then went up to the sitting room to take stock. PM felt that the Gulf had drawn into sharp relief for him both GB's strengths and weaknesses. When he was really motoring and setting out ideas for the reconstruction of the global financial system, you felt there was nobody else who got it so well and who could drive forward the change that was needed. But then at other times that very denseness was what made him so distant and unconnected from the public. He was never going to change though. As Douglas had said to me, we had to work with what we had. There was no point imagining a new GB would come along.

Peter was in a strong position. It was widely thought, even despite the yacht malarkey with Osborne, that his return had been a strengthening move. It had certainly helped finally put to bed the idea that the Blairites were out to oust him (even if some still were). PM felt GB had regained some of his confidence and I think some of that would be down to Peter. Yet whilst the polls were improving a little, and GB was improving in his execution, we were all agreed that there was still serious dysfunction at the heart. Peter got out his yellow lined pad and a fountain pen and started to take notes. We worked towards a discussion of what was needed to try to give him the best shot of a chance of winning. Peter felt that six months ago it looked totally hopeless whereas now there was at least some hope we could win.

I felt the odds were still against us because any benefit gained in being thought to manage the crisis well would be wiped out by real recessionary impact like lost jobs and firms. It was only because the Tories had responded so badly that we were in the position we were. A strong opposition would have done better than this. One of the main organisational problems was that he never got all his key people in the same room. So who would they be? Probably us three, or maybe Peter plus one of us two. Ed B, Ed M, DA. I said if he had any sense he would put DM in there too. But also – who would staff such a group? Our mutual sense was that David Muir was the best there. One of the problems was a whole set of layers of OK but not brilliant people. PG asked first Peter, then me, if we would want to run the election campaign. We both said no. Would you chair a planning group, he asked Peter, who said yes. What about Douglas? Philip felt he would be fine so long as he didn't feel Peter intended to steamroller him out of any position or authority. Peter said he had changed. He was not like that any more.

He was pretty down on Douglas and also on AD. He felt Alistair was just managing things along. E.g. when Peter said at Cabinet that the PBR was crucial to everything Alistair got defensive about it, said he felt like he was being set up. When I asked whether he really believed we could win, he gave a moderately convinced yes. He was moving to my view that DC was not the real deal. He felt Obama, 'the most emotionally literate politician of our time', would make all of them seem inadequate for a while. Good chat and we agreed that we would meet fairly regularly and seek to get proper ministerial groups going re election planning. Headed home. [Fiona school friend] Kathy O'Shaugnessy's 50th birthday. Henry Sutton [creative writing teacher and *Mirror* books editor] was raving about the novel. Watched *Newsnight Review*. John Wilson [broadcaster] chairing and fairly positive in the way he pitched the discussion of the novel. Anti-war Asian guy dissed it big time. Julie Myerson [author and critic] ditto. Ian Rankin [novelist] more positive but said it lost its way. Pretty negative overall.

Saturday 8 November

Off to Wolves. Lost 2–0 and Calum raging at the lack of passion of our fans, and lack of inventiveness. They were discussing the book on *Saturday Review* [BBC]. Much better than *Newsnight*. A theatre director who really liked it, even defending the flat prose on the grounds that it was about depression for heaven's sake. Watched *21* with Fiona, about blackjack. Kevin Spacey [actor] very good. Texted him to say he would do Peter M really well. Fiona thinking I should go low-profile again.

Sunday 9 November

David Muir sent through a draft of GB's Lord Mayor's Banquet speech, which was not bad. Matthew [Mills] had got through to the next round of tour school [US golf scholarship] by one shot yesterday and we went round to Tessa's then Strada to celebrate. He was really buzzing with it. Off to Spain again tomorrow and then off to the Australian Masters. Not doing enough at the moment. Decided finally to do my own website, possibly with a blog, Campbell on Cameron.

Monday 10 November

Mark Bennett and Mark Lucas came round to chat re the idea of a website. Mark B had been going on about it for some time, and he was right. He was full of stories about his time working on election in Virginia. Sounded fantastic. He had a picture of one of the crowds for an Obama rally with 'change can happen' in lights at the end of the park. On one day alone there had been 13,000 people canvassing for Obama in Virginia. Every aspect of the campaign was fabulous. Website discussion really enthused Mark L and we worked out we wanted something fairly simple. Speeches (ads as well as content). Charity. Politics. Blog. Sport. Media etc. Mark B to monitor and decide what debate to allow. Told Mark L I wanted to operate on a professional basis, not just use him. Had a separate discussion with Mark B re Volume 1 of the diaries and whether there was any way of doing it with GB there. He was strongly against, and I had pretty much moved to that position too.

The economic realities becoming worse, with talk now moving from recession to deflation and a lot of job losses being announced pretty much on a daily basis. F and Grace were out so I was able to watch GB's Lord Mayor's Banquet speech in full and in peace. I had done a note to David Muir first thing and it was interesting to see the bits they had taken in and those they hadn't. GB always seemed to resist really pointing up a strategic point. It was a good speech though, even if for me the topline and central argument were not clear enough. It was one of those speeches where he was expected to touch all the big foreign policy bases but he rightly did a lot on the world economy and struck a good tone on the US. Obamamania still going strong and his specialness was going to cause problems for all leaders for quite a while. Obama seeing Bush. Fascinating to watch the body language, e.g. Obama putting his hand on Bush's back. Transference of power visible. Felt a bit sorry for Bush who was being defined utterly negatively, security and economy. Obama just stratospheric. McCain still defending his decision to have Palin as running mate but she was a tactic that did in his strategy. Run later. Asthma bad.

Tuesday 11 November

Working on *Maya*, Rebecca having sent through seven chapters with her comments. Some were tricky but most OK. Of all the criticisms so far the flatness of prose was the one to take on board. Mind you, the *Saturday Review* discussion had pointed up the flatness worked quite well when dealing with depression. Fixed with Burnley to be able to collect duplicates for my lost in the post Chelsea tickets. Went on the bike, got them, then got involved in a rage incident on the way back with some sports car knobhead cutting me up. I opened and slammed his door so hard the window smashed. I cycled off but then worried I should report it. Spoke to Fiona, then Charlie F, then Gavin [Millar]. They both felt I was under no legal obligation if nobody was hurt but also that if the guy made a complaint and the police tracked me down, and it led to a prosecution, I would be in a stronger position if I had volunteered my involvement. Called Kensington desk officer who seemed pretty uninterested but said if

I felt I should I could fill in a self-reporting accident form. Went to Hampstead and did it there. Pretty daft though. Should not have got involved as it could easily have escalated.

Out to the Law Society for the second of my Aeolus after-dinner speeches. I did the Lions stories, amid Obama and other stuff. Felt on top form and it went down really well. Nice crowd. Also helped doing all the small talk beforehand even if it was a bit of a pain going over all the same old same old. A former Thatcherite said he had switched to us in '97, had been thinking of going back, but the Bullingdon Club stuff put him off.* He said 'It shows they are not one of us.' Good event.

Wednesday 12 November

Out to White City to do the first batch of local BBC interviews. Around a dozen and all mainly focused on the novel, with politics as an add on. A few said they had read it and liked. Far less cynical coverage than nationals. Whizzed through in no time. To Cactus [producers] for Richard and Judy. The switch from terrestrial to Watch Channel on Sky had seen their ratings dive but they were still influential on the books front. New format, in a fake bar with a few people, including a Prince Charles (60th birthday) lookalike. Interview fine. Conned into playing pipes but OK. Liked them both.

Off to Random House for the drinks do to celebrate *All in the Mind*. Grace told the story at the do of how she and Ella and Nina were trying to interest people in my book at Waterstones and a woman said she didn't like me, then went into mega apology when Grace said she was my daughter. Caroline made a nice little speech and gave me a framed copy of the cover and the *Guardian* cartoon from yesterday's digested read.

Chatted away but then set off for Chelsea. What an incredible night. Nobody really gave us a chance. But Chelsea, despite some of their top names playing, were misfiring a little and we rode our luck. Drogba scored first and then landed himself in deep water by chucking back a coin thrown out from our end. 6,100 Burnley fans there, making a lot of noise. Second half and extra time we were the better team and Ade Akinbiyi equalised. Into penalties and we scored all of the first four, they had missed one – Bridge – so Wade Elliott had the chance to seal it. He blasted over the bar. Sudden death. Michael Duff taking our first one. I realised it was his mum standing behind us. Nerves then relief. Then [Brian] Jensen saved from John Obi Mikel and we were in heaven. Guy in front had said earlier 'I

* Cameron, Osborne and Boris Johnson had all been members of the disreputable all-male dining club when all were students at Oxford University.

know you don't do God but He is playing for us tonight.' What a night. Grace and the cousins also there and had really got into it.

Thursday 13 November

Early train to Paris, re-reading Gillian Slovo's *Black Orchids* pre-interview and review later. Out to Ivry for book discussions. Photographer saying rumours re Sarko and Carla close to splitting. Almost certainly bollocks but apparently same source as said they were getting married. Dire traffic and eventually had to duck out to the Metro and just made it to the Beeb studios in time. Me, Gillian and three reviewers. Mine up first and it did OK. General points related to too much tell not enough show. A couple of them criticised the editing and I defended on the grounds that Rebecca had made similar points. I emailed her 'Hope you heard me defending you on Radio 5.'

One of the reviewers said it was a good book badly edited because there was too much tell not enough show. I said my editor had made exactly the same point and even managed to curb my excesses at times. Did pretty well though. Gillian Slovo was on. Said she cried at the end (while reading on a train) and it affected her deeply. Said I had tried to do something technically very difficult, tell six stories of very different people with only one linking character, and she thought it came off. Another reviewer said she found it uplifting. Also that she had never read a book by a man which so understood women, particularly re the horror of rape and prostitution. 'If it did not have his name on front I'd have thought it was the work of a great feminist.'

Did an interview with the Beeb Paris people on the French Socialists who were meeting this weekend to try to select a new leader. All the same old same old mess. No clarity at all. To the Residence, shower and change then meeting with Julien Vaulpre, Sarkozy's conseiller de l'opinion, who wanted a discussion on how we used polling. Also talked about the need for proper centralised co-ordination. I got the clear impression that they did not do that – not least because Sarko was very last-minute and not good at involving others. Julien said that his relationship with [François] Fillon, his PM, had worsened. He was still too hyper. I sensed from him, and from the meeting with Jean Sarkozy [son], that they were less confident than I expected them to be. Sarko Jr very dashing and charming. He was with his very quiet, shy but apparently fabulously wealthy wife and a UMP [centre-right party] colleague. My voice was going a bit after the football but it all went fine.

The main thing was a talk at the Embassy. I did maybe twenty minutes off the cuff, usual stuff re strategy, then Q&A. Nothing too exceptional though Jean asked me to advise them for the next term. I waffled a bit and said remember that je suis un socialiste. Again I sensed they did not do very basic stuff. Sarko asked me if I did not miss it. I said a bit but not enough to want to go back. I felt OK saying how I felt GB could win. Osborne going down badly with his own folk at the moment. Nice event. Peter Westmacott chaired well. Audience a mix of young and not so young. Signed a fair few books and the general mood was terrific. Dinner with Peter and Susie. GB had been there four times last month. He and Sarko often one-on-one. Said they heard terrible things about Sarko's personal habits etc. Could be vile to staff as well. His lateness at Verdun for the Armistice event with [Prince] Charles was not such a big deal here. It was all too common. Peter pretty canny re politics. Had clearly been helping GB get to a better place with Sarko. On the French socialists he felt they were no further forward.

Friday 14 November

11.13 train. Home and went through all the emails that I had left unanswered. Out to get Calum at Euston and off to meet Owen Coyle and co. at the Bull, Gerrards Cross. All still buzzing post Wednesday but trying to get focused for QPR tomorrow. Very critical of refs. Couple of US guys there re a possible football youth deal with Carolina. Calum really enjoying listening to them. Owen had something about him without a doubt.

Saturday 15 November

Went for a walk with Fiona. She was pressing on what I intended to end up doing with GB but I was not sure myself yet. GB was in the States at the G20 and still getting a good press on the economic front but bad on the Baby P situation post-PMQs.* The empathy stuff continued to let him down. Off to QPR. I'd met Ali Russell, QPR deputy MD, at the *FT* sports summit, and had arranged to go for lunch and then to the away end for the match. They had done the club boardroom-type place like F1. Fabulous food. Gorgeous hostesses wandering around taking coats. Passes round the neck – worn by all but Bernie Ecclestone. The Burnley directors were all down on a far table. I pointed out Barry [Kilby, Burnley chairman] to Bernie and they had a little chat. He was giving me his forcibly held view that the Olympics were going to be an expensive waste of money. He

* Concern was expressed by the public and in Parliament over a one-year-old boy who had died in London in 2007 after suffering more than fifty injuries over eight months despite being seen frequently by children's welfare services and NHS professionals. The boy's mother, her boyfriend and his brother were all jailed for allowing his death.

was wearing a brown polo neck. None of the QPR lot wearing ties. Lots of expensive jeans and shirts and cashmere. Flavio [Briatore, co-owner] pretty full of himself.

Sonia [Kilby] came round to the away end with us. Not bad turnout but a bit after the Lord Mayor's Show. One down but for second time in a week came from behind to win [2–1]. To Philip and Gail's with the boys. PG OK but lacking in energy. Chatted to Gail about possible next book. She was thinking maybe jump to the idea of political bestseller.

Sunday 16 November

GB called while Grace and I were in the cinema for *W*, the new film about Bush. Not a bad film. Oliver Stone [director] avoided the easy caricature. Grace said she quite liked Bush. Jeff Brolin certainly got some of the mannerisms and speaking habits.

Monday 17 November

I was in and out during the day then off to Smollenskys in the Strand for the London Labour dinner. Sukie Sohal [organiser] had got the place packed out and we had organised it so that I could also get to the LRF sports awards. Tessa introduced me and I did a mix of laughs, strategy and Obama as galvanising event. Did a big defence of Peter M which went down well. Also going for the Tories as vulnerable and us needing to hit them harder. Tessa seemed a bit down but she was telling me she was definitely going to stand again. The mood was pretty good, much better than even a few weeks ago. Odd that an economic crisis had turned things round a bit. But the fallout was still going to be severe and the battle ahead tough. But it was definitely on again. I went off to the West End for the LRF event. Nice do and I was in and out in forty minutes then back to Smollenskys for the Q&A and book signing. Really nice mood around the place. Got a lift home with Tessa. Those people love you, she said, because they know that when it comes to it you are Labour through and through and they know what you did.

Tuesday 18 November

Had the first really long chat with Natascha [McElhone, pregnant when her husband had died] since the baby was born. She sounded OK but heaven knows how hard it must be. She was amazed how the boys had adapted. She was still working when she could. But she still found it hard to talk about it and missed Martin so much. I was on the 3.05 flight to Glasgow and got to the airport way too soon. Terminal 5 seemed to be over its teething problems. Flight up a bit late. I was reading *Brothers* by David Talbot which was moving me much more towards Alex's view of a conspiracy theory on the [Kennedy brothers] assassination.

Donald picked me up and we headed to the City Chambers for the LRF do. Chat and sign a few books, then chair the evening. We were welcomed by a member of the Lord Provost's team who spoke as though Leukaemia was a country. The medics went on a bit too long. A young couple with a sick daughter spoke very movingly as did the father whose loss of a son led to him starting the Glasgow branch. The books had been purchased special deal and were going full price with the mark up to LRF. Ditto Donald's CDs. Out for dinner with Cathy and the marketing team to discuss rebranding. There was a real need, she felt, to extend the branding to include lymphoma. Back to Donald's flat. Smaller than the last one and a lot of building stuff and boxes still around. Also I was worried about his skin and breathing problems.

Wednesday 19 November

Out through dreadful traffic to the BBC for the second bout of regional radio interviews. Did about a dozen, all pretty samey and with the voice getting worse. Lunch at [businessman] Willie Haughey's firm, City Holdings. Nice new offices overlooking the Gorbals area. Celtic Park in view. Willie a good guy and who was clearly helping the party a lot not just with money but ideas. I did a lunchtime chat session with his board which seemed to go pretty well. Off to town. Popped into Costa Coffee for a coffee and someone at the next table was reading the book. Turned out to be the student who wanted to interview me for the student paper. Signed stock then down for the session. More than 100 and the shop said it was the biggest event they had done for ages. A handful of anti-war protesters asking very hostile questions amid all those about the content of the novel. Could have got fairly nasty but I think I dealt with it OK. Iraq was always just going to be there as a difficult and divisive issue. Amid the Iraq questions a lot of the others were getting really fed up with them and by the end of it a pretty positive feel.

To Hampden for the Scotland v Argentina match [0–1]. Even with all the hype surrounding Maradona's first match as manager it was not full by some distance and like all friendlies a bit lacking in passion. Saw Walter Smith and Gordon Strachan [Celtic manager]. Brian Wilson [former Labour MP] there as Celtic board rep. He said we were not surrounded by our ain folk here. Rangers dominated. Great reception for Maradona. Left early and off for a drink with Donald. Glasgow pubs so different without smoking.

Thursday 20 November

Another early start getting Donald out of bed to head to [editor] Mandy Rhodes's house off Byres Road to do the interview for *Holyrood* magazine. We went over loads of stuff. A bit caught up in her own world at the nexus of Scottish media and Scottish politics. Too much re the former. But we got through tons of other stuff, personal, political, historical, lots of the big issues and people of *The Blair Years*. As I did pictures in her front room, I was trying to find out if she liked or rated Salmond. More rated than liked. Into town to check in to the Radisson. I was still feeling rough and had not done any exercise for a week. Went to the gym for a while but still not feeling great and didn't push it. Susie Mackenzie [journalist] arrived at 2.30 and I had a couple of hours with her for her proposed book on GB. She was doing a portrait rather than a life story. It was difficult talking about him because I knew so much bad stuff which I really did not want to divulge so was trying to be totally supportive whilst not always being convincing. She said someone had told her GB was in awe of Balls which seemed odd. But maybe he was.

She said someone had told her a story that I had said to GB, persuading him to take jokes out of the Manchester speech, that he was never funny, never had been, never would be. Not quite true. She had interviewed JK Rowling in the morning. She said when she was coming on to see me, JK had said she wished it was the other way around because then she could ask about me. 'She said she would love to meet you.' I said the feeling is mutual and she said she would put me in touch. I asked if she liked GB more or less since having researched him. She said she had moved beyond that. She found the project interesting. She had never known anyone who provoked so many different responses and had so many facets to him. The plan was to flesh out a different side to him in the run-up to the election, but she was clearly beginning to worry about deadlines. She had seemed quite dour when I met her in Manchester but this meeting revealed a lively mind if by her own admission fairly naïve re politics.

Donald collected me to head to the Tiree Association annual concert at Partick Burgh Halls. I had been slightly dreading it, another night on show, expected to shine and sparkle and get the right tone and hit the right notes. But it turned out to be a really enjoyable event. As Donald said afterwards it would have meant a lot to Dad that we did it and the people were so reminiscent of him and where he came from. I had to speak for ten, fifteen minutes with a mix of Tiree reminiscences and general stories about my time in politics, then compere a few acts, Donald piping, accordion, flute, fiddle, bodhran, two singers. I felt a real part of the whole event and what it was about. Quite a few of the older people came to say they knew Dad, some that they were distant relatives. One had a copy of the programme for the same event in 1950 and there was a picture of Dad in a photo of the then Association committee. Also his uncle Hugh in full regalia as president. Really nice evening, went down well and Donald pleased with it. Fiona was speaking at the Cambridge Union against private schools and won.

Friday 21 November

Early train down to Manchester, in a freezing cold carriage, still feeling rough. Arrived lunchtime and met Calum for lunch. Collected at six and over to Southport for Labour NW fundraiser pre their conference at the weekend. Shaun Woodward hosting. The organisers had sorted a stack of books for sale and they went OK. I did a mix of strategy, GB doing better and why, and Obama as galvanising event. Q&A after the main course and it all went pretty well. I suppose there was a point to it and it did go down well but I really was feeling like I had dunspeakin' this week.

Saturday 22 November

Dave Edmundson collected Calum and me and very kindly drove us to Turf Moor. He had lost nothing of his enthusiasm and was really loving his work with the FL Trust. He felt a little distanced from BFC and clearly there were scars there from his work at the club. He dropped me at the new enterprise suite behind the goal. Louise Spencer [head of Community Sports Trust] took me up to meet the kids who had been on the Duke of Edinburgh scheme I funded. I hadn't realised they were going to be mainly special needs, some quite serious, and they seemed to get a lot out of it. I did a little speech then individual presentations and photos. To the boardroom for lunch. Poor game [v Doncaster Rovers, 0–0] ruined by the ref. Owen [Coyle] called afterwards, totally furious. Steve Thompson had been sent off for second yellow foul but Owen felt the other guy should have already gone for a foul which went unpunished. Home then out to [Fiona school friend] Mary Ross's 50th birthday. Some of her relatives giving me a hard time re Israel–Palestine. Also I went a bit OTT with one of them on private schools. Nice enough do but I tended to feel a bit too much on show at these kinds of events.

Sunday 23 November

[Former TB advisor turned teacher] Peter Hyman's 40th so up to Crouch End for the start of his do. I was first to arrive which meant I could have a proper chat with him. He was still loving the teaching. Now aiming to be a fast-track head. He was surprised that so few of the Blairites really got behind DM. He had been helping him and felt that we could all have helped more. I said I was not sure what he had planned to achieve. Also I felt he did not do enough to draw people in. Peter got that I think. We agreed though that the last thing DM should do now was hold back. He should be making big-hitting interventions. Good to have Peter back but now it was like he was the only other big-hitter. Nice do, though I left before any of the other No. 10 people arrived. Off to the Wolseley with Ed, to meet US publisher Peter Mayer. He was very American, a bit shambolic and difficult to pin down but Ed was sure he was the right guy for the novel. He liked it, thought it unusual and surprising. Now wanted us to generate supportive comments from people known in the States. Nice enough lunch. Heaving with people. So many mixed signals economically.

Monday 24 November

Off early for St Pancras with Fiona. Met Greg for a coffee. Sixty per cent full in first class on Eurostar to Paris. The banks collapse had been a disaster for them. Not a very nice day but we had a nice enough time. Took bags to the Residence then had lunch with the Seneses in an interesting little new restaurant inside a shop. They were both on great form. I was still feeling rough but not rough enough to get help. Back to watch the PBR. AD did OK but he had two problems – some of the big-ticket changes had been leaked in advance (according to the government by someone giving out stuff to the Tories who were then getting it out through third parties). Also his delivery was flat and as ever there was insufficient big-picture argument. The coverage was ruined by the Beeb's inability to accept people had an attention span longer than a minute. Graphics filling the screen. Tickertape re what Robinson and Peston thought as it happened. Osborne's attack was pretty strong and I felt the massive borrowing requirement would become a big problem.

Out to Mick Hucknall's flat next to the Eiffel Tower. Lovely place. Saw Romy [daughter] for the first time since she was born. Fabulous roof terrace. He was selling though because they had had an offer he could not refuse. Out to WHS. I felt these talks were going pretty well. The horrible weather kept the crowds down but the mood and the content were good. After the signing out to Sormani restaurant. Very expensive for what it was. Back by twelve. French media dominated by the fallout from the Reims vote at the weekend which had failed to sort out a leader of the PS. Martine Aubry [Mayor of Lille] had narrowly won over Ségolène Royal [outgoing First Secretary François Hollande's former partner] but it was not clear cut enough to be accepted and there was a lot of talk of challenges and ballot rigging etc.

Tuesday 25 November

Breakfast at the Residence. Peter Westmacott was positively raving about the feedback. Fiona and I had a bit of a wander. I ended up at Bert's café before heading – with too much time to kill – to Charles de Gaulle. Flybe plane with a couple of Manc and Scouse stewardesses who really did not like the young football team lugging on their bags. Flight nowhere near full. Another sign. Train to Manchester city centre, dropped bags with Calum then met the BBC Speaker team, and started to work up some ideas. It was looking reasonably interesting though still not sure this kind of TV was my thing.

Out to St Ann's Church for the Waterstone's event. Rector called Nigel [Ashworth], ex-psychiatric social worker so set it up well. I spoke for twenty minutes or so, including telling them the background to 'We don't do God.' Then a really friendly Q&A and a pretty long signing. Enjoyed it. It helped being in a Church I think. There was also a lively shrink there and she and I got a bit of banter going. Plus a reformed hack or two. Later did *Newsnight* – not terribly satisfactory because I could not really hear what Paxman and studio guest Nigel Lawson [former Tory Chancellor] were saying. I was trying to take it all to 'the choice' but there was a lot of 'death of New Labour' around because of the new top rate of tax. Got one or two OK points in but not great. Then lots of texts saying get a haircut. *Newsnight* driver took me back home to London. Got to bed 2.40 a.m.

Wednesday 26 November

Went for a haircut. PM and I had a little chat. He was feeling emboldened yet isolated in there. He was also sounding unconfident about the fallout from the PBR. The notion that it was the end of New Labour was growing. Not just the new top rate. As through this whole period, there was no real sense of big argument allied to forward vision. So the what-ifs tended to crowd in and undermine the forecasts. There was also something highly unconvincing about asking people to borrow and spend their way out of a mess created by borrowing and spending money we didn't have. I spent part of the day preparing for my Teach First [fast-track graduate teacher scheme] lesson at St Marylebone tomorrow. We had settled on showing them Obama's speech and analysing it technically. Found a couple of good articles which helped, e.g. one on Cicero, and which explained technical terms like tricolon, anaphora, epiphora.

Then out to Festival Hall. Fiona Phillips terrific as the interviewer and so nice. She was out of *GMTV* any day and exploring lots of options. The hall was about four-fifths full and the atmosphere terrific. DS and wife in front row. I did a reading and a brief opening speech, which seemed to go

OK. Then into the Q&A. Mostly re the book and mental health. Just one hostile – re Iraq – and even that was not too hostile. 'You are a decent man, why didn't you stop the war?' Good final blast with a load of questions in one go. The signing went on for a good while too and with a nice mood.

Thursday 27 November

Out to St Marylebone for the Teach First session. The teacher, tall, blonde, a bit anxious because they had been having trouble with the YouTube upload of Obama's speech. Brett Wigdortz, founder of Teach First, came along, ditto the deputy head and later the head, named Elizabeth Phillips. Really did not take to her. I seemed to have fired a bit of enthusiasm about Obama and his speech. She came in and said 'What had he ever actually done?' After another couple of ignorant barbs, I ended up asking whether she thought her cynicism about politics fitted with the teaching of citizenship. The class itself flew by. Intro, show the film, set a few tests re things to look for, discuss, then get them to write an intro. Alex Blair of *The Time*s was there, and said she found it fascinating, both the content and the way the girls responded so well. Most were enthused. Several really up for it. Definitely flowed and they got a lot out of it. A few stayed back to talk to *The Times*. Gave me lots of positive feedback then seven out of ten which Ella thought a bit harsh.

Went to see PG who was in good form. He was totally unconvinced about the PBR. Felt we were falling back again. Out p.m. to Savoy Place to speak and do a reading at a mental health event. Maybe 300 people, mainly psychotherapists. Did my usual spiel, the same reading as last night, then listened to some of the others before having to leave. Greg Beales, GB's spad on health, was very good. Alan Johnson had spoken earlier and committed the government to more choice of therapies. Yet it was getting no coverage at all. A growing theme at these kinds of events was the impossibility of getting good press for any kind of progress. Ian McPherson, director of the National Institute for Mental Health in England, slipped me his card and said he found the novel excellent, and it contained some major insights.

Friday 28 November

Fairly sniffy piece in *The Times* re Teach First. Quite different to what she said yesterday. Another example of how they felt they had to be at least partially negative to get in. Chest been bad for over two weeks now so finally went to see Bostock. Cathy Galvin had asked me to do a short story – a relatively new innovation – for the *Sunday Times* magazine so I started to think about that. Fancied going to see Rory in Oxford. Set off after speaking to him and we met for lunch before going to watch him play football, as a ringer for the Law Society. He seemed pretty happy and together. He was working hard enough. Last week of tutorials next week then all-out revision. He was set on his year travelling and poker playing.

Saturday 29 November

News agenda totally dominated by the terrorist attacks in Mumbai and continuing fallout over the arrest of Tory MP Damian Green by police investigating official information leaks. Drafted *Sunday Times* short story. Fiona and I left for Chevening [Kent estate used by Foreign Secretary]. I think I had only been there once before, for a conference, though it felt unfamiliar. Not sure that these places helped keep politicians in touch. It was dark by the time we arrived and the Colonel who ran the place was about to take guests on a tour. I ducked out. Fiona told David and Louise [Miliband] I was being anti-social, which I was. Down for drinks. Pictures of their wedding ten years ago on a big board. Mainly chatted to Ben Evans [designer] and Amanda Levete [wife, architect]. Douglas and Wendy Alexander both giving me the strong sense they felt the PBR had been a bit of a disaster. DA had done *Question Time* [BBC TV] from Basildon and said he found the hostility pretty strong. They were listening but not hearing. They did not buy our arguments at all. They felt the economy had gone wrong on our watch and they did not believe the solutions we were putting forward would work. Post-PBR the mood had definitely moved back a little.

I found very few signs of belief we could win. David Lammy [Universities Minister] said there was no chance at all. He just felt that the economic impact was too severe and that there would be a return to the reasons people did not go for GB once the immediate storm was through. Nice enough evening though truth be told I was not fully at home in the world of political intrigue and gossip any more. Added to which we got a call halfway through that Grace had got into an argument with the staff at Starbucks. Had a good chat with Will Hutton [political and economic journalist] who said he felt I had done a great job carving out a 'very honourable and interesting niche' post Downing St. Otherwise an evening of mainly small talk. Glad to get to bed.

Sunday 30 November

Up for a long walk in the rain. Chatted mainly to DM, David Lammy and his partner. Pretty gloomy re our prospects. David L in particular.

He knew Obama and there was no doubt the difference in style, passion, mission and purpose was hitting home. Not going to be easy. DM tended too much to criticise the government, direction and general strategy, as though he were not really part of it. Nice enough crowd and we had a perfectly good time but I was glad to get away. Just on the fringes of a depression I feared. Google alert sent over not bad review in *Newsweek*.

Monday 1 December

I called Tom Bostock about having the flu jab. He insisted that as my records once said I was allergic to eggs, he was very uncomfortable giving me the vaccine. He said if something were to happen and then it emerged it was on my records then even though I had eaten eggs hundreds of times, and given him permission etc., he would be in a difficult position. He said he would prefer that I went to the Royal Free [Hospital] to get proper allergy tests and let them do the jab. OK. Met Alison [Blackshaw, former PA to AC, now head of administration] for a cup of tea in Whitehall. She said things were pretty grim in there. The new open-plan No. 12 meant she was back in my old office in the bay window. She felt trapped by her own sense of being institutionalised. To the Royal Horseguards to meet Jeremy Heywood. Peter M had just been in there doing a business seminar. Jeremy seemed to have put a bit of weight on. He had a white wine. I had an orange juice and we had a very frank discussion.

We went over where I had got to with GB pre the last reshuffle. He said the Peter M business happened very late. It may be GB only finally went for it when I said no the day before. They had been sounding out the extent to which PM might get involved, and there came a point where Jeremy said only GB could have the conversation. He said there was a view Peter would only take Foreign Secretary. I said Peter would have given anything to get back in via the Lords. He had known from the day he was born that he wanted to die in the Lords. And I had sensed he had grown fairly bored of the Brussels scene. But so convinced were they that he would want Foreign Secretary that there was a little scoping work done on a new and bigger environment brief that DM might have gone for. He said Peter's return had definitely increased general effectiveness and he seemed to give GB confidence. But there remained real problems at the centre related to lack of political strategy and lack of clarity about who did what and where authority lay.

He said he felt he and Gus between them had the civil service machine working OK for him but the political operation was woeful. He did not know what they all did. Stephen Carter had been seen as hopefully being able to oversee professional systems but it just didn't work. He was bright in many ways but lacked the politics. Others did not give him a chance because they did not think it would work. He said it had taken a lot of negotiation and refused posts before Carter finally went with the Lords and the Comms Minister's job. Jeremy felt GB would keep going at me. He felt he saw PM, me, Ed B, Ed M and Douglas as the people he would want most to help with strategy. It was not entirely clear if he was speaking with GB's authority but at one point he suggested there could be another reshuffle in January and I should go in as Cabinet Office Minister in the Cabinet, based in the Lords.

He said GB was still thinking of putting out AD. He said No. 10–Treasury relations were terrible. I said who would he put in? Ed, he said. Which one? Balls. Re me I said if I really felt I could be the difference between winning and losing of course I would do it. But I was not persuaded. He said he knew I could make a massive difference, in terms of galvanising and leading and holding things together. He said I was one of the few people who could say difficult things to GB and he would listen. I remained totally ambivalent about it. Something pretty substantial was holding me back. I think it was a slight loss of energy and appetite plus a lack of respect for some of GB's people and operation. He asked me really to think about it as he was sure it would make a big difference. He did not feel I could go back as a backroom person as I was too big a public figure now.

We had a good chat for an hour or so. I said simply he had given me a lot to think about. Condi [Rice] was in No. 10 as Hillary C was being announced as Obama's Secretary of State. As I left for home I checked for messages. One was from GB asking me to go in tomorrow. He said he needed help with his speech for the QS debate and also how to handle the Damian Green saga. Ludicrously we had somehow allowed media and Tories to turn it into a great crusade for freedom and truth in the face of New Labour Big Brother. I called him when I got home and agreed to go in first thing. This was a case of Central Office getting a civil servant systematically to work for the opposition against the government at taxpayers' expense. We were losing the PR battle big time.

Tuesday 2 December

Cab in early and via 70 Whitehall to No. 10. One of the custodians made me a cup of tea while I waited for GB to finish a meeting with the Olympics people. He said that most days there was no real energy in the place, not compared with TB days. Victor Blank [chairman, Lloyds TSB] was in there for a meeting. 'I never thought I'd see the day when you were in the waiting room,' he said. GB came through with David Muir and we went through to the new open-plan office. He worked out there except when he wanted meetings. 'What do you think?' he said. 'Like a newsroom.' Indeed it was I guess. But it felt a bit odd. There was a lot of hot desking and also bits of most parts of No. 10 represented there. But it still felt strange for a PM to be out in the middle of a big room. His solo office was the old SCU [Strategic Communications Unit] office and we went in there to work on the speech for tomorrow. First he went into a big diatribe about the Damian Green fiasco and the various people who had fucked it up. He felt the cops were confident they would get a conviction and all that was happening was that Tories and media, for their own sakes, were presenting a totally dishonest and one-sided story.

I said they had to get after the Tories on it far more and make the point they were going at this as a way of not doing serious policy. Harriet had called a meeting with the Speaker [Michael Martin], and her office had somehow managed to send her email to a Tory MP so that set the frenzy off in a different direction. This was a major media wankfest now. But I got the sense of a No. 10 operation that was a bit hand to mouth and reactive. Jeremy was filling him in on what Gus and Jacqui Smith were doing. But it felt very ragged. We worked on the speech. He was complaining it would all get drowned out by the Green stuff. He was also saying 'As you know, these Queen's Speeches are always useless! Just a load of Bills on this and that.' The speech he had sent through last night was not that great but they had done a new version which was far better.

We worked on the anti-Tory sections. They had a good line re DC saying he got help from all the former Tory Chancellors who 'luckily still had their marbles'. We worked our way towards a 'yes we can' v 'no we won't' and the idea of the Tories still being old Conservatives, dogmatic, do-nothing, uncaring, though I felt it overdid the do-nothing. In between times, just the two of us in the room, we chewed the fat over other stuff. He repeated his offer to join the government as a minister. On Obama he was clearly not convinced of the *Team of Rivals* approach.* 'If there is a breakthrough in the Middle East, is it Hillary or Obama taking the credit?' I thought it was a small-minded point. Where I did agree with him was that there was a sense there were too many Bill C people around which was taking away from Obama as an agent of change and the future. Clearly also they were having some trouble getting into Obama.

He said he felt a bit let down by Bush. On troop numbers in Iraq, a White House official had let slip at an earlier meeting that they were not going to allow numbers to fall pre-US election. 'So we had been wasting our time.' He said when we were trying to get to host the G20 there was

* President Obama's favourite book, recording Abraham Lincoln's rise to the presidency and how he appointed his fiercest rival to the key Cabinet positions.

no real support from US. We had to build elsewhere. They stayed neutral. He thought Bush would go out quite a sad figure in many ways. I asked if he thought Iraq had been a bad idea. 'I support what we are doing.' He had to leave for Cabinet but wanted me back in to do more on his speech. I slipped in the back way and tried to avoid Cabinet as it broke up. Harriet came round to GB's office wanting to see him re her plans for a meeting with the Speaker who was going to make a statement on the Green business when Parliament opened tomorrow. Balls appeared when GB came back, so did Jeremy. Another confab on the Green affair, GB constantly repeating his story re the background, how awful and unfair it was etc. They just needed more political balls and fight. Back to the speech. Back to the same re-running of the same lines. Glad to get out.

Home to redo short story before off to Burnley v Arsenal. Alex had asked me to get a ticket for him and meet up for dinner. Snow once we hit the north but the match was definitely on. Arrived Turf Moor around 6.20. Alex already there with a hilarious posh flat cap. Up for something to eat. It was a bit public but I picked his brains re GB. He now felt that whatever happened the country did not want DC as PM. But I think, inevitably for someone in the top wealth zone, he was not taking into account the hellish economic fallout to come. Good atmosphere. Asked Alex what he really thought about Arsène Wenger. He said he rated him and respected him and he was good at a lot of things. But he sometimes wondered if he really had the mentality for a truly big club. He felt we were playing the only sensible way against Arsenal – high tempo. In their faces. Really good game. They had four one-on-one chances in the first half, a couple in the second. Our first goal after six minutes after ball broke from their first miss. Half-time we were all thinking if it carried on as before they would definitely score.

Alex telling me what he felt maybe set him apart from Wenger was that he did not mind dealing with the big super-rich players. He reckoned Rooney made around £12 million outside his actual wages last year, Colleen half that. Second half we played even better. Once we got the second goal, really felt it was going to be. Great mood through four minutes injury time, 2–0. Loads of messages coming in. Set off for home, dire weather. TB called. He was in the States, about to see Obama, Bush and others re MEPP. I told him I had seen GB and felt on one level better but still felt unstable. He felt the PBR had not really worked. Tories all that kept us up. They were OK on guerrilla and presentation, crap in everything else.

Wednesday 3 December

Out to the Royal Free for my allergy tests. The guy in the wheelchair from up the road was there too. Chatting to him about all manner of stuff. Turns out he was an early pioneer in family therapy. He felt I would never escape my past life and should not try, whatever I did. I passed out twice during the testing. First time after saying how squeamish I was and he was scraping my arm. Felt woozy, became conscious of how loudly I was breathing. Then out. Next thing I know five fuzzy faces and voices asking if I was back with them. Then half an hour later something similar though not quite as heavy. Home by half twelve. Fiona worried when I told her and I rested most of the day. Watched Spurs beat Watford. United hammered Blackburn Rovers so it was us, United, Spurs and Derby in the semis. Alex reckoned we would beat Spurs and get United in the final. He said the cap he wore at Burnley had been getting a lot of stick. Jason had texted him during the game and said 'Can you take that haggis off your head?' Out for dinner with Grace. She was tricky at the moment in that she got into scrapes. But she was such a big loving character that I could forgive her just about anything.

Thursday 4 December

Into LRF for meeting with Cathy Gilman and Josh Blackburn [friends] for a meeting re rebranding of LRF. Very helpful. Definitely needed proper research. Ian Grenfell [Mick Hucknall agent] contacted me out of blue re whether I would help Russell Brand re-brand and plan properly for his comeback strategy. Lunch with Susan at the Tate. Trying to persuade me I should not be disappointed re sales figures. She was pressing about the diaries. Felt the next one would be entering a tough market. That could have just been negotiating though. She also felt definitely do a political thriller too. Home then out to new Italian South End Green with Farthings and Kennedys. Really nice evening. None of them seemed to think going back was a great idea.

GB called asking me to help him put together a fightback strategy on Green. He then went into a big blame thing – the Speaker, Tories for wanting to make his life difficult, Harriet not doing it right, blah blah – but his real problem is a failure to have faced up properly to strategic and staffing issues from day one. I spoke to Peter who had sent me a text saying the whole thing was 'Keystone Cops'. That was exactly how it felt when I was in the other day. Fine working on the Queen's Speech but once someone came in to ask his reaction to Green they were suddenly off in all sorts of directions. There are some OK people in there, I said, but there are no figures who combine ability and authority sufficient to make things happen. Peter said he has you back which has given weight and ballast and a bit of guts. I said he's hoping to grind me down to go back but as you know I just cannot function surrounded by dysfunctionality. He is hoping you and I will just move in and sort things out. But life is far more complicated than that.

I advised him months ago on the need to identify, publicly, the ministers and MPs he was going to license politically to take forward a harder strategy. If anything things seem to me more hand to mouth not less. I said they had to be shaken out of this meandering, non-strategic, blamey, un-robust, un-tough, let the Tories run us ragged approach. I blind copied him in on an email I sent to Sue Nye, saying it was ludicrous the extent to which the Tories have been able to run the Green story to their advantage. We look all over the place whereas that is the charge that should be made to stick to them. Yesterday Boris Johnson, in a senior position on policing, was making political judgements and comments which could prejudice a police investigation and subsequent trial. An outrage yet we seemed to let it go by. I said the Labour voices have either been managerial and technocratic, or all part of the Westminster club saying how terrible it is that MPs get interrupted by policemen.

The whole thing has shown once more a problem I have been mentioning for some time – a lack of politicians with balls, judgement and a license to be allowed to display both. Lines to take are useless without a cadre of people at all levels able to put them over. The public only hear and listen to big points when these media squalls are going on. None of the media I have heard on this has seen ventilation for big political points. There was an opportunity here, not being taken, to put over some big points … that the Tories have nothing to offer on policy so try to make the debate all about things like this; that both Cameron and Johnson have shown their unfitness for office. We keep hearing MPs saying they have to be able to have confidential discussions blah blah which simply serves to alienate public from politics. But above all, I said when GB called to discuss, if there was one point you want the public to get from this it is that the Tories have nothing to offer the country so they leap on any issue that allows them to avoid debate and decision on policy, the economy, public services, things that matter to people in their daily lives. I said it had shown up once more a capacity problem in the political operation which seems to me to go deeper and further than one or two personnel issues at the centre. He said he was sure I could sort that. I said I was pretty sure I couldn't.

Friday 5 December

Slightly dreading big strategy powwow at No. 10. I was early and, as had happened more of late, allowed to let myself in through the Cabinet Office rather than wait for a duty clerk. The place was empty but for a couple of custodians, and strangely lacking in energy. Eventually I bumped into

Sue Nye up by the study. She was listening to the morning conference call. A table full of tea, coffee and plates of sausage-filled bread rolls beneath cellophane wrapping. I went into the study and waited for them all to arrive. David Muir was first. He had brought in my diaries and asked me to sign the book. I wished him good luck and said that if there was one message from the book it is that it is all hard work but worth it. It was a message more for him than, currently, for me. When GB came in he made a beeline, talked a bit about Burnley's win against Arsenal and how it was all down to Scots, asked if I thought he should call Alex re getting Rio Ferdinand out of training to do a knife-crime campaign launch, then sat down and went through a Saatchi explanation of how they had taken NK's strengths and turned them into weaknesses.

He wanted me to think of doing the same to Cameron. So good speaker became slick and smarmy. Young and fresh became inexperienced and a risk. The meeting started vaguely on time. Latecomers included Ed Balls, his tie undone round his neck, hair wet, eating a sausage roll. Douglas was late too. David Muir did a polling presentation based on focus groups and some public polls. It was not great but nor was it out of the game territory. He was fairly diplomatic and circumspect on GB. Very funny moment when he showed a wheel of attributes people associated with the leaders. One – which neither GB nor DC scored on – was playful. 'What is playful?' asked Peter M. 'That sounds the most interesting.' He was in his European look, red v-necked sweater under expensive suit. He and GB engaging pretty well. Part of the purpose of the meeting was for GB to get Peter and Balls in a proper discussion for the first time.

Balls had put on weight. Addressed almost all his remarks to me. Mentioned the press – particularly the right-wing press – in virtually every contribution he made. Defensive about his own policy area. David's main points were the pessimism of the electorate and the need for us to define clear bold challenges and deliver bold solutions to meet them. PG echoed that. They both showed that whereas health and education had been top issues in '05 they had fallen way down. A sign of success in some way but we had to get them back up. Economy was way ahead of everything. Crime not far behind. Environment also slipping as people moved to care far more about their own standard of living. GB's big point was the need to set everything in the context of globalisation, a changed world. There was a fair amount of agreement that the framing of new challenges was needed.

I suggested a process that worked back from the manifesto, and first agreed the questions we wanted then. I said they all worried far too much about the press day to day and it stopped them being strategic. PG made a similar point about the testing of opinion. He clearly thought they were too focus group-driven – quite a statement coming from him – and said 'We go to the voters too soon.' We were both saying they needed to decide the clear objectives for the future and go for them. It was odd to me how much things returned to a discussion of how the media behaved or reacted to things. Both David and PG were clear that the public were both more aware of media negativism and more dismissive of it. I felt it could be bound into an argument about patriotism. GB chaired the meeting OK, though he seemed tired again. He tended to default to an economy, jobs, public services message.

Re Balls I was not clear what he was saying. He was definitely speaking more for himself, less as Gordon's little echo. He seemed to be saying on the one hand don't move from the basic Blair–Brown position, on the other arguing for slightly more leftist positions. But he was not clear. And everything was lost in a sense of defensiveness because this paper would say this, this paper that. DJ was the best on the argument about how the media had changed and how we needed to worry less about them, more about our own message and then work out how to use all the new avenues to get it out there. Tom Watson also had an interesting contribution on how online government delivery was advancing and how that could and should be used to recast the influence people can have on their own public services. But apart from them, and Justin [Forsyth, strategic communications and campaigns director] who clearly was drawing on his Oxfam Campaigns experience, I didn't feel they grasped the new media landscape with any conviction or confidence. The tramlines were all a bit worn.

The economy was clearly the backdrop and GB was constantly referring to managing the downturn, planning the upturn. That was clearly right but we also had to watch – and this came out of the polling – that people did not look, as with Churchill in the war, to him for now, DC once we were through it. The language of wartime was beginning to come through. GB's other big point was that these complex global challenges required progressive solutions. I suggested as a strapline something like 'Turning a world of risk into a Britain of hope and opportunity'. I said a combination of economic pessimism and government tiredness had drowned out hope and energy and created the space DC had occupied. We had to get boldness of government, optimism and patriotism to build a sense of hope and drown out DC as an agent of change. It meant clearer government and political strategy. It also meant less playing to the media and more to the public. And a bigger sense of energy, team and attack.

I did not feel that much energy in the room though. Peter made several perfectly sensible points but I wondered if he was really in touch on this stuff. PG and I having argued for boldness, he said he was all in favour of bold so long as it was not something that went off in the wrong direction. He felt the PBR had been bold and may have been economically sensible (not TB's view) but the political strategy was not well handled. I thought he was buttering up a bit, possibly to Balls, with a bit of a negative tone re AD. GB said he wished the Treasury would do this, that and the other. PG said he thought that relations between No. 10 and HMT were better. Ed said he and Jeremy Heywood long for the halcyon days of TB–GB! Laughter. I was not terribly clear what Ed M's big points were. Something about progressive solutions but also – and I agreed with this – the need not to convey the idea we felt everything we had done was right. There had to be some sense of having learned from the journey, mistakes included. He felt we had to acknowledge failures in regulation and the borrowing boom. But he rightly pointed out the challenge now was to frame an offer for the future in an era of austerity and not, as before, one of prosperity.

I jotted out a quick list of things he could do – virtually cost free – on the new politics and citizenship front – compulsory voting, lower age of voting, citizenship in primary schools, volunteering in secondaries, PCC on statutory footing, right of reply. He nodded enthusiastically. I doubted it would go anywhere. GB wanted some deliverables out of the meeting. Ed M and Liam [Byrne] were tasked to plot out a course to the manifesto. Again I said work backwards. GB suddenly said he felt we needed a big Road to the Manifesto operation early in the New Year. We persuaded him that was far too early. It showed a little his desperation. He also asked DJ to do a note on new media and opportunities we were missing. And he said he wanted to work with me on shaping a new New Labour message in the context of globalisation. PG suggested I write out a new political message board. New Labour renewed. GB was definitely addressing himself more to the Blairite team than his old advisors. Balls sensed that I think.

Liam made a couple of OK interventions. Also I could not help noticing how much, from the back, he looked like a young Neil K. I scribbled as such to Sue. He was clearly finding it frustrating, as I had, trying to work the systems of the centre into something more functional. But I felt he had a good point about how the processes needed to be more medium- and long-term. Douglas did his usual stuff about how we secured 'permission' to address the future by better framing of the past. There was quite a lot of 'the real lesson from Obama' is but I'm not sure they really had thought through the real, real lessons. They were about authenticity, honesty, openness, real bottom up as well as leadership. This group did not have that it seemed to me.

At the end GB asked me to go through to the White Room. 'I'm sorry, I was tired, I wasn't firing on all cylinders.' I said it was quite useful as a meeting. He said 'The problem is the younger ministers have not risen to it.' The changing of the guard was going on, watched by a small crowd. He sat on the arm of one of the sofas and I knew another ask was coming. 'I really want you to think about it again. You can make a big difference. I need you to do more.' He was giving me the real hard stare. I felt that sensation I had sometimes seen with other people when faced with TB. It is very hard to say no to the Prime Minister. I said I would think about it again but I had no real enthusiasm. He said with Obama coming in, and lots of change in Europe, I could be a part of that. I walked out with him. PG was waiting for me. PG and I set off for his place. The taxi driver was clearly hostile and was trying to start a conversation about Labour. I said to PG I had to make a decision.

The meeting had not enthused me. Balls with his confusion of boldness and leftism. Ed M who, as Peter M said, sometimes made you think he could be TB and the next minute made you think he was Tony Benn. I said I did not really have the passion or the will for it. But it was becoming embarrassing. He kept asking me. I had to decide finally, tell him what it was, and not go back on it. We went through the options, later joined by Fiona. Lords plus Cabinet as Cabinet Office Minister. Proper job running the centre and in place for running the campaign. Downside the Lords plus glorified version of what I did. 2. Lords plus sport or Olympics. Would be OK if it really was that, but not sure it would be. Fiona felt it was all down to whether I had the will and the desire. I didn't really.

PG – and later Peter M – said it was obvious from that meeting why GB wanted me in there. Peter said if I went back, they would all defer to me and we could get some momentum going. He said what GB was doing was seeing if he could wean himself off the advice and advisors he had relied on for years. He needed to know he had this new and different strand of advice and that he could rely on it and do better with it. He was still not sure. PG was wavering between definitely go back and for heaven's sake don't. I went home and later picked up Calum from the station and we went to Café Rouge. Peter M called. I said he felt it was better than he expected but there was nobody owning the process. GB had not really led the meeting towards conclusions and delivery.

I texted TB and we spoke around 8. He was in New York doing lots of MEPP, JP Morgan. Had spoken to Obama and was definitely carrying on as envoy. On my situation he went through the options one by one. Cabinet Office felt bad, he said. Back to the centre. Media would really go for me. Endless questions from the Tories about what I actually did. He said he would really think about it and call back on Sunday. He was also of the view still that defeat was far likelier than winning and I had to watch my own position a little. He said in the end I would have to decide but he was clearly veering against. Went to the end of the William Ellis [School] quiz night. F and I getting on pretty well at the moment.

Saturday 6 December

Off really early to Egham Literary Institute. Whole weekend really working on *The Speaker* [TV series to find best young public speakers in the UK]. Briefed by a barrister, Liz Cunningham, who had given the six surviving contestants some help preparing their case. The plan was for me to hear their speeches, give them some feedback, then do a workshop looking at Obama's Chicago speech, get them to rewrite, then wheel in a real audience to vote on who was the most persuasive. They were all OK but could do a lot better. Gave them feedback and then the Obama session which they seemed to get lots out of. They really got enthused and took a lot from it I think. We got the Carling Cup draw as we were doing it – Burnley v Spurs, away first leg. Worst of all in some ways. The audience seemed to enjoy the whole thing. Had a good chat with a couple of students who ended up interviewing me for their student magazine. Did an interview on the day and some of the issues and then home. GB called to chase up the discussion re a new message on globalisation. Damian Green Westminster wankathon still going on.* GB really going at Mugabe [calling on world leaders to tell the Zimbabwe President that 'enough is enough'].

Sunday 7 December

Off early to Riverside Studios. Jo Brand [comedian], Jeremy Stockwell [actors' coach] and John Amaechi [ex-basketball player now educator] were the regular judges [on *The Speaker*]. I did a couple of interviews for the programme and then the website. Then into the show. Give feedback. Gave them all signed copies of the diaries. Out for dinner with Audrey and the kids, Fiona having gone to NI for her eleven-plus film.

Monday 8 December

Good reaction to short story from Cathy Galvin. Did a tidy-up in the study and letters etc. Started work on GB note but could not really get into it. My problem was an inability really to get enthused. I felt a deadness inside me at the thought of being more involved, and then a guilt at not wanting

* The Metropolitan Police defended the arrest of Green, a shadow Home Office spokesman, who allegedly had for nearly two years been supplied with documents leaked by a 26-year-old civil servant who said he thought they should be used 'in the public interest'.

to help more when everyone said I could and many said I should. To the dump with all the old novel drafts. Conference call on Thursday speech. Fixed Russell Brand meeting. TB called. Said he had thought about things. He was absolutely clear that I should not go back to the centre. It would be Lord Spin. The media would think I was there to be at war with them and it would be disastrous for me personally. Also it would set me up as the responsible person for failure. And I would end up in the Lords. So unless I had a real desire for the job the other option was an advisory role based at the party where I could help in an informal way, though he felt I should make it more formal.

He also felt the best thing I could do was to advise on policy direction. He felt there was a danger GB would try to get me to help put a good spin on bad policy.

He said what we need is new financial architecture not an end to everything that has worked and everything we've believed. He was scathing about Balls and said it was a real problem if Balls and Ed M and Douglas were still GB's key touchstones. And he was worried about Peter. 'He is so pleased to be there and helping shape the strategy, but he is not really driving as he would have done before.' He said if James P was in that group you would at least see the difference in the argument. He felt the public were confused – years of being told borrowing was bad and now it was the answer. It was really helpful to get his take on my situation and I was pretty clear now I was not going back or even going much beyond what I was doing now. Out on the bike but asthma bad. Bit of work then briefly to [businessman] Salman Amin's party. Chat with Stephen Carter. He said he really thought I should have gone back in with GB as a minister. Told him why I disagreed.

Tuesday 9 December

Walked to meet Georgie Thompson for lunch. She wanted to pick my brains on her Superchick project. She'd done Sky Sports News for seven years. Surely time to get out. Then to Kentish Town to meet Russell Brand. All a bit cloak and dagger. Neither of us particularly wanted people to know I was advising him. We met at his agent's office in Kentish Town, near where I had filmed some of the breakdown film. His manager came through first. Nik Linnen, northern, bearded, looked a bit like Brand. RB arrived a few minutes later. Door opened, 'Well, well?' he said in a 'Who'd have thought it?' kind of way. Really overdoing the pleasure, honour to meet you stuff. I was with them for two hours and he really grew on me.

The backdrop was the whole Sachsgate episode. I felt he came out of it better than Ross, that the whole thing was overblown and another piece of evidence that the Beeb management lacked brains or balls. What I think they wanted from me was some kind of reassurance that they were more or less doing the right thing. I did my objective, strategy, tactics thing, told them a few examples and RB seemed really taken by it. He loved the idea of getting above and beyond the media. Make sure you always know before they write about you what they're going to write. We went through the kind of technique you need to make sure the answers rather than the questions get heard. He had won a comedy award last week and dedicated it to Ross 'as a signal of support and friendship' and he seemed pleased when I said that looked like it was planned and it had the desired effect – he controlled the story and the coverage. He was quite political, said at one point Arnie [Arnold Schwarzenegger] was trailblazing for him and he was going to be the first British American President! He was bigger in the States than I realised.

He was about to go on a big UK tour. Brought in a couple of writers who wanted to say hello. Clearly a Labour supporter. Keen on how we handled ourselves. Asking very basic questions. Often would jump up, look at his reflection in the window, straighten his belt, sit down again. Must always dress like this. Unshaven. T-shirt, heavy metal jewellery, tight trousers, big black boots. Definitely a look. He went over the Ross thing in detail. Not planned, just went too far. They had no idea it would go so big. Once it did the BBC were hopeless. He had loads of stuff coming up. I said plan the media outcome for all of them. Also if shit hits the fan again, I went through how you can train yourself to say only what you want. Now, I said, the recent episode had put him into a higher league and he should exploit it. The feedback later was that they got a lot out of it. Mainly I think a bit of structure to things they were probably doing. He was more likeable than I expected. Totally open about his desire for fame, big houses, loads of women. Quite calculating too. But warm and funny, and beneath it all probably really insecure. Very funny about how ludicrous it was for him to be leading the news.

Wednesday 10 December

Time to get back into *Maya*. I remember Gail had said there will come a time when you'll want to stop talking about *All in the Mind*. I had definitely reached that. The BookScan figures were still ticking over and though the publishers seemed OK with it, I wasn't. Broke for PMQs. GB made a howler which reduced the Tories to collective hysteria when he appeared to say 'While we were saving the world...' Horrible moment and he did not recover that well because did not show enough humour or self-deprecation. I wanted him to say 'Oh dear, the sketchwriters have died and gone to heaven.' I went out for my first run in a while. Asthma dreadful. Ended up walking back from Camden.

Thursday 11 December

Into LRF for meeting with Cathy and Charlie Metcalfe, business guy who had been at that farewell dinner for Christiane and Jamie [Rubin]. His first wife had died from leukaemia. He had seen my *Standard* magazine piece saying I was working on a new fundraising drive and had contacted me via Matthew Freud. Good meeting in that he signed up to be one of the 50th anniversary supporters but also agreed to sell the idea to his rich Tory friends, and to sit on our investments committee, possibly with a view to chairing it if it worked out. Meeting with Roger Baker [director of press and broadcasting] on election structures. He was wanting my take on what he was hoping to put in place. I think he found it helpful but as with everything political at the moment, I was not firing as I should be. He seemed to be getting on top of things and said No. 10 was better than before. But it was still not right. Anyway, I think I helped him a bit. Off to Liverpool St, Andaz Hotel, for a ladies' lunch. Real prostitution this one. Julie Lynch had hired me for their conference in Brighton and then asked me to have lunch with the top twelve women in insurance. Nice enough and I spoke OK, no notes, OK Q&A, then gave out signed diaries. Think it was fine but it really was not work, or fulfilling. One or two of them really nice and quite sharp. Usual stiff Q&A, maybe a bit softer and there seemed to be some sympathy for GB and not much warmth for Cameron who was all over the papers today with his Christmas card, holding his disabled son, wife in trainers and no socks, potty in background. Pretty awful but it might work for him – only, however, because we had not got over the line that he was all spin no substance. Home then off to Wheatley. Calum already there.

Friday 12 December

Out for a run but again asthma kicked in after a mile or so and I walked-jogged back. Calum and I went to see Robert [Templeton]. Seemed pleased as ever to see us. And as ever I left feeling a mix of humility and sadness. Took Mum for lunch at the Sun Inn. Sky News on in the background. Really busy news day – de Menezes inquest open verdict, bad for the cops.*

* In 2005, Brazilian Jean Charles de Menezes had been shot dead by police at Stockwell station after being mistaken for a suicide bomber. The inquest jury reflected police claims that he had been lawfully killed and returned an open verdict, the most critical available to them.

Manchester voting No to congestion charge. Athens riots continuing after the cops killed a teenager. Mum on really good form at the moment though her shoulder was bad. Calum brilliant with her. Drove off to The Wirral. Checked in the Village Hotel. Briefly used the gym. Could not get going again. The party fundraiser was not well organised. It was very much a members-only event, the average age was way too high, there had been no outreach e.g. to business or local money or young members, and it felt a bit tired. Roger Philips from the Beeb in Liverpool was compering. He and his wife Mags great supporters. The book sales as a fundraiser went well, but generally I felt it was a bit of a waste of time. I spoke OK, did not do much humour, mixed heavy message with hope. Back to the hotel. Heaving with hen nights and Christmas parties. Thankfully I was in the extension.

Saturday 13 December

Gym for a while, breakfast, then off in the howling rain to collect Calum from Manchester station. Drove to Preston and met Frank Teasdale [former Burnley chairman] and Judith for lunch at Northcote. My idea and wanted to be my treat but Frank not having it. He was on fine form, full of mickey-taking and old tales. Not happy with a lot that was going on. Also felt even if we went up [to Premier League] we would struggle to put that many more on the gates. Calum and he joining together in major mickey-taking re my propagandist methods. Missed the first couple of minutes of the match. Had barely sat down when we scored, then two more inside eleven minutes. 3–0, could have been five by half-time but Southampton pegged back a couple to set up edgy finish.

Sunday 14 December

PG had been pressing me to go to church with him. Collected him and we set off for All Saints Margaret Street, not far from Oxford St. High Church. Incantation, incense. Lots of gay single men. Hardly any young people. Fairly full. Very beautiful music. Nice sermon too. Fiona texted to say TB had just been on telly explaining why I don't do God! It was a nice event and PG was obviously getting a lot out of it. He clearly thought I would go down the same path. Perhaps I would. I felt a pull at times but tended to pull away, or go for it more in theory than practice. We talked to the minister at the end. His sermon had been about the need to stress fundamental truths – especially in the light of all the economic stuff. Watched a fair bit of football while trying to work, then watched Sports Personality of the Year with Rory. He and I, and Calum up north, voting repeatedly for Chris Hoy. Expected him to come third but in the end he won by a mile. Also Dave Brailsford Coach of the Year and British Cycling Team of the Year, so a great night for them.

Monday 15 December

Denise Winn round to do an interview for her *Human Givens* [holistic treatment] magazine. Ex-*Mirror*, now a therapist and it was all about trying to get me to endorse what they did in a way. Had definitely reached the end of the road re interviews I think. Fiona McM round and we reviewed where we were. She had all the cuttings so I sent through a revised prelims schedule for the paperback of the novel. Ed sent a very nice email saying that I should feel very proud, as he does, on seeing the strength of the reviews. To City Hall to speak at the Stand to Reason [mental health charity] conference. Jonathan Naess [campaigner] had asked me to do a little speech and reading. Couple of hundred people. Running late. Spoke OK. They were selling for 11 quid and sold a fair few while doing an interview with Alan Beattie of the *FT*. Got asked by Mindapples [mind care education] to do my 'What is the staying mentally healthy equivalent of five a day?' I said sleep, family home, exercise, bigger cause, laughter. Not bad.

Very nice security doorman called Godfrey who came over and said 'You must go back to help Gordon. He needs you. We need you.' He said 'my people' will always vote Labour but a lot of people take everything for granted. He was really warm and intelligent and I had a really powerful sense of duty, also that it was as though he had been sent in some way. I was doing the signing by a door. He was in a chair just across from me. He waited till there were no people around. He said 'I can see just watching how people relate to you here that you would make such a difference. You did it for Tony. Now you have to do it for Gordon.' Tube home. Out with Fiona for dinner at the Commons with DB. A bit late. The place was pretty quiet. DB seemed pretty chilled for him. Still with Margaret [Williams] the GP. Three years now. 'Little lad' [Blunkett's son by the magazine publisher Kimberly Quinn] almost six. Taking him to Hamley's tomorrow before he heads to America. He said he had no desire to go back to government. 'He's not going to offer me Chancellor or Foreign Secretary.' I said I thought it was great Margaret Beckett had gone back to a lower job, there was not enough of that in politics. He kind of agreed but – obviously not knowing what was on offer to me – said 'Why on earth would I want to fuck around at the Cabinet Office or somewhere like that?'

He said what he would really like to do was work with me and Peter at the party. He said he reckoned the two of us were better known than any member of the Cabinet apart from GB. Also thought we connected with young people. He was down on Harriet and Douglas. John Reid and Carine [wife] came in with Doug Henderson [MP]. JR came over for a chat. Said they had loved the breakdown programme and thought it was really moving. Mainly football small talk and so on. Keith Vaz took me on a tour of his table. Also asked if I would go for a Leicester seat. Commons always impressive on one level but not enough to want to be there. Both DB and Vaz saying I should get a seat.

Tuesday 16 December

Email from Sue Nye asking if I had any ideas for the New Year message? I did a draft, but suggested rather than putting it out as a statement, he record it as a film on the No. 10 site, and just put it out there. If there is too much politics in it, do it on the party site. I said not to worry about comparisons with Obama. Do it in front of desk, not behind. Use autocue. The draft tried to bring together some of the lines that were coming out of the strategy meetings we had been having. How to get hope and opportunity for Britain in a world of uncertainty and danger. Optimism in the face of the big challenges – economy, security, environment. Talk up UK strengths. Free trade. Open economy. Global reach greater than any country of our size. Some of the greatest innovators and entrepreneurs, financial and social. We lead in culture and the arts. The best armed forces in the world. Steps on the environment. Big message on the economy, his role in leading through the most serious global economic and financial crisis of this generation's lifetime. How we averted catastrophe. What we do now. Warning of the continuing downturn and the various possible responses. Regulate and supervise better, and on a global basis, but not turn back on markets or turn inwards to protectionism. Reasons for confidence. Our people. Past challenges.

I also suggested he use it to tell the whole story, from 1997. There is a real danger if we let the economic crash define the whole era, it will wipe out all the political gains of past progress across the piece. Media and Tories will want to do that. He has to take the lead in making sure they can't succeed. Spell out the risks as well as the opportunities of globalisation. Education and innovation the key.

Felt a bit pissed off giving virtually a whole day to visit to Swindon school in advance but was in many ways glad I did. Tough special school. Mainly educational and behavioural difficulties. Kids excluded from a couple of mainstream schools. Real problems at home. There to hand over a Lady Taverners' bus donated by Stuart and Margaret [Le Gassick]. Nice head, good teachers. Some really nice kids but you could tell just looking at some of them they had crap lives. Some would end up in jail beyond a shadow of doubt. They sang 'Hallelujah' to us. Several obsessed with football. Good atmosphere round the place. Rewards for good behaviour system. Went for a spin in the bus. I did a little speech on the equal worth of all, how they all had a talent and had to let it flourish. One of the teachers, a Greek guy, said they could see the kids improve during the day, but then by the time they came back in the morning, it had all gone back again. I said to Stuart they were the kind of people that really deserved to be called entrepreneurs. And giving those kids a real chance was why you needed a government committed to helping the disadvantaged.

On the way back took a call from GB, on his way to Iraq, saying thanks for the note. Asked me to go in early on Thursday to have another chat. He felt the Tories had made a big mistake in getting themselves committed to cuts. Felt Cameron's blast at greedy bankers, even if *The Guardian* fell for it, was all about positioning without policy and not within a proper strategic framework. There was a new poll out tonight in *The Guardian* showing us up a bit and the Tories down a fair bit. He sounded OK. But the economic backdrop was getting grimmer and grimmer. I suggested taking Obama's quote 'two wars, a planet in peril, the worst economic crisis in a century' and using that as the structure for the new year message and trying to make central message world of risk and danger to Britain of hope and opportunity.

Wednesday 17 December

In with PG to a meeting at Freud's with Blue State Digital, the guys who built up Obama's online message campaign and fundraising operation. Two Americans and a Brit who worked with them on Ken's campaign. Very sharp and switched on. They explained the kind of thing they could do. Seemed so right for what we needed but we explained there was a cultural leap a lot of our politicians would find hard to make. Douglas was a bit late, and immediately started to express himself very cautiously re how we would need to integrate with what was already there. That may be right but we must not let it get mangled. I felt the online operation had to be central to everything we did. Partly looking at the stuff Mark Lucas had done for me. But above all the way Obama had empowered people to get involved. Yesterday everyone's inbox got a message from GB re Royal Mail. They said it was a waste of time and effort and counterproductive. It was top down, not a call for action. They believed properly done they could turn this into a money-maker for the party. They knew we were a different sort of politics and culture but confident nonetheless. I liked them. PG and I wanted them in ASAP.

Superb office block full of very bright people. That was clear from the atmosphere on the little tour I did with PG. Matthew F and I discussed me possibly getting involved with him in the New Year. Maybe speechifying and strategising on an occasional basis. On the political scene he said it was like the patient got better but he was still critically, possibly terminally ill. He felt when Obama came properly on the scene people would think why can't we have one like him when we used to a couple of years ago? But he felt the Tories were useless and still had a hunch Hague would be leader by the election. DC just too lightweight. Then *Newsnight* cultural review interview – chose *God of Carnage* by Yasmina Reza as best play, *I've Loved You So Long* best film, *Reluctant Fundamentalist* by Mohsin Hamid best novel and *Mules* by Winsome Pinnock, directed by Amy Hodge, best overall.

Thursday 18 December

Dermot O'Leary had asked me to do one of his first *Time Capsules* programmes on Radio 2. Kind of poor man's *Desert Island Discs*. Slightly different formula. Had to select one childhood piece of music (Donald playing a tune in honour of Dad on the pipes). First song bought or really loved during teenage years (Diana Ross, 'Ain't No Mountain High Enough'). Our song type thing (Randy Crawford, 'One Day I'll Fly Away'). Best song ('Ne me quitte pas'). Funeral song ('Quand on que l'amour') [both Jacques Brel]. Went to get diaries from PG. He thought the full version was much better than single volume but not publishable pre-election. Some – maybe 5 per cent of the passages I had sidelined – was not publishable any time. He felt all the characters came through as they are which is why it was bad for GB in particular. Melissa Benn round. Loved the novel and wanted me to sign several as presents for her family, including Tony and Hilary [MP son].

Main event today was GB's strategy meeting 4.30 to 6.30. He asked me to go in early but he was tied up with Mervyn King [Governor of Bank of England] and by the time he was out most of the others had been gathering. PG was trying to get a bit of bonhomie going but it was hard work. Nick Pearce [head of No. 10 Policy Unit] there for the first time. Also Damian McBride arrived with GB. I was sitting with Peter M. I scribbled him a note 'I thought you had dealt with him.' 'So did I.' GB apologised for being late. David Muir did a presentation which showed the gap with the Tories beginning to narrow, GB ahead on economy and some attributes but still not great. He had a slide showing 'DC no TB' which showed how far ahead TB was at similar period of his leadership. Cameron definitely more vulnerable than before. PG and I were pushing the need to build a team of MPs and others tracking him all the time. David said it was important we stayed focused on the need for action and the Tories as do-nothing party 'because people don't like it when the issue is borrowing'.

That was the thing I zoned in on, along with DC weak, when GB threw it open. I said you can't just walk round the issue. If it is real, it has to be addressed. We need an explanation for it. GB said the nearest we could get to was globalisation, difficult things now to build for the future. We went into a fairly tired and rambling discussion of general message and strategy. He seemed to be wanting slogans. The best was from Douglas. Help today, hope tomorrow. He did a poor presentation on the state of preparedness at the party which was little more than an analysis of how we lacked the finances to have what we had had for a campaign before. Liam Byrne did a very average presentation on the shape of the year ahead. He said he had prepared it with Ed Miliband, who was not there today. It was little more than a mini-grid of one thing a month we knew to be happening.

Peter scribbled me a note at one point: 'So are you moving in and taking over?' I said not without improved direction and leadership. 'How many people in this room would Obama have had on his B team?' Quite, he scribbled. GB at one point had his head resting on his hands on the table. He looked tired again. DJ Collins and Tom Watson did a presentation on digital and the internet which was OK but pretty basic stuff. They were quite strong on the need for better use of online, and the need to engage more in new forms of comms but it would be a big cultural leap for the senior politicians to get it. Balls was less flapping about today. Made one or two sensible points about the need to lay the ground better for bad events ahead. We could not be giving the impression there would be no pain, or that government could guarantee security to jobs or businesses. We were back to the need for greater clarity in medium- and long-term narrative. Peter said he felt we were explaining some things well, some badly.

Someone said Tony McNulty [Employment and Welfare Secretary] had been really good on *Newsnight*, great on substance and tone. 'Did someone send him a text to say thanks?' said GB. Sue, sitting next to me, started to do that. I felt is this how low expectations have got that if a minister does an OK interview we are all supposed to celebrate. I said it does not say much for the Cabinet. Ed Balls said 'He is in the Cabinet.' Is he? 'Well he attends,' he said. 'But half the government attends.' I did feel at these meetings a sense of us all saying the same things as last time. I was a little alarmed to see a pile of copies of my draft New Year's message and said to Sue we should not get into a writing by committee situation. Sue was the only woman. GB seemed to look to me and Peter and a bit to Ed and Douglas for bigger points. It was due to end at half six as there was the office Xmas party. I was hoping to escape. GB said he had a quick meeting with Victor Blank but could I wait around to see him before I left. Alison came in and took me to the state rooms where the office do was going on.

Chatted a bit with Sarah who was dressed as Santa. She had read my novel, was nice about it. Back in to see GB. He would not let go. 'I really need you to help me.' 'I am helping you, just not as much as you want me to.' 'I really want you to think again about coming in full-time.' I said his problem was he had found the one person in politics who really did not want to go to the Lords. Also I felt after the next election I would not want to stay too involved in politics. I told him too that I had some concerns up top about going back into it full-on. But he just wanted to keep pestering me really. Said he really needed me. 'Peter has worked,' he said, 'though I know you can never tell where it ends with Peter.' He said even at these meetings it was obvious how much I could give him and so he really wanted me to think about it. I said I would. I was relieved when Sarah came in and said he needed to go in for the group photos. He said he would be out in a few minutes. And he had another go. Said goodbye to Alison, signed a couple of books then off to meet Fiona. Bumped into Simon Walters [*Mail on Sunday*] on way out. 'You've got your work cut out,' he said.

Off to Matthew Freud's. Chatted with Ken Livingstone who was writing his memoirs. Piers M quite funny about his own fame. E.g. how Obama was trying to get his endorsement. Stuart Rose on how retail was worse than he had ever known. George Osborne and wife arrived. I asked him who was going to win the election. 'I don't know,' he said. He seemed less confident than previous times I had seen him. DC not there. He said he was in Yorkshire. F thought it was probably a diplomatic absence, that all the toffing with Freud-Murdochs not good for them. Peter M there. Chatting with George, a real toff when close up. Vulnerable. I asked Tim Bell same question – who will win and why? 'You. Because the others are fucking useless.' Les Hinton and Rebekah who said I was the only Labour person not vetoed by the people who were co-hosting her New Year's party. Never saw Elisabeth [Rupert Murdoch's daughter, Matthew F's wife] which was a bit weird. Dominic Lawson and wife. Peter Stothard re the need to stop the Tories. He said I really had to go back and help. Quite happy to leave.

Friday 19 December

Read Fiona's book on working parents. Clear sense of her being virtually a single parent. Caught a clip of GB's press conference on the news. He used a section from the draft message for the New Year re challenge matched by optimism which seemed a bit of a waste. Alison texted to say Simon

Walters was sniffing around about the meeting yesterday and Damian had given the line that it was about digital operation and could I speak to Michael Dugher [GB's chief political spokesman] by switch. Spoke to Dugher and Muir and told them absolutely no need to say anything. Their instinct too often was to say something not true.

Emailed Sue saying I received a call and then a text this evening to the effect that Simon Walters knew I had been at a meeting on Thursday and the line had been given by Damian McBride that this was a meeting about digital media, part of which GB attended. I said it was a ludicrous thing to say. I explained Simon Walters saw me leaving the building as he happened to be walking down Whitehall. I said nothing. Therefore he knew nothing about what I was doing there. It seems to me a simple line, if asked, that I regularly see people in govt, including in Downing Street, was all that was needed. Their line was untrue and counterproductive. I also told David Muir to instruct Damian, with whom I don't think I have ever exchanged a word, that he briefs nothing about anything I am involved in without talking to me.

Saturday 20 December

Off with Calum to Paddington. Syd Young met us and we went for lunch at the café near Temple Meads. A guy asked if I would recommend a book on politics for his mate for Christmas. Mine, I said. Suggested he get one from the station and I would sign which I did. Out to Ashton Gate, did a couple of interviews for radio. Game dire in first half but then really took off. They [Bristol City] went ahead with a penalty. We came back with two well-worked goals to win 2–1. Dropped Calum at the station then off to Keynsham. Urban Espresso café for a party members and non-members event. Spoke for about fifteen minutes, Q&A, mix and mingle. Signed up the very pretty girl working at the counter. She said she would join the party if I went back there for a cup of tea. This and the smaller dinner were fundraisers for Dan Norris [MP]. Dinner at [former TB advisor] Conor Ryan's house. A head and deputy head, two Labour candidates, an author, an interior designer. They were paying over the odds to meet me. Deputy head great on how we had transformed schools. Balls not popular with teachers though, they said. Dan and his lovely girlfriend Wendy drove me to David Mills's in Darlingscott. We had a good chat on the drive. He said his problem in the seat was GB. He did not have a big enough solid Labour vote. The area did not warm to GB as they did to TB and didn't trust him. He also found it difficult being lectured to about loyalty from a whips office rewarding disloyalty to TB. Wendy was working with the Russell Group of universities trying to get more working-class people to top unis. Felt we had missed a lot of tricks. They came in for a drink with David, Tessa and Jessie.

Later David admitted he was more worried than ever re the Italian court case. The prosecutor was calling for a four-year jail sentence. The judge was determined to get him as a proxy for Berlusconi. He said if it happened he would be a political prisoner. There had to be a huge fuss made about it. There was no evidence but they were determined to get him. I could see how shocked Tessa was, that this was the first time he had let the bluster go and said what he really thought. He looked terribly sad. I told Tessa he was obviously thinking worst-case scenario and not to worry more than she was already. But it was a big hit. She said the children must not know what he had said. He seemed now to be resting hopes on the process running out of time.

Sunday 21 December to 1 January

Long period not doing diary, and not doing much at all. Low-level depression on and off. No big dip, just not able to get up to much. Feeling a bit directionless yet not sure what big projects to take on. Watched the United world club final, sent Alex a congratulatory text afterwards. 'Worth it in the long run,' he said. Burnley's Christmas a bit of a disaster though, losing Boxing Day home to Barnsley [2–1] and away at Doncaster on the 28th [2–1]. Went with Graeme, Mikey and Jamie (brother and nephews). Graeme really wheezy. Much worse than I had been, but the cold had definitely brought on worse asthma added to which I was occasionally crapping blood.

The only political work I was doing was a bit of work with David Muir on the GB NY message. We cut it a fair bit. He ended up overdoing the idea of 'Building tomorrow today'. It mixed candour and optimism. I had never been sure of the merit of these messages when TB was there and was less so now. The idea when I sent over a draft was for him to do it to camera and release as film on No. 10 site. They did as a podcast instead but it did not quite work. Message not bad but low impact. GB didn't call much and maybe had got the message that I really did not want to be back full-time. The news was dominated over Christmas by the Israelis kicking the shit out of Gaza.* Lots of words of condemnation but there was not much to be done to stop them with the UN divided and the US still in pre-Obama limbo. TB low key. Not sure where he was but he needed to get his voice up on it.

* Armed conflict between Palestinians in the Gaza Strip that ended in a unilateral ceasefire after three weeks.

Xmas day OK, went to the Kinnocks and it did not get too heavy. Helle on great form. Seemed fairly confident of a coalition win at next election. Steve had got a new job with the Davos economic council lot and both of them seemed pleased he was doing something totally his thing. Having some great chats with the kids. Chris Hoy [knighted] main story in the [New Year] honours list. Managed to keep socialising fairly low-key. Out with Neil, Glenys and Rach to [film director] Hugh Hudson's. Neil and Hugh thought the film *The Queen* was a piss-take. Maryam [Hugh's wife] and I didn't. Hugh telling us re a film Mohamed al Fayed [businessman, father of Dodi Fayed] wanted him to make – Dodi [Princess Diana's boyfriend, killed with her in 1997 car crash] and Di, but there had to be portrayal of Philip as a Nazi! Nice enough night. Maryam off to States to make a film on aneurisms. New Year's Eve dinner with Tessa and David then briefly to Lindsay's. In the New Year I needed to sort health, crank things up workwise, get going on better promotion Book 1, complete 2 and finally decide re GB. Got in touch with Justin Langer to see if we could get him to be a face for the charity.

Saturday 3 January 2009

Out on the bike a.m. then off to QPR v Burnley with the boys. Up to the hospitality club for lunch and after chatting to Ali Russell and some of the Burnley guys for a while, Jamie and Harry (Redknapp) arrived. Had a good chat with Jamie. Interesting on how gangsters got into players at Liverpool.* Poor game. Nil–nil. Liked Ali Russell.

Sunday 4 January

Watched GB on Marr online. OK. Better tone and backdrop but still not great. Also I worried that they were not coming up with a persuasive argument on borrowing etc. Then turned on Five Live to find GB as a guest on *Fighting Talk*. He did OK. Then called me for the first time in a while and asked me to go to see him tomorrow. I felt the same dread I had felt before Christmas but also realised I had to do it. Couldn't not really. PG and family back from Jamaica so we went out to Marine Ices. Philip looking really well. Felt re GB that I should agree to a couple of days a week, advising on strategy etc., stepping up as we got nearer to the election.

* The father of Liverpool captain Steven Gerrard had revealed that his son had been terrorised and threatened with being shot by a known gangster who was trying to extort money from him.

Monday 5 January

Slept badly for some reason. Got the bus into town. Peter M called. Asked where I was. I said I was on a bus en route to seeing GB. He said I had to find a way of getting more involved. He felt GB was improving and that in part was the result of us all weaning him off bad advice on to good advice. He was very funny about going to Argos at the weekend to buy a new heater. He had to phone Ben Wegg-Prosser to find out how the whole Argos thing worked. I went in through the Cabinet Office. Cleaners and messengers always pleased to see me. Chat with Sue Nye. She said Peter went to their place on Boxing Day 'and had to be reacquainted with the kids'. GB was on the phone to [Recep Tayyip] Erdoğan [Prime Minister of Turkey] about Gaza. Balls was around as our meeting started. Lots of small talk about Christmas etc. On the Middle East he said he had spoken to TB yesterday. GB also feared Obama would not be as interested and committed on foreign policy as people might imagine. He felt the silence on Gaza might be less because of respect for Bush than because they could not work out the position.

We went round a few policy blocks and had a perfectly nice chat before we got to the point. He felt there were now clearer dividing lines on the economy. He felt he could persuade people this was global and that we had handled things OK. More important it was about the arguments and the policies for the future. He felt the Tories were weak on policy and could be exposed as such. But he needed my help. 'I keep saying, I need you to help me. I need you here.' I felt we were going round the same circles as pre-Christmas. He just wouldn't take no for an answer. He was back to the idea of the Lords again. I said no. Then suddenly asked if I would be election campaign director. I quizzed him a bit half-heartedly on finances, how things would work etc. But I was slightly losing the will to live and having said any contribution I made was through party not government I went along with the idea of going in to do something on those lines. Before I knew it, he was talking about whether to do as salaried or consultant.

He was basically asking me to do Douglas's job. I said how would Douglas feel about it. He said I think he would appreciate it. He said he intended to freshen up the government again before too long. He asked if I thought he should move David M to a domestic job. He seemed a bit lost where he was. I said he certainly needed a higher profile and should be more politically engaged but it should not be seen as a demotion. Then he was back to lists of who I rated. This was nonsense. I had been going on about the need to licence more ministers to be cross cutting and say edgy interesting things but most of them could walk down any street unmolested and unrecognised. He said he had been surprised how disappointing they were. It all pointed to me being there, he said, trying to generate arguments and get people to put them over. He felt Alan J was good, as did I, but got hurt by the deputy leadership contest [beaten by Harriet Harman] and was now a bit 9 to 5. I felt we were weak on women. He said re Tessa he felt she had become non-political because of the Olympics. It was all a bit tired.

I felt myself being trapped in though in part because I was in there for so long. When Bill the messenger brought in his lunch – it looked like a Christmas dinner – I thought I was going to be stuck in even longer. He was in generally OK form but was fixated on this idea of the difference I could make. I felt he overstated it. Also underestimated the extent to which it was the team that did the job not just me. He was asking me to do a lot of people's jobs. He said he wanted me to try to get on with Balls. I said it wasn't that I didn't get on with him but that I sometimes our judgements clashed too much. He also said he would like me to get to know Damian McBride. Again, I said I didn't know him but could only go on reputation. He said you'd like him. He loves football. He has acquired some of Peter's reputation for black arts and yours for strength with the media. He has a creative spark and we are short of those.

He finally had to leave to see a couple of new SB [Special Branch] guys, one of whom had worked with Straw. He said Jack loved all that dressing up as Lord Chancellor. Loved all the access to establishment figures. Went out with Sue. I said he had ground me down. Good, she said. I jumped in a cab. 'Been telling Superman what to say as he saves the world have you?' said the cabbie. We had a friendly but robust argument all the way home. He was really down on us. PG said last night there was a real danger the public just hit a tipping point with us. By the time I got home and told Calum I seemed to have agreed to a new job, I was feeling dreadful about it.

Spoke to PG and he and Georgia came round for a chat. I said the whole thing filled me with dread. He was asking me to go in and recreate a campaign machine that was not there. What were the politicians all doing? PG agreed it was unreasonable. Also felt I could get out of it still. The important thing was to work out a modus operandi and go for it. Peter M was at me the whole time, saying I had to make a difference and it was time to bite the bullet. I explained some of the reservations but he was clearly now cranking up all the time to try to get me in. As the day wore on I felt worse and worse about it. I spoke to Neil who said though he was less totally opposed than before he was still opposed. He said even at part-time you had the enemies going full-time. He felt the Lords idea would be a disaster.

Also spoke to Carol L who said the atmosphere inside Vic St was OK but there was no flair or drive or leadership. If I went it would fall on me very quickly. She said the taskforce leaders had been asked to do presentations to Douglas, Ray Collins [general secretary] and David Muir. For hers she said David didn't show, Ray was on his BlackBerry and Douglas was there for ten minutes. So hardly surprising there was no grip. She said the party would love it if I went in but it would be a bad move for me. I went to bed feeling really low. Spoke late to TB. He said he needed to think about it carefully but his initial instinct was that it was not a great idea. I would without doubt bring some order and flair to the operation. But the main issue was policy at the moment rather than politics. He said he found it admirable that I did not want to go to the Lords. But a party job could end up with me thinking the whole thing was a bit weird. He felt on balance not. Help but not full-time.

Tuesday 6 January

Barely slept, not a good sign. I said to Fiona I really felt I had to tell him I was not going to do it. I sent an email as follows. I said I was sorry to send a disappointing email but having reflected and spoken with family and close friends I had decided I cannot substantially increase my commitment. Partly because of outstanding other work commitments, but the reasons are mainly personal and family. I assured him they were not political and I would continue to support him. But they combined to ensure my heart would not be 100 per cent in the task. I had managed to get a different sort of balance in my life and was reluctant to give it up. Partly because of this I said I didn't share his own belief that I could make the kind of contribution I had in the past, which was in large part dependent on a 24/7 commitment and the building of a substantial number of other people into a team. I promised I would continue to offer him and his team strategic advice and to step up work for and in the party as an election nears. But he really had to understand now, full-time is not happening. I admitted feeling wretched saying it and asked him not to take it as lack of support for him personally, but I knew it was the right decision.

Peter M called again as I was getting ready to go out for the Spurs match. He had seen my email to GB. He said he felt both of us were approaching it in the wrong way. That there had to be an iterative process towards greater involvement not some kind of big bang. He said 'If I say to GB that it was not a total standoff but offered the chance of some formal involvement was that OK?' I said yes, but he has to give up on all these full-time job offers. The match was fantastic in the first half. The second half was a different story. They were better and we seemed to implode. A few fabulous moments but second half a massacre [4–1].

Wednesday 7 January

Another sleepless night. PG saw GB. Said he was a lot more relaxed. Told him he needed proper political operation, policy agenda and major attack on Cameron. Also that to get me engaged he needed to have others above, alongside and below me. Peter or maybe James Purnell. GB thought maybe DM. Got the French novel translation title. *Tout est dans la tête.*

Thursday 8 January

I had been sleeping so badly that I felt I should see DS. Went to his house. Explained that in general I had been OK but I was really agonising about the GB situation. He had battered me into submission but the moment I said yes I regretted it and now had got myself out. He said his assessment of me was that I had a really powerful instinct and where it was strong and sustained I should follow it. We were back to the clash between self and service. He felt if I was doubtful I should go for self and recognise I had given a lot of service. He would be worried for my mental health if I went back to a situation I was not comfortable with in which I was expected to deliver so much of the load. I felt better having seen him but knew I would continue to feel torn and guilty. Barnaby Spurrier [film producer] sent a great email saying his partner, just back from making a film with Robert de Niro, was really keen on *All in the Mind*.

Friday 9 January

TB called from Paris. He said someone had said his TV French had improved but it still wasn't as good as mine. He felt on balance I had done the right thing re GB. Clearly not sure whether his MEPP role was going to be sustained post Obama. In any event he was definitely still interested in the Europe job. He was worried that GB felt everything was all about politics and presentation, which is why he was so keen on Peter and me, not policy. He was worried they were, almost without realising, retreating from a New Labour position. There was a sense of a leftward drift but without an understanding of how they were losing people in the centre. He was sure Balls would be giving bad advice. What was less clear was whether GB still took it. He said the people in the States he spoke to felt the economy was going to get much, much worse. *Independent on Sunday* were on asking if I had been offered a peerage. I decided to say nothing but they kept at me. Eventually I said simply that I had always said I could not imagine myself in the Lords.

Saturday 10 January

Out on bike. David Mills sent through his statement for the court case. Worked on that a bit. He needed a couple of absolutely clear short statements for media pick-up and also needed to remove bits that came over as a bit flippant. Burnley v Swansea. Lost 2–0. A danger of our season imploding if and when we lost to Spurs after the second leg. Fiona and Grace out at the ballet so Calum and I went out and had a very nice chat. He was still pushing me to go back.

Sunday 11 January

Alex called re book royalties on the diaries as he was worried he was being ripped off with his book. Also that the credit crunch etc. was beginning to affect them too. E.g. although selling out, not as quick. He'd called because he was watching Cameron on Marr in his hotel room pre-Chelsea. 'Lightweight and superficial.' Not sure he could live in a country led by someone like him. *IoS* splashed on my so-called peerage rebuff to GB. Also fair amount of coverage for Milburn 'back' doing something on social mobility policy. Had a couple of chats with Alan who sounded like he was in a similar position to me. He was asked to go back – in his case maybe a Cabinet job – but he had told GB he'd made a lifestyle choice and he didn't want to go back on it. He felt a duty to help but no real desire, and although things were politically a bit better, he still felt the Tories were favourites. Georgia was out canvassing and then round to watch United hammer Chelsea 3–0.

Monday 12 January

Tried a run, in pouring rain, but asthma still creeping in. Ed had finally heard from Susan Sandon re Novel 2. We knew there would be a credit crunch impact on the advance but the offer was well down on the first one. In the end, I said to Ed, it wasn't about the money. I enjoyed doing them and they were just another arm to the profile. Added to which it looked like the first might be a film.

Tuesday 13 January

Off to Oxford with Rory. His last term. It had gone so quickly. Drove back, stopping halfway to write a couple of the key scenes. Then to Old Street for a meeting with the Marks and Dora, plus Stuart Till [Silverfish media chairman] re the website. Looking good. Needed a better rationale for it but instinctively felt it was probably the thing to do. Mark looking to work more for me on this. The Tories launched a poster on debt. No way this argument could be avoided.

Wednesday 14 January

Having chosen the records a while back, recorded Dermot O'Leary's *Time Capsules* programme for Radio 2. Enjoyed it. Five songs per a formula, five free choice. Lots of chatter in between. Wrote the copy for all the various pages of the website and started to give Mark lines for Facebook. Alex called for a long chat re my situation re GB. He felt I should get honoured in some way. I said I was not bothered about that. In which case you definitely did the right thing. He felt for the public I was a bigger figure than Peter M and that if I was back in in a big way I would be a magnet and target and if I didn't feel I had the team and the support it could easily go wrong. He felt help in lots of ways but not at the expense of my whole life. Really good natter on his own situation too. Still loving it. Still enjoying team building and the pressure.

Thursday 15 January

David Prescott round to record stuff for the Go Fourth website. There had been a surge of interest in Labour and the web following Derek Draper's launch of LabourList.org. So maybe it was the right time for me to get into all this. He wanted me and JP out doing campaign masterclasses. Lots of nice stuff on Facebook, Mark Bennett having got me on there after nagging for ages. Barnaby Spurrier and his very nice colleague Glynis came round. They really wanted to press on with *All in the Mind*. Both felt it was too good not to be a film. He had drawn a blank re TV but they felt it could make a British movie. Off to see TB in his office. He said he had never been working so hard and seemed to be travelling more than ever. Just back from getting his Presidential Medal of Freedom from Bush. You looked embarrassed, I said. Probably the best way to look, he said. Only in Britain could people think it bad to get recognition like that.

He said he was never happier than when out of the country away from our media. Yet he was clearly keen on the Europe job. Sarko was dead keen for him to do it. If Merkel went for it, it would be a done deal. GB might not really want him but he would not be able to stop that kind of momentum. GB was trying to speak to him on MEPP while I was there. They had a perfectly OK chat on where the Israelis were, what the Egyptians were up to. TB felt they were closer than people thought. He said to him he was with me. 'Tell him I'm still after him,' he said, laughing. TB was more sure than ever I did the right thing, felt he would expect me to do the whole job at the centre and without real honesty about the strategy. There was no honesty about it. He did not want to say he was giving up New Labour but in policy terms he was. You could feel the leftist instincts on some of the economic messages but on public services where was he heading? What was the direction on health and education? It wasn't clear.

He was pissed off with David M who had written a piece saying the 'war on terror' as a notion was misguided. He had been captured by the foreign policy establishment who wanted to say these groups were all disparate and unconnected. They might be, but the determination required to deal with them did require something closer to the Bush approach. He said it is worth pointing out September 11 was the last attack. Nightmare scenario for Obama is a softer approach followed by a hit. He was in good form generally. Frustrated at the envoy job as he felt he had responsibility without power. We bobbed around between domestic and foreign. He felt GB still had a chance but felt it unlikely. He felt DC was weak but might be strong enough. He also felt the economy might get worse.

On Obama he felt it was all a bit overblown and that he was not quite the Messiah figure he was being presented as. Also worried that he would be mainly domestic-focused. Did he want to be the first US President to distance from Israel? Did he want to let down Palestinians? No. So he might box and cox. He felt he was intensely political. Could be the business but not totally clear. Then to Freuds. First did Fox TV on Obama. Good interview though the guy was a bit odd. They're like Daleks these US TV guys. Then to watch PG talk about mood and watch a rather depressing focus group. NHS brand the top. Politicians the bottom. No link between the two of course. Usual moans and groans. All said recession not affecting them but then saying how they were changing their habits. Very down on GB but banks getting blame. Cameron nowhere. Then had a session with some of Matthew's clients.

Friday 16 January

Out to breakfast telly at Beeb on depression. Mark round to show me how to use Facebook. Got 500 friends in three days which he thought was pretty good. I did a piece for LabourList explaining my conversion to social media by reference to PG's theory that for me, today's irritation becomes tomorrow's obsession. Used to hate joggers. Now ran everywhere. Used to hate dogs. Now Molly on the sofa next to me as I type. Now the same with online malarkey. Mark B told me Facebook has the same population as the British Isles. And it felt like a foreign country the first few days as I attempted to navigate my way around it.

I still felt we should not imagine Obama won because of his superior use of online campaigning and messaging. That is only part of the reason. He won because he had a strong, clear, hard-headed, thought-through strategy; good campaign organisation; and the inspiring of ambassadors in every street and workplace. It was also a fabulously disciplined campaign.

So with the embracing of the new, he was also master of much of the old in terms of good political campaigning. Some of the press were saying I was 'leading Labour's online fightback'. God help us if so. But it was definitely time to get more involved in debate via the web. The flak and abuse was an irritant but nothing more. I was finding the general nature of the debates taking place really refreshing, whether on LabourList, Go Fourth or Facebook. There seemed to be a desire for a livelier and more open debate about politics than most of our mass media is able to deliver.

Saturday 17 January

The economic news grimness was growing. Calum and I watched Burnley get robbed at Preston North End on telly because of a dire penalty decision. Out at 5 to do a live Sky slot on Obama and the inauguration. Lots of comparisons with TB '97, euphoria etc., but I was highlighting the differences as well as the similarities.

Sunday 18 January

Calum really getting worried re his exams. Maybe he had been working too hard. I had a pretty quiet day, bit of exercise, bit of work. The build-up for Obama was really growing. Felt a bit for GWB who was being written up as the worst ever President. TB and GB both said he had been defiant, saying history would see things differently. If Obama softened in the war on terror, for example, and there was an attack, or if Iraq really started to entrench the progress, things could look different. The economic picture was getting worse by the day.

Monday 19 January

PG felt there was a chance of a real slide in public opinion and a shift to the Tories just because they weren't us, and we were the government. GB and AD were announcing a fresh and massive bailout for the banks amid growing economic grimmery. The full scale of the disaster at RBS under Fred Goodwin [CEO] was becoming clearer. GB had mentioned it when I saw him last week, and the notion Goodwin was a megalomaniac just desperate for more and ever bigger deals, who got carried away with his own importance and the scale of what he was doing. Bill Hagerty was round most of the morning to go through the '97 stuff from the diaries. We were still looking for cuts. Fiona was away at a conference in Bury so Grace and I had Audrey round making us dinner before I did an Aussie radio interview. Alex called, said he thought we could win even with the economic stuff.

Tuesday 20 January

In to Victoria Street for a meeting with Sue Macmillan, head of the new media team. Douglas chairing, Ray Collins, Marianna, David Muir, PG, Alicia Kennedy [party deputy general secretary]. Douglas was too much pointing to problem not to solution. He and David [Muir] had been to the States and seen a lot of the Obama people. Their report was OK. Basically said what we knew – that though they did brilliantly in the use of new technology, the key things were a strong and confident leader who knew his own mind, a united and hard-working team signed up to the same strategy, and real discipline and organisation. 'So we're fucked then,' I said, and to be fair they all laughed. But we did lack all of those things. Part of my problem with the old GB team was that they couldn't see their own role in the making of their problems. E.g. when Douglas referred to Obama as 'the nearest thing we will see to a political phenomenon in our lifetime' and I could see the TB people in there raising their eyebrows. Or when Douglas said to me, 'It will be hard no longer to have a friend you can pick up a phone to in the White House.' Sue seemed to me to be doing a good job with next to no resources. I had to leave early. DM and then GB called. He sounded very down. He said what shall I do about Cameron and Obama? What do you mean? Just so defensive. He thought the Tories would be able to make a sense of closeness between them, generationally for example. I said but you are the PM. It was ludicrous and showed a lack of confidence. He ran through why they'd had to do what they did with the banks [another package of measures to aid bailout of banks] yesterday. He was keen to emphasise that there was really no option, that the alternative was an enormous collapse.

I said to him he really had to – I had been saying this for ages – license a group of ministers and MPs to get off the leash on DC. David Muir and I had been saying get Alan Johnson involved. GB said he would. But I doubted it would happen. Home to watch the Obama inauguration. I watched it mainly on CNN. Amazing crowds. Great pictures of all the old Presidents arriving. Obama's kids looking great. Obama and the chief justice fluffed the swearing in. His speech was OK without soaring to the heights people had been hoping for. But the mood was terrific.

Wednesday 21 January

Stuart Prebble came round. Went over a few ideas for programmes. The one he liked best was based on the Rethink [mental health charity] report 'A World Without' re Churchill, Darwin, Florence Nightingale etc. – great historical figures who had mental health problems. Watched PMQs. Not a great mood right now. Set off for the Burnley–Spurs game. Alex came on wishing us luck and talking about all the injuries. He said he still felt if we got an early goal we could get something out of it.

Amazing match. Ground full. Most standing. Wild rain. Spurs poor. We were playing well. One up half-time. David Moyes and Sam Allardyce [club managers] there and when I had a cup of tea with them at half-time, both said they thought we could do it. Fabulous second goal by Chris McCann then the third by Jay Rodriguez. The place going mental. Extra time and if we held on we were at Wembley. Then Spurs scored, and that was that [won 3–2, but lost 6–4 on aggregate]. Back to Manchester with Calum, listening to a phone-in with Spurs fans all saying Burnley deserved to win. I'd never had so many texts from people wishing we'd done it.

Thursday 22 January

Left at 6, home just after 10. Economic gloom unlimited on the radio all the way down. Dinner with Moir Lockhead [businessman]. He had been with Andrew Adonis and was suggesting a plan for free travel for jobseekers. Been to US recently and was worried Obama, despite all the talk of small-time donations, had got tons of money from the unions and they would call it in with secret ballots on union membership. He felt the economy was going to get worse and worse before it got better. He said he really liked Andrew, thought he got transport inside out. He felt I was probably right not to go back.

Friday 23 January

I started the day with a big row with Fiona and Grace because they were having a go at me for being so negative. Also Fiona saying I underestimated how hard it could be for the kids that I was their dad. To Silverfish to record about fifteen different video blogs. It would be interesting to see if this website thing took off. Mark Lucas felt it was going to be very strong. Also David Prescott was pushing on with the Go Fourth stuff. The Facebook thing was taking more time than I expected and had a funny moment when Brian Jensen [Burnley goalkeeper] asked me to prove it was really me before he would become a friend. I asked if he was at training. Yes. I texted Steve Davis [coach] and said tell Brian this is me!

Saturday 24 January

The workload on *Maya* seemed to be heavier than with *All in the Mind*. Rebecca's view was that that was because it was potentially a better book. It was definitely improving but I wanted this to be the last main rewrite. Drew in the FA Cup against West Brom, equalising to go 2–2 in the last minute, so another replay. We had now played more games than any other club in the country. I was feeling a bit down. Probably a mix of things. We watched a couple of episodes of *The Sopranos*, including the one when Tony Soprano had bad depression. A bit close to home when he was wandering round the house in his bathrobe and going to bed during the day. 'That's a bit like you,' Fiona said. 'I don't own a bathrobe.'

Sunday 25 January

The *Sunday Times* had a story about four peers saying they could amend Bills for cash.* It had a horrible feel to it. The economic stuff was also getting grimmer by the day and GB was going into another major down phase. Out for dinner with Tessa and Jessie. Still feeling down though and all the chattering was doing my head in. It wasn't about them, but me, but I fear I was coming over as rude and irritable. They were worried about David though. Nobody really knew how it was all going to end. The other thing hanging over me was an old university friend who had been asking me to lend him money again, 8k this time for a project I feared was going nowhere and would be money down the train. I agreed to give him 5 but said he had to find himself a professional fall-back plan. I felt for him but my experience with lending was not a happy one.

Monday 26 January

Interview with Mark Brown from the mental health magazine *One in Four*. Very perceptive guy. Really got the mental health world, and especially what the issues were related to depression. I had a decent bike ride for the first time in ages but my asthma was bad. Yesterday's *Observer* had a piece on my Go Fourth blog which was spun up as me leading an online campaign. All a bit silly but it meant I should get more stuck in. I did a piece for Derek Draper's LabourList, blog-style re my technological uselessness and also DC not being up to it. It was OK and provoked a bit of response. Also Iain Dale [publisher, Tory parliamentary candidate] asked to be friends on Facebook and sent me an email saying Derek didn't get this online world, that it was too shrill and not conversational enough. He felt I got it in a way the others didn't. I called Andrew Adonis for a chat about Moir's idea of free bus and rail travel for jobseekers. He was keen. Sounded like he was loving his new job. Dead keen on high-speed trains. Felt the third runway at Heathrow

* Four Labour peers faced a police investigation into accusations that they offered to amend proposed legislation for payments of up to £120,000. After House of Lords inquiries, two of them became the first peers to be suspended from the House since the 1640s.

was probably right but not possible politically. On the Lords he reckoned the *Sunday Times* stuff was the tip of an iceberg. Felt the election difficult but not over. He was really pro all the stuff I had been doing on mental health.

Tuesday 27 January

Breakfast with Gill Morgan [*Times* magazine] in Shoreditch. She wanted me to try to interview Carla Bruni and Rahm Emanuel. Gill said morale was low in newspapers but she had found James Murdoch pretty inspiring when he talked to them about the need to understand they had a future provided they adapted. Car to Millbank to meet up with Hilary Caprani from Rethink and Sophie Raine from Frank PR. Doing a report on the World Without… report [part of mental health charities' Time to Change anti-stigma campaign]. Recorded the script then out and about filming. Relatively painless. Went to Watford v Burnley with Stewart Binns [film-maker]. Played pretty well but lost 3–0 on a dreadful pitch.

Wednesday 28 January

Really decent bike ride. Into town to see Stewart Till. As well as being chairman of Silverfish he was chair of the UK Film Council and had some good advice on *All in the Mind*. Nice guy. Went to Portland to see Bradders who had been helping on *Maya*. He, Steve Morris and Martin Sheehan [former No. 10 colleagues] all working there now. Tim Allan pretty chilled. He'd done well to build up what he had. Big and growing team, some good clients and some very bright people on his books. He had another go at trying to get me more involved. He had just lost a big contract with the FCO for G20. He was sure it was because No. 10 took against. To Euro PR firm HQ for a branding brainstorm re LRF. All fine. Name change definitely on. Just a question of managing potential critics.

Thursday 29 January

Working early before leaving with Fiona and Grace for [Grace's close friend] Tyler's mum Kim's funeral at Golders Green. Really sad. Tyler was holding it together OK, and she spoke well considering. Ditto Kim's brother and boyfriend. Had a good chat with both afterwards.

Friday 30 January

Out before 7 and off to St Albans for [former rugby player now with Saracens management] Richard Hill's Saracens event. He was really grateful that

I kicked it off for him. Packed house at fifty quid a head. Did my ten rules of leadership and then Q&A. Went down fine. Flogged a few books. Richard a top bloke. Worried about the 'British jobs for British workers' protest at Total [oil and gas company] in Lincs. That could easily turn bad. Off to Manchester. Negotiating with DJ Collins [communications director] re a Google event he wanted me to do. He was in Davos which he described as a party conference for the rich 'and not much contrition around' about the crash. He said the economic elites did not exactly do self-awareness and analysis very well.

Met up with Calum, pottered around then off to Swinton for the Hazel Blears fundraiser. She was on great form but basically thought we'd had it and post-election going to be tough. She felt GB just didn't know how to build a team. Good atmosphere, and quite a few candidates from around the area had come to do pictures. Did the Go Fourth weekly email. Someone there said she got it on her mobile ten minutes later. Did a mix of jokes and need to up our game in the speech. Felt a bit disheartened by Hazel's take. She was normally very upbeat but she seemed to feel we were done for. Bed by half twelve.

Saturday 31 January

Tried to go for a run but my asthma was bad. Out to the Lowry for breakfast with Alex. In the team room. Some of the players sitting around reading the tabloids – Rio Ferdinand, Michael Carrick, Darren Fletcher, Ryan Giggs, couple of the younger ones. Fletch and Rio came over to say hello and have a chat, but generally there was a very quiet atmos. Alex was talking about Glasgow old days and how the working class had changed. He had seen GB recently with Roy Gardiner [Man U director] and said he had found him better than he had expected. He could not see people voting for Cameron. But the economics were getting worse and worse for people. Talked a bit about gambling. He said betting was his big release.

Collected Calum and we headed over to Burnley to see Stan Ternent [former manager]. He was actually going to be at the game. He left Huddersfield because they had a rival operation going on under the youth side of things. He'd basically said back me or sack me and they'd sacked him. Ronnie Jepson [former Burnley player, now a coach] came over. Good Labour man. Not a bad match and we won it [beat Charlton 2–1] in injury time which was brilliant and made the journey home a bit better.

Sunday 1 February

David and Louise [Miliband] came round first thing with the boys. DM spoke of the government as though he were not really part of it. 'They're hopeless. There's no attack. There's no intellectual grip.' He said the Nick Brown school of politics had the upper hand, which made for a poisonous atmosphere. He felt even if DC was not great he was not so bad that people could not see him as PM. He was articulate and he was presentable and not daft. Polls bad. Economic stuff bad. Louise said she thought it was all over. DM seemed to think likewise. He could not see where the forward agenda was coming from. Louise was very down on Ed, said that whenever there was a family event they tended to avoid politics, because they felt he was on a different tack. Louise was sharp, and very ambitious for David, perhaps more so than he was for himself. Fiona felt he would never go for GB, even when it was obvious someone needed to.

Monday 2 February

Heavy snow overnight. Meetings being cancelled all over the place. Slaven Maric from the Balkan Youth Games in Croatia made it. They wanted me to be an ambassador for the games. He was a real character, very warm and funny. He said he had never been so nervous because everyone he had mentioned me to said I was intimidating, a genius, fearsome, scary, and I would rip his head off. His colleague had decided not to come because he did not think he was well dressed enough. Crazy. He showed me a DVD on the project which I said I would support. It was all about using sport to help poorer kids and also to bring countries together. I also fixed for him to see Nick Keller. They had built up something pretty good from a low base. Did a piece for the *Mirror* on the World Without… report. Doing a bit of Facebookery. I could see how people get hooked. Stayed in most of the day but later F and I went to the new Everyman in Belsize Park to see *Milk*. Terrific performance from Sean Penn, and brilliant on the way in a campaign you can never quite tell when change comes.

Tuesday 3 February

Working on the World Without… report, signing off press release etc. I finished the *Mirror* piece and then made a lot of changes to the report. It was all a bit pop history – basically saying Churchill, Lincoln, Darwin, Florence Nightingale and Marie Curie suffered mental illness and might not fare so well today. It was a perfectly good talking point and would help generate a bit more mental health debate in a different kind of way. I went out for a swim but my shoulder was crap. The media was full of snow post-mortem bollocks. GB was getting hit over his 'British jobs for British workers' speech of a couple of years ago as the demos in Lincs continued over Italian and Portuguese workers. He had rather led with his chin on that one, given some industries simply could not survive without bringing in these immigrant workers. I did a thing on it for the website.

Went into Silverfish for last-minute checks on the website and to record some new material. They'd done a really good job on it and it had a lot of content. Really looked good. Stewart Till there, very pleased. It could all end up much more costly and time-consuming than I planned for though. Still really cold. Home to listen to Burnley beating WBA [3–1] on the radio. Paltry crowd though – partly because we had had so many games, also the vile weather, but also another sign of the recession. The economic stuff was going to shape the next election for sure, and even though GB got plaudits for his handling of it, the fact is a crash on our watch, even if global, was bound to have electoral consequences, and the government likely to get hit hardest.

Wednesday 4 February

Into the West End to meet Sabrina Guinness [TV producer] to discuss the possibility of [Alexander] Lebedev [new owner, *London Evening Standard*] joining forces to do some fundraising for LRF. They did the Raisa Gorbachev Foundation, she having died of leukaemia. To the BBC to do an interview for Alan Yentob's programme on oratory. I think I vaguely made sense. Sue Gray [Cabinet Office] called to say they were going to have to make a decision on the claims made by [Martin] Sixsmith [former civil servant] for papers on him under the Data Protection Act.* Counsel had said we would lose a tribunal so the question was whether we gave them over without it. I had several pretty choice memos about him. She said if it led to an action the government would be responsible. She was pretty down about the scene generally. Still no real grip next door.

I went through for the latest GB strategy meeting. Same crowd – the Eds, Peter, PG, Tom Watson, Liam Byrne [Chief Secretary to the Treasury], the No. 10 people. It was not great. Polls had dipped further. This particular group was still not blending or being honest with each other except through the odd flashes of humour. The big question he was trying to resolve was when and how to signal a forward economic plan for recovery and renewal. Peter M felt the expectation would be on the Budget. I felt there was still a gap open for proper analysis and explanation to be followed by the highlighting of steps to be taken for a new

* Transport Department director of communications Sixsmith and press officer Jo Moore left their posts in 2002, Moore having described 11 September 2001 as a 'very good day to bury bad news'. Sixsmith was subsequently cleared of any wrongdoing and received a substantial payment in compensation.

economic settlement. It was a perfectly friendly meeting in some ways but as PG said afterwards it felt like we were all groping around in the fog. Miliband was saying we were in better shape than people thought, considering how bad the economy was and how much baggage we had. We were talking again about the need for a proper operation on Cameron. GB still saying Alan Johnson would do it. But this had been going for months.

PG said we had had a chance in December/January to kill DC and we didn't do it. GB was constantly going through his four stages – recapitalisation, getting lending going, etc. etc. – and said what we needed was a comms strategy. They were still too trapped in the day-to-day judgements. Some of the young staff people had OK contributions but you never left feeling that someone was going to pick it up and drive it. David Muir was looking a bit frazzled. There was still a sense GB listened to the last person he spoke to and Balls was the one who could turn his mind. GB had been signed up to a plan of events that amounted to a plan, but Balls seemed to want to stop or slow it. There was a feeling even among some of GB's closest people that Balls was starting to look beyond the time when GB was leader. Out to Camden Brasserie again to meet Brendan [Foster] for dinner. He still felt we were in with a chance because people did not like the Tories, but he thought the public just weren't going for GB.

Thursday 5 February

Most of the day at Bloomberg's judging the Sports Industry Awards. Generally I felt the entries were not as impressive as a year ago. Paul Deighton [CEO, London Olympics Organising Committee] spoke up on the need to honour the people who made the decisions on lottery funding, back to the Major era. Nick Keller was in a bit of a state because Virgin had sent him an email saying they could not do the free flights deal for Beyond Sport. I called TB in the States to get him to call [Sir Richard] Branson [Virgin Group]. He had just seen Obama at the National Prayer Club and made a big speech about faith. So as everyone had been speculating on whether GB, Sarko or Merkel would be the first foreign leader to meet Obama, up pops TB. He sounded very chirpy, agreed to help. We chatted away about this and that. He still felt I was right to be out not fully in. He was off to Miami then Abu Dhabi, then Australia to see [the Rev.] Pete Thompson [Anglican priest, TB friend and mentor] who was dying and [former Western Australia Prime Minister] Geoff Gallop's wife [Bev]. 'It's going to be the last time in both cases.' I spoke to Charlie [Falconer] and Gavin [Millar] re Sixsmith. Both thought not a problem. Fiona's book, final version, arrived. Looked good.

Friday 6 February

Got the bus in with Grace then met John Woodcock [GB special advisor] at the café in Waterstones. He was worried we were close to a tipping point. It was still all a bit dysfunctional. There was nobody doing what I did and driving the whole thing. There was a classic case of that today – we were heading in for a meeting with GB and the strategy team to discuss 'the plan for economic recovery'. Then came through an email from David Muir – 'Scrap the plan' – explaining that Balls had got at GB and now the plan was gone. John was still pressing me to go back full-time. I said I felt like I was being asked to go in, solo and without the team we built, to lift a load others should be lifting and setting myself up to cop it for their failure. 'I quite see why you might say that,' he said.

In for the meeting itself. Douglas texted PG to say he was snowed in, which given the snow had gone was pretty lame. There were actually no elected politicians at the meeting apart from GB. It meant we had a better and more honest discussion than last time because there was less game playing I guess. PG was a bit tougher in his message. He said it was 'not rocket science'. I've always hated that phrase. There was a lot the government was doing under the 'real help now' title and we just needed to do a better job of getting that communicated at every level. We were both saying there had to be a better explanation of how we got here, better explanation of where we were and where we were going. People understood it was difficult. They were needing to hear more big-picture and less initiative-itis. I feared if they came up with another grand plan it would backfire. But there could be staging posts towards it. PG felt the G20 was the next big staging post and we needed to build to that.

GB seemed a bit anxious about Obama, though. He worried he had a vested interest in trashing the last ten years, of which we were a part. GB was also clearly worried that the protectionist instincts of the US would come through as Obama tried to get his economic rescue plan through Congress. He was far better at explaining the background in these small groups. They had a plan for regional rollout of the 'real help now' documents, for communities and sectors, which was fine. PG was convinced there was a separate meeting structure though which had Balls, Whelan, McBride deciding what GB should do media-wise. These parallel structures were death, and one of the reasons I couldn't face being in there 24/7. He needed to be more rounded in the message and his execution of it. We were there for a couple of hours and at least it was better than the last couple of meetings. It was bizarre to think though that that was because there were no politicians there and because we could be more open and honest as a result.

I said for example that I had been worried at the Balls message last week that a great ideological divide had opened up and we were heading to big state v small state, classic spend v cuts situation. The Balls problem was real I think and when DM picked up on PG's point about the meeting being better without the politicians, Philip said 'That's because they're after your [GB's] job.' It seemed a given now, too, that Harriet was constantly setting herself up for a leadership campaign, though I wasn't convinced. It was all part of the paranoia. The mood was OK though and at least there was the outline of a plan if not a clear and agreed strategy. Got a cab with PG to Freud's to discuss how I might work there. He was keen and thought I would enjoy it. But I should not make a big deal of it. Popped out for lunch with Grace. Did the Go Fourth weekly memo really late with Mark. The website was getting a fair bit of debate. A few criticisms on navigation but it was OK. Was keeping up the idea of one blog a day and with a few vlogs on YouTube it was going OK. It was interesting how friendly people were and how, when someone got nasty about 'GB and his paranoia', the friends tended to kind of gang up.

Saturday 7 February

Rory decided he wanted to come with me to our game at Birmingham. Drove off and met Calum at New St. Lads' day out. The boys went off for a drink and I joined Karren Brady [Birmingham FC managing director] for lunch. She was doing some photos for *Marketing Week*. She had definitely become a little more self-obsessed. Going on about her column in *The Sun* and how they didn't value her and whether to go to the *Mail* for a lot more money. Not very nice re Alex McLeish [manager], said he was not decisive and he had brought in some duff players on huge wages. David Sullivan [co-chairman] there wearing an indescribably naff Ralph Lauren blazer. All talking about a do he had had at the Dorchester last night when Paul Anka [Canadian-American singer-songwriter] was singing. Burnley were terrific first half. Should have been four up half-time. One up. Then dreadful Steve Caldwell back pass. One all. Good atmosphere in the away end, and a bit of trouble outside. Really should have won it though. Nice chat with Rory. Mock exams coming soon. Fixed for *Newsnight* to film at Queen Mary [University] on Monday.

Sunday 8 February

Got my first new party member via Facebook: Joanne Sheppard. Sue Macmillan got in touch to say on her application form re why she was joining, Joanne said 'Because AC told me to.' The economy was still dominant media-wise but bankers and their bonuses really picking up as a big negative. The political fallout from the crash was going to be even worse if these fuckers showed no sign of changing their ways. JP was running a great campaign via FB [Facebook], sorting a big petition saying they should not take the bonuses. There was a lot of build-up to Fred Goodwin and the other top bankers at the Treasury select committee. The web thing was beginning to take a lot more time than I expected. Off with Rory, Gavin and Oscar [Fiona brother and nephew] to the United game at West Ham. Met up with Alex in the foyer at Upton Park, chatting mainly politics until he got bothered by rich autograph hunters. He could be incredibly rude to kids. Great goal by Giggs won it for United. Round to the Goulds' for dinner. Gail away. PG cooking. Georgia really going for the Erith seat. PG well, and chirpy.

Monday 9 February

To the uni to meet John Rentoul [*Independent*] and the Beeb team for the *Newsnight* report on Time to Change. Rentoul was in charge of the students doing a module on the Blair government. They'd had Lord Hutton last week, who had been scathing about the Beeb. I did half an hour on how history would see TB then hour or so Q&A. They were all doing different dissertations on aspects of the government so had their questions to ask on that. Nice bunch. Then did *Newsnight* interview for their package. Lunch with John and some of the students. Briefly saw JoP, who was doing the afternoon session. Really good line-up. Home to write and potter then out to *Newsnight* on the mental health report. JP there doing the banks and their bonuses. Pauline with him. We had a brief chat about how to take the Go Fourth thing going forward. Balls all over the papers, apparently having said it is the worst depression for a hundred years.

Tuesday 10 February

Mirror full page on Time to Change, bits and pieces elsewhere. All day on media. Starting with *GMTV*, then fifteen radio interviews. Got into autopilot mode quite quickly, blogging about it in between. Grace popped in for lunch then off to Alan Titchmarsh [presenter] at the Beeb. Liked him. Nice manner. Got the mental health stuff well. His show was seemingly getting 90 per cent share. Live audience, and I could sense they were really listening, especially when doing my own mental health stuff. Then to Richard and Judy. One of the best things to come out was the *Milk* analogy – me saying film showed how social change can take time but it does happen. Mental health discrimination the last taboo. Caught the news on the way home and the bankers were getting out their apologies at the select committee. Getting pretty good coverage for the report. Radio good. We really need to get real change going in attitudes though because this was good money Time to Change had to go with now. 16 million to spend. I did a note for Theo Bertram [GB advisor] pre-tomorrow's PMQs. GB needed to get a dividing line on DC being all words while he was action.

Wednesday 11 February

Good bike ride. Blogged re Obama and Lincoln being born on the same day, and how hard Lincoln would have found it to deal with the modern media. Blogs starting to get good responses. Also Mark putting vlogs on to FB. *New Statesman* asked me to guest edit. Thinking about ideas for that, including maybe Q&A with Alex.

Thursday 12 February

Fixing French trip for the book. Also taking a look at the proofs. I was really chuffed to see it in French. Celebrated with lunch at Le Flâneur.

Friday 13 February

I put up a blog on Boris Johnson's general obnoxiousness in the morning and it got a good response, largely because it was picked up by Iain Dale, Danny Finkelstein and others blogging. Getting a lot of feedback that LabourList was just a diatribe whereas JP and I were getting the need to be a bit nuanced. Dale in particular seemed to like the way we were doing it. JP really doing well on the banks stuff. Major campaign. I had a chat with Jon Sopel about the web and maybe doing a piece for *The Politics Show*. Decca Aitkenhead was pushing for me to do one of her G2 interviews.

Maggie Darling called and said the *News of the World* were trying to do over Alistair on his housing allowances. They had sent through the story they planned to write. She said it was factually wrong in several places but AD was worried and what should they do. I said it all depended on the facts. If it was wrong and libellous they had to get a lawyer engaged. AD was in Rome for the G7. I spoke to him late on for about an hour and it dawned on me he was thinking of resigning. I said you can't resign over this, unless you actually have done something wrong. I dug into the story a bit more and it was clear to me there was a big flaw in their story. They had assumed he had chosen his London home as his main home, rather than Edinburgh, as a way of getting more money. But up to '04 that was the rule for ministers. Since '05 he had been in Downing Street. So all they could really criticise him for was being dilatory for one year, certainly not corrupt.

Yet he seemed really down about it. I said this is the last thing you need, I understand that, but don't let your general low mood re the economic scene make you take this more seriously, or more darkly, than you should. He said he was not Jacqui Smith [Home Secretary], who faced similar problems [over 'second home' expenses] last week. He was higher-profile and he was a Finance Minister. It was different. I said – and I know Charlie was echoing this to him – that he was not seen as dishonest, the facts were too complex and the Tories would not really pile in. I called Gavin, who lined up a lawyer if we needed one. I said to AD he should sleep on it but it did not feel like the end of the world, and there was a risk he would turn a problem into a crisis by overreacting. It was annoying. They could probably generate a bit of bad publicity but I was convinced the rest of the media would not follow it up much, unless he signalled real worry.

I had a long chat with Charlie, who felt exactly the same as I did. There was such a spectacular lack of fight in the operation at the moment. Phil Bassett [advisor] was handling the *NoW* and agreed with me but did think they would do it big. We agreed we had to engage on the facts and let them know what they got wrong. It worried me too that AD was so down about it. Endlessly saying 'You know, you know', and blustering. Like most honest people, he really hated having his integrity questioned. I said I didn't believe reasonable people would. Yes, he said, but there are a lot of unreasonable people out there. Yes, I said, but it is wise not to make decisions based on what you think they will think. You have done nothing wrong. For one year, there was a minor oversight which you corrected as soon as you were aware. Sleep on it but for God's sake don't do anything daft.

Saturday 14 February

Fair few calls from the Darlings. It was a bit alarming the extent to which, on the basis of the copy sent over by the *NoW* last night, he had gone from 'This is tricky' to talk of resigning. He had said several times that he was not Jacqui Smith and that as Finance Minister this was more damaging. But both Charlie and I felt that apart from a possible accusation of being dilatory in not switching to Scotland as his main home immediately when the new rules came in, there was not that much to worry about. What had worried me more was the Meccano nature of the whole operation. I also sensed that he had not been keen to tell GB. There was little trust there these days. Phil Bassett was doing a good job dealing with the *NoW* and although he was sure they were going to do a story, he did not sense it was destined for the splash, particularly once the facts were engaged in.

AD sounded pretty down the few occasions he called from Rome. Maggie had a bit of spunk but she could obviously not command the Treasury machine, which seemed pretty useless.

I did a blog on Cameron intervening in the story of the thirteen-year-old dad.* I got a pretty good pick-up yesterday and today and I felt that DC was going for issues and talking points rather than policy. Mark Ferguson [AF's son] called from Jo'burg airport. They were refusing to let him in because his passport was full. I was out on a run but called Paul Boateng [high commissioner to South Africa], who said they were really strict on it. Bono [Irish singer] was turned back too. I told Mark he might have to come back home and leave the family there, but somehow he got in. Off to Burnley. Good match and we held on to an early lead. Should have been out of sight but at least it was a win against the leaders, Wolves [1–0]. Peter Risdale [Cardiff FC chairmen] was there to watch as Cardiff had a day off before their match at Arsenal on Monday. Agreed to go with him and Neil.

Sunday 15 February

Sunday Times News Review had a big piece from 'award-winning war correspondent' Christina Lamb on why she was sending her son to a private school, 'What's so wrong with WINNING?', usual self-serving mythologising about how there was no competitive sport in state schools. Did a pretty vituperative blog which got an OK response. I emailed it to [John] Witherow asking for space to counter the argument, having pointed out no editor used state schools and that explained the negative coverage. I think he thought I was joking. Spoke to Alex re doing the *New Statesman* as a way of putting down a marker on the format. Good mix of sport and politics. He was up for it. Great note from CF re novel. He was a terrific reader. Really saw what it was about but could also spot changes and analyse which were for the better and which not.

Monday 16 February

Jason Cowley [editor] and James Macintyre [political correspondent] came round to discuss the *NS* guest editing. Agreed a fair few ideas. Jason seemed a good guy, keen to sort the place out – said he had too many chiefs on comfy packages and not enough Indians capable of doing legwork. They were chuffed Alex had agreed to a piece. Got Sarah Brown

* The fifteen-year-old girlfriend of a thirteen-year-old Sussex schoolboy had given birth to a daughter. Pro-life campaigners praised the children for deciding to go ahead with the pregnancy and Cameron commented that the case raised 'worrying questions' about modern Britain.

to agree to do the diary. Fiona and Melissa [Benn] on public services. TB agreed to do a piece. I did a quick blog on whether it was OK for me to go to Arsenal v Cardiff or was that adulterous vis-à-vis Burnley. I got a car to the Emirates. Really nice Ghanaian called Edward driving, and he was so excited to have me in the car it was ridiculous. He was waiting for me in the street and when I went out he said 'Oh my, it really is you,' and did a little dance in the street. I went back in and got him the audiobook of the diaries. He was a total fan, of me and of TB. Said he was worried we might lose but that Cameron was a total lightweight. That was the line the public were on to I think. Got to the ground. Dinner with Risdale and some of the Cardiff board, and Neil. Wenger came up before the game and said hello. It was funny watching with Neil, because in addition to getting into the game, shouting and the rest, he also talked to the players the whole time as though he was the manager, and as though they could hear him. Calum and a few others messaged me to say the cameras had shown us sitting there and said I must be there spying for Burnley. Cardiff were shocking. Just didn't show up [Arsenal 4, Cardiff 0]. Fiona in N. Ireland for her education film.

Tuesday 17 February

I did a Facebook status update about going north to see Mum and how she thought the NHS was great after her operation. Got as big a response as anything, people saying get well. Also started to write a piece about the need for Labour to turn the satisfaction with the NHS into political support. Mum on good form. I went out for a run when news came through David [Mills] was found guilty and 'sentenced' to four and a half years. I spoke to him, Tess and Matthew. All in varying degrees of shot to pieces even though they had been expecting it. Appeal being considered. David sounded shell-shocked but said he still felt he would be fine in the end. Headed to Stoke Rochford, for a Labour staff gathering. About 150 party staff, mainly from the regions. I was struck by how young they were and also how white. I was in the bridal suite without a bride! Alicia and Roy Kennedy [party official] seemed to be in charge. Quite a good bunch at the top table. I did the main speech and did a mix of funny and serious. Did a big message about the need for them to get empowered and feel that they could take risks. But the mood was pretty subdued. I got a great response at the end but Phil Dilks [press officer] came up to me at the end and said 'We're fucked, I think.' I monitored the news a bit for David Mills. There was a fair few other stories going on so it went down the lists pretty quickly. Calum called during my speech with news of our last-minute equaliser against Coventry [1–1].

Wednesday 18 February

I did the plenary with Roger Baker [Labour press]. He did a presentation on the regional media. I tried to do a bit of big-picture strategy and also my top ten tips for leadership. I sensed in the Q&A a fair amount of exasperation at the lack of clarity on strategy or any real leadership. There was a great *Mail / Sunday Times* picture to be had as all their new company cars were lined up in a long line. I felt a bit depressed as I left. There was goodwill and enthusiasm but I sensed they didn't really know what they were supposed to be doing. I did a separate session with the regional teams. Again very young and looking for guidance and direction. Good response to blog on the NHS. A few of the right-wing bloggers having a go. Iain Dale positive re me and JP. Draper and LabourList getting a bit of a hammering.

Thursday 19 February

Peter M all over the press, having had a whack at the Starbucks boss Howard Schultz, who had talked down the British economy. Peter had said to two journos, 'Who the fuck is he anyway?' so it had all gone bigger than planned. I did a blog defending him and telling Schultz to buck off and leave Pedro alone. Texted Peter to read it. He said it had been a rare ray of light in a dark spell. 'When can I see you and Philip before I sink completely!?' I had an OK run. Long chat with Alex to go over the *NS* article. He didn't want to be too personal on Cameron. He was in the papers today as saying Chelsea couldn't win the League. He hadn't said it. David Meek had written his programme notes and he hadn't seen them. A bit annoyed about it. I had to go out for a couple of hours' filming with *The Speaker*. They had reshaped the programme I was in and needed more shots of me at the top.

Dropped me at Fredericks where I was meeting Charlie F for lunch. He was just back from [Mo Mowlam husband] Jon Norton's funeral. Really sad event, he said. His daughter had spoken very movingly. Charlie was his usual penetrating self. I thanked him for all his help on the novels. He felt, however, that I had to get back into the frontline. He said I should get a seat, win next time while the party almost certainly loses, then watch things get worse under the next leader ('whichever of the pygmies currently putting themselves forward it may be'), then go for the leadership. 'You should be Prime Minister,' he said. I was quite taken aback but he had clearly thought it through and was adamant. He said my current drifting was summed up by the fact I had spent the morning going round in a car in Camden pretending it was Egham, for the sake of a few TV pictures.

He said I had shown I had real political skills and could achieve pretty much whatever I set out to. Of the four people who effectively built our success, he felt Peter and I were the two least tainted in a way, or at least most able still to make a difference. TB had moved on. GB was being exposed. Peter had shown it was possible to come back with the past forgotten and I could do the same. I was popular in the party and I was respected by opinion formers as tough-minded and able. Nobody thought I was anything else. Yes, he said, there was a risk – Iraq, Hutton, drink, depression, but he felt I was in a better place than before. But the idea of Harriet or Balls or Cruddas? I had to do something. He felt David M was weakened. Maybe James but he was not sure. He really felt I was the person to do it. But when Adam Ingram [MP] and Maureen [wife] joined us for coffee, Adam said to me I was well out of it. He certainly felt there were no attractive options out there but he felt I would go bonkers trying to deal with the PLP etc. There was no point me going in just to be a backbencher, but things would move on very quickly. He was politely saying Charlie was talking cock.

But Charlie came back to it several times. He felt TB was not in a great place. He found it off-putting the extent to which he always had to say how busy he was all the time. He didn't think the MEPP role was sustainable and he was in danger of just looking like in it for the money because he had to make so much to pay all the people he was employing. He was such a sharp guy. He was also still very funny about people. He and Adam both agreed I probably wouldn't fit in the Lords. 'That's why you should go into the Commons. You are a bigger loss than you realise. I understand why you don't want to be a backroom person with GB, but you shouldn't be backroom with anyone. You should go the whole hog.' Chat with Alan Johnson re my mental health event in Hull. He was pretty scathing about Harriet. She was all over the papers at the moment, she and Balls looking like they were positioning for post-GB.

Friday 20 February

I blogged early asking for ideas for the manifesto and young people to write for my edition of the *NS*. To Gospel Oak Primary School to film the vlog for the site and Teachers TV [education channel], hitting back at the Lamb piece. I did an interview with Omar [Pallas, caretaker and football coach] about how we started the football club. Fantastic collection of trophies. Mark Lucas very good at getting me in the right frame for just talking to the camera. Guido Fawkes [political blog] had done a 'What's the point of AC videos?' but that's because they were on a separate YouTube account. It was not what people were seeing on the site. The Marks came back for a chat to review. Both felt it was going OK and we had ironed out a lot of the problems. Also that I had made a real impact which we could now develop. Mark B stayed to show me how to do Twitter and how to manage the comments on the blog. There were a few people who were literally never off the site. It felt a bit stalkerish.

Saturday 21 February

Fiona had a piece in *The Times* which led on me never doing homework and basically thinking women should be in the home. We had a bit of a row before I set off for Norwich. I did a quick blog re going to see Delia [Smith] for lunch. Drove to Carrow Rd. Lunch with Delia, Michael and her usual collection of family and friends. His mum a lot more frail than last time, ninety-eight now but still getting to matches. Delia's mum on great form. Eighty-eight, and still nagging me to stand for Parliament and take over the party. Delia said they had lost count of how many times they had watched the film of my diaries. Another woman there had left the party because she felt we were no longer left-wing and was now voting Green. Interesting chat with Delia about her faith. Like quite a few God people, she felt I did do God but didn't want to admit it. She said prayer was a mindset and she tried to be prayerful all the time.

Not a great match. We were poor first half though we worked a good equaliser. Should have nicked it in injury time. At the end I went through to see Charles Clarke, who gave me a hard time for helping prop up GB. 'He is going to lead us to disaster and when he does I will say I told you so.' He said my reason for supporting him at conference, to avoid chaos and lack of clarity about what followed, was a terrible reason. He was hopeless and even though a lot of the names being mooted were dreadful, anything was better than this. The hospitality guy asked me to do a quick Q&A, during which I spotted Phil Webster, who I had described as proof you could be a good journo and a good bloke. He said the government was worse than he had ever known it, really dysfunctional.

Sunday 22 February

Rebecca and I had had our first real spat-ette. My irritable texts about the paucity of chapters were followed by some from her. Then silence over the weekend, though she did send through a fairly large chunk, with a lot of good stuff. It gave me plenty to work on. I also went out on the bike and had a decent enough ride. I was conscious of getting slower though and of the knees hurting more.

Monday 23 February

Had an early run, blogged then did Decca Aitkenhead from *The Guardian*. Lots of joking around about how she had so many things to plug for me. She was really nice, funny, and broadly sympathetic. To Soho house to meet Frederique Andreani [French journalist]. She had the idea for a website for the French community in London. Not clear to me whether it would work but I was happy to help, even if it kind of added to the sense I was just helping lots of other people with their projects.

Walked to Random House. Good meeting with Rebecca to agree next steps. Then to a meeting with Susan Sandon and Rob Waddington [account director] re the paperback of *AITM*. The hardback had got into five figures plus, plus 7k of the paperback. Rob said it was an OK performance without being sensational. But he said only two hardback novelists had sold over a thousand in the same period, let alone ten. Smith's in Top 6. Waterstones doing as 3 for 2. So all set OK. Then SS sprung on me that they wanted to delay publication of *Maya*. They felt spring would be better. I felt a long wait but they said Ed had agreed it was a good idea. Emailed Ed, who said he did. Discuss later. The meeting then morphed into one on the full diaries, joined by Joanna Taylor [project editor], Bill, Mark B and the design guy Richard. Looked at some designs. They looked pretty good. Just needed better pictures. Gail popped in and said we would need some kind of sticker on the front that said these were the full works. You mean, uncut and uncensored, said Bill.

Tuesday 24 February

Poll in *The Guardian* had both Tory and Labour down two. Tory twelve-point lead. I did a blog saying they ought to be way further ahead and DC had not sealed the deal. To Freuds first to advise PG on his handling of the book [*The Monkey Cage*] by Stan Greenberg which was pretty spiky re PG. PG said there was a whole thing going on between Stan and Mark Penn [pollsters, over their respective roles in TB's final election campaign] in the pollster.com world. It was chuntering away every day and this was his contribution [to the dispute]. I felt it was a bit defensive and he needed to make more of the fact that TB in the end did pretty much his own thing. Then to see Matthew for a rather vague discussion on what I might do for them. We both saw problems as well as opportunities and agreed any contribution should be quiet. Get a project and see how it goes. Matthew said at one point I was the thinking woman's Piers Morgan and had to develop in that direction. Would get him for that! Mind you, Piers was doing really well by his terms at the moment. TV fame in the States. Now doing a big ITV show here.

PG was convinced I would really enjoy doing stuff at Freuds. Lots of good young people, lots of interesting campaigns. They both, in the discussion about the political scene, said they thought GB would quit before the election. I said that was as big a decision as any and if the thought was that he bottled decisions, that said to me he would stay. He may not be as strong as TB but he was not a quitter like that. I was talking to a quite nervous-sounding David Muir re PMQs. Georgia was still pressing on in Erith and wanted me to do an event for her. Home and checked the site and the Facebook stuff. Went for an eye test at Miltons. Walking back when some guy on a bike shouted, 'Blood on your hands, Alastair, pal,' as he passed. RTL were chasing me to get involved and help them prepare the case for a Channel 4 and 5 merger. The boss man called me a couple of times. Later watched United in Milan. Should have won but ended goalless. Alex sounded a bit nervous when we spoke later. He was also worried about having spilled a glass of wine on the sofa as Cathy was away!

Wednesday 25 February

I was having breakfast when David Muir called to ask for help re PMQs. They were expecting a real tanking because of Fred Goodwin's pension.* I sent over a bit of a half-hearted email. Then he phoned again to say DC's son Ivan [six, suffering from cerebral palsy and epilepsy] had died. It had not been announced yet but could I give some thought as to what GB should say. They sent over a three-line statement which was lacking in any real depth or emotion. I suggested making it much more emotionally charged. They had already said that GB would not do PMQs but later decided not to have PMQs at all. I was blogging then did a note to GB re his statement on Cameron. He was pretty good in the House. Real sadness for DC.

The *Sunday Times* asked for a piece building on the blog I did last week re Christina Lamb's piece about sending her son to a private school. Chat with JP re the Canary Wharf fundraiser we were doing tomorrow. The *Mail* diary ran a big piece on me.

Thursday 26 February

Meeting with Cathy at LRF. She was clearly thinking I was not as active as I used to be and was making a few cracks about it. It was probably true. I was feeling generally that I was too stretched by different people and organisations asking me to work for them for nothing. PG was chasing me re doing an event to help Georgia in Erith. Happy to do it. Doubtful she would win but she was showing a lot of guts. Several rows with the *Sunday Times* over the schools piece. They were asking for changes I was not happy to make. They wanted me to address halfway some of

* The former Royal Bank of Scotland CEO had said ministers had known for months that he had a £16 million pension pot and refused to give up any of a pension amounting to £693,00 a year.

the arguments I considered to be myths. I resisted and said it proved my point that unless the right-wing worldview on schools was followed then pieces tended not to get in. Witherow replied that all it proved was that News Review editor Susannah Herbert asked reasonable questions in an effort to make it more than a rant. The pictures were terrific, kids holding lots of trophies, but even though Sian Griffiths [education editor] was still fighting to get it in, I doubted it would happen. I was close to losing it with them. Then Cathy Galvin called to say she was unable to get the short story in either. She said she could not get a straight answer as to why. I suspect they just decided the education piece was too strident and so I would be persona non grata for a while.

Out to Canary Wharf for Labour fundraiser. I was due to meet JP (busy starting another online petition on the banks and Goodwin's pension). I did a ten-minute mix of a couple of jokes and then why we can win still. Good enough mood in there but a bit flat. GB came and did an OK speech mainly focused on the economic challenge leading to Obama visit. He said a few nice words re me, ending with, 'He does many things but whatever he does he is firmly Labour.' Chatted with Sarah, who seemed OK. Gordon just didn't do the light-touch stuff very well. JP virtually directed the speech at me, lots about us blogging and tweeting and whether he could say this and that. It went on a bit too long but was OK. Good buzz. Tube back with JP. Both lamenting the fact that it took two has-beens to lead the way in this online stuff. He said the problem was the younger ones did not have the personality. He felt GB was still frightened of his shadow.

Friday 27 February

Peter M had asked me to go to a meeting at BERR [Department for Business, Enterprise and Regulatory Reform] to discuss message for the ad hoc ministerial committee on communications he was meant to be chairing. First I had a session with him on his own and then with PG before we were joined by David Muir, Gez Sagar [Labour advisor] and officials from BERR and HMT who were going to be running a new cross-departmental comms centre on the economy. Peter's office had not changed much. Last time I was there it was for his departure. He was wearing a very Euro suit, kind of beige-brown, a monogrammed shirt and very expensive two-tone brown shoes. How are you, I asked, and he let out a very large sigh. Stressed. He plomped down on the sofa and gave me a few instances of where it was just very difficult dealing with No. 10.

He said he was pretty sure, without actually being able to prove it, that No. 10 had been responsible for leaking the details of Fred Goodwin's pension. He said it had had a calamitous effect in that Goodwin had fought back and leaked letters suggesting the deal had been agreed by [Lord] Paul Myners [Financial Services Secretary to the Treasury]. But the worst thing was that it was this kind of thing GB was concentrating on, not the big picture of leading the country through this dreadful crisis which, said Peter, was going to get worse before it got better. He had said as much to him. But he found he was the only one who really spoke to him in those kinds of blunt terms. Then there was the whole business of the lack of proper structures. They were still looking for an AC-type director of comms. They still needed a chief of staff-type figure. They had known that for ages but it still was not there. The comms had a series of people of varying ability and politics who all ran into each other because the status issues were never resolved. GB made them feel they were all equally important.

He had sent GB a note saying he had to unite his two spheres of influence (he defined one as being symbolised by him inside government, but which included me and PG, and another which centred on Balls). They were giving substantially different advice and he needed to fuse them, rather than have both groups thinking he agreed with them. He had written a note setting this all out and suggesting the current strategy group be GB, PM, Ed B, Liam Byrne, DA as ministers, me, PG and David Muir as support perhaps with Gavin Kelly and Justin Forsyth [No. 10 officials] as the best reach out to government. 'Do not add to it or it will become unwieldy,' he told him. But because he was basically asking him to confront the reality of divided strategic advice, he did not get a reply. Peter felt he would never change.

PG joined us and he felt that Balls had a veto on a lot of things that went to GB. Also that Whelan was more powerful and involved than was widely thought. GB could not rid himself of bad politics and bad advice. While he was there, I commissioned PG to review Stan Greenberg's book for the *NS*. The comms meeting itself was poor. I was not impressed by the Treasury guys. At one point they said we cannot really say we have a plan in case it doesn't work. When I asked if they had government worldwide locked into these new structures they looked at me like I was mad. When I suggested that No. 10 was the only place where centralised comms were ever really accepted across government, Peter got very defensive on their behalf, said it was unique for HMT to allow these kind of cross-government structures inside the Treasury 'because they had all the information'. I said if you are confident, fine. But I left them feeling unconfident it could or would work.

Gez set out a variety of conflicting statements that various ministers had used to describe the current situation. They showed a central problem – the lack of an agreed script. Peter said that was the purpose of the meeting. He said, in his best very funny piss-taking mode, that my website described me as a 'writer, communicator, strategist', so could I put my mind to writing the words to communicating a strategy that would bind in the whole of government? I said I would happily try but did we have a government capable of agreeing to it, sticking to it and implementing it? PG was the clearest both in terms of where the public were and what we should do. He said we needed a clear single-page script which we all stuck to. The public were confused and some were angry but all were looking for explanation and leadership. We had a discussion on the whole issue of whether there had to be some kind of acknowledgement of mistakes made. GB was terrified of anything the media could present as an apology or an admission the crash was 'our fault' as the Tories and their media would just use it to try and get him on the run. But I felt tonally we needed something. Maybe 'None of us planned or predicted this'. Of course we could have done things better. But even that PG felt would be difficult. It was not a very satisfactory meeting all round.

I felt a bit sorry for Peter. Maree Glass, his diary secretary, who had been with him for years, said she had never known him work so hard. He was being torn in so many different directions. GB was still very needy. He was key to the economic debate. And now Peter had Royal Mail on his plate and that [his proposal to partly privatise the RM] was growing in political controversy not least, he said, because of Harriet and others stirring on it. He felt the Harriet thing was real, a kind of deliberate and unsubtle positioning working in an inchoate alliance with Balls and Cruddas. I said to him the more I saw and heard the more I wanted to jump out of the window. I shared a cab with PG who was equally down about it. When I spoke to Peter again later he said to me I was underestimating the extent to which systems and structures we had built under TB had gone.

I worked on a message note while talking to him. I felt GB needed to get close to something very big-picture, even Churchillian, something that indicates both seriousness of the situation and a determination to get through for the long term. He needed to explain that alongside the upside to globalisation; sustained prosperity and rising living standards for British families, there had been a downside and Britain, in common with every country in the world, was being battered by economic storms. What started as a crisis for some, in the banking system of America, has become a crisis for all, in every economy in the world. 'None of us planned for it, nor predicted its scale or its impact' was all he needed to say by way of apology or admission. But he needed to be clear these unprecedented times will lead to change every bit as great as that wrought by the industrial revolution, and require determination every bit as intense as that called for in war. The storms are far from over. There will be further unexpected shocks. Things may get worse before they get better.

His role is to set out a route map through the change, to show the way forward to that better tomorrow. He needs to be clear it will come, but only provided we learn the right lessons and take the right decisions for the short, medium and above all for the long term now. He had a good story to tell in terms of his role in the crisis that had been action to protect savers and homeowners from the potential collapse of banks, and the steps to protect the most vulnerable and to help where we can those who lose their jobs. But he needed to start crafting a more confident message about the future, that out of recession comes recovery and out of recovery comes a Britain stronger, more secure, more in tune with the values of the new world now being shaped. Peter worried GB would see all that as too close to the admission of failure he didn't want to make, for fear the Tories would try to put all economic failure at our door. But they were going to do that anyway. His role was to show he got why it happened, had played a big role in dealing with the fallout, but had what it took to shape the future. This would actually play to his strengths and Cameron's weaknesses, if he could seize it.

He needed to set out the big choices – our choice to borrow so that we can invest in our public services and in the industries of the future. Our choice to ensure the markets become servants of the people, not their masters. Our choice not to face inwards but face out, to build the alliances we need knowing that this global crisis will require a global solution. Our choice not to dilute our commitment to the environment but to strengthen it. Our choice not to turn our backs on the poor but to stand up for them. Our commitment to help British firms and families survive the recession and prepare for the recovery, in which the qualities that made Britain great before will make Britain greater still. I worked on a note and sent it through. I also repeated that I was not making an anti-Treasury point earlier on the structures for comms. But in reality, in any crisis, there has to be more centralisation not less and I'm not convinced HMT has the capacity to drive all that is needed on this. I was more than a little troubled by their observation that 'you can't say there is a plan in case it doesn't work'. The reason I talked about wartime structures was because it needs that kind of intensity and that kind of drive through the government machine. Again, I was a little alarmed at the look on one or two faces when I said you needed government representatives around the world bought into this. I rather despair that some of the really basic stuff we used to do now seems to be considered an enormous effort by people who are meant to be brightest and best.

Facebook and Twitter were creating a lot more work than I imagined but I had to keep going with it. Give it a few more months. The site was getting decent publicity still – big spread in *PR Week* headlined 'King of Spin Goes Digital'. Out with Fiona to a restaurant in Wood Green for another party fundraiser. Several people who had been there last night too. Good enough mood. The candidate Karen Jennings [trade union official] lacked a bit of spark but the new post-Baby P Haringey council leader, Claire Kober, was terrific. I was on OK form. Did fairly basic speech, a bit of banter with Fiona, and then Q&A. Nice enough evening. Fiona in good form and a lot of support for her re education and parenting. I had reached the end of the road with the *Sunday Times* and having made a couple of tweaks decided no more and sent them an email saying the whole episode proved my point. All the points they asked for were to meet halfway their right-wing negative view of the state sector, which I was not prepared to do. David Muir sent through GB's US Congress speech which was pretty strong. Really good on the big picture, and on the detail of a way forward, and good on the history of the special relationship.

Saturday 28 February

David Muir called to say thanks for the note on the speech, and could I call GB in the car, on his way back from the Policy Forum in Bristol, to say I thought it was strong. He said he really values your and Peter's views on this kind of thing so tell him it is definitely in the right direction. I called and GB sounded on good form. He was laughing about how Peter M had gone straight from the private session to the cameras, and he was still enjoying himself, he said. I didn't tell him about how he came across yesterday – a bit beleaguered. We chatted a bit about football and then I said I thought the speech was really strong. I felt he could do even more history and there was a case for specific mention of Abraham Lincoln given where he was in the US financial crisis debate now. He said his main concern was how, without seeming to lecture, to send the message about the US needing to take greater account of their role to the wider world, the need for the kind of huge global package he wanted to present at the G20. I said what about praising Obama for recognising that what America did they did 'with and for' the world. Also, what about setting out the choice we have taken – and making sure they chime with the choices Obama is setting out too.

He asked me to keep thinking about toplines too. There was a lot of good stuff there though and if he delivered it well it ought to meet the moment. BFC a bad defeat at home v Sheff Wed. 2–4. Calum said we were dreadful. Out to the Landmark Hotel, where Man U were staying, to do an interview for MUTV. A wedding party was going on as the team arrived. Up to room 264 for a photoshoot with Alex for the *New Statesman*, to go with the interview we'd done for the issue I was editing. First in chairs, then me sitting, him standing behind, and he was in really relaxed form. He said he had got in industrial cleaners to deal with the red wine he spilled on Cathy's best sofa while she was away. Photographer was happy, though Alex was getting a bit grumpy after forty minutes or so. I stayed for a bit of dinner, chatting mainly football, and a bit GB v DC.

Sunday 1 March

Blogged on going to the League Cup final match, which led to a flurry on FB about what a proper fan was, and whether I should be going to a game involving other teams. Burnley fans out defending me. Out to the BBC to do an interview for Comic Relief on Time to Change. Usual stuff. Then home, bike, before Rory and I set off for Wembley. We were on the official United tables in the Great Hall as all the non-playing players came in. A good-looking Brazilian woman sat with us and it turned out she was [Rodrigo] Possebon's girlfriend. Complaining about the weather and him not getting in the team [Man Utd]. Talked for a bit and she ended up giving me her address to send *Os Anos Blair*, Portuguese translation of the diaries. May as well get rid of them somewhere and she said she was keen to learn about Britain. Chat with John Madejski, who was complaining the banks were as bad as ever.

Brian Mawhinney [former Tory chairman, now with Football League] was there. I asked if he thought we were fucked. He said as an expert in disintegrating governments, and the moment at which they cannot come back, I would say yes. He said all the positioning for the succession – more from Harman today with her saying Fred Goodwin would not get his pension – and the lack of a coherent narrative, it was all up even without economic meltdown. He accepted DC had not sealed the deal but felt he had time and was good enough. Poor game. Atmosphere not electric either but good when Spurs missed their penalties [Man Utd won on penalties after 0–0 draw]. We managed to get back in fairly good time. Did a bit of work on GB's Congress speech but it was in OK shape.

Monday 2 March

Fiona on *Woman's Hour* going on about me not knowing how to use the dishwasher again. Getting good publicity for the book though. I worked on the speech for tomorrow whilst also pottering. Did an OK blog on GB's speech on Wednesday. But it was interesting how the straightforwardly political stuff I did got next to no reaction compared with football or anything personal. Lunch with Sukie Sohal from the party, who was trying to say I should challenge Boris. Really bright girl. Doing a PhD while also working full-time at the party and having regular dialysis. She had a real downer on David M. Thought he was really arrogant and said that was a view shared across party staff. Interesting because it was rare that I picked up on him provoking such strong feeling either way. She felt we had no chance at all of winning. Home half eleven to do BBC WS interview on GB in advance of his trip to US.

Tuesday 3 March

Blogged on Fiona's book and got a big response. Humour making serious-ish points was definitely the way to go. Melissa said I should do comedy. Finished the speech for later. Out later to the ecobuild conference. Massive event. Roger Harrabin [BBC environment analyst] chairing my event. Did a newish speech on the principles of big change. Q&A not hostile. OK crowd. Bumped into Yvette Cooper [Work and Pensions Secretary] on the way in and also Clare Short, who had been on a panel. We had a nice enough exchange. First speech and Q&A for ages. Felt I did OK. Good on the big picture of topscale change and did lots re the need to ignore day-to-day and go long-term. Then up to Parliament Hill for Grace's acting masterclass. Really good.

Wednesday 4 March

Lots of messages about a namecheck on *EastEnders* last night, Janine Butcher asking Peggy Mitchell to let her run her campaign. 'Where would Tony Blair have been without Alastair Campbell?' On to Ben Wilson at the Beeb to try to get the clip for the website and maybe do a vlog on advice for her campaign (for Walford Council). GB was not getting a great press for the trip and I thought Obama came over as a bit arrogant when they were in the Oval Office yesterday. The media were obsessing at the fact there was no press conference, which was taken as a bit of a snub. Fixing RTL meeting. Figures for the site up again yesterday after Danny Finkelstein plugged it. Out on the bike. Lunch at Primrose Hill and a bit of a carb lapse, then into the Beeb to do stuff on GB's speech. Alina Palinamura [commenter] seemed to be on my site all the time, responding to everything, and was going into overdrive today, not least generating support on my FB page for the idea of me running for office. I was on with Sopel. Jonathan Beales and Carole Walker [commentators] were doing a lot of pre-speech blathering.

I did a pre thing on big set-piece nerves and also the lead-up to G20, then they cut to GB. It went well for him. Good response. Good argument and lines and rich in values and authentic GB. Touches of Bible in there too. Did a few minutes at the end and felt it was going down pretty well. Blogged to same effect. David Prescott sent over [Adam] Boulton vlog whacking JP for having a go re their blathering about the lack of press conference. I was finding a combination of emails, FB, blog, Twitter etc. hard to keep on top of. But felt overall it was going OK. *EastEnders* definitely a bonus. Peter M on for lines re speech.

Thursday 5 March

Out of the Boulton–JP row last night, I did a blog on the self-obsession of the modern TV journalist, how all they were interested in was their own opinions, questions and profile and not answers or the people they covered. Took in Nick Robinson as well. Got picked up on Sky blogs. Still pushing on *NS* stuff which was shaping up fine. Out first thing to Tesco's on Cromwell Road. *All in the Mind* was their book of the month. Driver very down on GB. Felt it was all over. Mark B had a good idea re me doing a piece for *The Sun* advising Peggy Mitchell. Also recorded vlog while at Tesco's. Cab to Victoria Street with a very nice driver who had been the one who told me 'quantitative easing' (money printing) was on the news. He seemed to think GB doing most of the right things but not getting a message through. One of several today who said I should go back.

Popped in to see Marianna. Her bump getting bigger. She said nothing much was improving there. Really going back to old-style union stuff. Fixing seats the old way. Whelan influential. Ray Collins old-style. Harriet difficult. She said people like her were desperate for me to step up and go for it. I said I wouldn't. Good comments on vlog. Lots saying funnier than Tory wit. Also lots on Boulton but more mixed. Went out for a walk with Fiona, Rory and Zoe, lunch at Carluccio's. Nice fresh day. Back to clear desk and pin down a few things before going out for dinner with F's book agent and wife, Jonny Geller and Karen. She gave me a fairly tough grilling on why I didn't go back and I was maybe too open in saying why not. He seemed a nice guy and was pleased with the way the book was all going.

Tessa was at the next table with Keith Mills [Olympics Organising Committee]. He and I had a little chat while Tessa said hi to Fiona. He said if I wanted GB to have any chance of winning I had to go back whatever the reservations. He put his hand on his heart and said 'Country needs you.' He said the Olympics was going fine and invited me down to take a look. He felt the Tories were really weak but at the moment did not need to be much more than that. Jonny quite interesting on publishing and what was going on. Big brand authors still getting too much. Trade petrified of Christmas.

Friday 6 March

Getting good reaction to the Peggy Mitchell stuff. Out to Freuds for the meeting with RTL and Dawn Airey re Five trying to take over Channel 4. Just as I was sitting in the foyer came the news that Peter had had green liquid thrown in his face by a Heathrow protester. Just threw it in his face and walked off. I texted him and he said it was OK but still stinging. I said the problem was he was the only one seen as having any real character. The meeting was OK but it was going to be tricky working out the boundaries for all this. When do I actively pursue this e.g. with Peter and Andy Burnham, or do I just stick with fairly gentle advice? I felt I was able to clarify a few things they needed to say and develop. Chat with PG and Greg then off to TB's.

Chat to Jason Cowley re where we were on the *NS*. Coming together well now. Took about an hour and a half to get to Wotton Underwood and TB's fabulous new gaff. I'd joked with him I was coming down to a shadow Chequers and it was a bit like that. Country roads. Big gates. Tables and chairs outside. His and hers studies with very nice paintings and furnishings. Big grounds. Cops with machine guns. Night vision cameras. Brilliant newly built gym with all the gear, Shearer signed shirt and a picture of TB and Bush. 'We email each other!' He was very solicitous of the driver and then we went in for a lunch prepared by the wife of the couple he had hired from Chequers. He was looking very fit though greyer and a bit thinner at the front of the face. He said he was busier than ever, probably travelling too much.

He went through the next couple of weeks. Here two days then Portugal, Jerusalem, Abu Dhabi, Dubai, Singapore, US. His dad was in a bad shape and was now in the home next to where Audrey was moving to. He seemed to be enjoying the work. Said he came across really interesting people all the time. Met the Sully Cheeseburger guy [Captain Chesney 'Sully' Sullenberger, pilot] who landed a plane in the Hudson and thought I should interview him about the decision-making process. TB agreed to do a piece on God. He was fascinated about the Alex piece I had done for the *NS*. He was fairly mellow on GB but felt the thing was going backwards pretty quickly. To be fair, he felt GB had got a handle of it all better and more quickly than the rest of Europe but he felt we were heading to something close to nationalisation of the banks and maybe sooner rather than later.

He had had an unannounced and fairly long meeting with Obama the night before his 'amazing' [annual] National Prayer Breakfast (4,000 people).

He liked him, but felt the economics were going to be really tough and if the Republicans got their act together, there was a risk he could be a one-term President. He felt a lot of serious credible people were not buying into his plans. The big fiscal stimulus, if it doesn't work… then what? He thought GB was doing too much that was a bit gesturish. The truth was the banks were basically bust and it was going to take government to protect them even more than they had already. The toxic stuff may be even more toxic than we realise. He was still a bit too starry eyed about the guys who were making lots of money effectively betting on things going right or wrong. He told me some long, complicated story about some guys who made three billion each gambling on the sub-prime stuff going wrong. We kept coming back to GB. He said it was pretty big of me to keep doing all this stuff I was doing but ultimately it was unlikely to turn it around. If Labour people seriously think Harman, Balls or Cruddas are the solution then we have really had it. Gone for a generation. I said the problem was once you're thinking about what happens when you've lost, you've already lost. Yet that was happening right now in senior levels. If you lose the will to win, you don't deserve to win. I keep saying provided we do a, b and c, then we can still win. But time is running out. Also, the tragedy of Cameron's son will take more time out of the real battle. He said Cameron was not that good but he may be good enough because we're bad.

I said someone at RH had been looking for a few cuts in Volume 1 and she wanted to take out some of the TB–GB stuff, of GB undermining TB, because it was 'so repetitive, like every day, every page'. TB said he had always thought if GB was either brilliant or impossible that would be fine. But he is both. Just impossible, he could have got rid of him. Just brilliant would have been fantastic. But he was both. When you look at the NHS and all the improvements, that was a result of the reforms he tried to block. And now he doesn't defend and promote the progress because he was against the measures and people in the system know it. On education Balls was putting his foot on the brake. Nobody apart from AD and Peter was really getting noticed on policy. The rest was all piddling politics. As for Harman, he said she is there because he helped her and he found it hard to believe she hadn't known about the pressure Dromey piled on over cash for honours.*

MEPP going OKish considering. Hillary doing OK. Re Obama, I said I didn't like the tone of his handling of GB the other day. He said he had been seen to see Hillary a few days after she was knocked out of the race and she said there was an arrogance to Obama that could be tricky. He was

* Labour treasurer and Harriet Harman's husband had said he was 'kept in the dark' about loans from wealthy individuals, and then accused TB of lacking respect for the party.

frustrated on MEPP because there was a sense it was his responsibility but he did not have the power. He would stick at it. He was obviously focusing more now though on his business and TB Associates. JoP was easing his way out of the bank to help run it. He wanted me to get involved in a couple of projects. He said CB had written to Fiona. 'Is it likely to get a reply?' I said probably. Leo arrived with Jackie. He was sweet as ever, obsessed about beetles. Very well dressed and funny. But he can't see him that much I thought.

TB said he hated being in Britain too long at a stretch because the media was so ludicrous and negative. We were still seen round the world as political geniuses, yet the press drove an agenda of being hated at home. I filled him in on all the different things I was doing and some of the nice things that get said amid the usual war criminal stuff. Like the kid who was doing a dissertation on Attlee and Blair being the best post-war premiers. Lentil soup, cold meats, salad and fruit. Then a walk round the grounds. Not quite Chequers but it felt the same. Huge dining room with a fancy table. Little statue of Harold Wilson. Some really nice paintings. We sat for another hour or so in the main room. Two chairs like for a bilateral. Sofas toward a fireplace. Big fancy clock. Steps up to a grand piano. Nice. Tasteful.

Back to GB. It could have been one of the great governments I said. We did a lot of good stuff and I can always defend it but it could have been great. He said yes, but there was another way to look at it. There are always different poles of power in a government. Everyone knew what they were and everything revolved around that. With me gone, he is the only major pole but the others are gravitating elsewhere and moving to the wrong place. He had told both DM and James Purnell that they had to understand that losing the party suddenly really matters. They have to start rebuilding the party now because it is going in the wrong direction. But David had lost his nerve and James was doing well on policy and had to start fighting politically better than he has. He said again I should do my best to help but it was probably hopeless.

I said lots of people were urging me to get a seat. He said I could easily get one but why, unless I was certifiable, would you want to spend your fifties on the back benches in opposition, which is where you will be? We had a really good old natter about all sorts of things. Very funny on Bill C and how Hillary's new job was cramping his style on fundraising. Also re Dacre. TB said they sent him a copy of his [GB-requested] review of the release of official papers and if I saw it they would have to tie me down. E.g. 'It has been said there has been an erosion of trust in public life – and I have to say I agree…' I said if Dacre got a K from GB, that was it for me, no more help. He said it was bound to happen. It was a disgusting relationship but that was his politics. He said if the switch had a sudden rash of calls – Obama, Murdoch, Sarko, Dacre, Merkel – it is not as clear as it should be what order he would take them in.

Left about 3. Back to get Calum from the station. Very funny about my new social media operation. Like my own Sky Sports operation. It was getting close to taking off. Out to Chinese restaurant near Baker Street for a Karen Buck [Labour MP] fundraiser. I was on good form. Used the line that if you think what's going to happen when we lose, you've lost. Matthew Taylor used a brilliant device to get money. If you don't give the twenty pounds, we don't publish the leaflet. If we don't publish the leaflet, a voter does not see the message. If he does not see the message he does not vote. If he does not vote we will not win. If we do not win the Tories do and progressive politics is lost. Good evening. Audrey happy.

Saturday 7 March

I didn't sleep well. Got up early and worked on the novel. Then blogged on Peggy Mitchell, a longer version of the piece in today's *Sun*. Ben Wilson [BBC] called to say the *EastEnders* people loved it. I did a long session on Wattbike [exercise trainer] before collecting Calum. Fiona was going to a conference in Oxford and Grace was out so he and I went to the [David] Milibands' for dinner. It had been their suggestion and I quickly realised he was looking for guidance and she was looking for me to inject a bit of courage if I could. He had lost his nerve after last year and was also clearly losing touch a bit. Even though he tried to make a joke of it he asked at one point who Danny Boyle [award-winning film director] was. He also seemed, despite being one of the first to do a blog, pretty ignorant about all the online stuff. I explained as best I could how I thought politicians should use it, and gave him reasons why it was all worth doing, but I think I was talking over his head. I said he had to raise his game and his profile. They all did if we were going to win and if we lost then the party was going to matter and he needed to be out there doing the business. If Harriet or Jon Cruddas were the solution we were fucked.

He said the operation had gone backwards in many ways. GB was still driven by the politics of damaging others, not building a team. He was still surrounded by ghastly people. DM seemed to think he was doing OK himself but he was quite defensive and Louise was pushing him quite a lot to be harder. She said at one point she sometimes worried he was just too nice. I was probably doing most of the talking and trying to get him to see how he needed to up the ante but he seemed strangely detached. His commentaries on the government were like those of a third person not a member. Balls was still the main influence. GB also bizarrely cowed by Harriet. And Whelan and co. all around the whole time. We had a few good laughs amid it all, for example my descriptions of TB's 'shadow Chequers', and Calum talking about how Neil had given him a really interesting talking to on the best way to beat people up. We had a bit of fun on Twitter, me saying I was having dinner with someone but as I got told off for name dropping I couldn't say who. Then offered a book for the first to guess it and a Twitter regular called Dean Perry got it after thirteen guesses. Nice enough evening but Calum also said he felt David was not as strong as he had been. He too picked up on the notion that he was coming over more as spectator than player.

Sunday 8 March

Fiona was on Marr. It wasn't really satisfactory as it was a paper review and too crowded and she did not get enough on the book. Peter M was on. As PG said, he was a class act at the moment. Mainly pottering around till we all set off for the Emirates for the Arsenal–Burnley game. Not a bad atmosphere in our end and we played OK but got done by three stunning goals. Did a bit of work after a kip then round to PG's. Tessa there, seemed pretty chipper. Filled PG in on my chat with David M. He said GB seemed to suck a lot of energy and fight out of anyone who might be a threat. The news was dominated all day by the killings of two soldiers in Antrim.*

Monday 9 March

Blogged on NI, recalling what we said at the time of the Omagh bombings and saying the reaction yesterday, unity on condemnation, showed how strong the peace process really was. Spent a lot of the day editing and rewriting various *NS* pieces. Started on an editorial warning against post-defeat positioning. Half a dozen pieces in by the end of the day. Coming together. The day seemed to whizz by then off to Hook in Hampshire for a speech tomorrow. Fabulous hotel, Tylney Hall. Felt a bit like Chequers. Watched the news, wall-to-wall NI, Shaun Woodward seemed to be handling it well.

Tuesday 10 March

Gym. Liam Byrne on the telly talking about the next phase of public service reform. The main focus was fast-track teacher training for the brightest and

* Two off-duty British soldiers were shot dead outside Massereene Barracks. Irish paramilitary group the Real IRA claimed responsibility.

best hit by recession. He did an OK job defending the record. I blogged on how refreshing it was to be back on health and education and how we needed to get back on the attack properly and I hoped this was the start. But it had fizzled out by the end of the day. There was just no fucking oomph there. GB kept saying that was why he needed me but how come they had lost the basics. This was not genius stuff we were talking about. Gill Edinburgh [Sussex Enterprise, Chamber of Commerce] met me in the foyer and took me over to the venue. She had led me to expect a bunch of real diehard Tory businessmen but they were a good bunch. I was on good form – did the basic leadership speech – and the Q&A was lively with a few funny moments.

I did a big defence of CB under attack from a woman in red glasses who was a verbalised *Daily Mail*. Signed books, then the usual last haggler surround, then off to Covent Garden. There to review *In the Loop* [political comedy film, a spin-off from *The Thick of It* TV series] for the Beeb's *Culture Show*. They'd planned for me to watch it with Armando Iannucci and Peter Capaldi but they seemed to have bottled out so it was me and Mark Kermode [film critic], the guy with the funny haircut. The film's PR Bronwyn Pyke was there trying to spin me and talk about co-ordinating any reviews I did. The trouble was I thought it was crap. It was like a very, very long cartoon. *The Thick of It* worked because it was half an hour at a time. I just felt it didn't work as a film. Mark tried hard to get me to say I was hurt or offended but in truth I was bored ten minutes in. No light and shade. Too lazy and one-dimensional in the portrayal of politicians as venal and self-serving. Mark said he liked the swearing but even that I found dull after a while. I ended up getting stuck into him because he said people were right to be cynical about politics. Got quite heated.

Bronwyn trying to find out what I thought. I agreed with the Beeb to say nothing and did a teasing tweet I was watching it to set up a teasing blog tomorrow saying I was gagged from saying what I thought. Off with Slaven Maric [Croatian friend] to Milton Keynes v Huddersfield. *NS* coming good. Kevin Spacey said yes to doing a piece on the economic benefits of the arts. TB copy coming. All going well. Met by Pete Winkelman and wife and Roberto Di Matteo's lovely wife Zoe and their daughter. She was telling me how Di Matteo approached her when she was modelling and how he never gave up. Pete such a bundle of enthusiasm showing us round. Hotel. 30k plans for the stadium. Good atmosphere. 10,000 crowd even with Champions League on the telly. Poor game. Over dinner he was urging me to get back in and help Gordon. He said you probably don't realise how popular and respected you are and how much people think you can change things. So even if you don't go back to that you have to do a big job. Run sport or something. Run the Olympics.

Wednesday 11 March

Call from No. 10 to go in tomorrow and he was clearly going to have another go at getting me in. Blogged on Iannucci film on the line that you can't spin a spinner, saying the film people were desperate to know what I thought and the Beeb people were desperate to keep me stumm. Also put in a line on the education survey I was going to do with Fiona's *NS* piece on education, asking all editors about their own schools and the choices they made for their own kids. I had been chivvying Dacre, who had first claimed he had not received the email, then that it was non-grammatical and then finally came back with answers. Eton. Tweeted I still hated the *Mail* but thanked him for replying. Knackered at end of day. Burnley two down to 4–2 against Crystal Palace.

Thursday 12 March

Blogged on social workers after hearing a terrific interview from Martin Narey of Barnardo's. Lord [Herbert] Laming progress report on review into Baby P today so doubtless there would be more Balls bashing of social workers. Working on cover options for the magazine. Bruce G round for a chat. Still felt F and I should think about Parliament and that I had to get more involved with GB. He still thought I should go in the Lords and really go central again. Great chat about stuff. Old times and new. He said you'd be hard pressed not to think we deserve a pat on the back about how we did things. Because these guys are clueless by comparison. Ministers were losing nerve, he said. To Soho House to meet Natascha. Looking great, and happy. Said she had grieved but never felt angry. Missed Martin terribly but did not get angry about it. We chatted about my situation and the charity stuff she was doing re Martin. Off to Notts. It was OK as a do despite being black tie. Quite a good crowd around me. No real desire for the Tories and more sympathy for GB than I anticipated. Home in the early hours.

Friday 13 March

Tired after a late night and not sleeping well. In early to see GB. Just the two of us in his office. At least he didn't just go on the job charge again as I feared and we ended up having a pretty good chat. He said Obama had called him after the trip and said he had no idea our press was so crazy. He sounded genuinely shocked by the coverage. He said the whole trip had been pretty good but it had made him more convinced than ever that the problem was not policy but comms. He went through the totality of what they had done on banking and the rest of the economy and it was huge. Other countries were following. But there was no sense of what he had done and what it could achieve. He said retail sales were holding up better than expected and it may well have had something to do with the VAT cut. But needless to say no credit. Told him I had seen TB at the shadow Chequers. He looked disapproving. 'I hardly ever go to Chequers,' which was not true.

We got on to the whole blog/social media thing and I ended up persuading him there was a case for getting the government geared up in a completely different way. Maybe have a dozen doing it all the time as a means of communications and rebuttal. He seemed genuinely interested, even if he could not himself do it. He was definitely up for change but could he drive the machine? I told him how deeply underwhelmed I was by the Treasury team at Peter M's comms meeting. They just lacked the drive and imagination. On recent ministerial shenanigans he felt Harriet was just naïve and Ed Balls was not up to anything. But naïve or not the strength in depth issue was a real problem and he had to start addressing it better. He scribbled away, jotting down key words I was saying.

I said last night's dinner showed me once more the Tories had not sealed the deal but we could not keep on saying the same thing. Eventually we would run out of time. I said he should not see new comms as a way of getting round the press but as an important strategic and political tool in its own right. Just make sure we have clarity of message and then be edgy with how it is put over. Great for rebuttal. JP was showing what you could do with it. Yet again we were saying how there needed to be more focus on health and education. Alan Johnson had done a presentation to Cabinet on the progress on the NHS and it was genuinely good. But where was the politics of it all? Better meetings than others recently but still a sense that the operation needed to be much stronger.

He had to go off so I had a meeting with Jeremy, Justin Forsyth, David Muir and Mark Flanagan [head of strategy] to go over what we had discussed. I agreed to go in next week for a brainstorm re Twitter etc. and how to use it better and more politically. Home to go through address book with LRF for Big 5–0 targets [trying to get fifty 50k donations for 50th anniversary]. Managed to finish draft 3 of *Maya*.

Train to Manchester with Greg Nugent. Straight to Piccolino's. Met Calum. Good night. Greg and Calum endlessly piss-taking. Darren Bentley [Burnley FC communications director] had got me to go up for Ladies' Day lunch at the Forest game so did a piece of whimsy re the idea of Darren saying the women wanted me ahead of the players weaved in with the idea I was going to do loads of stuff for Fiona like bake a cake, take dog to groomers, go for mange tout at farmers' market. They took us to a snazzy bar where I was a bit out of the comfort zone. Too high recognition, though it helped with the doorman asking us to go to the front. I was glad to get out. Just not my scene. I wonder if it was in the old days when I was on the booze. Probably.

Saturday 14 March

Out for a run early. Horrible litter around the place. Real mess and post-booze atmosphere. Texted Alex to wish him luck for the Liverpool lunchtime kick-off, and he sounded a bit pessimistic for him. Up to the Hilton for breakfast with Greg. Loads of Cockney Reds around. Peter M called, exactly as I was looking at the *FT*, which was leading on him spelling out the need to learn from the French economy. He was sounding a bit down. He said the whole scene just wasn't functioning as it should. He said we probably shared an analysis of what needed to be done but he doubted GB was capable. There remained good analysis and low capacity to make change. I said you sound a bit ground down. He said he felt it.

Cab over to Turf Moor for the Ladies' Day lunch. Real mix of really good-looking young women and some real perma-tan sunbed types. Did a little speech, with some friendly heckling. There was already a lot of booze going down. I watched United v Liverpool [1–4] on TV with Andy Payton [former Burnley player]. Great Burnley match. Five–nil. Forest hammered. Three of the goals were extraordinary. Given we had absolutely battered Forest, I felt a bit bad getting a lift back on [Forest owner] Nigel Doughty's helicopter. He was such a nice guy. As solidly Labour as ever, pretty much shared our views on the politics of stuff and felt there was still a chance we could see off the Tories, but there was not much time left.

Sunday 15 March

Suddenly spring seemed to be here. Warm and sunny so out on the bike with Rory. Fabulous when it was like this. Chasing the last few *NS* ideas and working up a comms plan for them. In the afternoon out to *The Age of Stupid* premiere. Not a bad film, and certainly made the case re climate change, but as I blogged later, I think people felt a bit manipulated by the whole thing. Loads of media. I was asked to do a clip with Franny Armstrong who'd made the film and I got an early sense it was more about her than the issue. It was an OK film but tried too hard in places to build in the broader political message, e.g. on Iraq, bankers, changing the political system. Then they pretty much ambushed Ed Miliband at the end with a big pledge card and a threat to vote anyone but Labour if we went ahead with Kingsnorth power station [Kent]. Pete Postlethwaite [actor] went off on one at Ed and said he would give back his OBE if we gave the go-ahead. Ed handled it fine, didn't over-commit but tonally in the right place.

It all felt a bit student politics though. I was asked to do another interview with Lizzie Gillett the producer, as we were leaving, and I said what I thought – that it was OK but for the bigger argument and the need to make political change not nearly as effective as Al Gore's film, *An Inconvenient Truth*. I also said they needed to think through the 'anyone but Labour' approach. I found Franny in particular too self-righteous. Grace was interesting about the whole thing. She was OK with the film. Thought it powerful and sad, and the device of looking back at a devastated world was a good one. But she said as we left 'I hate those people. Public school Lib Dems.'

Monday 16 March

Pottered a bit then into the *NS* to go over the proofs. Most of the stuff I had asked for had come off and they had done some great artwork. Writing the leader and tinkering with other pieces. Clear that Jason was genuinely looking to change things and with support could probably do it. Fixing the logistics to do a piece for the *Times* magazine on Keighley Cougars [AC's hometown rugby league team]. Gill Morgan said fees were dive-bombing, but I agreed to do it because I was keen to do it for the Cougars anyway.

Tuesday 17 March

Blogged on Iran, previewing GB's speech offering help with civil nuclear programme in exchange for supervision of the military. Most of the day in *NS* office. Mainly tinkering on stuff. Rewrote a few headlines. Vernon Bogdanor [academic] piece the one bit that was broadly anti-Labour, or at least warning we could be out of power for a long time. All coming together though. Off to Ipswich v Burnley with Rory and [family friend] Mike Lownes. Dinner with David Sheepshanks [Ipswich chairman] and an Indian guy who was offering to raise money for LRF via his driving a car in the East Africa Safari Rally. I liked Sheepshanks and he was totally charming with Rory and Mike. Great game. One up brilliant goal by Elliott. Should have made it two. They missed several sitters and finally equalised second half.

Wednesday 18 March

Blogged on contents of *NS*. Looking fine. Put out the front page mid a.m. and got a fair bit of interest, also *The Sun* and *The Times* were running extracts of the AF interview. Fiona thought maybe I should go back to journalism full-time. Not sure I wanted to. Best to keep the freedom etc.

Definitely a better mag than usual though and they seemed really happy with it. Kate Taylor who was doing *NS* press was in and fixed to do a bit of media tomorrow. Grace's parents' evening. Doing OK. Grace such a big character in there. Easy to tell which teachers liked her and which didn't.

Then out to PG's confirmation. He was being done at the same time as two others. I got there halfway through just as the water was about to be poured on their heads. It was a moving event in lots of ways. Not just that he was still alive. But the whole ritual felt very powerful, and he was clearly moved by it. It was hard to see me going the same way, and after we left I was still insisting he was doing it as a 'God insurance policy'. But he said he really felt that the closer he got to death the more he got from it all. There was a nice little drinks do, then home. PG and Gail seemed in good shape.

Thursday 19 March

OK coverage for the *NS* stuff. *Times* and *Sun* did the AF piece well. Most of the other papers picked up on various angles. Off to do *Week in Westminster* with Danny Finkelstein and Steve Richards [political commentator]. Really laid into Cameron and the media for giving him such an easy ride. Danny kept saying DC had changed the Tories' tone and that was important. But surely the tone had to be backed with meaningful policy change? Over to Radio 2 to do Matthew Bannister, who was taken with the *NS* piece on state schools and the media. Short phone-in.

Into No. 10 for a meeting on their internet operation. Mark Flanagan got this stuff pretty well. Justin and David Muir also knew there had to be a big shift in how the government, collectively and individually, thought about this. We brainstormed a bit. I said they had to be persuaded if they did not engage properly in this, they were done for. This was the key to getting their comms into a different place. They had some good ideas but it felt tired and I sensed their worries about whether they could deliver the ministers for change. I banned crisps from the meeting. Biscuits were bad enough. But crisps. Christ. And I said they should have a new rule – if you're late for a meeting, you don't get in. I felt every time I went in there that they were responsive to ideas but unsure about capability in making them happen. Peter M said much the same thing when I spoke to him on the way home later. He said the whole set-up was really frustrating.

Friday 20 March

Did LBC on TB and God then blogged early on how there were massive protests re handling of economic crisis going on in France which were being largely ignored here because they did not fit the UK media prism re everything being terrible for GB. Cue plug for the French publication of novel. Later out for dinner with Grace, Rory and Grace's friends at Freemasons. Rebecca sent through all her final suggestions on novel.

Saturday 21 March

Blogged on Cameron, and Danny saying he had 'changed tone' was the big breakthrough for the Tories. PG started to text later on about the *MoS* and *Sunday Times* doing pieces, possibly inspired by Whelan, about Georgia [Gould] in Erith. Told her she needed to get someone up in local media saying this was the right-wing press trying to stop her because she was going to be good for Labour and good for the area. *NS* still getting attention. Breakfast with Ed [Victor] to go over diaries, novel and Winning, then over to the Landmark to see Alex for a cup of tea. He said he had rarely seen so much crap as had been written about the Liverpool match. Football-wise he felt they outplayed them but [Nemanja] Vidić [defender] fucked up. Back home and worked most of the day on the novel. Burnley 2–1 win at Plymouth. United 2–0 defeat at Fulham. Grim for them. Media loving it. Out for dinner with Mike [former *Mirror* editor], Sandie and Kate Molloy. Late night at La Casalinga. Mike on great form. Telling us about a dinner he was at recently where someone he knew was adamant I was responsible for everything that was wrong in Britain.

Sunday 22 March

Suzanne Moore [columnist] in the *MoS* saying she was resigning from *NS* because of my guest edit. *The Guardian* were chasing so I gave a line that her claims to be of the heart of the left were somewhat undermined by the fact she was writing in a right-wing rag. Off to Keighley with Seamus Kennedy [photographer]. [Reality TV star] Jade Goody's death leading the news. Drove up, met Calum then over to the Cougars' ground. Met the chairman, the board, kids doing community stuff, in for the team talk pre-match, watched the match, back in the dressing room, Radio Leeds interview, then after the match I did the man of the match presentation, then just sat chatting with some of the players. One, Sam Gardner, had written a novel and asked me to read it for him. Good bunch of lads. Went to the mosque and chatted to a young lad Omar Khan. He said he did not agree with war but glad to meet me. Nice young man. Drive back. Home by 10. Enjoyed the day.

Monday 23 March

Spent most of the day working on the Keighley piece. Worked fine. *The Guardian* filled the whole of page 3 to follow up the *MoS* story on Suzanne

Moore quitting from what turned out, according to Jason Cowley, to be a job she never had. They carried my line re her credibility being weakened by her doing her bleating in a right-wing rag. Weird how an attack like that could still be thought worth a whole page. Blogged on Ken Clarke cock-up over the weekend re inheritance tax. Plus a little whack at Moore for claiming to be of the left while writing for the *MoS*. Clarke had seemed to cast doubt on the Tories' inheritance tax-cutting policy. I suspected it was a cock-up born of his laziness rather than an ideological divide. But it showed how weakly any Tory position was pinned down.

NS fallout still going strong on blogs and in print. Out at 6 to Millbank Tower for the launch of the Fabian Society book [*The Change We Need*] on the lessons from Obama. David Lammy in the chair, Will Straw [book editor], Catherine Mayer of *Time* magazine and Ben Brandzel, an American who was part of the Obama online campaign. Good event. Broad agreement that command and control comms was old hat. Need to shape new landscape. My main point throughout was the need for Labour to throw off their defensiveness.

Tuesday 24 March

Blogged on the Fabians plus running the *Guardian* correction saying Suzanne Moore had not had a position to resign from. Lunch with Tim Hincks [TV executive]. He had two ideas to propose. A big global grope on football analysing why England can't seemingly win the World Cup. And the idea of taking a bunch of working-class kids to learn a posh sport like polo or Eton Fives and take on posh boys somewhere. Nice guy. Still felt we could win but time running out. GB off on his pre-G20 world tour. Mervyn King comments on the inflation and depreciation of sterling causing a lot of problems – seen as a warning to the government re Budget and another stimulus.

Wednesday 25 March

Radio 5 on social workers. Blogged early on *In the Loop*, then set off for Manchester. Mark B emailed about a Kevin Maguire [political commentator] piece in the *Daily Mirror* having a go at Georgia over Erith. It was clearly from the same Whelan stable as the weekend. It had the fictitious line that I had called a local activist to say she was a future PM. First I emailed David Muir and Sue Nye to say if it did not stop I would do a piece on why GB could not wean himself off bad people and bad politics. Then blogged anyway saying that he had been spun, and it was going to need youth to help us win. Real bitterness in these people that was pathetic.

Then a bit of toing and froing with Conor Hanna [*Mirror* deputy editor] as I was making sure they knew the Maguire story was total horseshit. Did a bit of work, then down for the IoD speech I was there for. Dinner with Calum at the hotel. Saying he wanted to do politics. We were both talking to Georgia, who was beginning to feel the heat.

Thursday 26 March

Slept badly. Collect Calum and head home. Out later to Freuds for a session on the recession and the public with Asda and News International. CBI economist did a really downbeat assessment of the economy. We were going to watch PG doing a focus group – all women. Philip warned they would be in basic denial about how bad things were. They were. What came out was an innate optimism about their own lives, pessimism about the country. Family and community were more important than ever. Media not trusted. Brand pyramid put Obama top again. Supermarkets next. Media and GB bottom.

Rebekah Wade and Colin Myler [editor, *News of the World*] were both very defensive during the discussion which followed. Asda's Andy Bond more impressive. Interesting session. PG on good form, doing his usual flirting with middle-aged women in the group, which was slightly skewed by a very middle-class woman full of stories and info about shopping. What was also clear was the lack of a narrative about Britain and the direction for the country. At the pre-meeting with Asda I had said that I would not go boots flying on the press and instead say that they had taught people to be more sceptical and now they were more sceptical about them. But when it came to it I went in quite heavy. Stirred things up a bit. But I was saying to Asda they should think of their own TV station, mags etc.

Friday 27 March

Lunch at Langham Hotel with PG and Andy from Asda. We went over yesterday and the media defensiveness. Also his plans for a higher profile and how to get more involved in sport. Bit of a chat re politics and also the religious culture at Walmart [American retail giant, owner of Asda]. *Front Row* [BBC Radio 4] with Kirsty Lang. Nice interview about *The Speaker*. Out to watch *The Damned United* [film drama about football manager Brian Clough] with the boys. Liked it though not as much as I was hoping to.

Saturday 28 March

Blogged a review of Clough film. Feeling tired and a bit down. I had not been badly depressed for a while but I could sense it coming in. Also had really bad vibes about the week ahead, G20 London summit protests etc. PG came round to talk about Georgia's Erith campaign. He felt the attacks had cut through a little and people were starting to worry she was the divisive candidate. He said on the one hand people said they rejected smear campaigns. On the other they absorbed what was said. Gail had spoken to Sarah Brown about Whelan so hopefully that would stop things for a while but he worried the damage was done. PG in good nick but could look very tired all of a sudden. Set off at 5 for Chevening. Definitely felt a bit of a dip. David and Louise were putting the boys to bed as we arrived. Kevin Rudd and wife Thérèse Rein. Daughter Jessica and her husband Arthur Tse. Matthew Taylor. KR in socks with no shoes. When DM ticked me off for jeans and trainers KR came down in jeans and identical Asics trainers.

We had a long chat on GB's situation. He felt things were still winnable but there had to be a change of mentality so that people in the government and the party thought we could win. He agreed with me that there had to be better and more sustained attack of the Tories. Also that we had to get out of the 'fourth term hard' mindset and into the understanding that it was all about who seized the future – first post-crisis election with the understanding nothing much was going to be the same again. He had a very good manner about him. Calm and unflappable. The odd 'f' word thrown in. Looked you very much in the eye and analysed before concluding. I could see why people said he lacked charisma but there was a calm that was powerful. He really didn't rate Cameron. Felt he was a total lightweight. Obviously thought we should have done a better job of attacking him. David and, after he arrived, Ed both showed up the defensiveness and the sense of being divorced from the government. If I said they needed to do a, b, c they agreed. But I meant them every bit as much as GB.

Kevin clearly liked GB and to a large extent was on his wavelength. He asked what would be helpful to say on Marr in the morning. I said talk up GB's role and also that he is in the mainstream. Over dinner things were more policy-focused. Climate change – clearly he and the Aussies had this higher up their agenda I think. He was a more downbeat version of Clinton – very policy detail-focused but always explaining explanations too. His wife and daughter clearly close and bright. The son-in-law was interesting – Oz-Chinese banker, and very non-PC. Regularly throwing in a few right-wing critiques. KR looked like he was used to keeping him in his place.

After dinner back to a more political discussion. He really seemed to share my frustration at the state of our politics and lack of campaigning. He asked me to talk to his chief of staff about some of the ideas I had for new comms. He said he was thinking on the same lines re blogging, Twitter etc. but finding it hard to get his people to move in a concerted way. Lots of Obama – he had just been to Washington – and the feeling that things were now going to get tougher. But Obama was still doing lots of good campaigning stuff – not least use of new supporters to sell his message on the economic package – to good effect.

All asking the usual 'What are you up to?' And I was feeling more and more the sense that while people like him understood why I wanted to enjoy the freedom I now had, I should be more involved not less. I said the problem was – and I had seen it again with David and Ed – the will to win was there but the desire, hunger and belief were not. Both Kevin and David were on the Marr show tomorrow so, with the clocks going forward, they went to bed fairly early. Nice enough evening, a bit ruined by the kids squabbling at home and never off the phone. But Rudd definitely a good thing.

Sunday 29 March

Out for a walk through the Maze then round the grounds. Fiona said 'What a lovely place – you can see why they want to stay in power.' Watched Marr. Rudd was excellent. Good tone. Realistic. Set his own agenda. Turned questions to his advantage calmly and cleverly. DM was OK but there was definitely something too defensive about our politicians when they were on TV. Marr also had [Dmitry] Medvedev. Something very creepy about him. Interesting to see KR's wife and daughter's reactions. They felt he was more deferential. I said it was complicated because he looked like Putin. Chinese Ambassador also on. Good tone too. Blogged on the setting of expectations and Rudd's excellent tone. Home for lunch. Slept most of the afternoon. Definitely on a bit of a dive.

Out for PG party. Funny speech. Said he had popped round yesterday and – once I'd woken up – I said I hoped this party wasn't going to become an annual event. He said he rather hoped it did. TB, CB there as we arrived. F said she didn't see them. Very odd. TB spoke to the kids and was very into Rory's poker. Said he had been looking at old pictures for the book – today of Bibi Netanyahu and the two of us 'looking younger'. GB arrived later and 'How's your blogging?' had replaced Burnley as the opening gambit. PG's doctor, a guy from Stirling, spontaneously raised Kevin Rudd's interview and asked why our lot didn't do them like that any more. Margaret Jay (who loved the novel, she said, apart from Arta, my Kosovan character, who reminded her too much of noisy women on the bus). Ed was talking to Susan about *Maya*. Both had read parts of it and liked it. But in what she said, and her body language, she was indicating the cash for this kind of book was diving.

Nice chat with Ian McEwan. Good bloke. Grace liked him. [Lord and Lady] Hollick (saying GB just couldn't do it). Les Hinton (newspapers in real trouble), Freud (re an IVF doctor he was advising in a battle v the Beeb), Salman Amin and wife, GB (me trying to persuade him to get the government engaged in blogging etc.). Pat and Marianna McFadden (re pregnancy). Nice enough do. PG looked very tired towards the end. I was feeling down. Definitely diving, low.

Monday 30 March

Out to *Loose Women* at ITV. Something I always found a bit depressing about daytime TV. Audience of people with not much to do. False bonhomie and overdone excitement but the panel was not too bad and I had a bit of time to plug the book. Got a call from Rudd's office asking me to go for lunch at the High Commissioner's residence. It was really a continuation of the earlier discussion with Rudd. He saw it very much in terms of bypassing an increasingly hostile media which did not see its job as allowing politicians to communicate their message. I sensed Rudd felt there was not much buy-in across the government for the new approach he felt was needed.

He had seen GB earlier and they did a press conference together. He felt GB was too concerned about how he was seen, not least by the media, and he would do well to push it to one side. Also, he needed to make sure the crisis did not go to waste, to be and be seen as someone who understood it and reacted well to shape the future. We went round the block on messaging, Twitter, Facebook, lessons from Obama. He said Malcolm Turnbull had had it. The Republic question was not front of mind. He really didn't like the media. Said James Murdoch was so far up himself he thought he was going to disappear. Good chat. Lovely sunny day.

Cab back home to see the kids then out for dinner at the RAC with Peter Schmeichel and an Anglo-Danish lawyer friend. He had not wanted to say what it was about on the phone so once we had done the small talk and gone through for dinner, they explained. Big stuff. Basically they were putting together a deal to try to buy Man U. A mix of people with money round the world, 20 per cent of the shares for fans. They seemed confident of raising the money – Goldman Sachs were already involved – and that the Glazers [US family, owners] were ready to sell. They seemed serious. I said to them even so they were in a way the weakness of the bid as they had no relevant experience. They wanted advice on strategy and also what to do if it leaked. Best to get as close as possible to the truth, I said. The truth was Peter S was fronting a global consortium aimed at buying the club and giving it back to the fans. We fairly quickly got to the role of AF. I said he could hole the whole plan if he wanted to. The question was whether to take him on board early. I felt yes. PS felt probably. He felt AF would do it if there was money involved.

He also felt AF was part of the problem in planning for the future – he had been so successful that there was no real thought as to what happened afterwards. I felt AF would not be a backseat driver. Equally Peter felt it was important both to persuade him to stay but also to plan the future. We agreed to think it through but on balance I felt best to draw him in early. He could torpedo it anyway so why not take out one of the reasons he might – lack of involvement. To reflect. It felt a bit half-baked but the lawyer said if there was the money there it would go ahead. I emphasised too they needed to be sure of all the links in the chain, who needed to know the kind of media pressure they would come under. I liked Peter but was not sure whether this thing really had legs. I said don't even try to present members of the consortium as true fans even if they were.

Tuesday 31 March

Out at 6 for the Eurostar, off to Paris to promote the French translation of *All in the Mind*. Blogged early on expectations for the G20. Really building up now. I read *Le Monde* and was struck by all the little interviews around the place with people from different walks of life in different parts of the world, who all wanted different things. Message to the leaders – ignore the noise and make the decisions. I had bad vibes for GB though. Leaving London as the leaders arrived really brought home how my own life had changed. Part of me wished I was there at the main event. Part of me – probably the bigger part – was happy to be on my way to Paris to do my own thing. Arrived to be met by Agnes Chalnot [press officer] from Albin Michel and straight to *Le Fou du Roi* on France Inter [radio station]. The first of several 'only in France'-type radio shows.

I was now with Florence Godfernaux [publisher], middle-aged blonde, very beautiful in a middle-aged blonde French kind of way. She said *Le Fou du Roi*, presented by Stephane Bern, was one of the best shows – slightly anarchic. I was sandwiched in between an African band and a French rapper but got plenty of time for the book. Both Stephane and the reviewer (a guy from *Le Figaro*) were very positive, and the line of questioning was going to be focused so far as I could tell on how my political persona could produce such a sensitive book. But Tony Cartano, editor, had said we wanted it taken seriously as a book and that was happening. Had a bit of time at the hotel and then a series of back-to-back interviews. *Le Figaro* for a full-page profile plus pictures. Then *La Tribune*, then *Le Parisien*. Working out about 50:50 on book and politics. But the book was being well received.

Off to Canal Plus [TV channel]. On *Le Grand Journal* with Michel Denisot [host]. Kept a fair bit on the book. Also a bit of G20 and comms in general. Good programme, with a young live audience. Felt the French was holding up OK. Dinner with Florence in a nice old-fashioned brasserie. She is quite a character. Later to Karl Zero's political talk show on BFM TV, bald, big glasses, dyed black hair on the side of his head, quite edgy. Hates Bush. Showed him my GWB cufflinks. He said he wished there were people like me in French politics. I was getting a very interesting perspective from journos that Sarko was getting more and more dictatorial. And yet as I kept saying their press was so much softer than ours. Started to develop a line that a mix of the two was needed. That theirs was too soft, ours too one-eyed and negative.

Wednesday 1 April

Did blogs earlyish from the gym. One on G20 jokey on being bounced this morning by Sarko on Radio Europe 1. Sarko had summonsed the interviewer for the slot I had been booked into for a while. It meant I had a bit of a lie-in, gym then *Le Journal du Dimanche*, then *Ouest-France* whose reporter Roberte Jourdon loved the book. She had read it really closely and was really effusive. Then meeting with Julien Vaulpré [Sarkozy advisor]. Franck Louvrier [communications advisor] had gone to London with Sarkozy so had cancelled. Vaulpré was a bag of energy but also seemed to think things were not quite as good as the last time I saw him. He was also extraordinarily indiscreet e.g. telling me Sarko was becoming more and more dictatorial, using different means to bear down on journos, but also that he was not good at taking advice and being strategic. He was also clear that Carla was a bit of a problem, that Sarko was totally dependent on her, and that the staff did not get too close. Carla had also been important in getting Louvrier back in favour. He said the press was becoming more difficult (I saw plenty of desire to be so but not much in terms of outcome).

He was advising a strategy of more engagement with critics but Sarko was not keen. He wanted me to think of maybe working with him in the private sector. He felt governments and businesses just didn't get it and we could do really well. I said I was not terribly moved by that world. He also wanted me to think of something GB and Sarko could do when they were together in Paris in early May. Off to do two more TV news interviews, half book, half G20, the second one a bit weird as he tried to make the book link into the G20. Anyway, Florence was fine about it all. I was watching as much of the G20 coverage as I could, and the focus was on protests and a fair bit of violence including attacks on banks.

Meanwhile Obama–GB press conference tending to focus on fiscal stimulus, Sarko–Merkel on global regulation. Lots of focus on Obama and later the Queen as she hosted a dinner. Dinner with Florence at Lutetia [hotel] then to France 3 for *Ce soir (ou jamais!)*. Hour and a half and I didn't feel on form. French dipping a bit. Felt OK though even if I couldn't do much about the book. Tired. Early start tomorrow so did blog late, starting with Tony Benn observation that all change starts on the streets and whether these kinds of protests had any effect at all.

Thursday 2 April

Up really early and off to yet another only-in-France show, the morning show on France Culture [radio channel]. Ali Baddou presenting, and people wandering in and out to do little essays – philosophy, history, Middle East, my book – and then discuss. Ali and the resident reviewer, Alain-Gérard Slama, were both really positive, AG even seeming to talk in the same breath of Disraeli, Churchill, Hugo! He said the reviews in the UK were of me not the book, as though someone in politics was quasi-anti-constitutional to do a good book. Nice programme and I liked Baddou. Back to the hotel. Gym. Down for interview with *Courrier International* then long photo session with *Le Monde*.

Lovely sunny day. G20 deal done. GB looking good. Everyone saying it had gone well. Mix of stimulus and regulation and crackdown on tax havens. More money for IMF. GB's line was that it was the day the world came together to start to fight back. Then the best-looking interviewer yet, Marie Brette from *Le telegramme de Brest*. She had a lovely manner. Got a bit harder as it went on but she was really nice.

Up to watch all the G20 stuff. Email from Mind [charity] that I was shortlisted as 'Champion of the Year'. Summit ending well for GB. Real sense of sorting things out for the future. Also of inter-connectedness being the key. Protests close to the hotel meant I couldn't get to the France 24 [TV] interview but later to France 5 for *La Grande Librairie*. Hour-long, no breaks, and I felt the presenter, whose brainchild the programme was, had really read and liked the book. Some in the audience had already got the book which I signed as I left then stayed for a drinks do. Nice atmosphere. Out for dinner to La Closerie Des Lilas with Florence, the presenter and cartoonist and half a dozen of the team. One girl in particular really pushing me on whether new life could ever be as satisfying as the old. Lots of chat re Diana.

Friday 3 April

Blog on the question – could David Cameron as PM have delivered the G20? Concluded he was not Obama. He may not even be Hague. Michelle

[Obama] a real hit at a London school yesterday. Carla [Bruni] had not gone doubtless so as not to be upstaged. Protests now moved to Strasbourg for NATO. Protesters had made pretty big tits of themselves. Professional protests. Last meetings at the hotel then off to a pretty quiet Eurostar. All OK at home. Calum and I decided to head off to Mum's so as not to spend all day tomorrow driving. She was on good form.

Saturday 4 April

Did a little blog on a piece I saw in *Le Monde* yesterday, saying Stockholm and Hamburg were named as Europe's first green capitals, having beaten off Bristol among others. The blog seemed to be doing well, but it was becoming a bit of a grind, and not uncostly either. I could just about make the case for it but wondered if it was not a bit symbolic of drift. Did anything of what I was doing really stack up? Novel one done and while it did OK, and for some was really powerful, it did not cut it as either bestseller or high literature. Book 2 done (ish) but now almost a year till it was out. Politics on hold and where I was being more and more drawn in I was more and more irritable about it, feeling I was doing too much that others ought by now to be doing. I guess this is just the depression playing itself out, or in, God knows. But I was definitely feeling down about everything I was doing. Sunny but windy and went out on the bike. Set off for Derby. Good game. Terrific support for Burnley. One up then conceded well into injury time. Probably a fair result [1–1] but disappointing. All pointing to the play-offs.

Sunday 5 April

Blogged on Berlusconi keeping Merkel waiting on the red carpet as he finished a mobile phone call. His people were claiming he had been on to the Turkish PM persuading him not to block Anders Fogh Rasmussen [Prime Minister of Denmark] as next NATO general secretary. He added a lot of colour to the world's political scene, but you'd be a bit embarrassed to have him. Up to see Audrey's flat with Mum then off to Catherine and George's. George had decked up a tractor and trailer for a ride round the farm, Mum and Aud wrapped up in big blankets. Catherine on good form, felt AD had done OK on Frost. She said she was but a minnow and yet had no idea how we coped as we did for so long. Felt the pressures were just too intense and too many things going on. She said there were too many people who felt they were operating as I did, trying to hold the ring and be strategic but nobody had the authority or the ability. She said she was genuinely shocked at how dysfunctional it all was. That being said, GB was still doing OK out of the G20. Slight poll bounce in the *Sunday Times*. George felt strongly that Jacqui Smith should resign.* The No. 10 scene did not seem that much better.

Monday 6 April

Blogged on Obama, head colds (it said in the press he had a cold) and being woken in the night to be told North Korea had whacked off a missile. The blogs that were topical but with a bit of insight from having been there behind the scenes when things like this happened were the ones that seemed to get the best response. MPs' expenses were dragging on and Jacqui Smith was getting whacked again. GB should have taken Cameron up on his offer to sort it out together, even if he smelled a rat. It was all a bit ragged at the moment. Obama was still doing really well though apparently getting whacked a fair bit back home. G20 to Afghanistan summit, plus handle Sarko and Merkel, then Prague for huge speech on a vision of a world without nukes then Turkey and a speech to the Parliament saying they should be in the EU. Big bold stuff. Had a rare bust-up with Mum over her saying it makes no difference who's in power.

Tuesday 7 April

Definitely been fighting off a depression in the last few days. Low-level but definitely there. Took Mum to the station. I was starting, as I had with Dad a few years before he went, to wonder whether it was the last time. She was in great nick for her age but she was eighty-three next week and looked a bit frail as she walked off. Had had a good laugh with the boys after Calum asked her 'How had someone so sane produced four nutters?' I also noticed she had become more opinionated and full of little homilies. She and Aud were such bricks though. To Silverfish. Recorded a clip for Georgia in Erith. Then did a vlog on *The Speaker*, which was starting tonight. Blogged on it too. Did a vlog on the need for the manifesto process to be opened up to young people à la exercise we ran for the *New Statesman*. One on Obama and the need to give him time. Then one on Scotland and bagpipes re the theme of national identity, pegged to the film I was doing on bagpipes tomorrow.

Home to potter and redo the tribute speech I did for Frost before heading out for his 70th birthday party at the Lanesborough Hotel. I was due

* The *Daily Telegraph* had disclosed that the Home Secretary had made an expenses claim for the rental of two pornographic films, which had been watched by her husband and parliamentary aide Richard Timney.

to be the last speaker before David, after Ronnie Corbett [comedian], Tim Rice [lyricist] and David Owen [former Labour Foreign Secretary]. A bit daunting when I saw some of the people gathered for the drinks. Felt quite a Tory event (perhaps because of [daughter of the Duke of Norfolk, Lady] Carina's side of the family) though apart from Owen, [William] Hague, us and Seb Coe, there was not much of a political turnout. Long chat with Hague at the drinks. He felt the election could still be lost. 'Oh yes, we can mess it up.' Also, they did not underestimate GB's resilience. He would not give up. But he felt DC gave them something none of the others – himself included – had been able to and he also felt he was saner than all the rest – himself included. He asked if I was going back, then said 'The old warhorse will not be able to resist the sound of trumpets', then that I'd be welcome to join them.

David Mellor saying business was more interesting than politics. Victor Blank saying things were tough but all you can do is keep going. Liam Neeson with his kids which was nice. Billy Connolly [comedian] grey and svelte. Pamela Stephenson [psychologist, wife of Connolly] large and unfriendly – I was sitting between her and Emma Fitzalan-Howard who was Carina's sister-in-law. Liked her. Really inquisitive about the novel and *Cracking Up*. Michael Parkinson at our table. Matthew Freud saying I needed a proper monetising agent. 'You're talent not advice now.' Tim Bell – last time I saw him he said he thought we would win. Now he thought hung parliament. 'The country doesn't really want either.' The Palins. Andrew Lloyd Webber. Trevor Nunn who said he really cheered when he heard me say if all we do is denigrate our leaders don't be surprised if we end up with weak ones. Roger Moore [actor] and wife – amazing faces! John Madejski saying I had too much talent and I was frittering it. 'You need to decide to do something big, then do it.'

Speeches. First Corbett who did a very funny ditty. Then Tim Rice who was OK, mix of funny and serious, Owen on the family, which was really nice, then me. I wasn't on form and didn't really catch the moment. Depression not helping really. I tried to use his mentions in the diaries as a backbone because I was going to present him with the Arabic diaries as a present, but the stories weren't funny enough. A few good lines but felt best when I was being serious about his role in the history of our media and how much a part of our lives he was. But it didn't really work. Felt a bit deflated by it. Also knew from how many people came over to say I spoke well that I hadn't. Fiona agreed I had not been on form. Also, she said that it was a pretty Tory room 'and they don't like us like they did'. David's speech was his usual after-dinner stock. Very funny if rambling but it worked. Hanging around for a while then home with the Palins. All of us a bit bemused by some of the people but agreed Frost a remarkable bloke. Not at all pretentious or big-headed and always remembered people in his past. I felt surprised to have been asked to be one of the speakers again and I wished I had done it better. I liked David a lot, and felt I hadn't really caught him tonight.

Wednesday 8 April

Out after three hours' sleep to City airport. Blogged on Frost and the lessons to learn from him at seventy – stay enthusiastic, don't take yourself too seriously and have what Owen called an 'instinct for friendship'. He was due to interview GB this morning. Never stopped or slowed down. Flight up to Glasgow pretty empty. Bumped into Bridget Prentice [Labour MP] who said she was standing down. Clearly felt we were not going to win, and at fifty-six was looking for something else to do. Met at the airport by Rosie from STV, who was helping with the film I was making on bagpipes for the Scottish 'Homecoming' series. To the university to meet Donald and do a bit of chatting and playing. Chancellor, Ken Calman, came down and asked me to do a big speech there next year. Bane of life. Happening more and more. Donald and I playing Scotland the Brave and Rowan Tree which were the easiest copyright-wise.

To the National Piping Centre. Fairly high faff factor but enjoyed it. Lunch then meet Roddy MacLeod. Played chanter with some really nice kids, one American, the rest Scots. If only all kids had a genuine sporting or musical passion. Good chat with Roddy then he played a jig in the museum. Certainly getting the ingredients for a decent piece for *Made in Scotland* [Scottish TV series]. Also for a blog. Staying at the City Inn, bit plastic but convenient. Out for a run but got asthma. Dinner with Mick McAvoy and Paul Charles from STV. Good blokes. Shared much of my analysis re TV. Wanted me to think about a series of authored pieces on subjects of my choice.

Thursday 9 April

Out at 7. Blogged in the car to Fort William re JP at seventy, after *The Sun* had a story yesterday asking if he was Britain's laziest MP. Driving up with Rosie and Sarah Howitt the producer. Stopped halfway for me to drive and chat while filming. Taking the piss about how all programmes had to have journey and jeopardy. Good bunch though. Nice drive. Lovely message from Fred Michel [News Corporation lobbyist] re *All in the Mind*. Getting good reviews in France too and he was raving about it. Met up with the Lochaber Pipe Band. Warm-up, tune, play in car park then march down to the waterside. Good sound and stunning scenery. Woman pipe major and quite a few girls in the band. *Oban Times* snapper down there. Did a team photo then I set off for Conaglen [rented house]. Got there just before Fiona and Grace arrived. Nice to get away again. Stuff winding down a bit.

Friday 10 April

Out on bike. Blogged on pipes and national identity. Out for a walk. Greg [Nugent] and Karan arrived with the boys. Later Mark, Lindsay and Hope. Day spent pottering mainly.

Saturday 11 April

Up early and did an hour on the bike out past the ferry. Stopped halfway to do blog on language, and whether English would always dominate. Pegged to putting up the interview on *La Grande Librairie*. Used the taxi driver in Paris on Arabic-French, learning at school and whether English would always be the dominant language. Long walk. Lunch. Later with Rory, Grace, Ramsi [friend of Rory] and Hope for a dip in the river. Bloody freezing. Damian McBride resigned over emails to Draper suggesting running smear campaigns against Osborne and DC. GB's words pretty heavy about it. Burnley win at home v QPR [1–0]. Definitely in play-offs now.

Sunday 12 April

Blogged on McBride, pretty condemnatory, main point that it was not just unpleasant but ineffective. Biggest response yet. Hits and comments. GB called but as there was no reception, I didn't get the message. Tessa and David arriving in time for dinner. Tessa anxious about being spotted. I was beginning to feel a bit dragged down by noise etc.

Monday 13 April

Got another message from GB so called him. He said he was worried that the story would become disunity rather than him dealing with it. He said this all happened in January, now he had dealt with it, Damian had gone and my blog of yesterday was being taken as criticism. He said he knew it was bad but we had to be careful not to let the Tories keep it going right up to the return of Parliament. I had already blogged saying I thought GB should have apologised to Cameron and the others who were mentioned. It was important that someone was getting right to the bottom of it, and also that he made clear, in terms people accepted, that he had no truck with it. I suspected he was worried that they would then get him on to an apology for the economy, but I said I felt it would do him no harm at all to apologise to DC. It would point up the difference.

Charles, Sarah and Donald [Kennedy] arrived. Nice little boy. Real chip off the block. GB called again, said he would think about an apology. He said the *Mail* were trying to make it all about me. Let them, I said. He needed to make the right decisions to limit the fallout. The feedback from everywhere was dire. Not quite curtains but not far off. Tessa said TB would see it in part as a vindication, as he was done in by these people. Lots of articles beginning to appear on there being two Gordons. Good GB who had a mission to change the world. Bad GB of Whelan, McBride etc. Tessa said he had had all the conviction sucked out of him by Balls and his coterie. Charles was on good form. Scathing re the Lib Dems. Felt leading the party was to a large extent a waste of time. All that effort for so little. Enjoying being Rector of Glasgow Uni. Doing media – e.g. in the same film series as me for STV, doing one on the Caledonian Canal. Generally having a nice life.

We went for a walk and he was picking my brains about stopping drinking. He said he didn't drink as much as people said but he had been drinking enough to worry about it. I asked if he ever worried about it. Yes, from time to time. Did he feel it affected his basic ability to do the job? Sometimes, yes. Did he ever start out to have maybe one or two but end up absolutely smashed? Yes, but not all the time. I said my basic take was that if someone was worrying they had a problem, they did. I asked if he was worried what other people would think if he admitted it? He said he didn't feel it ought to come to that. He could maybe just cut it down and get on top of it. I said that is fine if you think you can, but do you? 'Och aye, I think so.' He asked me how I had managed to stop. I said, well, in the early stages I had no choice because I was in hospital, and unless I wanted to hunt around for neat alcohol I wasn't going to find any.

I said Dr [Ernest] Bennie had made me realise I had a problem and once I had that insight, even though I was tempted most days, I realised I had to deal with it. And then when I got into it, I started to take a lot of strength day by day without drink. Then after a year or two I felt like it was a big achievement and I loved it. 'But you have the odd drink now,' he said, and I said I did, and I don't know why. I wished I hadn't. But it shows you can control it, he said. Maybe, but that might be because generally I am on more of an even keel. I am an addict and back then alcohol was one of my addictions. I said if he felt he had a problem, he really ought to try to stop, and it was hard to do alone. He nodded and drew on his fag. I said you're smoking too much too. Aye, I know that. I felt he was holding something back, that he wanted to tell me something more. In the end I just said 'Listen, if you think you're an alcoholic, you need to admit it and face it.'

I said are you worried how your constituents would deal with it? Or the media? Or the party? But he didn't really want to engage beyond asking me what I did, and two or three times he came back to this point about me having the odd drink. He asked if I thought he could do that. I said I just don't know. But you remind me of what I was like when I first started to worry I had a problem. I kept looking for the things that told me I didn't. 'So don't do as I do… do as I say!' We both laughed, then started to head back to the house. 'Anyway, it's been good to have a wee talk about it.' I said any time he felt it would help to do that, I was happy to be there for him. And I said if he really felt maybe he needed to go cold turkey, I could find him the people and the places, and I said I was confident he had enough public support and reputational strength in the bank to make sure it landed fine. 'There is only one question that matters,' I said, 'and that is if you think you have a problem, and if you want to deal with it.'

Once we got back in, he was asking me to explain all the blog, Twitter, Facebook stuff. Showed him how I did it and said I would get him a session to get himself going. He could really benefit from it in such a rural seat, but he was not convinced. Nice lunch then Easter egg hunt and a chat re general Scottishness. He said GB had called him in his first week to sound him out with his GOAT [government of all the talents] plans but he wasn't interested. He said he felt Gordon sounded a bit desperate and wasn't really clear why he was reaching out. He thought I should be a rector somewhere, that I would love it.

Tuesday 14 April

The days just rolling into each other. Three meals and bike, golf and chat, and a bit of reading thrown in. More arrivals today – Zoe, Jessie [Mills] and Louie [boyfriend], Grace's friends. I was really struggling on the depression front now and isolating myself a fair bit. Went for a long bike ride, also a long walk, trying to fend off depression but by dinner time it was pretty hopeless. The final trigger was a row with Fiona about all the people and the twittering and the fact that when Calum and I said we were going into town it suddenly became a big excursion. I went for a swim and felt a bit better but not great. I just wanted to sleep but couldn't.

Blogged on McBride being a setback not a crisis. Several of the papers had run extracts from yesterday's blog and Charles said it was quoted on the radio too. JP called from China. He said GB had called him and asked him to ask me, without saying he'd asked him to do so, to desist from comment. JP said he felt the whole thing was dreadful and he wanted to say something. *Today* had bid. But we agreed better that he did something on his blog. David [Prescott] organised a question and he posted an answer basically saying Draper had to go [for supporting McBride's idea]. David Mills was reading *Maya*, which was good because he read it so keenly and had good points to make. Dinner but then straight to bed. Depression at seven, even eight out of ten. Really shit.

Wednesday 15 April

Woke up really depressed. It had been building for a while and was now pretty set. Definitely seven out of ten, maybe eight. Empty stomach. Lethargy. Neither wanting Fiona there nor wanting her not to be here. Dry mouthed, sweating, eyelids heavy. All the usual but worse. Thankfully Rory wanted to do a long bike ride so we did the long route to Fort William which took care of the whole morning. Loved talking to Rory as we cycled along, and felt it might get me lifted out of it. Top boy. We rode along together for the first hour or so then he went ahead. Some fantastic bits when the wind really came in behind me. Scenery awesome as ever, some lovely birds flying over the water, and normally that would lift me, but for some reason it was saddening me even more. Rory doubled back then we headed back via the ferry and I had one or two suicidal thoughts. I could tell Rory could tell something wasn't right, so I just talked to him and tried to talk myself round. But I was feeling like real shit.

Back for lunch but I was finding any and all talk really difficult, and I could feel Fiona's tension and anger with me rising too. I went for a kip, then did a blog on yesterday's *Guardian* story that climate change experts were very doubtful a rise in temperature could be kept to two degrees. I referred to the dream I had last night of the North Pole melting and a white tsunami coming towards us. Email from Ed saying Susan Sandon was trying to drive down the advance for *Maya*. I wasn't really that bothered about the money, but I loved the way Ed seemed to fight as hard for what was always going to be a small advance as he had when he was doing the deal for the diaries. He said he just loved the doing the deal bit. David Mills had read it and had some good ideas for improvement. He really read it well though. Felt it would appeal to women. We went clay pigeon shooting. Feeling we had too many people up there. In truth it was usually the political voices who got me on edge. I went to bed as soon as I could without it seeming rude. I think it was obvious to everyone though that I was not in great shape.

Thursday 16 April

Tessa and David off after breakfast. Another wonderful sunny day. Tessa said Calum had said to her I always picked on the people I like best so she should take it as a compliment that I was having a go at her wittering about jam recipes and seaweed baths! We went for a longish walk before breakfast and she was quite interesting re GB. She said he was probably a conviction politician when he started out but the conviction had been sucked out of him. She saw Balls as a problem. He fed on GB's insecurities and made him fear people he didn't need to. They had run this kind of negative politics against us the whole time and we had tolerated it in the interests of unity and keeping the show on the road. But now it was a culture and he could not wean himself off these people. He was like an alcoholic. He knew it was wrong but he couldn't stop himself. As for Balls, she felt he was now less a GB disciple and more striking out for himself. But for some reason GB could not see it.

I was still feeling really down. Daily blog becoming a bit of a grind and not always sure it was worth it. Churned out something or other, about some of the arguments on Facebook which were getting quite personal, not about me but about some of the commenters, particularly Alina. Went into Fort William for a swim but still struggling, really struggling. It was not the full works but a mix of emptiness and anxiety. An Aberdonian Arsenal fan was quizzing me about Soccer Aid in the changing room. He was pretty amazed I was there, I guess, and we chatted for a few minutes, all football, a bit about the area, and I was hoping it might help re-centre me a bit. But I was feeling quite edgy a lot of the time and as soon as he was gone, I just plunged again. After I swam, I just stood in the shower for God knows how long, hoping that if I let enough water run over me, somehow the depression would wash out of me. Fucking madness really. Part of me just wanted to be able to react as everyone else seemed to be to the fact we had a few days in a nice place with lots of people who were having a great time.

Fiona reminded me last year had seemed to have had the same effect. I'd forgotten that, as I often did the big ones. This felt like it was a big one. I was constantly looking to be on my own, partly because I could tell how much I was irritating Fiona and how the others were worrying about me. I felt my voice weakening as well, which is always a bad sign. And when I'd stepped out of the shower, I realised I had been crying without even realising it. This was not good, really fucking dire. PG sent me through Georgia's draft speech for the selection and though it was OK, I gave him a few ideas to strengthen. She had done it herself, and he was really proud of the way she had developed in the last few weeks. It was unforgivable that GB had allowed – or in any event not stopped – Whelan operating against her down there. Even amid all the talk of people disapproving of smears, more smears were being taken and run at face value. The media storm over McBride could not have happened at a worse time. Plus *In the*

Loop must have thought they had died and gone to heaven to have all this going on as they were in major promotion mode. I was getting lumped in as usual. One or two said I should take it as a compliment. I didn't.

Friday 17 April

Blogged on the Hillsborough memorial service [20th anniversary of football stadium tragedy] and how now WAS the time to debate bringing back standing at football. There were a few comments saying it was very bad timing, but I was making the point that grounds were better, hooliganism was under better control, and a return to standing could actually be another fitting memorial, for it would show we had changed for the better. Also, though it was always claimed a return would be disrespectful to Liverpool fans, the Kop almost always stood. Andy Burnham had been heckled at the Anfield memorial which was pretty grim for him. I really felt sorry for him, especially as he had pushed hard on behalf of the families. I also noted that the papers I saw headlined it as 'minister' booed. In other words, not known well enough by name. It was definitely a problem that so few of our ministers were well known.

JP called. He had been in China for a few days and was due to see GB later today. He said he was planning to tell him that he needed a clear-out of the stables, and he had to get his ministers in gear. He had spoken to him a few days earlier and said GB seemed genuinely shocked when JP said Whelan had told him about the Red Rag plan ages ago. We agreed on analysis and some of the solutions but worried whether GB could actually turn it round. There was near invisibility of proper message or strategy. Jacqui Smith was pretty much silent on G20 policing, which was raging on.* Ed M was not really driving on climate change. DM had lost his nerve, he said. AD was quiet. Peter M was at least trying but apart from that there was not much doing. Heaven knows what morale was going to be like when Parliament came back next week. JP sounded pretty fed up. He said of course it's what we all worried about. He does the G20 stuff better than anyone but we all know he has these ghastly people all around him and this is where they take him.

GB had finally apologised [re McBride and Draper] but what a messy tortuous process. First of all, insisting that McBride and Draper had just been juvenile. Then when McBride went, trying to make out it was a big deal that the government had acted. But as I said to JP, even when I was

* On 1 April, a man died at the protests after being hit and thrown to the ground by a baton-wielding police officer in riot gear. Ian Tomlinson walked away from the incident only to collapse and die a short time afterwards.

speaking to GB the day after McBride left, there was a hurt rather than angry tone and he was more worried about unity than doing the right thing. Grace and her friends left p.m., along with all but Rory, Calum and Zoe. So really quiet for our last night, which was nice. I took a call at dinner time from Margaret McD and then from PG about the tampering of the Erith postal votes in Victoria Street which meant tomorrow's vote was being postponed for two weeks. Margaret adamant it was organised by Trots, those who did not want Georgia to do well. PG said the same, that they were pretty sure she was going to win and this was a real attempt to thwart the process. I felt for Georgia, who was doing this for the right reasons but would be feeling pretty wretched about things. It was needless to say being presented as a negative for her. PG said she was doing OK and toughing it out, but it was not easy.

Saturday 18 April

Up early, tired. Did a short blog, free of politics, re the Wattbike and whether muscles had memories, before we set off. Fiona feeling sad about leaving. She loved it up here, and so did Molly. I was glad to be heading home though. I had no idea why I had plunged so badly but I needed to get back I think. We listened to the [Tony] Benn diaries audiobook on the drive south. Parts of it were amusing, like his conversations with Ted Heath [former Tory Prime Minister] and his attempts to fix washing machines and other sundry housework stuff. He obviously got down about Caroline not being there, and adored his kids, though. Hilary only seemed to get mentioned when he was being promoted. I got the sense that he quite liked me, really disliked TB. He always seemed to see the worst point about TB and tended to take any opposing view from wherever it came. He was quite nice about me, even around the time of Iraq and my resignation. He was though angry with the MPs for failing to land a blow on me at the FAC [Foreign Affairs Committee].

He described the ludicrous scale of the coverage of my departure well. There were times he came over as self-obsessed though, for example his exchange with Clinton – it was all what he said not what BC said, which was a bit odd. But the journey passed more quickly with him for company. Fantastic scenery right through Scotland and the north of England, with perfect light showing off the hills. Erith quite big on the news along with Alice Mahon [former MP] quitting the party and continuing complaints over the policing of the G20. We dropped Calum in Manchester then got home by 8. A guy at the petrol station at the bottom of the M1 wound down his window and shouted 'Hey Alastair, you do know Labour's finished now, yeah?' It was beginning to feel a bit like that. PG had done a group. He said they just failed to see GB as a leader and they were willing to quite like Cameron and maybe give him a go.

Sunday 19 April

Blog on Budget, billionaires, Balls and Susan Boyle. It was really just a kind of review of the papers, weaving in the main elements. I pointed out that normally the Sundays pre-Budget were full of it but McBride and police were getting the space. The *Sunday Times* splashed on a story that Balls had effectively been running the so-called smear unit using McBride. He had denied needless to say but it was clearly well sourced. I simply said that if he smeared me – I was in the list of their 'targets' – I had not been aware of it. Re billionaires, it was the story about [Lord] David Sainsbury [former Labour minister and philanthropist] becoming the first Briton to give a billion to charity. And finally a reference to Susan Boyle who had been an instant global sensation after singing on *Britain's Got Talent*. Piers M and [Simon] Cowell [judges] loving it. They had been dismissive and sneering – because of her looks – until she sang. She was a phenomenon indeed. I said the lesson for politicians was authenticity. It got picked up in a few places.

Neil K was on Marr reviewing the papers with Carol Thatcher [daughter]. He was excellent on smears etc. Also stood up against her defending herself for saying golliwog on TV. Philip was clearly a bit more worried about Georgia but she was keeping on keeping on. David Miliband came round with the boys. Louise was working. We had a good old moan about the current state of affairs. He said it had a horrible feeling of inevitability about it. They were GB people in charge and they were bound to have done something like the smear stuff they were being done in for. It was GB's making. GB claimed he wanted to get back into the bigger picture but the truth was he tried to hold everyone down. If you had an idea, it would be shot down. If you said something out of the ordinary, it was a leadership bid. And it was Balls who drove it.

I said he needed just to ignore what everyone said and get out there. Likewise Ed M needed to develop a really strong voice on climate change. GB could not carry this alone, even if he thought he could. He became the nth MP to ask me to do a fundraiser, this one the South Shields lecture with Alex F. At the moment every time I was asked to do something like this, my heart sank. It was the result of optimism and enthusiasm being driven out of me by the whole GB operation. I said that when he had been trying to get me back in, one of the big reasons I didn't want to was his key people. McBride may have gone but the rest were there. Hateful people, he said. The antithesis of what we actually believe in.

Monday 20 April

Did a blog on the way the coverage of the G20 police was developing. They were becoming the latest to be on the receiving end of a totally negative prism. Feeling odd these last few days. Anxious. The bids on Iraq and the UK troops coming out were not helping. Lots of bad dreams too. Feeling a lot less sure about things I had been sure about. Could we have done differently? Even if it was the right thing did we do it in the wrong way? How true was it that we did all this because we wanted to ourselves, and how much because of the US and in particular Bush? Train up to Preston. Changed at Preston and did the little train to Burnley. Drink with Calum, bite to eat in the boardroom, then watch the match. Won 1–0. Sheff U fans poor. Team hard but not skilful. Great atmosphere. Lift back with Ray Ingleby [vice-chairman] who was intimating that if we did not get promoted we could go into administration.

Tuesday 21 April

Blogging become a bit of a chore. Did a bit of whimsy on the fact that the Great Wall of China had been discovered to be 180 miles longer than thought. I was spending too long pottering about dealing with some of the internet stuff. Drifting a bit. Novel more or less done. Speeches not quite right. Into Freuds for a meeting with and about Georgia's campaign. Saw Matthew first to say how sorry I was about his dad [writer and politician Sir Clement Freud]. He had had a great press after he died. Matthew said he went quickly and with no real pain and had been doing interesting things to the end. On me he said I should 'yield to the fact you are talent not advisor'. He said I was one of those people who divided – some people loved me, others hated me, but I was not the type to get ignored. It meant I had the opportunity to make a real difference. The better known I was, the more I made. The more I made, the more I could do for e.g. leukaemia and mental health.

Georgia meeting with her, PG, Nicola Howson [Freud executive], Margaret McD, John Braggins [Labour campaigns staff]. Georgia seemed OK but a bit subdued. We agreed we had to somehow clear her out of the negatives attached to her, including her attachment and connection to us. Matthew F popped in at one point and was really clear which helped distil what we had been discussing. We agreed she needed to find ways of getting through to members who she was and what she believed. Had to be her and personal. Had to be getting out the line that it was about new politics not new / old Labour. She felt the members were OK but the worry was more and more that the media negativity would make people just will the thing away, not stay engaged or enthused. It was ironic that she was being smeared and briefed against via anonymous briefings to papers running editorials saying it was time to stop the smears and nasty briefings. There was also a tension with John B, who did not agree with us that we felt there had to be some pushing back on the lines of attack against her. He felt only the members counted. We agreed she should write a very personal letter to them.

I said to PG she seemed a bit down but he said that was because when she was not out there with the public, she reserved her energies. It was totally unfair how because of her connections she was being portrayed as something she is not. Thought about Calum too and how, if he did decide to maybe go into politics, he would probably have more disadvantages as advantages from being my son. Mind you the disadvantages were more media than real. But it was hard for GG. Gail really down about it all too. Bike. F, Rory and Grace went to see *In the Loop*. Grace loved, Rory liked, Fiona fell asleep. I went with them for dinner first and then home to watch the Liverpool 4–4 draw with Arsenal. Rory was convinced my text updates were a wind-up.

Wednesday 22 April

Blogged on how different things might be if the same pro-football tone of football coverage was matched by a pro-politics coverage of politics. Partly based on the contrast between *Newsnight*'s coverage on MPs' expenses last night, where the tone bordered on nihilism, and the excitement of the coverage of the 4–4 Liverpool v Arsenal match. Big build-up to the Budget though yesterday GB had done a website video announcing big changes on expenses which got a lot of coverage.* I worried though that it had the feel of something that would unravel. All a bit tactical as ever. Odd to miss the Budget but I had agreed to open a new MIND resource centre in Hertford. Fabulous sunny day. Managed to catch PMQs on the radio as we drove down there. Cameron going on the figures. Borrowing numbers were going to be absolutely dire. Nice enough event. Good turn-out and I did a little speech and then a reading and Q&A. Mental health related, mainly. Told the basic story of the breakdown.

Dutch guy Henck van Bilsen who was a CBT [cognitive behavioural therapy] specialist and really interesting and passionate about it. Totally positive about what the government was doing for mental health. Nice

* GB announced the scrapping of the much-criticised £24,000-a-year second-homes allowance among a package of reforming measures. The second-homes allowance was to be replaced by a daily attendance allowance of up to £150 a day tax-free, which immediately drew hostility within Parliament.

woman called Karen gave me a lift back. Psychiatric care. Used to work in Holloway prison. Got back to pick up on the Budget. 50p tax top rate. Huge coverage on the scale of the economic crisis. Basically in for a long period of tax rises and spending cuts. Cameron did pretty well. Caught bits and bobs of news and discussion. Pretty dire. Getting harder and harder to see a way back and even with the dreadful figures they were still not really acting with candour and setting out the scale of the challenges. Alistair did OK presentationally but with such a bad hand he was going to be hammered. And of course the press would go into overdrive re 50 pence tax rate for high earners. Mind you, less focus on the point about a manifesto breach [50p tax band] than I had expected. But the general tone of coverage was bordering on contempt.

Thursday 23 April

I listened to Cameron on the media and felt he did OK. He was strong on message, weak on specifics about what he was going to cut, but OK in explaining why he would not be yet. PG said the public were definitely turning to him a bit. They just didn't see GB as a leader. It was all grim at the moment and he was not doing the things we had been agreeing for ages ought to be done. I was finalising a SNCF [French state-owned rail system] Paris–Brussels train gig for the week after. Very French. 'J'aime le train' – people speaking on different main train routes about why trains were great. Fixed to see DS because I was not feeling right still.

Endemol sent through two treatments for a couple of series ideas – a probe into why England didn't win the World Cup. And the idea of taking kids from a tough estate and training them to take on posh kids at posh sports. Definitely needed something like this and it would be worth doing. Out for Bill Hagerty's 70th birthday dinner at the Bleeding Heart. Bloody black tie. Nice do though. Martin Rowson [cartoonist and writer] did a very nice speech. I was sitting with his wife who was a wills lawyer sorting out wills which were disputed. I felt it would make a good middle England TV series. Syd and Jackie with us too. Penny [Stott] there but we did not really get the chance to talk.

Friday 24 April

Did a blog on Ed Miliband's clean coal announcement yesterday plus the IOC's very positive assessment of Olympics preparation.* The weather

* No new coal-fired power stations would obtain government consent unless having equipment to bury at least 25 per cent of gases now and 100 per cent by 2025.

was fabulous at the moment so I was getting out on the bike a fair bit. Went to see DS. I told him of dreams where he was asking me to read letters I had not written. He said that probably meant there were things I wanted to say which I had not. Or things I needed to tell him which I had held back. So I told him of all the anxiety and incertitude I now felt about Iraq in particular. Were you rethinking fundamental position, he asked? I don't think so. I could argue the line and defend every step at every stage. But I was troubled. The idea of the inquiry and having to go over it all again troubled me. The fact I still got attacked so much, when ministers did not, annoyed me. Also I constantly asked myself if we could have done things differently.

Did we do the right things in the wrong way? Were we too worried about the Americans? Did we just get stuck on tramlines and couldn't get ourselves off them? Was I arguing what I believed or what it was my job to say I believed? Was it just that things hadn't worked out that made me anxious about it, or something more fundamental? It was confused and confusing. He said anxiety usually meant there was some change going on. Perhaps I was re-evaluating. He also felt the McBride stuff will have churned things up in me a bit. That was right. I resented being part of that. It had made me less keen than ever to go back. I was pottering mainly but then out late p.m. to meet Peter M and PG at Philip's. Peter arrived and we had the usual joshing about before we went upstairs to the sitting room, Peter took out his pad and asked what we thought. I think we both thought it was all over. PG felt we should be thinking a bit about how to help PM position himself. Of course we would help GB and help the party but he felt there was really no chance of coming back from this now.

The debt figures were horrendous. Our big strength – economy – was pretty much gone and it was hard to see how we got it back. Added to which people did not like GB and did not trust him. I said I had no enthusiasm for being back in there. I told him the story of GB's call about McBride and his trying to use JP to get me to shut up. Also the fact that he had said to me earlier 'The two people I would really like you to get on with better are Ed Balls and Damian.' It seemed Peter has also been urging an early apology. He felt on his own position that it was better than expected. But the politics and lack of strategy were hopeless. He felt he had made a mistake in not standing up against the new top rate of tax. It may have made no difference but he now felt it was just a mistake. He denied it had been done for tactical positioning and to get the talk off all the big bad figures. The aim was genuinely to raise money. PG said when he had seen AD he had said do not listen to any polling on individual measures. The public would say it was fine to tax the rich but the only people who would make a noise were those affected.

He said he felt there would be three groups – a GB group, mainly ministers plus us if we would, to do overall strategy. Douglas heading the election taskforce structures. And him doing a longer-term election strategy group. But it was likely Balls, Harman and others would have to be on that. Harriet was clearly a bigger power in the land than I realised. They had to take her seriously. I said as things stood I was happy to feed in thoughts and ideas to him as part of his political preparation of that group but I was not going to commit to much more. PG did the usual thing of saying I would eventually do a lot more but I was not at all sure about that. I did not feel enthusiasm. I also felt we had been going to meeting after meeting, saying the same things, hearing people say they agreed. Then nothing happened. GB maybe just could not do it. Peter said Balls never ever disagreed with him. Yet they both knew they wanted to track different courses. He felt Balls still had the ear.

We were all saying apologise about the McBride emails. So who was saying don't? He also felt the expenses 'solution' was just a muddle. He did not think it through. Peter had encouraged him to be bold but had no idea he would do it in such a cack-handed way. It was nice to see him and a good chat in many ways. But the whole thing felt fucked. I said at least he was going to end up where he always wanted to – in the Lords and with lots of room and time to do new things. Philip was able to see a next generation take over. I would only be happy when I was out of the whole thing. He said we would all end up working with TB – 'You watch.' Out for dinner at Melissa Benn's. Husband Paul cooking. Told F on the way about the discussion with DS. Nice evening. Really liked Melissa. The other couple, from Richmond, had seen *In the Loop* and hated it.

Saturday 25 April

Partly because I did not have much time and partly because I was still avoiding the Budget I did a second blog on the marathon, running extracts from the 2003 diaries. Incredible to have done it when the war was at its most intense in a way, just as we were realising we were not going to find WMD, and yet got no adverse reaction. I really did wish I was running it tomorrow. Off to Waterloo with Calum to head to Southampton v Burnley. They were down already having had ten points deducted [breaching insolvency regulations] so were going to be up for it bigtime.

Spotted on the train by a couple – he a Scots accountant, she a dentist – who were quite chatty. Calum excellent in judging people as ever, felt he was a bit of a creep in that he basically agreed with pretty much anything I said, but probably voted Tory. A Blairite Tory I would say whereas she, on the occasions she looked up from *OK!* and *Hello!*, came out with pure

Middle England bollocks of the worst *Mail* variety. Too many people who were going into dentistry were of 'this colour' she said, running her finger on a pale brown Costa Coffee cup. 'Can't brown people fill teeth then?' I asked. 'I'm not saying that, but you know what I mean.' 'Not really, no.' A few bitchy comments on Cherie. Then it kicked off when they raised the cost of their kids' school fees. I went off on my 'state schools better, private education a form of child abuse' kick, and said their selfish decisions had an impact on others. Got into a decent heated argument without falling out too badly. The carriage listening in, Calum shaking his head, probably at them for their views and me for getting stuck in.

A Burnley fan, working-class background but Oxford-educated, joined in on my side but then said he sent his seven-year-old daughter private because his wife insisted. Divorce her, I said. Most of the carriage were listening now and some of them started to laugh. I walked to the ground and met David Bull [with whom AC had co-authored a book, *Football and the Commons People*] who had interviewed me for the programme and sorted tickets in the away end. Met Lawrie McMenemy who was leading an appeal for cash. Swapped stories on how big a twat we thought Rupert Lowe [former Southampton chairman] was. Big and very big. Nice enough atmosphere but amazing to think a club like this was in such trouble. Upstairs for lunch. Steve Coppell [manager of Reading] arrived. He was watching us in case he got us in the play-offs. I had met him a couple of times but never really talked to him. There was a dry wit there that did not come over on TV. Talked a bit about how videos had changed the job of managers. He still preferred to go to games but it was possible to watch any game in real time or get it edited for the things you specifically wanted to see. I could see, in a way that did not really come over on TV, why players would respond to him.

Gail called, very anxious about Georgia. She said she hated politics more than ever and just wished Georgia was doing something else. I said the hard thing was realising there were people in the press and in both main parties who hated us so much they wanted to hold it against our kids too. But she would come through it stronger and she had the qualities to succeed, and she should not worry too much. The great thing about Georgia was that she was a genuinely nice person, genuinely talented, but also she thought the best of people and that would actually help her through this. To the away end. Good turnout. They were the better team and we were lucky to get a point though in the end we had the chances to win. 2–2. Pitch invasion by Southampton fans which turned a bit nasty with coins and missiles getting thrown in.

Got a lift back with Andy Hodgson [Burnley fan, TV auctioneer]. Peterborough up automatically. Congratulated Darren [Ferguson, manager]. Sent a text to Alex after they overturned 2–0 down to win 5–2 v Spurs to say 'Good day for Ferguson family.' 'Yahoo! What a day,' he said. The day was a bit ruined by Preston's late winner at Birmingham which meant we still had to get something out of the game v Bristol City on Sunday. I also made the truly horrific discovery that if we finished sixth, the play-off was moved to the Friday which was when I was due to be in Portugal. Nightmare. Started to try to unravel. Calum and Fiona went to see *In the Loop*. He didn't rate it.

Sunday 26 April

Good chat with Andrew Adonis about railways pre my Paris event. As a transport nut, he loved the idea that the French were so into their trains they had a 'J'aime le train' day and got people like me to speak on trains! He was laughing away, asking how mad people on a British train would think things were if the announcer piped up that the French President's ex-spokesman was in the buffet bar doing a speech about British Rail. But he did say he thought 'J'aime le train' was a great idea and we should do something similar. I wanted to quote from his speeches and also get the facts to show why we were jealous of the French railways. He was as full of enthusiasm as ever. Facts and figures pouring out, and he had some great lines for me too, and some good pointers to the history. On the general scene he said he kept busy with transport and tried not to think about the rest of it too much. He felt the problem with the top tax rate was that New Labour always tried a fair share for all and in this context it looked like we were putting the burden on one group of people. I read Cameron in the *Sunday Times* and did a little blog on his use of the word 'independence' to describe the civil service, suggesting he would get himself into trouble if he confused it with impartiality. The press was dire on the Budget. The debt figures were just so overwhelming, plus there were lots of stories of people threatening to leave the country because of 50p tax. GB was failing to get his way on expenses. It was not a good scene. Lovely hot day. Out on the bike. Rory home for a bit and had a laugh with him though I sensed he was getting a bit nervous about the finals looming.

Monday 27 April

Michael Foster [talent agent] round for a chat. He was keen to work with me in getting a proper agreed strategic approach to TV. He felt I had all the attributes but it had to be thought through. He felt Paxman's style was past its sell-by date. Piers was successful by his own lights but the style was too tabloid for me. I could devise formats or ideas between them that rested on my being serious but funny, committed politically but (particularly if we lost) no longer part of the government or even governing party. He was sure the celeb thing would blow out and there would be a market for more serious TV. Agreed we should both mull. I was not as motivated to be on TV as people like him felt I should be. Ed V felt he was OK but he put lots of backs up. I liked him more though, and the fact Annie Robinson spoke so highly of him was in his favour. To Paddington for a cup of tea with Slaven Maric, who was wanting me to commit to dates for Croatia. Out for dinner with Grace. Love her to bits. So funny. Wish she would work a bit harder but she is basically going to be fine. Big, big character.

Tuesday 28 April

Finally blogged on something specific on the Budget, namely how to explain the new top rate. Be open about it being a manifesto breach. Link it to the extent of the crisis. Extraordinary measure for extraordinary times, not a signal of a shift against enterprise. We understand the link between inward investment and tax rates. Also the need for more candour in admitting we cannot be sure about forecasts. I think I managed to avoid it being taken as a big whack but it was hard to make a proper defence when nobody in the government seemed to be.

To Freuds for a meeting with Matthew Freud, Nicola, Dawn Airey and Sue Robertson [Channel 5] re where we were on the Four–Five TV merger (or not) situation. When Dawn said Cameron had basically made clear he was in favour of it as a step to privatisation, I said that was the thing that allowed them to get stories going that would rattle a few cages. She felt Andy B [Culture Secretary] had basically decided on the BBC Worldwide solution [merger] for 4. I said this would allow you to get people higher up the chain interested if DC was suddenly looking like he had made a strategic choice to be the tough man – raise money and look for cuts. But it was a sign of how power was shifting that even I was advising them to take account of DC's position and use it to put pressure on the government who, according to Dawn, were changing their position hour to hour.

Home then set off by car to Nottingham for the second of the 'Evening with Eddie Izzard' [comedian] events for the party. Coates Building at the University, 550 people, mainly students. Good group of Labour students helping organise it. Eddie a good guy. Very pro-Europe and thought (now forty-seven) he would try to get elected to the European Parliament within fifteen years. We were sharing the platform with Lilian Greenwood, PPC [prospective parliamentary candidate] for [Nottingham South MP, standing down at next election] Alan Simpson's seat, who was OK if a bit uninspiring. She seemed very nervous about facing a big audience but did fine. Eddie had done one of these in London with Ed Balls and Tessa and had more planned for the coming days. He quizzed us separately for a bit then opened it to questions. It went particularly well when we did the quick-fire answers at the end. Bounced around from WMD to funny moments (e.g. TB in Japan earthquake gear) plus being asked to impersonate people. Eddie was quite eccentric at the start because we did it in French. Good event.

I had been worried that being a university there would be a lot of anti-war hostility. What little hostility there was came more from Tories on the spin thing e.g. 'Your vendetta against the BBC'. Eddie was an interesting guy and I took seriously his statement that he would one day stand for office. He also took what he was doing seriously. For example he wanted to go for dinner to have a bit of a post-mortem, and get my thoughts on how he could improve it. He was grateful for the idea of the fast crossfire bit at the end, which I had first used on [former ITV political editor] John Sergeant's recommendation ages ago, and which he intended to build in to other events now. We went to a place called Amores in Beeston. Boss man clearly a big Labour supporter. Chuffed we were there. Wanted photos as I left. Eddie off to do a gig. He said he was basically paying for the Labour tour by doing gigs after the event. His big thing really was Europe. He had an idea to run across the whole of Europe capital to capital even though he barely ran now. Left around half nine and home by midnight. Good response on Twitter. There was a lot of passion and enthusiasm among those students. If only we could catch that enthusiasm politically.

Wednesday 29 April

Did a long bike ride in great weather then pottered, mainly working on future speeches. Went to Hampstead to get a few presents for Grace. Lunch with Fiona at the little café opposite Boots in Hampstead. Henry Kelly wandered by. He said he was bored with the travelling back and forth to Reading for his radio show. He felt the political game was totally up for GB. The Gurkhas row was the latest disaster area and expenses were still rumbling on.* A few calls from MPs saying post the Gurkha defeat it felt like the end.

Thursday 30 April

Easy blog first thing as David Prescott asked me to do one on JP going back on the road for the Bank Holiday weekend. Out to Kalendar for Grace's birthday. Tessa, Jessie and Audrey joined us. Tessa was saying yesterday it really felt like the end. To the *New Statesman* to sign books for those who got

* Campaigners demanded UK settlement rights for all Gurkha soldiers and the government agreed to revise settlement rules. But these turned out not to guarantee settlement for all Gurkha veterans. Opposition parties and rebel Labour MPs backed a Liberal Democrat motion that all Gurkhas be offered equal rights of residence.

them as part of a subscription deal. Jason said the reverberations were still being felt from his asking me to guest edit. But the sales had been good and the attention fantastic. I walked to the Commons for a meeting with Andy Burnham. The place felt a bit dead. Andy was in OK form but like DM – who I bumped into as he was preparing to do a statement on Sri Lanka – almost talking as though the government was them not us. He said on a personal level GB had been good to him. For example he called the minute he was booed at Anfield and said he was right to have gone. When there was something about his wife's illness in the press, he was straight on the phone. But when I said I had told GB he needed to license the younger ones to get out there with new arguments and be a bit edgier he said it just was not happening.

He remembered when TB called in the younger ones and said just that. But with GB there was a safety-first thing. Added to which he felt Harman and Balls were trying to get GB to choke off progress by others. We had a good chat about sport and he asked me to head up a manifesto team to bring in outsiders to work on campaign. As with everything political at the moment I felt a mix of duty and non-desire clashing immediately. Part of the worry was that GB would see it as me getting back on the pitch. Andy felt that sports policy was in a good place. Also that he had lots of good people who were ready to come out for us but they needed organising. Nice guy. He was glad he went to the Anfield memorial despite the reception as it opened up the issues. I bumped into Vince Cable [deputy leader, Liberal Democrats] on the way out and had a little chat. I said what's it like being a popular politician? He said it won't last. He said he was reading my novel. A bit of mutual flattery then went our separate ways. I told Freuds the Five plan for Four was a dead duck.

Home to get into effing black tie again then off to the Sport Industry Awards at Battersea Park. 1,300 people. Good chat with Ron Dennis [Maclaren former Formula 1 team principal] first in the bar then over dinner as I was with him. He was getting a lifetime achievement award. The Soccer Aid crowd were there, asking me to do the next one.

I presented the leadership award to Dave Brailsford and chatted on stage with MC Martin Bayfield about read-across between leadership in sport and politics. Chat with Jonathan Edwards and Sally Gunnell, and Michael Johnson who has real charm and charisma. Loads of people asking about Burnley. It became a running joke with Dennis as one after another people came up to ask if I was confident we would go up.

Friday 1 May

I had been looking for a reason to blog on the book of poems Charles Wardle [Tory MP] had sent me, written by his bipolar daughter Sarah while sectioned under the Mental Health Act. I tied it in with the appointment of Carol Ann Duffy as poet laureate, dealing with the lies, allegedly briefed by No. 10, that TB and I had blocked her in the past because she was a lesbian. Out for a meeting at Endemol with Tim Hincks and his team to go over the football idea. Felt OK about it. Telly not totally my thing but I definitely needed some new projects to motivate me at the moment. The political scene was going from bad to worse, in large part because of poor leadership and organisation. Lovely hot day so went for a long bike ride when I went home. Jessie round and had a massage. Legs in good shape but asthma bad. Would get worse as hay fever season kicked in.

Saturday 2 May

TB called first thing. He had been in around a dozen countries in almost as many days. Home for a day then off again to Jerusalem. He had been in Freetown [Sierra Leone] and then out to the country. He said he had never seen poverty like it. He was sure we needed a different model for development and he was sure he could generate the support for it. It had to be about liberating them to run their own affairs more, less charity. He sounded shocked by some of the things he had seen. The President [Ernest Koroma] had also asked if he could help set up proper comms system so he hoped I would go out with him on a future visit. JoP was still attached to his bank but also doing the business side of things for TB. On the GB scene he felt he was probably fucked. When he heard about the 50p plan he felt immediately it was a huge mistake. Anyone who was well-off was already being inundated with ideas of how to avoid paying it so it would raise peanuts. As for those who would pay it, they were influential and they would use it to say New Labour was dead.

GB had trimmed and allowed himself to be pushed into a wrong position. He felt Peter M should have done more to try to stop it but he was feeling isolated in there at the moment. The reality was that we had allowed myths to develop and the truth was coming through now. Added to which he could not cut himself off from bad advice. I said I had not been doing much but did he [TB] think I should cut out altogether? He felt no, people realised I was doing it because I was loyal to Labour and it was important people saw the Blairites stayed loyal. But when I said I was off campaigning up north with JP, he sounded bemused. 'That is loyalty indeed.' I said there was a worry the whole shooting match – his legacy included – would disappear down the plughole if things went on as they were. He acknowledged that but said it was hard for anyone to blame us for recent events.

Drove north listening to Akon and then Man U at Boro. Two–nil. Another big step to the title. Got to Keighley a bit late, thanks to a succession of crashes on the M1, but JP was even later. I did a little speech with party members, introduced by new candidate Jane Thomas, then JP arrived and he did the same. Charles Clarke had said he was ashamed to be a Labour MP. JP had given him and Blunkett (who had called me protesting he had been taken out of context) a whacking. But there was something a bit tired about me and JP being the ones out campaigning and defending GB and the government. JP was good at it though and we got a good little crowd going in Keighley town centre. Did a little stump speech but I was going through the motions a bit. I did a piece for the *News of the World* which was OK but later we heard Hazel [Blears] had done a piece for *The Observer* talking about the government's 'lamentable' communications. What on earth was she thinking of? Ego or a genuine attempt to destabilise? Who knows?

JP's big point was 'Stop complaining and start campaigning' and in his usual tub-thumping ramshackle way he was visiting a lot of places and making an impact. But the mood was mixed. One or two hecklers. He saw them off pretty well. We both did a bit of telly. Blogged, then off to Leeds for a party members' rally. Richard Corbett MEP and Hilary Benn also speaking. Had a nice chat with Hilary who felt things were not great but not as bad as they might seem. Nice man. I was impressed by his little speech too. Realised it was probably the first time I had seen him speak outside a Commons or TV environment. I did my usual rah-rah which went down OK, then JP asked me to stay back – I was rushing off to Manchester – and he did a really warm tribute. He said I had always given him good advice, that it was almost always right, and that I was a team player, Labour through and through. I certainly think he and I were showing it was possible to be of the old regime without doing in the new. Left them to it, then headed to Manchester to meet Calum. JP still had the passion but he admitted to me he felt GB just didn't have what it took to turn it around. Out to the Italian near Calum's, getting nervous about the match tomorrow.

Sunday 3 May

I didn't sleep too well. Did a quick blog re Hilary Benn and the need for the ministerial team to be more visible. He had also talked about the need for more confidence and how JP had been brilliant in taking on [John] Humphrys and rebutting negativity yesterday. Hazel's attack was leading the news and John Woodcock called in a bit of desperation. 'Christ on a bicycle – what do we do?' He said Hazel had withdrawn it, or at least said it was not intended to attack GB, but the damage was done. There was a feeling of lack of control, headless chickenry and no big policy agenda to fill the gap. I advised big-picture focus medium term, a bit of rallying round short term but understanding we were into a frenzy mode so maybe just let it blow out.

Over to Frank Teasdale's and out for lunch with him and Judith. First home-end sell-out of the season. Good atmosphere and great win [over Bristol City]. Four–nil so we were definitely in the play-offs, against Reading. Also other results conspired to make sure I was OK getting back from Lisbon. Took a call from John Madejski to go for dinner at the away leg. Long drive back but it was amazing how much quicker you went if you won. Disaster for Cardiff who missed out on one goal. Decided to do a blog for the morning re whether Cardiff could become a metaphor for Cameron. But it was all whistling in the wind. Cameron was being handed it on a plate. Some of our lot looked like they were losing the will to live.

Monday 4 May

Rory back for a birthday and also Tuesday's match. Had a great chat with him. Frank had said yesterday that Calum was 'turning into a really good lad'. They both were. Also Grace was really funny at the moment. Out for dinner with R and G, F out at the ballet. I could not watch the news – it was like a car crash. Harriet saying she would definitely not stand as leader. Frenzy mode setting in though. Watched *Endgame* with Rory – account of the secret talks leading to the end of apartheid.

Tuesday 5 May

Blogged on the *Endgame* film and contrasted Thatcher's lack of role, and indeed her obstinate position, with the hagiographies to her in the weekend press on the 30th anniversary of her first election win. Read her book – the section on South Africa – where she was basically saying her approach led to Mandela's release. What was interesting about today though was that our problems, and the ease the Tories had in exploiting them, it was in some ways the result of the Thatcherites having continually defended her record in a way we did not. Off on the 24 bus to Victoria Street to speak to the party staff. Douglas was chairing it and we had a little chat beforehand. He was yet another one who made things sound as though he wasn't actually part of the government but an outside commentator. They were great at saying how bad things were. Hopeless at solutions.

To be fair to him he was caught between all the madness going on in there. GB was still mainly listening to Ed B, pretending to listen to Peter M, trying to get both working together but in reality he had twin strategic paths. I said unless he chose one and stuck to it, he was fucked. He had to decide a course and chart it out. He could not keep being so tactical and event-driven. Mine was the second of these party staff sessions. PG had done the first and Douglas said he had been very visionary and big picture. He wanted me to talk about the rhythm of the day in a campaign and also give them some hope. Afterwards Carol L and others said I had managed to do that but I didn't really feel that. I felt it was all a bit downbeat and sad. I did make the point that the Tories had not sealed the deal as we had in the mid-'90s. But as I said what needed to be done it was obvious that things were not being done because of the lack of leadership being offered. Hilary Perrin [Labour staffer] spelled out the hard truth – what are we actually saying about the forward offer to people? I gave my best answer but it was not great. DA said next to nothing. Afterwards Ray Collins [general secretary] and Vanessa Bowcock [fundraiser] were pressing me to get involved in the 11 June dinner. Elton John had pulled out.

Home to potter around for a bit before meeting up with Rory and heading to the Emirates for the Arsenal–United Champions League semi. Our tickets were not in the away end proper but a section for United corporates in the main stand. Les Dalgarno [AF's lawyer] there, Mark F. Jason [Mark's twin] had gone back north because Darren's ex-wife and kids had been involved in a terrible accident. Park scored to give United an early lead. Ronaldo free kick. All over. Great night for Alex though considering everything else going on.

Wednesday 6 May

Meeting with Prebble. He had read Volume 1 of diaries and liked it. But he thought we might need to broaden it to make a series. Maybe tell the whole story of the Blair–Brown relationship. Or make it more thematic. He wasn't sure it worked in the same way as *The Blair Years* had done because so much of it was further back. We agreed to mull. To the Waldorf to meet Michael McAvoy [TV exec] to discuss maybe doing a programme on the media and the way it had changed and the damage it did. Nice guy but again not sure it was where I wanted to be. I was really tired at the moment.

Thursday 7 May

Didn't sleep well. Ended up getting up even before the alarm and did a bit of work. Off to Heathrow and I blogged in the back of the car on the musings of an insomniac night. Liked it. It was probably just another way of avoiding talking about politics at the moment as it was all so dire. The plane was a bit delayed but we got to Lisbon roughly on time. Met by Berto and Sofia who were press officer and editor of Bertrand, who were publishing the Portuguese translation of the diaries. They were nice but clearly did not share my control-freak punctuality. As a result we kept running late. To the Four Seasons Ritz. Lovely room. Fabulous pool. Then to a conveyor belt of interviews. The first guy almost as obsessed with football as I am. Second one longer questions than answers. Third nice guy but very hostile re war. All a bit long.

Off to a beach restaurant to meet the guy from news agency Lusa who was obsessed with the Azores summit [2003 council of war hosted by President George Bush, with Prime Ministers of UK, Spain and Portugal] and [José Manuel] Barroso's role in particular. He reminded me I had described Barroso [European Commission President, former Prime Minister of Portugal] as pompous which also came up later on TV. Same old same old most of them. Then a guy called João who seemed to have read everything I had ever written. Even had little printouts of recent blogs. Nice guy. Gave me a lift to the next one. By a lake. Huge fat guy. Boy had he read the book. Easily the best informed about Britain. Radio then two long telly interviews with a couple of older guys who had both covered Britain when Thatcher came in. Getting tired but did OK. Swim then out for dinner with the girls and a guy called Eduardo from the publishers. OK food and a succession of musicians performing Fado, a Portuguese music style (Fate).

Good chat with Alex Ellis, the Ambassador, who gave me some good tips on how to handle the Portuguese. Bit of an inferiority complex. Obsessed with how they were seen from abroad. Bad taste left over from the McCanns.* There was a lot of racism flowing from it – them saying we could not take care of our kids. Us saying they could not organise a police inquiry. Did about seven hours of talking by the end of the day. Knackered but still didn't sleep well. Some really good responses to the insomnia blog but also some saying it was 'blood on hands' guilt re Iraq.

Friday 8 May

Swim, breakfast, blog on Bhutan. Had seen a piece in yesterday's *International Herald Tribune* re Gross National Happiness index as the key indicator for government policy impact.† Also quotes from the government

* Three-year-old Madeleine McCann disappeared in May 2007 from her bed in an Algarve holiday apartment, where she was staying with her parents, Kate and Gerry, and her two-year-old twin siblings. Despite investigations by the Portuguese police and Scotland Yard, she has never been found.

† A phrase used in the 1970s by the fourth King of Bhutan, who claimed Gross National Happiness was more important than Gross Domestic Product.

comms guy on the negative impact of the media so I threw in a bit about how any happiness strategy would require us to get rid of the *Daily Mail*. Down to do the PricewaterhouseCoopers event. Good crowd. Did some funny TB stuff, rules of crisis management, the five crises we had endured then how well the world was doing re the current crisis. Good lively Q&A. I still found it possible to explain how we could win but time was running out.

Telegraph had got hold of all the MPs' expenses and the media were going into meltdown on it. GB and his cleaning bills. Hazel [Blears] and several second homes, one at a time. JP and mock Tudor beams. Straw's council tax. The *Telegraph* had the lot and were going to eke them out day by day. Disaster-ville really. Anji was back from the States and said there was a real fin de siècle feel here whereas in the States the same problems were being met with energy and hope. Two more interviews, then out to the airport. Tired. Really tired. Maybe the no-carb diet needed to change. TB has mentioned some fifty-plus Wellman pills he was taking, which he said he would get for me. We were missing each other by a few hours which was a shame. Home by 6 then out with Fiona and Rory to the Freemasons [pub restaurant]. Fiona and I argued about the [Work and Pensions Department] inequality figures. Got very heated, her turning it into a full frontal, saying we had failed on the big things, and fucked up because TB got too hooked on the foreign policy stuff.

Saturday 9 May

The expenses scene was getting worse. I did a blog trying to balance genuine shock at some of the things being revealed – which really were shocking – whilst not getting picked up too much by the media in a way that would be damaging for GB. I did say though he had made a mistake in not taking up Cameron's offer of all-party leaders' meeting and they should now publish them all soon to stop the *Telegraph*'s drip-drip, which was holding politics to ransom. I spent a bit of time writing my French speech for next week then off to Burnley for the play-off first leg [against Reading]. Managed to get a fair bit of work done but I was having a bit of a blind spot on the novel at the moment. Maybe needed to leave it even longer. No great rush I guess. We collected Calum at the flat in Manchester and set off for Burnley. Everyone very nervy in the boardroom. John Madejski arrived and we had a little chat about stuff. He thought the expenses row was a fuss over nothing. Good atmosphere but we were not great in the first half. We kept plugging away though and eventually won a penalty which Grezza [Graham Alexander] put away. Real feeling we could do it now.

Sunday 10 May

I didn't particularly want to blog on expenses again. Justin Forsyth in No. 10 sent me the *Mail on Sunday* story claiming GB on YouTube [fighting recession message] had been my idea, presumably briefed by Whelan and/or McBride. Did a little rebuttal and then a piece on Obama's brilliant speech to the White House correspondents' dinner. Comic genius. It wasn't just that the lines were good. They were brilliantly delivered as well. Fiona was away at the Fowey book festival meeting lots of old friends from down there, so Audrey was round to cook lunch etc. She was suddenly looking more frail and not so on top of everything.

Monday 11 May

Out early doing breakfast telly and radio on Mind's 'Get it off your chest' campaign on the need for men to be more open re mental health problems. To Westminster to do a photocall on it with [Lord] Melvyn Bragg [broadcaster, novelist], Stephen Fry and a Heart Radio DJ the snappers kept asking to move out of the picture. I felt sorry for him and we had a little chat. Popped into Millbank to do *You and Yours* [Radio 4] then home to get ready for Paris. At St Pancras I took a call from Rebekah Wade who said Tom Watson was suing them over something they said during the McBride saga and she was not going to settle (she thought the *Mail* would) but if it went to court she would go for the whole government big-style. I made a half-hearted attempt to tell her that was unreasonable but I could not be bothered with it really. I wanted nothing to do with the press and not much to do with the politicians right now. I was avoiding getting sucked into the whole 11 June fundraiser at the moment. I sent Sue Nye a little note re Rebekah's threat to which she replied, 'Oh lordy.' Must be a nightmare in there at the moment. Lots of reports of GB going crazy and throwing things around. Staff morale dire. Justin F had asked me my view and I said GB had to do more than he had done so far and give a sense he did actually get it. He did a speech which at least did a bit of that but Cameron was looking fleeter of foot. Very odd hotel in Paris. Had a kip then out for a long run.

Tuesday 12 May

'J'aime le train' day [railway PR operation]. Turned out to be perfectly enjoyable but a bit surreal. With Frank Bernard from SNCF. Hostesses in red suits drumming up interest. Down to the restaurant bar area to do my little speech and Q&A. Thank God for Adonis. Had some good stuff from him, and the train stories, especially the convoluted history of the Channel

Tunnel, and all the different arguments used against it, went down well. Frank said he accepted our tribute to French railways but we were doing better re cultural change to respond to the challenges of the environment. Really quick, clean, comfortable. Did the same speech on the return leg, Q&A OK, though ended weirdly with a guy asking if I was involved with TB and Bush in covering up the truth re UFOs. When I said no, he produced a mass of documents from a plastic bag, and thank God one of the hostesses managed to stop him coming to sit with me. Nice enough event and the French team with me seemed to like it.

Eurostar back to London. Not remotely full so still struggling. Home then out with the boys to Reading for the second leg. I had dinner with Madejski and co. Tonight he was fulminating about expenses so he had changed his tune since Saturday. Great atmosphere in the away end. Poor first half but two wonder-goals in the second half saw us through. Absolute bedlam in the away end and the fans refused to leave for ages. Real feeling we could go all the way. Round to the boardroom to congratulate our lot and commiserate with John and Coppell, who was very down and, reading his body language, about to quit I would say. We left about half eleven and just after midnight they announced Steve had quit. Got home and did a blog on it – there is absolutely nothing like football for that kind of night. Buzzing.

Wednesday 13 May

Into Google HQ near Victoria to sign 450 books for their conference next week. Nice chat with DJ Collins. We had both had similar reasons for resisting GB's blandishments which included the 'truly horrible' people who worked for him e.g. McBride, Whelan etc. He felt there could have been recovery but he just did not do strategy. Lunch with Calum before he went back to Manchester then did Sky Sports News on last night's match. Pottered mainly, then watched United win at Wigan. One more point and they'd done it. Rory worrying about his exams a bit.

Thursday 14 May

Two-blog day – charities and recession, then trailing the PEB [party election broadcast] whacking Cameron. It was a Tory boy hitting a punchbag cut with real people warning of what he would do. OK without being brilliant but a lot of the responses were quite negative about it. The expenses stuff was getting worse by the day. Today Andrew Mackay [MP] quit as DC aide and Elliot Morley [Labour MP] was in real trouble over claiming for a mortgage that had already been paid off. Absolutely dreadful and getting worse. GB always slightly behind the curve. His apology had followed DC's. Firm action was not as firm as DC's. He was losing the grip. I had also noticed in France the sense of him and the country being a bit of a laughing stock. Long bike ride – but I was putting on weight again – then out with Grace to the Mind Awards. I set up the photographer to pretend he was from *Heat* magazine and ask if he could take her picture. She almost fell for it. Loads of snaps and small talk then the awards. I had a feeling I would win. Nice enough do. I was announced as the winner ['Champion of the Year'], and apparently it wasn't even close. Did an OK speech, told the crack Grace had made to Fiona re 'Talk to me like that again and I won't even mention you in my first BAFTA acceptance speech'. Otherwise just very nice about the charities and their campaigns, and I was really glad Gracie was there. We went off to meet Fiona at the Camden Brasserie.

Home to change then off to Euston for the sleeper. Bumped into Ed Balls and an aide coming down the platform. He asked how bad I thought things were. Bad, I said. Probably terminal. It was true all the parties were damaged by the expenses scandal but we looked worse and we were not handling it well. 'So Tory Britain then?' I said there was not much of an alternative at the moment. This was to some extent filling a vacuum. But we were expected to be better. He said he had been urging the *Telegraph* to run something on him because people were assuming they had something to hide. It turned out, and I got a text from Mark B while still on the train, that he and Yvette's 'flipping' of second homes was one of the *Telegraph*'s stories for Friday. I assumed he would feed back anything I said to GB so I gave no indication of any change of heart about going back. On the contrary I was feeling pleased I had said no, if profoundly depressed by what was going on. He said he had been doing a party meeting in Coventry and it was hard to get people motivated. I said we could still do it if we shouted about the record, the Tories and the future. He said that was pretty much what he did. On to the train, kind of glad I had nothing to do with it. Had a sleeping pill and slept OK.

Friday 15 May

Off the sleeper, got myself a coffee and waited for the car. Blogged in the car on the Mind Awards. Huge number of congratulatory messages on Facebook last night. Nothing in the papers of course. Lovely scenery. Arrived Crieff Hydro. 350 people at the Scottish social workers' conference. Did a bit of humour, redid my blog pro social workers, then advice on how they get themselves a better image, then an OK Q&A. Nice enough event. Clear to me though that the SNP were still doing really well. Car to Edinburgh. Read the latest instalment in the *Telegraph*. Dire stuff. Shahid Malik resigned as Justice Minister. Loads of people reading the Tory papers at the airport. Lots of pissed people heading to Spain for hen nights and stag parties. Plane late back. Tired all the time at the moment. Called Alex to say good luck for tomorrow. Incredible achievement to get yet another title.

Saturday 16 May

I blogged a revised version of my *La Repubblica* piece on Berlusconi, taking in the fact that he had dismissed their ten questions about his relationship with the eighteen-year-old girl as a hate campaign. It was extraordinary how only *The Times* and *La Rep* were going after the story, e.g. getting hold of the girl, because the rest of the media was controlled by or influenced by SB. Off to Lewes with Fiona. Can't believe on the day of the United v Arsenal game that would see the title decided I was going to the Charleston [former home and meeting place of the Bloomsbury Group] Festival. I was trying to be nice but failing miserably and getting grumpier and grumpier. She loved all that Bloomsbury stuff. Met by Alison and Michael Farthing [former London neighbours] and we were then taken on a tour of the house. Some lovely paintings and artefacts and interesting stories of the Bloomsbury set but not really my scene. Lots of expenses talk over lunch and although outraged people were also worried it was all going too far now. Nice chat with Alison who said they were both enjoying their new life [Michael now vice-chancellor of Sussex University].

The main event at the festival was Vince Cable, Will Hutton and Robert Skidelsky [economic historian] on Keynes. Four or five hundred people in there. All in the main middle-aged middle-class. I was keen to see Cable and try to work out why he had the appeal he did. I'd met him recently and had a chat which gave me some insight but getting a good look for an hour and a half would be a better guide. Plainly dressed. Dull-looking. Dull voice. But he spoke clearly and simply on complex issues. He did not patronise or claim to be right about everything. He was modestly amusing. Modest and authoritative. He was warmly received. But his biggest asset was not being in government. For example, at one point he made clear he did not tell the whole truth on tax if interviewed on TV and nobody batted an eyelid. And he admitted we were better off out of the euro. It was as though he were not treated like a politician. Skidelsky interesting and both of them felt solutions were moral as much as economic.

Will Hutton lively and stimulating but he had an infuriating habit of taking his glasses on and off every few seconds which made it next to impossible to concentrate on what he was saying. Nice chat with Simon Fanshawe [writer and broadcaster] but he felt we were probably fucked. GB was no longer speaking to the public in a way they listened to him. Off to the Farthings' lovely new house. Nice chat with Michael about new lives, his and mine, then off to Brighton to see Illtyd [Harrington] in a hilarious gay hotel. Men trotting in and out to go to the sauna. Staff wearing pants. Illtyd frail but not as bad as we feared. Facing up to a risky op though. Nice enough day though F and I did get on each other's nerves a lot. Home to watch *Match of the Day*. Didn't miss a great game [Manchester United 0, Arsenal 0] but good celebrations. Amazing achievement [second hat-trick of Premier League titles with United] by Alex.

Sunday 17 May

Blogged on Cable, trying as hard as possible to be objective, analysing why he was so popular. Got a pretty big response for a weekend. Did a piece on cycling for *The Times* while riding on the Wattbike. Pressure really building on the Speaker [Michael Martin] to go. MPs putting together a motion of no confidence. Slight feel of scapegoating to it but it was being so badly handled. Cameron stealing a bit of a march on GB but still not that great. The worry for Labour was that it did not really matter what we said or did now. The country had decided to go for change.

Monday 18 May

I'd flogged the idea to *La Repubblica* of a series of articles on the Champions League, partly to justify going there and did the first, a piece on Alex, drawing a fair bit on politics and also his particular style of leadership. Good laugh with F over the fact that for the first time I managed to make a bank payment transfer on my own – to UEFA for the [Champions League final] Rome tickets. Out on the bike and the sessions on the Wattbike were definitely helping to up the pace and stamina and efficiency, I think. Then just pottering really. Had done a blog on how the media could only deal with one frenzy at a time as though swine flu had been cured by MPs' expenses, which got an OK response. I was working on *Maya*, somewhat half-heartedly, when I listened on the radio to Michael Martin, who did a dreadful statement, no real contrition or forward strategy (a few meetings with leaders) and he was then taken to task by a succession of backbenchers. In truth he was probably a goner, the first Speaker forced out in 300 years. There was no sign of the expenses situation abating at all.

Tuesday 19 May

Mary O'Hara came to do an interview for Guardian Society re the Mind Awards. I suppose there was a danger that I was going to get drawn more and more into mental health charity stuff which would both piss off LRF and also eat more into the time I was giving to causes without a real strategic approach. We went to the Odeon Swiss Cottage to see *State of Play*. It sort of made me wonder about whether I wanted to be a journalist again but there was so little of that kind of journalism left.

Wednesday 20 May

As the expenses row roared on I did a blog on the lovely Hansard book that had been sent to me recently, in which parliamentarians and others who had worked there, like me, chose their favourite Commons speeches. I had gone for John Smith's speech when he did Major as the man with the non-Midas touch. There were still good speeches but the media never reported Parliament except when it was a scandal or crisis or it fitted their pre-ordained agenda for the day. Mind you, there was so much bad stuff coming out of the expenses coverage still. It was dire. It was hard to defend politics at the moment but I did say if Parliament reformed so must the media. Later, at Alison [Blackshaw]'s farewell in No. 10, both Nick Robinson and Andy Porter [*Daily Telegraph*] said they agreed with a lot of what I was saying. But how? Nice do for her. I did an OK and quite funny speech and it was nice to see a lot of the old No. 10 faces. Chatted to Lizzie McCrossan, Pam Green [secretary], one or two others who all said it was horrible there under him. That we had warned them a bit but nothing prepared them for the rudeness and the boorishness and the lack of respect. Wendy Abbs [former duty clerk], now a teacher, said the place fell apart when we left. Alison loved the evening which was nice. She got signed photos and letters from Major, TB and GB. She loved that kind of thing.

Then off to Royal Society of Medicine for the end of the memorial to Martin Kelly. Natascha looking fabulous and holding it together though she had been crying a bit earlier when the boys spoke. Rory home again to revise and I had a nice chat with him later. He was working really hard at the moment.

Thursday 21 May

I was due to head to Edinburgh and on the way to Heathrow went to the place in Oxgate Lane NW2 which had left a collection card for a redelivery. It turned out it was a scam designed to get your credit card details. Did an email to Trading Standards. Had a bit of time messing around at the airport. Noticeable how many people were reading the *Telegraph* and the *Mail*. *Telegraph* still running page upon page of bad expenses story. I was in front row but sandwiched between two women, one reading the *Mail*, the other drinking whisky with her lunch. Got a cab into town. Driver very friendly. Asked if I got fed up of people like him recognising me and wanting a chat. He felt the MPs' expenses situation was bad but that it would pass because ultimately everyone fiddled what they could. I said the MPs were meant to be different. 'Aye, but no' that different.' Thought TB good, GB less so and running out of luck. Staying at the Sheraton. Did a bit of writing, then a swim and off to the dinner at the EICC [conference centre].

Nice guy next to me, Mike Hussey of Land Securities [property company]. They'd asked me to do a number on change, which I adapted to do a lot of off-the-cuff stuff on the need to defend politics or else we had had it. The usual funny stories went down really well. Once they warmed up a bit they were applauding as I went through. Q&A OK, though the questions were tough – guilt re David Kelly for example, spin, contempt for Parliament. For once I left feeling it had gone about as well as it could. It still did not add up to much though. Hazel Blears called me earlier on Margaret McD's instigation. GB had described what she did re her tax affairs as 'totally unacceptable' whilst saying of Hoon and Purnell that it was OK. I said to her that she needed to ask him direct whether she was being softened up for the push. Also she had to make clear to him that her position was untenable if he was using words like that. She said Peter M had said the same.

Friday 22 May

Car to the airport and another packed plane south. So many conflicting signals re the economy still. The plane landed early and I was hanging around for a bit in the sunshine waiting for Rayan [Benyamin, driver]. Approached by a woman editing a magazine who wanted an interview. She said she thought TB was cool, GB sad. The taxi driver in Edinburgh earlier said something similar, 'It just doesn't work.' And I was struck last night by the viciousness of the desire of a couple of people – both said they had voted for us before – to kick him out. It was hard to see a way back now. Even before the expenses it was hard enough. But this was doing real additional damage. Joe Irvin [GB advisor] called me. He said they had got our MEPs to agree to a number of changes which would make things there more transparent. And which would be in contrast with the Tories. I said I could not see any way of making the expenses story a positive and it was far better that GB got on to a big-picture place of major reform and constitutional change. Joe said he would pass that on and GB would want to speak to me later. No. 10 called with him when I was having my hair cut so we couldn't really speak. I was pretty grateful for that. Off to see DS and part of the discussion was how in a way I just wanted out of the whole thing. It really wouldn't bother me if I had nothing to do with it. I felt bad about the way good people like Chris Lennie [Labour deputy general secretary] were pressing me to help with the June fundraiser and I just so lacked any enthusiasm. Similarly when ministers called as they did for advice, I did not really want to get involved at all. Said to David I was not feeling overly depressed, just down and a bit unfulfilled.

Saturday 23 May

The piece on Keighley rugby league team appeared in *The Times* so did a blog on the two ends of the sport financial spectrum. Them, and Burnley playing in a match [play-off final] worth 60 million quid in TV money to the winner. David Triesman called to say he had spare tickets in the royal box if we needed them, but I already had loads of tickets for the Burnley end. We had a chat about his current situation at the FA. Sounded down. Said he felt a lot of support for what he was trying to do but [Richard] Scudamore [Premier League CEO] was a total control freak, the Premier League was so powerful they could block pretty much anything they wanted to. He said he felt tired and drained. It was very political and he could do with picking my brains on it. Audrey came round to cook for us, which she loved doing. Later watched Robert Carlyle playing Hitler in *Rise of Evil*. Terrific performance. Really scary to be reminded of the link between economic decline and the rise of extremism.

Sunday 24 May

Out on the bike early. Lovely sunny day. Then back to read the papers and do a quick blog on the different ways Bush (quiet, low-profile) and Cheney (all guns blazing against Obama) were handling themselves out of office. Told the story of Cheney snarling at me for saying when they say democracy people hear Americanisation.

Monday 25 May

Up early, quick blog titled 'Only one birthday present that counts' on the match. Sorted tickets out for everyone going then got a lift with Sky to Wembley, as they wanted me to do some pre-match interviews. Even at half twelve the place was heaving. Went into the Wembley Suite lunch. Listened to the speeches then out to the stadium. Jimmy McIlroy, John Connelly and Adam Blacklaw [former players] just behind us. Good atmosphere in the build-up though then got a bit tense. Lovely sunny day, not as hot as yesterday. Fabulous goal from Wade Elliott, and the place went mental. We never really looked like conceding. Loads of messages coming in. Last few minutes unbelievably tense but we hung on. Terrific celebrations on and off pitch. Never seen so many smiling faces as we came out.

Did Sopel on the BBC News channel live, a piece for *The Sun*, lift home with Gavin [Millar], watched the highlights, then out to the Marriott in Duke Street where the players were due to have a party. As I parked the car I bumped into Clarke Carlisle [player] who was on the phone to his mum, and said 'Hold on, Mum, I've got to give Alastair Campbell a big hug.' Barry [Kilby, chairman] in dreamland. Sonia ditto. Owen Coyle was very cool, and there were rumours he was set for Celtic. Fiona had never met him before and said she really didn't take to him. Sandy Stewart [assistant manager] saying he loved doing it for all the people who had supported the club through the bad times. He asked if it was better than the elections. I said I never enjoyed them because you were always on to the next thing. He said he got that totally. Whereas this you can just enjoy. Steve Davis [coach] agreeing with Fiona I should do a book on Burnley's year in the Premier League. Left to go to the Camden Brasserie then home to watch the highlights again. Great day.

Tuesday 26 May

It had still not fully sunk in that we'd won and were going up. The council had asked me to present to homecoming and trophy presentation at the town hall, so Rayan collected me and a hungover Calum at half eight. I was due to go to Rome today ahead of the Champions League final, Alex having got me tickets, but had pushed it back and did a piece for *La Repubblica* on why I was going to Burnley because it was a bigger better story. They ran a headline on it about how Man U providing the riches and Burnley the poetry. Lots of texts and calls and a good response to a blog suggesting the highs were all the greater when you've known so many lows. We dropped Cam at Manchester then on to Burnley. There was a real buzz around the place and, after the torrential rain I woke to in London, warm sunshine. Went to the gym at the club then over to the town hall. Good banter with the crowd who started singing 'You're only here on expenses'. On which – I had a quick chat with Kitty Ussher [local Labour MP] who had taken a bit of a battering over her new ceiling and comments about why she needed rid of the Artex. She said it had not been as bad as I might have thought when out canvassing but she hinted if the local elections were truly terrible she would know if it was going to be fatal.

The plan was interviews to around 7, when the open-topped bus was due to leave Turf Moor. Council chief exec Steve Rumbelow, whose idea it was to invite me, went out first to introduce me then I went out and led a rendition of Ee-I-ee-I-o… The noise was pretty amazing. The crowds filled the street and went as far as the eye could see, both directions. The bus emerged at the top of the road and I went into wild commentary mode. Fabulous reception for them. The players came in and had a little drink in the mayor's room before we brought them out to the balcony in groups. Then the board, then Owen and staff. I put Owen on the spot and asked him to say in front of all the fans that he would not go to Celtic. Best that can be said is that it was a diplomatic answer that came back. He said it was a hypothetical, and he looked pretty pissed off to be asked. Darren [Bentley, Burnley media manager] asked me to go back to the club on the bus but I was worried about getting back too late. Nice call from Barry [Kilby] on the way home on how grateful he was I made a fuss of them as well as the players. Directors do tend only to get stick but ours are a good bunch and it was as much Barry's success as anyone's. Lovely day. Did a blog on the way back and was home by midnight. I really wouldn't have missed today. It meant so much to the town and the area.

Wednesday 27 May

Stuart Le Gassick arrived and we set off for Heathrow. The only election poster I saw between home and the airport was one in a window. Big contrast when we arrived in Rome. Posters everywhere. We had breakfast in Gordon Ramsay's place at the airport, and a chat about the political scene. Amazing how many people, in a mainly friendly way, were basically saying GB was finished. Flying economy but I was offered an upgrade when I got on. Said no because Stuart was not covered but I went up front for a chat with Bob Geldof and his very pretty colleague from his Africa campaign, Eloise Todd. He was going to the match (supporting Barca) but also seeing the Italian government on Africa and wanted my take on how to handle Berlusconi who was 'fucking useless and delivering fucking nothing'. I said he was vulnerable at the moment, at least more than usual, and he should go for it. He said that was his instinct too but lots of people were advising him to go easy and not alienate. I said SB responded to pressure and I recommended a strong line like 'I don't care what his relationship with the girl is but the real moral question he faces is…' etc.

Bob was scathing re GB, said he had tried to be reasonable but he was hopeless, just not a leader. He had lots of good qualities but lacked TB's leadership skills. What would have TB have done on expenses – yeah, it's terrible, here's what we're doing, now let's focus on what really matters e.g. the economy. We carried on in the same vein in the car into town. Eloise really bright too, very political, close to despair about the current scene. Boiling hot day. First to the wrong hotel, then the right one, Eurostars International, met Stuart's friend Shukri al-Braik [entrepreneur]. He reckoned Shukri's oil and gas interests brought him in £200 million a year. Chat was all about big money, e.g. buying football clubs, private jets (PJs) though Stuart's promise of one had been bullshit.

Then out to the match by car. The usual UEFA over-complication so we ended up walking miles round the ground before getting to the right entrance. Stadium impressive if a lot smaller than Wembley, and United seemed to outnumber Barca a bit. Real sense of scale when you saw the hundreds of snappers being shepherded around. United started well, and for the first few minutes were on top. Then [Nemanja] Vidić let in [Samuel] Eto'o and that was it. [Patrice] Evra gave the ball away for the second goal. We left before the trophy presentation to get away. In fact, we were trapped on the bridge as thousands of United fans did likewise. Still getting people saying well done re Burnley. Very funny scenes of street traders selling beer in defiance of the alcohol ban, running in groups every time the cops came by. Off to the hotel then ran into Nancy and Bob [Geldof], dining separately, at the same restaurant. Nancy all over me. Stuart's eyes popping. Bob with a load of Chelsea pals. Amazing how quickly the feel that there had been a big game on evaporated. A bit of horn-blowing but that was pretty much it. No real atmosphere. Nancy pushing to see TB. Texted him and he agreed. Did a piece for Friday's *La Repubblica* on how Alex would react to defeat plus a blog for tomorrow briefly dealing with the match then drawing the contrast with the ample evidence in Italy that there was an election campaign on. Posters everywhere. Our politics totally defined by expenses now and nobody challenging properly. Bed around two. Text message from GB saying well done compering the victory parade!

Thursday 28 May

Out for a run, down by the Coliseum and round by the Senate. Lovely warm morning. The city had been pretty well cleaned up, scaffolding coming down, barely any evidence of Man U or Barca. Caught the English papers on a newsstand. All very down on the team. Alex will be gutted. Texted but didn't call. Breakfast with Stuart and Shukri who were working on whatever deal they were doing, then to a shopping centre near the airport they were thinking of buying. Bumped into Jason, Mark and then Darren [AF's sons] at the airport. All said AF was OK but the whole team would be feeling down over the summer. On the plane I was next to a nice chap from Vodafone. Interesting take on expenses – he thought it was going too far now. Nobody good would want to go into politics if it carried on like this. Rory had been pissed off to miss our game and United's because of exams but in a way it was easier now because they so did not deserve to win. He didn't really want to talk about it – back focused on the revising.

Friday 29 May

Interesting email from Elvis impersonator Mark Wright who suggested MPs publish diaries for last four years alongside their expenses. Not sure it would work but I used it as the peg for a blog on the need to stand up for politics. The problem now was that GB, Cameron and Clegg were all vying with each other to see who could shout loudest on constitutional reforms whereas actually it needed someone to show some leadership for politics and politicians. Geldof was right about how TB would have handled this. A growing and worrying sense not just that we would lose but that we were finished as a political force. Out with Grace. Sort of shopping but bought nothing. Nice just spending a bit of time with her. Really enjoying the bike at the moment but it was just too hot for May, surely.

Saturday 30 May

GB called as I was reading the papers. The usual football small talk, then a sort of political discussion. He said he was struggling. He felt he had a plan and a strategy but it was impossible to penetrate the wall of noise on expenses. 'Some of what's gone on is indefensible… Fraud.' Fiona was in the kitchen, mouthing 'Tell him he has to go', while I was trying to avoid saying anything. Do you have any thoughts, he asked. I said there had to be found a way of getting above it. But how, he said? I was conscious of saying nothing much. I wanted to tell him what I really thought – that he had had it and a lot of it was down to certain realities coming to horrible fruition. But it was easier said than done. His confidence must be close to rock bottom and I did not really want to make it worse. But he was still playing the blame game 'I had no idea … People should have told me…' He said he would like me to go in 'and discuss what I might do for him'. I could not have sounded less keen.

I said I was tied up most of the week but free part of Tuesday. Come in Tuesday, he said, obviously I would like you to think of doing the things we've talked about before, but if not, we need to work something out. A few weeks without contact and I had felt better within myself, despite the horror of watching the whole thing implode. He had a way of taking me down with him. As he spoke, I longed for the call to end. When it did, I wanted to find ways of getting out of the whole thing. Fiona said you have to tell him. He has to go. Someone has to tell him. But it would only have impact with him if it was done publicly and then I just become another voice crying in the wilderness. Truth is that someone else probably would be better but it was not absolutely clear. There really was something tragic about these calls though. Almost pleading, yet I felt unable to give what he thought I could. I went out for a long bike ride in searing heat.

Sunday 31 May

I called Alan Johnson to get a sense of whether he was up for making a move against GB. Even accepting that he might be a little coy, my sense was he had no such intentions. He was giving all the reasons against – GB was the best man for the economy, he had been very good to him, and most telling of all in a way 'I don't want to be Leader of the Opposition.' There was definitely a feeling that he was the only one who might be able to change things, start to turn them around. Michael Portillo had a big piece to that effect in the *Sunday Times*, which led on a story, unclearly sourced, that GB wanted Balls as Chancellor. The sense of *Titanic* and deckchairs would be strong. GB was showing no leadership on expenses. Worse, he thought he was. Alan said it was because people knew health was doing OK, plus he had come up smelling of Chanel on expenses, that had led to the fresh bout of speculation on him, added to which his call for proportional representation had put him in a camp marked reform.

We had a very nice chat, in which he admitted things were dire but he did not see himself as the solution. I texted TB to ask if he thought it was time to tell GB the truth. He was at home – up before the FAC on MEPP tomorrow – and we ended up having a long chat. He felt it was not time to push him out because it would mean an election whatever happened and it would be a wipeout in the current situation. He said the whole thing was horribly predictable. We had kidded ourselves that he might grow into the job but actually his weaknesses had come to the fore as much as his strengths. When TB had said it was time to start defending MPs and politics, he might as well have been talking a different language. GB just said the media were in full cry. TB said it may be his prejudice, and he knew it was mine, but we had ceded power to the media and GB had ceded more. It made for dreadful governance. Cameron was not great. But he didn't need to be. It was almost visceral what people felt about GB. McBride had been a bit of a turning point because it drained moral authority from GB. But the big one was the fifty pence top rate. That gave them all an excuse to turn, those who had not already. It was bad economics and bad politics and what did he gain from it?

He had talked to Peter M yesterday but felt he was confused really. On the one hand he said GB was continuing to take two strands of strategic advice. On the other he was saying Balls might be better as Chancellor. There was a big inconsistency there. He felt Johnson might be better in the short term but frankly he was not a Prime Minister, not least because he didn't want to be. And though DC was not great, he did not have to be. There was such a desire for change and he could give it. As for me he said he felt I should avoid getting dragged into doing anything I really didn't want to. We knew he was not up to it and just had to help as we could without getting sucked in. You could give all the advice in the world but certain fundamentals were not going to change. Fabulous response to the blog. On Facebook the biggest yet so decided to do another whack at the BNP for the morning. I finally settled down, after a fabulous bike ride out to Potters Bar and back, with a nice cooked breakfast in Chipping Barnet, to *Maya*. Quickly whizzing through to try to deepen and enrich in certain parts.

Monday 1 June

The block on *Maya* had lifted and I was up at 6 to do another fifty pages on the edit. GB had done Marr yesterday and was doing the rounds again today. He said on *GMTV* he had made inquiries about Susan Boyle of Cowell and Morgan.* He was the PM for God's sake. I used his anti-BNP letter on the blog but it was hard to be supportive. Also apparently on *Today* he put me and Peter in the same bracket as McBride re controversial spin doctors or whatever. I set off for Stratford to meet Godric [Smith, director of communications] and a press officer, Ben, for a tour of the Olympic Park. Fabulous to see it coming together. Recalled (first for GS, later for a blog) the process of decision-making, how it was all a bit 'yes but/no but' until Team GB's letters came in urging TB to go for it. The stadium was looking great. Felt great. Went for a salad on the lawns by Canary Wharf with Godric. He felt GB was finished. It was worse than Major. A lot of people liked Major even if they didn't rate him. They neither like nor rate GB.

The Susan Boyle newspaper billboards – GB calls re her health in the Priory – the latest. He felt strongly that I should avoid going in there. Maybe the time to tell him the truth. PG felt the same. TB though felt if he was going to go in the autumn that might be better. Alistair D was in trouble. Albeit small sums he had fucked up on expenses and was having to pay back a few hundred quid. The sight of all these MPs being caught out on minor oversights and major fiddles was dire. Great to see Godric

* Singer Susan Boyle had been beaten into second place on the TV show *Britain's Got Talent*, on which Simon Cowell and Piers Morgan were judges. She had subsequently been admitted to a clinic, suffering from exhaustion.

who clearly loved his job which was better paid and less stressful than what he did before. God it was hot at the moment.

Tuesday 2 June

Another hot day. I did an hour on the bike then worked on the speech for tomorrow. The GB situation was building up media-wise. Also it was now rare to find anyone who had a good word to say for him. Into Soho to meet Deborah Van Bishop from BBC NW on doing a half-hour documentary on Burnley. I was not sure whether the film was going to be worth the hassle. Could be another project I was driven to by others, not strategic, but I guess it would be kind of fun. We talked over key moments and key people though of course it was going to be tricky getting decent match footage as Sky were so possessive. Anyway, she went off to draw up an outline plan. Then to the Gay Hussar for lunch with Sylvia Sheridan [businesswoman]. The place had not really changed. A very loud Nick Cohen lunching with Francis Wheen. Bill Hagerty in there too. My session with Sylvia was mainly listening to her. Down on politics but still wanting to help the party. She was very down on GB but that seemed to be near universal at the moment. She felt so much of the problem was lack of leadership. Even the expenses situation could have been dealt with if there had been leadership. Hated Balls. Felt the idea of him as Chancellor was madness. Wanted some of the older big beasts like Blunkett back in there. I sort of tried to persuade her to buy a table next Thursday but I was losing the will day by day.

GB had been due to call me in today but he didn't, doubtless because he was dealing with the fallout from Jacqui Smith announcing her departure [as Home Secretary], and I was just relieved. Met up with Tom Baldwin who was over from Washington ahead of coming back permanently as chief reporter [of *The Times*]. Nice enough chat but again he was looking to me to explain what was happening at the centre and I couldn't and wouldn't. I wanted out of it all really. The daily blog was becoming a bit difficult too because I could only go on so long without it being so obvious I was avoiding the subject. In to the FCO later for a little reception in DM's office for the Great Run [road running] series. Brendan [Foster] full of common sense as ever. He felt GB was finished. People had seen enough of him. Most didn't rate him. Those that did didn't like him. He was not going to recover. DM felt pretty much the same, said Cabinets recently were weird as people did not really say anything, and just avoided the subject.

He asked if I thought Alan J would do better, which I took as an indication he was not thinking about it himself. I said probably but you can't be sure. If a successor was forced straight to an election we would still have all the expenses stuff hanging around and this horrible anti-politics feel, and it would be a meltdown. But the other danger was we just limped on and GB dragged us ever further down. He said he veered to that view. Meanwhile news came through that Ed [Miliband] and Justine had had their baby so that cheered him up a bit, but my God the mood was grim. Dick Caborn there, saying we just had to tough it out. I feared we were past that. We could be talking total wipeout without substantial change. And the truth was a lot of this was happening pre-expenses. Clearly he would use that as an excuse but it wasn't going to wash for long. Nice little speeches and vids re the run and its growth around the world.

Wednesday 3 June

Lots of calls on *The Guardian* calling on GB to go. The media really had become the opposition even more than in our day. Early train to Hull and did blog on how *The Guardian* was all about attention-seeking in an era where impact was all that counted in journalism. To be fair they did a biggish number on Cameron's loony friends in Europe but it was small beer compared with expenses and the sense of crisis surrounding GB, about to get worse with Hazel Blears suddenly announcing she was resigning [as Secretary of State for Communities and Local Government]. I had no idea until doing interviews after my mental health speech to Hull Business Week. Good event and in the Q&A every question was about mental health. Did half a dozen interviews which were also mainly about mental health with a bit of GB thrown in. Really good do and I felt I was on form re the issues, stigma and discrimination, my own story etc.

Alan Johnson's agent Kath Lavery was chairing it and was very down about the political scene up there. Yet Hull felt so much better the little bit I saw. Problem was people had stopped listening. It felt like the political class was capitulating all over the place. Did a book signing, photos, more mental health interviews then got the train home via Doncaster. Hazel's resignation had set off another day of frenzy. Ignored calls and emails from all the main broadcasters. Amusing interlude when Janet Street-Porter [journalist, broadcaster] got on and had a row about having the wrong ticket. Ended up calling the ticket man a jobsworth but he held his own.

JP was back from a Council of Europe trip and wanted to meet up. We were chatting through various scenarios and concluding GB probably ought to go. He felt everyone had really tried to give him the benefit of the doubt but it had not worked. Far better to get the pain of working out a future leader and future direction now rather than waste the first two years in opposition while the party tore itself to bits. I said I had come to pretty much the same view but the question was how you did it without some kind of buy-in from him for a transition. If he just dug in it would be hard to push him out. JP felt that if there were a real head of steam he would have to go. He was also appalled at the lack of a campaign in there. He wanted to do a piece criticising Harriet Harman, Douglas A, Hazel and Caroline Flint [Minister for Europe] who should have had a proper campaign. He had asked Harriet for the strategy and she back came with a postcard-worth of old dividing lines.

He was pretty scathing about them all but deep down felt GB just did not have the leadership skills needed to bring people together and govern and campaign. He was intending to see him and say that he could not support him unless there was real change. We had a good chat but it was pretty depressing in that we both basically felt the game was up. He was not sure Alan J had it in him, will-wise or ability-wise, but agreed he was the only one currently on the scene who might be able to make a difference. With Hazel quitting it was meltdown time on the later news. Hard to imagine a worse backdrop to the elections tomorrow though in a way it would help GB because it would add to the list of outside-factor excuses they could trot out. I went to bed pretty down about things. Torn between the desire to do something to help and the desire to turn my back on the whole thing.

Thursday 4 June

I did a blog on the trip to Hull, the fact that people there were saying we had effectively saved the NHS and how that was more important than moats and the other expenses scandals for which we were going to get battered. Fiona was running the committee rooms out of the kitchen and there was a steady coming and going of people helping do polling station work and knocking up. But it was hard work. One new member though. I was pottering upstairs and had the idea of a French TV show. I was not that keen to get even more high-profile in the UK, but felt my French was just about good enough, also that their media was more serious. Started to put out a few feelers. I was certain we would want to spend a lot more time abroad if the Tories got back. Conference call re the Sedgefield mental health event next week.

Finally finished *Maya* rewrite. Out for an early dinner with Grace before watching the BBC documentary on the *Calendar Girls* which was really helpful in advance of the [charity] event next week.* The new calendars were selling well. Then at 10 p.m., as the polls closed, a genuine political shock – James Purnell had resigned via *The Times*, *The Sun* and *The Guardian*. They carried his letter to GB saying he made a Tory government more

* A group of Yorkshire Women's Institute members who produced a calendar with nude photographs of themselves to raise money for leukaemia research.

not less likely. Then Graham Allen and Barry Sheerman [MPs] were on echoing the call. It looked like the beginnings of something concerted. GB had Ken [Livingstone] defending him on *Newsnight* – not sure if it helped or hindered but it was one of those rare nights when you went to sleep really not knowing what might happen in the morning. I had seen no evidence that GB was thinking of throwing in the towel but perhaps if this was the beginning of something, who knows?

Friday 5 June

The election results were if anything worse than expected. But in a way James, unless others were coming out against GB, had cemented him in because the others were going to have to come out and profess their support. They were also able to criticise Hazel and James for the manner of their departures, Hazel for the silly 'Rocking the boat' brooch she wore, James for doing it via the papers. I texted TB, Peter M, DM and PG saying 'What now?' Peter said 'A wounded leader fights on.' He called and asked what I thought. I said I felt GB was simply not going to be elected PM and the longer this went on, the more weakened he became. That being said, I realised if he went there would have to be a hasty leadership election followed by a general election in which we would be wiped out. But he really could not go on like this. Peter was adamant the centre was getting better, that GB really was taking on board some of the things we had been saying. I was not convinced.

I said he (PM) held the key in many ways. Publicly and privately he was seen as really significant and that gave him a power he did not have before. He needed to work out how best to use it. For what it is worth, I said, that probably means working out how best he can leave, in as dignified a way as is possible, and let someone else – probably Alan J – take over with as much time as possible before an election. And even with that we would probably lose. We were having quite a serious chat before he cut off hastily, saying GB was on the line. TB said things kept coming back to the basic problem – he is not and cannot be a leader. In a way it was all so predictable. He had made strategic and policy errors at every turn. The Keynesian stuff had been fine but limited. He had not widened his circle, Peter M notwithstanding. And he just could not communicate in the way that was required. None of these things were going to change. Yet he agreed with me that it was hard to turf him out now without his consent and without an immediate election. He was in no doubt something would give but agreed James, without any follow-up from others, had shored him up.

Peter had been key last night, calling round those who might be tempted to follow James to say it would mean an immediate election. DM called, sounded a bit shell-shocked. He was worrying far too much about the papers saying he was a coward for not going for it. He had to think about whether it was the right thing to do, and if not what was his argument? I felt the only excuse he could give was that all the 'what then?' questions were not thought through. He grabbed for it, which was a sign he was a bit desperate, I felt. I sensed he was feeling like he ought to seize the moment but finding the reasons not to. He said it was obvious what had to happen but it was not clear how to bring it about.

The local election results were now unfolding alongside a reshuffle. Alan J to Home. DM out supporting GB. John Hutton announced he was going but he was out quickly defending and supporting GB. I found myself watching 24-hour news for the first time in yonks, and pretty gruesome it was too. They really smelled blood now, but I kept thinking if he did not want to co-operate with a departure plan, he did not have to. His immediate test was to get a Cabinet together which he managed. He would get panned for putting Alan Sugar [businessman, media personality] in the Lords as an enterprise tsar! We ended up losing every council we fought. MPs really were going to hit the panic buttons now. Tessa back in Cabinet [as Cabinet Office Minister]. David Mills came round for a cup of tea while I was watching it all unfold and I said I thought she should have resigned.

There was now too big a gap between what people were saying privately and publicly. That included GB too. There was a contempt for him among some of the media at the press conference later. When he denied he had wanted to replace Alistair D with Balls, for example, they all knew that was not the case. His efforts at banter were dire. He did OK on forward big picture but there was a sense of someone hanging on to a job nobody thought they could do. It was a nightmare knowing what to blog about these days. I had got myself locked into doing something every day and it was getting commented upon even that I was getting later in the day before posting. I thought the whole point was do it when you felt like it. Did one echoing some of JP's criticisms of the non-campaign, which were put to Harriet in various interviews. They went on about how they had been out around the country but the truth there really had not been a campaign worth the name. Calum home after his exams. He had very good judgement about people and about mood. He had always said GB not a leader. He also felt there was nobody to step up. All so depressing.

Saturday 6 June

The papers were a bit of a warzone for GB. There was an over-the-topness to the coverage but it was not clear he could get his head above this. The Sugar appointment was slammed. Also some lack of clarity about

Glenys Kinnock's appointment as Europe Minister which GB had had to admit in his press conference he had been forced into because Caroline Flint – now on a bit of a media rampage – had refused the same job. He had calmed things a bit and at least now could head off to the D-Day landings commemoration in Normandy. But even that had been fucked up with the row about whether the Queen was going or not, and he was the only man capable of making Prince Charles, seated alongside him, look more tortured. Also to have Obama there looking great, calm and relaxed, cannot have helped.

He spoke OK but got booed by a small group of veterans, and also said Obama when he meant Omaha. Tired, stressed. I didn't have a clue what to blog about. I wanted deep down to say he had blown it and could not defend these results and should make way for someone who could rebuild. But that was a shot to be fired only once. Mark came to the rescue with the tale of how they won their by-election in Lambeth. I was intending to start pushing the need for more activism and local campaigning. I had no desire for it myself. Out for a long run in the rain, first for months, and really enjoyed it, but felt it after.

Sunday 7 June

Feeling really depressed about the political scene. Did a blog on how the frenzy may have been so frenzied on Friday that today's European election results will not be so dramatic. But it felt dire. There was a contempt in the papers that I think went beyond anything we had endured. Also, not sure to me how much of it was real and how much media hype. Today did not feel good. Set off with Audrey, Grace and Molly for Oxford to meet Fiona, who had been at a meeting, Rory and Zoe. Rory had had one bad exam but felt he was in good shape. Just two to go. Took Audrey to show her his room then had a wander round town. Rory and I went to Caffè Nero and were just chatting when a customer came over and asked me to sign a page on which he had carefully written out 'I was Tony Blair's pornographer-in-chief.' Declined. Out for lunch, nice enough time and good for Rory to have a little break. But every time I thought of politics, I just sank a little more. I said to Jamie [Naish, nephew] in places like this I always reckon I can pick out how people might vote and I would say we were in two in ten if we were lucky zone. Wish I had a pound for every interview bid I ignored.

Several mentions on Twitter and FB of Peter M's interview on Marr. He really had developed such a better manner. Pushed back well, said what he wanted to say. Did not let Marr boss the course of the interview. Watched the election results come in. Worse than expected and the expectations were about as low as they could be. Chat with Peter. I repeated that the best place to get to was an agreed transition. GB just was not liked and it was not going to change. Other parties of government were doing OK – France, Italy, Germany, Poland. The centre-left getting hit. But we were wiped out in parts. Behind the Tories in Wales. Way behind the Nats in Scotland. Behind UKIP overall. And two seats to the BNP. Horrific. In a way a lot of the sting was taken out in advance by the reshuffle and the chaos of Friday but this was just too dire for words. He could not stay in these circumstances. Equally he would not go.

Monday 8 June

I slept badly, and woke up feeling sick. The BNP wins were really revolting. Also their vote in numbers terms actually fell. It was the collapse in our vote, particularly abstentions, that won for them. I sent round another round of 'what now?' texts. Peter said we rally round the leader and tell MPs calling for him to go we will wipe out what little support we still have if this goes on. Lots of coverage for his Marr *Show* 'masterclass' but mixed in with Charlie saying he had to go. Fiona adamant now I must not support GB let alone help any more. But I still did not feel I should say he should go. This required a bit more thought. PM was keeping his cards close to his chest but he did not push back too hard when I said the ground had to be slowly prepared for as dignified an exit as could be planned.

TB was in Norway. We had a long chat. He felt it was now totally unsustainable but could not be rushed. The sense had to build, without any of the key figures being seen to push it, that there would be a space opening up later in the year if there was no real and lasting improvement. He felt very strongly there wouldn't be. He was being found out. He just could not lead. He should have been more rigorous on the economy, more inclusive, warmer about the past and the record and he should have stood up for MPs, not allowed them to swing. There was no fightback apart from rallying round and saying he would see it through. It was all about strategic direction and it was not there. He felt there was an outside chance GB would see it, but accepted there really was no dignified way of going out when it was being made so clear it had been a failure.

Had a similar conversation with Neil, who saw that he was not cutting it but of course it was more complicated for him now that Glenys was in there as a minister. Neil started out by saying the MPs trying to force him out were bovine and politically braindead. I agreed but only up to a point. I said he had to go before an election. People kept saying things could not get worse but they could. There was a visceral desire to kick him out. He said where did it come from? I said we were all guilty of trying to say there were simple obvious truths when in fact the reasons for votes and swinging votes in particular were complex. But I felt there was something in his character that made for a dysfunctional centre and people sensed it. They also felt he was now reaping the whirlwind of the kind of nasty politics that got him there. He said we both had access and when we used it we were probably saying much the same thing, hearing him agree and then not change much. Agreed to get together in the coming days not least to advise Glenys on how she handled her position in coming weeks.

David M called after I texted him. He said he felt there were a few who could be mustered for a final blow but if a word got out it would be crushed. He did not want to say who but he wanted me to work out when best to do it. Pre-conference? Pre-pre-conference? After? My instinct said limp on a bit and eventually go to him and say he had to maybe announce at conference he was going, followed by a contest, followed maybe by spring election. Text from David S saying 'Are you OK amid the chaos?' I said it was depressing but was trying as best I could to stay out. Good, he said. Blog on how BNP actually lost votes so the question was could we turn anger into activism and get the stayaways out to vote. The PLP turned out fine for GB but it could not go on like this. The media quickly took the line that the crisis was over but there was a danger that the public would just think it showed us being more and more out of touch.

Tuesday 9 June

There was definitely that 'post-crisis' feeling around the place, and GB was through it for now. The calls from the ministers were slowing again, and I suppose now they were going to have to live with what they had. David M called. He said he was getting hit in the press for being a coward, and maybe they should have gone for it but the truth was that meant immediate election and wipeout. He said there were people who were ready to make a push in the autumn and that might be the best thing now. Deep down, I don't think there were many people who thought we could win. 6 p.m. train to Darlington for the mental health conference tomorrow. Met by a nice psychiatrist called Lenny Cornwall who drove me to the hotel. Stood as Labour councillor in unwinnable ward. Too late for dinner. Went to the gym and then bed.

Wednesday 10 June

News leading on financial pressures on the NHS. Quick blog on the need to protect mental health services. To Hardwick Hall [Sedgefield] for the event. More local media. Then the speech. Lenny's presentation included a really interesting 'disease prestige' league table which had heart attacks, leukaemia, spleen rupture at the top, and the mental illnesses at the bottom. Did a very personal and pretty powerful speech I think – not easy in a roomful of shrinks – and the Q&A was good. Lively and a sense of them saying they got something from it too. Quite a lot of anti-media feeling. My train got back in just as Mum's arrived from Retford, home briefly, then out to the Noël Coward Theatre for the night with the Calendar Girls. Did a little speech at the *Good Housekeeping* reception in the upper circle, a few words on Lindsay and Ellie and childhood leukaemia death rates, then out on stage with the original Calendar Girls.

Did a really good Q&A, Angela Baker on general story, Trish Stewart on original idea, Lynda Logan hilarious about Prince Charles writing to her, Chris Clancy on her nerves at nudity, Beryl Bamforth on being the oldest. Elaine C. Smith, one of the actresses in the play, said they were watching backstage and felt 'How do we follow that? They are hilarious.' Something really nice and authentic about them all, very different characters, strong but also individual, worked as a team. The play itself was great, a mix of funny and sad. I watched it sitting next to Lindsay and it was emotional when the husband – John – died, and when the stage filled with sunflowers at the end. Really good show. After party, chatted to a mix of the real CGs and the actresses, then we struggled home through the melee caused by the Tube strike.

Thursday 11 June

Out early for a trip to Psychiatric Intensive Care Unit in Liverpool and a speech to the National Health Confederation, bumped into Alan Cochrane [Scottish political journalist] at Euston, chat re Scottish politics. He said the BBC was getting [late leader of North Korea] Kim Il-sung-like in its coverage of Salmond, who was getting more and more bumptious. Worked on the speech for NH Confederation on the train. Met by a bloody huge Chrysler, watched by a queue of people getting into taxis. The driver told me Ronaldo had gone to Real Madrid. At last. Arrived at Rathbone Hospital and taken by Nick, the big bald guy who led the team, and Anne Evans, the service user who had asked me to go, into the PICU (psychiatric intensive care unit). Great facility. Designed in part with the help of service users.

Quite a few people turned out to show me around. Held up to eight people. Four at the moment. One bipolar, who wanted to take a picture with me and the Liverpool team, rushing around everywhere. Another speaking in tongues, really disturbed. Nurses fantastic. Incredible system for drug management. Fantastic advances. Why was there never any recognition of progress in the NHS politically? Lots of signed messages and letters from stars around the place. Average stay around eight weeks. Fantastic co-operation with service users and carers, down to the design of the windows by patients explaining what they mainly threw at them – TVs. Had lunch and another chat with the team, then off to the Arena. Pretty humbling to see the work these guys did. Like the team of nurses walking with the lad speaking in tongues.

Steve Shrubb and Lisa Rodrigues from Mental Health Network met me. Good people. Said Andrew Lansley [shadow Health Secretary] went down badly yesterday. Burnham OK today but nervous. Several hundred at conference, and I was on form. A few scribbled notes, just wandered round the main points – challenged the NHS to sign up more to Time to Change – only 12 per cent of the different parts had done so. Read out blog comment re NHS as employer. Did my usual stuff then a reading, then Q&A moderated by Sarah Montague [broadcaster]. She wanted to do a mix of health and politics. Audience really liked it when I laid into the way the media covered politics and public life. Had a whack at Cameron for slapping down Nadine Dorries [Tory MP] over her remark that the expenses scandal would lead to a suicide. Really good reception plus they were all getting free copies of the novel.

Off to Lime Street then home, doing bits and bobs. Picked up by Rayan with Mum and Audrey to go to Stamford Bridge for the party fundraiser. All a bit depressing not least because they had not really shifted the tables like they had hoped to. Pretty well organised but felt flat. Also lots of non-paying ticket holders. Went to the home dressing room for the VIP bit. Had a chat with Alan Johnson who was definitely not up for a challenge. When we talked about the record and how to defend it he seemed shocked when I made suggestions about how they might take things on. The whole evening I had the sense of the fight having gone out of people. There was not the same energy as before. GB came over to the VIP reception and we had a bit of a chat with Eddie Izzard. Neil and Glenys were at our table, with PG and Georgia, Lawrie McMenemy [ex-football manager] and his very nice Geordie wife. Glenys saying she still had not talked to Peter M.

PM was very much the one people seemed to want to see and Carol Linforth was taking him round tables. I had a little chat with him but it was all a bit networky. Tanni Grey-Thompson introduced GB who overdid the self-deprecation a bit. Quite good after that though. Said there were four pre-conditions for winning which had not been in place – economy in right shape, politics in right shape, choice with the Tories, policy debate. He said he was confident we could have all that in place for the General. Went down OK. Mum said it was the best she had ever heard him. Did a tweet on that which got a pretty big response. Richard Darlington and another spad came to lobby me re going back. They said things had actually got worse in terms of direction and co-ordination. I explained why I was not going back. I also said their own ministers had to do more and start to seize some of the space. They looked a pretty tired lot. Virtually all the non-politicians were saying we had no chance.

I was glad to have taken Mum and Aud but the combination of the whole thing feeling a bit flat, and the constant badgerings of people saying I had to do something made me glad to get away at around 11. Mum really enjoyed it. Calum felt the mood was just really poor and so few of the politicians had any oomph or presence. Also Eddie Izzard's speech was a bit odd. Really short after a long intro.

Friday 12 June

Texted TB to ask if he was going to the 'zoo' that Rebekah Wade's wedding threatened to be. He called. 'I have found a very urgent need to do very urgent business in the Middle East.' Cherie was going but he was glad to be out of it. Didn't think GB should be going. Did not want to be in that media swirl even for half a day. On the general scene he said GB was pretty much 'eviscerating the party'. He felt that though Peter might be in charge of presentation, policy was the problem and that would be Balls getting GB to play to his worst instincts. He felt that the Budget had been a turning point. That GB had ceded too much post-expenses. It was ludicrous to turn it into a big review of the constitution. He felt there was probably no coming back now, that it was too late. He still felt we would be better with someone else but hard to be sure. Blogged on Liverpool and last night, with GB's four key points.

Nice hot day, F's hay fever really bad. We set off for Althorp, [Earl] Charles Spencer [brother of the late Princess of Wales] having asked me to kick off the book festival he ran, and got there just before dinner. A drive lasting a few minutes to get from the gates to the house. Met by the housekeeper and shown to the King William room. He had slept there in the seventeenth century. Huge family portraits everywhere. Big four-poster bed. Huge shuttered windows. An old-fashioned toilet seat, literally a seat. En suite bath – literally just the bath in a cupboard. Dinner was a barbecue, including game, local and organic said the very friendly chef, which was delicious. Charles Spencer a very diligent host, moving around between little groups chatting.

We had a long chat with his latest girlfriend, a young widow called Bianca. She was from Cornwall, so we chatted away about the West Country. Artist Robert Lenkiewicz her stepfather. Very pretty. Three young kids. Charles seemingly a real ladies' man. Michael Dobbs [writer and

Conservative politician], who had put on loads of weight since the last time I saw him. Working on a play about Denis Thatcher. Stanley Johnson who was very witty and extraordinarily like Boris [son] to look at and to hear. We pushed him a bit re Boris's view of DC. No love lost I would say. Fiona asked him if Boris wanted to be leader. Oh yes! Tell me anyone in politics who doesn't? Then discussed whether it was possible to do without being in the Commons, which led to a discussion about whether Peter could be PM. Good chat with Bernard Cornwell and his American wife Judy. He had done fifty-one novels! Extraordinary. Very clever guy. Brit turned US citizen, an Obama-voting Republican. Quizzing me on what I wanted to do with the rest of my life. Clearly thought I should be back in there. 'You don't want to be a novelist, believe me.'

Saturday 13 June

The shutters in the bedroom were so tight I kept waking up, thinking it was the middle of the night, worrying about lack of sleep. It was only when I went for a pee and saw there was sunlight coming through the roof that I realised we had slept in. I had been hoping for a run through the estate, but there was only a bit of time for breakfast before my session. Fiona McMorrough told me my event had sold out first, and there was a big crowd waiting when I arrived. Did a gentle interview then Q&A. All pretty straightforward, mixing book creativity and politics. All OK. Enlivened by Stanley J getting up to ask what was vaguely intended as a hostile question but it wasn't really and in any event I was able to make a big thing about who he was and how his question was so vague I could pick and choose which parts to answer. Otherwise all the usual really. Very white middle-class middle-aged audience, as most of these festivals are, but enjoyed it OK.

Did a signing, when one woman, who had seemed very friendly during the event, came up and just said 'One word to you – David Kelly.' I said that was two words. OK, she said, conscience. Let it be on yours. I said have a nice day and carried on signing. Did a few photos and a chat with the local paper, then went to see Fiona at her session before we went for a walk to see the island in the lake where Diana was buried. Nice peaceful scene. Only family and Nelson Mandela had actually been to the burial site, but there was a memorial with a silhouette and a quote from her about her work for others, and a quote from Charles from the funeral speech. Lunch chatting to Bernard Cornwell's wife, then him. He was keen to keep in touch. Very interested in politics. Pro-TB. His next book, he said, had fifty-four members of one Scottish regiment and thirty-seven were called Campbell.

We set off cross-country for Chipping Norton for Rebekah Wade's wedding. TB had decided he was urgently needed in the Middle East. I called him and said if he could get out of it, so could I. Too late, he said, only one of us could pull out without it appearing rude. Both GB and Cameron were due to go. I thought it was sad and a bit pathetic that the party leaders felt they had to go. Nobody could pretend this was friendship; it was bowing down before Rupert. At least TB had the balls to say fuck it even if in fact he wasn't really and CB was still going. He said to me that Cherie had been 'ridiculously nice' about me at some event she did but there was little evidence of it when she saw me. Cut me dead, didn't seek out Fiona who was hating the whole thing even more than I was. The ceremony was by a lake at the foot of a hill on the Sarsden House estate which, DC told me at the reception, used to be owned by Shaun Woodward. We had gone from old establishment to new in one ninety-minute drive. We parked up for as long as we could to delay going down to the throng. Bumped into a snapper. 'Are you on duty official or just papping?' 'I thought I was invited but now I'm here apparently I'm not welcome.'

Murdoch and Wendi Deng [wife] down by the lake. Dacre talking to Jack Straw. I had a brief chat with Osborne who said 'Bad week for the Blairites.' I started to say there was no such thing any more, just Labour, but he rather cleverly cut me off at 'No such thing…' 'Exactly, they've had it. At least Purnell showed some balls.' Sought out Frank Warren for a chat, again asking me to a fight. PG and Gail. I didn't realise till I heard people congratulating her that she was in the honours today as a DBE! Asked PG if he was now Lord Dame. Said to me I was probably the least famous person there. Said he was quite looking forward to Cameron as PM because he would really go for him. As the ceremony began I was at the back with Piers Morgan so we did a bit of a running commentary. 'I thought Susan Boyle would be here to lead the singing.' 'Do you like her?' 'I love her – she is making me even more famous in America.'

The ceremony was under way, Rebekah in white, which set Piers off again, Charlie Brooks the groom barely visible behind a pillar. Then we heard the sound of heavy cars. Oh God, I said, GB arriving late and loud. He and Sarah appeared at the top of the hill. He clearly thought about staying there or even heading back. They walked slowly down about two thirds of the hill. Ten yards from DC. Neither said the Lord's prayer, I noticed. GB looked deathly pale and was chewing methodically. God, he looks terrible, said Fiona. Jeremy Clarkson, wearing a white suit, did the reading. It was one of those events where people were constantly scanning the audience. Not that many politicians. Lots of Murdoch people. Not many celebs. Lots of his friends I didn't know. There was a bit of milling around then we all headed to the house about a mile away. A fairground had been set up to add to the surreal nature of the day.

We parked up, walked over and the first person I met was Murdoch. Very friendly and chatty. He said on expenses that it would lead to permanent change and probably go too far. More down on GB than the last time I heard him speak. Still felt the Tories not up to much. Pretty warm on Obama though he said business was beginning to have concerns, though he felt at the moment he could do no wrong. 'As you know though – the higher you go the harder you fall, so maybe it will get rougher. For now, he's doing well.' Fiona and I were talking to Kirsty Young and Nick [Jones] her husband when DC came over. I asked him if he thought the general election was in the bag. No, he said, the swing we need is big and in electoral terms it is still a mountain. He said you guys achieved it when you didn't need to. We need to achieve the same sort of swing to win. Things can still go wrong. He said the expenses thing had reduced Parliament to a state of shock. These were people who had been minor celebs locally, never got much national attention and now they were going around being accused of being crooks. It was hard and lots more would decide to move on.

I said he appeared depressingly non-complacent. He asked if I was back in harness? No, he is not, Fiona chipped in. Good, he said. 'Keep him there. He is too good.' He seemed to have more presence than the last time I saw him. Also later, when the two of us were alone talking about the media – I had said if he won I would help him do something about them and he agreed things were getting worse not better – Murdoch and Gail came over to join us. 'What are you two cooking up?' asked RM. 'Just talking about the future of *The Independent*,' lied DC. I sensed he was not that keen to engage with RM. I wondered if in fact he might do something. We talked about spending and investment. At the NHS Confederation, Lansley had suggested 10 per cent cuts and GB had really gone for it on Wednesday at PMQs. I said I would be surprised not to see you come out with specific cuts and he said yes, they would. Osborne joined us and at one point RM said to DC 'When you're in power…' 'Did you say "When"?' I asked. 'Yes, I did.' DC said the deficit was now so huge it was impossible not to think in terms of cuts and he was clearly confident it could be a plus.

Murdoch said the cuts would have to go on for years. Dacre hovering. Straw as well. Fiona very chilly with him. Tessa and Jessie, James Harding and his very nice girlfriend Kate. Matthew F never far from RM's side. Long chat with Clarkson. He was so right-wing as to be off the scale, but it was easy to see why he was so popular, because he had a charm and sense of mischief that went with it. There were several hours between arrival at the reception and food, so Fiona and I decided to make a run for it at 7. Otherwise we would be there all night. Glad to get away. Home to get something to eat then I watched the incredibly moving BBC4 documentary on families of soldiers killed in Iraq and Afghanistan. Very moving, mixed too in terms of whether they thought the war was just and whether their loved ones died in vain. Brilliantly made and parts of it had me in tears, like the kids who pretended their dad was still there at their birthday parties.

Sunday 14 June

Bike ride then out with Rory and his mates to Lord's. Ireland v Sri Lanka then England v India. Whoever invented Twenty20 cricket was a genius. Both matches exciting, especially the second one. India fans easily outnumbering England's and at times the atmosphere was more like a football match. Sitting in the Mound stand next to an Indian caterer and restaurateur and then Tony Lit, the candidate for the Tories who got into bother because he had been photographed with TB at a Labour dinner. Seemed quite a nice guy. Rory drinking too much and almost got into a fight with a twat just in front of us. Good day out though. Doubt England will win this series, even though they won today.

Monday 15 June

I slept badly. I had been fretting on and off for a while about the Iraq Inquiry. It was partly not wanting to go through it all again but also I would have to immerse myself again too. Stewart Wood had told me at the Chelsea fundraiser that it would be announced early this week, maybe as early as today. He sent me the draft words yesterday and they seemed to me to be heading for the worst of all worlds – sessions in private but some could be in public. Stewart said GB felt he had to tip the hat in the direction of openness whilst protecting national security. It was classic fudge though, which would satisfy nobody. I said if he felt a private inquiry would do a better 'lessons learned' job, then better to defend that as a point of principle. I learned TB was making the same point via JoP. I asked Matthew Doyle if TB was intending to say anything. He said if it was a public inquiry – Clegg and some of the victims' families had been calling for that over the weekend – TB was under instruction to go on the attack and ask who ran the country, the government or the media. GB was changing the text to the last minute. To be fair he went for the hard line and held to it despite a lot of attack in the House.

I popped round to see PG who could tell I was nervous about the whole thing. I said the problem was at the time of all the other inquiries I was totally immersed in it all. I would have to re-immerse myself fully. He asked me what I really thought. I said I thought we did the right thing in the wrong way. Also that whilst TB genuinely believed in what he was doing, and we all thought the WMD threat was real, I had a nagging worry we had been dragged along by a bunch of right-wing Americans doing it for all sorts of reasons, not all good. He felt I had to get a position close to that for the inquiry. We agreed GB had been OK but he would get panned in the media. Peter M called a couple of times saying could I calm TB down. He said his latest emails were hysterical. Also spoke to JoP who said if it was public TB would go ballistic. It would basically be saying that it was being done for the media, not to learn lessons. I texted TB in Gaza to say he did fine but even in his reply I could sense he was pissed off. If they have to have one, fine, but if is going to be of any value it should not be a media-fest.

On the general scene PG felt it was all over. The moment may have passed to get rid of GB. He was not going to change. But everyone else had been so weak too so it was all pretty hopeless. Blogged on cricket, Iran – huge protests after apparent election rigging – and a brief line on Kim Howells's hilarious letter in *The Times* about the need for the Cabinet 'assisted places scheme' youngsters to put a sock in it. General feeling DM may have damaged himself fatally with his 'I almost resigned' interview in *The Guardian*. Called Kim and we had a good chat. He said everyone in the PLP would rejoice if I went back and sorted them out but they understood if I didn't do it. Trying to help Grace with her maths. Made a bit of progress but I would be a hopeless teacher.

Tuesday 16 June

Slept a bit better but not great. I had drafted a blog on the Iraq Inquiry and sent it to PG and F. Both felt I should not get into argument or detail. So instead I did another one on mental health, pegged to my giving evidence to the Speaker's panel [parliamentarians] in Parliament later this morning, with a couple of pars tagged on saying it was not a black and white call whether to have the inquiry as public or private. Surprisingly, *The Times* were saying there should be no inquiry. It was extraordinary though how these inquiries took on a life of their own, and unless they totally fitted with the hostile agenda, they got panned. I said to PG it was like with Hutton – when he was putting the government through its paces, and the media was feasting day after day on bad news for us, the judge was a man of unimpeachable integrity carrying out an important public inquiry with rigour. When he reached a judgment which their coverage had not led them to expect, and which certainly they didn't want, he was an old establishment fart who couldn't see the truth when it was staring him in the face.

So it would be again, that unless an inquiry reaches the judgment that critics of the government's Iraq policy want, it doesn't count. What was happening now was that the critics were getting their retaliation in first, criticising the scope, the length, the conditions and the membership of the inquiry. Nick Clegg started yesterday from a position that Iraq was Britain's biggest foreign policy failure since Suez. He has decided that. So have much of the media. It is a point of view, not a fact. It is also a point of view that allows little room to take account of the considerable progress made in Iraq in terms both of democracy and everyday life for many Iraqis. Considering recent elections in Iraq, the democracy point sits well alongside what is currently happening in Iran. I had been really touched by the BBC 4 documentary at the weekend which was based on interviews with the families of service personnel killed in Iraq and Afghanistan. It was their story, simply told, and it was TV at its best, with next to no commentary because none was needed.

Nick Clegg said yesterday he was speaking for the families. It is true that some of them are strongly opposed to the government action. Some are not. Some believe the government did the wrong thing. Some do not. Some believe their loved ones died in vain. Others do not. Equally, I suspect some would want an inquiry to be held in public, while some would not. The day-to-day media will be pretty universal in the condemnation of the government's decision to hold evidence sessions in private. But the inquiry has the task of establishing fact, examining many aspects of a complex situation, helping the government to learn lessons. It is not there just to feed the 24-hour news machine. Whether the inquiry was to be in private or in public is presented as a straightforward decision by those who think it should be in public. How can there be any argument against that? But it is not that straightforward, and I thought GB made arguments which at least deserve a proper hearing. This was going to be my fourth inquiry related to Iraq. Two were in public, one – the ISC [Intelligence and Security Committee] – in private. All three were testing, but this was the big one in a way. I wrote a blog on it all but Fiona and PG both said don't post it. They were probably right.

Cab in with Calum. Up to the café by the Boothroyd Room. When I thought of all the nerve-racking inquiries I had done this was pretty relaxed. Small crowd, maybe half the MPs there, a handful of journos, mainly sketchwriters. Chatted to Andrew Sparrow [*Guardian*] who said he liked my blog. He felt JP and I were the only ones on the left who got this new media world in the way a lot more people on the right did. Bumped into Julie Kirkbride [Tory MP to Bromsgrove]. She was looking great despite her recent problems on expenses.* She said she felt really hurt but what could she do? She had to move on and set up a new post-election life. She felt she had been done in because she was a woman making typical arrangements for kids. There was still a real men's club feel to politics. I said, and made the point in evidence, that I thought the political classes had been very poor in defending the good they do as the leaders vied for toughness. And DC had been wrong to slap down Nadine Dorries for saying she was worried someone would kill themselves.

I did my usual stuff. Tribute to Anne Begg [Labour MP] and David Blunkett but said they were not defined by their disabilities. It sent a powerful signal though. So it would if people with mental illness did the same. OK Q&A. Not sure there was much they would get out of it. Home, bike in lovely weather then potter around. A few bad comments on the blog re Iraq but mental health stuff well received.

Massive row with Fiona later after a teacher called to say Grace had not handed in some work. We blamed each other. I had to go out to a big LRF event at Somerset House. Did not feel up for it but it went really well. Current and potential supporters. I spoke about why I got involved, how good the charity was, then interviewed Patrick Doyle the composer, then Joe Smale [leukaemia survivor] and Prof. Ghulam Mufti, who was terrific on how progress in survival rates was down to LR. Nice event. Photos after. Geoff Thomes there too. Emma Watson, who was Henry Hodge's doctor and said he was in a really bad way. Michelle Lineker [mother of leukaemia-surviving son] who introduced me to a guy from Kinetic [branding agency] who made me think we should go for Sky as bikeathon sole sponsor. Really liked Michelle. Iran boiling over but the authorities were going to crush it by the looks of it.

Wednesday 17 June

Fiona and I still not on speaking terms so I hid away upstairs and worked on a new speech for the conference on post-conflict comms I was speaking at next week. Chatting to the Beeb about the Burnley film. Out later to the Oxo Tower for Murdoch's summer party. One of those anyone and everyone dos. Phil Webster and Danny Finkelstein. Phil saying he had never been busier and he could not remember things so bad politically. Chat with Matthew F who felt things were getting worse. Dawn Airey spitting

* Expenses irregularities involving two homes and the employment of her sister as her secretary at taxpayers' expense caused Kirkbride to announce that she would stand down at the next election. Her husband, fellow MP Andrew MacKay, resigned from his post as aide to David Cameron and also stood down as an MP.

tacks at the Four–Five decision [merger proposal cancelled]. Good chat with James Murdoch mainly about my new Wattbike. Took him the guide and he definitely wanted one. Trying to get him involved in the bikeathon.

Spent most of the time chatting with Dave Brailsford and Roger Draper [CEO, Lawn Tennis Association]. I think they were quite surprised at the way so many of the politicians came over and the very frank discussions we had. Like Charles Clarke, with son Matthew, telling me he thought I was a disgrace, that I was one of the few people who could bring GB down but I was helping the party walk headfirst into a train crash. He was very funny with it, pointing and jabbing and saying Charlie thought I was a disgrace too but then said to Matthew 'I love this man. He has brought me down and laid me low at times but he is a big and honest character and I love him.' He asked me if I had been helping GB in recent weeks. I said no, not in recent weeks. He said that is a very significant statement and I believe you because I think you, unlike Peter, are not a liar.

Peter was there, looking like the big panjandrum. I was chatting to Rebekah and Murdoch who when he saw Peter said 'Ah Prime Minister.' Slightly uncomfortable conversation with Richard Wilson [former Cabinet Secretary] trying to engage but both probably feeling we managed to rub along OK but did not have much in common. Next head of army [Chief of the General Staff], [General] Dave Richards, came up to make a point of saying how good TB was over Sierra Leone. General [Richard] Dannatt out today saying the Iraq Inquiry should be public. GB starting to wobble on it. JoP had said to TB that he would. Nice chat with Liz Murdoch re *Maya* and also the idea of me doing a French TV show. Florence Godfernaux pretty keen on the idea too. Ed less so.

Thursday 18 June

Blogged on the attacks on Romanian families in Belfast, then a whack at Ed Balls for his interview on *GMTV*, when he seemed to be distancing re the inquiry, saying his 'personal' view was for something more open and transparent and also saying we should have taken more time with Saddam.* Classic diddling. He was always first on the phone if anyone veered from the GB line on the economy, and recently leading calls for unity. Got a text from him within minutes of blog going up. He said he had been totally supportive of GB and did I want to see a transcript? I got it over. In fact, it confirmed my view. He was diddling on the inquiry and on the war. I didn't like attacking a member of the Cabinet but it was so blatant.

* More than 100 Romanian families were evacuated from their homes after being subjected to racist intimidation and violence from a group of 'racist thugs'.

Texts from JoP and TB that GB was beginning to back down over pressure. John Major and Robin Butler were going vocal, with Butler planning to go up in the Lords and say that it should be in public. It was ending up, as we said it would, with the worst of all worlds. Iran still going huge but the authorities were beginning to clamp down harder.

Dropped a line to John Sawers who had been announced as John Scarlett's successor [as chief of SIS]. Off to the Beeb at TV Centre with Rob Jones and his team from USP [production company] to do a pitch for the 606 [football radio show] contract at Five Live. OK bunch of guys in the team but I didn't like the middle management type plus the head of the station who were hearing us. I said I thought the show had become flabby, needed to be more focused and strategic with better talking points and planning. They asked some reasonably tough questions. I was moderately keen but would not be too bothered if it didn't happen. Rob thought they would ask me to do some whatever. I called Charlie F to tell him about Henry [Hodge] being ill. Ended up talking about Burnley, Kitty Ussher having been sacked [as junior Treasury minister] last night over her expenses claims re flipping. There had been a rash of calls and messages saying was I going to go for it. I was thinking about it, though probably would not go for it.

Charlie and I agreed to meet for lunch and I scribbled a list of pros and cons on the paper tablecloth at the Camden Brasserie. Main pros were mission and purpose, full-on existence again, chance to make a difference. Main cons were loss of freedom and variety, big hit on earnings, but more than that was the freedom point plus right back in the frontline. Charlie said there was also the pro that I could become leader of the party and PM. I stand and win the seat, but the party loses overall. Another leader takes over. Loses next time. I take over. Win in nine years' time. PM at sixty-one. I didn't share his view I could do it, but he was insistent. He said if you look at any of the people being touted as leader, you are a bigger figure. Most important, he said, you have leadership skills and those are what are lacking currently. He was off to Sunderland to do *Question Time*, the programme having gone through twenty-two ministers who said they couldn't do it. After they realised CF was on, No. 10 offered John Healey [Housing Minister], but CF decided to stick with it.

Got a call p.m. from Anna Hodge saying Henry had died. Really sad. All the memories of John dying came back. Sat there crying while writing a short tribute and an appeal for the blog. Later to the Commons – amazing how many of the coppers mentioned Burnley – for the Journalists' Charity event out on the terrace. I was doing it as a favour to Chris Boffey and Bill Hagerty [charity trustees], Q&A a 'cash for questions' with Robert Peston and Alan Duncan [Tory MP]. All the obvious questions

– expenses, and was the story overdone, on which I said yes. Duncan did a good defence of MPs and the need to halt the anger which had become hatred, and Peston said he quite liked MPs. On the Iraq Inquiry, I said that for some people it made no difference whether it was public or private – unless the government was found to have been wrong, there were some who would not accept it, just as they did not accept Hutton. I was conscious of becoming quite cantankerous, a combination of being back with the two worlds I was doing my best to leave behind. It was a mix of heavy and light-hearted with Duncan very funny. I had a proper chat with Peston, and found him more engaging than when he was at the *FT*. He said he had watched *Cracking Up* on my website and thought it was a really important film. Also thought I should do more telly.

Did a few photos then scarpered to meet F, the Macleods and the Bridges, at Marine Ices. Catherine said, as she always does, that she had no idea how I did the job for as long as I did in the way I did. She was full of stories of GB's erratic behaviour, not least vis-à-vis Alistair D. Everyone knew he wanted to get rid of him for Balls, which is why it was ludicrous of GB to claim otherwise. They had big arguments re the whole cuts v investment debate, with AD arguing – sensibly in my view – that we had to admit there would be cuts to some public service programmes. GB went off on one of his rages, spitting eggs and bacon at him so that AD said calm down and finish your breakfast and then we can discuss this. Catherine said I should only go for Burnley if I really wanted it and if it was a step to leadership. I should not do it out of duty, because I had done enough on that front. She was appalled at the way the No. 10 operation was run, said they still ran everything based on negative lines. She was worried that the public sense of GB and Labour being dishonest was now being compounded by the way the cuts investment argument played out.

Friday 19 June

I dashed off a quick blog re ideas from three readers – Jane Appleton suggesting I make an LRF tribute fund for Henry. Interesting comment from someone who kept trying to post positive comments about me on the *Mail* website on why the newspapers blocked anything that went against their line. And one from a woman asking me to help young people spin their CV, e.g. cleaner becomes hygiene officer etc. I guess it was another way for me to avoid the main political picture. I'd noticed that whenever I got on to charity and asking for money, the response was low.

I met Richard Darlington [Douglas Alexander advisor] and Polly Billington, Ed Miliband's spad, at Costa Coffee in Belsize Park. I was very frank. They were looking to me to go back to get a grip of the whole thing, but it had gone beyond. I said there had to be more leadership at every level, and if it was not coming from the very top, they had to get their own ministers to be more engaged. What did they do all day? They agreed there was a sense of ministers being busier and busier departmentally as a way of displacement on the politics. They said there was an assumption that at some point I would go back and Peter and I would run the show. But I was more clear than I had been for a while that I was better off out of it and that while I could make a difference I wasn't convinced it would be so fundamental as to change course. They were full of stories of how dysfunctional everything was – there had not been a spads' meeting since the third week of May. The spads were mainly without politics anyway. I said there was a limit to what they could do about GB, but they could change their own ministers.

They needed to shake them up. Douglas had to start shaping the campaign now. I was probably too frank but I felt they were all heading for a slow-motion car-crash disaster and they needed to do what they could to get a grip. But at every level of the organisation things seemed to have gone backwards. So much was about lack of leadership. I spent the rest of the morning emailing round trying to get money for the Henry appeal. Steve Richards's [*Independent*] column said I had been involved with JoP in persuading GB to go for a private Iraq Inquiry. I dropped him a line to say it really misrepresented my position and later did a blog saying what I had actually said – that I was worried it had to be one thing or the other, that they would end up with the worst of all worlds if they did not have a line and stick to it. Steve accepted what I had said and agreed he would correct it some time. It was obvious GB was going to get pushed into changing his position. The Tories were pursuing a strategy of signalling agreement then doing something different when it went public.

I emailed Stewart Wood, Jeremy Heywood and later Gus O'Donnell to say that as the line seemed to change, as ministers were expressing personal views, and as someone was briefing out against us, I would like to see the written briefings the government was using. Meanwhile Guardian Online reported me from last night saying that it would make no difference to critics if it was public or private. Gus called later. He said he was feeling very sore and aggrieved. He had done what he thought GB wanted – a Franks-style inquiry.* Yes, he had selected the committee and agreed on format, but GB had to defend it. Instead he was sheltering behind him and preparing to change tack under pressure. He said that things were dreadful in there, they just rolled from one mini disaster to another and

* In 1983, Lord (Oliver) Franks had conducted an inquiry, held in private, into the Argentine invasion of the Falkland Islands.

were totally lacking in strategy. He felt on policy there were good things happening, but on strategy and political comms, it was hopeless. We had a good old whinge to each other. He honestly didn't know where the inquiry would end up now. On Robin Butler calling for it to be public, he said 'He told me he just wanted to tweak the government's tail – I hope I don't end up like that.' He knew GB was volatile and erratic but he had been worse of late. Peter making a difference but not enough. Balls at it. No. 10 not functioning. Rory back from Oxford for good.

Saturday 20 June

Another displacement blog, on the British and Irish Lions in advance of the first rugby union Test in South Africa. Figures always low when I did not do politics though, especially at weekends. Matthew Doyle called to say someone was out briefing some of the Sundays that TB pressed GB to have inquiry in private. I had really had it with that lot now. It was all about blame and nobody standing up for anyone else.

Sunday 21 June

Rory and I to Lord's for the Twenty20 finals. News still dominated by Iran. Great seats at the back of the upper Mound stand. Moir Lockhead and his sons arrived. Good blokes. Lots of chat re Burnley – elder son Sean was a United and Rangers fan – and then settled down to watch the cricket. We were rooting for Sri Lanka as the team that had not lost and because of [Tillakaratne] Dilshan who till now was player of the tournament. Out for a duck. Sri Lanka poor with the bat and Pakistan cruised it. Good event but a bit anti-climactic.

Monday 22 June

All day home on and off, admin, a few chores like sending out books etc. The political world was focused on the election for the Speaker. I did a blog basically saying I thought Margaret Beckett was safest bet, bad news if an Old Etonian – George Young – got it. John Bercow [renegade Tory MP] might be 'baby out with the bathwater'. He got it in the end. What was fascinating was to see how obviously gutted the Tories were that he got it. Later [Sir] John Chilcot [inquiry chairman designate] wrote to GB saying he had already decided the inquiry should be in public where possible. It had all unfolded pretty much as I had predicted. GB pushed around by anyone. He was saying Chilcot should consult other party leaders – in other words do late the groundwork he should have done ages ago.

Tuesday 23 June

Blogged on the Speakership and why I hated Eton, which had had a few comments yesterday. Facebook page getting all sorts of random debates sparked by my blog at the moment. Worked on the speech for tomorrow. It brought home how out of touch I was on basic questions re Iraq. I was going to have to immerse myself pretty deep. Chilcot saw Cameron and Clegg 'on PC [Privy Council] terms' but Clegg immediately out to say he was pleased TB and GB would be witnesses in public. Weakness at the top being exploited. This whole thing was now going to play out across the election landscape. Hopeless. Lunch with Sue Gray who, to my surprise, felt really strongly I should go for Burnley. Like Charlie she felt that I could go as far as I liked. She felt they were badly in need of direction and none of the people at the top at the moment could give it. I was taken aback how strongly she felt but I found myself again giving the cons perhaps more forcefully than the pros.

She was full of stories of how dysfunctional it all was. Gus was feeling very sore about being hung out to dry. The reshuffle was hilarious at times. All the names on a giant metallic board. Peter kept going in and moving the best people towards his team. Tessa good to have around. She liked Purnell, liked Ed M personally but felt he was weak. Ditto DM, both more and less impressive. The juniors not cutting it. If I went back I would be walking into whatever I wanted. I said I had decided about not going back to the centre. Burnley was tempting in some ways but I did not really want to get back into the frontline. She said Peter had shown it could be done. I said he was different. The status and titles meant something. They meant nothing to me. Back to do a bit of work, then out on the bike. Blistering hot. Florence Godfernaux on re Canal Plus idea for regular show once a fortnight.

Wednesday 24 June

The Iraq Inquiry vote, which was preceded by more U-turns and concessions to make sure they saw off the Tory motion.* The thing had panned out exactly as we predicted. Take one line, feel the heat, cave in. I was speaking at a strategic comms/post-conflict conference organised by Albany [communications specialists]. I was up for two slots, part of a Q&A panel with [General Sir] Mike Jackson and Edward Mortimer, ex-UN, a.m., then a keynote and Q&A p.m. The conference was opened by Nik Gowing [TV journalist], quite an interesting presentation on how the speed of comms was transforming the world, and how slow the decision-makers were to

* Calling for assurances on how much would be public and for MPs to decide its terms of reference.

react. The kind of reasoned analysis more in the media needed to make. Q&A was OK, with Jacko and I probably agreeing more than he expected us to. My main point was that despite it all the leaders and decision-makers had a lot more strategic space than sometimes they realised. The speech was my usual guide to strat comms and crisis management with specific focus on Kosovo, September 11 and Iraq.

Quite a lot of cynicism about what we had actually achieved – including from Robin Clifford [former Kosovo Force spokesman], who had been pretty obstructive in Kosovo and who now was telling me we did not achieve much. Ex-Ambassador from Bosnia complaining about TB's visit there in the late '90s, that we did not spend enough time there. Quite a few interesting points on the nature of communications for example the difference of our and US language on democracy. Nipped out halfway to deal with emails and Hilary Caprani [mental health campaigner] came on to say Tory MP Mark Harper raised my evidence to the Speaker's conference at PMQs. Heard quite respectfully and with a few hear hears. Off to Hampstead to try to sort my phone which was cutting out whenever I used it at home. Watched a bit of the Iraq debate. Government won the vote but had woefully lost on the handling of the issue. Sent TB a message: 'Object lesson in abject handling.' Some very heavy attacks on him from our side.

Thursday 25 June

Spotted a line in John Kampfner's piece in *The Spectator* – mainly about how Peter had persuaded GB to go for a private inquiry for TB – that 'Blair and Campbell' had prevailed on [Lord] Butler to water down his [2004] report. I had had nothing to do with it and was not even there. Sent an email to Matthew d'Ancona [editor] complaining and asking for an apology and donation to the Henry Hodge fund. He spoke to Kampfner who stood by the story and said his sources were on the committee. By then I'd spoken to Gerald Shamash [lawyer], Gavin [Millar, QC] and Charlie, all of whom felt it was serious and I should see it through. I also had calls out to Butler to make sure he was on the same page, and the lawyers thought it was defamatory of him too as it suggested he had succumbed to our blandishments. At first d'Ancona seemed pretty bullish but by the time I had finished my speech, I checked in with him to see where we were on it and he had caved in on all points. Apology, as drafted by me, donation to LRF, total acceptance they could not stand up the story. Gerald felt I could easily have pushed for more. Matthew being reasonable so I decided to be likewise.

The speech event in Manchester was a lot more enjoyable than I expected it to be. Ed Roddis the comms guy had been messaging me on Facebook and wanted me to do a big number on leadership and strategy. They were a good crowd. Chartered Institute of Public Finance Accountancy. Basically a bunch of accountants. But they were lively, very responsive. Enjoyed the Q&A, especially the woman. Victoria Armour, who said her question was 'Can I have a free copy of your book?' I ended up agreeing to cycling with both to her home in Twickenham. I was asked direct if I would stand for Burnley and – even though I was getting more messages urging me to go for it – I said no. I had done my bit, valued my freedom etc. The organisers were really chuffed with the whole thing. Said best yet.

Train journey back enlivened by bumping into Helen Worth [actress]. Thirty-five years in *Coronation Street* and she said she still loved it. Reminisced about the TB visit years ago. She was still basically Labour but she was disillusioned. She was very nice about TB and about me but felt things now were dreadful. Good chat, about her work, my work, families, acting. Liked her.

Friday 26 June

Did a little blog on two nice surprises – Cipfa being interesting and meeting Helen Worth. Without being critical of GB's ludicrous line on spending I made the point that there seemed to be very little appreciation of what was being said. Yesterday the finance directors present had all been saying they were planning for cuts but there was no leadership at all on the issue from government. Set out for Bill's in Chiswick to work on his edits of '98. Got there early enough to go out to Twickenham to deliver the books. Cleaner au pair type there. 'Thanks for keeping your promise,' she said. OK session with Bill, then had lunch at the place opposite.

Cycled to Chelsea to see Helen Worth and drop books there too. She lived alone in a small, nice house. I rang on the bell and when I said it was me she said she was naked with a face pack on at the top of the stairs. It certainly broke the ice. We sat out the back and chatted away about stuff. She seemed very chuffed I had gone there and delivered the books. 'Can I read the novel first?' She had a lovely manner, very thoughtful, also seemed totally centred in her life, who she was, what she was for. Cycled home, did a bit of work then Tessa came round for dinner. Meanwhile mini disaster had struck because my new phone had come and Fiona, having thought all the numbers were saved to the computer, discovered they were not. So I'd lost hundreds of numbers.

Saturday 27 June

Got Rayan to take me with Calum, [friends] Roland and Keir to Wimbledon. Roger Draper had sorted us LTA hospitality, which meant we had nice food, a place to escape the tennis which at times was dull. Alan Milburn announced he was standing down so I did a blog on that and urged parties to go for youth amid all the churn. The boys were really good fun, Roland full of banter, later drinking pints of champagne and chatting up the stewardesses. Cam was good with both of them. Really good mates. The tennis was dull until Andy Murray v Viktor Troicki when Murray was superb. Different class to how he was a couple of years ago.

Sunday 28 June

Did a quick blog on Murray, suggesting the reason some people didn't like him was less that he was Scottish than that he was a winner, obsessive about winning. Then worked the whole day on the '98 editing. I got through it more quickly than I feared I would. Fiona thought Rory was a bit low after the exams and not sure what he wanted to do with himself.

Monday 29 June

To the Lanesborough to meet Tony Hollingsworth [producer, campaigner] who wanted to pitch to me three ideas – media and political consultant to his 'Listen' global media awareness campaign on children's poverty; be a non-exec of the company managing it; present a documentary on Mandela and music. His campaign was pretty well put together but I did not feel overly enthused. Nice enough guy, big driver of change, but I wasn't sure this was for me. What was at the moment? As with Beyond Sport, where I did what Nick asked me but without any real energy or drive. Rory gave me a lift to King's Place for the event in memory of Henry. Full house. TB, CB, DB, Harriet who spoke pretty well, David and Louise, Tessa and David, lots of MPs, judges and lawyers. Some good tributes and a lovely photo album display set to Bob Marley. The plug for LRF was on the back so that should raise some money. Margaret looking pretty shot.

Worked on the train to Preston, having missed all the GB–DC exchanges on spending, GB having set out his 'Building Britain's Future' document. Got a cab to Stan [Ternent] and Kath's, who were on good form. He was a lot mellower, happy for Burnley, feeling we had a fair chance of staying up. He was a bright guy, astute about politics, picking my brains on GB and both of them seemed to think he was not really up to fighting the pressure for 'Time for a change'. We weaved around between football and politics and books. Stayed up pretty late, Stan in full flow with some of his old football stories. My favourite was about John Bailey, who boasted to his Everton team-mates he had landed a big four-year contract in South Africa. 'What about apartheid?' someone asked. 'All sorted. Three bedrooms overlooking the sea.' Did a blog on Henry's funeral, referring to TB's black eye [gym accident].

Tuesday 30 June

Watched Balls on Sky. What he said was probably this side of OK. But he looked awful. Kath spotted it, said he had poppy-out eyes and did not look trustworthy. Full-on day. Started with a run, then back for breakfast. To Turf Moor for the first day of filming for the Burnley doc for the BBC. Ged Clarke, a Geordie, the director, who was good on attention to detail but it meant quote a lot of hanging around, so I got irritable through the day but I think we did get some decent stuff. Did Rachel Brown, Burnley-supporting England women's team goalie, Tony Livesey, Burnley-supporting broadcaster, then went to Tattoos Inc, to watch a tattooist called Helen putting a club crest on the leg of a fan called Gareth. In the next chair a guy was having his whole back painted. He said it was an addiction.

Local paper came to do something on me being there, did a chat, then lunch before doing Barry Kilby at the ground. Barry chatted away OK then took me to the boardroom area which was being refurbished. Did Andy Payton [former player] – who hours later would be interviewed by cops over cannabis plants in his house. Then Stan, who was good on the gulf between the various leagues e.g. I said if Man U was a scratch golfer, what was the championship? 24, he said, maybe 36. Stan was really nice about me, what I had done, what I did for Burnley, and said he thought I sometimes underestimated what and who I was.

Wednesday 1 July

Slept in so missed my planned morning run. Feeling tired. Alina had commented on Facebook that the blog had become less political. I emailed her to say well spotted and it was because I had been feeling very disillusioned about the government. Calum was working at No. 10, going through the correspondence. He said there were a few letters saying he needed me back. Breakfast then to the club. Good session with Martin Dobson and Paul Fletcher [players from the '70s], mix of serious and funny. Then Jimmy McIlroy [player from '60s] sitting in the stand named after him. Nice chat. Seventy-eight, and said he had never been more excited. He also said he used to look at me and wonder if I was mad, doing all-day journeys to watch a football match.

Train home, did a bit of French with Grace, then out to the Drill Hall to record *Chain Reaction*. I'd never heard of it but it was basically a radio series where A chose to interview B who then became interviewer and picked C to interview, and so on. They wanted a comedy connection in every interview so I would have to pick a comedian, probably John Cleese. Frank Skinner had picked Eddie Izzard who picked me, and we were recording the two back to back in front of a live audience. Frank and Eddie were already there chewing the fat in a hot, hot studio which would get hotter when the audience came in. Eddie was going on about his running exploits – he had done his first 26-miler as a training run. He was going to run across Britain. Also was going to play Madison Square Garden. It was only since getting to know him a bit that I realised how big he was. He was huge, and in many different parts of the world. He now had almost as many Twitter followers as Stephen Fry.

Frank was pretty laid-back, quite laconic, basically Labour, picking my brains on GB and what was going on at the moment. Eddie was a firework, shooting off in different directions the whole time. I liked him but sometimes wondered quite how his comedy worked. He could ramble a fair bit, and Frank played to that a bit when they got to their interview. We had a little break then I was on with Eddie. He steered off a lot of the political, and basically focused on my background, questions of identity, then depression and mental illness more widely. The producer, Sam Bryant, seemed happy with both. I was covered in sweat by the end of it.

Thursday 2 July

I was pottering mainly, sketching out a few ideas for next week's speeches, then waiting for Cathy [Gilman] to pick me up to go to Celebrity Speakers agency in Burnham. I was getting a bit fed up with how much I was doing that was all bitty, and this fell into that category, though to be fair to Cathy she had said no when they asked me to do it and I had said yes under pressure. We chatted over a few things on the way, then did a little Q&A and pep talk re the mindset of fundraising before heading back home. Tim Kerr-Dineen [personal friend] on with a story I did not really understand about the wife of an Iranian who had been beaten up and Tim thought the spooks would be interested in his laptop re Iran–Iraq arms dealing etc. He was garbled and not clear but eventually I did a note for Tom Fletcher at No. 10 who could decide whether to pass on to the spooks or not.

Out with Fiona to David Frost's party. We ended up chatting mainly to Charlie F and Margaret Jay. Usual crowd, lots of old Tories, a few royals, film stars like Michael Caine, loads of TV people, Cameron, Charles and Sarah Kennedy joined us for a bit. We bumped into Peter M who after a bit of small talk asked me to sit down on a bench with him. As Fiona said later, he was 'trying to create a moment' and there were certainly lots of people looking over as we chatted. He said he needed to know when and how I was coming back in? I said maybe I wasn't. I felt no real desire or drive and recent events, including some of the briefings against, has confirmed me in that. I was not convinced much could be done to avoid defeat. Maybe, he said, but we could stop it from being a total wipeout.

Cameron was across the way, Rebekah Brooks and others hovering around him. She came over at one point to take a picture. Others came over, asking what we were up to, so it was hard to chat properly. But I did glean Peter and Shaun Woodward were at odds, that he did not especially rate him, but GB had given him some kind of role on strategy and he not Balls was the one pushing hardest the line on spending – which I had suggested was at best incredible, at worst a disaster. If the Tories were any good, they would be out of sight by now. He said he would like to have a proper chat about what I might do. Stayed another twenty minutes or so, just a succession of those little fleeting chats then off we went. I was on the cusp of a big dive, I could feel it.

Friday 3 July

Caroline Gascoigne [Random House] sent over a new *Maya* cover. Worried it was a bit downmarket now, though it had been my idea to make her beauty much clearer. TB was photographed getting an Anglo-Indian award from Peter M, so his black eye was out, but with none of the old frenzy. I did an interview with the *Daily Record* on the STV film I'd done on bagpipes. Jim Murphy [Labour MP] was on asking me to do a fundraiser. He said apart from Peter, there was no showbiz factor in the government and that was why they all wanted me for these dinners. He also said at one point 'Why are we so useless?' Fiona wanted me to go out for dinner with Shawn Slovo [friend, screenplay writer] and Victoria [Bridge, neighbour], but I was feeling down and went to bed.

Saturday 4 July

Did a blog on Bernie Ecclestone, who had said in *The Times* he preferred dictators to democracy and that Hitler got things done. He seemed to give the impression he was led astray re the Final Solution. Out later to Rachel and Stuart's for a surprise party for Glenys. I was feeling pretty down and not up for it, so I was glad the kids were coming. All their old friends there – Derek and Eva [Tatchell, friend of the Kinnocks], Alan and Ann Keen [MPs] (who seemed pretty shell-shocked by the expenses fallout), Colin and Barbara Parry [Glenys's brother and sister-in-law], Arlene McCarthy and Michael Cashman [MEPs]. Steve, Helle and the kids there. Camilla really friendly, sitting on my lap teaching me Danish and when she ran off, saying to her mum 'Save my place.' Helle wanting me to do an event for her in Denmark. Glenys really moved when she came in. Not sure I had seen her cry before. Nice do and she seemed to love it. Steward Wood [GB advisor] there later. 'Have you forgiven us?' he asked, re the inquiry.

I said I just felt it was dreadfully handled and trying to shift the blame when the fallout came about the possibility of it being private was just wrong. He said he thought Chilcot wanted as much of it as possible in private but some of the others were feeling the pressure and worrying about criticism. He did nothing to dispel a picture of No. 10 as dysfunctional and GB being pushed around by different strands of advice. He seemed to suggest Shaun [Woodward] had been behind some of the briefing. He felt GB saw Shaun as the one who best understood the Tories and he was definitely listening to him a fair bit. He said Peter had got his revenge in the Sundays, apparently pinning the tax and spend line on him. He said that when I ran the No. 10 comms the Treasury used to say I was unable to keep control of extraneous briefing whereas anything out of HMT was controlled and organised (quite an admission given how much poison went out). But they genuinely did not know where the stuff about TB and me trying to stop it from being public came from. He asked if I thought they had had it, and the Tories were in. I said probably.

Sunday 5 July

Out on the bike to see Jamie Rubin. He and Cristiane were renting a flat in Holland Park. Nice to see them both. Her sisters were there too, and her 96-year-old dad who said he always liked my style. Jamie and I went for a walk to the park where he told me he had had a bad time. He had supported Hillary, without really going for Obama, but when it came to it, and she was made Secretary of State, a little group of 30–40-somethings around Obama blocked both him and Sidney Blumenthal [former Bill Clinton aide]. Also, Hillary did not really fight for him. He had clearly been expecting something big if Hillary had won, and something at least substantial and interesting once she became Secretary of State, but that was not now going to happen. He seemed very down about it, and also thought that it was in part jealousy of his profile, and of Cristiane's fame, among some of Obama's people. He said they were a petty crowd. He felt Obama was pretty much in control of all the big policy shots and Hillary was very nervous about doing anything that might upset him. We chatted about the GB scene and he felt I had done right in staying out. He felt it was probably unfixable. Also I had a reputation as a winner and had to protect that.

Monday 6 July

In to see Jonathan Powell in his new office in Dover Street. Very flash. His boss was some mega-rich American commodities broker who had got rich on silver and basically liked to surround himself with people that made him feel like he was really important. JoP was working for him as a base and then doing stuff for TB, going round the world. He was travelling too much. Not seeing the kids enough. Also doing some conflict negotiation work. As for Sarah, she had written a play which was basically based on her, JoP and TB re Iraq, with lots gleaned from hearing his phone calls. The National were looking at it. Wow. He was going to have to get ready for some publicity out of that. We chatted about the Iraq Inquiry. He was sure our diaries would be subpoenaed – certainly mine. He thought Chilcot was basically weak, the others on the panel would be tricky and they would let the whole thing become a monster growing out of control. He seemed in OK shape if not terribly fulfilled. He thought TB had still not really adapted. He loved being feted. Meeting world leaders. Feeling he was still a PM kind of figure.

Off to lunch with Nigel Doughty [businessman] at his office near the RAC. Same age as me. Semi-retired. Basically venture capitalism. Seemed pretty pro-GB and also seemed to think we could still win. I bumped into [Sir] Malcolm Rifkind [former Tory Cabinet minister] on the way out and it was clear he did not recognise me when I said 'Hi Malcolm.' 'The face seems terribly familiar,' he said. Then he seemed hugely embarrassed before we laughed and then chatted away for a bit. I had forgotten he had become an MP again – in Kensington and Chelsea. He said his was the only seat where it was the constituents who left for the country at the weekend, rather than the MP.

Tuesday 7 July

Out to Civil Service Live [annual cross-department learning event]. Did an OK speech, OK Q&A, then book signing that went on for a while. Big event. Nice enough do. Had a little chat with Gus. Others coming up to ask me to do other events. 'This is what it's like,' I said. 'Want to swap?' he said. He would sign books and I could have a proper job again. Home to work on speech for tomorrow. Alex F on asking me to help sort Antonio Valencia's visa. He was in Ecuador and it had run out.

Wednesday 8 July

All day at the Beyond Sport summit. Nick Keller had done well putting it together. I did a speech, Q&A, two workshops, so basically a whole day and no mobile reception. It was good when it got going but I was beginning to feel with these things it was too backward-looking. Then a guy from Leicester who had founded What If. He told me afterwards he thought the 'new' in New Labour was the single greatest act of strategic comms. The thing was running late in part because so many Third World visitors but they were a great bunch and to be fair to Nick they had put a good conference together. Lunch with Kate Garvey who wanted to pick my brains about a pre-Copenhagen climate change campaign.

I got away around 5 and was planning to get straight off but started to get calls about a *Guardian* story on an out of court settlement with Gordon Taylor [Professional Footballers' Association] by the *News of the World* re phone-hacking. I did a quick blog saying there were questions for News International, the press more generally, the police on the earlier inquiries and of course Cameron because of Coulson's role. Andrew Neil was straight out saying it beggared belief that Coulson would not have known if it was widespread. I texted Peter M to say they needed to go for this big-style. They were not fielding ministers which I thought was a mistake. They wanted me to go up but tonight it was not possible as I was heading up to Mum's to see Graeme and Mikey [brother and nephew] before they headed back to Poland. Going pretty big on the news.

Thursday 9 July

Off to Lancashire for Barry and Sonia Kilby's wedding bash, but first I did another blog on Coulson, making much the same points. I had a stack of media bids so after speaking to John Woodcock [Labour official] I arranged to do the rounds at the Inn at Whitewell where the reception was, late p.m. JP was one of those who was alleged to have had his phone hacked so he was out and about in Cumbria. I ended up doing the Beeb at the top of a hill in Lancashire prompting a load of 'Heathcliff' messages. I said there were questions for the paper, the PCC, the cops and Cameron. Really trying to take it to a question of Cameron's judgement. Some of the hacks thought he would end up going but I suspected not. The media as a whole would not keep this going too long. Then [assistant commissioner John] Yates of the Yard popped up and in a pretty weird statement said that they were not reopening their inquiries. Also that it was not true JP's phone had been hacked.

The only response I got from News International was a text from Fred Michel 'Attention á qu'est-ce que tu racontes aux medias amigo' ('Be careful what you say to the media, amigo') and a very snotty message from Rebekah. Arrogance. They really did think whatever they did was OK. That being said, Fiona pointed out there was something unsatisfactory about my interventions. Either I was in the fray or not but it looked odd doing it from the middle of a moor. I suspected bridges with News [International] were burnt. It would be interesting to see if they pulled the plug on the cycling tie-up I was trying to sort between the charity triathlon team and Sky. The wedding went fine. Loads of people saying we had had it, that they voted for TB but not GB. Bed half eleven.

Friday 10 July

Up early and out on the bike to the top of the hill. I was troubled and angry re Fred Michel's text but would leave it for now. JP called, and later Gerald Shamash [party solicitor] on all the various legal things that could be done now. JP had a call from Yates yesterday just before his own statement and JP felt there was something very odd about it. Fiona felt News and Coulson were still in some trouble though later NI put out a pretty strong denial. Off to Gawthorpe to watch Burnley training for the documentary. Alex called about *The Guardian* as he was named today as another phone hack target. He had a barrister on the case and was obviously going to talk to Gordon Taylor. We went back to Turf Moor to do pieces to camera, then off to the town hall to do a quick interview with Steve Rumbelow, chief executive, about the impact on the town of getting to the Premier League. He was very disappointed for Kitty Ussher but also said she might have been in bother. He felt sorry for her in a way because not everyone had taken to her. Partly the Southerner thing, partly the fact she came via an all-women shortlist. We both agreed she had seemed a bit detached and distracted the night of the victory parade.

Off to Fletch's [Paul Fletcher] in Rawtenstall. Nice old farmhouse dating back to 1640. Beatles stuff everywhere. He and Sian both Beatles fanatics. Chatted loads of football and politics. Another one who liked TB but not GB. Some great old stories about his playing days. He and Steve Kindon practical-joking. My favourite was tying an old rope to a tree near hotels where they were staying, then asking a waitress to take out carrots to feed a non-existent 'club mascot' Shetland pony. Cue panic when it wasn't there. Really good bloke, and clever. Not just the stadia but some of the ambitions he had. A Chinese guy was trying to buy half the club and Fletch was pushing for a university of football to be there. Chatted away till late. Blogged on great moments of the day. Also did a line contrasting the speed of Yates's announcement there was no point reopening the hacking case, and the length of the cash for honours probe.

Saturday 11 July

Out on the bike first thing, then breakfast and a walk round Rawtenstall with Fletch. Set off for Bradford, where we were playing a pre-season friendly [v City]. Good Burnley turnout. I met up with the TV guys and we went for a cup of tea which I spilled down the front of my shirt. Thank God I had another one. Very rusty and lost 2–1. Hung around at the end to do pieces to camera then set off for home. The news was dominated by the growing numbers of deaths among UK soldiers in Afghanistan.

Sunday 12 July

Knocked off a quick blog on the triathlon I was doing today and Fiona getting the Fred and Anne Jarvis [former National Union of Teachers general secretary and late wife] award for education campaigning. The cab driver taking me down to Dorney Lake was from Kosovo. Really warm. He said we were heroes in Kosovo, not just TB, but me, Jamie Shea [NATO], Jamie Rubin. Everyone there knew what we did, he said. His kids went to Gospel Oak and he said he could not believe we used the same schools as Kosovan asylum-seekers and refugees. It was odd how people found it strange we should use a local school. Had a good chat. It was annoying to see the amazing facilities at Dorney Lake – this was Eton's rowing college. Pretty tired at the end but did reasonably OK. Definitely slower than I used to be.

Monday 13 July

Did a blog on the various military situations we had been involved in and urged GB to use the G8 statement today to set out the whole picture. He didn't really do it. The country, or at least the media, was going through a major emotional reaction to the recent deaths in Afghanistan. They were all really sad, and three of the eight were just teenagers, but war was now covered as though death and injury would never happen. The issue was becoming whether we had enough helicopters out there and GB was looking a bit shifty about whether there had been a demand for more, and for more troops. The head of the army, Dannatt, looked like he was stirring a fair bit. I was feeling tired all day. Not overworked so a bit odd. Perhaps unwinding to the holiday.

Tuesday 14 July

Telly idea came in. Political animal. Kind of reality TV show for politics. Sounded awful. Maybe I did need some new projects though and maybe TV was the thing. But I usually found it strangely unfulfilling. Did a blog on climate change, Ed Miliband doing the renewable energy strategy tomorrow, and focused on a Berlin brothel giving a discount to people arriving by bike or public transport. Out to Triandrun with Rory to get bikes fixed, then did a really nice ride around Essex. Back to get his degree results. 2.1. He was pretty disappointed.

Wednesday 15 July

Watched GB at PMQs under pressure on Afghanistan. Hopeless at pushing back on Cameron's opportunism, which was dreadful. Lunch at the Phoenix Palace to map out next novel. Caught out in rain at Edgware Rd. Buxton [music and literature] Festival on asking me to stand in for CB because she had swine flu.

Thursday 16 July

Longish bike ride and was well into it before I realised I had forgotten my helmet. In fact, I only realised when I stopped for a coffee, checked my phone and someone had tweeted that they saw me without a helmet on a hill. Charlie F called and I met him for lunch at Christopher's. Still at me to stand for Parliament. He clearly felt I was slightly wasting myself which maybe I was. He loved the *Observer* picture of me and Peter M at Frost's party. Lots of chat re the usual old stuff – Peter M, GB, TB etc. We wondered whether Peter might at some point move against GB. He thought of all of us TB felt the most removed from the UK scene. Glenys had come out and openly said yesterday that TB was UK choice for EU President, which was probably a mistake. Re GB Charlie felt he was getting worse and yet the Tories were nowhere near home and dry. He felt I would have to go back at some point, otherwise it would appear disloyal and offhand. He still felt the Burnley option was the right one for me.

He was on good form though we both confessed to slight feelings of driftology. He recounted how Margaret B had told him she always preferred GB to TB, politically and personally, yet when she reflected on her career, TB had always been straight with her and treated her well, whereas GB had treated her abominably. Off to see Gavin at Doughty Chambers to plan an event for Henry Hodge. We agreed a panel of Dominic Grieve [shadow Justice Secretary] and Charlie on the human rights act would be best. Home, then out for dinner with Mary McCartney [photographer] and her bloke Simon Aboud. Something really nice about her, and he was a good bloke too. She was agonising about schools and we were trying to persuade her to take her son out of private school. Talking loads re the celeb culture bollocks. JP bumped into Armando Iannucci in DC after watching *In the Loop* on the plane. He said Malcolm Tucker was me with less swearing. Started a load of Twitter activity.

Friday 17 July

Blogged on there being no hiding place on Twitter with my bike ride yesterday and JP in the States. Pottering about in the main. Avoiding big decisions and activity to do with the government. Eddie Izzard and Karon Maskill, his promoter/assistant, came round for a drink and with Fiona out at Tessa's we ended up going to the Camden Brasserie. He was very good fun, pretty wacky, really revved up for his big run, dead serious about going for an elected position at some point. We were pretty cagey re GB but he was still of the view we could win. He didn't think people warmed to Cameron on any level. The run was going to be 1,000 miles. He had designed a new flag for Northern Ireland – green plus doves – because he didn't want the Red Hand [historic symbol].

Wednesday 26 August

Writing this at the end of an incredibly long holiday. A month. I kept a few notes on the BlackBerry as it unfolded, but we were away so long they fell off the end of my badly set email queue. I also lost a couple of chapters of a new novel, in the same way. Maybe it was not meant to be, though Gail was pressing me to promise my next one would be political. It is annoying to have lost the chapters, and the diary records, but maybe holidays are best remembered not day to day but as a whole. We went out earlier than usual because the Tour de France was going up Mont Ventoux and we wanted to be there for that. Calum was the only one travelling with us as Grace was at Nina's in Cornwall and Rory was flying out with his mates, Charlie, Harry and Ramsi. We stayed at an OK hotel on the way down and had a nice enough time but I was conscious of a bad depression looming. I have no idea why, and so often the start of a break is the time for a bad one, but I knew it was going to be bad.

It was lovely to get to Puymeras and the Tour was great, especially when Jeremy Whittle [cycling journalist] managed to wangle me a pass to drive to the top on the Malaucene side, so we parked up and walked a few miles down. Found a spot next to a guy with a TV in his caravan and watched that before the top guys arrived. Great spectacle in many ways but passed us in no time. Cycling fundamental to the holiday. Rory and I doing pretty big rides most days. Did Ventoux twice, then Malaucene. Rory gave me a minute for every year and every kilo I had on him so got a 57-minute head start but he still beat me. Did a couple of four-hour rides too. My piece on Puymeras for the *Telegraph* was reprinted in the village newsletter and Roger the mayor invited me to the soirée d'amitié for village friends. The depression peaked about four days in. I wasn't enjoying the place like I normally did. Eventually virtually collapsed one day when I got back after a long bike ride trying to chase it away. All but Fiona were out. She was very nice about it but felt in hindsight it was a mini breakdown. I spoke to DS a few times and he sent out some pills with Julia when she came out. I was in better shape after a week or so I guess. But it meant in some ways the first week was wasted. I tried to start up a couple of novel ideas but didn't really get going.

Local MP Thierry Mariani finally got me to the opera at Orange which we really enjoyed. *Cavalleria Rusticana*. Then took to listening to it on the big climbs. Mariani just been appointed Sarko's rep on Afghanistan and Pakistan. Bit of a man in a hurry and very right-wing. Lovely daughter Solenne who looked about twenty but was in fact just fourteen. The other guests were interesting, a left-wing senator who had stood as an independent and had lost several fingers of one hand, and a guy called Étienne Mougeotte, a big deal at *Le Figaro*. More interestingly for us though he was one of Arsène Wenger's best friends. He had been over staying with him for a few days. Said Arsène had turned down a fortune from Real Madrid because he was determined to take Arsenal further. Loved living in Britain. Very interested in politics. More right than left. Mixing up eating in and eating out. Not sleeping well.

The Iraq Inquiry had first annoyed me, because of the woeful way No. 10 handled it, then worried me simply because I was not on top of the detail like I used to be. Had a chat with TB who felt Chilcot was trying to be responsible. He thought I had nothing to worry about because all my issues were in a sense dealt with. The question would be preparedness for the aftermath. I felt the mood had so changed that they would want to be pretty critical. As for the political scene generally – dire. GB low-profile. A bit of a farce with a succession of different ministers reported to be 'in charge' while GB on holiday. Harriet, Peter, Alistair, Jack Straw. A big flurry on health after Daniel Hannan [Tory MEP] attacked the NHS on Fox News. I did a blog on that. Otherwise gave it a pretty long rest. After Rory's mates left we had a week with just the five of us, which was really nice. Then Zoe and Sissy out. Finally Nina and Ella. By then I was more chilled. Had also been back to see Burnley beat Man U in our first home game in the Premier League.

I had been speaking to Alex before and agreed we should meet up for a drink after but I knew he wouldn't be up for it. It was some time before we had a chat about it. When we did he said he still felt we would struggle. Thought our fans were brilliant considering we had so little possession. Talked to him about Pini Zahavi the Israeli football agent because TB was asking for Nicky [son], who was getting involved in some football agent work. Pretty mixed response from around the place. I was getting into the AOL [online service provider] column on Burnley and enjoying it. Did the first before we left and another five during the holiday. Also some media at a studio in Avignon. PG was there for the last few days and on good form. He told me GB had charged Tessa with the task of getting me back. I was moving more and more to not wanting to get involved.

Tessa called and it was clear PG was right. I just didn't have the will to get too involved. Good chat with TB who had reached the view that GB was just hopeless. 'It is beyond rescue. And the tragedy is that on policy and on strategy the Tories are entirely beatable. I could beat this lot easily.' He was still asking me to get involved in some of his overseas work. Euan [Blair, son of TB] determined to go into politics. Currently at Morgan Stanley. TB keen for Rory to go to the Sports Foundation. Main dilemma of holiday was whether to go back after the United game. Did so with Cam and we had a good few final days. Decided to do the GNR and was doing a few runs when we got back.

Thursday 27 August

Out all morning up round the North Circular filming for *Watchdog* re the postal scam. Talking to a victim, then to Westminster to talk to Trading Standards. The card in the letterbox scam was the key to a bigger scam, using the credit card details given in the first to pay for full-page ads flogging non-existent goods. Working away but fairly half-heartedly. Dinner with Tessa at Kalendar. Still chipping away about me going back. I just felt the whole thing was dire. The handling of the Lockerbie bomber was the latest lack of leadership issue.* Hiding behind the Scots when he should have been defending the idea of improved relations with Libya.

Friday 28 August

Did a longish run, maybe ten miles plus, and was tired for the rest of the day. Out with Calum to see London Skolars v Keighley Cougars [rugby league]. Wild night weather-wise but Skolars won and so were through to the challenge final play-offs. Home before Grace and chatted late re that. Shocked.

Saturday 29 August

Out to Chelsea. Met up with Danny Finkelstein and his son Aaron who had adopted Burnley as his second team. Poor turnout and it transpired we had sent loads of tickets back. Poor atmosphere. We did OK for half

* The Scottish government was heavily criticised for freeing Abdelbaset al-Megrahi, who returned to a hero's welcome in Tripoli.

an hour but their superiority really told after a while. Lost 3–0. Fiona at the Edinburgh book festival so Aud round for dinner. Tried a little run but energy crashed.

Sunday 30 August

Managed a slowish one hour forty run. Ought to be OK for the GNR but not definite. Grace grounded. Went with her to see Audrey p.m. Not really motoring. Could not have another period of drift. Fiona back from Edinburgh. Lockerbie still rumbling on.

Monday 31 August

Bank Holiday. Another longish run, over an hour, and felt not bad. David M came round for a long chat. He wanted advice on how to position himself generally and more specifically how to use his conference speech. He saw no way we were going to win. We were at 25 per cent in poll after poll. GB did none of the things needed to improve our standing. There was nothing to suggest things were going to change. The economy might be picking up but we were not getting the credit. He felt we could get wiped out. It might be possible to limit the damage with a change of leader. Best would be voluntary. The only other way would be through the threat of irresistible force. He felt if he, Alistair D, Peter, maybe Jack, all said he had to go he would have to. But even he was not sure e.g. Peter would do so. It was impossible to have a conversation with Harriet because she was so gabby. The Eds would fight for him, especially Balls.

Harriet's position was unclear. Alan J was keeping cards close to chest but maybe deep down knew it would not work. Harriet was the only one who had an organisation as she had already run and won a campaign. He said GB only listened to people he feared and that basically meant TB, Peter and me. If we all said he had to go it might have an effect. 'He doesn't listen to us. We are just the people who do the photocopying. I don't think there is anyone round that Cabinet table he fears.' He did not think GB really understood how bad things were. He did not do empathy. He did not get real polling. As to why he would fight on, it was bad enough being defined as such a bad Prime Minister. Was he really just going to disappear? If we lost, he becomes the worst leader too but at least goes down fighting. Sarah definitely pushing him on. He didn't know how to attack the Tories. We chatted a bit about that.

He asked for help with his speech. I reluctantly said I would but it really was reluctant. I said I was not even sure I would go to conference. Last year I got too sucked in with all the propping him up. All it did was help prolong the agony. He said the reason to get involved was to try to help stave off total wipeout. On policy he felt we were OK but GB was so erratic. E.g. his recent visit to Afghanistan. He was not there long enough for anything meaningful. He went because people thought he should, not with a real purpose. I felt it was not possible to make that much difference. Putting in tonnes of effort might yield a few ounces of improvement. We went round in circles a bit. Fiona popped in at one point and said afterwards she felt DM seemed a bit out of touch on the domestic scene in particular. She said to him you all just have to make him go. Out to ESPN in Chiswick. Guest pundit with Alan Curbishley [former footballer and manager] on their new Monday Review programme. Did OK but the other AC obviously dealing with most of the stuff because of football expertise. Had a good chat with him off set. He was convinced we would stay up.

Tuesday 1 September

Calum doing his exam. Out for a run. Henry Mee round to do photos and sketches for a portrait for his next exhibition of '30 people who shaped the age'. Old-fashioned haircut. Trendy jacket and bag. Liked to natter away. Did stills and sketches over a couple of hours. Then Prebble round to go over a few telly ideas.

Wednesday 2 September

Fucking BlackBerries. I had another stack of diary stuff, maybe ten days' worth and it just disappeared along with a load of emails I had kept. Fiona had been saying for ages to get a new one and she was right. So doing this from a mix of memory and calendar stuff. You forget all sorts of things though, from what's in the news to what you've done. Sky launched a thing to get a leaders' debate going and said they would empty-chair any of the leaders who didn't show up. Cameron and Clegg said yes straight away and had probably been set up for it anyway. GB was still getting whacked over Lockerbie and was going to have to take a hit on this too, assuming he wanted to keep options open. John Ryley, boss of Sky News, did a really arrogant pitch on it and I decided to do a blog pointing out it was not as obvious as they might think. Truth is if it was going to happen, best sorted quietly between parties and broadcasters. The mood politically was pretty dire. A sense of fatalism. No fight. GB not picking up much at all. I was getting briefed up on the *Pop Com* [French TV media show] topics for the show tomorrow, mainly how different countries dealt with swine flu, in comms terms, and politicians' holidays as Obama's had seemingly been controversial.

Thursday 3 September

Out early for Eurostar. Picked up a copy of *The Independent*. Funny story about the wife of the Japanese PM who believed in aliens and all sorts of other stuff. Eurostar fairly full, certainly more than last time so maybe things were picking up. Paris a bit grey. I was booked into a Radisson near the Périphérique. Did a bit of work then out to the studio to meet the *Pop Com* team. Seemed an OK bunch. Also did a sports programme so as well as talking about some future ideas we also chatted about that. Victor Robert the main presenter a nice guy who was clearly being developed by the channel. Met the admin people to finalise payments etc. then back to the hotel for an OK run before dinner at a crap restaurant near the Périphérique.

Friday 4 September

Raining so went to the hotel gym. Treadmill broken so went out. Got soaked but had a good run, up by the Parc des Princes stadium and then on a 200-metre three-lane running track near the Stade Français ground. Enough for a blog on respect for sporting facilities and how that could be part of the 2012 Olympics legacy. Back to hotel, chilled for a bit then to the recording studios as St Cloud. Very big set, fairly high-quality production. Makeup man fussing over me, including putting on mascara. Got a big response to a tweet asking how to take it off. The show went fine I think though there were too many of us for the main discussion on flu – me, Jacques Séguéla, advisor to successive Presidents, Marc Gentilini ex-Red Cross and a spokesman for the interior ministry. Also the discussion was not focused enough on the comms issues. They all seemed happy enough with it but I sent them a note saying it needed greater focus and clarity, and giving them a few specific ideas.

Florence Godfernaux came to watch the recording, then she and I went for lunch. She was very switched on and keen for me to build profile there. She felt it would lead to lots of work offers in France. Also agreed to send her *Maya*. Did another quick blog at the end of the day, having got back to catch up on GB's speech on Afghanistan. Typical Beeb coverage, all analysis no content. Really annoying.

Saturday 5 September

Up early to set off for Keighley Show. I was taking Audrey, picking up Mum on the way, then Audrey's old friend Muriel. A real furore being whipped up in the States about Obama speaking to a school on Tuesday. The health row had been getting more and more intense, but beneath it all there were two things going on – the Republicans never lying down, never stopping. And an unspoken racism. Doubts about his legitimacy as President were all about that. Listened to GB's speech to the G20 Finance Ministers on the way up. It was standard stuff but there were definitely signs of things picking up. Keighley Show was fine, if a bit disorganised. Plenty of people who remembered Mum and Dad. Ann Cryer was president and she and I chatted away during the lunch. She was clearly quite confident Jayne Thomas could succeed her OK. Did a fairly standard after-lunch speech, mainly about Dad, then a bit of judging and then off.

Sunday 6 September

Sundays carrying stories of the Beeb asking Nick Griffin [leader, British National Party] to appear on *Question Time*. Blogged saying Labour should reverse policy of not appearing with him and put up a strong and effective minister. Even though most commenters agreed in general there were far too many saying where were we going to get a strong and effective minister from? Out for dinner with Ian Kennedy [friend, academic lawyer], who was pretty low after Andrea [wife] leaving him. Made me realise that however much we get on each other's nerves from time to time, life without Fiona would be totally grim, and sad.

Monday 7 September

Off to Newcastle, working on speech to the Entrepreneurs' Forum on the way. I was staying at the Hotel du Vin. Brendan came round for tea and we had a good natter about things. He was more down on GB than ever, just felt he was not a leader and never would be. He was not going to change. Maybe I could have made a difference but he was doubtful. He felt I really ought to help DM, saw him as the one who would make a difference. The EF dinner was at the Baltic Centre, Gateshead, and the backdrop down the Tyne was so impressive I couldn't resist a little tweet saying the place was transformed since the Thatcher days. Got a good response though with a few saying parts were still awful. Nice enough crowd. The president was clearly a raving Tory and had plenty of digs at the government in his speech. I gave a few gentle digs back. I did my usual leadership speech which went down well. Good response afterwards, including a woman who said if I stood for office she would get involved. I knew deep down I was not going to but equally I felt I should. I seemed to be able to strike an empathetic tone denied to most of our current leaders.

Tuesday 8 September

Went for a long run along the quay, hour plus, then blogged on transformed inner cities, plus a bit on last night's Q&A. Home for a bit then straight out for a black-tie dinner, the Lloyds List shipping industry awards, at the Royal Lancaster. Pretty right-wing I would reckon. Editor was a guy called Tom Leander, an American, and I was also sitting with an Aussie woman, also from Lloyds List, and the head of the International Maritime Organization. Good reception at the end and in fact it was a bit tricky to leave.

Wednesday 9 September

Blogged, one of my best yet I think, on the beyond parody speech by Cameron yesterday, re lower salaries for MPs and taking away MPs' food subsidies. Plus the beyond parody piece by someone called Tara Hamilton-Miller [former Tory advisor] in the *Telegraph*, re how cool the Conservatives were. But nobody was going for him. The media tickled his tummy. Our lot just sat and twiddled their thumbs. It was tragic to watch. Michael Dobbs popped round for a quick interview for a radio programme on the impact on politics of the Brighton bomb. I was pretty much of the view the balance between security and access was OK. But he was clearly getting more views suggesting it was going too far the other way. I finally, finally signed off the final, final *Maya* version. Out all p.m. to a meeting with the agency doing the rebranding for Leukaemia Research. They were all a bit slow and pedestrian and we pretty much ended up where Cathy and I had suggested ages ago but she seemed to want to do the meeting as part of the internal politics. Ran back. Had got a few half-decent runs under my belt now.

Thursday 10 September

Did another blog on Cameron, this time more focused on the need for Labour to do better on the record and better at going for him. He really was getting away with it now. I was getting regular postings on Facebook from someone who wanted Peter M to take over from GB and who was offering herself as his wife. I emailed PM in China to tell him. He asked when I was going to explain how to win an election. I said it was unwinnable now without major and probably impossible changes.

Friday 11 September

Breakfast with Ed Victor at the Honest Sausage. Flare-up with a Yank whose dog kept coming over to our table. 'Do not kick my dog.' 'Well, get it under control.' 'Brits and dogs! And rude people.' Ed was convinced I should do a political book next. Also that we should look to do the diaries very soon after the election. And that whatever I do I must not go back to the party in a big way. He was looking pretty good, had had his 70th and was pretty much in the clear health-wise. Still doing loads of work. I popped in to see PG who was back from the States. Usual groundhog discussions – how bad it all was, how we should not have anything to do with it, but then he wields out a new poll and wonders if I want to read it with a view to giving the party advice. Chris Lennie chasing me for various things – to chair a fundraising group of big donors. To do more stuff myself including more with Eddie Izzard. I just did not have the appetite to do it on anything other than my terms.

To Carlton Gardens to see DM. We sat in one of the big rooms and went through his conference speech. OK in parts. Hardened and sharpened it. He needed to position himself as the moderniser who also defended the record and showed a bit of fight. But he was going to be speaking on the Thursday when everyone would have left. The mood was going to be so flat. He now talked as though the only question was how bad things would be and whether we could limit the Tories to one term. We did some OK work. He was interesting on Afghanistan, felt that the US had no clear strategy and did not readily take advice on one. He felt eventually there would have to be talks with the Taliban to divorce them from Al Qaeda. Also [Hamid] Karzai [leader of Afghanistan] was a real problem, weak and ineffectual and if not personally corrupt, surrounded by it. It was going to be hard to maintain support. GB seemed OK but like all of them a bit becalmed, resigned.

Off to meet Alex at the Landmark, up in his suite. He seemed a bit tired. He was confident enough about the team, felt the league title was between him and Chelsea. He was a bit down on Rio Ferdinand, felt he was spreading out in too many directions, going a bit Beckham-esque, just as Becks was getting back more to football again. Loved Wayne Rooney. Said he and Colleen [wife] would make £16 million off field this year. As for himself, another couple of years then take a position as club ambassador. Re GB he said it all reminded him of Brian Kidd. OK No. 2. Less so No. 1.

Off to meet Audrey and then go to visit Leo Blair [TB's father] in his Highgate nursing home. He seemed thrilled to see us, would not let go of my hands and kept saying the few words he could get out. 'Bloody hell', 'God Almighty', 'Well...' Interesting that the picture he had by his bed was him and Hazel, the first wife, not Olwen. Nice enough place but it must be so awful not to be able to speak when he clearly was OK in most other ways. Texted TB to tell him we'd been and he seemed pleased.

Saturday 12 September

Good run round the Heath then off to Liverpool. Worked on the piece Ken Livingstone had asked me to do for his *New Statesman* guest edit, on the Tory press love-in with Cameron. Major Alzheimer's moment en route when I realised I had left the match tickets at home. Thankfully I was meeting Kenny Dalglish for lunch and he was able to sort me duplicates. Got to Lime St, cab with an Evertonian desperate for us to win, then up to the boardroom. Off to the away end from where we witnessed something of a battering [lost 4–0]. Did my AOL column on the train back. Rory had a better time at the Spurs United game. United won 3–1.

Sunday 13 September

PG sent over poll and a note. Working on speeches then to the Everyman [Theatre] to see *The September Issue*, the fly-on-the-wall re Anna Wintour [editor-in-chief] and *Vogue*. Harmless enough though felt she had a few issues. Dinner at Bacchus with the boys.

Monday 14 September

Worked on and off on my first column for *Le Figaro* on authenticity being the key to comms in modern politics. Got a couple of books at City airport, then lunch, enlivened by a Russian waitress telling her colleagues who the greatest goalkeepers in history were. Flight up fine, car to One Devonshire Gardens then out for a long run around Glasgow's West End. The hotel was meant to be the new 'in' place, a collection of houses knocked together. Nice enough I suppose. Jim Murphy [Secretary of State for Scotland] was down at the political Cabinet in London earlier but came back to collect me and head out to Clarkston for the fundraiser I was doing for him. He was pretty scathing about the Cabinet, said it was just the usual random points. 'Jack Straw tells the same story every week. It is government by anecdote.' I asked him what the main GB point was and he said it wasn't clear.

Peter M went on about the need for greater humility in communications, Harriet did her usual women and new politics stuff. 'I didn't bother to speak as it was pointless.' He seemed pretty jaded, felt there was no chance at all of getting back into the game, and all that we had to play for was keeping opposition to one term. We were like a tired bunch of people who had no empathy and no understanding of people. He said it was not just GB though he was clearly the biggest problem. He felt all of them were weak. Apart from Peter, there was no box office at all. He was very funny re Pat [McFadden] who said he went round the country apologising for not being Peter M. Jim hated his current job. He had turned it down three times, saying he needed something else to do alongside it, but in the end decided why would I waste all my time and energy preparing for defeat? He reckoned he would be DM's campaign manager if there was a contest, but he felt DM would not go for it if he thought there was going to be a long period in opposition.

Tessa had called me earlier and she also felt it was now all about limiting defeat and trying to stop the party going crazy afterwards. Jim said the party in Scotland was virtually dead. He reckoned he would make more money fundraising than the rest of the party put together. Re what he did, he said he marked Salmond. He had tried to warn GB that the Lockerbie decision could not just be ignored. He had had several meetings with him and GB had just said we were best staying out of it. And then he wondered why he got dragged into it. It was pathetic. The other thing Jim was trying to do was have a referendum on independence on the same day as the election. He and Douglas had both said to GB that obviously they wanted to win but if they didn't then it made sense to get the question dealt with at the same time. He was sure we would win and then it was settled even if we lost [power]. He felt with a Cameron government Salmond would find it easier. There would be no strong Labour voice in a campaign. He seemed really fed up with everything though still jaunty in other ways.

Went to his house for a cup of tea. Both dad and wife unemployed, and he said he was useless at sorting stuff like that. I hadn't realised Jim came from quite such a working-class background. The dinner went fine. Donald came over to play the pipes. Usual higher-value donor reception then in for the dinner with my speech before and Q&A afterwards. Spoke well, really trying to fire them up to believe we could still win because the Tories were not up to much and the Nats were not as good as our defensiveness would suggest. I had a whole load of people asking why I didn't stand. They felt in the main that GB had had it and even for the ones who liked him that was the elephant in the room. Jim did a little speech at the end and was incredibly nice about me, my role, and values. Every time I did these events I felt I ought to be right back in the fray. But did I really want to go back? The fact I hesitated so much surely meant no. Jim drove me to the hotel. He was already talking of GB and the government in a kind of future past tense.

Tuesday 15 September

Blogged on something Jim said last night about voting SNP being a way to help Cameron get elected, and worked up the line about DC being

Salmond's Trojan horse for independence. It was not really taking off at the moment but it was going to come and I had no doubt Salmond was hoping for a Tory win. *Sunday Mail* editor read it and liked it, asked me to do a piece. Got the train to Edinburgh. Approached by a guy who said he was in comms and started asking me loads of questions. Said it was like a rock fan bumping into a rock star on a train. Nice enough guy, wanted to come to the speech tomorrow. I was staying at The George, but the room wasn't ready so I dumped my bags and went for a haircut at Toni & Guy. 40 quid! A record. Did a long run out through Leith, lovely sunny weather while London was lashed by storms. Tweeted was there a nicer city centre when the sun shone? Not many. Ate in then out to watch the United game in Turkey. Bit of a non-day but at least I had been getting the miles in.

Wednesday 16 September

The Tories were running with a leak of a Treasury paper on cuts, which they were saying, and the media was regurgitating as, GB having misled people. What they did not do was explain exactly what it was. The comms conference was fine, did an OK speech mainly on world of change plus leadership. Lots said afterwards they had wanted it to go on for longer. Tom Kelly there, had a little chat with him re the lack of comms strategy in No. 10. Met Simon Pia, Iain Gray's press guy. Seemed OK, ex-journalist, fairly experienced but struggling to get Iain to do the things needed to raise his profile. Added to which – and I was hearing this all the time – there was no real direction at the top, UK-wise. They felt Salmond was potentially vulnerable on the economy. But they had a real problem with the BBC which was effectively nationalist, while the bulk of the media now ran an anti-Labour agenda.

Lunch hosted by Platform PR which included Fiona Ross, ex-STV [political correspondent] who said she was in despair about what was happening. Equally she felt it had been entirely predictable. GB just could not lead. Got all big decisions wrong. It was hosted by a woman from Inverness whose husband was head of the Highlands Health Board and was telling me alcohol was the big problem there and getting worse. Changed in the cab, packed flight down, got home by half six and went out for dinner with Grace, who was on great form. Working harder at school and had learned from recent events.

Thursday 17 September

Did another blog on Scotland suggesting that Salmond was hoping for Cameron to win and England needed to wake up. *Sunday Mail* asked for a piece on the same theme so worked on that too. Pottering around clearing up after three days away then out to Avalon to meet Jon Thoday [managing director]. We went through a few ideas and he was keenest on the idea of me as a more upmarket Piers for the Beeb. I also floated the idea of a me v Piers 24-hour programme. Plus maybe sport. Slight problem in him wanting to take care of everything – speeches, books etc. Not sure we would get on that well but he did have some decent clients. Lots of comics. Ran home about six miles but painfully slow. Out to Kensington for the Durrants [media company] dinner, which I did so LRF could get free media monitoring. Some OK people there. Good crowd and Jeremy Thompson [Durrants] said afterwards he got a stack of thanks emails etc. He felt best yet. Maybe because I did more media analysis.

Friday 18 September

I had been hoping to do John Cleese as my *Chain Reaction* interviewee, and he was up for it, but he had been insisting on doing someone as his interviewee someone not very well known, and as the argument went on with the BBC he said eventually 'As I am unable to agree to interview Wayne Rooney or the Pope, I'm afraid I won't be able to take part.' I went for Alistair McGowan [impressionist, comedian] instead and spent the first part of the day scripting out the shape of the interview. Long and rather irritating conference call about a speech in Jersey next month. They were clearly quite excited by it and determined to make a big palaver about it. Research call from *Watchdog* which was also developing palaver potential. Way beyond what we agreed to at the start. Then a call with Ed [Victor] and Stuart [Prebble] re options on documentaries re the full diaries. Stuart felt the Beeb would only go for the full TB–GB story.

Went for a little run then out to see TB. He did his usual 'never been busier' spiel, reeled off all the countries he was about to visit, went over some of the stuff he was doing in China and the Gulf. I was surprised it wasn't getting more media attention. He was basically advising governments and businesses how to deal with governments and on a potentially bigger scale than others had. He said he was enjoying it but I had a sense of him running away from things. He hated being in Britain because of watching the government and because of the media and the way they still went for him. He was due to see GB later and he was clear that anyone would be better. But he did not intend to say so. He said he had told Peter M that for the first time he really was at a loss to know what to advise. He felt we had left a perfectly good and serviceable political position and thrown it away. The idea that a rush to Keynes was the answer to the economic situation was ridiculous. But none of the contenders had really emerged and the chances are we would just limp on to a dreadful end.

He was almost in a 'can't be bothered' mode. He was not really going to get drawn in too much though GB had asked to see him later today. We chatted over the rumour that GB was on anti-depressants. TB was always shocked when I said I sometimes used them but to be honest I hoped that GB was using them. Jim Murphy had said something about him being a lot calmer and chirpier 'but still unable to engage in any meaningful way'. TB said he still talked to Peter who was 'desperate' and he talked to David but he was not sure he had the whole range. TB felt sure he would be better and change might give us a bit of space. He felt the Tories were low grade. The worst thing was that the media had politics back where they wanted it – Tories in power with Labour in for the odd burst. All under attack. He was pleased I had gone to see his dad. I had the sense of him being on a different sort of treadmill. He wanted me to help him with his Kuwait work and also see some of the MPs from the new Japanese government when they were over. He set off to see GB and later told me it was all a bit weird. GB was up for taking advice but he did not really know what to advise. He also felt that the atmosphere in No. 10 was odd, close to being dead.

Later out to the Beeb to record my *Chain Reaction* interview with Alistair McGowan. I didn't really take to him at first but in the interview he was terrific, not just funny, weaving from one voice to another, often while describing the technique he was using, but also clever and making some really interesting points about politics, environment, culture. I loved the fact he said he couldn't do Cameron despite having tried. 'Is it because he doesn't stand for anything?' I asked and it got a decent response. We recorded forty-five minutes, during which he must have done dozens of voices and also told a few good stories. They would definitely have enough for a decent half-hour. Home to get a massage pre the Great North Run. Fiona out at the opera.

Saturday 19 September

Whacked off a quick blog on what it said re Cameron that McGowan couldn't do him. He had said 'All that comes out is an upper-class whisper' which was a lovely line. Train to Preston. Frank Teasdale met me, we made it in good time and I went to the boardroom for lunch with Barry Kilby and co. The atmosphere was pretty good for a lunchtime kick-off. We went one up against the run of play. Sunderland equalised and at half-time I thought we were heading for defeat. But both Niall and Stan Ternent, who I saw for a chat, reckoned we might nick it. Second half was totally different. Two goals from David Nugent making his home debut and away we went. 3–1. Hundred per cent home record.

Helen had sent me a car from the GNR and I did my AOL column on the way up to Newcastle. Rory and Calum had both been up helping, and really enjoyed it. I was at Brendan's table for the usual pre-race dinner, next to the chief exec of the New York marathon who was a very impressive character and evangelical about the power of sport to do good. Dick Caborn and I were doing the usual winding up of each other and of Brendan about his dual role as race owner and Beeb commentator. Nice do though as ever. Bed by half ten to watch *MotD*. Burnley looking even better in the highlights.

Sunday 20 September

Lovely sunny day, as it always seemed to be for the GNR. Out on the bus to the start with Dick and family, and Phil Brown [manager] and his Hull City entourage. Rory made the point Phil could have promoted any charity he wanted but wore a Hull shirt with 'Brown 1' on the back. Did a bit of media, lots of hanging around, then set off with my usual chaperone runner, Graham. Started OK, then slowed a bit, ended OK despite a bad blister after six miles. In a bit of a state at the end. Did over 1.52 but took off a couple of minutes for interviews. Got the foot seen to, then helicopter into town. To the hotel to watch the end of the Manchester derby [v Man City]. 4–3 United deep in injury-time winner. Alex looked as happy as I've seen him for ages. The train back had a fair smattering of runners. Also had a chat with Sting [singer] who said hello when I made one of many trips to the loo. Very nice bloke I thought. Saying how much he had enjoyed the experience – he had been the official starter – telling me about the new album he was recording in Durham Cathedral, asking what I was up to etc. Got home and Jessie was there to do a massage. The blister had spread from side to sole. Really nasty.

Monday 21 September

Out first thing to Finchley Memorial Hospital to get my foot seen to at the walk-in centre. Pretty quick and efficient and at least after going barefoot on tiptoes I could come out wearing shoes. I was limping though and my hip was starting to hurt a fair bit. Douglas had a big interview in the *Telegraph* in which he said he hoped I went back, but I was getting more not less resistant really. GB was not doing bad on one or two substance issues but people had widely given up on him. Out p.m. to Benchmark for a meeting with Nick Keller and Tanni Grey-Thompson to talk to her about how she could improve her public speaking and up her rates. Really liked her but there was too much backward-looking in her speeches as currently worked out. Gave her a few ideas. She was interesting on the subject of the politics of the Olympics.

Tuesday 22 September

My piece on authenticity had appeared in *Le Figaro*, getting not quite as much attention as [former President of France] Valéry Giscard d'Estaing's novel, *The Princess and the President*, which was about a President's affair with someone clearly based on Diana. Out to SW1 to meet Chris Lennie and Vanessa Bowcock [Labour officials]. They wanted me to chair a new fundraising group. They said my cred was higher than ever and everyone felt I was the person to do it. I went through very frankly the reasons I was reluctant – LRF and the potential problems there, but above all not wanting to get sucked in further than already I was. Of course I knew Chris well but I barely knew Vanessa at all and perhaps I was too frank, when I was talking about the way GB and his crew operated and why it made me worry that even a huge effort would only make marginal change. I agreed to help with preparing their case and also with the odd meeting etc. Though they thanked me for my frankness I think they were disappointed.

Off to meet Bradshaw at Costa Coffee. After a bit of small talk we got down to working on AD's speech. It was OK without being brilliant. But Alistair was in a better place than most of the ministers, the vast bulk of whom were invisible or useless. It was really beginning to annoy me that so few of them made any impact whatever. Home then off to do the voice-over for the *Watchdog* film. It was OK, if a bit cheesy in parts. Nice girl called Ros doing the sound who was a runner so I bored her with stories of my blisters which had now led to a limp because of all the weight I was putting on one side. To the Beeb at White City for the programme itself. The usual ridiculous hanging around. Had a good laugh with Annie Robinson as ever. Did the film and also a bit of a consumer discussion. The air conditioning was a bit of a nightmare and I ended up feeling a cold coming on. By the time I was home, I was sure of it. A bad one.

Wednesday 23 September

Feeling rough, and a bad day for it. Two speeches at a BT Connect [telecommunications] conference at Wembley during the day, and an awards ceremony in the evening. I did a quick blog on the media double standards kicking in again e.g. a warning by an ex-MPC [Monetary Policy Committee] member [David Blanchflower] that unemployment would go to five million if the Tories got in, which barely registered. Likewise GB being presented with the World Statesman of the Year award as the UN gathered, for the annual General Assembly, barely registered. The Wembley event was fine if a bit odd as the speech was in a central holding bit surrounded by lots of stalls and activities. Mainly computer and hi-tech stuff and as part of the deal I had to go round and talk to all the people on the stands. Mixed picture on the economy. Most thought things were picking up but that it was going to take a long time before all was well again. Some fascinating new stuff there, e.g. a tiny hand-held video recorder and a where they showed off incredible special effects which they could put to all sorts of different uses.

I did a fairly long interview with Channel 4 re social networking, in a box overlooking the pitch which was being dug up. Tired after it all but only had half an hour at home before heading out to the Royal Lancaster for the *Regeneration & Renewal* magazine awards. Again freezing air conditioning. Black tie, fairly boozy, but I was on form and it went pretty well. The lifetime achievement award was to Professor Anne Power [London School of Economics housing specialist]. I was sitting with her over dinner. She was a close friend of the Hodges so we talked mainly about that, but also about the scene generally. She was but the latest to say she could not understand why we appeared unable to fight back. She felt GB has a lot of strengths but was unable to communicate. She felt I should go back and help him but she understood why I was reluctant. Really nice woman and she made a lovely little speech when she got the award. I was still feeling rough though and glad to get to bed around half eleven.

Thursday 24 September

Feeling rough, rough, rough. TB had asked me to see some MPs and officials from the new Japanese ruling party so I went to his office and in trooped seven or eight Japanese guys – one woman – to give me their cards, sit down and pick my brains. The main guy was an MP clearly close to the new PM [Yukio Hatoyama]. Others were civil servants. And one party strategist. Plus a brilliant young interpreter. Brilliant in that he appeared to be able to take in several voices at the same time. My main point was strike while the iron was hot. They asked for a really detailed analysis of my own operation and how we dealt with personnel issues, crisis management etc. They were pretty smart I thought, and clearly keen to apply some of the Blair government lessons. TB was clearly in demand to give advice on governance and these guys were taking notes on really basic things, like they were revelations. Nice enough bunch though. They asked me to go out to Tokyo to talk to the party people there. The impression I got was that the new guy was serious about reform, but it would be even harder for them than it was for us.

Then to LRF to sign letters for the Stephen Fry event which was proving a harder sell than I thought it would be. Then the short hop to Galliard [healthcare communications company] to help them brainstorm on a pitch to drug company Roche for a contract to promote Herceptin as a treatment for stomach cancer. Not really my thing but I gave them a few ideas and also tested some of theirs to destruction. Annoyingly one of the people in the meeting tweeted that I had been there. Home for a kip, feeling bad still, before heading out to a new restaurant in Islington to meet Tessa, Jessie and co. Tess was in a bit of a state re her mum, also David was clearly worried about the state of the Italian case. Did a blog earlier on the relentless trivial agenda coming from the UN for the UK media – snub by Obama, GB asked if he was blind, if he was quitting blah blah. If we got the press we deserved then Britain did something very wrong in a previous life.

Friday 25 September

Up at 6. Off to Eurostar. Blogged in support of Roy Hattersley's call on ministers to fight harder for what they believe. Arrived and straight to Saint-Cloud to record one-on-one with Victor Robert re Giscard's novel. He had let it go for a couple of days with the idea he had had an affair with Diana. OK discussion. Hard to do humour and I was plugging my own book as a way of saying that this was a story of book promotion nothing more. Then headed for Ivry for meeting re books etc. Tired and feeling rough as hell.

Saturday 26 September

Consistently blogging on the theme of media double standards and getting OK responses. GB sent his speech through and I did an OK note I think. I was pleased that one of the central themes was the fightback. The whole party needed to get off the back foot. He had done fine in New York and Pittsburgh but our media had got it into a trivial agenda, lots of blah. It was beginning to feel a bit like things had been with Major in his latter days. But at least the speech had a bit of fight in it. Worked on it for an hour. I liked centrality of the FIGHT. I said the theme of the whole conference should be about the nature of that fight, and his speech should be the highpoint of that.

He had a line about 'fight fight fight', but I said he needed to think through how they will use the [Hugh] Gaitskell [former Labour leader, who used the phrase 'to save the party we love'] analogy against him. I liked the analysis of how the Tories miscalled the call of the century at every turn, and suggested he end with 'And it is because they were wrong, wrong, wrong that we must fight, fight, fight to stop them getting their hands on the levers of our economy once more.' I said if you think that works, the 'fight fight fight' line could be used in different ways at different points in the speech, e.g. 'And it is because we believe in the NHS that we must fight, fight, fight to ensure the Tories do not get in to reverse these changes and make their cuts.' Or in Europe. 'And it is because we know Britain must stay strong in Europe that we fight, fight, fight to make sure every man, woman and child knows what a Tory European policy looks like – racist, homophobic, at the margins of power.'

Of course it is possible to overdo, but if he went for it once, it was likely to be the topline, so there was a case for really hammering it. He called a couple of times, accepted that the conference and the speech have to be the point at which the mood of defeatism and inevitability is turned. The party needs to feel that he really believes winning is possible. That means no politics as commentary in the margins, but absolute ruthless focus on the importance of the fight. There was probably too much anti-Tory stuff, and I suggested ways of getting them stripped down without losing the message. I was also trying to think of ways of turning DC's support in the press into a weakness for him, rather than a strength. I said there will come a point where the public thinks the whole thing has gone too far. The people have to decide who wins, not the press.

There would be something very interesting, and clever, about GB saying DC being popular with the British press is a sign of weakness not strength. There were parts of the speech though – particularly the mainstream middle-class section – that read too much like an attempt to pander to the *Mail* agenda. And I hated the way he wanted to bum up Sugar/Cowell/[Simon] Fuller [TV entrepreneur] stuff as being about giving young people a chance. It came over as trivial. This has to be a big speech, on big themes, challenges, heavyweight policies, I said. Don't throw in things that risk weakening that. Putting Cheryl Cole [singer and TV personality] and Duncan Bannatyne [entrepreneur and TV personality] into a conference speech? No. He needed to build up the section on optimism about Britain. The Tories and the media (I said you should run the two together in this) run Britain down all the time. Yet we have so much going for us. All of these sections should be really personal.

He sounded up for it. The schools and hospitals sections felt unambitious. He was risking losing the focus by pushing too hard on ID cards – big story, be careful how big it goes. But there was plenty of stuff in there, the question was whether it was where people wanted him to be right now. I felt he had to be on really big challenges, and the contrast between experience and substance v inexperience and style. Climate change. Terrorism. Economy. I felt the main things he had to play up were the concept of the fight, the defence of record / values as the key to a forward agenda, big challenges v small politics, GB v DC.

David M had sent his speech through too. It had gone backwards. I had the sense David had lost his bearings a little and didn't really know what he wanted to say. His first four pages were on Afghanistan, which was perhaps inevitable, but that was half of a speech that was going to need to get him back on the domestic pitch. Alistair D's speech a bit better. Peter M sent his through over the weekend and in its own way it was the best of them. Witty and personal and also with a bit of fight. Off to Spurs with Calum. As at Chelsea a pretty poor turnout though OK noise, even as their goals started going in. Our four away games had now gone 2–0, 3–0, 4–0, 5–0. At this rate we'll lose 20–0 in the last game of season.

Sunday 27 September

A whole week without exercise. First the foot, then the cold. Umming and aahing about going to conference. Each time that world impinged on me, I wanted to push back. I watched GB on Marr. He did well enough and showed he was up for the fight. Marr asked him at the end about his eyesight and the anti-depressant rumours, which was pretty low. Did a quick blog, serious politics 1, low journalism 0. I could tell that GB was uncomfortable answering but he did OK dealing with it. Peter called asking when I was going down there [Brighton conference]. He too thought GB did OK, and also that we had to work up a proper line of argument re the role the media, especially the BBC, was playing in setting the backdrop for politics. Everything pointed the whole time to Gordon loser, Cameron winner.

The Sundays showed up the problem in a way. All the papers going big on various lines, interviews etc., but there was no coherent theme linking it. Peter on *ST* mag cover with his dog, and a story flammed up by them about him saying he would work for the Tories, Alistair in *The Observer* saying they had lost the will to live, Harriet on women, JP saying we were concentrating too much on women and not enough on campaigning. No clarity. I felt by the end of the day though that at least the sense of a fightback was there. Decided overnight not to go to Brighton. I just couldn't face getting sucked in to all the media stuff and all the 'What you up to, when you coming back?' Not to mention the late night speech process for GB.

Monday 28 September

Kirsty [McNeill, GB speechwriter] had sent another draft through. I worked on it for an hour or two and sent through a note. It was much better, and clearer, less cluttered. I suggested a new opening, starting with the idea of being in a fight. How it is the fighters and believers who change our world. He called and asked if I could do a line-by-line write through. Some of the sections were strong, others really weak, and I suggested some fairly big cuts. He was trying to cover every base. I quite liked the paragraph I had done yesterday – 'If you change one life for the better, you change one family. Change one family, and you change a street. Change a street and you change a town. Change a town and you change a country. Change a country and you can change the world. Conference, this Labour government has changed the country for the better, we have changed the world for the better and do not let the Tories or the cynics make you think otherwise for one single second of the fight ahead.' I still thought the tone of the politics/exes section was too negative, and I was worried there was nothing on sport, and suggested he look forward to the 2012 Olympics either in the 'what's great about Britain' section, or one of the things they said would never happen.

I did not want to get sucked into the speechwriting process madness, but I now had GB, David M, AD and Peter all asking for help on their speeches. I had tried to put in some ideas for all of them. GB's draft was tighter and better but it still lacked either driving argument or really purple passages. He had thankfully dropped the awful passage where he was going to be asking Simon Cowell, Alan Sugar, Cheryl Cole and a few other celebs to advise on the whole youth opportunity thing. Whether or not to do TV debates was in and out. PR [proportional representation] not clear. A few big announcements but not well explained. AD's was fine, much better than last week, with a bit of decent explanation and a bit of fight. David's had gone backwards and lacked passion or colour. Peter's was by far the best. Funny, wise, full of politics. He turned himself into a metaphor for the party – if he could come back so could the party.

I was mainly working at home with the live [conference] coverage on the Parliament channel in the background. Watched AD who did fine, and later Peter who was terrific, really got the place going. I had been blogging on the importance of fightback and it really came through that there was a bit of fighting spirit in there. The party loved it though and so everyone was trotting out TB's line that his project would not be complete until the party learned to love Peter. We had a chat later and he said he felt really relieved but still anxious about the week. He was finding it hard to get any kind of real discipline imposed. He was pleased his own speech had gone well. The media, as ever going from one extreme to the other, said it had electrified the conference, till then a bit depressed and downcast. Fiona was doing a fringe meeting so it felt even weirder that she was going off and I was staying home. Went out for dinner with Rory and Grace and we had a nice enough time. I was still so bloody torn though and it didn't help that whenever politics was really high-profile as now, people kept talking to me, either as though I were still there, or urging me to get back.

Tuesday 29 September

I'd been having problems with my nose and went to see Bostock, who was pretty clear I had had a return of polyps. He went through my notes and I was amazed to discover it was more than fifteen years since I had them done. He was on good form, largely because he had found a new girlfriend. But he was still saying the NHS was hopeless. Inefficient and for all the talk of choice not really focused on patients. He said he was surprised – but pleased – I wasn't in Brighton. He felt I was in good shape. Peter Schmeichel called for a chat and said he really thought I should get back in the frontline. It was so obvious what they needed, someone who could communicate and fight. They looked a bit lost. He had seen Helle and thought she was in with a chance. I did a few last-minute suggestions on GB's speech though it was almost certainly too late to make a difference. I went to watch it at Silverfish so that I could do a video blog straight after which worked pretty well. As a speech it did OK without being brilliant. Sarah introduced him but went on too long. There was a terrific film at the start, of great achievements by Labour down the years, but then Sarah, then another film in which GB appeared as a talking head. He was OK in terms of delivery but it felt flat and flabby at times.

Fiona was there sitting with Philip behind Neil, Glenys, Eddie Izzard and Sarah's parents. She and PG both felt it was OK but not much better. I did the vlog mainly on fightback and also the big policy substance but it was not one of those speeches that really wowed people. Then later the news agenda began to switch when *The Sun* announced they were switching from Labour to Tory. In truth they had gone a while back but the media were loving it. If anything it was an even bigger thing than the switch to us in '97 when in truth because of the way the media had changed it was probably less significant. But try telling that to the Beeb. Radio Five called while I was in bed and I did a chat with Richard Bacon [presenter] trying to downplay it a bit, and also making the point the Beeb had more to worry about from a Murdoch–Tory alliance than Labour. But it was one of those stories that the rest of the media would lap up.

Peter called, said Rebekah [Wade, CEO News International] – 'Is she dim or manipulative or both?' he asked – had called him frantically trying to get hold of GB to tell him before it was out on the news. Peter had told her to relax, that nobody would take it too seriously, not to worry. Classic Peter. She was obviously a bit worried about GB–Sarah reaction but they were a ruthless bunch and would do as they were told. Gail was adamant it was James [Murdoch] not Rupert who was the driving force behind it. Peter sounded a bit more subdued, felt GB's speech was OK but had not really cut through as planned, and would not move the dial.

Wednesday 30 September

The Beeb were leading on *The Sun*, which was pretty ludicrous. GB was doing a morning round of interviews and sounded a bit ratty. He was using some of the lines Peter and I had agreed last night, about people not papers deciding elections, the need to focus on policy choices etc. but he will have been hit a bit by it. Mark Bennett called and said I ought to get out there a bit because heads were dropping and people were overreacting.

I went to Millbank and did half a dozen or so interviews, trying to make a bit light of it and also run the line that getting an easy press was Cameron's one big success. There was a pretty big response to the blog, and a lot of hostility to *The Sun*. Some saying they would rejoin or join the party because of *The Sun*'s arrogance. But the rest of the media were just running in their slipstream. Bumped into David Blunkett on the *Daily Politics* show, where I was saying the public were not as interested in the media as the media were. As we came off the set, with people still around, DB just said apropos of nothing 'It's not great out there.' The worst thing about it was the sucking of oxygen from the fightback and the substance of GB's speech.

Thursday 1 October

Did another bit on *The Sun*. Into Random House for a meeting with Gail, Ed, Susan and Caroline. We agreed to do the full Volume 1 regardless of the election result, probably in June. The rest would depend on the result. Agreed we would maybe edit Volume 4 next so that it could be given to the Iraq Inquiry if needed. To the Brewery in the Barbican for a rehearsal of the Pharmaceutical Society Digital Media Awards. Nice crowd organising it including [awards chairperson] Rachel Farrow who was funny. She asked me about my porn writing and by the end of the evening we had agreed to have a competition for charity to see who could get sex story published first.

Nipped out to Mike Molloy's art exhibition launch in Belgravia. Lots of old *Mirror* guys. Lovely to see all three of the girls [Molloy's daughters]. John McEntee [diary columnist] saying that [columnist, author and playwright Keith] Waterhouse's funeral had not been packed which really surprised me and made me wish I had been able to go. I liked some of Mike's pictures and thought about buying one but Fiona wanted to see first. Back to the awards, which were pretty well organised. I did a mix of anecdotes and a bit of rah-rah and was OK without being on total top form. Lots of Labour people there but there was still huge resistance to Gordon, with still no enthusiasm for Cameron.

Friday 2 October

Rayan collected me early and we set off for City airport. The guy checking tickets at security followed me through and was virtually begging me to go back. He was Asian, said he was lifelong Labour and 'I am really scared the Tories will get back. You have to stop them.' He felt DM should take over. This kind of approach was happening more and more as people faced up to likely change. There was hardly anyone on the flight to Jersey, maybe fifteen mainly elderly people. When we landed it was not as warm as I had expected but pretty. I was met by Trudi Roscouet, who was organising the dinner, and a cop who was chairman of the group I was speaking to, Institute of Chartered Secretaries and Administrators. They were two very diverse characters, he quiet and calm and methodical, she excitable and loquacious. Both nice though and we had a long drive round the island on the way to the Hotel de France. They were clearly proud of their non-party-political political system – 'a coalition of independents' – and also felt a little bit defensive about all the talk of tax havens, offshore etc. as they apparently did better in a recent IMF report than the UK.

I checked in and changed before heading to meet the Lieutenant-Governor, Andrew Ridgway, at government house. I had not realised he was the same guy I had met in Kosovo. He was then a senior officer working with General Sir Mike Jackson, and we chatted away a fair bit on that. He had a classic public school establishment-type chief of staff who had been there eighteen years. Ridgway was a nice enough type and was really helpful in filling me in on local issues and history, what to avoid and what to promote. We reminisced a bit about Kosovo and also on the importance of the whole comms scene. He was very strong on the line that Afghanistan was a war that had to be seen through to the end. Typical government house. He had invited me to stay overnight but I felt tomorrow's early start meant best to stay in a hotel. Nice guy though and we had a good chat.

The one major downer of the trip, as I feared from the conference call it would be, was Cameron Macphail, the Scottish banker (rhyming slang allowed) who was to interview me at the dinner. He had come up with a ludicrously complicated format supposedly based on different debate and quiz shows. It included pretending questions had come in from people with funny names! I ended up at the pre-meeting saying that it was not going to work and we needed to change it. 'But all the work I have done,' he bleated. I said all that mattered was the outcome. I had done stacks of these events and this was not going to work so I was not going to let it happen. He had all sorts of nonsense lined up. He was also of unutterably boring voice and ponderous manner, the worst sort of person for a lively after-dinner Q&A.

I went for a run and afterwards told Trudi I wanted it sorted so that the thing was changed. After I was pretty rude and heavy with him, we agreed Trudi would bring me a collection of audience questions and I would work my way through them. Into the black tie then down to the reception for loads of photos and small talk. At the dinner I was seated between Ridgway and the local LRF people as we were the chosen charity for the raffle. Nice atmosphere. Trudi had had a quiet word with Macphail to the effect that I was worried the Q&A would be a disaster if he tried to control it. He was a disaster. We went up together and he did a long unwitty intro, which ended with me playing the pipes for a couple of minutes then a few dull and ponderous questions before I decided to grip it. The guests' Q&A session went well once I had cut him out.

Saturday 3 October

Up before 6, car to the airport and off. The plane was busier than yesterday and the one from Gatwick to Manchester pretty well packed. Did a blog going over some of the funnier questions from last night, with a few whacks at the Tories pre-Manchester conference. I had done the 'My Week' column for *The Observer* which along with the blog I used to say Marr needed to show similar attitude to Cameron. I used the piece to plug the Stephen Fry event as well as run around the block re Peter, *Sun* switch, Ridgway and Kosovo, Jersey. Worked OK I think. Bumped into a Burnley fan coming off the plane. Turned out to be the brother-in-law of council leader Gordon Birtwistle, Lib Dem candidate for Burnley who was picking him up so gave me a lift to Turf Moor. Bit of a disaster as we left the airport when my laptop fell out of my bag and the on/off button smashed. Gordon seemed to think their week went pretty well, that ours was not great and that GB was never going to shift the feelings against him.

Got to the ground fairly early. Everyone seemed a bit nervous about Birmingham. Richard Scudamore from the Premier League was there, first time since a League Cup tie against Oldham thirteen years ago. He was a pretty tough character, smart. He said he listened to 'the Caborns of this world' going on about community and grassroots 'but what do they mean? Football is a collection of clubs that's all.' He spent most of the first half on his BlackBerry though to be fair it was pretty dull fare. Second half a lot better and we won 2–1. Did my AOL column on the bus to Manchester. Calum and I went out for dinner at Santini's. Too many Tories around.

Sunday 4 October

Slept in, but up in time for Cameron on Marr. He was OK without being brilliant. Under pressure he looked a bit peevish and his line on the Lisbon Treaty was weak.* The Irish had voted yes now and yet he was trying to face both ways, including the ludicrous line that he did not want to say anything that undermined the debate in Poland and the Czech Republic. He was given a fairly free hit on welfare reform and his so-called big bold plans. Poor on spending and jobs. Not happy when asked about his wealth. Calum was watching and said he thought he was quite good at not answering questions and just leaving an OK impression. Train to Warrington and walk to the [rugby league] stadium. Three play-off matches with Keighley v Oldham the middle one.

I was taken down to do the coin-toss on the pitch. Real mix of nerves and aggression down there. Good match though in warm sunshine plus drizzle. Keighley won 28–26 and lots of happy Cougars were celebrating as we headed for the station. Good sporting weekend though I was feeling bad because Fiona had said she had felt lonely at the weekend, Grace out as usual, Rory away doing a race in Sheffield. Back by half eight, dinner and bed. Tories getting a bit of grief on Europe but in the main he was getting OK coverage. I did a blog late on re Cameron really not having answers and not enjoying difficult questions. Another day in which several strangers had urged me to go back. Fiona was beginning to think I should too. PG felt we should maybe set up a pro-record and anti-Tory campaign from outside.

Monday 5 October

Out to the Beeb to do two hours of local radio tying in with BBC Headroom coming up to World Mental Health day. Thirteen ten-minute interviews, half and half live and pre-record, with a pretty good run at getting over

* EU agreement to amend the constitutional basis of the Union.

the main points plus loads of book and website pluggery. Even since the last round I did for Time to Change there was a shift in tone and attitude on the issues. Only one – Stephen Nolan in Belfast – tried to make it about Labour, GB etc. The demand was certainly there too with another twenty or so also wanting me to do one. Cab to St James's to meet Robin Janvrin for lunch at a little Italian restaurant in Crown Passage. He seemed pretty happy with his life, three days at HSBC doing corporate sustainability etc., trustee on a few bodies, including on a charity fund set up for [Princes] William and Harry to raise and allocate money. Reminisced a bit about working together. Talked about the movie *The Queen* on which we shared the view that TB and the Queen were presented as real characters while the rest of us were caricatures. He felt the royals were in good shape, stable and OK. He liked William, said he was sensible. But he was also pleased David Manning had this guidance role in there.

He clearly thought GB was not a patch on TB and that the Tories were going to get in by default. We agreed to meet up with David Manning. Texted David Miliband to say he must keep going to make Europe an issue this week. Did a blog at King's Cross on the need to do a better job of defending the record as a way of showing what the Tories would dismantle. Ridiculous that they had not been hit harder over e.g. scrapping New Deal [Labour programme to reduce unemployment] or Sure Start [Treasury initiative to give children 'the best possible start in life']. Train to Leeds. Unlike yesterday's from Warrington, which was heaving, I had a carriage to myself. Got changed without going to the loo! Cab to the Armouries. *Yorkshire Post* there to do an interview on the theme of the speech, the changed media landscape and how to manage it. The 'online reputation management product' being launched was Profiled.com [personal branding website] and the guy presenting it was Steve Wainwright who was quite nervous about the whole thing. I did a big-picture context-setting speech on the nature of the modern media and how I defined strategic communications, then he did the sell. It was an interesting enough idea – that you take control of your own internet profile and try to make your own version of your profile the first thing people find on the web.

About 130 people there and some seemed impressed, others less so. I stayed for the drinks for a bit, then headed back to the hotel. Went for a run then picked up an M&S salad and went back to watch *Newsnight*. Boris and Paxo [Jeremy Paxman] had a pretty good bust-up. AD had announced a pay freeze for some top public servants and the Tories had trailed an announcement in Osborne's speech re raising the pension age. But for me the most interesting moment was when Michael Crick [*Newsnight* political editor] chased down a load of candidates who were a modern version of chinless wonders. They refused to open their mouths about Lisbon.

Tuesday 6 October

Did a quick blog on the *Newsnight* chinless wonders then set off in pouring rain on the drive to Sheffield Children's Hospital to accept the cheque from Dransfield Properties for the Big 5–0 campaign. The hospital hierarchy out in force, and I was picking up a fair bit of pro-Labour anti-Tory messages. We did a few snaps and then looked at a research programme upstairs before I had to leave for Leeds. I was keen to see Osborne's speech. No TV at the [West Yorkshire] Playhouse so nipped next door to the Beeb and watched it there. I was amazed how little interest there was. Nobody had it on so far as I could see and nobody but me was following it. It was OK by his own terms but I felt it was pretty average. The issue was going to be the extent to which he got credit for toughness as opposed to lost support for specific measures.

I did a pre-record on various things, mainly mental health, for the drivetime show, then back for lunch at the Playhouse. Arranged to go for a run, down by the canal, back for a shower then listened to the other speakers at the conference (Institute of PR) while blogging on Osborne. Did same speech as last night, a bit livelier. Nice enough event. Lots of them tweeting as I did it. Good instant feedback. David Muir emailed and then called asking if I would be part of GB's pre-PMQs team. Hard to say no. I definitely thought things could still be turned against Cameron though and that their conference was not going as well as the media would have it. Home for dinner, both Rory and Grace there but Grace complaining I was away too much.

Wednesday 7 October

Off to City airport with Rayan. Picked up at Glasgow and driven to STV for *The Hour* to be interviewed by Stephen Jardine and Michelle McManus. She was really nice, warm and friendly and bright as well. Definitely Labour. The other guests were Jim Kerr of Simple Minds – he and I nattered mainly about football – and Gerry Marsden [both singers] who was saying how awful the Tories were. I had two dinners to go to on the one evening, first at the Radisson for the Insider Elite [business] Awards, then a fundraiser for Mary Galbraith [Labour candidate] in Bishopbriggs. Donald was piping at both and looking really well. Stephen Jardine was hosting the first one. I had a bit of a bust-up with a Tory twat at the start who asked me as he arrived if I would be apologising for the state of Britain. Gave him all barrels. Had blogged earlier on Cameron claiming to be pro-Union yet in his 'English votes on English issues' playing into the hands of the Nats. When I did the speech, to a fairly Tory audience, I did a big number of how he did not cut it and on the Union point there was a lot of nod-along going on. I was on really good form, usual funny stories which went down well then my leadership ten points which also went down well. Dinner with the sponsors but managed to get away by quarter past nine.

Lift with an ex-cop named Bert. Drove through Michael Martin's seat and then Mary's constituency. Good crowd. Nice atmosphere. Sold loads of books, well over 100. Spoke pretty well. I did a few jokes then a big thing about how and why we could still win. Mary chaired a Q&A. At both events I was asked why I did not stand for office myself and it was a question I kept being asked. Maybe I should. And maybe I should go back for the campaign. Still didn't feel it in me. Really felt able to motivate and enthuse though, in a way hardly any of our politicians could. Did a bit of a whack at Nick Robinson for calling DC PM in a two-way earlier, which I said was a mindset as much a mistake and also Richard Dannatt who had been announced as a possible Tory minister in the Lords. Chris Grayling was blindsided on it and at first attacked it as a GB gimmick not realising it was DC who was hiring him. Late back.

Thursday 8 October

Blogged on Robinson and Dannatt and their slipping tongues. I really felt Dannatt was wrong, that he should not be allying himself to any party so soon after he had been in the military. It put in perspective some of the undermining of GB. The flight down was delayed. Home in time for Cameron's speech. It was OK technically but there were too many contradictions. His big argument was against what he repeatedly called Big Government yet his portrayal of Britain as basket case was set alongside expressions of support for lots of things the Big Government had done – minimum wage, Sure Start, devolution etc. It was a speech tailored at the media with his personal stories. But it reminded me of TB on a bad day when he hadn't really worked on the argument. The media was mixed on it. I recorded a video blog saying I felt it was still game on. But as I said on *Channel 4 News* there had to be some real fightback from Labour. I asked Peter M who had been in charge of the week. He said he had been in Korea and Japan. I said it had not been sharp or clear enough. There were mistakes and weaknesses going unpunished. Too many of them.

Friday 9 October

Justin Webster round to interview me for a Spanish TV documentary on Aznar. Blathered away and they seemed to find in useful. Conference call re the npower event next week. Kate White [LRF] round to go over Credit Suisse pitch next week. Worth 300k if we got it and she reckoned me doing the pitch might make it. Obama announced as the winner of the Nobel Peace Prize. Major surprise. Surely premature? I wondered if TB would have won it one of these years, for Ireland, but for Iraq. TB and GB with the Queen etc. at the St Paul's service for Iraq troops. [Archbishop of Canterbury] Rowan Williams's speech was taken as a dig at TB. Some on the blog took it as a dig at me.

Saturday 10 October

Just before dinner TB called. He had been over for the Iraq service and the papers had a fair bit both on Williams's speech, taken as being critical of him, and a soldier's father who apparently refused to shake his hand at the reception then went to the media and told them. He felt it was a set-up, said most were fine but it was obviously a bit upsetting. He said the service had been very well done and the troops seemed fine with him. He was calling effectively at the behest of GB. He said he really wanted me to go back in some kind of major capacity. There was a Lords list coming up and he thought I should be on that. I said I had no desire to go to the Lords for the sake of it. He agreed it should only happen as part of a job that required that. He felt GB would offer me pretty much any job I wanted to get me in there. He said he would not discourage me if I thought I should. I said I was in the same position as before – willing to help but not willing to take the whole show over.

I felt with him I could make a fair bit of difference and we were usually on the same wavelength. With GB you put in massive effort for minimal change or advance. I honestly worried I would go crazy in there. It angered me that they had not filled the gaps left by our departure and were just waiting for me to turn up one day and say OK I will do it. I had a better balance in my life and I was doing a fair bit already. What he wanted was full-on commitment which I could not give. TB understood all the reasons, also said that he was speaking to him more and trying to help and I sensed he had promised GB, as had Tessa and others, to try to get me to go back. He asked me to think about it, said he would go back and find out just how desperate they were and speak again on Tuesday. Even that exchange left me feeling a bit ground down.

He also admitted that even though the Tories were not up to much and had exposed flanks, Cameron was probably good enough to beat GB. Too many people had given up already. Simon Lewis [No. 10 press] called to ask what I thought they should do about the lobby briefings. He said the US trip had been ghastly, the Obama snub story cooked up because they were all in a fit of pique about something. He was doing the briefings and did not feel he was making mistakes but equally nothing good came of them either.

GB, as I knew from one of the conference drafts, had been thinking about overnight scrapping it but we both felt that had to be thought through. I said Simon needed to speak to Peter and Douglas and get a shift in the balance of story making and briefing to the party not the government.

Sunday 11 October

David M was doing OK on the Tories and European extremes but apart from that there was little sign of the follow-through from conference season, added to which expenses were coming back as an issue because Sir Thomas Legg's letters to MPs post-audit were due.* I went out on the bike then back to catch Bertie Ahern on Marr, as I was seeing him later at Cheltenham [Literary Festival]. I caught the paper review with Jane Moore [journalist] and Robert Harris [novelist]. They and Marr said they felt the media was getting tougher on the Tories. Could have fooled me. Set off for Cheltenham, working on Bill's Vol. 2 edits on the way. Arrived at the racecourse to meet up with Bertie. On good form. He seemed to be walking very stiffly though. Doing the usual mix of post-PM stuff while remaining an MP. Very warm re TB publicly and privately. He said he thought [Jean-Claude] Juncker [Luxembourg Prime Minister] was the one to watch out for re the Europe job [EU presidency]. Didn't rate Cameron but he felt GB was, even if unfairly, in trouble.

A few hundred there for the session. Went through the book fairly chronologically and we seemed to be a pretty good double act. Good mix of light and heavy. Clearly not keen on [Gerry] Adams or Peter M. Liked McGuinness. Spoke well on how he felt his sacrificed his marriage to his work. Waffled a bit on whether he fancied being President. Worried about the economy. Generally we whizzed through maybe ten OK questions, a signing then off to my own event at the town hall. Did a UTV interview on mental health, then Radio Gloucestershire, then into the session. Q&A mainly political and lots of worry about the Tories, also lots of applause for my usual whack at the two-way pundits. Also announced, on the basis that Obama had won the Nobel Peace Prize (premature said Bertie), that I had won the Nobel Prize for Literature for my next novel.

Monday 12 October

Lovely day so went out on the bike for an hour before heading for Oxford to do the Labour Students. Really good turnout, much bigger than last

* Sir Thomas had been appointed to chair an independent panel to examine all claims relating to second-homes expenses allowances from 2004 to 2008.

time. As usual I was feeling a bit pissed off when it came to it but they were a good bunch and I felt quite enervated by it by the end. I did half an hour without notes, my usual mantra on record, attack, policy etc. Took maybe fifty questions in the Q&A, mix of political and personal. I sensed a lot of bright people who were maybe more up for the fight post-Tory conference than they had been before. A fair bit on Iraq and the bulk were unconvinced I think. No doubt at all that the anti-Tory feeling was the one to hit. But as Chris Lennie said, apart from me and JP, and DM on Europe, nobody was going for them. Fiona nightmare journey to Cheltenham. Body on the line on the way. Eventually they sent a car for her and Simon Schama [historian].

Tuesday 13 October

Up half five to do the 6.20 slot on *GMTV*. Trumpeting new results showing 91 per cent childhood survival rates as a result of a fifteen-year testing programme funded by the charity. Managed to plug Big 5–0 and mini plug the Stephen Fry event, which was now close to being sold out. Could never quite get my head round the early morning atmosphere of *GMTV*. Seemed a bit lower manned than usual though. To the County Hall hotel, for breakfast with Andrew Rawnsley, who was doing another book. Amazing how shaky my memory was e.g. had no memory of being in Sedgefield on '05 election night. Rawnsley was one of the better ones but it was all a bit relentlessly personality-based and trivialising. He felt I stayed too long. Thought JoP and TB withheld news from me re Kelly coming forward. He was way too interested in how I got on with Cherie. He had clearly spoken to a lot of people. Not sure I helped that much. TB had been very funny about his own book. He said once it got past 2003 he was a bit lost because my diaries had triggered his memory all the time.

To the Inn on the Park to meet Catherine McLeod. She was full of horror stories about GB. He said that in Pittsburgh he had been in a total rage the whole time because of 'snub snub snub'. He was also pretty much at loggerheads with AD who wanted, with Peter's support, to be much more open about the need for further visible bearing down on the debt. She asked if Balls 'had something that made GB scared of him'. Why? Because Alistair would get him to a better position then Balls would push him back. She said she had no idea how I managed to hold the thing together. Ollie Robbins [director of intelligence and security, Cabinet Office], the former private secretary to TB at No. 10, had been asked by GB what the operation needed and he had said 'a Campbell and a Jonathan Powell'. She confirmed GB's obsession with getting me back. He had said to AD he would be fine if only I went back. It made me less not more likely to want to do it.

She said what amazed her was how little you actually knew as a journalist, how different it was on the other side. She said AD had really had his eyes opened. He had never been tribal, and he had always felt there was a good as well as bad side to GB but he had seen a lot of the bad recently. Disorganised, bad-tempered, but convinced everyone was out to get him. Alistair was loyal, she said, but had been taken aback by some of it. He had never made threats but before the last reshuffle he did make clear he would only be Chancellor or out of the government. She asked if I thought he should behave a bit more as GB did to TB. I said no, because it was not his nature. But they should be drawing up big plans for medium- and long-term comms and education on the economy, involving other ministers, especially Peter.

Both she and Maggie Darling had lost weight, which she said was deliberate rather than stress. Lovely sunny day so I walked to LRF to see Cathy and meet up with Kate White before heading to Canary Wharf for the pitch to be Credit Suisse's charity partner. Six charities getting ten minutes to pitch and ten minutes' Q&A. British Heart Foundation, Over The Wall, a deaf charity, Alzheimer's, breast cancer. Fairly typical charity people, nice, but also pretty competitive. Surprised to see me there I think. Definitely worked with the twenty or so people judging the pitches for the three to go to a shortlist and a vote of the staff. Kate pretty good and I felt we were going down well. Said in the car I would be amazed if we didn't get it.

Cab to Royal Horseguards, meeting with Denis Hickie [former Ireland rugby international]. Now right out of rugby, had been involved with the Yes campaign on the Lisbon Treaty in Dublin and really enjoyed it. Now looking for similar kind of work. Nice to see him. Definitely a cut above your average sportsman brains-wise. Then finally over to 70 Whitehall to help GB prepare for PMQs. Bumped into Desmond Bowen, ex-MoD, who stopped to chat. Amazingly he was retired and now doing a bit of this and that, including as counsellor to security service staff who were worried about going off the rails. He said he had just got his letter re the Iraq Inquiry and he was probably going to be asked about aftermath planning. I wasn't aware families of soldiers were seeing the inquiry today and he said they had apparently been questioning legality, and saying they wanted TB tried as a war criminal.

TB called me not about that but about another chat he had had with GB and also with PM saying they were desperate for me to go back and help and would facilitate anything I wanted to make it happen. I was taken through to GB's little room near the Cabinet Room. Douglas was first to arrive who gave me a dreadful report on where they were – no money, a third of the staff they had this time last parliament, call centre closed, no money for direct mail, Ashcroft money pouring into Tories in next few months. He also seemed very down on GB still. He said he had been hoping Peter would grip the centre and sort the basic dysfunction but he seemed unable to do so.

GB came in, very warm in that loud way he has, and we went through to the Cabinet Room. His Clare Sumner [former private secretary to TB] was a tall guy I didn't know but who seemed pretty good with GB and had done a lot of preparation. Also Nicholas Howard who had been part of TB's PMQs team, Theo Bertram and later David Muir. GB went straight into a thing about the leaked Treasury document, the one that suggested the need for 10 per cent cuts after he had said there were no plans for any such cuts. He was clearly a bit obsessed with it. Douglas said he needed to say there were all sorts of documents and pieces of advice but ultimately ministers decided and this was rejected. They clearly thought Cameron would go on general integrity issues e.g. also ask if it was true Dannatt had asked for 2,000 troops.

I wasn't sure they would think Dannatt was the thing to go on. I said we should stand back and agree what was going to be the aim for three months of PMQs. What did we want to say about GB and what about DC? There had to be a strategy, not a piecemeal approach. But he kept going down the thicket of specific questions first. The official was pretending to be Cameron and when he said – which he did three times – 'Why didn't the PM even mention the deficit reduction plan in his speech to the conference?' GB snapped back 'I did, why are you saying that?' After the third time I said for God's sake if an official can get under your skin how easy is it for Cameron to do it? GB said he hated the public schoolboy sense of entitlement that Cameron exuded. He went off on one – how have we got a situation where we made the right calls on the crisis and the Tories made the wrong calls but we get no credit and they get such an easy ride? I said he had to stop thinking about the media and also stop worrying about Cameron. Get above it all.

We agreed to try to make one question a professorial explanation of the deficit reduction plan, pointing to more to come in the PBR, then another re better than expected jobs figures tomorrow, only going to the anti-Tory dividing lines later. He seemed to get it for a while, but then would go backwards again. At points he would have his feet on the table and put his hands over his face, at others he would get up and stomp around the place. He also had a statement on Afghanistan after PMQs which we talked about a bit. I asked if even so Cameron might do Afghanistan in PMQs too. GB felt not, Nicholas felt yes, especially as GB would be starting by reading out thirty-seven names of all the soldiers killed during the recess. He seemed OK on the arguments about that as we went through all the different options the military had put – he was announcing another 500 troops tomorrow, as Obama continued to deliberate about whether to send another 40,000.

The meeting went a bit round in circles and Douglas and I were trying to get him to fix on one major line about the Tories being 'wrong on the recession, wrong on the recovery'. I said they should be doing more to get David Blanchflower's views about the Tories out there, but they were all so defensive. Theo said the lobby see him as a Labour voice. I said fuck the lobby. The public don't know who he is. GB was a very difficult guy to brief. He went off again this time about James Murdoch and went through a whole range of policies – Sky monopoly, Ofcom, BBC top slicing – where Tory policy followed Murdoch and explained the *Sun* switch. Again I tried to say to stop worrying about it but it was hard to shift his mindset. After 100 minutes I said I had to go because Fiona was waiting for me. I said before leaving that he needed to get above the noise, talk to the public not the House. He said the noise was unbearable. I said speak to the mic and then the public hear you not the noise. Don't let DC rile you and explain what is happening. Let him do soundbite, you do serious. I was glad to get out. The pressure to go back was going to come on again though, that much was clear.

Peter M texted to ask how it was. I said difficult. He was paranoid and defensive. He was too lippy about AD and cuts. He was resistant to strategy. PM texted back to say he had heard I had helped on all those fronts. I said OK but understand that when I go in there I have an immediate desire to get out again. Fiona was at the Parenting Institute reception upstairs. I missed Sarah who had told Fiona of a really unpleasant meeting with CB last week when she had come in for a breast cancer reception but had been rude and difficult. I chatted to Alice Thompson [*Times* political journalist], who is so right-wing she is off my radar, and Mary Riddell [*Daily Telegraph*]. They asked if my tie was one of Samcam's and I didn't have a clue what they were talking about. I said my mum got it from M&S. 'Oh, Sam [Samantha Cameron] loves M&S.' Left for home and really glad to get there. I felt sorry for GB and knew I ought to want to help more but today showed me again he was expecting me to go and pick up a disorganised demoralised dysfunctional operation that his leadership had in part created.

Wednesday 14 October

Out earlyish after a quick tweet on what I was going to be doing during the day – namely the npower climate cops SOS competition. Ten teams of ten kids trying to devise and implement the best green campaign. Some good some less so. Bumped into [Lord] Michael Jay [chairman, Lords appointments commission] who was with the German npower chief exec

Volker Beckers. Had a little chat about what we were both up to. He said you could tell GB did not have anyone doing what I did. He said the civil service always needed clear direction and it was not there. He felt it was all a bit sad. We reminisced a bit then I had to go and do my speech plus Q&A (one deliberately bad, one OK) with Konnie Huq [TV presenter], who was quite a livewire. She had done a piece for *Blue Peter* with TB and wanted me to find out if he remembered her. He did.

The kids were fairly bright. Hardly any non-white which annoyed me. Some really sharp. Good ideas – e.g. writing books to greenify primary schoolkids or turning a cycle path out of a disused railway line. Some seemed a bit slow on the uptake, others got what I was saying straight away. Went round the tables one by one and tried to advise. Then a stack of interviews upstairs – we were at Shakespeare's Globe [theatre]. *Sunday Times* has dropped life in the day – presumably political. Same old same old stuff but it was OK. Home and did a quick blog on it saying I was inspired by the kids' passion. Up to a point.

Thursday 15 October

Out to the Home Office to speak to their senior staff about leadership. I was pretty frank re how difficult we had found parts of the civil service. There were some good and bright people in there though and I think they took a fair bit from it. They certainly said so. I felt it was all so obvious yet so few people got this stuff about strategy and clarity and the importance of the understanding of the big picture and everyone's place within it. Then out on the bike before heading out for another bloody pro bono event, US Democrats Abroad. The problem was the constant asking of the same questions and me having to sound fresh. Catherine Mayer [*Time* magazine] was interviewing me, then Q&A, and it was all fine really but I kept on setting out what I saw as our strategy whilst they kept asking why it wasn't happening and why I didn't go back to make it happen. It was all fairly friendly though they were mainly anti the war and wondered why we got so close to Bush. There was a lot of media negativity about Obama so I did a big thing on the need to keep seeing the good and understanding it was important for all of us he did well. Then to a second event for them, more exclusive, at the swanky St John's Wood home of a venture capitalist who was really into what I was doing for Leukaemia Research and wanted to help.

Friday 16 October

Blogged on the Democrats meeting and the observation made in a question on how Cameron's so-called progressive conservatism was modelled on Bush's compassionate conservatism. Ended up doing three blogs, that one and two on the outcry over a Jan Moir piece in the *Mail* about Stephen Gately.* In between finished reading [diaries] Vol. 4, I went to see Rachel, Neil and Glenys. Neil seemed pretty chilled though both of them were down on GB. Glenys said she had no idea it could be so dysfunctional. There was nobody at the centre holding it together. Rachel said the reason she and the others were keen for me to get in there was because GB did not really listen to a lot of the people advising him. Neil felt we were looking at hung parliament territory at best. Yet the Tories were just not that impressive and were there for the taking. Glenys said there was a huge amount of disloyalty around. Amazing to hear all the talk around the FCO for example. She was quite pleased to have been moved from Europe to minister for Africa, UN etc. but that too had been handled in a chaotic way.

By the time I got back I had caught up on the big response to Jan Moir's article in the *Mail* on Stephen Gately, which was provoking a huge anti-homophobic reaction. I did a blog on it, pointing out this was about Obergruppefuhrer Dacre not Moir, and later another one doing line-by-line analysis of her statement attempting to say she hadn't really said what people were saying she said. Bollocks.

Saturday 17 October

Did a phoner for *Soccer AM* re tomorrow's Burnley–Blackburn match. Actually feeling confident for once. Latest nonsense for GB was his refusal to say in a webchat with Mumsnet [website for parents] what his favourite biscuit was. He can't win. If he had answered there would have been a load of stuff about why he chose that biscuit blah but it was probably going to end up worse, and *The Times* had two biscuits on the front page – Cameron and Clegg's choices – and an empty plate for GB. Meanwhile there seemed to be divergent voices on whether we should engage with Nick Griffin on *Question Time*, Peter Hain writing to the Beeb saying that as the BNP's constitution had been declared illegal, they should not be allowed on.

Sunday 18 October

Off early with Rayan for Blackburn. Did a couple of radio interviews and also chatted to Joe Hewitt about the World Cup for Street Child [global

* Following the Boyzone band member's sudden death from an undiagnosed heart condition at the age of thirty-three, Moir wrote a column claiming that a 'dangerous lifestyle' was the real cause of the death of Gately, who was gay. The Press Complaints Commission was immediately flooded with complaints.

campaigning monument for street children]. I was spending too much time half-helping people and not enough on big projects of my own. Met Calum at Mill Hill station then down to Ewood Park, where I had to get a security wristband and get escorted to the away end. I don't think I had ever seen so many cops at a match. One came up and said 'Get three points today. Hate these bastards!' Our fans had had to come by coach from Turf Moor escorted all the way, and it meant we were outnumbering them during the players' warm-up. Good atmosphere, but it was downhill all the way, lost 3–2. I left a few minutes early, missed our second goal. Good job I got away. Not a nice feeling coming out and I was glad to have Calum's Scotland hat as a mini disguise. Still got a bit of lip and kept moving. Cops had their work cut out after the goals too.

Got away and though the traffic was bad in London made it for a good part of the Leukaemia Research reception pre the Stephen Fry event. Sold out. Did 606 from backstage then intro'd the event with pleas for Big 5–0. Great reception for Angela Baker [real-life Calendar Girl] when I announced her. Ed came on to tell his story, then Alan Yentob to introduce Stephen Fry. He was so popular it was ridiculous. The clips were great and SF spoke so well. Lots of funny moments, good serious moments too. Stephen such a nice guy, and talented. My favourite bit when he said John Cleese told him 'You'll never make it while you're so nice and polite to everyone.' 'Yes, you're so right!' 'You see what I fucking mean.' Good on his past, family roots, mental health etc. Dinner with Mick [Hucknall] and Gabriela afterwards but I was feeling a bit down. Not helped when Grace called to say she had left Fiona's keyring with all her keys in the back of the cab. Mick had been raging re reality TV, Cowell's influence on music, the dearth of real talent and was in a fury about GB calling Cowell to ask after Susan Boyle.

Monday 19 October

Blogged on GB not being able to win – slammed for not saying what his favourite biscuit was, slammed for entering the Susan Boyle debate. And how the trivialisation agenda suited Cameron. Fairly blank diary. Did a bit of work p.m. but fell asleep at my desk. Not been sleeping that well. JLA [speaking agency] called with a last-minute bid to do an awards ceremony tonight as someone had pulled out. But we had plans for dinner with Rory and Zoe and family for their birthdays. Rory thought we were mad to turn down the gig and so did I but F was in a right old strop. Nice enough evening but it was so wearing when we were not getting on after the big row we had last night. Tearful call from Tessa who would talk endlessly with her take on the political scene, then the moment I mentioned

David she would fear the worst and start crying. I spoke to David too who sounded very down about things. Said though that if the worst came to the worst he would probably get house arrest in Milan, not clink.

Tuesday 20 October

Blogged on Dacre–PCC again, saying even he must realise his K has gone, and the story of OUCA [Oxford University Conservative Association] and the racist jokes at their hustings which led to the university demanding they lose the U bit of their title. Yet the new OCA was now affiliated to Tory Party HQ. Into No. 10 via 70 Whitehall, and up to the study. The place felt very quiet as I pointed out to Michael the messenger. He said the building had lost its soul, which was a pretty heavy observation. GB came in a few minutes later and before long he was onto a full-on Murdoch diatribe, James in particular. He said people had to wake up to what was happening – the birth of a new establishment, a rich set throwing their media weight around and trying to run the country from Oxfordshire where they all met at weekends. Did I see the *FT* yesterday? No. Well, just take a look – there are five major policy issues Murdoch is concerned about, and the Tories have gone with them on every one of them. It is actually a form of corruption.

I said he could either moan about it or take them on publicly so the public were at least aware, but it was a big call. He said he was up for taking them on because it was just wrong. I said our weakness was the sense people had that we spent a lot of time trying to get them on board. He said in a sense what TB and you did was reach a deal, that they said they supported us but in fact *The Sun* in particular still pushed a very right-wing agenda. Now they were open about it and hoovering Tory policy. I said I had always wanted to take on the media as an issue but TB was against. He seemed surprised and kept coming back to that, asking if I was serious about taking them on. I said if he went for it he really had to go for it, knowing how hard they would come back at him, and he also had to go for 'your friend Dacre'. 'He's not my friend,' he said, adding that he felt Dacre was weakened, that when the media decided not to go after Coulson they were bowing to the *Sun*/*Times* agenda. He said he had written a speech on this and would send it to me, setting out why the Tories were wrong, also pointing out it was a dangerous moment for the BBC. But of course they were so busy following the right-wing media agenda they were too busy to notice.

On biscuitgate, as I had taken to calling it on the blog, he said he had never actually been asked the question, that it was all got up by Tory wives – he meant Sarah Vine [wife of Michael Gove, shadow Secretary of State for Children, Schools and Families]! As for PMQs preparation, peppered with constant returns to the Murdoch question, we mainly went over Royal Mail, where we agreed he had to get to an argument against politicisation of the dispute [over cuts in jobs and services], Afghanistan and the Territorial Army cuts – which he was sure were leaked by someone close to Dannatt – and the economy, where whatever happened he had to start using the line we agreed last week 'Wrong on recession, wrong on recovery.' He was clearly feeling down at the scale of media attack, said it was all a strategy to present him as not normal, not human. Even Sarah was used in it – the line being that even she could not make him human. I had to leave after about an hour for the Doughty Street Chambers event. Peter M, David Muir and others said I was making a difference but I think he was conscious of me not being pulled in too much.

The Doughty Street event – a debate on the future on human rights in memory of Henry Hodge – went OK. Maybe fifty people there and we raised more than 10k. Dominic Grieve spoke first, just from notes, fluent, slightly playing to the audience. He used a very different tone to his conference speech and Charlie F went for him on that. Polly Toynbee was chairing, but the questions from the floor tended to be meandering and non-forensic, and so I think Grieve will have been quite pleased with it. His main line was that they would operate within the ECHR [European Convention on Human Rights], not repeal the HRA [Human Rights Act] – which I thought Cameron had said they would – and that indeed they would add to it. Good event in many ways but I was shocked how prolix the lawyers were in Q&A. It must be all that standing up in court being paid by the hour.

Out for dinner afterwards to Vats [restaurant] – me, F, Gavin, Charlie, Margaret [Hodge], who was pressing me on what Labour should do and why I wouldn't go back to run the campaign 'and save the party I love'. Charlie and Margaret both felt there would be another heave against GB. The general feeling was Peter would not move. They all thought a combination of DM and Ed M was the best, definitely not Balls and Cruddas, that Harriet would not run though I was not sure of that. Gav felt we were to blame for the space given to the BNP because we had let down the working class. Griffin making news today by saying the generals who had attacked him for trying to ally himself to the military should be tried for war crimes like the Nazis.

Wednesday 21 October

Based on the conversation with GB yesterday, I did a quick blog on biscuitgate, he having said he was not even asked the question. Also a bit on

BNP v the generals. A number of former military top brass had attacked the BNP for trying to ally themselves to the military. Nick Griffin had responded by saying Dannatt and Mike Jackson were war criminals. Griffin was getting huge build-up in advance of his appearance on *Question Time*. I walked into town, had a bad haircut just off Tottenham Court Road, then met Natascha for lunch at the Soho house. She was looking great and seemed to be in good form. Chatted a bit about her work, *Maya* and why she found it so difficult. Maybe it felt a bit weird for her, being a film star. She was keen for me to see the boys [her sons] and talk to them a bit. I was starting to go through Volume 1 of the diaries again to see just how bad they were for GB. The nightmare scenario was publication amid him trying to hang on as he negotiated to lead in a hung parliament situation.

Thursday 22 October

Lovely cold sunny day so I went out on the bike round Regent's Park. Later I popped into the Belgravia gallery to see which of Mike Molloy's paintings had gone. I bumped into Michael Grade who earlier had been defending the Beeb over Griffin's appearance on *Question Time*. He was looking at galleries too. Had a little chat about his current life, then wandered off to the Wolseley for lunch with Howell James. Now head of comms at Barclays. He said he knew next to nothing about banking but he had learned fast and was enjoying it up to a point. He picked my brains on what the bankers should do about their [much-criticised] bonuses. I said there had to be something – possibly a self-imposed windfall tax – which showed to the public they got the outrage. If not there had to be a major defence of the case for banking mounted. He felt it was unlikely.

He was his usual gossipy self, full of warm words for TB and less so for GB, whilst for Ed Balls, he had something close to total contempt. He felt the whole post-TB period had been woefully handled, that Stephen Carter was not a good choice because he did not understand the brutality of the politics. He nonetheless felt that the Tories were not really up to much and that the game was still on if only GB could get back into it. The problem may be, however, that just as people stopped listening to Major they have stopped listening to GB. He told me a very sad-funny line from Major, a couple of days before '97 polling day, turning to Sheila Gunn [press secretary] before he had to make another 'We can win' speech, saying 'I deserve a fucking Oscar for this.' Howell felt JM never really thought he could win through the campaign. He said the Tories always underestimated TB and so they failed to adapt when he came along. He said he missed the centre and would be surprised if I could resist the pull back, though he understood why I was reluctant. Some of the GB stories, he said, e.g. his obsession about the media and the need to do something about them, were eerily reminiscent of Major.

He is always good company. He had not seen much of Peter but was loving the fact he had come back to the place he wanted to be and had established himself so powerfully. Pottered a bit p.m., more diary work then after dinner watched *Question Time* with F, Rory and Calum, who was back for R's birthday. It was all fairly predictable, but I feared it was better for Griffin than the media judgement was likely to have it. The headlines were probably already set even before he did it. It is true he is not greatly articulate and prone to saying stupid things. But he was aiming for a fairly narrow constituency and with some fairly clear points which he more or less managed to get through. Added to which there was a sense that the rest of the panel, including [David] Dimbleby, and the audience, were ganging up on him.

Jack Straw, as I feared he would be, was poor. He was given the first answer to the first question – about whether it was fair of the BNP to hijack Churchill's image for their own purposes. A free hit if ever there was one. He waffled poorly, got in a couple of claplines but was not strong. His later answer on immigration, and whether our 'failure' had anything to do with the BNP's relative success, was even worse. Dreadful. Chris Huhne [Liberal Democrat] wasn't bad. [Baroness Sayeeda] Warsi [shadow Minister for Community Cohesion] for the Tories wasn't dreadful. Bonnie Greer [novelist] OK. But as an event, whatever the papers were going to say, it served Griffin's purposes. I had been intending to do a quick blog, hoping to say it was a disaster for him. It wasn't though. It was a disaster for everyone else, or for politics. The Beeb will have been happy with the ratings if not the protests etc., but I was a bit alarmed by it. Liz called late on to say Donald had been taken to hospital.

Friday 23 October

Out for a bike ride then back to do a blog warning Labour not to inhale the media line that last night was terrible for Griffin. I didn't criticise Jack personally but he was bloody poor. The coverage today was now moving towards a sense of backlash against the Beeb and the other parties. Griffin was playing the underdog quite well. Lots of hits on their website. The Beeb were defending themselves but not sounding too confident. Nice evening out at Camden Brasserie for Rory's birthday with his mates. Liz heading to Glasgow to see Donald in hospital. Doctors thinking toxins round the brain. I was thinking maybe reaction to drugs or lack of drugs, as he had been saying he had been feeling good and might have stopped taking them.

GB called about his idea for a media speech. He was clearly wanting to do it and probably being held back by lots of people in there e.g. Stewart Wood who sent through the speech. He went over exactly the same arguments as the other day. It was probably not a good idea for him to do it but he was clearly getting more and more frustrated. I said he should aim off a bit on my own view of some in the press, and make sure he took other advice too. He said he really felt they had to be challenged. It sounded like one of the arguments I had with TB, only this time we were agreeing with each other. If anything I was trying to get him down off the ceiling.

Saturday 24 October

Set off with the boys for Burnley. Finished reading Volume 1, which was pretty bad for GB, without being totally devastating I guess. I still wouldn't fancy it if it came in the middle of a hanging on to power scenario. Five-hour journey. Great start. Steven Fletcher goal. But Wigan much stronger and we lost 3–1. 100 per cent home record gone. Quick drink with Frank Teasdale, then off to Manchester. Dinner with the boys at the restaurant near the flat. Italian guy telling me he loved TB, would always vote Labour, but with GB we were finished.

Sunday 25 October

Breakfast then off to Stocksbridge for Rory's [cycle] hill climb contest. Seriously steep hill. And serious hill climbers. He got himself sorted then we walked the course. Tough. A bloke asked if I was doing it under a pseudonym as my name wasn't down! As if. Rory started OK then faded a bit but he was glad to have done it. Parts of the course were so steep I don't think I could have done it without coming off. We found a pub with a telly for the Liverpool v United match. United didn't really show up and Liverpool deserved to win. The pub filled out with a stack of pretty hard people, including a woman with a dreadful loud cackle. Made it back for dinner then Mum, Liz and Kate [niece] arrived, Kate staying for the week to do work experience cum research at HemiHelp [charity for children]. Mum clearly a bit worried about Donald.

Monday 26 October

Took Kate to HemiHelp then pottered a fair bit during the day. Mum and Liz having a good old witter and later went to Audrey's. They did not seem to get why I sometimes found it irritating constantly to get asked to do charity and speaking stuff. I also noticed Mum getting more and more opinionated. The Europe President job was picking up. I still felt it was unlikely TB would get it. David M had put his weight behind it yesterday but was a bit daft I thought in saying it should be 'someone who stopped the traffic'. PG was trying to get me to get more behind DM, felt I should not be propping up GB. Today, post-clocks going back, was reckoned to be the most unproductive day of the year and it felt that way.

Tuesday 27 October

Alex called as I was walking through St James's Park. He thought Rory should really make a go of going for coaching qualifications. He felt GB was in trouble and too many ministers behaving as though we'd lost. Up to the study in No. 10. GB bounded in, asked if I had seen his draft speech on the media. I said I had. I thought it was an OK argument but probably not for him to make. Re PMQs he was off on one about the MoD's 'piddling' announcement of £2.1 million for Territorial Army training. He said there was a campaign from within – 'I am at war with the army, not just public opinion on this,' he said. He called up the spad who deals with MoD and laid into him. 'Never known such incompetence' blah. Not great leadership. The problem was if we gave more money the MoD just moved to the next thing, he said.

Douglas and I were clearly there to try to manage him towards better positions than the civil servants and Theo Bertram would then write up for him. He was not easy to manage. I thought James Bowler [civil servant], the guy who did for him what Clare Sumner had done for TB, was pretty good with him but GB tended to go off in all sorts of directions. I said he needed to try to do a different tone. Don't let DC get under his skin straight away. Maybe agree and half accept some of his points but then get to 'Wrong on recession, wrong on recovery'. He asked if I could go in tomorrow. I said I couldn't. He went off to the NEC so Douglas and I stayed and gave them some ideas on how to change GB's style. The key was to be more relaxed and dismissive. GB overweight again. His shirt a mess. Thick black felt pen going hammer and tongues the whole time.

To the park to meet PG for a chat and a coffee. He felt with GB as leader we were heading for meltdown. Maybe under 200 seats. DM would put us back in the race. But how to get there? TB texted asking if I thought, if it looked like the EU job was not going to happen, he should pull out quickly. I felt yes. PG felt no. Nice chat, a bit meandering then home to meet Grace and go for lunch with her. Into town for the Leukaemia Research Bikeathon Awards. We were all a bit – in fact a lot – pissed off because Alzheimer's won the Credit Suisse vote. Also part of the day, at Theo Bertram's request, I'd been doing a letter to the *FT* on Osborne's credibility gap as a result of trying to do both the election job and shadow Chancellor. Got a good response for it and they did a news story on it too. They rightly said there would be hollow laughter at Tory HQ but it made a point pretty well.

Wednesday 28 October

Blogged re Osborne, elaborating on the *FT* letter, broadening it to Cameron confusing strategy and tactics. The TB Europe [presidency] situation was really hotting up. I spoke to JoP, who reckoned 40/60, which was pretty pessimistic for him. Merkel was playing her cards close to her chest. Sarko was quieter than before. Others were becoming more aggressive and Juncker was out saying he would do it. Steve Morris suggested I do something on it so we started to sketch out a blog for tomorrow. Cab to Random House for meeting on the diaries' schedule and *Maya* publicity. I was still worried about the nightmare scenario of GB being mid-hung parliament negotiations when I came out with all this. As Bill said it was not good for him. Still going over titles.

Bumped into Charlie Falconer on the train to Newcastle. He was going to the same event to do the pre-dinner speech before Eddie Izzard, Tony Robinson [actor] and I did the after-dinner. He was as ever gossipy and funny and probing re all my meetings with GB. Re TB he felt it was unlikely he would get the Europe job. He was still at me to get a seat and go for the leadership after the election after next. He was more persuaded of my skills than I was perhaps. He was enjoying his law firm and his work as chair of RDA [Regional Development Agency]. Still missing the big stuff though. The event was at the Hyena Comedy Club. Charlie's ra-ra speaking style not as good as his conversation but he is popular and can get a good response. Eddie, as at Chelsea, was brief and not playing it for laughs which I think disappointed people. Tony came over as a bit Dave Spart [*Private Eye*'s fictional left-wing activist] and in the Q&A he and I had a few mini rucks about what I saw as having cake and eat it positions, e.g. of course loyalty but people should always say what they really think.

The format didn't work as well as it should. Answers were too long and lots of people couldn't get in. The tone set from the panel was too heavy and Eddie was more Dimbleby than Izzard. I liked him though and let him in on the idea I had been having about doing a series on comedy, culminating with me doing a show. Interview comics and writers and then try to do it myself. He thought it was a terrible idea. He also thought it was like saying I want to be a Premier League footballer. Not sure I agreed but it would certainly be a risk. I did a bit of book signing then off. Long chat with David Mills who sounded very down. So was Tessa. She had warned the kids he might have to go to jail. Matthew had said something very wise – one day it will all be behind us and we can start again. Donald still in hospital and Liz trying to get his drugs situation sorted. He was being moved to a Glasgow psychiatric place, Gartnavel.

Thursday 29 October

I did a blog re TB and the Europe job focused on his qualities and what it said about Cameron's judgement that he would seemingly prefer a Luxembourg federalist to a Brit. But the sense was, as the summit started, that it was moving away from TB. Steve Morris was sending me points all day. JoP asking for ideas to regain momentum. I suggested an open letter from Bill C. TB said he was getting his ass kicked by all and sundry. I said he was now in 'in for a penny' mode. I had breakfast with Brendan. We had our usual mutual moan about things. He was very pro-DM. He felt I should try to get Alex to go and talk to the Cabinet and give them a lesson in teamwork and strategy. But I was beginning to worry the thing was all lost. Brendan said he had seen my letter in the *FT* and it made him think 'Right, this is obviously part of something bigger because that's what Alastair does and there will now be concerted argument by ministers. But there was nothing.'

He said he had been on my blog a few times and noted the number of people saying the same – why was I seemingly alone in going after the Tories? He felt GB was ultimately not up to it. People sensed that all the stuff his critics had said about him was true. Always liked talking to him because he was bright, not slavish and with good ideas. He still felt we could just about hold on but was sure it would be easier without GB. Got the train back, working on my seven favourite books for Emma Mitchell at Random House. Going for *Madame Bovary*, *Richard II* (plus in same mention Stephen Greenblatt's book on Shakespeare [*Will in the World*], David Storey's *This Sporting Life*, *Sputnik Sweetheart* by Haruki Murakami, *The White Lioness* by Henning Mankell, *Team of Rivals* and *The Clarets Chronicles* [Burnley FC history]. Cab to Islington for the meeting with Paul Farmer from Mind. They wanted to pick my brains on policy, and the best way to influence the manifestos, also how to deal with the Tories if they won, Time to Change, general positioning. I felt they were in quite good shape but needed sharper edge and greater clarity on priorities.

Friday 30 October

I was talking to JoP a fair bit re TB and Europe, as the leaders met in Brussels. The mood seemed to be swinging away from TB. I did a few lives from home – Beeb, Sky, Radio 5 – to put the case that if it was meritocratic he would walk it and it would be Europe making another mistake if it went for a small figure. JoP felt that Merkel would be looking for an EPP [European People's Party] figure and maybe for David Miliband as the Foreign Minister figure. I felt on good form but also that he was now facing an uphill battle. I tagged a bit onto my blog about Rory seeing Liam Gallagher [rock star] give a *Big Issue* seller fifty quid last night. I had tweeted about it and it got a huge response. *The Sun* had used part of yesterday's blog re TB which made me wonder if they were not going to be as all-out pro-Cameron. I might be whistling in the wind on that. I could not help thinking the Tories were still vulnerable though, as I kept meeting people who would make a point of saying they didn't want them and they wished Labour could get their act together. TB was starting to flap a bit I think and later in the day said no more media. I'd suggested they get Clinton to do a piece extolling his virtues. He agreed to do it and Bradders and Steve Morris drafted.

Saturday 31 October

The State Department kyboshed the Clinton piece. Really annoying. He said he always went through them and thought they might have gone for it, but no. It could upset one or two relationships. All the mood music from Brussels was negative vibes. TB was clearly a bit fed up. To be honest I couldn't really understand why he was so keen. Set off north around half eight, to Burnley with Rory. Big game and a lot of focus on whether Phil Brown [Hull manager] would survive. Darren Bentley took me over to the Jimmy McIlroy stand to say a few words to the women at Ladies' Day. All dolled up and a few well boozed up already. *Match of the Day 2* were filming there and it was pretty wild. Or at least it would be. Did a little interview, then through to the Foundation Club to do a little Q&A in there. All the big calls went against Hull. We won 2–0 but I ended up feeling a bit sorry for Brown. Did my AOL blog on sympathy for him and surviving the bum-pinching ladies.

Off to the Velodrome at Manchester. Good night's cycling with Chris Hoy winning more World Cup golds. The boys enjoyed it. Good chat with Dave Brailsford. He was keen to keep in touch so I could maybe advise him a bit on how to handle Sky and the changed media scene for him. I chatted to Chris Boardman who was complaining the cyclists were spending too much time on the commercial side of things. Did a medal presentation. A handful of boos but a nice evening all round and back to see *Match of the Day 2*.

Sunday 1 November

Blogged on Stephen Fry who had yesterday tweeted he was bowing out from Twitter because someone had said his tweets were boring. I did a blog on depression, saying he should tweet or not as he sees fit. Good response. We set off in vile weather, which did not change all day, for Glasgow. I was keen to see Donald myself. He was in Henderson ward at Royal Gartnavel. He was in better form than I expected. Had a little chat with one of the nurses, who said he was doing fine now he was back on the clozapine. He had been totally haywire when he arrived but had stabilised. He said he didn't remember bits of it. She wanted to talk about my novel, and politics. We went to his flat to check everything was OK with the car and the house, then out for lunch at the restaurant where his lodger Joe was chef. The boys were great and I was glad we had gone even though it meant a 410-mile drive back. Pretty knackered by the time I got home. Glad I had gone though. Another fabulous NHS facility as a result of a Labour government.

Monday 2 November

Blogged on a survey showing only 15 per cent of Brits said they cared about global warming and its impact. Down from 26 per cent pre-recession. Lowest of twelve countries surveyed. Used it to highlight contrast with how much people cared about who won *X Factor*. Ed M texted to say he liked it and would send me text of his next 'educative' speech. But it was going to be an uphill struggle pre-Copenhagen [UN climate change conference]. Long bike ride then pottering and preparing for tonight's charity event for Camp Quality [charity for sick children] at the Comedy Store. Really tired after yesterday's driving so had a rare p.m. kip before heading out. Interesting bunch of comedians. All middle-ranking, I guess. They got a bit antsy at my taking notes, worried I was going to use their acts on the dinner circuit. Chatted with Dominic Holland and Milton Jones, who had the best one-liners, about the comedy scene generally. Michael Macintyre the current king. Earning millions. Ditto Eddie, who they said had been touch and go for years but suddenly made it big-style. Lots up in the 80–100k bracket but it was hard. And they worried about losing their material to others. I had done my usual batch of funny stories which went down OK but I could see pure stand-up was a very different thing. Not impossible though.

Tuesday 3 November

Did a blog on Alan Johnson and immigration, as he had done a speech yesterday admitting people had real and justified concerns, also that we had made mistakes. I also backed him on his sacking of [Professor] David Nutt, the drugs advisor, on the basis that advisors advise but ministers have to decide.* Out on the bike in lovely autumnal light but it was way too hot for this time of year. Then to Portcullis House to get sneaked through to the shadow Cabinet block to see Andrew Mitchell [Tory shadow minister]. A lot greyer than the last time I saw him. Had a couple of special advisors in with him, one of whom had asked him why on earth he was seeing me. He told them the story of when I did a magazine piece picking six young(ish) MPs I predicted would go all the way to the top – Major, Blair, Brown, Mo Mowlam, Portillo and Mitchell. He told them too that I had later said 'Five out of six ain't bad.' His office walls were covered with pictures, mainly of family and constituency, and some visits, also him behind DC on his first PMQs when he said to TB he 'was the future once'.

His tables were covered with development books which he insisted he read. He said he loved the international development job. Cameron let him get on with it. He said they had both been grateful when I had blogged DC had been right to visit Rwanda at the time of floods in the UK. He clearly read the blog quite closely. He was not in the inside circle, hardly surprising seeing that he had run David Davis's [leadership] campaign. But he felt DC had done a good job. The circle was DC, Osborne, Steve Hilton [strategist], Ed Llewellyn [chief of staff] and Andy Coulson. Hague one ring out. Gove close in socially but same place as Hague politically. He said it was very much like the TB operation. Small and tight-knit group. He was sure they would win if GB stayed, less so if he went. He thought if he went it would probably be a hung parliament. There was not that much confidence around. He also felt the next parliament would be unmanageable in lots of ways. There would be stacks of new MPs and they would regard the old ways – including whipping – as vestiges of a failed old guard. Some would be good. Some would be terrible. But it was not going to be easy.

He reckoned the best-case scenario was 30 majority and that would not give them that much control. He felt on our side Ed M was more attractive as a candidate than David M. Harriet hopeless in many ways but she had stuck at it. Peter doing well and the Lords loved being drawn to him. He could not really understand why I wouldn't go back but then when I explained he sort of got it. We had a nice chat and when at one point he said 'You don't really think Cameron would be a disaster,' I found myself pushing back but unsure if I really meant it. He said that when I did the diaries in full the real charge against us – the Blairites especially TB and inner circle – is that we let GB become PM knowing in our hearts he would be a disaster. There was something in that. But even now it was

* Nutt was sacked after criticising government policies and claiming that ecstasy and LSD were less dangerous than alcohol.

not possible to be sure that if GB went what followed would be better. We ate a sandwich and I drank a tea from a polystyrene cup while he sipped Coke, and he seemed to want to keep talking.

Off to the Royal Horseguards to do another Japanese interview. Then to No. 10 and up to the study. GB came in first. He was looking pretty heavy. Also glum. I asked how things were. 'Oh, you know.' He said he had been making calls trying to get support for TB in the Europe job 'but it was difficult'. Merkel basically wanted a Tory. Some of the left people didn't want TB because they thought he was not really one of them. Zapatero would do what Merkel said. Sarko was not really willing to give up a whole load of capital on it. So it was not easy. He was probably wanting me to feed back the message he was trying. But the main message was that he was failing. We chatted as others filed in – James and Nicholas from his parliamentary team, Ed M and Douglas, Theo [Bertram]. Nicholas Howard had given me a funny scary moment earlier when he had said new [Iraq] dossier documents were going to be released under an FoI ruling. He sent them through. Then said in fact they were published at the time of Hutton.

GB told me that he had just heard five UK soldiers had been killed in Afghanistan, seemingly by someone dressed up as an Afghan cop. We agreed it would dominate PMQs and he should turn it into a mini statement. He also had the problem of the memo written a few days before a soldier, Lieutenant-Colonel Rupert Thorneloe, had been killed, in which he had warned of inadequate supplies and helicopters putting them at risk of IEDs [improvised explosive devices]. He got the note over from the MoD – which he said was leaking like a sieve – and got right into the detail. DA and I were trying to get him back on the big picture. He was also worrying about Karzai who had been reappointed President and the whole thing – our troops dying to prop up a discredited regime – was sapping public support. He did at least say he ought to make another big speech on Afghanistan. I said he needed to be explaining the whole time. He clearly wasn't that plugged in to Obama. He was asking us why we thought Obama was taking so long to decide whether to agree to the military's request for 40k more troops – if we were taking so long we would be crucified, he said. He reckoned Obama would fly from Oslo to Afghanistan. I said it was tricky to collect the Nobel Peace Prize then announce loads more troops.

He kept asking what we thought Obama was up to. Douglas was very good on the big picture and on the detail for Afghanistan. But these five deaths, which sounded unusual, were going to make things even more difficult. The other issue we discussed was the Kelly report on expenses being published tomorrow. He did not think Cameron would go on it.

If he did his line was to push it off to the new Independent Parliamentary Standards Authority. James said Ian Kennedy was going to head it. I said 'Oh my God, he is a really good friend.' 'A mate like John Scarlett?' said DA. Even bigger. The general feeling was MPs would have to take all the recommendations. Cameron would claim some success as some of the things he had been calling for were in there. Andrew Mitchell had told me he had said to the shadow Cabinet that the political class were like the Germans in 1945. In retreat, and they would not be able to advance until reparations had been made. GB felt much the same. He was now raging at some of these people who had been put into these positions by him. He was scathing about Nutt. But he was scathing about anyone who was meant to be an advisor and who did anything other than totally support whatever he said at the time.

Wednesday 4 November

It was beginning to pick up that Cameron's media policies were all basically designed for Murdoch and doubtless in part explained the *Sun* switch. I knocked off another quick Cameron blog. It was definitely the case that the glow was wearing off him. If only we had a real operation against them, he would be in a lot more trouble. Off to the National Portrait Gallery for the trustees' dinner as guests of [Sir] Nick Blake [High Court judge, friend]. Peter M there as an honorary trustee as NPG policy network president. Didn't really have much time to talk to him. Looked around the Beatles to Bowie exhibition with the Janvrins. Some pretty good stuff. The people running the place were perfectly nice but it was without doubt an establishment event. Black tie. Lots of sirs and posh voices. Yet even here little enthusiasm for the Tories. I was sitting next to Carol Lake from JP Morgan, pretty livewire-ish who was passionately pro us and against them.

Thursday 5 November

I had a little dig at Trevor Kavanagh at the end of a blog on Cameron. The main part of the blog was about a picture in *The Guardian* where Cameron was standing on the Tube writing as he travelled. I asked if anyone had ever tried it. Re Kavanagh he had been on the radio re DC's Europe speech saying people understood why there should not be a big fight with Europe when people were more interested in jobs and the economy. They always were. Other sceptics angry at Cameron's retreat on the referendum. Out to do yet another Japanese interview, this time TBS TV. Japanese interviewer but his English wasn't great, so Jason Priestly did a lot of the talking. I was genuinely surprised by the level of interest in my advising them.

To the Royal Garden hotel where I was due to speak at the awards for the Guild of Architectural Ironmongers (basically the people who do any metalwork on doors). Nice enough bunch. I was on really good form and did a more stand-up style in parts to see if it worked. Q&A pretty good too. One or two hostile – 'psychologically flawed', Iraq. Possibly a bit glib when asked if I thought 'we' should invade Iran. I said I had not yet been briefed on the Guild's military wing, but I would advise against. I had all the usual feelings of negativity about this kind of thing – being a mix between comedy and political recollection. But it went down well and I had a few at the end, one of them really passionately, pleading with me to stand. Charlie F had been saying for ages if I went into Parliament I would quickly become a big figure and then possibly a contender for leader after next, assuming GB would be gone soon. But I still couldn't see it. And, as Bruce [Grocott] said yesterday, the regime for MPs was going to get tougher and tougher and I would have to give up a lot. I wish there was someone I could really talk it through with to help me reach a definitive decision. At the moment I was pleasing nobody, least of all myself.

Friday 6 November

GB, as we discussed on Tuesday, was doing a set-piece speech on Afghanistan. The five deaths he learned about on Tuesday had become public and led to more 'bring the troops home' calls. His speech was fine, though the Tories were straight out with a 'mixed messages' attack, namely that he was saying we would not walk away but also saying Karzai had to measure up or we could not support indefinitely. It was all a bit scary though and Charles Guthrie and [Admiral Sir] Mike Boyce [former Chiefs of Defence Staff] were out attacking again. I did a blog saying GB was right to keep setting it all out. Also we had to learn lessons from Kosovo. And Obama had to sort out and decide a strategy. He was taking far too long to respond to the military's call for a 40k troop surge. There was a danger, as Shaun Woodward said when I saw him later, that he was morphing into Jimmy Carter [former US President]. Indecisive on this, Copenhagen, gays in the military, health. Too defensive in the face of all the right-wing attacks.

Grace was off school, possibly with swine flu. I set off for the north-west. Traffic dire. Five hours in total to Knowsley Hall. Worth it when I got there. Beautiful old stately home in fabulous grounds. Good setting for the St Helens Chamber of Commerce dinner. I took in four tricky words from people at my table to weave into the speech – caravan, cheeseburger, schnitzel and Rhodesian. Managed it. I asked Shaun if they wanted laughs or serious. He told me – and I announced at the start – that Peter M five years ago had done serious 'and he does not have happy memories of the evening'. So I played it mainly for laughs with a bit of anti-Tory thrown in. Lots of photos then Shaun and I went to the main sitting room for a chat. First, he said NI was a lot more precarious than people might imagine. It might be that at some point GB would have to bring the thing close to collapse. They were obviously worried it looked like dumping on the TB legacy. I said that was less important than doing what you had to do.

He said [Peter] Robinson [First Minister] was not a leader. He spent all his time looking over his shoulder. Also he and McGuinness did not get on. And they were worried Adams resented McG's role and relative popularity. It was hard to see the whole thing holding together. I said he should speak to TB and JoP but I was sure they would agree that if it required more bold moves, they should be made. On the GB scene, he said he felt there would be no challenge. The expenses scandal had drained them all of risk or courage. He felt the only line for GB was to be the doctor who could get the cancer removed, and not worry about whether there were better looking surgeons and prettier nurses everywhere. Like me, he felt that if Labour could only get their act together, the Tories were still beatable, that a hung parliament was possible. He asked what I thought should happen. I said my usual – attack, defend the record and promote an agenda that means something to people. Equalities bill and constitutional stuff would not cut it. Also create a proper dialogue not top down. And build the team. All the things I had been saying for ages, but without any sense it was bringing about much change.

GB felt I had to be back there but I worried it would just lead to more of them peeling off and doing even less. Shaun was hugely suspicious of Peter, felt he was promoting himself at the expense of the government, more interested in lining up a job than doing the one he had. I said that was unfair, that Peter had brought some ballast to the operation and was one of the few out there with a profile and a message capacity. The younger ones were nowhere, though DM and Ed M had improved recently. I was quite taken aback by just how negative he was about Peter. Perhaps he wanted to be the right-hand-man strategist. I had always found him pretty good but none of them were team builders. I said ultimately GB needed to build the team and he could no longer do it by separate conversations with half a dozen 'key people' in different rooms. They had to be under the same roof and arguing out the same strategy, not pretending to.

Again tonight, people telling me the problem was New Labour was no more. Even now these people would back TB, or some would. But they had a real problem with GB. It was pretty clear cut. Even as we were speaking a guy who said he worked for the NHS came over and told me I really had to stand. So did Shaun's St Helens MP colleague (David Watts). We must have talked for close on an hour and it made me feel even more that GB could not do the necessary. And yet I found it very hard to say that upfront to GB himself. Unless there was a Plan B, presumably around DM, we were probably stuck with him.

Frank Warren called. He wanted to put on a bill of fights, including a title fight, for the troops in Afghanistan. I put him onto the right people at No. 10 who seemed to think it might be a goer.

Also talking to Emily Hands who was now in charge of Afghan comms strategy. About time someone was. She acknowledged it had all been a bit piecemeal. We talked through what might be done but the truth is it had to be internationalised and Obama and the US had to get their act together. [Sir] Ian Kennedy [chairman, Independent Parliamentary Standards Authority] called after doing a briefing which the press were taking as him moving away from [Sir] Christopher Kelly [chairman, Standards in Public Life Committee] (on expenses and ethics). The *Telegraph* were also on to both of us about our friendship, including when he was our phone a friend when Fiona and I did *Who Wants to Be a Millionaire?* I thought it might be a smallish inside-page thing. Turned out to be the splash including a picture of me and Fiona taken as a TV grab. The papers were getting more and more ridiculous. He and Andrea both sounded a bit jumpy though.

Saturday 7 November

The *Telegraph* was even more ludicrous when you actually saw it. They carried my quote saying I had been disappointed he didn't get the answer re Skylab when I called him as phone a friend. And that he was his own man who knew his own mind and would do well any job asked of him. I had the same sentiments as part of my blog, laced with piss-taking of the *Telegraph* of which there was plenty more on blog, FB and Twitter. Godric said it was the best example yet of a diary story turned splash. Brendan called, said 'You must be a true legend if you're getting front-page treatment for a quiz question asked four years ago.' Ian and Andrea getting worried though. At one point he said he felt low and demoralised and said to Andrea he wondered if he should not have taken it. He was going to need to be stood up in the next few days until the current interest faded. He felt that the media had sensed he was not just going to take Kelly as gospel, that he would be working out what was needed to fund a modern legislator.

Set off for Manchester and after dropping off Calum's bags at the flat did the BBC religious department's interview re TB for the programme they were doing on him. Nice enough interview and got over everything I think. Texted TB to ask him if 1. He could get the Europe job and 2. Was there any chance GB would win the election? He said 'No to both.' He called, said there was maybe a tiny chance re him and Europe but he felt it was unlikely. On GB he said he could sit down and write him the strategy that could lead to a win, but GB could not do it. Or even if he did, he did not really believe it. It was like the speech on Afghanistan. He said the right things. But he did not really feel it deep down. It was like the New Labour thing. He did not get it. And he was not really going to change. Nor were the public. They had given up on him. There was a settled view that he was not a leader.

The reason I could survive even after Iraq, he said, is that people will forgive you decisions they disagree with so long as you decide and so long as they understand where you're basically coming from. With GB they sense he is all about tactics and winning and they know he is indecisive. It is not going to change. He did not intend to rock the boat and he didn't think Peter would. As for DM, he felt he had gone up in standing a fair bit in recent weeks and he was pretty sure if there was a contest he would get the leadership but he didn't think it would happen. Met Calum from the station and off to Man City. We had a place in the players' car park. Sightseers looking at all the players' OTT cars. Wags arriving in blacked-out limos. Great match. Two up. 3–2 down, 3–3. Good material for the AOL blog.

Sunday 8 November

Slept badly because wankers in the top flat in the house opposite had a late and loud party last night. To Kalendar for breakfast. I bumped into Andrea. The *MoS* had done a piece on their marriage bust-up. I spoke to Ian to say I still felt best for him not to get involved too much in day-to-day rebuttal. Try to stay above it. It would blow over. Hague was asked about it on Marr and said he did not think friendship with me ruled him out. What mattered was his ability to do the job asked of him. I worried, however, there was a danger they made a bit of a crisis out of a drama. Out to a restaurant near Euston to do a fundraiser for Frank Dobson. Nice enough mood, sold a fair few books and I felt on pretty good form. Used the famous McEnroe quote – show me a good loser and I'll show you a loser – to condemn the fatalism and the defeatism and set out why I thought we could still win.

I was introduced by Dobbo who said that if I was broken in two the word Labour would be written in the middle. He said he always felt I was the one Labour voice in No. 10. I responded by saying TB was Labour too! Raised over a grand which was not bad for a small restaurant though I did point out Cameron was doing dinners which pulled in millions. Had a good chat with some of the younger ones about their experience campaigning for Obama, which they felt the party was not using well enough. Mind you, Obama was beginning to take a hit for all his dithering on Afghanistan and climate change.

Monday 9 November

The Sun led with a huge 'Bloody Shameful' headline and a story about a badly written GB letter to the mother of a soldier who had been killed. She was complaining about him misspelling her name, plus messy writing etc. One of those stories that was going to stick. Spent the morning writing my speech for the *Rail* magazine dinner on Thursday. Spoke to editor Nigel Harris who was totally effusive about Andrew Adonis as Transport Secretary. Said he was the best ever. Good chat with Andrew who gave me some great lines. Boundless energy and enthusiasm and he was a real help for the speech. The truth was, however, that I really was going to have to stop prevaricating about whether or not to help GB properly and get on with it either way. I was not exactly wild with enthusiasm. Plus the book deal complicated things further. But I really hated the Tories, and felt strongly they didn't deserve to win. And I was going to have to decide soon. F thought no to No. 10, yes to party. Really good bike ride.

Cold and crisp round Regent's Park. Bumped into Geoffrey Robertson [human rights lawyer]. He was out having a constitutional, he said. He had had Sarah [Brown] round for dinner last night. He felt things were pretty grim there. He had been lobbying hard on the McKinnon case, said he worried the guy would kill himself in a US jail and it would be devastating for GB.* He said I had to go back full-time and help him, because he could not do it with the people he had around him. He needed a strong and clear hand there to keep an eye on everything. E.g. the kind of thing that was all over *The Sun* today. He felt GB had a lot of strengths and they were not being put over to the public e.g. the fact that he had led the world in the response to the economic crisis. Nice guy and very bright.

I was starting to get loads of messages from Ian and Andrea. She had been harassed. Ditto Tom [son] who said he was worried he had let himself get drawn in too much. Ian was leaving long messages on my voicemail and I sensed he was at the end of his tether. He said he was prepared to get shot at himself but he was not prepared for Andrea and the kids to cop it. I said it was not pleasant but it was only the *Mail* and the *Telegraph*,

* Gary McKinnon, an Asperger's Syndrome sufferer, had hacked into Pentagon and NASA networks from his home in the UK, and faced charges in the United States of computer fraud. America asked for him to be extradited, but many thought he should be tried in a British court, where he would receive a more merciful sentence.

it was not raging across the news and if he quit he would make himself a bigger target.

He was also annoyed at the sense that he was merely there to rubber-stamp Kelly. He said he was not in the media world or in the world of their values and he would not buy the line it was a victory for them if he went. But when I spoke to Andrea she said there was a subtext that he was looking to show her he was standing up for her. Sheree Dodd [communications consultant] called. She was working for the Speaker, who had spoken to Ian and was clearly worried he was going to walk which would leave the whole thing in tatters. Ian said he would sleep on it but he sounded very down. Switch called asking for his mobile because Harriet wanted to speak to him. All a bit of a drama and I could see why he might want out but he had to stick it out.

Tuesday 10 November

Fiona had decided to put a carpet into my office so I had to clear out a load of stuff in the boxes on the floor. Managed to throw away a whole load of stuff but ended up with dust all over my throat. *The Sun* were still motoring with the story about the mum of Jamie Janes, who complained about her name being misspelled in a letter and had recorded a call from GB, so it was beginning to look even more like she was being exploited for the *Sun* agenda. Pretty vicious stuff. Topped up the interview for *Easy Living* [magazine] on my favourite books, then off to meet Nancy for lunch at Locanda Locatelli. She was recovering from a lost voice and sounded husky. She was tactile as ever. She was pressing me re whether I would go back and I went over the pros and cons for a bit. She was having trouble with Sven and had hired Fiona Shackleton [solicitor] to sort out her money. She was still keen to support Labour.

Walked to Westminster. I bumped into Vernon Bogdanor who said he could not understand why so many of our people seemed to have given up the fight. He did not think Gordon had but he felt many of the others had. Yet it was there to be won. And he felt we had to make it a battle of the progressives v the rest and with a much bigger focus on the past. GB had led the world out of recession and the Tories had to be portrayed as a risk. He was spot on. He felt that a hung parliament was no good because it meant halfway to the exit. I went for a cup of tea with Carol Linforth, and the usual story of a beleaguered and yet also becalmed party machine lacking leadership or energy. She said there was next to no proper link-up with No. 10 and no real preparation for the campaign. She felt I had to go back. They were all assuming I would go back in some major capacity. But she could tell my heart was not in it.

To No. 10, first for a session with David Muir and Justin Forsyth. They said today had been a bit of a roller-coaster emotional day, because GB had done his monthly press conference and it had taken them ages to get him into a decent frame of mind to deal with questions about *The Sun*. He managed to get above it and did fine, they said. He had spoken to Murdoch, who had apologised to him over the editorial (accusing GB of an underlying disregard for the military), and to Rebekah. She had done the usual stuff about not being on duty at the weekend blah. David said he was pretty tough with her. I said he had to get over the message that they paraded as friends of the troops but did so much now to undermine them because of their hatred of us and their determination to be proved right re the Tories. They asked for general advice. I said they needed to develop a squad of general big-hitters. They were clearly having trouble mobilising people. Alan J for example.

DM had done a great job on Europe but was sometimes reluctant to broaden out, they said, which was not my sense. Burnham and Liam Byrne were up for it but they were not seen as big beasts. Harriet and Balls willing but doing their own thing. They rated Yvette [Cooper]. They felt DA and Murphy saw problems everywhere. Whingy. Peter good but even he was very down at the moment. I said they needed a psychological jumpstart to get the mindset that they could win. Justin said it needed me to go to a political Cabinet and give them that motivational talk. I did not leap at the chance. But the sense of fatalism they were dealing with was too strong. Justin said the other problem was that they were not me – they could not really get ministers out in the way I did. And GB was not TB. His authority had been weakened and they were not all of them committed to now but looking to the future. They didn't deserve to win then.

I gave them advice as I could, then GB arrived. Looking heavy and tired. He was not as fired up about *The Sun* as I thought he might be. Angry at Rebekah's pretence that it was not personal. Angry at the Beeb too for putting on the Jacqui Janes tape recording without knowing where it came from. Angry with the army for the way they were allowing this to become 'government v army'. I said the problem was a lack of internationalisation of the strategy or the comms so that it looked like it was all down to him. Obama had still not decided. He said there was a major debate going on in the States – his political people were advising this was another Vietnam. His military were demanding another bigger surge. I said I felt his speech last week went well and now maybe he should do one on the invisible threat we were dealing with. DA said in the US media there was a greater understanding that this was about success in attacking the Al Qaeda leaders in Pakistan.

Hard to see what Cameron would go on at PMQs. I reckoned a mix of issues showing lack of clout or leadership. Hard for him not to do

Afghanistan on Armistice Day. He would not get into the letter. DA was picking my brains on the way we could multilateralise comms and also how we got a proper sense of strategy being put over. Obama so important to this but he did not seem to take the Brits that much into account. Also on the Tobin tax, GB had been done over by Timothy Geithner [Secretary of the US Treasury] who had said he would support what he was saying but then went against it.* Get a grip of those Yanks, I said. 'What, like you did with Bush?' We always knew what he was doing, I said. The mood was OK considering and the media feeling seemed to be *The Sun* had overstepped the mark and there was some sympathy for him. But I remembered Dennis Skinner's observation that nobody ever voted for a victim. It was certainly the case that if pity was the over-riding feeling, you'd had it. The one thing you had to give GB was his resilience. But the team-building skills were weak.

Before the meeting I called switch from the study. 'I'm back,' I said and they all squealed when Carol announced it. Then I said it was a joke. But they told some horror stories about the way he treated e.g. typists, duty clerks etc. Not good. I chatted with him about Ian and said he needed a high-level message of support, or else he would still go. GB had said to me 'You have to make sure he doesn't quit. And he has to do Kelly.' I said it might not be enough. Jumped in a cab. Asked me about Burnley. It was actually beginning to take over from politics as the main thing from cabbies. To the Camden Brasserie to meet F, G and R and wait for TM [Gibbons-Neff, son of Fiona's best friend in the States] and his girlfriend Caitlin who was studying at Queen Mary's. TM was so young-looking, and small for a Marine. But he had a toughness about him. Pretty sharp on the war, happy to talk about what they got up to but also pretty good on overall policy. He said there was definitely a view that the Brits were not as well-equipped as the Americans.

TM had a great memory for our holiday in France, when they were all kids and he and Rory had a fight. He said he could remember when we were driving down Mont Ventoux and Grace was asking what the worst swear words were and I said 'platform' so everyone was going round saying platform for ages and she thought it was hilarious. Fiona pleased we had managed to see him. Back to more Ian and Andrea. Her mother and neighbours in the States had been doorstepped. At least he had not quit but he was sounding very on edge indeed. So was she, though I think she had a better sense of it being worse if he quit.

* Suggested by American Nobel Laureate James Tobin as a tax on conversions from one currency to another, it had been broadened into a tax on all share, bond and currency transactions. The UK government opposed it.

Wednesday 11 November

Did another blog on *The Sun*, based on the fact that in the *Mirror* the soldier's uncle had said his sister was being exploited politically, and that GB deserved an apology. *The Sun* had definitely overcooked it. Peter M was on the *Today* programme and though I didn't hear it, he was apparently pretty strong and spoke of a contract between the Tories and News International. It was going to crank up. I got the transcript and it was all very Peter, and good. Lift from Rayan out to the airport. He said 'Please, please, you have to go back. Look, I have a tear in my eye because deep down I know that you can be the difference between winning and losing. You must, really you must.' All a bit heavy for me but I was certainly feeling that pressure more and more.

GB called as I arrived at the airport and we went over the Afghanistan stuff again. I was convinced Cameron would have to go on it, because it was Armistice Day. When it came to it he did training and youth unemployment – figures out today – and according to David Muir GB had his best PMQs for ages. GB wanted advice on best lines for Afghanistan. I thought the one we discussed yesterday – weaken the Taliban and strengthen the government – was what he had to get over, plus a sense of the invisible enemy of terrorism being prevented. He was genuinely angry at the way *The Sun* focused on all the issues of our military and not the Taliban etc. I told him the line from my diaries, RC and I saying that if today's media had been around during WW2, we would all be sitting around in lederhosen eating sauerkraut.

I was still unsure about my stand-up plan. Had a bit of time to kill so went to the gym in the hotel. Nice hotel in Heerengasse [Vienna]. Newish and modern. Beautiful girl at reception. The telly was wall-to-wall coverage of the suicide of German goalkeeper Robert Enke. Watched a heartrending press conference with his widow Terese. He had had depression for years. I did a blog while on the static bike and found myself crying. I wrote that none of us can really ever know what was in his mind as he decided to take his life. But in truth there had been times when I worried that if my depressive waves had not stopped when they did, God knows. The last really big one was the summer. There were TV pictures of Enke after his last game on Sunday and I could tell in his eyes something was wrong. But why should any of his colleagues have thought he might? The one thing I feel David [Sturgeon] had really helped me get was the insight that it does pass. I got a good response to the blog, and it was timely with Mental Health Media Awards coming up.

This Week [BBC TV] were trying to get me on for tomorrow re *The Sun*. I said yes provided that as well as doing *The Sun*, we would also do mental illness. Did a couple of interviews, first with a public policy mag, which was fine, then the foreign editor of *Der Standard*. I took a bit of an instant dislike to the guy and ended up being pretty aggressive and dismissive with him. He was all spin, Iraq, TB and Europe not being trusted. He also had what Mum would call a sleekit look. When he asked about *Forum* [magazine, to which AC had been a contributor when young] and what the difference was between porn and politics, I went off on one. A bit heavy but he really was an irritating little shit. The event I was there for was a speech and Q&A with government spokesmen and advisors. I did my usual strat comms stuff. The questions were largely about how we actually managed change, quite specific on meetings and decision-making processes.

One guy, from the finance ministry, said I was 'the godfather of spin, the reason many of us do the jobs we do'. Another asked was it a problem that I became as famous as TB? I said I think if TB and I walked down a street here now… and before I could say 'he would be the only one recognised' someone shouted 'Nobody would know either of you.' I told the story of how we won something from Viktor Klima [former Chancellor of Austria] when he was rotating EU President by doing an interview with *Kronezeitung* [newspaper]; which had the headline 'Dickes Lob für Klima' ('Big praise for Klima' from Blair) and how this thereafter became known as the Dickes Lob strategy whenever we used public flattery to achieve something from someone. It was interesting the extent to which we were still seen as one of the best in terms of political message. The guy from the lobbying company that had invited me, Lukas Wiesbeck, was a really nice young bloke, bizarrely a huge Newcastle fan.

I felt the evening went pretty well. I was a bit angry with myself for losing it with the *Der Standard* guy but his bosses seemed OK. The *Sun* story had been pretty big there. GB had told me that the Austrians were leading the fight against TB for Europe in many ways so I did a big thing about how it was a mistake. The foreign ministry spokesman said afterwards he agreed. But he felt Iraq and the fact we were not in the Euro, allied to the fear of such a big figure doing it, meant it was probably not going to happen.

Thursday 12 November

Didn't sleep well. Never did in new hotels. Gave up at half five and went for a run round the city. Really nice place. We should definitely do more of this kind of stuff with the kids. Then breakfast with Lukas, his boss, the boss of *Der Standard* and the spokesmen from the finance and education ministries. Finance was Conservative, education was Social Democrat. They felt that my speech was right in theory but it was hard to deploy strategy clearly in a Grand Coalition situation. They gave me some examples of where it was impossible because the coalition partners were working against each other. The finance guy was apparently quite a big cheese within government comms – a bit bumptious but OK. He was boasting about how he had used Twitter to screw an important announcement planned by the Greens. Slaven Maric and the head of Croatian TV had come over for a meeting so we had a little chat. Slaven doing the usual network stuff, who he had seen, who he wanted to. Wanting to get me out there but the original plan had foundered on the back of the recession. Back in time to go out to the Heath for filming for tonight's *This Week*, on GB and *The Sun*. Then out to Simpson's for a speech to a dinner hosted by Nigel Harris of *Rail* magazine. I'd done a specific speech based on Nigel and Andrew [Adonis]'s calls and it went down pretty well. One or two a bit hostile but by the end all pretty much eating out of hand. Another group not terribly impressed by the Tories. But GB remained a big issue, even if the *Sun* thing had backfired on them.

Off to Millbank to do *This Week*. Andrew Neil very friendly, Portillo less so, [Diane] Abbott [Labour MP] even more unfriendly. Portillo wearing way too much makeup. Googling himself. Portillo went off on one about me abusing the media, followed up by Abbott and in between an OK chat with Neil. Abbott and I had a few sparky exchanges e.g. when she asked if I would be going back to help and I said I probably helped more out of the job than she did while doing hers. Knackered though and need to be up early. Fred Michel texted to challenge the assertions Peter M and I had been making re there being a deal on policy between News Corp and the Tories.

Friday 13 November

Quiz night at school. Conor Gearty [LSE academic] the new quizmaster. Did well. He'd been to a dinner at Chequers recently. Said he found GB really tired. Yet also thought serious people were turning against the Tories.

Saturday 14 November

Woken by a text from No. 10 asking if I would do a conference call with GB at 9.30. I called switch to ask who with – Douglas, Ed M and David Muir. Saturday morning used to be a regular stack of calls. This was a rare intrusion, but I did not much fancy it. I called in nonetheless. He wanted to let off more steam about *The Sun*. He said he had been told 'You were brilliant on the Andrew Neil show' (DM will have told him to say that). But he wanted to know where I thought it went now. I felt they would calm it for a bit but then come back worse than ever. He agreed with that. He wanted to keep the argument going about the idea of a deal on policy. I said it had to rely on more than assertion. We had to get journos and MPs on the case, or even better a major documentary, so that it really opened up. At the moment it was too easily dismissed as politicking. We then got on to the lines of attack for the Queen's Speech. He felt that the legislative stuff was OK but in truth what was needed was proper attack. The line that they were 'wrong on recession, wrong on recovery' had to be sustained.

He said were we saying they were basically right-wing? Were we saying they concealed the truth? Were we saying they did not get the reality of people's lives? We were saying all those things. He got into an argument about which one. I tried to set out a way in which all became part of the same attack. We were on there for around an hour. Eventually I said I had to take Grace somewhere. There was something too depressing about these conversations – the constant whinging about the media, the references to Coulson and deals with *The Sun*, the repetitive conversations on old points, the explanations of policy we had all heard before. David Muir kept telling me I was making a real difference to the operation. Godric had volunteered that though he still thought the country had decided against him, his performance at PMQs had really improved. Fiona and I set off for Suffolk to see Ian Kennedy and the boys at their house out there.

Much bigger than I expected it to be. The ceilings were a bit low, and I banged my head a fair bit. The boys had grown up a lot and we had a really good chat about all sorts of things. Ian was clearly still very upset about the marriage ending and made repeated references to it. The boys were rallying round pretty well. He had got over the wobble re the IPSA job. But he was not keen on Kelly and was determined to set his own agenda. His analysis was that Kelly had looked only at the rubble whereas what was needed was a proper assessment of what the modern legislator needed and what was justified. The problem was a lack of political leadership, so they all competed for the lowest common denominator. He said there was a former judge on the interviewing panel who gave him a hard time for not telling them about being my 'phone a friend' – 'like it mattered'. He said there had been a few digs from the same source till eventually he said hold on, no more. Wild and windy day. But we had a nice time and I was glad we'd gone. It seemed to cheer him up.

Sunday 15 November

Out on the bike, a few dozen laps of the Emirates. Back to watch Fiona on Adam Boulton's programme debating with Toby Young [journalist] his plans to start a new school in his area. Then did a blog saying she trounced him. Led to him posting comments back, then Fiona, after which I did a jokey posting on her split infinitive and missing apostrophe, which sent her off on one. Pottered a bit then went round to Philip's to see him and Peter M. Peter M already there, with his Brompton [bicycle]. Gail looking tired but making tea for us. We settled down upstairs. I took off my shoes. 'Yes, good idea,' said Peter before stretching out. I asked him where we were. He said not in a very good situation. I said can we win? He said almost certainly not.

He had had a chat with DM after the Cenotaph ceremony last week. He said David had asked him the same question and was somewhat taken aback when he gave the same answer. But when David asked him what it meant in terms of what he might do, he said he would not lift a finger against GB. He then made a joke about how he could not stop others though if he happened to be abroad. He said their conversation was interrupted by Harriet who was 'unusually Delphic'. He felt she did not really think GB could win. It was her entreaties to him about the need for proper election structures that had led to him setting up a new election ministerial strategy team which PG would present to tomorrow. This was the ostensible reason for our meeting, to talk through what he would say. But it went a lot wider. PG now had a settled view that GB could not win. He felt there was a danger of a big defeat. 'Carnage.' He had done a few focus groups recently and there was an overwhelming mood of pessimism and a feeling that GB could not do it. Whilst the media may have rallied to him a bit over *The Sun* and the letter, to the public it was just one more sign that he could not do the job.

He said they would at least listen to us if we had a change. He said DM's name emerged quickly when people talked about that prospect. He would definitely limit defeat and might get us to a hung parliament situation. Peter had an equally gloomy assessment. He said we had all been waiting in hope that GB would improve. But whilst he had many qualities and on a good day he displayed them, he was basically incapable of change and the public had decided that whatever he was he was not a leader. He said that of all the people in the office, none, with the possible exception of Leanne [Johnston], really had faith in him any more. People worked very hard and worked long hours but they felt they were propping up a dead horse. He said very few members of the Cabinet retained faith in him. I said if that was the case, he must at least consider following through the logic of what he was saying. If we thought there was the possibility of GB seeing that government, party and even he individually might improve as a result of change, and if there was now a genuine alternative, then surely he had to think that through in terms of it being something he might help to bring about.

I said I had always been clear that he could probably only go if it was voluntary. I felt a process in which he stayed while a new leader, hopefully David, was elected, was the best thing that could happen. But I agreed if it was just another bruising battle in which he did not want to go, then it was a disaster. PM felt David had improved hugely but he was still not sure if it was a route to guaranteed improvement. But he did believe that with GB we had had it. He said he had been shocked at how badly he treated people, how dysfunctional the office was. At times – as on Friday after the by-election win and the sense he had seen off *The Sun* – he could be calm and lucid and clear-sighted. But too often he just raged the whole time. He said that because it was now an accepted fact – however untrue – that he had betrayed GB in '94, he felt he could not do so again.

We went round in circles and eventually agreed that what might have to happen was that DM, Harriet and Alan J were prevailed upon to go to see him to say in their judgement he could not lead them to victory, and he should consider his position. They should not say they would resign and they should make clear they would not be making it public. As to whether they would, who knows? But he felt Harriet had shifted a fair bit. Also, Balls was 'no longer a Brownite – he is a Ballsite'. Peter was still not sure whether to believe Harriet's statements that she would not stand. He also had another go at persuading me to go in – 'It is fun, you have a platform and you can pick and choose when you go.' He looked a little overweight but given the workload and all that was on him, he looked OK. He said the ministerial group meeting tomorrow was him, Harriet, Alistair D, Alan J, DM, Douglas A, the Eds, Jack Straw. But there had to be a 'de facto' strategy group and he wanted that to be us three, DA, Ed because of the manifesto, David Muir and the agency. That was the thing he wanted me and Philip to sign up to. We said we would, but we both felt we did not want to get drawn in more deeply. And we both felt it should not exclude going to GB and for once saying what we really thought.

I said when I went to the meetings in No. 10, the minute I got there I wanted to get out. Also I felt if we were all admitting it was a lost cause, surely we had to do more than join the sleepwalk to defeat and disaster? But I realised it was hard and agreed it was not certain that what followed would be better. PG felt I had to do more to help David. He felt I was allowing myself to be used. But so was he now. We joked about Peter briefing as we spoke, via BlackBerry, that the old team had been reassembled to back GB. I was surprised at just how negative he was re GB. As well as the ministerial strategy team there was to be a daily Victoria Street meeting to take forward what was happening in the government, and he felt he should chair it rather than Douglas but he could not do it every day. We chatted away for ages and it was all very friendly and warm. But there was something dreadfully depressing about it too. He and David Muir were seeing Coulson and Ed Llewellyn to talk about TV debates. He found Coulson 'a bit intimidating'. Why? 'He is very direct and has that working-class menace lurking.' He said he reminded him of me a bit, that he was one of those people able to get inside other people's heads.

Monday 16 November

Out to Kalendar for breakfast with Nick Keller. He was quite interesting on the political scene. Felt we had done better in the last six months but that he could not bring himself to vote for GB. 'I don't want to vote Tory. I'd switch back if Miliband was there.' Alina had sent me [Obama campaign manager] David Plouffe's book [*The Audacity to Win*] which I was really enjoying. It also brought home how important the psychology of the person at the top was to the nature and tone of the campaign. It was the opposite of the way GB operated. I was working on my speech for TalkTalk tomorrow and there were some terrific little summations of campaigns and campaigning which I intended to use. I dropped him a line saying how much I liked it. Otherwise a bit of a nothing day. GB called for help on his QS speech but I was off form and unenthused. I was going into a bit of a dip and he was not exactly the best escalator out of it.

Tuesday 17 November

The party had announced that Mark Lucas's film from conference, *Against the Odds*, on great causes won by Labour, was to be our Queen's Speech PPB. So a victory for Twitterer Ellie Gellard [student activist], in support of whom I had blogged at the weekend. Did another one congratulating her, and also on Hague for helping to block TB [from presidency of the European Council] and deliver a federalist like Herman van Rompuy [former Prime Minister of Belgium], who was out calling for new EU-wide taxes. Neil called. I read him out some of the key Plouffe sections on leadership and teamwork. He loyally defended GB and said it was the majors and adjutants who caused trouble and who should be made to read that. But the tone was set from the top. I was getting lots of bids on the QS but decided against. Also had decided not to do *Question Time* this week. Out on the bike trying to chase the gloom that was falling. It wasn't a bad one but it had the potential to be. I told F up front so she pretty much left me alone.

GB called a couple of times. I gave him a good line on inheritance tax – the first tax cut where the people proposing it know personally all those who stand to gain. He was at that stage of running the same arguments at me the whole time. It was like TB but without the lightness and humour. He basically wanted reassurance which I tried to give him. His problem was that a lot of people had stopped listening. Another death in Afghanistan. Obama signalling slowdown on Copenhagen. The Tories were starting to run the line that the QS was all about politics and not the interests of the country. [Lord] Strathclyde [Lords opposition leader] did a briefing saying they would block bills in the Lords. GB called again and we went through some of his attack lines. I said focus on social care, banks and jobs, and hone the attack on inheritance tax. My LRF event went fine. GB called before, and again afterwards. 'How's your charitable work?' he asked. 'Fine. How's your political work?' He said dreadful. He was still trying to get the EU job for TB but it was not on. He could get the Foreign Minister job which might in some ways be more important.

Headed home, but feeling down. DM called as he was heading to the airport to fly to Dubai then Kabul. We had a pretty frank conversation. Agreed that as things stood the game was up. That a change might make a difference. That he was the only serious option. He was still clearly a bit tempted by the EU job [Foreign Minister] but had pretty much committed to staying in UK politics. He knew that I had doubts about whether he had the full panoply and asked me to speak to Louise later. On GB he felt that nothing had really changed or improved. The PLP was paralysed because of expenses. Ministers were part-time. There was no teamwork. The campaign was not there. He felt he had a body of ideas and policies that could get us back in the game. He did not believe we had lost the battle of ideas but we had lost public and media opinion. We were looking tired and ragged. He felt he had it in him to get us on the pitch.

I told him what I had said to Peter, that it needed a group of them, without publicity, to tell him what they really thought. He said the only people GB respected or listened to were TB, Peter M, AC and PG. He didn't listen to the Cabinet. He said he was torn about the Europe job but he felt we had started something in Britain and he did not want to run from it. Later Louise called. She had a slightly different take. She felt he was still tempted because Europe would be a big and interesting job and he would do it well. They would probably stay in London at least for the first year while DM set up in Brussels and basically lived on a plane. The big question was whether there was any chance that GB would go. She felt if there was, he had to stay around. I felt that if he did then DM was the only possible successor but if it happened after defeat anything could happen. She said she knew I had doubts. I said they were in the area of his manner, an aloofness with real people that could quickly be defined as arrogance. She agreed he needed to work on that.

I said he was basically a good man and clever and a team player. He needed to be clear in his demeanour that politics was about great causes for improving people's lives, not an intellectual pursuit for the few. She felt he had improved a lot and that he was up to it. She felt the situation was hopeless as things stood. I read her some of the lines from Plouffe. 'Everything GB is not.' She said she felt I had to go and tell him the truth. I said all that would happen is erosion of confidence allied to delusion that I was plotting for someone. There was only a point doing that if there was a bigger plan. I felt it would need him, Harriet, AD and Alan J (whose views on all this appeared to be unknown) to go and tell him he was leading them to disaster. If he did not listen, well there you go, they were right to worry about the impact of regicide. She said there were few people they could talk to. But in the end DM had to decide first re Europe – pretty much overnight as the summit was soon. And then re what to do if he stayed. Not easy.

Wednesday 18 November

GB called as I was in the car going down to the TalkTalk event in Sussex. He was back banging at his typewriter. There had been another soldier killed in Afghanistan so that was going to be the start of PMQs. Went over his lines of defence and attack. Tories out saying it was a waste of time etc. Then TB called. Started jokily, asking how 'Buuuuuurnleeeee' were doing. The purpose of the call was Europe. He asked if I thought he should take the EU Foreign Minister job if asked. I felt not. I had never really understood why he was so keen on the No. 1 job so why would he go for the No. 2? He said his instinct was no, but GB was keen and he wanted to check with me. He said he had actually felt a bit of relief when the No. 1 job went away. He was building up something really good, he was enjoying it. He said the stuff he was doing in Africa probably helped as much as anything he did in power.

Then he came to the point of the call. He said they would definitely welcome a Brit in the job, especially if the top job went to a 'midget'. He said if not him, there were only two names they would consider – David or Peter. GB wanted TB to do it in part so as not to lose David – which would be seen as a sign DM felt we couldn't win – or Peter – ally, plus key to the campaign. TB had said to GB that I was more important to a campaign than Peter. He felt it would be good for the UK if we could land that job and he should do what was best for the country. But he could see the downsides all round. He felt DM was definitely against. I said so did I but Louise made me think he was persuadable. GB clearly felt Peter would be a bigger loss than DM because he had asked TB to have a go at persuading David to do it. TB felt DM was better staying because he still felt there was a chance things would open up and GB would not be there for the election.

He felt DM had come on a lot. He felt Peter's departure would not be such a blow because it is so clearly such an important job. He would do it well. Its size would limit the sense of any 'flouncing out'. He said he had told GB that if Peter went, he would persuade me to do more for him. I said 'If you think I am running that campaign, you are wrong. That is de-fin-i-tive.' He said 'I'll put you down as leaning marginally in favour then,' and laughed. I said it did my head in every time I went in there. He said he would help. But that would be the kind of outside big-picture strategy help that I was looking to do. With Peter gone I would be even more under pressure to get right into the centre. He clearly was going off to say he was trying to persuade DM but actually try to engineer PM into it. Would there ever be a time when my life was not revolving around the various movements of TB, GB, PM, PG et al? Probably not.

The TalkTalk event was at Goodwood Park Hotel, so nice drive through the Sussex downs. I had never really had a proper chat with Charles Dunstone [chairman, Carphone Warehouse]. Liked him. Charles came through to fill me in on the nature of the event – key TalkTalk people, they had been successful beyond what they had really envisaged and now were planning the next steps. I did my spiel on world of change then ten steps to leadership, initialised on a postcard. Went down well. Could always tell when I was on form. Used a fair few quotes from Plouffe's book. Good questions in the Q&A, then through for a finger lunch. Charles rightly spotted that GB failed on most of those leadership tests I laid out. TB and Obama succeeded. It was a lot of it about temperament and psychology. He said he was himself prone to panic in a crisis and not always getting head above parapet. He felt GB needed help and he could see why he wanted me back in but understood the reluctance. Asked if I'd be interested in non-exec directorship when they go public. Enjoyed the meeting, then set off for home.

David Muir texted me to say GB nailed Cameron with the line I gave them on IHT. I surfed around a bit for coverage and the neutrality suggested to me GB had won. Set off for Wembley and the Street Child World Cup fundraiser. About 450 people. Joe Hewitt [organiser] really effusive about the help I'd given in getting a few people there. I did interviews and a few pictures with Mandy, a South African street child who was now helping organise the event. Nice enough do. Off to Archer Street in Soho to join a bit late the TB Team '94 gathering. A bit of an odd and scratchy affair. TB and Peter were both consumed with tomorrow's Brussels summit to decide the new top EU jobs born of the Lisbon Treaty. TB had now accepted that he was not going to get the top job and had decided against the High Representative job. But he seemed possessed of the idea we should fight to get a Brit into the post. I sensed he was scheming, probably for Peter, maybe for something further down the track, or to get Peter in as a way of weakening GB for DM.

Europe's No. 1 choice would be David but he had decided he was going to stay and try to get GB to go. TB was now pushing for Peter who was really keen, partly because it was such a big job but also as an exit strategy from GB and his current situation. But GB would not let him go and if he did not back him, it was not going to happen. The other name in the frame seemed to be Cathy Ashton [European Commissioner]. TB and PM said GB would only agree to Peter's name going forward if he could guarantee that I would go back and run the campaign. I was clear it was not going to happen in the way they wanted. Earlier I had received my Iraq Inquiry letter which had depressed me a bit. JoP had had his too. TB said he intended to be very robust about the policy. Sally Morgan – who had not received a letter – David Hill [former Downing Street communication director] and I all felt TB was being a bit too relaxed about how it might go. We felt that it would be tough and that they would really go for him. I was feeling I had to start researching pretty soon. TB had called Louise earlier to try to lean on her re DM. The dinner was all a bit scratchy. Tim [Allan] and PG not there. David M was in Kabul for the Karzai swearing in. Sarah Hunter [spad], Kate Garvey – who had lost loads of weight, James Purnell – who had put it on, Mike Craven all there.

JoP, rarely for him, had had too much to drink. His main refrain was that GB had to go and that I had to stop propping him up. Anji was pissed as well and was saying the same thing more violently. I said if there was a plan, fine, but if it was just people mouthing off, it would lead nowhere. Later I gave Pat a lift home and he felt that DM was definitely moving. He said the government was paralysed. Nobody thought that they could win with GB. There was so much denial around, mixed with a sense of fatalism, and expenses had shaken their confidence. But he did feel DM had grown and something might give. We did the usual quiz thing – which my team won – but it was not quite as harmonious and friendly as in the past. Kate said part of it was that apart from me and PM, who were still in there with GB to different degrees, they had all moved on. Pat, apart from being happy with his baby, was more downbeat about things than ever. Email exchanges with Piers, who agreed to a very good quote for the front cover of *Maya*. Random House and Ed very happy.

Thursday 19 November

I was due in Grantham, at the Belton Woods hotel, for the CCPR [Central Council of Physical Recreation] conference. Chief execs of sporting bodies. I was definitely on form on the speaking front at the moment, even if it felt a bit of a waste of my time. GB called a couple of times to thank me for help on the speech and to say he wanted to see me again 'to discuss how we can best use your help', so he was on the charge again. Rachel K told me that there had been a discussion about how they could get me in, up to and including a Cabinet seat and a place in the Lords. I went for a swim then headed to Mum's. Got a call from Simon Clifford, the football guy who had helped Clive Woodward in the past. He said he had been approached by the *Mail* about Nicky Blair, digging into his work as an agent. Simon said he was a big fan of mine and of TB's, because of politics and also because he was a major depressive. I called TB to alert him and kept him in touch.

Mum was in good form, though she did appear to be even smaller. We had a nice chat about various things whilst watching the live concert at the Albert Hall for Children in Need. Finished the Plouffe book. I should distil and send to GB to emphasise the importance of the leadership psychology of a campaign. But maybe he just could not do it. *L'Express* had asked me for a piece on Sarko and Obama so I worked on that for a bit. The EU summit dinner finally agreed on Herman van Rompuy as the new President and Cathy Ashton as the high representative. So not the big voice for Europe that was envisaged.

Friday 20 November

Left after breakfast and headed home. Dentist then lunch with Tom Baldwin at Black and Blue. He said that *The Times* was changing for the worse and he was finding it hard to get anti-Tory stories in. His piece last week on Tories failing to attract celeb supporters was turned into a piece saying nobody liked politics. He was reliably informed also that Samantha Cameron was pissed off with the extent to which Rebekah Brooks now felt she should be spending time with them at weekends. He really felt I should get back in, said I ought to be at the peak of my powers, stopping the Tories get back in. Cup of tea with Adam Sherwin who wanted to leave *The Times* in protest at their coverage and work for the party. I recommended him to Chris Lennie. Cumbrian floods dire. DM text saying GB should go in January with a big consensus push.

Saturday 21 November

PG saw Peter M who was by all accounts very pissed off that GB had blocked him from going to Brussels and as PG said 'The one thing that will get and keep Peter offside is if you block or stall his ambition.' In the afternoon settled down to watch Burnley v Villa on the internet. Real wild weather but we played pretty well, early lead sadly thrown away near the end [1–1]. Then we set off for Kingston, dinner with the Molloys at Penny Stott's. Sad to be there with no Richard. Penny still used him as her main point of reference in conversation. Mike was on great form though alarmingly right-wing on some issues. Not surprised when he said they had the *Mail* and the *Telegraph* delivered and he read the other broadsheets when he went out. Lots of the usual reminiscing re *Mirror* days, Maxwell etc. Glad we had made the effort to go, even to the extent of missing a home game, and getting to bed – for us – really late.

Sunday 22 November

I woke up early and went down to potter for a bit. *The Observer* had a poll putting the Tory lead at 6 per cent which could either be a blip or a possible weather changer. PG came round for a cup of tea, knowing that David M was coming round at 12. DM happy to see us both together but PG felt it was better I saw him alone. He thought we needed a really honest conversation. PG was in no doubt GB had to go. He said he had made that clear enough when he presented to the Cabinet strategy group last Monday and said that the country wanted change and renewal and neither main party was felt to be offering it. He was just back from the States and was feeling tired. I showed him a couple of the emails GB had sent me – dreadful spelling, mix of upper and lower case, full of nonsense. Yesterday a long one with a stream of invective aimed at Cameron on IHT. It was not at all clear what he was intending to use it for or what I was expected to do with it.

I had been pressing him yesterday to go to the floods in Cumbria and today he went and got a good reception in the terrible situation, where he seemed genuinely concerned.* PG was pretty clear that without a change we were in possible meltdown territory. It almost didn't matter about Cameron because he would get in by default. He also felt Harriet had definitely shifted her position and believed GB could not win and had to go. He was not sure about AD but my sense was Alistair had just about had enough. He felt we – and particularly us two – would be judged harshly for the way we had helped GB to succeed [Blair], whilst adding that it will be easy to say in hindsight but I don't know what else we could have done at the time. He was also worried that lots of the civil servants would go running for cover in the Iraq Inquiry and that they would be gunning for TB and the politics of it all.

* Record rainfall caused flooding in parts of Great Britain and Ireland throughout November. In Cumbria, many people were forced from their homes and hundreds had to stay with friends or relatives or spend nights in reception centres.

He went off amid a thunderstorm then DM arrived a bit later. He was definitely a bit steelier than usual. He said there was no doubt GB had to go and the only question was how. He felt that the best way was for TB, Peter M, PG and I to tell him, as the co-founders of New Labour, that he was heading for disaster and the best thing for country, party and himself was to go. I said I would be up for it and so would PG but I felt PM would not and TB would be unsure how to play things. He also needed to think through what happened if we did that – which we would do without publicity – and then he stayed. Then he and other members of the Cabinet would have to go to him and say the same thing. 'What you mean he'd put a gun to the party's head and blow it up?' Well, he might. He felt Peter M was unlikely to move against him but he did know the situation was untenable.

As for the others, he did not want to go into that. But he admitted Ed M could be a problem. David had been telling him for a while Gordon had to go but Ed was being told by some he should go for it too. I said we may have to take you for dinner at Granita's. He didn't seem to find it very funny. I said does Ed think he could do it? He said we haven't really talked about it, but he is quite shifty about it. I said 'If you can't square your brother people will wonder what chance you have with the country.' DM had clearly thought about it all a lot. He said his pitch would be that the Blair–Brown era was over and we had to put forward a new agenda focused on innovation economy, education back as the main priority – Balls would have to be moved or even removed – green, constitution, crime and ASB seen from the responsibility side of things, maybe Europe. We agreed though that Cameron had rather neutralised Europe or at least made it less neuralgic. He was pretty compelling as he went through it. He was a better communicator than GB. He was also able to engage people better and understood the need for a proper team operation.

He said he was getting a fair bit of policy work done in various 'small cells' but obviously did not want too much down in writing. He said Harriet seemed sincere in not wanting to stand as leader herself. She would be key in gauging voices elsewhere. None of this could get out or there would be a real problem. Equally he had to understand it may just come to an eyeball-to-eyeball moment and he had to be clear how he would deal with that. He said if GB asked him his view direct he would say he felt he had to go. If he was asked on the media he would have to try to fudge it. He was pretty determined though, said he had given up the chance of a top job on the world stage which he would have done well because he did not want to see the Tories beat us when they had not really won the arguments, and because he believed there was a chance of stopping it happening, or at least getting to a hung parliament.

I asked if he had spoken to Hillary [Clinton] who had been gushing about him in an interview. He had. She felt we were doomed with GB and would try to help if it came to it. He kept coming back to what I could do to help. He felt it was in the area first of speaking to GB honestly and then preparing DM's pitch for a leadership and then general election. I said if we went as a group – assuming he would even allow a meeting to take place – he would simply feel we had gone again him because deep down we always had been, and he might well just sit tight. So DM had to think through Plan B or possibly a mix of old hands and current Cabinet. He felt a majority of the Cabinet wanted this to happen but of course he could not really cast around. Also he was being advised he could not be part of such a delegation himself, that it would harm his succession chances. I was not so sure about that.

It was clear Peter Hyman, Andrew A and James P were talking to him and he wanted to bring me in, whilst understanding I would continue to talk to GB. 'It is in nobody's interest that he falls flat on his face. In fact, if the plan is to get him to go in a dignified manner, it is better he does well in the House for example, so I think you should carry on giving advice on that.' He accepted there was a major problem at the idea of a second unelected PM but he felt it would have to be ridden out. He would in short order set out plans on the economy, a proper war footing re Afghanistan, maybe a national unity approach, then to the other domestic policy stuff day by day. He asked me where I thought he was with public and media. With media I felt he was in a better place than a year ago and was seen by serious people as being a serious and competent player. By the public, though his profile had risen, it was still not huge, not part of the national consciousness, and that it was a bit geeky and policy wonk. He said he did not intend to be anything he wasn't – I liked that – and that he should probably be the serious man for serious times GB had promised to be, and he would resist the celeb stuff. I also said that whilst trying to rebuild media support he also needed to rise above it.

Both with him and PG I was talking up the Plouffe book and saying the psychology of the team was key – clear leadership, team building, risk and no blame culture. He felt he could do all that, certainly more than GB had. We went round and round like this for a couple of hours. Fiona was popping in and out, brutally frank, saying they had all fluffed it last time and now they had to make it happen. David said GB had been given the time he wanted and it had not worked. The unity argument no longer held the same sway. He admitted to being worried about the impact on Louise and the boys, but said in the end he had to do his best. He seemed pretty determined. We agreed to keep in touch. He was doing the QS debate tomorrow then off to Bermuda with the Queen.

Monday 23 November

I was definitely going into a dip, possibly because the Iraq Inquiry was starting tomorrow so the build-up was in full flow. Gilligan had a front-page *Sunday Telegraph* lead story purportedly based on leaked memos of the internal MoD review with which he was seeking to show both that we had prepared in secret and that we were unprepared. The right and left media were going to go for us now and already Chilcot was having to defend himself as being independent etc. I also sensed TB was planning to get a bit more focused. JoP felt that some in the intelligence and military would seek to push things TB's way. He said every review of every war showed people trying to do the blame game. Good piece in the *FT* on business groups criticising Tory plans to decimate RDAs so with GB, DC and Clegg all speaking at the CBI today.

I had not spoken much to GB who had sent me through the speech. He called a couple of times when I was out on the bike with Rory and I just couldn't face it. Out to see John Feehan [CEO, 6 Nations British and Irish Lions] at the Paddington Hilton. His big thing with the [David] Davies report [on free-to-air listed sporting events] was the proposal that the Welsh games of the 6 Nations should be free to air in Wales. He said in the digital age it was as good as saying anyone could watch. He said his main aim was 'to keep the BBC honest', that they could not really get a fair price for the rights without real competition and he was not convinced this would deliver it. I said where I thought the government and Tories were on the consultation, suggested they prepare an economic case to put for a different approach and agreed I would help with it.

Home to work a bit but I was feeling demotivated. Tweeted a bit about the biased coverage of the CBI speeches, exacerbated by an extraordinary late Beeb bulletin – not a word on the CBI speeches, but a Nick Robinson puff piece on Osborne and his green economy plans. Nice chat with Fiona re where I was on things – could not decide on anything. Troubled re GB, troubled re Iraq, not really motoring on anything for the future. Maybe time to start a new book. Long chat with John Woodcock [Labour Co-operative candidate] who had been selected for Barrow and joined the queue wanting me to do a fundraiser.

Tuesday 24 November

David Owen, ex-*FT* now freelance, called asking if I had been approached to help with the World Cup bid because he said it had been mooted. News to me. The news was wall-to-wall Iraq Inquiry. Protesters wearing TB, GWB and GB masks with fake blood on their hands. Chilcot seemed fairly measured. I caught some of the first session with Peter Ricketts

[Foreign Office] and others. Chatted with JoP who shared my concern we were vacating the field and so critics could set the tone for a 'whitewash' unless TB was really gone for. I went to see Bostock for a repeat prescription and he was full of black humour about the inquiry. Worst possible day to see him, the usual rant about Iraq and how I could have stopped it, and I probably felt guilty, and also about the NHS. I spent the morning reading my evidence to Hutton as a way of trying to get back into it. There was so much I had forgotten.

I was going into a dip and the Iraq situation was going to hover between pressure and stress. Bostock definitely not helpful on that front. Bit of a 'served you right' tone. I was dreading going into Downing Street. Usual fannying around to get in and a former Treasury guy was in the entrance asking loudly if I was due at the inquiry. I said I hope not today because if I was I was late. Up to the study where GB was already in with James, Theo, Nicholas and a woman I didn't know. She was a bit starey-eyed and seemed to want to focus on messaging. We were pretty sure DC would go on floods and maybe then the economy as there were more not-great figures around, and also as they were pushing a green economic agenda though not very convincingly. GB was really keen to keep the IHT attack going. He also wanted to link it to fox hunting. 'These are his fucking priorities.' I said he had to be careful not to go OTT or let them come back with a class war thing. Best to stay focused one at a time for now. Let others build that kind of picture.

Theo said the *Mirror* was planning a splash on how much the Tories stood to gain from the change. Theo kept pushing at it but I think we held him off. He was also very wary about linking floods and climate change. It now looked like Obama was going to Copenhagen but there was no sense of a deal in the offing yet and it seemed he was only going as a drop in when over to collect his Nobel Prize. We all thought the whole Nobel thing was a bit odd anyway. I was always struck by how little GB seemed to know about Obama's plans e.g. what and when he intended to set out re Afghanisation. I felt I was there really just to calm him a bit, keep him focused and try to help the team pin him down on answers. He said the Supreme Court was due to announce a judgment on OFT [Office of Fair Trading] v banks tomorrow and he felt if it went the right way he could get up the banking reforms as an on-your-side issue. He seemed to have put even more weight on. Bruce popped in, we had another run round the circles then I made an excuse about having to go to the Mental Health Media Awards and off I went.

I stopped to see the new Thatcher portrait which she had been in to unveil yesterday. It was impressive, a terrific likeness, especially the eyes. I got a cab to the awards and interestingly both this driver, and the one who took me to Whitehall earlier, asked if I was going to the inquiry and said they were on TB's side. 'All too easy in hindsight but I wrote to him at the time and said I supported him. We'd let Saddam get away with it too long.' Not much of that in the media coverage and a lot trying to undermine the people on the inquiry as a way of leading them to feel unless they really go for us, and TB in particular, then it is a whitewash. I was also getting messages on Facebook from people worried about the story in *The Observer* that judges felt there was a war crimes issue to face. I watched a bit of the proceedings and my sense was they were going to be thorough and tough, especially on the politics of it all.

We did a few vlogs at BAFTA [British Academy of Film and Television Arts]. First on Cumbria floods pre-Copenhagen, a before and after re the award I was up for, and a thing about *GQ* putting Cameron and Osborne ahead of GB in their power list. Nice crowd for the awards. There was definitely a better shortlist in all the categories. A British-Iranian comedian [Shappi Khorsandi] was compering and she really was funny. Gave me a good line for my speech too as she had a gag about shagging a fish and when I went up I started by thanking the sign language interpreter for teaching me how to say shagging a fish with my hands. *Cracking Up* was up against some really good films, Terry Pratchett [author] on Alzheimer's, Fiona Phillips on her dad's dementia, two others that were really good. I was pleased to win and quite emotional. Thanked everyone, including Mind and Time to Change and said we were near a tipping point. It was a nice event. Tweeted proud to win and got a good response. Relatively few jibes about Iraq at the moment considering how high-profile it was.

We raced to Philip and Gail's party and just got there for the end of her speech, having missed PG and Peter. Nice do, mix of politics – Sarah and CB both there too – and books. Susan Sandon saying publishing was in real trouble. Generally the books people seemed as depressed as the political people. David was away but Louise was there, looking pretty tense I thought. It must be a bit of a nightmare for them at the moment. The GB thing, and also the Ed thing if it was true – and she was sure it was – that he felt he might have a go if David did. Peter Hyman was clearly of the view that those of us who were helping GB were giving him the credibility to endure and survive and it was a dreadful mistake.

Rebekah Brooks made much the same point when I assailed her, only half in jest, about what a bad thing she had done in going for DC. She said we all knew GB was dreadful and he couldn't do the job, and they had supported him long enough, and we had had plenty of chances to get rid of him but didn't and it was all our fault. She could not believe Peter stood by him. Fiona felt she was a little bit rattled but I am not so sure. They basically thought GB had had it and that was that. Douglas was alongside, saying not a word. I had a quiet chat with Peter M who felt things had got worse not better. The dysfunctionalism was dire. He had really wanted the Europe job because it was the only way he could get out, but GB had blocked it. He also thought GB was behind some of the bad stories about Peter – 'Make me Foreign Secretary, says Mandelson' – at the weekend.

We sat down on the sofa and he said he felt I was giving GB ballast and keeping him calm. He felt I should carry on doing that, but that when the New Year came and it was still not clear where things were heading, and there was a move, that I was one of the people who had to 'summon up all your courage and…' 'Tell him Peter says you have to go,' I said. 'Noooo… You will have to do that.' I said that I was worried that the Iraq Inquiry was not going to be straightforward and that TB's reputation could really take a hit and we would all get hit with him. He said the inquiry was a classic 'GB–Woodward operation', worst of all worlds and now it means it will dominate the start of an election year. Hopeless. It was a nice enough do. Gail and the girls looked really happy. I was a bit worried how tired Philip looked though.

Wednesday 25 November

Another bad night's sleep. The coverage of the inquiry was advancing as we assumed, picking over anything that might be deemed bad for us, e.g. today WMD intelligence that was patchy and sporadic, including a report just before the invasion that Saddam had disassembled chemical weapons. Then Stuart Prebble came round and we had a chat over a few options – comedy, on which he was keen but I was still mulling, military and mental health, maybe based on a few interviews with former soldiers, plus I wanted to do one on Robert Enke. He was also quite keen for me to do *Grumpy Old Men*. Out to Bayley Street to record an interview for Piers Morgan's review of the year. They were full of how big he had become and how powerful within ITV. The interview was with a producer, all pretty superficial, Obama, banks, Peter M, war but also *X Factor*, Susan Boyle, Jacqui Smith's husband etc. Bit of a waste of time. I told Ed it was just backscratching in exchange for Piers's front-cover quote. But when they told me the others they were doing – Kelvin MacKenzie [former *Sun* editor], Max Clifford [publicist], Fern something – I thought what am I doing here?

Home to do a bit of work then out to Latimer Road W10 to meet Stewart Binns and record a voiceover for the new *Rhapsody in Claret and Blue*, official Burnley DVD. We were at the film for a couple of hours or so, then out for dinner. Home to watch *Inside Sport* on depression in sport, based on interviews with Marcus Trescothick [cricketer], Neil Lennon [footballer], Frank Bruno [boxer] and John Kirwan [rugby player]. Excellent. I got a letter from the inquiry support team in Whitehall about when to go in and see what I needed to read.

Thursday 26 November

Bad night. Lots of awful dreams. Needed to see DS soon. Marcus Trescothick had talked last night of the various bits of build-up to a big one and this was definitely stress building. While on the train to Devon, I did a blog on the media blackout – apart from *The Guardian* – on the Andy Coulson bullying settlement.* Imagine how big it would have gone had it been me at the *Mirror* and the case happening when I was with TB. It was a lovely cold sunny day. Quite a lot of water lying around in the West Country too which got no coverage of course because Cumbria was so bad. Geoff Lakeman met me at the station in Newton Abbot and we set off for the Palace at Torquay. A bit geriatric and in need of a refurbishment. We had afternoon tea and chatted away a bit about old times and also what his kids were all up to. He was clearly really proud of the boys [all musicians]. He filled me in a bit on Chris Meyer's evidence to the inquiry which sounded self-serving and full of quotable clips. The problem was that everything was gearing towards TB, including the question of legality. I had a swim before changing for the dinner. Torquay and District Medical Society. They wanted me to do stuff on mental health, which went fine, then Q&A, in which all manner of things came up, but not Iraq. Signed a fair few books, then bed by half eleven.

Friday 27 November

Alzheimer's moment on the way to the station when I realised I had left cash and laptop in my room. Made the train though. Reading novel on the way to Paddington then met Adam McCarthy [Australian diplomat] for lunch at a Chinese restaurant. On the inquiry he felt what was the point? It would discover that once the Yanks were definitely going, a few countries like ours and yours felt they would have to go to. He had been to the party conferences. Felt ours was subdued but felt we were still in the game. Felt the Tories tried to be non-complacent but they were cocky.

* Matt Driscoll, a sports reporter at the *News of the World* during Coulson's editorship, was sacked while on long-term sick leave. An employment tribunal awarded him £792,736 for unfair dismissal and disability discrimination.

He was not sure they were up to it. Nice guy and with a pretty good take on things.

[Sir] Jeremy Greenstock [former UK permanent representative to the UN] was doing the inquiry today and his carefully distancing lines were first that it was 'legal but of questionable legitimacy' and also that he had threatened to resign if we went without a new resolution. Day by day the diplomatic class were pointing the finger more and more at TB. Cab to TB's office for meetings to go over where we were on the inquiry. TB had decided he was best going first in the New Year, to stop this drip-drip build-up and take it all head-on. He was also planning to see [Lord] Peter Goldsmith [former Attorney General] and Straw. JoP was worried about being accused of collusion. But we had not been asked not to discuss and they would assume TB was likely to want us to be offering advice. Matthew Doyle had been to see the inquiry support team. There were 133 boxes of key Iraq papers. For obvious reasons they could not all leave the building. We would have to decide what we wanted to see. As things stood we thought the idea was public hearings then private as they went in detail over documents. CR read out a passage from one of TB's notes to Bush. 'Poodle-ism,' said JoP.

I asked JoP to think seriously about what we said if asked to hand over diaries. JoP said he had been. He would rather they didn't. My situation was complicated by the fact that RH wanted to announce my Volume 1 as early as next week. I sent over a note saying it was not a good idea. I was hoping in a way that the inquiry would have so much paper already. In fact, my diaries did a better job of supporting TB's position certainly than any of the witnesses so far. Snakes. Meyer's evidence got less coverage than I thought it would, perhaps because the media thought it was self-serving too. Also George Foulkes [Labour MP] was out and about yesterday saying where are the Iraqis, why no Ann Clwyd [Labour MP, supporter of military action in Iraq] or [Baroness] Emma Nicholson [former MEP], is it just a procession for prima donnas like Meyer? JoP seemed pretty nervous. Matthew said that John Muir, ex John Scarlett's private office and now in the Cabinet Office, seemed very well disposed. But it was obvious from the evidence so far that the civil servants were going to look after themselves.

TB was the one everyone seemed to be gunning for. I said the position I felt most comfortable with was that TB decided we had to stay close as a way of maximising influence. People could criticise or not. They could feel he did or did not exercise influence. But that was the strategy and I was happy to support. We were hampered by divisions in the US and also by assumptions made about their competence. JoP said he felt much the same but TB would not necessarily want us out there saying that. Another problem we had was that right and left in the media were now against and barely any voice was out there saying we did the right thing. It was all a bit grim and I could not help thinking the committee would feel duty-bound to go with the flow, whatever the truth or whatever views they actually held.

Saturday 28 November

Out with Calum and his friend Jack to West Ham. Five–nil down. Back to 5–3. Pretty crazy stuff. Home and did a bit of reading of my diaries to start the process of getting my head together re Iraq. I was probably looking at mid-January.

Sunday 29 November

Read first 200 pages of Vol. 4 of the diaries. Chatted with Gail about a RH announcement and agreed it was the last thing we needed right now. She and PG were both livid with GB. Could not believe how badly the evidence was going and how nobody foresaw it. Matthew had said something similar yesterday, that No. 10 people were now running round asking why this was going so big at a time Cameron was in a bit of trouble. Dick Caborn called about a Steve Byers idea for a group of ex-ministers gunning for Cameron. He said these diplomats were old-school Tories. They were sometimes better at class war than we are. Rawnsley did his column on IHT and how the Tories had miscalculated the politics. He outed me as the author of the line GB used last week, about it being the first time the proposers of the tax cut would know personally all who stood to gain from it.

Iraq Inquiry slowly shredding TB according to the Sundays. Dinner with David Mills, Tessa and kids at the Italian in South End Green. DM was pretty down about things. They had obviously decided to think the worse now, to say that he was almost certain to go to prison. The evidence was non-existent though, so he was still banking on the hope that there would be nothing on which to convict Silvio so there could be no way he was innocent while David was guilty. The kids seemed a bit subdued. A few pieces in the Sundays on the inquiry, mainly focused on mandarins shredding TB's reputation. *MoS* splash on TB allegedly bullying Goldsmith with the help of Sally and Charlie F, after Goldsmith had written saying there was no legal base.

Monday 30 November

I went for a swim which was great but later got the usual nasal reaction. Out later to RADAR [Royal Association for Disability and Rehabilitation]'s awards for disabled people. I was presenting the award for best fictional media – won by *EastEnders*. I was sitting with chief executive Liz Sayce and a few mental health people. John Bercow was presenting an award and he and I had a chat about various things. I said the leaders had bent over too far on expenses and they needed to stand up for politics. He said maybe we should hire you as a consultant 'but I don't suppose we can afford you.' He told me Sally [his wife], who was standing for Labour in a council election, was keen on getting a seat. I said the party should jump at it. He said he was very supportive of her ambitions. 'Of course, you know about wives with an independent streak.'

Also chatted re the expenses business Sheree Dodd and I had talked over and he seemed grateful I had kept Ian K on the park. Trevor Phillips [chairman, Equality and Human Rights Commission] was there and wanted to chat about the political scene. There was definitely a feeling of things not going too well for the Tories at the moment, however bad they were for us. I stayed for the other awards, notably young disabled person, won by Riam Dean who had successfully sued Abercrombie & Fitch when they made her work out of public view because of her false arm. David Manning was the main witness at the inquiry and did rather better than the others had.

Tuesday 1 December

With Obama due to announce 30,000 more troops for Afghanistan, I blogged on that, including *L'Express* magazine piece on his relations with Sarko who was refusing to send more troops. And I added a bit on Cameron who was doing a speech on health and safety based on tabloid tales e.g. kids having to wear goggles to play conkers. What a tit. Set off with Rayan and Jeremy Clarke for Bolton for the NW IAPT (improving access to psychological therapies) conference. Jeremy was a shrink and mental health specialist, for whom I had done an event a while back. Nice enough guy but it was always hard to work when someone else was in the car. I was reading TB's WMD statements and main speeches. Also Charlie called about the Goldsmith 'no legality' stuff. He said it looked like it was coming from Peter G himself but surely it was not in his interests to say he allowed others to change his view. Charlie had clearly been following the evidence closely and felt it was bad for TB. The mandarins were carefully and quite cleverly putting the boot in. He felt we had to think through a bigger strategy. That was the position I was getting to. The need for big points. There was little sense of Iraq in the inquiry. Saddam barely figuring. The human rights abuses. The murders and the brutality. The chemical and biological weapons we knew about let alone the stuff we didn't know about.

The IPAT event was at the Reebok. A few hundred people. Met the 'It's a goal' people, then did a few photos and shifted lots of books. Mark Easton of the Beeb was compering and I had a twenty-minute slot where I did my usual stuff, then a reading, then Q&A with others on the panel. Raced back to London for the bizarre Piers Morgan dinner at the Mandarin Oriental. The celeb aristocracy. Main table had Piers, Simon Cowell, Alan Sugar, Jordan, Amanda Holden [actress and TV presenter], Freddie Flintoff and later Sarah Brown. Cowell definitely the main man. When he went out for a fag every smoker seemed to follow. I was sitting next to Tracey Emin. We did half an hour on the war then half an hour me trying to pull her back from the Tories. She said the war made her blind to other good things we had done. It was all so anecdotal though. Nancy there, whispering she needed to see me.

Piers was in his element. He presented awards called the Morgans e.g. for thickest celebrity, most modest celebrity (Sugar), worst loser (Joe Calzaghe) [boxer], best person (Freddie who said he had enjoyed listening to Piers fake laugh at everything Simon Cowell said). Christine Bleakley got one, Lily Allen for insults, Sarah for stand by your man, and a lifetime achievement award for Simon who then took the stage to say these had been the vainest and most pointless awards in history. Quite an odd evening. Piers said he had probably spoken to me more than any other person there down the years. He had totally landed on his feet though and went through all the various knockbacks in his career. Quite creepy to Cowell but the sense was Cowell had some sway over all of them.

Wednesday 2 December

Reading more Iraq stuff when GB called. He wanted lines for PMQs. I gave him 'Domestic tax policy for Notting Hill, global tax policy for non-doms who pay nothing at all.' Checked Zac Goldsmith went to Eton and said he should say their policies were dreamed up on the playing fields of Eton. Did another blog on Cameron and why the Tories were flatlining. Watched PMQs and GB pretty much hammered him. Cabbie taking me to lunch had it on the radio and said the same. Tessa called to say everyone was saying they assumed I was back. DM called later and said he had been a lot better but the fundamentals had not really changed. Cameron did look a bit wounded though.

Lunch with Natascha which was really nice and also helpful because she got my head in a better place on the inquiry. She felt whatever doubts I had now were irrelevant. I should stand up for what we said and did then. She opposed the war but she believed us when we said we were doing what we thought was the right thing. She could not understand why so many people had turned against TB. She liked the way Obama took his time. She thought I should try to get almost philosophical about leadership and government. But basically she felt I should be strong and clear and give no quarter. I said to her later she had really helped. Also had a nice chat about the kids and how I was being much nicer to Fiona, even if going through the diaries reminded me of how she added to the pressures on me at the time.

To the Cabinet Office to meet John Muir and Andrew Brewster from the Iraq Inquiry support team and a couple of lawyers from the Treasury solicitors to go through the basics. Legally they said I was entitled to support at public expense and they would come into use when and if we were told about criticisms. I basically just wanted to get their sense of what briefing I might need. They had dug up a fair bit already. None of them had a good word to say for Meyer. Goldsmith was the only one using his own lawyers. John took me to Admiralty Arch [archives] where I met the guy who was in charge of the 133 files. He showed me their systems and basically said if I gave them an idea of what they wanted they would dig it out and I could read it in there. Previous witnesses had been spending between two and seven days in there. Amazing how much stuff there was and how much I had forgotten. Lots of messages about GB trouncing DC. Worked on my speech for Rheindahlen and then more reading in.

Thursday 3 December

The papers had a few bits and bobs re me 'being back' though Downing Street were able to say I had not been there yesterday. Simon Lewis was probably not aware that I had given GB the lines on IHT, non-doms and their policy being dreamed up on the playing fields of Eton, which DC apparently hated. Read through my evidence to the FAC of six years ago. Pretty word-perfect but it was a pain having to get my head round all this stuff again. I was getting into the habit of reading it all on the exercise bike. Jessie [Mills] came round. I was telling her about Natascha and her advice. Spot on, she said. Defend then not now. I did a couple of radio interviews on so-called class war, LBC, R2. LBC also raised Coulson and bullying so I got stuck into that too.

Friday 4 December

World Cup draw day. Twitter trending topics almost all to do with it by the end of the day. Worked on a piece for Elle about me and Fiona, enduring relationships, with decent plug for book. Blog figures higher than for ages. People picking up on the profile stuff re PMQs e.g. big piece in *The*

Indy today: 'He's back'. Nick Robinson and a lot of the right-wing bloggers picking up. Lots of Tory commenters too so it was getting through to them. Did today's blog defending Sally Bercow [wife of Speaker Bercow], who had done an interview on her days as a boozy one-night-stander but who more importantly had whacked Cameron and today's Tories. Out on the bike. Alex called, hungover from Aberdeen. He had been at some do and it turned into a late-nighter, and he felt rough. He had been watching videos of us; he thought our defence was weak and we could struggle.

I read FAC notes and dossier memos while watching the draw, then to David S for an hour. Helpful. He felt I was bound to be anxious and stressed but felt I had been through it all before and I would get through it again. No. 10 were playing down my role which as Peter M told them was silly. It should neither be played up nor down. PG's test results were in – all great. I went to see him and he was so chuffed. I could see the relief pouring out of him. He had been more worried than he let on. We chatted about the inquiry. He said people were so desperate to see some leadership that if we stood up and defended it properly there would be a sigh of relief in many places. [Mike] Boyce was at the inquiry yesterday. He said that he had been taken aside and asked to give a 'glass half full' account to TB. He had told the *FT* that it was me. News to me but it got followed up in a few places. I had always been quite wary of Boyce. GB called asking me to see him on Monday. I said they had to refine the class attack, was all fine provided it related to policy and values.

Saturday 5 December

Blog re Boris and Waddles, as I called her, what with more revelations in *The Guardian* yesterday that he had not been wholly frank about the efforts to appoint the ghastly Veronica Wadley as London arts supremo. Greg Nugent collected me and we set off for Portsmouth v Burnley. Chatting away re the usual stuff – Olympics going well. Eddie Izzard's visit had been terrific, he said. Also re GB etc. He still wanted to help. Also had others to help. Real old-fashioned ground and surrounding area. Great Burnley turnout considering it was lunchtime and on telly. We played OK and should have been well ahead by half-time. We were the better team but lost 2–0.

Sunday 6 December

Cameron's fourth anniversary as leader so did a blog on that, asking people for their key images, thoughts, moments, policies. Focused on the difference between strong environmental image-making early on and the paucity of green voice or message pre-Copenhagen. GB sent through big speech he was making tomorrow on public services. It was too long and list-y and needed more big message. David M called round for a chat re the GB scene. He felt the fundamentals had not changed. There was a feeling of a mini revival because the economy was looking a little better, GB had made no big mistakes and the Tories were not doing as well. But he still felt the general view was that with GB as leader we could not win. Harriet, Jack and (so he thought) Alistair all thought the same. He felt Harriet and Jack at the least were willing at some stage to go to GB and say he had lost the confidence of Cabinet, PLP and party. He accepted that this could only happen if there was some kind of GB buy-in. Neither of us have seen the slightest sign from GB he might go along with it. He was sure that we would do better without him but accepted that if GB decided not to budge it could be very, very difficult.

The situation with Ed M was interesting. The Guardianistas had been talking him up and Ed was definitely thinking that if there was a leadership election after a general election defeat he might fancy his chances. DM said he had been levelling with him about his own views and for two years had been trying to persuade him GB had to go. But he was also sure Ed would not betray him to GB. I was not so sure about that. He was seeing him tonight. They had to sort it out. I also felt DM could and should be more involved and engaged in broader thematic and domestic policy arguments. E.g. Tories and running Britain down, British character and the need for optimism. Trust. Teamwork. Big themes that could show he was not just a very competent Foreign Secretary but had a voice and a locus that went much broader.

He still seemed up for what he called openly a putsch. But equally he seemed to me no clearer as to how it might come about. The big question was whether they would have to make the threat to resign and see it through if he didn't budge. He said Harriet was bullish. So was Jack, though terrified of anyone knowing he was even thinking in these terms. 'Don't put it in your diary.' He felt Ed was in some ways a more political animal and OK with the idea that you have periods of government and periods of opposition. He had spoken to TB who was willing to offer help and support but not to precipitate. I said we needed to find out subtly – and maybe TB could – whether there was any part of GB that knew some of them were thinking like this and what he would do if he did.

Monday 7 December

No. 10 called first thing to say GB wanted to change the time of our meeting because he wanted to have an hour. I suspected it meant a full charge at me again. I filled up with the usual dread. I did a blog on *The Guardian*'s front page which was being reprinted in forty-five countries on different front pages, pre-Copenhagen. Good old-fashioned stuff but with a bit of impact as the summit started. Rayan collected me and we set off first to Belgravia Gallery to collect a painting for Fiona's birthday, then to No. 10. GB was at his desk in the outer office, working on a screen filled with gigantic letters. We went into my old office, now his, and sat down to chat. I was conscious of trying to stretch things out so we did not have too long on the point I knew he would want to raise. I said I was going to the NATO ARCC [High Readiness Force] conference in Germany. 'What are you doing that for?' he said. Maybe they think I have something to say, I said.

Within no time it was all about how the establishment was trying to do him in. He was still wound up about Dannatt. He was also convinced that lots of them were up to no good with the Tories. He was sure Dave Richards (CGS) was a Tory. He said his daughter worked for the Tories. I said I felt the military were pretty good provided they had strong and clear leadership. He was down on Obama. He said you guys, and so could he, could get straight through to Bush any time of day and night and he was pretty open. Obama was different. It could take days to set up a call. He also didn't involve people too closely. We were all a bit of an irritant to Obama. He had his eye on the domestic scene all the time and did not make life easy for us. On Sarko, I told him the Plouffe story about how Obama added Paris to his D-Day anniversary visit itinerary at the last minute so as not to offend him.

GB said Sarko was likeable but currently all over the place. He was worried about his ratings and not sure how to reverse them. I said that was despite having far greater media control. He said Sarko was convinced all the media were against him. We got on to PBR big messaging and also lines for PMQs. I said he should try to get up Copenhagen and use the line DC was 'All wind and no turbine.' Also on the deficit we just had to keep taking it back to their priorities. I also thought he should build up Alistair D but he seemed reluctant and kept going on, without a hint of irony, about all the leaking and 'the Treasury speaking with a different voice'. 'Perish the thought, that the Treasury might be doing its own thing and not being led by No. 10,' I said and to be fair he laughed. It was a perfectly pleasant chat and he scribbled a few thoughts as we worked on lines and arguments. But I kept wondering if he didn't have better things to do.

Eventually he got to the point. 'So what more can you do for me? I really need you to do more.' I said I accepted it was not satisfactory as things were. But I also said I did not want to commit full-time. I had always been clear about that and my position had not changed. I said I was reluctant to get put into a meetings structure with people I was not that keen on. I said he needed to trust his ministers more and give them proper responsibility. I detected he was down on Peter. 'I think he is finding the workload really hard.' He said he felt Douglas A was a serious player with a good mind but the media did not take him seriously. Harriet was obsessed with a small number of her own issues. He did not respond to my suggestion that David M should be encouraged to do more on the domestic front. He just looked down. I wondered if maybe he realised, or at least sensed, DM was still pondering the prospect of a pre-election change at the top. The younger ones were dismissed in quick order. The usual stuff. Which is why he felt I ticked the boxes. I said it was not going to happen. I would do more but not as much as he wanted. Then he was back to trying to have someone who could be his cipher. We agreed he could call me at any time but he said he did understand why I was not so keen to get back sucked in full-time.

He asked if TB had spoken to me. 'He said he would ask you to do more.' I said he had, but he also understood where I was coming from. I also felt I was being used as a bit of a pawn when TB realised he was out of the top EU job and then felt it had to be David or Peter. GB said Peter was a bit silly, calling round governments to see if he would get it. He agreed TB was in part pushing me to go back so GB would agree to Peter going. In the end he felt Cathy Ashton was fine. I raised Iraq. I said how on earth have you all managed to ensure the inquiry would dominate January. Why? he asked. TB for starters, I said. Me, Jonathan. We're all up in January. He seemed genuinely surprised but realised it would be hard to get heard above the noise it would create. Then back to another tale of the establishment doing him in. By the time I left I had been in there nearer to ninety than sixty minutes. I felt I was in the right position for me but could tell he was pretty disappointed with it.

Home then off to Terminal 5 for the flight to Dusseldorf. Paddy Ashdown [former Lib Dem leader], who was also speaking tomorrow, and Kate Silverton, who was going as guest of the ARCC commander as part of the military's schmoozing, were also on the flight. I was working through all TB's public statements on Iraq policy and felt my position on it all becoming clearer and stronger. There was very little not to stand by. His dossier statement for example was if anything understated. Collected by the military and taken out to Rheindahlen. Pretty major military camp, soon to be shut down and transferred to Gloucestershire. I was staying in one of the nice houses in the grounds. I had time for a quick change then off to the dinner. Very male. Totally white. Lots of baying voices and pinkie rings. I remembered JoP's quip at the Palace farewell to Robin Janvrin. 'We have failed in our mission.'

I was seated between Beth Cole, the tiny but sparky director of the

US Institute of Peace, and a posh-boy general who was the EU's man on defence. She and I had a good chat re US politics. I was picking up from the generals a really strong feeling that Obama did not do a very good job with his speech and surge announcement, that he was facing both ways and the hint of a withdrawal date was overly political and also a sign of weakness to send to the other side.* I said I was equally concerned that he did not properly consult and engage with allies, who he would need as things got tougher. She said she would like me to get in there and talk to them. She felt they might actually listen. I was not persuaded.

The guy on the other side told me he was a major Eurosceptic and remained so after a couple of years there. But he did see some of the good it did. He had worked with Paddy [Ashdown] in Bosnia who later told me he thought he was full of bullshit which I had kind of sussed. He did however think really highly of David M, had seen him in various settings and had got more and more impressed. He felt DM had a good feel for how the power structures were changing. Mark Laity [former BBC defence correspondent, now a NATO spokesman] there so we had a bit of a chat about old times during Kosovo. He said he had never forgotten how I had virtually single-handedly changed NATO comms during Kosovo but now, with him on my side of the fence now instead of, as then, with the Beeb, he felt it had gone back. It became a recurring theme of the trip and I decided overnight to harden up my message.

Paddy wanted to go out for a fag and a chat on the domestic scene. He felt the election had got interesting again, that GB had improved, Cameron had gone back and the result was not clear. He felt a small Tory majority or a minority government – provided Labour did not lurch leftwards in defeat – could be really interesting. He thought Clegg would not support the Tories because they were so far apart on so many issues. He did not think he would prop up Labour either, that Clegg would feel 'If the public are kicking them out the front door we cannot help them in through the back.' He said he genuinely felt Clegg would not play the coalition game. So a government would have to limp through a dire economic and political landscape. He seemed to quite rate Clegg but thought we were barking up the wrong tree if we thought he would go for the Tories. 'Nobody will let him.' I was stunned to learn Paddy was sixty-eight. He looked great and walked tall and with a stunning head of hair still. He also went down well with the military. There was even a new acronym for international jobs requiring a mix of military and political – ALF – an Ashdown-like figure.

* The President announced the deployment of 30,000 more American troops to Afghanistan and the intention of pulling them out a year later. 'This has to be a surge,' he said.

He was quizzing away re TB, CB, GB, what I thought David would do. He was pretty keen on Ed, felt he had done well on climate change. He remained fascinated by TB. He put him in the 'good' list of PMs. Thatcher was the last 'great'. 'My big beef is that he let Gordon stop him doing what he wanted to on Europe and the euro,' he said. And he did not really believe in the constitutional programme, not like John Smith did. He felt his greatest achievements were Ireland and 'on Kosovo, persuading an American President to put American troops on the ground to fight and win a moral war we would otherwise have lost.' He felt on Iraq that there was an element of hubris, that TB, having got Clinton to bend to his will, thought he could do the same with Bush. But his problem was not Bush but Cheney and Rumsfeld. Tell me about it.

He was himself involved in trying to resolve marching issues in NI and also still clearly taking calls on Bosnia. He was due to do *Question Time* from Wootton Bassett [nearest town to RAF Lyneham, repatriation centre for armed forces killed in Iraq and Afghanistan] on Thursday and we agreed there was developing a dangerous distance between politicians and military and public. If everyone went to Wootton Bassett and just pandered there would be a problem. Dannatt was also doing the programme and from Richards down there was real anger at what he did in getting so closely involved with the Tories.

Tuesday 8 December

Up for breakfast with a guy from the RCDS [Royal College of Defence Studies] who had just written a book on Hitler's general, Field Marshal Erich von Manstein. Had a really interesting chat on that and also on some of the themes in my speech which I was able to harden up even more with their help. All very down on Obama. More up on Bob Ainsworth [Secretary for Defence] than I expected but still felt it should have been a top-rank minister. I kept hearing again and again that the problem was a lack of the strategic comms I used to do. General Sir Peter Wall was there, recalling to his friends the time we met in Basra when he asked as TB visited a school what the *Sun* headline would be. 'Iraq schools better than ours,' I said. He was due up at the inquiry too and we had a mutual whinge about that. Liked him. Richards who was one of the speakers and his speech was a bit glib. Then Martin Howard [ex MoD official]. Now he was a senior guy at NATO and gave a pretty depressing picture of how the place worked, or didn't, and its many shortcomings.

Then Paddy who spoke well and without notes though at the end of the day I cannot remember what he said much, beyond a few anecdotes and quoting Kipling. To be fair though he was an impressive speaker and I'm just tired. I felt my bit went OK – very basic urging to get the concept of strategic comms and to engage with it properly, not as an add-on. They were a good audience. Lots of nodding at various points – e.g. military would do less media if they let professionals run it for them. Dangers of gap with politicians. Culture of negativity. Worries about Obama going it alone. Damage of Dannatt. Then the four speakers up for a panel which again went fine, all of us on the same themes. Mark Laity said I failed to understand how different and how much harder Afghanistan was. But in part because the leaders and governments were not doing the basics, I said. It had moved back.

Paddy said only Obama could fix this and actually he could fix it pretty quickly. I was quite taken aback by the hostility to Obama. As for GB he was not at all popular. I chatted mainly to Wall over lunch, then got changed and headed off to the airport. I had quite enjoyed it. I had another good chat with Paddy at the airport. He said that TB was terrific in lots of ways. He could not understand why TB had put up with GB so long. 'Whoever said he was psychologically flawed was right.' Really quiet airport and fairly quiet flight. Felt tired, much more so than when I was flying the whole time. Shared a car with Paddy from the airport. 'Is there a new pact?' the driver said. I had had him before and after we dropped Paddy at the Lords he said to me we should keep going on the Murdoch–Cameron axis, based on the fear of a Fox News here.

Wednesday 9 December

Did a quick blog re Alistair D, basically saying that his quiet authority and decency had helped in the recovery. But it was going to be a really tough day for him. The numbers were not great and I sensed in talking to people in Nos 10 and 11 that there had been a fair bit of skirmishing and rowing going on, with Balls persuading GB not to be too specific on the cuts etc. GB was pretty down on the Treasury and I got the impression he saw Alistair as something of an enemy, even though whatever he was up to was a fraction of what we used to have to put up with from GB's Treasury. I walked to Camden Lock and met David Davies [former Football Association executive] at the Holiday Inn. He seemed to be in the same position I was – if something good came along he would go for it, but it was hard to know what it would be. He was a kind of special advisor to the guy in charge of the World Cup organisation in South Africa. He felt I was right not to be going back full-time but also right to be helping a bit. There was definitely a mood against the Tories, or at least not too pro.

There was no signal in there and the second it came back the phone went and it was GB, wanting to talk about PMQs. He went endlessly over the same small number of lines, e.g. the one I had suggested re Cameron being all wind and no turbine. He also had a line about DC having said to the *Wall Street Journal* he wanted a flatter tax system and he kept going over the same line again and again. He must have been on twenty minutes and I had very little to say, partly because I had read nothing. He said he was grateful but I can't really think why. He was definitely more interested in him and PMQs rather than the positioning from the PBR. I said he should try to trail it for AD.

I got home for a meeting with Tony and Angie Russell of the Project Breakthrough art therapy group. He was bipolar, quite an edgy character. Alan Milburn had suggested they get in touch. Tony said he felt if I would get involved and engaged they could go on leaps and bounds. He said they just could not get any media interest at all. They did a magazine and coffee-table books, all based on art and photography. I agreed to help promote them but said I couldn't give too much time. Later sent emails to a few people re media, publishing and exhibition ideas. Tony not keen on the charities and clearly thought Time to Change was a waste of time.

I watched PMQs and the PBR. Calum texted halfway through PMQs to say he thought GB was like a man reborn. I felt some of the lines worked OK, others less so, but Cameron was definitely dented a bit at the moment. Alistair did OK on a pretty horrific wicket. Osborne did OK on an easy wicket, though it was quickly pretty apparent that there were some difficult questions for the Tories too. David M came round after ten to return the Plouffe book I had lent him, and to chat over where we were. He felt AD had done OK but that it was very Brownite, i.e. diddling all over the place. There was no big clear message. There was no real honesty about what was required. I asked him about his meeting with Ed M, the evening I last saw him. 'It was difficult,' he said. He does not think GB should go, and he thinks that if he does go after an election defeat, then it is not totally obvious that DM should be PM. 'Bloody hell, not another Tony–Gordon scenario – and even worse because you're brothers!' He nodded, said it was not too good a scene, was it? I said if you can't get Ed on board it is tough. He said it had been a difficult discussion but also friendly and fraternal in that they agreed family ties were more important than any political divisions.

I asked about the rest. He said that 'partly your fault' there was a feeling GB was in a better position, even if in truth the fundamentals had not changed. He was sure Harriet was ready to move. He intended to talk properly to Alistair. Jack S was clear something had to give. I said there are not many there I would walk into the jungle with and he needed to work out, really work out, where people were. He felt that if this was going to happen, it had to be in the next few weeks, possibly even Christmas. He went over his spiel again – Blair–Brown era over, policy agenda a, b, c. He wanted me to think about how all that could be developed. When he arrived around ten past ten he said no to a cup of tea because he said he was not staying long. It was 11 before he left. He was certainly more impressive these days but I wasn't sure he really had it in him to take this on, and force GB out. As for the stuff with Ed, it was a re-run of TB–GB with the brother thing thrown in. Everyone saw David as the senior, but Ed was clearly intending to run against him.

Thursday 10 December

The press were pretty scathing about the PBR. Questions too for the Tories and I did a blog on that theme. Cab to TalkTalk to see Charles Dunstone. I called Sally [Morgan] on the way as she was a non-exec on Carphone Warehouse and he was going to ask me to be similar for TalkTalk. She said she quite enjoyed it largely because he was a lively and interesting character. He told me she was his best non-exec because whenever the board was in a bit of a panic, she would basically say it was nothing compared with stuff we had been through. He talked me through his plans to reshape the company and have a separate TalkTalk board which he would chair. It was an impressive story, how they had gone from nowhere, with nobody really even noticing them, to be one of the big ones in the sector. He said, as they always do, that the workload would be fairly light, maybe seven board meetings and a few conference calls when things arose that were deemed to be tricky. He was obviously I think looking to me to be a voice of calm and reason when others were apt to lose their heads.

He was interesting on Simon Cowell and their sponsorship of *The X Factor*. He felt Cowell was a genius. Everyone knew he orchestrated and manipulated everything yet even when people saw that they didn't seem to mind because it was actually pretty wholesome family TV. As for the music industry claiming he was destroying real talent his supporters would say he was reinventing it. The genius was in knowing what the public wanted, also knowing how to work the media and knowing the kind of mix of personalities that would really work. Money for board membership 45k. I said he needed to be happy he could live with the baggage I bought to it, and he said he would think through it. He reckoned we could wait till post-election if it was easier.

On the Tories, he said he was at Freud's country place recently and Cameron came in. He just didn't fill the place. Like a public schoolboy fop. TB filled a room. GB had a certain strength and stature that made him at least interesting. Cameron had neither stature nor much interest. After an hour or so, we agreed both to think and decide in a week or two. I said I was at least interested whereas with most offers like this I wasn't. Piers calling a couple of times as he was on *Question Time*. Yet when I watched it later he appeared to be disappearing up Dannatt's arse. It was Paddy who went for the General for his being a Tory too close to his being a serving officer, and if Twitter was anything to go by Paddy who seemed to go down best. Out on bike later. Lovely cold day. John Sawers at the inquiry but mainly on the aftermath.

Friday 11 December

Out to see Bostock first thing to collect the vaccines for my flu and swine flu jabs. He said he was getting out soon and going to do part-time Harley Street. Said the NHS was finished. Pretty agitated about Iraq. Someone had put a comment on my blog about how the media were doing to Chilcot just what they did re Hutton, namely picking bits of the evidence to suit their agenda, but not presenting the whole picture or even part of the whole picture. I spent part of the day reading Hutton and the accounts of the meetings with Kelly confirmed that. He was supportive of the dossier. Maybe I should go for the media again when I gave evidence. If they had behaved differently Kelly would still be alive. If we had not had to deal with all that maybe there would have been more focus on aftermath. Caroline Gascoigne [Random House] called re inquiry and said we needed to discuss what we would do if we had to hand over the whole thing.

ENT appointment with Mr [Robert] Quiney. Polyps eight out of ten. Almost certainly need surgery but he wanted a scan first. [U2 manager] Paul McGuinness's party in Notting Hill. Ed there. Mark Ellen [journalist, former band colleague with TB in Oxford University band]. We discussed the idea of Ugly Rumours getting back together for Comic Relief. Then Sinead Cusack [actress] and Mollie Dineen [documentary filmmaker]. Both blasts from the past. Nice to see them both. Sinead telling me I was a hate figure for the revolutionary left. Mollie telling me she felt there was unfinished business and she would love to see me again to try to work out why it had been so hard to make that film [PEB] back in '97. Went to bed at ten and suddenly started veering wildly between hot and cold. Teeth chattering. Body burning. Texted Bostock who said it was OK, definitely not WMD! He was OTT at the moment and maybe I needed an ordinary doctor–patient relationship.

Saturday 12 December

Did not feel well enough to go to the Fulham game. News dominated by TB's interview on his faith with Fern Britton, in which he said even if he knew there were no WMDs he would still have felt it was right to get rid of Saddam. Sparked a mini-whoosh for the day. I had deliberately said nothing on Iraq pending the inquiry but maybe there was a case for engaging. I watched the dull and scrappy Burnley v Fulham match. We did OK to get a point. Still feeling rough.

Sunday 13 December

TB's interview on faith was interesting and I felt he did OK. But some pretty majorly vile responses on the web. Fiona off to get the Christmas tree while I rested and tried to recover from Friday. Still felt a bit out of it and wanted to be on form for going out with Grace tonight to see Miley Cyrus [singer, actress]. Really annoyed when a packet of fags fell out of her boot. We set off for the O2 by Tube. Had a bite to eat not realising that there was going to be a fabulous display of food in the suite which, I discovered on arrival, we were sharing with Boris Johnson, his wife and two daughters. He was on good form, very jovial and funny about the ludicrous nature of the event. Rob Hallett from AEG, who was promoting Miley's tour, was good fun too, very cynical about the whole thing e.g. saying to me at one point, 'At least in ten years you'll be able to say to Grace you used to like that Miley Cyrus crap.' He felt she was an aggressively marketed average talent, but there were almost 20,000 people in there screaming their heads off.

The music was instantly forgettable. Her brother Trace was the warm-up act and also did a duet with her in which he appeared not to sing. But the funniest bit of the whole night came when Rob mistakenly assumed Grace was in the meet and greet party before Miley went on stage. In fact, it was meant to be Boris and family but we all ended up going. Interesting to see all the backstage stuff but then we hung around, chatting to some of her team. Boris said at one point 'Can you confirm that we two giants of modern politics are standing in line, waiting to shake the hand of a seventeen-year-old we had never heard of till our daughters asked us for tickets?' He said what shall I say to her? I said ask her the nature of her relationship with Hannah Montana [Cyrus's character in hit TV series]. Eventually she came through. She was pretty much in the zone and Grace later said she thought she was stuck-up. But what a pain it must be to have to do these kinds of meetings just before going on stage.

She was introduced to Boris who then introduced her to me as 'This is my deputy.' 'Nice to meet you mister deputy mayor.' Rob Hallett was loving it. Back to the suite to watch it. Chatted to Boris's wife [barrister Marina Wheeler] who had seen the Fern Britton programme on TB. She said she 'fell a bit in love with him again' having 'fallen out of love' over the war. She said she quite enjoyed Boris's job – 'Much better than being an MP's wife.' Boris was talking about his brother Jo who had been selected for a safe Tory seat and how he still hoped his dad would get one. Reminisced a bit re the Althorp weekend. 'I bet you liked Charles,' he said. 'Your sort in many ways.' God knows what that meant. He was quizzing a bit re whether I was back, whether I did the 'playing fields of Eton' line and went off on quite a funny riff about that. Berlusconi hit in the face with an ornament in Milan by a mentally ill guy.

Monday 14 December

Interview with Paola Stringa from *Il Sole 24 Ore* magazine. Usual stuff on spin blah. I liked her. Very dismissive of Silvio who was all over the front pages today. He looked pretty hurt and fired up. I did an hour on the Wattbike reading more of Hutton. I'm not sure it was good for my temper. Reading it through made me almost as angry as I was back then, because of the idiocy of the whole thing. I had not read it that closely when it came out but, for example, Kelly was supportive of the dossier, and clear in the interviews with MoD Gilligan had embellished everything. Out for lunch with Rory, who had split up with Zoe. Out later to the Beeb to do an interview with John McGurk for a BBC Scotland programme, *Out of the Hot Seat*. I didn't engage on Iraq but I felt myself being tired and not feeling quite up to the mark. I wondered if the inquiry was stressing me more than I let on. Copenhagen was getting bogged down.

Tuesday 15 December

Meetings at Tower Bridge re the books. Haircut. Annoying and quite upsetting incident at a café in Belsize Park when an old guy came over and said 'Aren't you one of those war criminals?' I said nice to meet you. He said truculent bugger aren't you? Then complained to the owner I was allowed in there. He stood in the doorway and said 'Sometimes you people have to be told.' Talking to Lionel Barber about a possible column in the *FT*. He agreed it should be non-predictable and non-overly political.

Wednesday 16 December

Reading Hutton again. I had to work out exactly what to do in relation to preparation. Got Mark B to put up the front cover of *Maya* on FB and Twitter. Ben Evans [friend, director of London Design Festival] came round at 2 and we set off with Rayan for Burnley. Ben thinking that DM should go for it. Not sure he would though. Traffic grimmish but made it to record a BFC corporate video pitch. Dinner with Paul Fletcher to discuss his idea for a football university. Might need government support. Great game. We gifted Arsenal a lead, got back in with a penalty, then could have stolen it in the second half. Good point. Home by 1.

Thursday 17 December

Lunch with Tim Hincks [TV exec] at Camden Brasserie. Still trying to get me to commit to some kind of programme. Also volunteering to help the party. He was working with Cowell on a possible link-up and he was interesting on him. Said he genuinely was in pursuit of global domination and would be desperate for *X Factor* winner [Joe McElderry] not to get beaten by Rage Against the Machine to No. 1. He was still keen for me to do something with kids and aspiration. Or something political. He left at half two then I saw Denis Hickie and his mate about a festival they wanted me to speak at. Problem was it might come at the height of the election. Then Dara O'Briain, the Irish comedian and broadcaster, to discuss an idea called Political Animals, a Sugar-style elimination contest where I am the judge type. It had something to it but it was annoying that everything had to be made to fit one format. Went out for dinner with F and Calum after picking him up from Euston. He was on good form after getting his essay out of the way and very wise. Listened to a fascinating interview with Max Mosley [former Formula 1 motor-racing executive] on his experience with the media. Tweeted I agreed with a lot of what he said.

Friday 18 December

I did a quick blog on Copenhagen as climax neared. Suggested there would be tears, tantrums and a deal of sorts. It didn't feel too good though. Obama was having a few harsh words about the Chinese. Lots of countries were feeling excluded. The Danes were coming over as a bit hapless and incompetent. I went to the Cabinet Office to start going through some of the files for the inquiry. Read TB's notes to Bush. There were a few embarrassing lines, more of the poodle nature than any policy problem. But it all kind of fitted the line I was developing about him doing maximum support for maximum influence. There was one note where he set out a lot of 'what if' possible problems, and they were remarkably prescient.

TB's notes were well argued and were probably having an OK effect on Bush at the time. Were they all really going to be published so soon after the event? They had dug out about half a dozen files and I got through about half of them in the two or three hours I was there. John Muir seemed a nice guy and seemed also to share my view that the whole thing was a waste of time and money. Chilcot was clearly feeling the media heat a bit, having yesterday given a little pre-Xmas homily about how much they were uncovering and how contrary to some reports TB would give evidence in public. It said to me they were starting to be stung by the constant sniping that they were all establishment figures not giving witnesses a tough enough time.

Round to Grosvenor Square. Meeting with TB, JoP, Catherine [Rimmer], Anthony Measures [researcher], Nick Banner [advisor], Matthew Doyle and Victoria Gould [diary secretary]. JoP pointed out there could be no collusion re evidence. I made the point I wanted to use Catherine R as before. Also if Anthony was going through all the papers for TB we were entitled to expect him to look out for the things he felt we should see before we gave evidence. TB was as robust as ever. He felt the whole thing was a disgrace and classic GB. He should have toughed it out and insisted on a Franks-style committee. He felt that damage had already been done to US relations and more would be done if Chilcot tried to publish a lot of the papers. He intended to give as good as he got, point out that a combination of WMD, the regime and the importance of US–UK relations meant he had to do what he did. What's more it was absurd the inquiry started at 2001 as though prior to that Iraq was a benign country and the problem began when he and Bush invaded. Likewise you could have all the debate about DfID [Department for International Development] or State–Pentagon divisions but the real problem with the aftermath was Iran and Al Qaeda making sure there was mayhem.

He said if we had found WMD on entering there would be no inquiry. If there had been no targeting by Iran and AQ there would be no inquiry. What would the inquiry establish – that we took a decision we believed to be right, that lots of people disagreed with it, that they are not content just to say we were wrong, they have to say there was deceit when there was none. Also I had seen in one of his notes the accurate line that the Iranians had worked out if they promoted mayhem we not they would get the blame. Vic was worried there would be protests not just outside but inside and she was not sure the inquiry really understood the need to avoid public outbursts inside. She felt I was bound to attract some as the most high-profile TB advisor up before him. I felt confident on the arguments and the facts but presentationally we were in a different place to '03. I said to TB that reputationally he was taking a hit. He said he did not feel it anywhere but Britain.

I said he was ex-PM here and the inquiry was here. He seemed OK about things and intended simply to say he took the judgement that it was the right thing to do and he still does. Saddam gone. Kurds, Marsh Arabs. Democracy. Influence in region e.g. Libya giving up WMD. It was a useful meeting if only to get a sense of his confidence. I said I felt they would want to press us on US divisions because a criticism will be that we took too much on trust. Even on that he was back to the point about Iran and AQ. We had a little chat afterwards. I'd told them about the 'war criminal' exchange and although there was lots of 'I hope you told him to fuck off' when there was just TB there he said he was sorry I was still getting grief on his behalf. I tell you though, he said, one day we will be proved right and judged to have done the right thing. I had noticed in one of his notes to Bush the observation that Roosevelt had to promise not to get involved v Hitler to win an election. Yet today it seems so obvious America had to.

JoP seemed nervous. TB seemed more confident about the legal position. But there was clearly someone on Goldsmith's behalf feeding stuff out. He would damage himself if he said he didn't really say what he thought. TB felt the mandarins were behaving outrageously. I said I intended to preface everything with 'as I have said to the previous inquiries'. I was only there because of all the Beeb stuff really. If they thought I was expert on anything it was strat comms, how the media operated, and TB, and I intended to make some fairly big points on all three. I intended to say too that the media were trying to rough them up. Hutton was taken aback by the whitewash attack. That is the punishment you have to take for telling the truth. TB and JoP were planning to devote three or four days to preparation. I would do more. Partly because things were quiet at the moment. Partly because it was so important reputationally.

Saturday 19 December

To Retford with Audrey to see Mum. I'd called Audrey last night to see if she fancied it and we had a really nice day out. People-watching on the train. Mum thrilled Aud was there too. We had lunch at Trent Port, then went to see Robert Templeton who was downstairs with all the old folk. So depressing. Mum, Aud and I all agreed we would prefer to be put down than to end up like some of the really sad cases there today. Robert seemed pleased to see us but how the hell he had endured that kind of existence for so long was beyond me. Back to Mum's. Liz and the triplets came up. Audrey had a great time. She was raving about it all the way back while I read a stack of Hans Blix [former UN chief weapons inspector] reports.

Sunday 20 December

Rory and Cam out late so it was a hungover Cam I set off to Wolves with. Met Trevor Beattie and Facebook friend Jas – I had said on FB I had a spare ticket because Rory wasn't coming – at the Britannia Hotel. Good football chat. Trevor saying he was up for doing more for the party in the New Year. He and Eddie Izzard were intending to get together and target certain seats with cash and activity. He felt the Tories were looking a lot more vulnerable. Copenhagen fallout was dominating the agenda. Yesterday had not gone well. Too many of the politicians were out and about like commentators, always a sign it had not gone according to plan. Trev came in the away end which was decent of him. We were not that bad but two defensive errors led to two goals, we missed loads of chances and that was that. Calum went back to London while I drove to Tessa and David's in the Cotswolds.

The weather was turning pretty grim. Eurostar was fucked by the weather too, with trains having got stuck and a big angry backlog growing. I had a good chat with David about the inquiry. He said even though he had been anti-war he was appalled by the inquiry, the way the mandarins were behaving and the way it was being reported. He said he hoped I would be myself, make a lot of big points and show a bit of strength. Over a fabulous dinner – David was such a fantastic cook – he talked through his case. The last hope was the nine-strong panel on the Supreme Court. But he had resigned himself to the worst. He might get house arrest. But he was probably going to have to have at least some time in jail. He also had a massive fine to pay which he could not afford. He was remarkably robust considering. I said he should write a book about it all. He felt a novel based on it was better. But he was not sure he could write well enough.

We talked a bit about politics and the general position. Tessa felt there was a general recognition we would do better with a new leader, but no real appetite. She felt she and DM were the only ones who would really go for it. Harriet was pissed off and felt GB was a disaster but she didn't think she would do anything about it. Balls saw his own interests as being tied to GB and in any event was happy to strive away and be Leader of the Opposition. Jack felt he should be leader and was busy telling people he would be in with a chance but expected to get rinsed by the Iraq Inquiry. She asked me if I saw any sign GB would move aside. I didn't. We're basically fucked, she said.

Monday 21 December

David woke up keen on the book idea, asking for help with a plot. He had some fascinating characters to put in it and regaled us over breakfast with some of the colourful Italians in his tale. He was amazingly robust about the future. I took their dog for a run in the freezing cold. I really was so much slower than just a few years ago. Went past the place from where I called Phil Webster back in '03 to get his take on whether to leave or not, which had been one of the surprisingly significant moments. And here I was six years later on a long run with the same things going round my head – TB, GB, Iraq, inquiries.

Fiona went home via Dalesford. I set off but various accidents and weather situations meant I was multiply diverted and didn't get home for ages. Rory out again so we had dinner with Cam who was now doing his dissertation with the same intensity with which he had recently been revising. Eurostar were in a right old mess though general weather horror was taking off. I spent a couple of hours reading the Butler Report.* Although there were criticisms of us, as with the Blix reports there was plenty in there that stood up our approach. Every time I read about the fucking 45 minutes stuff though I was just angry that I was being hauled over for this crap again.†

Tuesday 22 December

Working on the Iraq stuff. The sculpture of Molly I had commissioned for Fiona's Christmas present was ready.

Wednesday 23 December

Nice present from GB arrived, a little hardback book, with a little message from him, containing Obama and Lincoln's inauguration addresses, and a little speech by [Ralph Waldo] Emerson [American essayist]. They were clearly putting careful thought into their presents. We'd already had one from Sarah which was a bits and bobs box with a No. 10 door on it, and a tree decoration of the door inside.

Thursday 24 December

Did a blog on the desire of some – F and G – for a white Christmas, alongside others – me – desperate for the weather to turn because of football. Pottered around, reading and chatting then went to get Fiona's present from Kirsty Tinkler [sculptor]. She'd done a really good job of Molly and it would go down well. Worried about all the kids for different reasons at the moment.

* Lord (Robin) Butler's 2004 review of intelligence on weapons of mass destruction.

† The government dossier on Iraq included the later disputed claim that Saddam Hussein could deploy WMDs 'within 45 minutes'. Lord Butler's inquiry was to conclude that the 45-minute claim should not have been made without more explanation.

Friday 25 December

No snow other than little remnants on the ground. We did all the presents – dog went down well – then out for a walk to meet Lindsay before we collected Audrey and set out for the Goulds'. Nice to have them here for once. PG back to his manic self. He'd done an itinerary for the day – toasts, quiz, a one-minute speech by me on cheerfulness. Great food cooked by Gerard. Kept pretty clear of politics. Watched some of the old holiday videos later. Really odd hearing the boys' voices as young kids. Also the one in Majorca where I was pretending to make a film about Peter M trying to organise a plot against John Smith to install GB. Peter camping it up big-style though it was amazing the extent to which it gave a taste of what was to come. E.g. talking about JS's health, me saying TB, Peter refusing to admit he was rooting for GB. All done comically but clearly even back then, it was all about that handful of relationships. I texted him in Morocco and got back a very barbed message re GB.

Saturday 26 December

Got Rayan to drive Calum and me to Burnley v Bolton. Hardly any lorries on the road and we did it in three and a half hours. Finished reading Butler and was starting on re-reading my various evidence sessions. Got to the ground for lunch. We were beginning to slip down the league and could have done with the win. We should have got it too but it was another 1–1. Four in a row at home, so focused on that in my AOL column. Filed on the way home. Neil, Glenys, Audrey round for dinner. Glenys full of the usual tales of dysfunctionality at the centre. She felt however that it would be madness to get rid of GB now, also that DM was not ready. She thought he was bright, capable, hard-working, but she felt he did not really understand what it was to be political. Neil said he was still a wonk not a politician. She said DM was a bit nervous a lot of the time, e.g. always rubbing his tie on his face in meetings. They were both keen on Ed M. Felt he had more empathy.

Sunday 27 December

David Miliband called, wanting to make arrangements for us to go down to Chevening. He said there was total inertia now. Harriet had gone from thinking GB had to be forced out to saying that it would be too messy and in any event the polls seemed to be improving. Jack and Alistair would not lead a charge. Alan Johnson would not even take calls or discuss the issue in any way. So it was pretty much impossible. I said he had to decide one way or the other and if it was not going to happen he had to throw himself totally into the campaign and emerge as the man with the energy and the ideas to pick up the pieces if we lost, or one of the key people who helped stave off defeat. He was clearly thinking beyond the election though and felt we could not pull it around. I sensed he had been thinking it would all just fall into his lap but life is rarely like that.

Monday 28 December

Called Bill Kenwright [theatre producer, Everton chairman] for a pre-match chat then Calum and I set off by train for Liverpool. C more revision, me more Iraq reading. We had been planning to meet up with Andy Burnham but by the time we sorted our tickets and grabbed something to eat at the ground we decided to go straight in. We were right in the front row, Burnley fans on form but Everton subdued. Until we lost a man, Stephen Jordan sent off, then they got two late goals. Really disappointing. David Bradshaw had been at Tranmere and we met up on the train. Nice to talk to him. Still furious at the way the media covered everything, especially Iraq. Back to another Grace drama. All been at Harriet's house the other night. Had trouble getting some boys to leave. Called over some Gospel Oak boys who ended up stealing a phone and Grace's wallet. Fiona wanted to call in police. Turned out one of the boys was one she had argued not to be expelled from William Ellis. All the kids giving us a few sleepless nights at the moment.

Tuesday 29 December

Fiona and I went for a walk and she was quizzing me about how I intended to approach the Iraq Inquiry, as she said it had implications for her and the kids too. I said I really didn't want to talk about it. I would work it out for myself. I'm afraid that even with the passage of time I did not consider her to be on my team on this one. The scars still ran a bit deep. BBC NI called to say Iris Robinson, DUP MP, MLA [Member of the Legislature Assembly] and wife of First Minister Peter Robinson had announced she was standing down because of severe depression. I did an interview and later did a blog. Then more Iraq reading. GB sent over draft Christmas message which was OK without being inspiring, then we set off for Chevening. None of the kids wanted to come so it was F and me.

Ben Evans and Amanda were coming too and Ben was clearly seeing it as a chance to advise DM on how to get himself in a challenging position – literally if pre-election, less so if after an assumed (by him and most others) defeat. We arrived as the boys [David Miliband's sons] were finishing their tea. Did the usual 'What did you all do for Xmas?' routine and it was not long before we were picking up on the negative vibes about Ed M, especially from Louise. When she and Fiona were giving the boys a bath later, she was apparently even more scathing. Ed had been busy cultivating the Guardianistas so that when Copenhagen failed he was somehow seen as a success. DM and I had a chat before the others arrived. He felt there was such inertia and defeatism that nothing was going to happen. He could do something dramatic, yet he did not believe people would follow. Harriet had moved back to a position of fearing the division would damage us even more. Jack S was looking at his own position. My own view on that was that he was in some ways content just to have been someone who survived as a Cabinet member through the whole time.

Alistair was fed up with GB but would not move. Peter was probably fed up with him too but equally would not move. I asked if he regretted not taking the Europe job. In a word, yes, he said. He felt GB was a disaster all round. He can't lead, can't unite, can't persuade, can't deliver a simple strategy and stick to it longer than a couple of days. On the war, he said the truth was GB was not a war leader and so whilst he went through the motions of what he thought a war leader should do, he simply was not up to it. The troops knew it, and the public knew it. He said his opinion of Bob Ainsworth had risen – he was clever, politically astute – but not a Defence Secretary. He was a chief whip. He said that on political strategy there had been no real discussion so people followed what they thought was a strategy, or they argued in public, as over the class war, so-called. DM felt the playing fields of Eton jibe had been a mistake because the Tories were bound to take it to class war. Only if we let them, I said, which we had, with a succession of ministers saying on or off the record that they did not like it because it cut off aspiration.

It was a classic case of your opponents reacting better to an attack, so that eventually the attack blunted and died. The reason the Tories and their media supporters called it class war was because it stung. DM had been busy trying to press the Chinese to stop the execution of a Kentish Town cabbie who had been done for heroin smuggling but who was bipolar.* The Foreign Minister had not even taken his call so we were left in the position of just complaining via the media without any chance of impacting upon the outcome. There were more hopeful signs on the Iraq hostage Peter Moore.† On the inquiry, he felt it was right to hold one but that the handling had been cack-handed. When he told me the date of the

* Taxi driver Akmal Shaikh was convicted of drug smuggling. Despite campaigners claiming his mental disorder demanded clemency, he was subsequently executed.

† Moore, the only known survivor out of five British hostages captured by Shia militants in 2007, was released in Baghdad.

Afghanistan conference – 29 January – I realised that was the same day as TB's evidence session at the inquiry. He felt we had to be open and frank about mistakes made but felt that the inquiry was drip-drip damaging TB and the government.

Ben and Amanda arrived and we were back into chitchat and the political stuff only restarted over dinner. DM looked a bit diminished. At one point Fiona asked him what set him apart from the others. He delivered a rather trite thing about believing in opportunity. She said anyone would say that. GB says it all the time. Nobody listens, he said. We said he was in urgent need of proper organisation. I felt he had thought it would all fall into his lap. But Ed Balls was nothing if not organised. His brother Ed was organising at least at the media level and that was helping him to build support in the party. We sort of cut to the chase later on and I said what I thought, which Louise said afterwards was unbelievably depressing.

I said David was seen as able and competent, and in many ways an attractive figure. But he did not do the touchy-feely stuff well – his brother was better – and there was a feeling he did not like getting his hands dirty. I was not suggesting a GB-style operation of undermining the leader, but he did need to up his game and get involved in far more than foreign policy. If he had decided there was no chance of unseating GB he had to throw himself unequivocally into the fight to win. If we won, he had to be seen as one of the reasons. If we lost, as the person who had shown guts, leadership, values and ideas for the future. But it was not going to fall into his lap. There would be a moment where he and Ed M were going to have to decide whether they went for it or not. 'I will book Granita's,' I said. 'It's not there any more,' said Amanda. DM was nodding along to a lot of what I said. So was Louise, especially when I said he needed far stronger people round him, and he needed a network of supporters and message carriers round the country.

I asked what contact he had made with the new candidates. He said they were being invited in for a chat on how foreign policy could help them in their campaigns. I said you can bet every one of them will have had a letter and an offer of support from Balls and Ed M. Don't forget that while we developed our political skills under TB, they developed their campaigning skills under GB. So – Balls in particular – it was about the black arts. DM was right not to get into that, but he did need – without being disloyal – to build a better sense of who he was and what he would do. I felt if GB fell under a bus he would probably get it but if it was after a defeat, it was not so sure. He had to really want it and have the operation to go for it if Ed M was getting himself into a better position. He nodded at that too. Fiona asked if they could envisage running against each other. He said not. I said don't rule it out, at least to yourself. Louise looked a bit lost.

There was a lot of black humour about what Hague and Ffion would do with this place. We were joking too about the tablecloth which they had not cleaned over Christmas. I said the cleaners were off pressing Hague's suits. It was a nice evening but a bit depressing. I gave DM a flavour of what Neil and Glenys had been saying. He said he had tried to persuade Glenys GB had to go but she was having none of it. Fiona pointed out Neil of all people would feel supportive of someone subject to rumours and challenge-plotting a few months before an election. On the argument that if John Smith had gone for it [leadership] we might have won in '92, I said it was maybe an optimistic assessment but I felt the public tended to get the point at elections. When Thatcher came along Labour and the country were tired. Change was needed. When she went, the country wanted change but was not sure about us yet. So they went along with a caretaker figure for a few years until we were. They gave us three shots. Now they are pretty fed up. But they don't like the Tories much, so they may well produce a hung parliament.

Clegg becomes important. The debates become important. Above all we have to fight like our lives depend on it. Then we went back over all the things we knew needed to be done but which were not. A moment of light relief when he described what happened at a Cabinet meeting if they all turned up. Over thirty people entitled to attend. Rosie Winterton. Pat. He said Pat had tried to start a discussion about Lords and other political reform last week and GB had just shut him down. I wasn't keen to stay too late and so we left around ten after the usual accusations that I was being rude in being so direct about wanting to leave. Fiona said in the car she felt it was all a bit dispiriting. He didn't seem to have the strength or drive for it and they were both clearly thinking they had made a mistake in turning down the Europe job. It was also going to be very rough at the personal level if he and Ed were set at odds. It seemed pretty inevitable to me.

Wednesday 30 December

I went to Fiona's surgery to register as a new patient, having got a letter saying Tom Bostock was about to retire. He could be a pain but I would miss the very personal care. E.g. I had to explain he had always kept my notes at home, and he tended to send repeat prescriptions after a text. This was a more modern but less personal practice. A guy in need of drugs medication was having a bad time. Lots of old people. I had to do my blood pressure on a machine, and go to the loo to give a sample. Still, maybe it would be better to get on a more normal footing. David Muir sent me a message re the planned Tory poster and press ad blitz and alerted me to a piece by Jack Straw in *The Indy* warning that the Tories were planning to buy the election via billboards bankrolled from Belize. I did a quick blog on that. Someone sent a message saying I had come third after Tom Harris [Glasgow Labour MP] and LabourList as best left-of-centre blogger. Right-wingers voted top though. Had a nice chat with the boys about how bored I was and how I needed a new challenge, maybe a film.

Thursday 31 December

A few messages re last night's Piers Morgan review of the year on ITV, where he had apparently got heckled when he said, in the context of the story of David Beckham advertising underpants, that I was a big dick. Probably shouldn't have done that interview and was also wondering whether the Morgan quote on *Maya* might put cleverer people off. He was certainly everywhere at the moment. Went into Admiralty Arch to have another Iraq session. Last night's programme was the first thing the women on the desk mentioned. Went through more of TB's notes, David Manning–Condi Rice calls, Blix meetings, more dossier stuff. John Muir came over with some classified material and told me en passant JoP had booked in for ten days!! I raised my worries about security inside and outside the inquiry room and he undertook to talk to them again. I would be the first identifiably Blair person and there would be more attention than for the others so far. Went for lunch at the Trafalgar. Turkish waitress very flirty. After a visa. Did a bit more Iraq then home. Had a bad cold and could do without going out. But in the end we had a nice evening. Tessa and David at the Wells Tavern, with Rory and Matthew [Mills]. I wound up our cleaner to believe Matthew had come out as gay over Christmas, which, given her old-fashioned views had kept us going for a day or two till Fiona told her it was a joke.

David was in good form considering they were all thinking he might be in clink this time next year. We steered off politics expect when David asked if I had agreed with Tessa denouncing the class war strategy. I said no and we had a discussion about that. Also whether there was any chance GB would move. She felt not but equally she said she intended to say to him he ought to go to help save fifty seats. She said she could not have it on her conscience that she did not even raise it. Fiona gave a pretty candid assessment of our dinner with David. Really glad the boys were there and we could switch to sport fairly regularly. Back home for a drink and to listen to Jessie's songs then up to Kite Hill to watch the Embankment fireworks. Lovely bright evening. Pretty near full moon. Tessa said they had been filled with dread about tonight but said they had loved it. Got to bed and felt like death warmed up. The sooner I could get a nose op the better.

Friday 1 January 2010

Polyps getting really bad. Ditto writer's block. Just couldn't get going. Maybe it would come once the *Maya* launch was out of the way. I was getting nice emails and messages from people who had read *AITM*. We hung around the house most of the day, then out for a walk with Aud and a cup of tea at Swain's Lane. Sense of things gearing up for loads of political activity in the coming days.

Saturday 2 January

Fiona's birthday. She liked the painting I got, which she hung in the hall. Nice to have one of Mike Molloy's pieces in the house. Kids all there first thing to do presents then she and G went out while Rory set off for Manchester and Calum and I drove to Milton Keynes [FA Cup, MK Dons 1, Burnley 2]. All the talk was of Owen Coyle and whether he was on his way to Bolton. Brendan Flood arrived as we were heading to the away end. I had a brief chat and he said Coyle had said that he would like to speak to Bolton if they made an approach. That meant he was going so far as I could see it.

Sunday 3 January

TB called re Iraq having just read some of the official papers as he had finished the first draft of his book. He did not sound like he was much in the mood for giving anything. He said this was the revenge of the establishment. 'You have to understand we were pretty iconoclastic. They can cope with traditional Tories and old Labour, but they found us hard to handle. Now we're gone they're quite keen to bury us. So you have the right-wing media who know only New Labour could or can win... the left who hate us for not being old left... and the establishment who have their own reasons to want something more manageable...' He felt Chilcot would be reasonable. The only question was whether, because of all the pressure, they would feel they had to be more critical than otherwise they would be. He was clear in his own mind that what we did was defensible based upon what we knew and thought. He also felt that history was being rewritten to an extraordinary degree, that there was no sense of Iraq under Saddam being a terrible problem. He felt tonally that we should be very calm, not at all petulant.

He did not think they would go for me over all the old stuff. I was not so sure. He thought they would be viewing me as much as a commentator as a player. JoP might get a harder time, he felt. On the aftermath he was back to repeating a lot of the points from the other day, re Al Qaeda and Iran. He was also still convinced history would prove him right. As for Goldsmith he said legal opinion on this kind of thing is often political opinion. Are we saying it is only legal if Chirac said so? He was sure I did not have much to worry about, that it was all going to be gunning for him and he said he intended to be totally robust. He felt people had contempt for the likes of Meyer for the way he behaved. Work on *Total Politics* interview on mental health. Otherwise really just getting through the day. Doing lots of French with Grace.

Monday 4 January

Had a lie-in so missed the Sky launch of the Tour de France team. More French with Grace. GB called a couple of times but I was really steeping myself in Iraq now, making notes, reading the evidence of others, some of the Hutton stuff. I had probably seen enough of the papers and it was better now just to reacquaint myself with the general story and detail and try to work out where they would come from. I felt we were not too bad on the build-up but would get hit on going too soon because the Yanks wanted it and not doing enough on the aftermath. GB had done Marr yesterday and was still on austerity v aspiration–investment. Papers all suggesting Balls has beaten Peter M re strategy. I texted Peter re how he was and he said we needed time for a proper chat. *The Times* splashed on the idea of TB being a liability for the election campaign because of the Iraq Inquiry. Included lots of quotes from Blairites said to be pissed off with GB over it. P.m. out to the ENT hospital for a CT sinuses scan. Good treatment. Quick, helpful. Definitely had bad polyps. Up to see Bostock for antibiotics for the gunge in my head. Very sad at leaving. Said he was being forced out by politicians. Scathing re our record on the NHS. Chilcot announced my date for the inquiry which triggered a few bits and bobs on media. Loads on Twitter.

Tuesday 5 January

I did a blog on Cameron's little wobble yesterday. Alistair had done a big number costing the Tory pledges and talking of their black hole – classic old-fashioned stuff. Cameron had changed his mind on marriage tax allowance and had looked shaky. First blood was the feeling. All day on Iraq prep. Catherine R getting into it for TB. She was getting into that mildly angry mode I remember from Hutton. I was making notes then doing other people's evidence. Nightmare. It was actually quite helpful though to have all the evidence online. GB called for a chat re PMQs. He didn't sound too chirpy considering people were saying we had started the year better than we ended the last one. He felt the Tories would go on the US–UK seeming spat re the intel on the guy who tried to blow up a US plane on Christmas Day.* What was obvious to me was that the relations with the White House and parts of the system had just gone.

It cannot have been because of Obama, surely? He said Obama was quite tricky, only really cared about his own position. Someone inside the security services was briefing to damage the UK. He sounded a bit paranoid about it. On Cameron, I said you had to get back on to him about the marriage wobble. I had said on my blog that it took time to get them on inheritance tax, this had taken time too, but it had damaged them. We worked out a line with variants on 'I do'. He asked me to go in tomorrow. I said I was immersed in Iraq so no. He said he felt he had done better last session as a result of our sessions so he hoped we could continue. He had said on Marr the Eton thing was a joke. I said they had to stick to the notion that Cameron's ordinariness was fake. People were not warming to him and we had to capitalise on that. I was reading Sawers and Manning till late. Aftermath was going to be the main issue, and also why we did not give the inspectors longer.

Wednesday 6 January

Another 8 a.m. to midnight session on Iraq. Getting a better feel for it. Meyer's evidence appalling. Self-aggrandising nonsense. Political too. Greenstock better, though with a lot of criticisms. They always exempted themselves. Boyce better than I expected. Really went for Rumsfeld and [Clare] Short. Did talkSPORT [radio] re Coyle – he was now on gardening leave – and was a bit heavier than my column. Terrible snow. John Muir was checking security for my appearance. Also the inquiry had asked for papers the conspiracy theorist blogger Chris Ames [journalist] had asked for, which were being held under Freedom of Information. Apparently they didn't even exist. Reading [Major General] Tim Cross [former officer commanding theatre troops in Iraq] who had a devastating account of the non-aftermath preparations but who did say that I had helped him. Catherine said the list of areas for TB was enormous. GB called half eleven and I was not able to take it. Tried to get him back before PMQs where he was apparently terrific again.

But by then David Muir had emailed me to say Hoon and Hewitt were going to call for a secret ballot of MPs on whether he should stay as leader.

* A Nigerian had tried to ignite an explosive device on board a transatlantic Northwest Airlines flight as it approached landing in Detroit. A White House official described it as 'an attempted act of terrorism'.

It was never going to work. I started to get bids but I wanted to carry on with Iraq. I was finding it quite helpful to read all the various different bits of evidence. Working too much at the screen though and starting to feel quite stressed. The reaction from party activists to the so-called plot or coup attempt was pretty angry. But ministers were slow – much more so than when James Purnell resigned – in getting out there to say they backed him. So he was wounded again but not fatally. Of course lots of people saying too that Hoon had been involved against TB too and that Pat was moving on and was mainly in the private sector. Johnny Hornby called to say he felt Peter and I were the only two who could shift him and we had to do it. Worked till gone midnight.

Thursday 7 January

Peter M called first thing. He said he didn't know what to make of it, but he felt GB was badly wounded by it. He said as it happened he and Balls were not getting on as badly as the press were saying but he did feel there was a problem with the PBR, and he did feel that sometimes GB was not using him but managing him. He did not have a core team or corps d'esprit. He had different types of relationship with different people and he tried to manage them all. Lots of people had indicated their unhappiness at the way he worked, lots had been given assurances he would change but of course nothing would come of it. He was not capable of changing. He said he felt very confused and strange about the situation and he knew people were looking to him to draw the sword as it were. But he would not do it. He could not do it. He understood why people felt GB should go but he could not help bring it about. Nice chat, felt a bit sorry for him. Felt a bit sorry for GB too, though Fiona said – she was halfway through [diaries] Volume 1 – that GB deserved no sympathy. Conference call with TB team in Kuwait re helping on their project. Then back to Iraq. Inquiry now chasing Iraq comms group papers. They were clearly going to go for sofa government, systems not right I think. Did a longish blog on the so-called plot-coup, talking about Alan Clark's point that they hated each other more than us. Someone on FB [Facebook] said the same was now true for us. I argued it wasn't and did a hit on DC. But GB wounded and so was David M.

Friday 8 January

I was on yet another Iraq prep session when Charlie F called. Straight into it. Into tough questions, namely we had said we would go to the UN but we knew if we did not get our way we would invade. I loved the way he just peppered the questions. So bright and so on top of detail even after all this time. He was such a top bloke. Agreed to come round later. I set off for Grosvenor Square to see TB and his lot. Catherine R told me that the list of areas for questioning went on for ages. She was beginning to get on top of a major briefing operation, with Anthony Measures, Nicholas Howard, Ian Gleeson [policy official, FCO], and some guy who had been in Iraq. JoP there already. TB really pleased I was signed up for the work in Kuwait. I felt the areas the inquiry were going for were Crawford and some kind of unspoken deal with TB, legality, aftermath, semi-detached DfID and whether we got enough out of the US given what we gave them. He was in pretty dismissive mood and I said he had to get into a different frame of mind. Told him which transcripts I thought were worth reading.

Tim Cross really pretty devastating account of lack of planning. I felt we could get to a different place – namely that the US–UK relationship mattered per se. Also I intended to defend strategic comms and what they might dismiss as spin. He was intending to spend a fair few days reading up on it. The more I thought of it, the more hardened I became against conceding too much and I know he was in the same place. He was commissioning all sorts of work to be done and I was now more focused on doing my own long narrative and working out all the points I wanted to make. I said to Catherine afterwards do you think we will ever be free of it? Crazy that I was seen as such a big event in witness terms compared with those who did the invasion or the aftermath. It was all about TB and I intended to defend him fully. Had to work out how much to go for those running for cover. We didn't go into the detail of what any of us would say but I felt there were a few arguments he had to start thinking about.

TB felt JoP might get a harder time than I would. I could not see my temper lasting three hours of dossier bollocks. I needed to get on to the political stuff too. Intended to ask them direct if they planned to go to Iraq. Also point out how we did use comms to get at least some grip on the US machine. Afterwards TB wanted a chat about the latest shambles at No. 10. He said the Afghan problem (no political plan and no end in sight) was in part because people knew he was not totally up for it, and also because they did not have the kind of relations built in at every level. He said he hated what was happening to Britain. Politicians going round apologising for being in politics. No leadership. Always pandering. Media that hated New Labour on the right because we won and on the left because we did not do all the old madness. Problem was the PBR was a return to old Labour. GB had never really believed in New Labour and he was not going to change now except tactically.

He said he feared that deep down we were a pretty old-fashioned country and the old forces of conservatism were waiting to return. We were opening the gate. He had noticed a bit more antagonism towards him with the Iraq stuff in the air. Abroad he felt it was a given that this was a good government and we were a success story. But the right wanted to bury us so we never came back to win again and the left were just the usual wankers who could not understand realities of power. Matthew felt if I was asked for my diaries I would have to give them.

Home with Mark to go through all the papers and work out how best to prepare my briefing. Charlie around, which was really helpful. As he fired the questions, I felt pretty good. On the internet people were starting to have 'askalastair' tags. I had now gone the whole week doing pretty much nothing but this, apart from a bit of traffic on Coyle. Also the Iris Robinson story had taken an amazing turn. It emerged she had tried to kill herself after an affair with a nineteen-year-old, and later emerged she had sought friends to provide financial help for him to start a business. I was reading Colm Tóibín's *Mothers and Sons*, but it was hard not to think the whole time about Iraq. I would be fine on big picture, but they would be hoping to catch me on detail. David Miliband called on his way to Pakistan. He said the Hoon thing had nothing to do with him at all, and he was sure Harman was to some extent behind it. He was watching to see how it panned out but this idea that he launched it then bottled it is just wrong. I said it should not change his strategy. As I said at Chevening, he had to get stuck in politically, and soon.

My fear for him was that his brother was emerging as a more politically acceptable contender for anyone to the left of us. He said Cabinet had been absurd. There they were, a couple of days after a mini implosion and GB just talked about which councils he had talked to about salt and gritting. Tessa later told me she had been to see GB on Monday and had said she was not saying she would resign but he had to think honestly about whether it was not better all round that he went. She said she was quite calm and measured but it ended in him saying 'I want you to understand I asked to see you, not the other way round.' She said it was like talking to someone who was ill. He just did not engage on a human level. She said she had dinner with Harriet the same night and asked if she knew anything of the Hoon-Pat H plot which she denied, but unconvincingly. She felt they were all making a point to GB in a different way but it was not enough.

Saturday 9 January

Desmond Bowen seemed to get quite a hard time at the inquiry. Not sure how much I should read and read and read. So hard to know where to stop. Some of the sessions seemed pointless. Tessa called, said she had been at a dinner with Dearlove last night, that he sent his best and seemed pretty supportive. Just a question now of honing and polishing in my head.

Sunday 10 January

Re-reading Hutton and going through my aide-memoire. News came through that Steve Davis and Phil Hughes [Burnley coaches] were also going. I sent a 'shocked' text and then one saying I felt Coyle had behaved appallingly and people felt sad and let down. Coyle called me, said he had seen Piers Morgan's column attacking him, which also said I had nothing good to say about him. He went through the whole story, did a big number on how much he loved the club, how he was really upset but he had had to put emotion to one side and made a decision based on football. Yes, I said, but that choice has ramifications for other clubs, including the one that gave you a big chance. He said it would take five, ten years to get Burnley to where Bolton is. I said you had a five-year plan. He said it was not about money but he had to think about his own position. He said he saw Brendan [Flood] like his brother, also that he valued all the relationships we had and he knew it had been a team thing and he was only the figurehead. Even all this he described as being about him rather than the club. Said he understood how the fans felt when a manager they had taken to left. He was the first to leave. Everyone else had been sacked.

He said he could have said all kind of things about the club but he didn't because he loved the club, the fans etc. I said it didn't feel like that to a lot of them. He said he was doing a press conference tomorrow and would say he believed we could stay up. I asked if he would take any players and he gave a pretty weaselly answer, namely not in this transfer window. Micky Phelan [former Burnley player, Man Utd assistant manager] felt we could use Coyle's departure to give us a real lift and he reckoned someone in management would really fancy it. Felt best to get someone with a bit of experience but said there were very few to choose from at the moment. Phelan said it was important to get someone working-class and tough who really got the place. Re Iraq said I should parachute into the inquiry with 'I'm innocent' on the parachute.

Monday 11 January

The last full day of preparation. Mark B came round and while I did a two-hour ride on the bike, he put together a folder for me. I felt pretty much OK on the main arguments and the points I wanted to put over, and also fairly on top of the detail. I had probably not read enough of the papers, but I was OK on most of the main stuff. I read the Hutton report again, also my evidence to the FAC. Managed to get through a fair bit then it just went all a bit word blind. TB called a couple of times just to say stay calm and be proud of what we did. GB called too, said all the best, apologised once more for it being in public. I was fairly brief because John Muir arrived with a few new papers to see.

Had a long chat with John Sawers to refresh my memory re the ORHA [Office of Reconstruction and Humanitarian Assistance] time, and my attempts to help Paul Bremer [chairman] improve his comms. Also getting help from SIS and Julian Miller re nuclear timelines, *The Guardian* having said that I had sought to change the dossier to bring it into line with the US. All bollocks but took up more time sorting that. Sawers really enjoying himself as C. 'Just had lunch with the Saudi king. Did I say I was in Saudi?' Also saying that he felt he could actually make new things happen. Wanted a chat at some point about the public profile of the Service. Helpful, and I said I was pleased he had stood by basic positions when he gave evidence. Then it was just a case of reading and re-reading and being more and more focused. Truth be told I was probably OK. Lots of messages coming in. Liz sent me Psalm 56 which had some lovely lines about being pursued by slanderers and enemies trampling on me all day long. The same old friends from Hutton days getting in touch with loads of messages. Dozens saying stay calm. Mum worried. Cam very philosophical about it all.

Tuesday 12 January

Woke up fairly early and went up on the bike for about an hour, just flicking through my folder and listening to Elvis. I revised a few details and committed a bit more to memory. Rory was up early ready to come with me. I thought it would help keep me calm. Grace really funny about being a witness too. 'What I intend to say to the court.' There were a few cameras and reporters in the street. Rory went out with my bag then got Rayan to come out just as I opened the door. 'Do you expect tough questioning?' someone asked. 'Tougher than yours,' I said. 'Will we hear anything new about the dossiers?' I said have a nice day and got in. Traffic was heavy and Rayan had to do some pretty nifty driving to get on our way. John Muir called to say there was no major protest and a few cameras. In fact, there were dozens, far more than I remember for Hutton. Lots of security but it took a couple of the plain-clothed guys to get me through.

Met at the Cabinet Office by Jackie Fraser [PA to Gus O'Donnell] and taken up to the little witness room next to the main inquiry room. Water and fruit, tea and coffee on demand, a telly, three or four blue chairs and a little glass table. Various members of the team came through at different times. Margaret Aldred [civil servant], who had warned me already they may want more than the allotted three hours, to agree how John Chilcot might present that. She also let slip that they could not believe how little Mike Boyce had prepared. Rod [Sir Roderic] Lyne [diplomat, inquiry panel member] who, as Rory put it, was 'all best mates', and we talked a bit about past stuff. He reminded me at one point we had asked him to do a job for us in Iraq. He said he was sometimes at a loss to know why he had taken this on. Martin Gilbert told me he had just seen a 1920s (unsent) letter in which Churchill was complaining to Lloyd George that 'There is scarcely a single newspaper … which is not consistently hostile to our remaining' in Iraq. Anyway, he was very friendly and the whole atmosphere was fine. It was lovely having Jackie to look after us, not just because as Rory kept saying she was so pleasing on the eye, but because I knew her so well and she was solicitous and friendly. Security came in for several discussions about exit and eventually we agreed I would leave out of the front but they would get them all corralled.

I flicked one more time through the folder, did another round of 'What are the toughest questions?' then before too long it was time to go in. Small, airless room, every seat taken. A few hacks to my left, alongside the stenographer. To my right the inquiry support team. The panel closer than I expected them to be. John Sawers had said that of the panel Chilcot was fair and reasonable, Lyne had gone for the mild Rottweiler role, [Sir Lawrence] Freedman [military historian] was the best informed of the other three, [Sir Martin] Gilbert [historian] was friendly, [Baroness] Usha Prashar [crossbench peer] out of her depth. I had exactly the same impression. Lyne did most of the tougher questioning. Freedman was quite intensive on the dossier, and I suspected was not keen on so-called blurring of politics and intelligence. Lyne's main points seemed to be about sofa government, and whether processes were adequate, whether there had been a fundamental shift at Crawford – I pushed back all day on that – whether GB was properly involved, DfID's semi-detachment, whether we could have given inspectors more time, all moving in and out of the debate all day.

I was pushing all the time how September 11 changed the context, how TB had always worried re Saddam, how we were deliberative and cautious and trying all the time to resolve diplomatically but with the clear threat of force. I did not feel weak on argument or on detail. Once or twice on the dossier and on 45 minutes I got a bit tetchy but otherwise pretty calm. Grace had given me a pen top to jab my hand but I only used it once and that was because at one point I was feeling the airlessness and could sense myself losing concentration. They were polite but fairly rigorous. Lyne had a little pop – 'Be serious' – when he was asking about my loyalty to TB and I said if TB asked me to jump off a building I wouldn't do it. But it was all fine really. Prashar kept asking the same lame question – like whether I agreed with TB – Gilbert not talkative and when he was he was interested in comms issues. I got over some pretty strong messages re the need for strat comms in these situations, and I said at the end there was a danger of learning the wrong lessons. We had to communicate properly in these unusual times.

There was a break mid-morning, an hour for lunch and another mid-p.m., so the three hours turned to six. I had no idea that it was going so big on the media till the break when I got loads and loads of messages. Alex had called literally as I was about to walk in at 10. At half eleven or whatever time it was at the break I forgot to turn off my phone and it pinged as I sat down. Turned out to be Harry Redknapp wanting to give me his take on [Brian] Laws and [Sean] O'Driscoll [potential Burnley managers]. Anyway, it was OK and they did not seem too offended. For the news they seemed to be getting excited at the TB notes to Bush – which were not new but the media were determined to say they were – my making clear TB's pledge that we would 'be there' if the diplomatic route failed, and the defence of the dossier. It was coming over OK but with the usual slant and addiction to whooshery. Tweeted that I was having a sandwich and God did these hacks talk some drivel. Most of the voices up were the critics – Gilligan around the place being treated as an independent commentator not a player with a vested interest. [Nicholas] Witchell [BBC] used the phrase 'confident and robust' which was very close to the words Georgia had said when we had dinner with the Goulds on Sunday – 'calm but robust' – which I had scribbled alongside TB's five Chicago tests on the inside of the folder.

It was for some reason more gruelling than Hutton even, perhaps because it was impossible to be so on top of the detail though I don't think I screwed up. The only possible exception was when I only half listened to a Lyne question re JIC [Joint Intelligence Committee] assessments when I thought he was saying would TB have still said 'beyond doubt' re the intel if JIC assessments had made clear it was not beyond doubt? I said no but reading the transcript later I realised I thought I was being asked whether TB was entitled to say beyond doubt even if those words were not stated. I decided to sleep on it but thought I should probably write to clarify, even if that part did not seem to be getting picked up that much. It was great having Rory there, and he was keeping me up to speed re BFC (definitely moving to Laws now) and Mark was a terrific help. He was kicking himself that he had not brought his camera to do a vlog. Everyone seemed to think it was going fine. TB texted a couple of times. Like Liz he had texted a couple of prayer and Bible refs. I had Psalm 56 in my inside pocket. Cherie also sent a message.

Then all the real old friends – John Bailey from primary school, several from university, loads from my old No. 10 team, the party and PLP and, as the day wore on, loads from sport – managers, lots of the [British and Irish] Lions. Hundreds of texts by the end of the day. Hundreds of tweets and FB emails. Media monitoring said even on the usually hostile sites there was a lot of support. I did feel strong in there and said to TB if only GB would show some fucking leadership and understand that even if he or positions were unpopular, people would respect you for defending them. It was a sign of how badly he was seen that it should even be deemed of note when I said he had been closely involved. Indeed, the Beeb were even saying it was the last thing GB would want to hear. Peter M sent some nice messages saying how good it was to see some non-jelly-like communications. All very encouraging.

I started to tire towards the end but when I went over my main points checklist, I had got most in. I was maybe too defensive of the US but I did want to say that all this running for cover and blaming the Yanks was just wrong. I thought about saying they should call media witnesses as they more than us were the cause of the trust problem. Indeed, their distorted coverage through the day showed that up well. By the last break I felt in control enough to say 'What's to go?' and once I was in the last lap it was fine. Chilcot came through with Margaret at the end and said he was sure that would be it now. He had given me the chance of another day and I said no, I would rather keep going till midnight. They had all been friendly though I think Freedman was a bit offside and I could see a number of areas for potential criticism being lined up.

Security had sorted the exit OK. I kissed Jackie goodbye at the lifts then went to the car which took an age to get through the swarm of cameras and hacks. One tried to open the door but the cops were doing a good job. We got home and now messages were flooding in. Charlie was doing media amid all the usual antis. It was leading everywhere for the rest of the day, and most of the papers, until the earthquake in Haiti. The Beeb were on the usual agenda but at least a strong clear message came through. Fletch [Paul Fletcher] sent a good one about seeing them off and ought to be proud. Donald said his special forces pals had loved it. So amid the blah, as TB and Godric both said, there was strength and clarity. As Rory said at one point, there's a lot of good friends out there as well as all the wankers.

It was nice to get out to the theatre, up in the Comedy Theatre balcony to see *The Misanthrope*. Funny and entertaining and though I was wired and becoming exhausted, I enjoyed it. Tweeted later that Keira Knightley would be a good *Maya* and decided to send her the book in the morning. Meanwhile Tim Hincks seemed up for buying it for telly. Got back and sat up late talking to Calum with the news on in the background. He said he thought people would respect me for standing up for TB and for saying I was proud we got rid of Saddam. And he thought even if the papers didn't like it – Charlie had warned of 'opprobrium' in the morning – real people would think I was telling the truth, saying what I really believed. The media think people don't like you, he said. 'You're one of the reasons people hate the media.'

Wednesday 13 January

Trying to sort backlog. Didn't sleep well. Too wired. I got up around 5 and had a bath, writing a longer than usual blog about yesterday. Pointed out the nonsense of them claiming there was some great revelation in the TB notes, of which there had been several references in my diary, and to which David M had referred to in giving evidence, or the fact that GB and TB discussed Iraq. He was the bloody Chancellor. Did a bit about how I prepared, also the amazingly kind messages people sent. Media monitoring said though the papers were shit, there was a grudging respect, and a lot more support on the web than usual. Barry Kilby called to say Burnley were going for Laws and to thank me for all the help through the week. He said Laws just nicked it on personality, also on results to budget. I texted Laws and also did a blog later and a video blog welcoming him. Suggested on Saturday that he come to the away end just before kick-off.

I was still pumping a bit with adrenaline. There was no real way of getting away from it either, as I had to sign the transcripts, and the media were still chasing. Reading the transcript, it looked like I was saying it would not have mattered if the JIC had made clear TB could not say 'beyond doubt' which sounded like I was saying it didn't matter if the JIC told TB he could not say that. I asked if I could do an addendum to the evidence. Also wanted to make it clearer re the question of whether Jack Straw saw TB–Bush notes. By and large people seemed to think I did fine. Then an unbelievably depressing call, and subsequent PMQs, from GB. He said he had seen some of the coverage and everyone seemed to think I had done well. I said it was ridiculous that I was up for twice as long as the military who led the invasion. And he said 'These committee people just don't know how to stand up to the media.' Fuck me. This was from the man who said one day it would be private and the next caved in to create this circus. He asked where I thought it went now. I said when any of the big names went up it would be huge for a day. When TB went it would be enormous. Then it would go away.

I said what I hoped yesterday showed was that if we defended ourselves strongly and without defensiveness then even on difficult policy positions it was possible to win respect even if people did not support us. GB kind of grunted. Then we exchanged a few lines on Cameron and airbrushed posters (his face for election posters) but later when I watched him, he was weak on Iraq. Clegg asked him why he would not give evidence before the election – which in my view he ought to, and he did a number about it being for Chilcot to decide. Then when he was asked about my saying he had been involved in policy-making and did he agree with what we did blah, he got up and did a totally defensive thing about the aftermath. It was a free hit to defend the policy with energy and conviction. And he pandered. I turned off the telly. It would not get picked up, but it was such abject leadership.

I did a note to David Muir, saying both that I agreed with Clegg and why GB's answers had been so bad. Unless we defend the record then an important campaign plank is not laid. I sent it to Peter M and Jeremy Heywood who had been on saying after yesterday he was more convinced than ever that I should be back in there. I said it was clear that GB wants to be distant from the policy (an impression reinforced by what I thought was a really weak answer to the other question on Iraq today – it was a free hit to defend the policy robustly instead of which he went into concessionary mode on aftermath planning). I said I thought with a lot of people this reminds them of the charge often made that he was not there when the going got tough. We have nothing to fear, on this or any other part of the record, being strong and confident, and defending ourselves properly. If we go around looking like we feel we have something to hide or be ashamed of, people sense weakness.

Of course the media are ridiculous in thinking there is something newsworthy in me saying GB (who was both Chancellor and a member of the war Cabinet) was involved in the policy. But the fact they do is because they never saw him or see him as having been so closely allied to it when TB was there. Also, on the point about whether he does it before the election, Jack S was going up soon so it is not tenable to say there are reasons why GB cannot or should not do it pre-election. I said that would apply to Jack Straw too. We have a situation, because this is all being played out publicly, where when Hoon, Straw, Goldsmith, Jonathan Powell and others go to the inquiry, let alone TB, this will wipe out everything else on a fair number of days. And every time we will be reminded GB is not going till after the election. It is a no-win situation.

I felt he should do it around the time TB does, be and be seen to be totally supportive and properly defending and explaining the position, from 1998 to the present day. It gets it out of the way. It gives the tossers the chance to mouth off for a day or two and then it goes away. I said I really felt today's handling of the issue showed weak leadership, almost amounting to embarrassment. I have been saying ever since GB took over that if there is not proper strategic defence of all aspects of the record, the good and the not so good, the easy and the difficult, then a key plank of the campaign will not be laid. I had said to GB earlier, that contrary to the rubbish peddled by an agenda-driven media, large sections of the public, even if they disagreed with the policy, will be supportive of a strong and principled defence of it.

Chris Lennie called, said that yesterday had given them all strength. I had loads of MPs on saying the same. Long chat with Charlie who did his usual brilliant analysis. Felt I could not have done much better but I was always going to get a shit press today. I couldn't be bothered with it. Looked at the *FT* and *The Guardian*. Got a few tweets saying why wasn't I suing the *Mail*, whose splash headline was 'Shameless, unrepentant and still lying'. Piers had sent a text last night, saying we would never agree on Iraq but I had done brilliantly in defending the indefensible. A few more like that. TB called a few times, said everyone was saying e.g. Catherine that with the possible exception of him, nobody else could have done that. He said it felt good just to hear and see some strength. Nice message from Cherie.

TB keen now to get me more involved in the governance stuff. Out in the snow for lunch with Caroline Daniel [*FT*]. Liked her a lot. Divorcee, pretty in a posh military daughter kind of way, and really bright and quite funny. Turned out I had met her years ago when she worked for GB. She said her first week was the week John Smith died. She thinks she threw away the envelope on which GB had scribbled 'Granita 7.30'. She said she always felt it should have been TB, also that like a lot of people she ended up not enjoying working for GB. She was not an Ed or a Charlie. She was doing worthy papers on the information superhighway. So eventually she got out, got into magazines, then *FT*. We had a nice gossip but also got to some serious talk about the paper. She said there was no regular column but I could write regularly in different parts of the paper. She asked me to write a piece developing on the themes at the inquiry on learning the wrong lessons on comms for Afghanistan. She was clearly friendly with loads of military types, and also put me back in touch with [Lord] Charles Guthrie who was in the middle of doing a piece for them. We agreed I should write regular stuff for her and then in other parts of the paper too.

The coverage of yesterday was pretty big and fairly predictable, though TB and others said what came through was strength and at last someone defending the position rather than running for cover. Chatted to JoP and TB re the atmospherics and tried to assure them a bit about what it was like in there. It was odd how unaware I felt of the other people in the room. Very different to a select committee.

JoP sounded a bit nervous. I wanted him to take off his beard because judges don't like beards. I sent him, and later Jack, my folder, because I thought it could help him. Back to more transcript reading and trying to clear my desk. Up there for hours, listening to Elvis. Starting to calm down.

Tim Hincks sent me a message saying he was hooked on *Maya*, and he wanted to buy it for telly. Quite exciting. The cover looked fabulous and I was chuffed that Grace was reading it and loving it. I sent a copy to Keira Knightley saying I loved her performance in the play and also saying I'd love her to read the book. Sent to Piers too. Cam was going through his usual pre-exam nerves. We stayed in and had dinner but then I was back working till midnight or so. Kind of wanted things to get back to normal. Turnbull was at the inquiry today and was laying into sofa government, legality issues and whacking me for whacking Clare Short. Another mandarin who showed why TB wanted his own people around him not the mandarin class. Only Manning, Sawers and [Sir Nigel] Sheinwald [UK Ambassador to the US] had shown strength. TB said he was sure the whole thing was the revenge of the establishment. Called Sawers to thank him for his and his staff's memory! I finally sent my changes and asked to be able to do addendum, and also said media should be called to the inquiry too.

Thursday 14 January

I sent a note to Brian Laws saying I was always happy to help him, and also suggesting he walks right to the away end at the start of the match at United. Had to sign off the transcript today and ended up sending a note of clarification. It was bound to get a bit of adverse comment but I thought it sensible to clear up various points. Confusion about whether I was saying Jack Straw saw TB notes to Bush before or after they were sent. I called Jack S to check if what I had said on the Bush notes was accurate. He said he felt I did well, and he agreed it would help to see my file so he could think about preparing. He intended to do an opening statement. On the notes he said he saw them after they were sent, which is the question Lyne had asked me, but as I had introduced the concept of who saw them before they were sent, that muddied it a bit. Jonathan had reminded me that the worst note – 'with you whatever' – had been softened to 'count on us', and the rest of the content really underlined the overall approach we had been setting out. Jack seemed to have good recall and also to be onside, though there was bound to be a different emphasis. He asked a bit about how it had been, and how the panel shaped up. He was sounding less nervy than sometimes he did.

Caroline Daniel had put me in touch with Charles Guthrie and we fixed to have lunch. When he called me back he said 'Is that my SAS colleague?' and laughed. He said it was good to see someone defend the government and TB and the military will have liked my evidence. He said he shared my assessment of Meyer. We went to the Wells for lunch with the boys and just nattered a bit but Rory was very down about the whole Zoe scene. Godders called for a good natter. Lots of messages still as people digested the press. Spoke to TB and Jonathan a couple of times. TB felt it could not have gone much better. He said we need to help JoP and make sure he doesn't say anything daft or disrespectful. Conference call with TB's team in Kuwait, more than an hour, to talk about how the government there should launch the Vision 2030 report. The reports they had done were superb, both in analysis and recommendations. It really was a plan to transform a country and a government. Of all the different consultancy things I had looked at, this was the most interesting.

I felt the best way to launch was via a major *FT* pull-out, then TB at their Cabinet, then PM, deputy and son of Amir [Sabah IV] present to the public with TB endorsing not leading, with chapter-by-chapter release to fuel debate. Stephan Kriesel [TB advisor], the German guy in charge, was super-bright and also quick on the uptake of plans I suggested. Peter Hain called pre-*Question Time* to pick my brains and I gave him what I saw as the main big-picture messages, and immediately felt his defensiveness. 'As a member of the Cabinet I'm not sure I should say the media are the cause of the trust problem.' I said their defensiveness in the face of a distorting and hostile media was one of the reasons they were in bad shape. He texted after the event to say it was awful and Dimbleby didn't let him put an argument. They never do. Worked late on various things, still trying to clear the backlog. Did an hour on the bike last thing to help me sleep.

Tessa and Jessie came round and there was a real sense of foreboding re David now. Also some of the things we had been saying needed gripping still hadn't been done. I sent an email to Charlie, copied to David and Jess. We should enlist David's MP, John Maples, to help. We should ask someone like Geoffrey Robertson to write an article making clear that if Italy had a proper legal and judicial system, this would not have got as far as it has. We needed some Italian journos on our side. And we needed to find out from our Ambassador what support David was entitled to if the worst happened.

Friday 15 January

Cameron doing a national security speech and had a pop at me about dossiers/intelligence, which was quite helpful for the *FT* piece, in which I would make the point future leaders would have to use intelligence. I wrote a long and funny blog re Dacre and homoeroticism at the *Mail*. Got a huge response. Charlie said it was better than suing and I had to keep it up. Got loads of responses to the Dacre blog, including one from Balls, who said the *Mail* was always attacking him too, so did he also fancy him? I couldn't help pointing out how GB has courted him. Piers urging me to do more and saying he would get feedback from the *Mail* crew. *Times* mag photographer came round and we did a couple of hours on pix. Emma [Mitchell, Random House] there too so we could plan media for the *Maya* launch. Matthew having said TB might do C4, *Newsnight* and Marr after his evidence, I kept in back pocket whether to do proper interview rather than just the papers.

Part of the morning at Grosvenor Square to help JoP prepare. Everyone there felt Tuesday went well and they wanted to hear loads of background and colour. Harry R's text message 'Hey Al – why you getting all this effing grief for getting rid of the guy with the moustache who killed people?' went down well. Chat with Matthew re media plan for TB. Grilling JoP. He seemed to have got more on top of the detail. He just needed to be very careful with words. E.g. the way he spoke it sounded like he was saying we did WMD because we could not do regime change. The thing to emphasise on why memos were ordered to be destroyed, and only one kept in No. 10, was because of all the leaking going on. I felt he would be required as I was to have more than three hours.

He was adamant about not shaving off his beard, as he had been at Hutton. He said he intended to be as low-key as possible but he worried he would say something silly. He felt he was a three-star witness, I was four and TB would be five. I briefed him on the room and the make-up of the panel. Of course I had forgotten he was a close friend of Lawrie Freedman's. Finally signed off the transcripts and Emma took in my signed letter. Did a bit of writing p.m., then we had dinner and watched *Invictus*, the film about Mandela and the Springboks. Loved it. It actually made me feel maybe I should have taken the Sports Minister's job, as it reminded me again of the power of sport to do good and inspire men and nations.

Saturday 16 January

Texted Alex re *Invictus*, then there followed a long exchange about Mandela, Africa, books and finally today's match [Man Utd v Burnley]. He had watched the video analysis and felt we were too open at the back and would struggle. Nice to set off with all the kids, all wanting to go for different reasons. Rory and Grace in the back, R helping G's revision, Cam in the front preparing for Monday exam. I had my Rheindahlen speech and was working on the piece the *FT* wanted re Afghanistan and the point I had made to the inquiry re the comms situation. Mark B following up the Dacre stuff with a YouTube video with Dacre going mad as Hitler in *Downfall*, falling in love with me.

Off to the ground. Good reception from people, including United fans, especially at the end. A woman whose son was in the forces said she was proud to know me. I was struck by fantastic disabled facilities just in front of us, including a guy on what looked like a major support machine. Brian Laws came to the away end as per my email and it went down well. Great atmosphere all day. Played well first half and had two great chances to take the lead. But once they scored we feared the worst. Never a 3–0 match though, and players kept going all day and so did fans. Front row a good place to watch, and our fans were getting a good reputation. We went to see Alex after for a drink and a post-mortem. Clive Holt [director] very complimentary about the inquiry and Chris Duckworth [director] on the Dacre blog. Bumped into Laws with Darren Bentley as they went to do the media. He seemed a nice guy, pleased with how we played but worried about not taking chances.

Fergie on great form. He usually is after 3–0. Alex and I talked loads of football, a bit of film and books. Also had Everton City on in the background. Loves David Moyes [Everton manager], but as for Man U former players – [Carlos] Tévez no brains, one-season wonder. [Louis] Saha no brains, oh for God's sake don't let him take a penalty. Grace had never seen him in full flow before and was laughing her head off. Cheered up Rory too. We lost but great day and all the kids enjoyed for different reasons. I was suddenly really tired and kipped a bit on the drive back.

Sunday 17 January

Big and largely positive profile in *The Observer* by Gaby Hinsliff. Also, according to a few texts and emails, being discussed on Marr. *Sunday Telegraph* had on front a story re me being 'forced' to issue a garbled apology to the inquiry. I took the two pieces as the basis of a blog. Said the *Observer* piece was largely positive and insightful but rebutted the line re *All in the Mind* getting stinking reviews by listing some from the back of *Maya*. I was determined to plug it every day between now and publication. I put up the exchange with Lyne and my whole addendum. Interestingly very little follow-up. Also finalised the *FT* piece. Was really pleased with it. It would make a good speech somewhere. Tessa and Jessie came round. They were both anxious and as 25 Feb neared so the reality of what might happen to David became more stark. Jessie was pushing her mum to grip things we had agreed at Christmas e.g. John Maples getting involved as local MP, a press campaign re how it would not happen if they had proper judicial system, Ambassador and so on, plus medical report. I emailed Charlie F and TB.

Jack Straw sent through his note to the inquiry. Classic over-detailed wood for trees. I read it quickly but decided to take a proper look tomorrow. Rory out with Audrey and later we all had dinner and he seemed better. We had done a bike ride together earlier after which I did him a note re his own plans on the football front. I was still feeling pretty wired. The huge coverage had in a sense brought back the upsides and downsides of being right in there. It was not really clear if I was going to get stuck back into the campaign and interestingly GB had not been in touch since my email to David Muir about him going to the inquiry pre-election. He was unlikely to like the piece on Afghan comms either but I really felt strongly about it.

Monday 18 January

Still not sleeping and waking up tired. Did an hour on the bike to try to get a bit of energy flowing. Mark put up the Dacre *Downfall* video on the blog. OK response though a few saying I was as obsessed with him as he was with me. Went through Jack's note in detail and sent over a couple of memos which I blind-copied to TB. Most important was defending the overall approach and decision even though WMD did not materialise. Also he was leading with his, or my, chin in including Kelly as part of the passage on trust. I pointed out we were cleared and the trust issue was a media point. Also sent him my notes which he said were 'ace'. He texted to say he had taken all points on board.

I thought he was right to do a detailed note, as it will help frame their questions and allow him hopefully to take them through a coherent narrative. I think the big point he is making is this – we saw Iraq as a genuine threat, based on his record and our experience, a threat which had to be confronted, particularly in the light of 9/11, that British policy was always driven by the determination to resolve the issue peacefully, but that there had to be a credible threat of force to make diplomacy work, and if the diplomatic track failed, the threat had to be carried through. That seems to me a pretty strong prism through which his evidence is heard. I told him my experience of the inquiry was that they give you the chance to make a point and their questioning was firm but reasonable. I also felt he needed to be clearer that even though no WMD were found, it was right Britain played a part in forcing Saddam to face up to obligations, that right to the point of invasion, he could have chosen a way out, that the world is well rid of him and Iraq a better country now.

I strongly argued against him using David Kelly as part of the argument on trust. I was not even asked about Dr Kelly, and if anyone was going to be expected to talk about his death, it was me. There was a full inquiry into his death and the government was cleared of all allegations against it. The trust issue in my view is as much about the media's refusal to accept or ever even to report fairly and dispassionately about Hutton or Iraq more generally. I said I did not believe he needed to mention it at all and said it will be used against us significantly, by the media not the inquiry. Do not play the media's game for them.

I chatted to TB before and after JoP giving evidence. He did OK, got some strong arguments over. His answers were really short and clipped. He was probably a bit vague at points but he was generally OK. Defended the position. Did not give hostages. No fireworks. TB said the whole thing was actually a disgrace. Everything was through a paradigm that said the war was a mistake and it was a disaster. He did not accept either of those things. He was going to defend it all the way through. He said I had drawn a line and shown the policy could be defended. He intended to build on that. He said the Cabinet Office was being ridiculous (though he had people helping on the qt) by saying he could not have papers after the time he left. His argument, which he was building with the Brookings Institute, was that he needed to have access to build the case on Iraq pre and post.

We discussed the merits of a prior statement and agreed he should do one. It would help frame his argument and frame their questioning. And if he decided not to use it, it would in any event be useful for his thought processes. Lyne went at JoP on the line re intel 'growing' case so he needed answers on that. What we got from giving support by way of influence. TB said long term the people who would come out well were those who stood up for what we did. Janice Turner round to do an interview for *The Times* re *Maya*. It was initially meant for the mag, but they wanted to do for the Review this Saturday because I was so in the news. She liked the book and we had a good discussion about the themes from it re fame. She ended up reading the sex scene to me, which I tweeted about. I think it was a good interview. Gave her a kicking re using private schools, all the bollocks she talked about statism, and *The Times* shifting rightwards. Grace loving book which was really nice. She was reading twenty to thirty pages every night then quizzing me in the morning. Made a few calls re David's case. I was fearing the worst.

Tuesday 19 January

The figures for the blog had been pretty big, now getting back to normal. Did a quick one on Alistair D, who had another solid interview in the *FT*, and compared with Michael Gove's incomprehensible teaching reforms – 'unashamedly elitist' – of yesterday, plus a couple of interesting pieces in the *FT* – candidates being sent on a 'green re-education programme' and a Nick Timmins [public policy editor] article on how they were changing child poverty measurements for a 'richer matrix of measures'. Sent a note to GB on using it for PMQs. Only the Tories could want a richer child poverty measurement. Out for lunch with Natascha. Gave her the book and we had a laugh about casting her as Maya – 'but I'm thirty-eight!' Chatted loads re the inquiry. She had been instrumental in settling my mind beforehand and was fascinated by all the detail of the thing. Walked to the Royal Horseguards [hotel] to meet Fiona Mactaggart [Labour MP] to hand over books and signed whisky. Nice reception from the staff and a guest – Asian I think – came over and said I did brilliantly at the inquiry. Fiona said likewise. She said the lack of leadership at the moment was desperate.

Over to No. 10. Cabinet Room with GB, Bruce, James and Theo. We worked on various lines about all the policy stuff Cameron had done this week – e.g. crime policy without mention of prisons, DNA or CCTV. Also the child poverty stuff, education and economy. It was all a bit thin. GB seemed to have taken on board my note about going to the inquiry. Showed me a letter he was sending to Chilcot saying he was happy to give evidence before the election. I still felt he was best to go up all guns blazing saying he wanted to do it and explain why it was the right thing to do. He said it's OK for you, you've done it and it went fine. I said so will you but it is a mindset issue. Geoff Hoon seemed to have done OK. None of the frenzy surrounding my appearance.

You got the feeling they were really just waiting for TB now but I said if he did it too that would pretty much get it out of the way until the election. It was clear they were going down some fairly critical paths and there would not be many strong voices standing up for what we did. Jack, judging by his notes, was clearly going to do his agonising and his differences as the topline, piling more pressure TB's way. GB was also working on a security statement for tomorrow. He seemed in OK shape but as Bruce and I agreed afterwards, there was something really tortuous about the process. Round and round in circles about what to say to fairly obvious questions. Meetings that could be done in half an hour took three times as long. Home to finish *FT* piece, which Caroline was happy with now.

Wednesday 20 January

Did a few tweets through the day re going to Arsenal v Bolton. Lunch at the Freemasons with the guys from General Electric on the dinner I was doing for their comms guys. Their spec for the speech was right up my street. Comms silos etc. Crisis management. Nice guys and ought to work fine. Out with Cam to the Emirates. Pathetic away turnout. Bolton two up but eventually turned it round to win 4–2. Great news in a call from Fletch. They were getting Fun88.com [online gaming] as a shirt sponsor. Could not put logo on kids' shirts so did I want them to have Leukaemia

Research? Fantastic gesture. More good news – *Maya* was *Time Out* book of the week and a line asking if I could be the new Jeffrey Archer. Tweeted that he would be flattered.

Thursday 21 January

FT piece looked fine. 'We have learned the wrong lessons from Iraq'. One of the first messages was from Dave Richards, Chief of the General Staff, saying thanks and how much he agreed with it. Out to Camden Brasserie to meet Lorraine Candy [former *Mirror* colleague] from *Elle*. She loved the piece on marriage. She wanted me to be an agony aunt for young women! Not sure it was me but it was intriguing she thought like that. She said I knew about work, relationships, pressure and they were young women who wanted it all. Said I'd think about it. Nice to see her. Reminisced a bit about *Mirror* and *Today*. Kids and all that. She had not changed at all. Told her how TB had really been freaked out in '94 when we did joint leadership interviews with him, then JP and Margaret Beckett and she told me she liked him the least. Grace braces off so that was the source of excitement as we went round her school for parents' evening. Doing a lot better. If only she worked hard and had done throughout.

Out to Scott's in Mayfair for dinner with Ben Evans and Amanda [Levete]. She was really positive about the inquiry evidence – Jack had been tricksy as expected today – and desperate to read *Maya*. She and F both very against agony aunt idea so kept winding them up about that. Ben was still wanting me to help David M but I felt he might have missed the moment, and the thing with Ed was going to be a real problem for him. If it was a month or two ago it would have been him but he had thought it would fall into his lap. That never happens. F pissed off when I told her Janice Turner had asked why we didn't live in a grander house!

I sent a message to No. 10 on the way GB's stance on going to the inquiry pre-election was coming over – very defensively. He needs a line out there saying he positively welcomes the opportunity to state the case as to why Britain was right to take the action we did, how despite all the problems Iraq a better place etc. Jeremy sent me a message saying GB agreed and they pushed back a bit at the eleven o'clock, but it was all running badly for us. Lot of revenge going on – revenge of the mandarins, and of the media. Did a blog on Labour's map re job stats, going through all the important places in my life and showing that everywhere there were fewer people out of work than under the Tories in recession. Obama went big against the banks yesterday [attacking banking's risky trading practices] and that was dominating the political agenda here too. Obama really getting whacked at the moment and looking like he was struggling.

GB had sent his letter to Chilcot saying he was happy to be called pre-election and that now looked like it was happening. The press were straight on to building it up as a problem for him but in fact it ought to be a way of doing a proper defence and then taking it a bit out of the arena. I had a bit of a worry the inquiry team was now enjoying the attention too much. Catherine R was out in the Gulf and said I had made a real impression by being fearless and gutsy. Sally M was on saying 'I have to rant!' She thought GB was crazy going for it. I said I felt it was probably the right thing on balance.

Saturday 23 January

Janice Turner's *Times* piece came out OK. Headline a bit naff 'I'm 52 but look 35' but the copy and pictures were OK. A bit narky in places but there was loads re the book and she certainly made it sound interesting. I was a bit hacked off that she lumped Greenstock in with Meyer as arse-kissing mandarins now running for cover and dropped Jeremy a line. There were some strong lines in there though and the general reaction seemed OK, including the guy who was in front of us at the football. The match [Reading 1, Burnley 0] was pretty poor and I spent most of the second half working on my AOL column. Really odd how we could be great one day and crap the next. Tuesday really going to be big now though. Calum met Laws's daughter in a London bar later. Small world. He would really have been hoping to get a win out of today. Guy behind me was asking if I was doing Soccer Aid again. Legs beginning to fade on me! Home to potter then watch *The Informant*.

Sunday 24 January

I was thinking about a piece on fundraising for the *FT* but I turned it into a blog re the way Cameron's poster launch had been undermined by air-brushing and also the piss-taking of anti-Tory versions which quickly hit the internet. The Dacre vid was getting a fair few plays. I emphasised the need for greater focus on local campaigns. Did a PS on a bizarre piece in the *Mail on Sunday* re *Maya*. Said it was sexed up and made it sound a lot raunchier than it is. Also had some factual errors. Designed to be a bad story for me but actually probably shifted a few copies. Out on the bike I bumped into Chris Chataway [former middle-distance runner and Tory MP]. He said he thought I had been 'gutsy' at the inquiry. We agreed to do the GNR again. Amazed when I got back to discover he was seventy-nine next week. Tweeted how athletic he still looked when running.

Did a bit of admin and worked on a speech. Big build-up to TB now.

Round to Charlie's for a meeting with him, Alan Ward [lawyer friend of David] and David [Mills] to go over David's case. He had what he called a 'clincher of a point', namely that the original court and the court of appeal were adopting different timescales for when the bribe was paid. I kept saying I didn't really understand it, Charlie seemed to get it, Alan got it but was dubious that it made that much difference. He got pretty sharp with David at points, told him to get his head out of the sand, kept saying he ought to be out there influencing the lawyers and their arguments. David was always finding reasons to be hopeful but there were moments when he looked pretty crestfallen. We agreed not to do an article, as it was not possible to guarantee a journalist getting the tone right, and a lawyer might piss off the Italians. Agreed also that there could be no government-to-government dialogue.

Charlie had sounded out Ed Chaplin, our Ambassador in Rome, who felt it was a non-starter though he was more open to the idea of an article. We tried to pin David down on arrangements for the 25th but he was clearly not that keen to think too much about all that. Said he would sort when he saw the lawyers. But he was looking pretty down. The sense we all had was that it was reaching the end of the road and nobody felt terribly hopeful. It was going to be hard to keep his spirits up for the next month and the sense I had of Tessa was that she was pretty crushed by it all. I also worried David was putting too much hope into the point he kept saying was a clincher. I was not so sure. Also at every stage of this process he had seemed confident it would end and it never did.

GB called a couple of times while I was there. Called him back when I got home. The usual 'How's Burnley doing?' and an attempt at a bit of small talk, then into my thoughts for his press conference tomorrow. Cameron had decided to pre-empt and do one an hour ahead. David Muir had sent over a too long and not too brilliant script focused on too many things. I suggested he narrow it down to the youth unemployment plan and have a big message on the recovery. But it was all a bit same old and lacking in energy. And he seemed to lack confidence in going properly for Cameron. I said the dividing line you had to get to was serious man of substance who may lack charisma but led Britain well through the recession v a PR lightweight full of flim-flam. We then had several minutes of how flimflam would be received and what people would take from it. I said he should use some of the attacks we had prepared for last week's PMQs and that meant a re-run of that whole conversation again. It was so hard to get him to pick up quickly on a point. I had been planning to watch a film with Fiona and Grace but he was on for over half an hour and I couldn't get into it so went upstairs to do some work.

Monday 25 January

Working on speeches then watched Cameron and GB at their press conferences. Cameron did a bit on the economy and a bit on ethnic minority candidates. Pretty light questioning. But he did have a sense of zest and energy. I find his manner irritating and the gaps in policy are huge. But it is not impossible to see him as Prime Minister. The press were pretty easy on him though he got pushed a little bit on tax rises and spending cuts to deal with the deficit. He was asked why he didn't tweet so I did a quick tweet 'DC's first tweet. Nice easy questioning. Avoided questions on tax rises spending cuts. Backtracked nicely on Edlington'. Then a blog on how he might have answered all the questions in tweets. Watched GB and although he did a lot of what we had agreed, inevitably there was a lot on foreign affairs, Ireland, and there was a lack of energy in there.

Philip, who was doing focus groups tonight and asking me for lines to test, said he was like 'anti-matter', draining energy out of everyone in the room. GB was due to head out to Belfast too because the power-sharing plans were under threat. Out for dinner at Charlie and Marianna's. Long discussion of David. Tessa popped round for half an hour. She was being weighed down by it all now. She looked pretty wretched. Felicity Mostyn Williams [friend of Falconers and Blairs] there too. She was very anti on Iraq but felt I had done really well. Said the intellectual powerhouse of the country really wanted TB brought to book. Chatted re Cherie too. She was shocked when Fiona said how much CB seemed to loathe me. Home by half eleven and Grace was on the last five pages. She insisted on reading the end out loud. When she finished she said 'Five stars, Daddy.' I was really chuffed she liked it so much. Somewhat troubling piece in the *FT* on Chilcot being part of a Butler attack on 'sofa government' etc. and lots of examples of so-called bad policy-making, very much the Butler mandarinate agenda.

Tuesday 26 January

I knocked off a quick blog on the Bolton v Burnley game tonight. Big one, focused on Burnley fans going to be giving a hard time to Coyle for having left us. Really feeling the build-up, which too often leads to nothing but let-down. To Random House for a legal meeting on [diaries] Volume 1. Martin Soames [lawyer], Bill and Joanna Taylor. Martin said he really enjoyed it and though he assumed there would be a smaller market than for *The Blair Years* he felt it was richer, and it was fascinating to see so many gaps being filled. He said the big change was the new picture of GB, when the stuff I had taken out about him was back in. He also felt that CB had made her demands for privacy less credible as a result of her own book. He did a long note on the general issues and then maybe ten pages of specific stuff that he went through. Most of it was manageable. E.g. he was worried about me saying JP went 'AWOL presumed pissed.' I said it was fine, that JP wouldn't object and him getting pissed at the *Spectator* awards was an annual event like the Queen's Speech. Other issues were all a bit in the 'life's too short category' so I let a few go. He thought there were some tricky TB–GB confidence issues but as they were both PMs there was a strong public interest defence.

It took longer than I feared and I was a bit late for a meeting with Matthew Freud. He wanted a chat about some new things he was working on, but first about his whack at Roger Ailes [channel chairman] and Fox News 'journalism'.* It was a pretty gutsy thing to do especially as he was not doing it with Murdoch's knowledge or support. He said sometimes you really did have to say what you thought was right. He felt we had totally had it re the election. Also that the way we had all propped up GB was like a family that knew there was abuse and incest going on but nobody wanted to say anything. He felt the Tories were lightweight and not very good but the media were cruising with them and GB and co. just did not have what it took to fight back. He said he had had a word with Sarah but admitted it was always difficult to say what you really thought about things.

The stuff he wanted to talk about was interesting – social networking was transforming media consumption. Twitter and Facebook etc. were deciding for you. Traditional media less important. He had developed a news centre-type operation for some of his corporate clients. Also for the Olympics they were proposing a news hub-type operation which had all the news products packaged for low budget and lazy journalism to take. But because of the quality serious media could take it too. He wanted to pick my brains on whether it would be possible to take that approach to the whole of government comms. Become a main news provider. I said it would only work as a replacement rather than a modification of current systems. Get rid of the lobby. Get rid of silo comms in departments with massive teams etc. Go for it as a new and streamlined centralised operation.

The mandarins would hate it. The politicians might fear it a bit because of the aggro. Current media would object. So it could probably only be done by a new government and I was not sure the Tories would have the balls. But he had a big idea there and I would help flesh it out if he wanted. He also had the idea of a kind of think tank operation out at Burford. He wanted someone like James Purnell to run it.

* Freud, who was married to a Murdoch daughter, Elisabeth, told the *New York Times* that he was 'ashamed and sickened' by Ailes's 'horrendous disregard of journalistic standards'.

Popped in to see PG who had done a couple of groups last night. He said they all saw the contrast in energy. The real anger was down a bit but it was not a good scene. Cameron stronger than we sometimes like to think. Off home to see Audrey for a bit on her birthday, then Calum and I set off for Bolton. Did a bit of speech work with a view coming up, then arrived at the Reebok [stadium] with an hour to go. As I feared the big build-up meant big disappointment. Not bad atmosphere though not great considering. Massive Burnley turnout, lots of Judas chants for Coyle, but once Bolton scored the place deflated a bit and in the second half we didn't really have a chance.

I left bang on the final whistle but there was a bit of trouble going on outside the car park I had to cross to reach Rayan, and I ended up having to leg it when I got spotted by a load of Bolton fans. Wrote my AOL piece on the football pain equation on the way back – it was so rare that massive hype met massive event – then kipped. We were in the bottom three for the first time. Fuck it. David Muir called to ask if I would brief GB in a series of meetings to prepare him for doing a TV thing with Piers Morgan. Inquiry had lawyers as witnesses who said the war was illegal which was getting a lot of attention. The build-up to TB becoming circus-like.

Wednesday 27 January

Blogged on a very good *Mirror* interview with Peter M. He was still capable of putting over a message, and anyone reading it would at least know what the government was trying to do. I was following the various twists and turns of David Mills's paper to the Italian [Appeal] Court of Cassation, with Charlie and Alan W commenting in detail. Also trying to sort the website bookshop launch. I cancelled lunch with Jeremy Heywood to go to [*Express* film critic] Ian Christie's funeral with Fiona and Audrey. At Golders Green. There was no God but loads of jazz and some nice speeches. Eighty-two, same age as Dad when he died. He and Bob [Fiona's dad] had been such good friends, and he was a terrific clarinetist too. It was horrible to think Mum and Audrey couldn't have so many years left. Very much a musician's funeral. Home for a bit then to No. 10 to see Jeremy. Peter Goldsmith at inquiry was on in the background. I had watched bits and pieces of it through the day and he seemed to be doing fine. They were being as rigorous with him as any of us but he seemed to hold up OK, certainly defended the final decision and also pushed back on the idea he was bullied. Jeremy said he thought I did brilliantly at the inquiry and it reminded him of what we missed. He said there were some reasonably good people in the building but nobody with authority to make decisions on the political or comms side, and nobody really to stand up to GB. He said on the government side he actually just got on and did a lot of GB's stuff, to prevent things becoming a complete mess.

GB had in some ways improved but there remained no clear and core strategy. He did not involve his ministers in anything like a team-building way, and so they all did pretty much what they felt like doing. Either had their own agenda or were totally lazy. He had a few horror stories on GB's lifestyle e.g. he was no longer going to Chequers – I had heard elsewhere that he had fallen out with the people there – so he stayed in No. 10 some weekends, barely slept, tapped away at his computer or phoned people. He was confusing activity with leadership. He was also looking tired because he was tired. He didn't eat well. I said you're asking me to come back to help look after a dysfunctional child. He was asking me to pick up bits of his – GB's – job. I was very frank, said that I was not enthused, that I felt some kind of loyalty and I hated the Tories but I felt maximum effort would yield marginal results. He said I had shown in the PMQs preparations I could make a difference and he thought I should look after the main events between now and a campaign and during a campaign.

I said there was a fair bit of revenge of the establishment around, and I was too neuralgic to come back into government at this time. He said he felt a few months ago it would have been fine but accepted that now it probably wasn't. He was also very concerned that so little of the political work was being done. He said 'This is kind of none of my business but for example what is the strategy for dealing with the Lib Dems? There doesn't seem to be one.' If there is he said he was unaware of anyone doing anything. Yet surely there was a chance that there would be a hung parliament, and GB would only be able to stay based on them? Yet they did nothing to think that through. We went round and round for an hour or so and he said he just felt things would be a lot better if I was around more. I said I could not really up things from where I was at because it would not be good for me and I would not be productive. I was now feeling bad on another front – him basically saying it would help him to have me around, not just GB, Peter etc.

Then to Peter M's Cabinet Office office for an election planning meeting. PG, Douglas A a bit later, Sue Nye, David Muir, Patrick Loughran [PM advisor], Justin Forsyth and Ben Wegg-Prosser. Peter set out a few questions on what kind of feel we wanted for the campaign, what the other bits of the campaign would consist of outside the debates, how we would get GB's game up, etc. We had quite a good discussion on the need to be more authentic and real. Said he had to admit to vulnerabilities, speak to the truth about certain situations, starting with the Piers interview. PG's groups had shown that the downbeat unenergetic feel to his comms was a real problem. He had to get life and energy but also connection and empathy. Ben said that we had to realise people now took emotional connection for granted. Whether it was an influence of the reality TV/*X Factor*-type thing, or the social media stuff I had been talking about with Matthew Freud, I don't know, but he was right, it had changed. Also, TB had been able to do this instinctively, up to a point so could Cameron, even for all his poshness, but GB really struggled with it.

I told them what Mum sometimes said – that she thought GB would be a great PM in the radio age – lovely deep voice, needed time to explain, looked tortured but didn't sound it. I gave a few examples of where he could answer things differently. E.g. if asked whether he really wanted to be leader in '94 – say yes. Admit it rankled. But get on to the point that it was the right choice and only then to what we have done as a government. He had to tell anecdotes that were real. Talk about his family, his loss, his values in a way that didn't sound planned and formulaic. Douglas seemed sceptical. He said GB was fifty-seven, his whole life he had hidden feelings and been a political animal. TB had always had more of a real life. GB hadn't really. Both Peter and PG said afterwards it was a really good meeting. I thought it was pretty poor, but they said by comparison with most it had been terrific.

Sue was clearly struggling to know what kind of campaign to put together. David and Justin went on about how GB 'came alive' with real people, but both PG and Ben said it did not really come over like that. DA said I was the one who had to try to unlock GB's more human side but he said it in a 'good luck with that one' kind of way. I suppose there was a danger that in trying to be more human it came over as phoney and rehearsed but he could not carry on as he was. Peter said we had to deal with what we had whilst also trying to make it better. Justin had us laughing when he said GB had not been shouting at the staff or rampaging round the office for weeks – 'Progress!' I left for home before they wound up, to watch United beat City in the Carling Cup semi-final. Texted Alex to say well done. He said it was one of the great Old Trafford nights and 'we have put them back in their box'.

Thursday 28 January

Did a composite blog – a news blackout on a story that there had been a massive rise in disadvantaged kids getting to university, the kind of Labour government success that people should know about but which the media finds boring and inconvenient for an anti-agenda. Praise for JoP's role in the peace process and a trailer for TB at the inquiry related to the slanted and one-sided coverage, which was picked up immediately by LabourList. We were back to Hutton-style, only print the stuff that damages and confirms what the papers already think. BBC not far behind. I'd persuaded the *FT* to let me do next week's arts diary to plug the book so I worked on that, then pottered a bit most of the day. TB called p.m., said he felt pretty well set. He had read my evidence through and said he was grateful still to have me on his side. 'You just put it so clearly and with so little defensiveness.' He said the more he had read the papers the more persuaded he was we did the right thing.

He said the danger was actually coming over as a bit delusional because he believed that so strongly. But he intended to say that not only was it right from the 2003 perspective, it was right for now. He was persuaded that the Iraq Survey Group findings confirmed that, even if they found no WMD, because the interviews with scientists and others all confirmed strategic intent and ongoing work. I said the way to avoid looking delusional was always to be clear that at every stage we knew there were other ways to go, but that we made decisions we believed to be right and he stuck by them. He intended to admit with regard to the aftermath that there were a lot of lessons to be learned. But equally that we had planned for all the things we were advised to expect, and which did not materialise. He was right on top of the detail but intended on the big argument to echo the point that the inquiry was already making difficult decisions for the future more difficult. We had a laugh about the excesses of the build-up. At one point he said 'Maybe I'm mad but I am more convinced than ever we did the right thing.' I said 'Hold on while I get my diary … scribbles … 28 Jan, TB calls on eve of Chilcot inquiry appearance … admits … "Maybe I'm mad."'

Friday 29 January

Mini flare-up at home over something or other. Going through a getting on each other's nerves phase. Down to the lockup in Kentish Town where we were storing hundreds of copies of *The Blair Years* which Rory was selling through a new website to raise cash for the party. It was definitely a good setting for a scene in the next novel. All these people, all backgrounds, some presumably criminal, some just storing because no space at home, but it was a whole other world. We had bought a stack of books cheap and were planning on selling them and giving the mark up to the party and mental health causes. Maybe I was looking for ways to help GB short of doing what he wanted me to. According to Carol Linforth, I was among the top three most asked-for speakers for fundraisers, so we would be able to shift loads there too.

I stayed in all day apart from that, did a bit of work but mainly I was watching TB at the inquiry. Heavy police presence and he got there before most of the protesters. The blather industry was in full cry all day long. He did pretty well. Rod Lyne was trying the hardest to get into him. TB agreed with me later Freedman actually the most irritating, telling people when they were right or not. Chilcot didn't ask much but TB felt he had in part provoked the little heckle and booing at the end of the p.m. session by doing a big number which essentially led to asking TB to express regrets. He should have said something about the dead, but I could sense he was both knackered and irritated and so just wanted to get out of the place. He was very good on big picture but also on detail. I watched it mainly on the inquiry website so as to avoid all the noise around the edges, the news channels constantly cluttering the screen with other stuff, including their fucking running commentaries.

I did a blog at half-time saying he was defending a judgement well. The key point for me was that in the end he made a judgement and some agreed and some didn't. He was held in for a fair while afterwards and I called him to say well done. He was pretty angry at the whole thing. 'It is a disgrace the way they are running this,' he said later. He felt Butler was behind some of it. 'People who devoted their whole lives to closed government suddenly wanting to hang everything out there so long as it damaged us not them.' He felt he did fine but said he found it very tiring. He had not seen any of them in the margins, he said, whereas I think four of the five had made a point of coming to see me. He felt they would go to criticism on several fronts but his point was that it would become harder and harder to take difficult decisions, if their conclusions were reflected by the lines of inquiry. He said he felt at least he had put out bigger arguments but he felt the whole thing was up in lights again and a large part of the media and establishment had no interest in fact.

It was all now about revenge for the establishment, and for the right it was about trying to bury New Labour. Catherine called on her way home and was pretty steamed up. As ever she and her team had done a great job and at least he hadn't been too ring rusty, except for the non-expression of regret for the deaths of soldiers and civilians. He said he realised immediately but he felt if he had – and this is what Chilcot was angling for – it would have been taken as an apology and would have totally skewed the overall message. So he felt better to seem hard and unflinching than play the game that was being played. As well as TB wall-to-wall the other big news was the lifting of a super-injunction which allowed the media to report that John Terry [Chelsea captain] had allegedly had an affair with [former Chelsea teammate] Wayne Bridge's ex-girlfriend. It would add a bit of spice to tomorrow's match at Turf Moor.

Saturday 30 January

Good review of *Maya* in *The Times*, once you got through the psychobabble about me and TB. Some good quotable stuff for the paperback too.

Set off earlyish to head to Manchester to pick up Calum and go for lunch. Lunch at the understaffed Little Chef just outside Burnley. Big crowd at the away end to greet Chelsea's bus. [Roman] Abramovich [Chelsea owner] not there because apparently the arrangements did not meet the liking of his advance team. Good to see Steve Atkins, now head of Chelsea press, who I knew from his days working for the government in Washington, and who I always remembered as a real pro. Good atmosphere. Lots of abuse for Terry but the Chelsea supporters were pretty good. 'Let's Stick Together' with the line from Bryan Ferry about very sacred marriage vows was playing as they lined up in the tunnel. They were better than us but also not on top form. Anelka scored first half. We equalised through Steven Fletcher but then Terry scored the winner. Would have been great to get a point but it was getting tougher and tougher to see where points were coming from. Frank Teasdale told me there had been complaints about my swearing and standing – both from people behind and alongside!

After the game I was doing a Labour fundraiser. Did an off-the-cuff speech then a Q&A dominated by Iraq which got a bit nasty when the wife of an Iraqi – who was also the mother of Kitty Ussher's researcher who had organised the event – started trying to shout me down. This inquiry was definitely stirring everything up again. Did OK but it was not a great mood other than when we did Tory bashing or football. A group of Manchester students there and I gave three of them a lift home. Really bright and committed – Ben Furber, English student Talia and politics student Lauren. Real passion for politics. Got to Calum's flat in time for end of *MotD*. Worked on the blog for AOL, mainly about Terry.

Sunday 31 January

Woke up before 6 and decided to set off for home. Snowing and quite difficult till the Midlands. Filed AOL blog from a service station. Did one on the Manchester students, and the importance of activism, and especially the line from Talia that her family and friends would vote Labour because 'every time I see them I give them a reason to'. Pottered around a bit on *FT* arts column. Edgy and snarky review in the *Sunday Telegraph*. Peter M sent his car to take me to No. 10. GB wanted me to go over his preparation for Piers. Terrible traffic both ways so we were a bit late.

Up to the study to find GB looking tired and his hair a bit dishevelled, Peter in his usual mega-smart casual clothes, Justin, David Muir, Kirsty McNeil and Nicola Burdett [advisor]. We both emphasised that this had to be a different kind of interview, that though he liked him Piers would press and probe and he would expect answers. More important, the audience would only listen if he was authentic and interesting and did not just lapse into politico-speak. We went straight into it, with me as Piers. He looked seriously overweight at the moment. His eyes were almost closed. He looked pale and his hair seemed greyer. I started off with John Smith's death, moved to relations with TB, bullying of colleagues, ambition, why he was unpopular, also did Sarah and Jennifer [deceased daughter]. He was quite moving about the baby's death, but the rest was very formulaic. E.g. re Sarah when they first met. 'We had an interesting conversation.' He said – without being convincing – that he thought the party chose the right leader in '94.

We went round a few areas, at the end of which Peter said 'Well that was all fine apart from one thing – most of the answers were not truthful.' GB said what do you mean and Peter did a very funny 'Oooooh, Tony and I got on soooo well! Did I ever want to be PM or think I could do it better than him? Noooooo. As for making sure ministers did not get into a position to rival or challenge me, it honestly never ever crossed my mind.' Sarah had joined us at the end of the 'interview' – which had its light moments e.g. when I said 'Don't call me Piers' 'OK, Piers.' She looked a bit defensive when Peter and I were both suggesting he should have answered every question differently. It was all too non-empathetic. He said something about Rawnsley – whose book [*The End of the Party*] was in the *Mail on Sunday* and had stories of GB losing his rag – and I said that this interview would be seen by more people than would ever read Rawnsley so get your eyes above it. It was such hard work to get him to see things clearly and act though. 'I did say that,' he'd say if you suggested he say something different. 'No, you didn't.'

Peter got very testy too with Kirsty when she tried to defend some of GB's answers. The stuff on Sarah was truly terrible. He just didn't like talking about feelings. We also said there is nothing wrong in talking about ambition. Only then will people listen to the stuff he thinks is important. I asked if he thought Piers-type viewers wanted to hear about how he handled the Asian and Russian economic crisis. I was desperate to get away for the football but he then asked me down to his office to talk about his [Commons] Liaison Committee appearance. The desk was covered with papers all with his mad scribbling. He wanted to talk about the Tories and the idea they were 'living a lie' on policy, like Cameron telling gay campaigners he had never voted against their agenda but now it emerged that he had. I'm not sure he had taken on board much of the discussion upstairs and maybe Peter had been a bit OTT. But the truth is if he just did another over heavy, slightly faux ordinary man-type interview it would backfire.

When I had mentioned to Fiona that he was thinking of doing Piers, she was appalled, said he should stop trying to address perceived weaknesses in personality and comms and focus on strengths, particularly economy. I noticed how surprised he always seemed when I met the No. 10 staff, e.g. Garden Room Sally today or Anne the messenger, and I always stopped to talk to them. The *MoS* today had loads of stuff from Rawnsley's book about his treatment of staff, and he was in a strop about it. But the truth is he did bully some staff and did not treat them well. He had to use the Piers interview to hit a new stride in comms. But I doubted he could. It just wasn't his thing. Justin was agitating to get away for the Arsenal game at the Emirates and GB seemed to want to hold me back and chat about the same stuff. I wondered if Sarah had been persuaded by Piers to do the interview and she had persuaded GB. He did not exactly look up for it at the moment.

Shared a cab with Justin to the Emirates and then home. Justin seemed OK but knew his limitations, as did David. They looked to me and Peter to persuade GB to their views and approach, but it only worked up to a point. PG called as I was watching Arsenal v United. He said Mark Lucas had to make five films for GB without having a clue what to put in them. Alicia Kennedy [GB aide] said they did not even have a basic strapline for campaign literature. Good news in the polls though. A definite closing up, in part economic but also a sense that the Tories were not up to much. The defacing – real and online – of their half-million-quid poster blitz had definitely backfired and would be making them think again about the next phases. Back to watch United batter Arsenal. 3–1 but could have been more. Fergie a happy man.

Monday 1 February

After a long time faffing we finally got the 'buy books raise cash for Labour' scheme launched. Looking pretty good I'd say. Steady flow through the day, alongside a lot of abusive messages from people not buying. But it felt OK and manageable. Also Rory came with me to the One in Four mental health conference* at University College Hospital and we shifted a fair few, this time *AITM* first, *TBY* second, *Maya* third! Some good five-star reviews on Amazon. Spent the morning doing interviews. A rather drippy Liz Grice from the *Telegraph* who did a bit on the novel, and said she loved the denouement, but mainly wanted to do same old same old. TB–GB. Role in election. Iraq Inquiry etc. etc. Similar with a nice woman from *Metro*. I allowed her to stay even though she told me it was now owned by the Mail Group. She seemed to get the book better than Liz but still wanted to do loads on Iraq. Going to be like this the whole way through.

* Campaign based on research suggesting one in four people in the UK will suffer a mental health problem at some point in their lives.

Fiona and Ed thought Chilcot had helped in a way because of my higher profile. But I was not getting a clean hit as I did with *All in the Mind*. Email from John Muir asking for my views on three documents Chilcot wanted to declassify. The mental health event was good. Did my usual spiel without notes and a fifteen-minute Q&A. Out for dinner with F, R and G. Rory picking up a bit I think. Grace doing better work-wise. Missing Calum as ever. He called wanting a ticket for Leeds v Spurs. Called Harry [Redknapp] who was great, going on about making sure he got two in good place so that Calum could sit with his mate. The Terry story was still bumbling along. It was looking tough for Terry. Iraq Inquiry was the military complaining about the preparation and cost-cutting.

Tuesday 2 February

FT led on 'manufacturing surge'. Tories in a bit of turmoil re shifting position again on tax and spend. It was looking a bit better for GB. But he was off doing his Westminster elections reform thing – AV – today which was a bit of a disaster I would say.* Biased I know, and later wound up by Bruce, but I couldn't see much merit to it. Did a blog contrasting GB's year – saving us from depression, and Cameron's – policy confusion and half a million down the drain in wasted posters. Clare Short laying into us big-style at the inquiry. She got an ovation leaving, which showed the kind of people going there. Basically said Cabinet was misled, TB lied, Goldsmith leaned on etc. Live all day but not massive across the whole media because of her cred problem. She had a couple of pops at me but it was mainly a story of her feeling TB misled her and she was foolish to trust or believe him. Witherow and a colleague were going to Ed's to read Vol. 1 [for potential *Sunday Times* serialisation]. In to 70 Whitehall for Peter M meeting re election. Not a bad discussion but there was no real sense of a campaign coming together. PG had done some more groups and felt that Cameron was more vulnerable.

We ran over some of the lines that might work against him. The lack of substance and policy was beginning to bite. Also the feeling that he felt he did not need to do much and had a sense of entitlement to the job. I said once more that there had been a craven cave-in re so-called class war. The public were ahead of the media on the Cameron negatives. David and Justin both very defensive re GB who was picking up a bit at the moment but still needed to improve hugely if he was going to have a chance. Through

* The Prime Minister announced plans to reform the voting system, seeking parliamentary approval for a referendum on scrapping first-past-the-post in favour of the alternative vote (AV) system.

to the Cabinet Room for a PMQs meeting – GB, Bruce, Theo, James Bowler, Nicholas Howard and me. Not easy to work out where Cameron would go. We had to do more to draw attention to his failure to raise the economy. We had some good lines on how he was in a total muddle since the weekend at Davos and the whole business of tax and spend shifting ground. There had to be a sharper attack and we went round in circles re whether it was no policy or a threat. The threat came from their inability to decide because of division, inexperience and incompetence.

It was all a bit round and round the houses, especially re the business of AV and when he came to it and why now? Truth is it was hard to see it as anything but a pre-election shift to a pro-Lib Dem position though it risked being classic please nobody. GB looked really tired again. Constantly hiding his face in his hands. I said to Bruce afterwards it was crazy how we kept going through the same arguments again and again. I was glad to get out and go for a walk in the park before joining Fiona and meeting Neil, Glenys and Rachel, and Hugh Hudson, at the Cinnamon Club. Dire service. Hugh in OK form though very down on politics. Felt we were crap but the Tories were crap too and so it was going to be a choice of evils. I got a bit steamed up at points about the inquiry which was becoming more and more a media-driven witch-hunt. Neil was on good form in part because he was not really engaged politically so seemed to prefer to talk football and kids which suited me. Rachel as lovely as ever. She was pretty scathing about the No. 10 operation. She wanted me to go with GB on Saturday [to Piers Morgan show] which I think would have been a problem. She said the upsides beat the downsides. Nice enough evening but I felt tired out by GB and hated being in the Westminster village.

Wednesday 3 February

PG sent me some interesting focus groups on Cameron, very interesting as public far more negative than the media. Jonathan Freedland [*Guardian*] had a piece today saying Cameron was a mess and when were the media going to say so? Signed more books a.m. which Rory sent off. He seemed to be enjoying it. Finished the diary for the *FT* arts section, then similar for *Public Servant* magazine. Worked on the speech to financial networks in St Paul's for tonight. Watched PMQs where Cameron went on [former MoD civil servant Sir] Kevin Tebbit's evidence to Chilcot re GB guillotining spending which made it hard for GB to stick it to them on the economy. Wall of noise so he could not really get into it and his attacks did not really land. Cameron was looking a bit jauntier.

Did blog on the groups' findings re DC then out with Rory and Rayan to the conference. Speech was my standard comms fare with a bit thrown in on the banks and their handling of the crisis. I was on good form and it definitely had an effect on book sales. Good event, well organised. Rory having a laugh on the way back about a woman there who was right in my face. I think the boys sometimes thought it both funny and also a bit weird when women were so clearly up for it with me. OK piece in the *Telegraph* both re me and the book. Ann Clwyd at the inquiry so needless to say a news blackout on that, as she was totally onside.

Thursday 4 February

Publication day but apart from a PA print and TV interview at 10 not much to do today. I did a quick blog on a virtual launch party which was at least funny and got a bit of pick-up. Basically a piss-take of the book launch party world. Good response. In to No. 10 to see GB and do another Piers session. He had spoken to Piers, as had I. Piers and I both trying to persuade him that he really had to speak in a totally different manner. Had to open up as he had not before. Also had to give colour and depth. Piers was keen for him to look good but would have to be pretty tough with him. GB first wanted to get me geed up re the idea of going for Cameron as an enemy of the middle class. Child trust fund etc.* Also obsessed again about the Murdoch agenda and the Tory policies on a whole range of issues. Did the interview [rehearsal]. He was better than last time and was actually crying a little after a chat about their lost daughter. Good on the boy with cystic fibrosis. But still weak on TB and Sarah.

As for TB, GB still could not really get anywhere near the truth on it. I said at the end it was better but it was still not quite there. Bad body language, not light on his feet, not really pushing it. Good on his accident and his blindness, but for example when he said he knew a lot about adversity, and I asked what he meant, he went on about the economic crisis. I gave him a pretty direct analysis. He had watched the first one and agreed it was pretty bad. But I think his team thought I was maybe too direct and hard with him. I didn't mean to be but I was pretty clear he had to raise the game before Saturday. Briefed Piers who clearly wanted to help him do well but it was hard sometimes. Out to the GE [General Electric] dinner. All their comms people from around the world. Good people, really bright some of them but my God the red tape attached to invoicing. All had a signed *TBY* and I took a stack of *Maya*s which also went quickly. Liked them.

Gary Sheffer was the main US guy. A Republican but pretty reasonable

* If victorious in the election, the Tories planned to scrap CTF, Labour's flagship children's savings scheme.

and hated Fox News and Sarah Palin. A lot of them thinking Obama was struggling and might be a one-term hit. The Brits and Irish thinking things were turning a bit re GB. Questions on Diana, Ireland – another rocky phase at the moment re justice and policing – and a bit of Iraq but not much. Clare had had a bit of coverage in the US. TB's had been huge, mine quite big but it was not enormous and their feeling seemed to be why are we having it? I was on very good form speaking-wise at the moment. Home late and caught Charlie on *Question Time*. Ghastly line-up – Clare, Galloway, Theresa May, Melanie Phillips. We had had a long chat earlier and he was on pretty good form. He was a bit too nice to Clare for my taste. Hard to tell how Iraq was playing out. The antis were probably even more anti but TB and I had both had a pretty good response. He said his mail was hugely supportive. He was also sure that strength gave you a lot even if people disagreed, though he wished he had said something about the dead.

Friday 5 February

Good review in the *Mirror*. Also yesterday's *Standard* not bad and today the ghastly Jan Moir had a piece about how women journos fell at my feet. Did a blog on a Scottish *Daily Mail* piece Mary Galbraith had sent me which was vile about Cameron. First of several tweets – on that, then Moir and how clearly she wanted me to save myself for Dacre. Nice lunch with Caroline Daniel at Roast at Borough Market. She wanted me to do a memo to Cameron, which could be fun I guess. She felt they were more vulnerable and that though GB was not going to change much he was looking stronger. News dominated by Terry dropped as England captain and MPs facing prosecution for expenses fiddling. Caroline pretty frank re her colleagues. Good piece in the *Mirror*. *Indy* 60-Second interview.

TB called ahead of his interview for the Piers–GB show. He said he was happy to do it and thought it was me who had been pressing for it. Not so – Peter, I think. He said he would be fine but he actually felt angry about the whole thing because the Tories were useless and beatable and if only we had stayed as New Labour and also fought harder for the record, then we could win again. I did feel the mood was shifting a bit though. NI got sorted re policing and justice. Did a couple of tweets re Cameron apparently bombing at a big fundraiser the other day.

Saturday 6 February

Chat with TB re his interview. He had seen my *FT* piece and the reference to him wondering whether I had not been right all along that he should have got rid of Clare. He said if he had she would have been more dangerous. In fact, he had destroyed her credibility by keeping her. He had spoken to Silvio re David's case. Silvio said the whole thing was about getting him. Politically motivated. But there was very little that could be done. TB said why can't David get it delayed till they know if Silvio will run again because they cannot really do one without the other. He said the chat about GB for Piers's show went OK but it was tricky. Tried his best to be warm and supportive. Not easy. In the country for the weekend but he said he was always glad to leave.

Set off for Burnley with Rayan. Such a big game. West Ham as desperate for the points as we are. I worked on the sports colleges speech for next week on the way up.

Messages first from David Muir then Piers that GB did well in the interview. Apparently very emotional about Jennifer Jane and Fraser's cystic fibrosis. Admitted to a kind of deal with TB and the feeling he was going to move over earlier than he eventually did. Piers really pleased. Both David and Justin said GB had really benefited from the rehearsals. He was more open and frank than ever. Piers clearly set for a big publicity fest. E.g. saying the *MoS* were splashing on GB crying (though it seems he didn't really). Over to Burnley and had a nice chat with Fletch. Terrific game. One up through Nugent. Danny Fox debut sealed with awesome goal. They pulled one back but we held on. Made for a good AOL piece though I had no idea how many people read this stuff. Got home by 9 having done a fair bit of work and a fair bit of thinking re Marr and Boulton tomorrow.

Sunday 7 February

Didn't sleep too well, worrying I had to make sure I did not lose my temper today. Marr and Adam were up there among the people who could get under my skin just for breathing when I was feeling a bit stressed out. I didn't want to get too stuck in. I had thought through all the tough questions yesterday – including the one Marr asked first on Iraq. I felt OK in the car on the way in, if a bit wired. Nice to see Emma shortly after arrival. Chatted with Alan Johnson as we sat for top of the show shots. Alan feeling as I did that things were moving our way a bit. Cameron not really on the main stuff at the moment. Marr got under my skin when he said, with obvious resonance to the dossier, that I was there to talk about my 'latest work of fiction'. The fairly short bit of the interview on the novel was fine. As soon as he turned to Iraq, as expected, he started with the question about my clarification to Lyne about whether I had said TB could justify saying Saddam 'without doubt' had WMD if the JIC had said categorically he didn't.

As he talked I felt myself feeling a bit weak and anxious. I could feel the asthma from earlier in the morning coming back. I sort of answered a couple of times but I was conscious of feeling odd, almost out of body, and I was worried I was going to get aggressive. I eventually had to stop to compose myself. All kinds of things were racing through my mind – shall I twat him? No. Was Mum watching and would she be worrying? I thought at one point 'I had my last breakdown relatively privately. This is live on the fucking telly.' It wasn't a breakdown but it was fucking weird. It was like I wasn't there. At one point I was saying to myself, this is a long fucking silence. I also knew my voice was going to be weaker when I did speak. I managed to get something out, about TB being an honourable man. Then when he referred to 600k deaths survey as backed by the UN – a lie – I was kind of back in my stride. But I knew it was a 'moment'. I somehow managed to hold it together to the end. I thought again about hitting him but left. Emma was waiting in the green room. 'Fuck me,' I said, 'that was fucking weird.' I felt totally fine again but knew it was going to be seen as a big moment.

Once we got out of the building, the calls and texts started. I called Fiona. She had already spoken to Audrey who thought it was really powerful and human and it needed saying, the line about them settling scores and pursuing their own agenda. Fiona was nearer the mark. She felt it was a kind of mini breakdown moment and that people would think it revealed real doubts about Iraq beneath the swagger. Loads of the usual suspects started to call and text. Charlie … 'In admiration'! Godric saw later and he and Julia [wife] thought fine. Dave Brailsford – 'There are cunts and good guys. Ignore the cunts and listen to the good guys. British Cycling and Team Sky right behind you. All the way.' Mark B said the reaction on social media was pretty positive though I wondered if that was the kind of sympathy that doesn't really help. The hatred of some on the right pouring out. Hague subtly twisting the knife. Fiona's friend Jo was staying with us and felt it was fine because it was so human. Some of the commentators straight out saying it was either a deliberate ploy to provoke sympathy or a testbed for the more emotional GB on Piers.

Piers called later, very funny, saying we had had a brilliantly laid plan to make GB more emotional and have a big media campaign to drive the numbers on. 'And then you come on blubbing and the whole thing is blown out of the water.' Matthew Freud 'is this some kind of blub strategy to make people feel sorry for us and stop the slimy Cameron getting in?' Loads of phone-in bids. Decided to do none. To Sky for Boulton. Darren Murphy texted to say I should use it to explain why I got upset. I did. I think deep down it was a feeling of injustice, strange as it sounds. It's hard to keep being called a liar when you know you didn't, and I think we had reached that point where for some people it didn't matter what we said, because they had made up their minds so may as well say nothing. It shot a hole in my general belief though, that you can get a message out over time.

Adam was fine. A fair bit on the novel, and also gave me the chance to explain why I had got upset. I decided to work on a blog to explain why I think it happened. Used the context of the GB–Piers interview. I wonder if it had been a Tony Soprano panic attack or not. Long chat with TB. He sounded worried at first but the words were fine. It was the body language that made it an issue. Catherine and MD both came on re Marr's 600,000 body count. TB also wanted me to get up the line re child mortality etc. Once the texts got into three figures I stopped replying. Blunkett and Jack S – back at Chilcot tomorrow – were very kind and supportive. Peter M called, said they are hateful and I did fine. PG watched it in the States on iPlayer and also felt it was fine.

Loads of traffic saying it was not really authentic at all. But people who knew me knew. Loads of the old No. 10 people. Alison put on Facebook 'I used to like Marr but now think he is a scumbag'. Lost count of the 'Are you OK?' messages. Lots of people asking what this inquiry is for. Piers cheered me up with a couple of funny calls, taking the piss and suggesting the whole thing had been a ploy. I just don't know what it was. But it was a first, for sure. As ever it was really close family that mattered.

The Ashcroft funding issue was definitely building up, and I sent a note to GB, said Cameron had made himself vulnerable by trying to get into GB over money stuff, expenses and so on. A well-aimed attack would hurt and resonate. 'There is only one question for the RHG [Right Honourable Gentleman]. Has his bankroller from Belize – Lord Ashcroft – delivered on the pledge made as a condition of the peerage his party fought for to become tax resident in the UK? Yes or no? He might like to talk tough on expenses but when it comes to sleaze then every day Ashcroft funds his campaign he is up to his neck in it. And in seat after seat around this country we will make sure people know he is trying to buy votes with money we do not know for sure he is entitled to have.' I suggested a backbencher ask him to do a review of the tax status of all major donors to the parties.

Fantastic email from Natascha who had seen the Marr thing – said I did brilliantly, that she could never have stayed so calm. She didn't feel I ranted or lost control. She was being nice, I know, but she said she was sure he would have felt foolish and embarrassed after the programme, because he didn't get anywhere with his 'accusatory, empty line of questioning'

Massive traffic on site. Gail, Susan, Caroline all sent nice messages re authenticity etc. I got to bed around 11 but could not sleep. I will never be free of questions because the antis have no interest in the answers.

Monday 8 February

Yesterday had gone big on the news, Stephen Nolan phone-in last night, Nicky Campbell [Radio 5 Live] today, but not as big in the papers as I had feared. Had interesting chat with Fiona first thing. She felt my demon was always pushing me subconsciously to make myself the centre of attention. I said I could be out there far more than I was. She thought it was more complicated than that. She felt I should actually explain yesterday in the context of a pressure situation. Nicky C had an hour-long phone-in 'Do you feel sympathy for AC?' and though they had a lot of people saying no, and coming out with the usual shit, there were some good defences – people saying that others didn't like me because I was good at my job and always fought. I did an hour on the bike and did another blog on Marr based on the false claims made about casualty figures. TB called on his way to the airport – on his way to the States to see Bill and Hillary among others – and said I should also see the note on child mortality rates. He was clearer than ever that this was now a media out of control, driving its own agenda, and that they felt they could push everyone around. He said he would love to buy a paper and turn it into a weapon of mass persuasion against the prevailing media culture.

I felt with the public it was not too bad. Dozens of private messages on FB and Twitter. Lots of history rewriting going on. I was still feeling a bit wired but had so many good omens on the way to Richard Bacon that I was fine. Richard seemed a really nice guy. Did an interview that was a lot on yesterday and I tried my best to explain it. All the different things going on inside my head. Mum. Whack the media. But basically that I had just had enough answering these fucking questions from cunts who would not last five minutes under the kind of scrutiny we take for granted. We did lots on that, lots on the book, but also a fair bit on the current political scene. Felt a lot better after it. Then off to do clips for *Newsnight Review* about what we were seeing and reading etc. Simon Mayo pre-record. Similar to Bacon. Nice guy. Liked him a lot. Did a bit on bagpipes as well as the book etc.

Café to meet Grace then home and out for dinner. Grace said she had told someone on the Tube reading a *Standard* piece on me breaking down that it wasn't true. The kids were brilliant at the moment. Watched *Newsnight* and there was a discussion on emotion in politics, with the Marr thing as the peg. More important George Young [shadow Leader of the House] and Gove were both asked re Ashcroft. They were getting more vulnerable on this. GB had been attacked by DC though over the MPs who had been charged and had done the classic thing of trying to go for a pissing match. And they were suspending Gerald Shamash [Labour solicitor, AC's lawyer]. Outrageous and weak.

Tuesday 9 February

Did a blog on *Maya*, reviews, then warned the Tories Ashcroft was brewing as a problem for them. I sent an email to GB on how to get this going via PMQs. That was the place for it now. He needed to go hard. Still feeling tired and still getting lots of messages and concerned calls. Not sure how it was helping the book or not. Gerald Shamash had been suspended from his role as party solicitor because of his representing the three MPs charged over expenses. It was a classic kneejerk response to Cameron's cheap shot expenses attack on GB. GB claimed to me later he did not know anything about it which I found hard to believe. Gavin drafted me a tough letter to Ray Collins [general secretary] which I sent over and also organised others to do likewise. It was another Peter Watt-type thing at a time we needed all supporters, especially good guys like Gerald. Ray Collins saw him later and assured him they would get back on an even keel. He admitted he had been hasty and was in part worrying about media headlines etc. Bruce G said women thought I was about to cry on Marr, men thought I was about to hit him. Out to *Loose Women*. Lesley Garrett [opera singer], Kate Thornton [TV presenter], Coleen Nolan [former singer, TV presenter] and Jayne McDonald [singer]. Met Ian McKellen [actor] in the green room, on talking about *Godot*. Lovely guy. Got him to sign an autograph for Grace and he did a little drawing.

Nice atmosphere around the place. Also Kate Thornton totally up front about being Labour, as was Lesley. Jayne was doing the broken Britain line but she said to me afterwards it was an act and she was actually Labour. Did a fair bit on the book but also Iraq, Marr and the election. Managed to get in some good whacks on the Tories. Lunch at a café in Grays Inn Rd. Brendan called for a major rant at Marr and a solidarity call. To the Beeb to do 'inheritance tracks' for *Saturday Live*. Chose 'The Atholl Highlanders' as the song inherited from childhood and chatted away re childhood and 'Quand on n'a que l'amour' as the one I wanted to leave behind. Nice interview.

Then to No. 10. Emma very excited to be getting a tour while I went to GB's PMQs meeting. Thinking of ways of getting up Ashcroft. Cameron becoming more vulnerable on this now. GB was a bit back with head in hands re things. Could not seem to get into how he could go for it. We kept saying he had two objectives – get up that he never does the economy and lodge the words 'Ashcroft scandal'. Theo said Ashcroft was asking for every email etc. from the party under Data Protection Act. Info commissioner had attacked the Tories' failure to be open about his tax status-peerage questions. He was clearly going to get litigious about it all. I did a tweet re Cameron saying if 100k people signed a petition for an issue to be debated they would allow it. Started a thing to get 100k re

Ashcroft status. JP on to it. He was also worried about Piers interview. He said it was gruelling and that he was not sure it would come out well. I was sure it would. In there for an hour. A few good laughs but he seemed weighed down again.

To Craven Cottage. Fabulously friendly club. Lovely chat with Martin O'Neill [Aston Villa manager] who was watching us. Said he had just listened to the Simon Mayo interview. Fascinating he said. Seemed a good guy. Agreed straight away to Rory going to Villa to take a look at their training. We played badly and lost 3–0 but the fans went off on a fifty-minute 'Brian Laws' claret and blue army' chant. Brilliant support. Players seemed amazed but didn't lift the performance. I did a couple of signings in Waterstones and Hatchards earlier and both said the book trade was not picking up at all.

Wednesday 10 February

GB called first thing when I was on the Wattbike. He was going on about some poster the Tories had launched re a so-called 'death tax' arising out of something Andy Burnham had said in a green paper yesterday.* It was another sign of how out of touch I was on the day to day, in that though I was aware of the issue – vaguely – I had not really followed the Tory response. However, I felt he could use anything the Tories did tactically, especially posters, to push the line that we were serious policy and they were presentation. We went over the same lines from yesterday and he sounded OK. I caught most of PMQs and I'd say it was a score draw. Cameron went on the social care 'death tax' as expected. GB pushed back OK but didn't really land blows. It was also not one of those subjects you could use to accuse him of avoiding the economy. And despite a couple of possibles, he did not really get Ashcroft up in lights. I did a blog on Ashcroft and Cameron's '100k petition means we would debate any issue' and so did a little piece on media double standards.

Out to MTV to record *Angela and Friends* for Sky One. Liked her [Angela Griffin, actress]. Real warm personality. Classic daytime telly – her and three friends on a sofa, me as main guest, second guest an American woman who called herself a 'flirtologist'. Lots of hanging around but Philippa Kennedy [journalist] came in to do an interview for *The National* [UAE newspaper]. We both managed to avoid doing too much of the 'good old days'. She pretty much shared my analysis of the media too. They were

* Burnham had denied that the government was planning a £20,000 fixed and compulsory inheritance levy to pay for social care for the elderly. The Tories had produced posters claiming the 'death tax' would be instigated.

all asking about Marr. Felt on form with Angela. She said on air she had never voted. I said I was going to make it my mission to get her to vote. Afterwards she said she would, and she'd vote Labour 'because I cannot stand Cameron'. Lots of nods around the studio. Nice enough crowd. Sent an email to the programme to say I'd happily go back to debate why people should vote. Home with Emma, planned next phase then worked on speech for tomorrow. Out for dinner with R and G then watched *Downfall* with Grace after dinner. She was pretty affected by it I think.

Thursday 11 February

Did a quick blog on sports colleges in advance of the conference I was due to speak at in Telford. Set up a dividing line between people who do because they think they can, and the National Movement of Whingers and Cynics. Set out some of the facts and contrasted with the Tory years, and ridiculed IDS pretending we had gone backwards on this. Up with Rayan and Rory. Fabulous event at Telford. [Baroness] Sue Campbell [sports administrator] such a star and so warm and welcoming. I was on form too and could feel a lot of warmth there. A good example of where you could take the media negativity and turn it to a positive. I did think maybe I should have gone with GB's Sports Minister plan. Sue said we had done a fantastic job on education and also on sport and the Tories got neither.

Did a bit of kick-ups with three girls from Manchester. One of them had just won a scholarship to the States. Opportunity written all over her face. Really nice day out. Rory enjoyed it too because he could make all sorts of sports connections. Back too late for his Hackney coaching. I was out to a Ham n High [Hampstead and Highgate] CLP meeting. Did my usual standard speech re the three planks of the campaign. Also told the story of the conference today – delivery coming alive – and how they needed to use social networking to get more young people engaged in campaigning. Pretty tired and old bunch who needed shaking up a bit. Annoyed me because I spoke to them a couple of years ago and said next time I came I wanted to see some young people there.

Friday 12 February

Nice message from Alan Pardew re Marr, Iraq, Burnley and offering to help in the campaign. 'This inquiry is becoming a witch-hunt,' he said. TB was a bit pissed off at the way the GB–Piers interview was running. 'What is the point of stirring up all this '94 stuff?' I said it was fine, that it would not be possible to avoid talking about their relationship, and that it was best to get close to the truth – yes, he wanted it, yes, he felt there was an understanding. Only if he said that would people listen to other stuff. It was a bit high-wire but I was sure all that counted now was actual viewers making and passing on instant judgements. I worked on a piece for the *FT* on social networking and the election, how instant reactions were going to matter more than the pundits, and how the Tories' posters were now all going to get defaced and distorted online. Jamie Redknapp called with heads up re the Sky show I was doing tomorrow, *League of Their Own*. He was clearly not really in his comfort zone, said I would be fine because it was all about quick wit.

Cab to Chelsea to see Roy Greenslade at the Marsden. He was looking better than I had expected him to. Home tomorrow. Positively raving about the NHS. Small world – it was Michael Farthing [AC's gastroenterologist] who had made him get seen properly. He had watched the whole of my Chilcot appearance and felt it went pretty well. We kind of stayed off the war though. Then round to see Natascha and the baby. Nice chat on relationships. She said when Martin died she was amazed how many of her friends suddenly started to tell her their marriages were not great. She said whatever ups and downs Fiona and I had, we would definitely end up happy we stayed together.

David Muir sent through a note on the rehearsals for debates. Michael Sheehan, US strategist, was coming over next week. GB was now asking me to be Cameron, having been Piers. The most important thing was to try to get under GB's skin. For GB it was about energy. PG in the snow in the States having one of his 'isn't life amazing' moments.

Saturday 13 February

To the Beeb. Clive Anderson [presenter] was OK, fairly friendly if a little uptight. Lovely to see Emma Freud who was the guest interviewer and who was also making the film on Aznar I was in. I went first, ten minutes or so, then music from Stornoway, Oxford graduates who asked me to say how good they were on their DVD. Emma F felt Clive spent far too much time on Iraq, spin, TB etc. and not enough on the book. Maybe I was just immune but I felt it was OK. To the pub for a drink with Emma Freud. She had a lovely phrase re Matthew [brother]. 'I sometimes worry he is moving to the dark side.' I defended him because of all the pro bono stuff he does and also because of his whack at Fox being a disgrace. Her daughter about to have major spine op. She seemed OK and told me lovely story of how she was going to tattoo a small zip on the end of the scar.

Home for a bit then out with Rayan to Pinewood Studios. Met Georgie who took me to the [*A League of Their Own*] set where Jamie [Redknapp] and Freddie Flintoff were practising on the gym rings. John Bishop and

I had to do a minute on the power plate. All a bit overdone. E.g. half an hour with gag writers who weren't that funny. I guess Freddie and Jamie needed them a bit more than Bishop who was a proper comedian or me who was meant to be quick on my feet. Too much hanging around. Managed to get a haircut from the makeup girl. The show was a mix of *Question of Sport* and *They Think It's All Over*, more the latter. Freddie seemed a nice guy, very bluff and quite funny, and wanted to chat about depression.

James Corden [comedian, actor] was the presenter, seemed OK but a nasty streak there. He made a crack about my book sales figures making up for people losing their lives in Afghanistan. The audience didn't like it, and the oxygen just got sucked out of the place, and he ended up apologising, eventually coming over to me, I think having been told to in his earpiece. He said it was OTT now let's forget it happened. But the mood changed. John Bishop also having a few pops. Quiz-wise we won and Bishop noticed I was taking over the team. All a bit of an odd set-up. Sky clearly determined to make it work. Good captains image-wise. Teams of writers. Jamie said the second one – with a different audience – was not as good. It was another venture into the celeb world I don't much like.

Sunday 14 February

Out on the bike and got a puncture. Bit of a Valentine's Day laugh giving F and G the WAGs' perfumes from last night – there had been a question about which WAGs had their own perfume brands and they gave me a load of them. I watched the Piers–GB interview. Piers will take a few whacks for being a bit soft. GB did OK. Definitely better than he would have been without all the preparation. He was fairly relaxed. A few of the stories seemed a bit contrived, but it was generally OK. Papers would kick it but drafted a blog on how, as with TV debates, the judgements that mattered were being made live by viewers, and communicated live too.

Monday 15 February

Lunch at the Camden Brasserie with Charles Guthrie. Looking a bit closer to his age – seventy-one – but still on good form. He shared my view re the Chilcot inquiry, that it was a waste of time and was just an excuse to beat up TB. He felt Lyne was the one to watch. 'A born troublemaker.' Didn't like Margaret Aldred [inquiry secretary] much either. He was defiantly pro-TB, felt he was a good man who wanted to do good and who did. He was not sure we had been well served by Dearlove. Still very anti-GB but said he was being 'a good boy' because belatedly GB had at least done some of the things he had asked for. Good gossip about some of the characters we dealt with and we had remarkably similar views. Meyer a tosser. [Sir] John Kerr OK. Tebbit oily. [Lord] Michael Jay [FCO civil servant] clever but did not really change the place. Manning and Holmes top drawer. Sawers hyperactive but good. I made a tweet out of something he said about Dannatt – 'He only listens to God and God is not sound on defence.' Great to see him though and one of those really enjoyable reminiscing lunches.

Out for dinner with Douglas, David Muir and Michael Sheehan who was over to help coach GB for the election debates. Quite a diffident and not terribly prepossessing guy but he was recommended. Expensive too, by our standards, though probably not by theirs. 20k for the trip. We chatted away re GB and some of his characteristics. He was prickly, bad body language when not speaking, allowed his loathing for Cameron to show, too keen on stats not arguments, talked about the government and him in particular as the solution. Also probably underestimated Cameron. Talked a bit about Clinton, Obama and some of the others he had been involved with. David, DA and I went round our usual analyses. Douglas very down on GB at the moment. Felt he was being held afloat by the rest of us but not really raising his game that much. Also felt there was a stubborn 40 per cent for the Tories and they were not going to fall much below that.

Tuesday 16 February

Up early for Kuwait call on my trip in March. Good clever people but they were clearly facing cultural and political resistance. To No. 10 for a day of debate preparation. I joined the end of GB's breakfast with Michael Sheehan. He had quite a good manner with him. Pointed out the importance of understanding GB was always on camera, the need to have the right look at all times. Once we started he showed us how the same person – him – looked slightly different in the flesh to how he seemed on the screen. He was very direct with GB who was not taking to the whole exercise well. Started to quibble about the way David Muir and co. had negotiated it. Once we started I was at the middle lectern as DC, Theo Bertram to my left as Clegg, GB to my right. The first question was on the economy. We had a one-minute statement – GB was totally lacking in energy. Then a minute rebuttal. Then free-flow. I just hammered the deficit the whole time and after a few minutes he stomped away and said we should take a break. His body language was dire. We literally had to show him how best to stand and what to do with his hands.

DA said to me at one point – he has all these people trying to help him and he could seize on it as an educational thing. But he can't stand not being the best or cleverest person in the room and so is ungracious and stroppy. He did get better but it was so easy, even when pretending to be DC, to get under his skin. He kept saying to me 'He won't be like this.' DM said yes he would. He will take it all to deficit and character. He will be quite personal. Sheehan had some good ideas for taking a line and turning it. E.g. when DC says he is in denial. I don't deny this I don't deny that etc. We got through half a dozen questions and exchanges and he was definitely a bit better later on. Sheehan taking us back and forth through GB's answers. Some good. Some terrible. Energy a problem but presumably that would be fine with adrenaline. Theo pretty good as an irritating Clegg. Sheehan telling GB OK to use old lines but not to be afraid of using new ones. DM said Obama's team always knew what he would be saying because they would test it.

Lunch was fairly light-hearted as GB went off to do other stuff. Came back after half an hour and we got going again. I was really hammering some of Cameron's toughest lines. GB the problem not the solution. Old Labour. Tax and spend. Hoarding power. Old-fashioned. GB became obsessed about our perceived defensiveness on the deficit. He felt we had to defend the deficit. We got the deficit because growth stalled. We will get rid of it via growth. He felt there was an economic orthodoxy which had to be challenged. We must have spent half an hour on that. Sheehan did not really get into content but said sometimes the style could allow you to shape the content. He was very professional but also quite technical. I asked him where GB figured in the lexicon of reaction. Pretty typical, he thought. Most did not like having to be coached. But I reckoned this could pay dividends.

GB was looking very jowly and overweight again. Sheehan asked him whether he liked or disliked Cameron. GB said he did not like him. He felt he was not a nice man. I said it was more that GB resented the idea he wanted to oust him. He needed to be a bit more gracious towards him, take him by surprise, also surprise people. Sheehan said he needed to be expressing anger for others, not for himself. He had to make sure he was always speaking to and for people. Sheehan picked up quickly on the way GB always sounded like he was saying what he was doing, but it had little to do with people. They were always 'they' not 'you' or 'we'. He certainly had a good observational style. He felt there was some stuff to work with. I had to leave at 2 for Alan Titchmarsh then for Ian Wright [former footballer turned presenter] on Five. Sublime to ridiculous in a way. It was odd being asked the whole time whether I missed being in there still, when in lots of ways I was.

Kelvin MacKenzie was at Titchmarsh, going on about papers being irrelevant, also the anger now coming out of programmes like *Question Time*, also how he preferred GB to DC who had no idea the hatred there would be for him if he won. Obvious he hadn't read the book so it was all a bit same old same old, e.g. Marr, being hated blah. Off to Sky to record the Ian Wright show on Five with Gloria De Piero [journalist, potential Labour candidate]. Lots of hanging around, chatting to Duncan James [singer], ex of Blue, who was worried about his spots. Ian really warm and friendly and great at talking up the book. Gloria looking a bit too dolled up but nice as ever.

Wednesday 17 February

Meeting with Chris Corbin [co-owner] at the Wolseley [restaurant]. I had no idea it was so busy during the day. He was a trustee of Hammersmith Hospital-based charity Leuka and wanted to talk about possible tie-ups with LLR. To BAFTA for a chat with Stewart Binns who wanted me to make a series of social commentary-type films. He was sure it would only get commissioned if I was behind them. To Waterstones to meet Chris Lennie and Vanessa Bowcock [Labour party official] to discuss a TB–AC fund-raiser for big donors. Gave them a bit of a fill-in on yesterday's events. I was totally ambivalent about the situation. Knew I had to help but hated the way I was being sucked in more and more.

To Peter M's meeting which was a bit dispiriting. PM, PG, DA, DM, Justin, Sue, Ed M, Patrick Loughran. We had a chat about yesterday, which went on for half an hour and was largely DA and I saying we found it a bit alarming, DM and Justin saying he would get better, PM saying it was early days. Sue was getting anxious about not really knowing what she was meant to be filling the campaign with, what kind of ideas and events. They did not really even have clear ideas for the main themes. Justin said they had an agreed half-page script for the event at the weekend, largely being seen as the launch of the campaign, but GB and Kirsty McN would 'fiddle with it to the last minute'. I was glad to get out. PG said it was like a social services case meeting where we all swapped notes on how worried we were about Gordon.

Thursday 18 February

Bike whilst writing speech for tonight. Calum 2k debt on service charges on the flat. Plunged both of us into gloom. Alex called for a chat. He was asking why GB did Piers. Felt Piers was a tit. I said GB had to clear away a lot of the negativity before anyone would listen to the policy and message stuff. Alex had put a big bet on us to win, felt young people in particular would not go for Cameron. He felt we should do more re class. Also reminded me he had said early on GB should admit he was hopeless at communication and just do the big serious stuff. He said he was sure Burnley were going down, probably with Bolton and Portsmouth.

Out later to RBS in Bishopsgate, a dinner for the telecoms and media customers. I was on form and afterwards Sir Philip Hampton, chairman, said I should redo my business model. I had given them the kind of free advice Brunswick [business advisory firm] charge millions for. I was giving them the message that they had to set out their own stall and stop being so defensive. Yes there was bad stuff [branch closures] that had happened but they were part of the recovery. Also chatting to Andy Green ex-BT. Said he had never known such scant enthusiasm for a change to the Tories. Felt if we had an attractive leader, things could be different. Also that the Iraq Inquiry was really bad news all round. Home by 11. Not as bad as some of these events. Stopped by someone on the way out – not a bank person – saying he was a big fan, thought the Tories were beatable. There was definitely more of that kind of thing around now.

Friday 19 February

10.10 train to Retford. Spent the day at Mum's. All siblings there. Mum looking pretty good. We had lunch at Trent Port. Graeme not in dreadful shape but not good. Donald seemed a lot better than last time I was up. Home for dinner. GB had a better day, with sixty economists coming out in the *FT* in two letters broadly in favour of the government strategy against the Tories.

Saturday 20 February

Out for first run in ages. Really stiff afterwards. Good interview with Douglas in *The Guardian*. GB speech at Warwick on 'future fair for all'. I did a blog bringing the two together. Calls started coming in with bids re GB from the Rawnsley book. Focusing on his behaviour, bullying of staff and such like. It was going to fly, I feared. I sent a note to Peter M and David Muir, saying I was worried about the tone of their rebuttal. For example on *Newsnight*, the Peter M clip plus JP in full JP mode would have made people think 'bullies', rather than the opposite. Also, they risk getting caught on a hook in which anything which emerges to suggest he has shouted or bawled at anyone is taken as 'proof' that any allegation is true. They had to get over the line that yes, he has a real temper on him but he is not guilty as charged and more important he would be a better PM than DC.

Sunday 21 February

Another longish run, including the Highgate hills and afterwards I felt even stiffer. The Rawnsley stuff was running pretty big. That much was obvious from the calls last night. I sensed the reaction was going tonally wrong. They were in over-denial mode. Best to say he had a real temper but this stuff was OTT. I didn't see Marr but seemingly Peter did pretty well. However, some woman named [Christine] Pratt [chief executive], all twin set and Tory jacketish, came out and said No. 10 staff had called the National Bullying Helpline. Book plus media interest plus denial and now 'real person' element needed for frenzy mode. The Beeb were ramping it even before her intervention and when she did intervene there was just blanket acceptance. Only later did it emerge that she worked two doors down from the Tories and that the website had Cameron and [Ann] Widdecombe [Tory MP] as the first things you saw. Added to which her husband had a vested interest in the issue.* I meanwhile did a quick blog headlined 'Great stuff in *The Observer*' – the poll showing the lead down to six. Rawnsley extracts showing GB role on the economic crisis.

I sent over a note to GB suggesting he take it on the chin and use humour right at the start of PMQs this week. 'Mr Speaker, this morning I had meetings with ministerial colleagues and others. In addition to my duties in this House, if honourable members shout at me too much in the next thirty minutes, I may later be calling the National Bullying Helpline.' Rayan collected me at half ten and we set off to collect Calum at New Street in a sunny Brum. To Villa and into the ground and the very odd experience of Burnley fans cheering news of Blackburn goals against Bolton. Snowing up there. Sunny with us and off to a great start with a Steven Fletcher goal. Villa were not great in the first half but picked up in the second half and tore us apart. Eventually lost 5–2. Lots to write about in my AOL blog which I did on the way to Hampshire.

Speaking at the Nomura [investment bank] strategy away-day pre-dinner. Hilarious to see a big group of bankers trying to do tie-less. None of them much rated GB or us but I detected no enthusiasm for Cameron and George Osborne at all. It was still game on if these guys couldn't be persuaded. The Q&A threw up more hostility to the sense of a shift away from New Labour. I said there wasn't but they had to understand whether they liked it or not they were in a more political environment and the Tories had to make a case better than they had till now. Home by half twelve.

Monday 22 February

The bullying stuff was still running big. I felt GB should go out, maybe even do a press conference, and do a bit of real passion, but say there was

* Mr Pratt owned a company offering to provide specialist advice in resolving company–employee disputes to which the charity made referrals. Following Mrs Pratt's public allegations about Downing Street staff, the charity's patrons resigned and the NBH, of which David Pratt was chair, subsequently lost its charity status.

a difference between being driven and being a bully. I knew he wouldn't do it though. It required instinct and the ability to ride a wave and that was the stuff he was poor at. It was certainly becoming a frenzy though. Arrived at Broadcasting House, where the phone-ins were raging with it. Then a lead story about Cameron 'calling for an inquiry'. Into what for fuck's sake? The reaction around the studio made me think his intervention could be a bit of a turning point on it. Did a blog later saying it said more about DC than GB. The problem of course was that the general sense was true – he was vile to staff sometimes and his politics was of the bullying sort. Good interview with Robert Elms [BBC London presenter]. Enough on the book I guess. OK on GB.

Watched *Newsnight* later. JP losing it with Rawnsley. [Lord] David Steel [former Liberal Party leader] excellent on 'Is this what our politics has become?' Did a tweet re Steel being excellent and JP doing well to get in the [Andy] Coulson bullying angle. Mind you evidence of how much Cameron had the media up his arse that he could talk with a straight face about bullying when Coulson's bullying at the *News of the World* had cost them £800k.

Tuesday 23 February

PG rang worried we were getting in the wrong place on GB bullying etc. He felt I had done a lot to get GB and his operation into a better position, in part because I had a deeper integrity than GB's modus operandi. He felt it was all a bit Nixonian. Everyone round GB knew that these kinds of stories were true. He said I had always been really angry about the stories of GB being rude to the staff. I said I attacked the Tories and defended GB on policy but was careful not to defend him too closely on character. PG said the subtleties would be lost. He felt I was being used, and that GB was becoming dependent in a way that would be very draining. He really felt I needed to get in a better place on this. I did a blog doing just that, namely saying GB did have a temper but the question was whether he was a better PM than Cameron was and I believed he would be.

I went in later first for a meeting with Peter and his strategy group, then GB re PMQs. Sue Gray heard I was there and came through for a chat about what Gus [O'Donnell] would say to the select committee tomorrow. The tough question was whether Gus had ever said anything to GB which might be seen as reining in his behaviour. And also if Gus had spoken to Rawnsley. Rawnsley was virtually saying as much. Gus did not want to issue a blanket denial I sensed. Yet later GB said to me Gus had said he would do exactly that. Sue said Gus wanted to say he did talk to the PM about how to get the best out of people – which would be taken as confirmation. She said the weekend had been fairly hellish. When she called switch to say thanks she said they were almost overwhelmed because unlike in our time there was precious little basic politeness and team building. The mood around GB's operation was a lot more negative than in our day.

Peter M's meeting was really tired. He was late, distracted because he had just done an interview saying something he shouldn't have re Major. Sue Nye had an election grid which seemed to consist of lots of blank days. One just had 'Angela Merkel' in it. Hopeless. To be fair she kept trying to get guidance. She wanted advice on where to put the big things. She was also being told by Jeremy they could not take a government plane to the US for Obama's nuclear summit if it came after the election period had effectively kicked off. Then a discussion about when to do the manifesto launch. Peter was adamant that it had to be before the first debate so as to give GB a platform. PG, Ed M and I were not so sure. I felt we needed to hold back as much as possible. Some discussion re how and when to use TB. I said it was not a clean hit. Sue felt probably play in early to see if it worked and then maybe do again. Philip emphasising how important the team was. We had a chat on how to use these economists who had been writing to the *FT* in support of our rather than the Tory strategy. I had the idea of a PEB in which they read a rolling script so the same message came out from a 'we the undersigned'-type parade of economists.

Through to the Cabinet Room. David Muir had said that GB had gone into withdrawn mode amid the Rawnsley fandango. I threw in a few jokes about bullying and he sort of engaged but he was definitely down again. I had wanted him to start with my joke re 'If honourable members shout at me, I will later today call the bullying helpline.' It was not possible though because he was going to have to start with seven deaths in Afghanistan. There was a dreadful report due at 11.30 tomorrow on failures in Mid Staffs Hospital Trust and the feeling was Cameron would go for that with a few bullying gags. I felt there was a case for GB having a pop about Coulson. He said it would not become an issue and it might be demeaning for him to do it. But the Culture, Media and Sport select committee report on phone-hacking was out tomorrow and there was never a better time to get Coulson up in lights. We went round in circles, on bullying, NHS, and a few other issues and after an hour I got away. One of the messengers really nice on the way out. He said he was worried about me when he saw me on Marr. 'Don't let the bastards get you down. You're a better man than the lot of them.'

Wednesday 24 February

Guardian ran a fair chunk of the piece I did for them yesterday on the DCMS report [on phone-hacking]. Needless to say, only *The Guardian* were going big with it. Also Alistair D had got another story going. He got verballed by Jeff Randall on Sky into saying GB had unleashed 'the forces of hell' when he talked of the recession being the worst in sixty years and also wondered aloud why Damian McBride etc. had briefed against him. Fred Michel, as happened the last time, sent a few text exchanges re my 'not objective' *Guardian* piece. Later Rebekah sent one saying she assumed I did not want to do business with News Int over the diaries. I said it was entirely up to her if she thought me saying what I thought meant we could not do business in future, if Coulson was a Labour figure he would be shredded, and the appeal of my diaries was me observing as I saw and commenting as I felt. I told Ed I would rather not deal with them than feel any sense of being beholden.

Fergie yes to sponsoring Rory to coach at the Street Child World Cup in South Africa. Ditto Piers and a few others. I sent through a few lines for GB re Alistair. Cameron mixed Mid Staffs then Alistair.* 'It's the nearest he has got to raising the economy', not a bad line. I said earlier GB would get strength from standing up for AD. He did OK. Good line from Cameron 'If they get any closer they'll be kissing.' Nil–nil draw really. Could have been worse. I did a bit of tweeting around PMQs re the odds on Cameron doing policy. Later watched Milan v Chelsea. Grace made dinner and said she wished we could vary our holidays a bit.

Thursday 25 February

D-day for David Mills. Tessa had called last night, clearly nervous and said she would like to have breakfast with us at Kalendar today. So Grace, Rory and I walked round with Molly, waited for Fiona after her swim, and had a nice enough time. Trying to keep her spirits up really. It was going to be one of those days of horrible seemingly interminable waiting. At least by the end of the day they would know one way or the other. But it did not make the time pass any more quickly. Audrey called after listening to LBC and asking if I knew re the story about Cameron in the *Mirror* being bottom of the class in his prep school. Chatted to Ed re diaries serialisation. Witherow had come up with an offer of 50k per book, which wasn't worth the aggro it would be. Of course it was possible that as I had had a pop at News in *The Guardian*, they would not take it in any part of the group. It didn't really bother me. I would rather have less money than not say what I thought. Some pretty testy exchanges with Rebekah about

* An independent inquiry reported that the Mid Staffordshire NHS Trust had become driven by targets and cost-cutting and that hospital patients had been left 'sobbing and humiliated' by 'uncaring staff'.

it all. Stop operating like a mafia. PG called a couple times still worried about how we would come out integrity-wise with helping GB.

Out to [Lindsay Nicholson's daughter] Hope Merritt's school, Queen's College in Harley St, to do an interview with their project – a documentary on mental illness stigma. They were a nice enough bunch, not as private schoolish as I expected and pretty clued up on the issue. Hope did the interview and was pretty good as a questioner. Matthew [Mills] called as I left and pinged over a story from Reuters which said the prosecutor wanted to drop the case against David because it had run out of time. It seemed too good to be true. I called Charlie who said it did indeed look like it meant exactly what it said. That was later confirmed just as we were going out for dinner to the Italian at South End Green. Matt and Jessie really emotional and excited, David quite flat, almost as though he was in shock. It looked like a face-saving formula for the Italians – they did not acquit him but he would not be jailed. Tessa really happy. TB suggested he say in the statement that he would have won on the merits of the case. I said to David just quit while you're ahead so he put out a short statement saying how he was pleased and could now resume a normal life. Not massive on the news which was also pretty good. I worked on the Burnley speech for the Jimmy McIlroy dinner on Saturday, did a bit of thinking on the political scene which I sensed was still closing for us.

Friday 26 February

Lunch with Mariella [Frostrup] for her new column in *Observer* Food Monthly. She really is lovely and I know sexy voice is a cliché but that is exactly what she has. We chatted about loads of things but as with so many of these interviews we got a bit bogged down on Iraq. She was clearly sympathetic but felt a lot of people just could not understand it. Also said some of her friends – all anti the war – nonetheless said they found my appearance at the inquiry impressive. She was quite intrigued on why I was getting into the whole social networking thing and we also explored my ambivalence about fame. Nice enough time but had to shoot off for a meeting with Dylan Pereira [TB associate] and others at TB's office. They were picking my brains on strat comms, all pretty basic and I sensed the project – which he was backing enthusiastically – was not going as well as expected. Popped up to see TB who was looking a bit tired. We had the usual chat re GB. He still felt despite the polls closing that it was unlikely he would win. But he accepted there was movement, at least in the mood. Told him some of the lighter moments from the Piers preparations and the Cameron debates. He was due to see him soon and seemed to be dreading it.

To Home House for a Leaders in Sport evening with Fabio Capello [England football team manager]. David Frost, David Davies, Mike Forde [Chelsea FC advisor], one or two others I knew among a very white middle-class middle-aged audience. Capello was interviewed, not terribly well, by the boss of the company who put the event on. No questions on Terry and Bridge, which after Bridge had announced he was not going to the World Cup, was pretty poor. Fabio's English was still not great. He gave some OK answers about leadership but it was very general and I didn't have much sense that he really thought about it. He also gave a very odd set of answers on penalties, very non-leadership, almost saying you had to leave it to the players on the day. As it was now virtually impossible to win a World Cup without penalties at some stage it was not much of an answer. He was quite funny and charming but not really as impressive as I had expected him to be.

Off to Groucho's [Soho club] for David Mills's celebration party. Charlie, despite not being too well, did a little speech. Ditto David. All his kids there, a few friends and he still seemed quite down. Went to an Italian restaurant where I was getting grumpy at the poor service from an Italian Malcolm Tucker lookalike. David seemed almost in shock. Tessa said afterwards she was sure they would end up together, but she was not sure when. She still loved him but it had been such a nightmare it would take time to get over it all.

Saturday 27 February

Off early to head to Burnley. More private polling showing slight narrowing. Calum not feeling great. I was guest again at Ladies' Day, said a few words and also sold a few books. Bigger event than last year and not quite so wild but a few who were pawing a bit. Lunch with Barry and Peter Storrie [Portsmouth CEO], Pompey having just gone into administration. He seemed to think they might be able to appeal. Played OK at times but gave away two crazy penalties and the second one did for us. Bumped into Brian Laws at the end. What do you do, he asked? You can train all you want but if players make bad decisions like that… Did my blog for AOL then round to the James Hargreaves for the Jimmy McIlroy testimonial. Loads of old players there, most of the team of the '70s, a fair few from the '60s. I was next to Jimmy who said he was embarrassed to be taking people's money yet when it came to his speech basically said you'd have to wait till the main dinner! I based my speech round Fletch wanting me to say he was the greatest Claret of all time then going through the others in the room.

Nice evening and I was on good speaking form. Ditto Fletch. Late night though. Bed at 1ish, which was late for me. I did a fair few weekend tweets on Tories not being in good shape and the gap was further narrowing according to the *Sunday Times* poll. Two points on eve of their spring conference.

Sunday 28 February

Up at 7 for a cup of tea with Fletch then set off for Wembley. Cameron on Five Live. He has real energy but he does not really connect and I felt what he was doing was raising the questions people have, without giving the answers. I had tweeted re journalists saying the Tories were jittery and then did another one about Cameron seeming to say 'people' in answer to the question about what was the worst part of the job. Vile weather on the drive down but got there in good time to meet Grace and head for the Football League lunch. [Lord] Brian Mawhinney [former Tory MP, chairman Football League] came over for a long chat. Amazingly we stayed off politics and just did football. He did an OK speech, his last. Chatted to Gordon Taylor about the phone-hacking situation. He was a bit defensive on why he settled but he was such a good bloke I didn't complain too much.

Not a bad game. Villa up early through a pen, Owen equalised then went off injured for Rooney who scored the winner. We were right by them as they came up for the medals, Gracie screaming at Alex. Car broke down in the bloody car park. Two and a half hours waiting for the place to clear and the RAC to come. Good reaction to this morning's blog which Godric drafted, on the news blackout on the NAO [National Audit Office] report saying they were on track and on budget for 2012. Caught some of the coverage for Cameron's speech. He did OK without it being brilliant.

Monday 1 March

Cameron really did have problems at the moment and they got worse when Ashcroft finally came out, pre-FoI release of his assurances on the peerage, and said he was a non-dom. Most of the media doing it big but interesting how many did not. Pottered a.m. then went out on the bike with Rory. He felt I should go for my own TV show. Fiona felt I should be going into Vic Street and No. 10 more and helping them get after Cameron even more. Sent a short note to David Muir re GB at Chilcot. Strength the key. JoP contacted me saying Ari Fleischer [former GWB White House press secretary] was trying to help the Glazers [Man Utd owners] find a UK spokesman or PR group to help their image here. I put him in touch with Tim [Allan] who was pretty grateful. Suggested he get going with a plan ASAP. Never much took to Ari and he sounded as dry as ever. Said he was still in touch with Bush whose book was out in November. Chatted a bit about old times. He had gone very much down the consultancy route.

Tuesday 2 March

Fiona had done a piece for the *Radio Times* which had the old line about me being useless round the house. Some of the papers picked it up. Did a bit of a light-hearted blog rebuttal on her claim that I had once deliberately broken the Hoover so as not to be asked to do it again. Out for breakfast with Fred Michel at the Wolseley. He was a bit late so chatted a bit with Tina Weaver and Jo Revill [both journalists]. Tina now living with Richard Wallace [*Daily Mirror* editor]! She felt the Tories were vulnerable and that we should not back away from class as an issue. Fred a nice guy but hard to reconcile the nice guy with the ruthlessness of News Int. He agreed Rebekah lacked subtlety. He felt James was not as out-and-out ideological as some thought. Was keen for me to see the *New Yorker* piece which was just out on the Murdochs. Said Matthew's whack at Ailes and Fox had been 'difficult and interesting'. He felt *The Times* and *NoW* were still up for grabs in terms of the election. They were clearly a bit worried about the recent polls and I said they needed to reposition in case.

He was very pro-me. He agreed Rebekah could not understand how I could do a piece like that in *The Guardian* and put at risk a serial deal. Alan Yentob [BBC director general] came over – Mark Thompson was setting out another strategic vision paper today – and he and Fred ended up having a bit of a ding-dong about things, Alan saying if they had any sense they would embrace the BBC. He felt it extraordinary the extent to which the Tory policy was now dictated by Murdoch's agenda. I said get stuck in a bit more then. Nice to see Fred though and I sensed he would repair a few fences. Maybe not.

To the Ivy Club to meet Nancy who was back from a trip to Cuba and later seeing Sven to try to resolve their financial differences. Nancy wanting to help more. Called Fergie re the Glazers situation. Still not talking down the Glazers though he said the ticket pricing drove people crazy. To Random House for a meeting first with Caroline – TB's book behind sked – and then Joanna Taylor on pictures. I had found some good ones. The production schedule was right on me now and I had really not focused on it. It would have to be printed by 26 April for heaven's sake. Bumped into Gail who said if needs must it could sit in the warehouse e.g. if we felt there was going to be another election.

Home then out with Rory to Thurrock for a fundraiser. Good night. Loads of books sold and money raised and lively event. I did it as a no-notes, walk round the stage job and seemed to go well. I did twenty-five minutes, whacking the Tories plus social networking, then Q&A, book signing till fairly late. Sent an email to Sue Nye etc. saying this was the kind of event GB needed. Doubted they would go for it. Finished fairly late but it was a good do and I felt chirpier about the mood.

Wednesday 3 March

I did a blog on last night and how and why the mood was changing which it was. The Tories just had not thought things through. I was about to leave when Geoffrey Goodman called to say Michael [Foot] had died. I felt so annoyed I had not been able to go to visit him with Fiona and Neil last week though she said he was barely able to recognise or converse. I was due on the Sky Book Show so drafted an obit in the back of the car despite the driver rabbiting on. I couldn't really call anyone because he was talking so much and was clearly a gossip, telling me all the famous people he had driven. The show was fine, Mariella F said she was quite disturbed reading my sex scenes and said she found it a bit revolting to see sex written by people she knew. Also that *Maya* was crying out to be a film which I said would be on the paperback cover.

Sky sent a car to take me to Millbank and did a few tribute interviews to Michael. The blog obit seemed to be going down well too. Said to Fiona I wonder how many times we will be asked to do tributes to dead Labour people for the rest of our lives. Bumped into Neil at Sky who was in a way relieved. He said he had found it quite upsetting to see Michael so weak and frail and not really there. Home to potter a bit, then watch England v Egypt, channel-hopping to Scotland v Czech Republic. Both won. Out later to *Newsnight*. Doing a disco on Michael with Hezza [Michael Heseltine] and [Baroness] Shirley Williams [Lib Dem peer, former Labour MP], but had a mild meltdown, identical to during the Marr interview, as the titles opened. Thankfully there was a five-minute film. I told Paxo, who was incredibly nice about it, said did I want to lie down, also that if I was not right he would just ignore me. I used the inhaler, which thankfully this time I had with me, and just about got it together for the chat. Did OK but it was all a bit Tony Soprano and a warning to take it easy.

Thursday 4 March

Kicked off the day with a burst of local radio interviews on Michael. Did a quick blog re Ashcroft on his birthday and lack of judgement of the senior Tories who failed to deal with this issue. Said TB and team had been obsessed with dealing with all questions before the campaign. They needed Melon heads like Charlie and Derry [Irvine]. Tom Baldwin came on, ostensibly re Ashcroft – he wanted to get TB to say something, which I later tried to get, without success. Ashcroft still a problem because Liam Fox [shadow Defence Secretary] had said Cameron knew only a month ago re Ashcroft being a non-dom.

Cameron as a bit flaky was coming through. Mind you the strategy group meeting was not that great. Not impressed by Ed M who was always saying what good ideas there were but was never really picking them up to drive them. GB had insisted on doing a big speech next Wednesday on the economy and they were all very down on the idea but actually I felt it could work – Budget date plus arguments. There was still not enough really to get people going but it was building. To Victoria Street, more people and a bit more life in there. Marianna said the more I went in the better because most of the people there had not done a campaign and at least I was a grown-up. Off with Rory and Patrick Loughran to Dulwich fundraiser for Tessa. Packed out and a good lively crowd. Spoke well. Q&A fine. Auction terrific. Got four figures for the signed pieces of legislation e.g. Minimum Wage Act. Raised twice what they had planned for. Nice evening and the mood of activism was definitely there. Gave Tessa a lift home. She seemed so much chirpier than a week ago!

Friday 5 March

I spent most of the morning working on the intro to Volume 1, partly as a way of trying to shape a line for any leak or announcement. I sent it to a few people and PG and Ed both felt it was too defensive about the fact of publishing, that I had nothing to be embarrassed about at all. Susan felt it was too much about now not then but I felt I had to square the circle between publishing a book which would not be that good for GB, and also helping him try to win again. I rattled off a quick blog on the Dulwich fundraiser, focusing on the fact that the big-money items were those raised by signed bills and Acts which emphasised delivery. Lovely message from Tessa who said she had raised enough to fund her entire campaign. Liaising with TB on details of MF funeral though when I heard the list of planned speakers – Bruce Kent [Campaign for Nuclear Disarmament], Helena [Kennedy] maybe, Mark Seddon [left-wing journalist, former NEC member], Neil of course, GB doing a poem – it sounded like the kind of event he might not be welcome at. It was still the case that the left preferred gallant and principled losers to pragmatic and modern winners.

I was working on the book intro while watching GB at Chilcot. He did well. Good tone. Upfront re right decision but alongside considerable empathy for troops and families. Also pretty strong on funding and hit back at the generals and chiefs who had been saying they did not get enough. Jeremy sent me a nice message saying he was glad I had prodded them into doing it pre-election. Liam Fox was shrill and OTT in his response. A bigger problem emerged later with news of an attack by Boyce that GB was being disingenuous in his evidence. TB felt it sounded like it went fine 'because he showed some leadership'. Halfway through I did a note to Stewart Wood to say GB was doing very well. Really good when he looks relaxed and confident. Mustn't let Lyne irritate him. Needs at some stage to make big point re the importance of leaders being able to take difficult decisions.

I think it would be very powerful if he said something about the scale of the decision, and the scale of the job. 'Perhaps now, I am one of the very small number of people who does know what it is like to have to make decisions of real magnitude, as Prime Minister. TB was faced with a truly enormous decision, which yes, was also a decision for Cabinet and Parliament, but he was the Prime Minister and had to lead this country at that time. Having succeeded him, and having been involved in dealing more closely with Iraq since, I am more convinced than ever that we did the right thing and for the right reasons and that history will be kinder on this than many are right now. I also believe we must learn the right lessons not the wrong lessons, and one lesson is that ultimately, for all the advice and the competing opinions leaders are given, they do have to lead, and now and in the future that will sometimes involve making difficult and unpopular decisions.' I was still agonising about the book. Philip was sure it was the right thing to do. Fiona felt even the worst stuff was not lethal for GB. GB off to Afghanistan.

Saturday 6 March

Buried in the *FT* story re Ashcroft a line that Cameron would require pay details of all civil servants over £58k to be published. Did blog on the double standards alongside a *Guardian* piece on training Tory candidates. Reading through the GB stuff in Vol. 1. Ed told me *The Times* – probably Phil Webster – were looking at it next week. To the Emirates. Never really looked like anything but defeat and yet as they missed chance after chance we nicked an equaliser and for a few minutes looked to be in with a chance. Crap atmosphere. Arsenal not quite there. 3–1. Back to watch United win at Wolves then off to the airport. Texts re polls showing the Tory lead up again but it was still single figures. Bumped into Ann Clwyd, who was looking older yet still flying around the place. Off to Kuwait too. She said she felt the inquiry was one-sided and there was no real understanding of the Iraqis' place in all this. She struggled to keep GB engaged and interested and felt we had not told well the story of Iraq's progress. Good woman. Took a pill and slept most of the six-hour flight.

Sunday 7 March

Met by VIP service – like the old days because of the TB connection – and taken to a lounge while immigration was sorted. Stephan [Kriesel], the head of TB's operation there, had been on the same plane and we chatted as we drove to the hotel. It was a much bigger operation than I had imagined. Some of the top management McKinsey-type people involved. Got showered and changed and headed to Seif Palace where TBO had an OK suite of offices in the basement. Team meeting. Maybe about twenty people. I did my usual spiel, a bit about TB and how to get the best of him. The day was then a mix of meetings there, including some interviews for the comms director of the new unit planned for the PM's office. There was a sense the Kuwaitis, and in particular the PM and some of his people, were resistant to any change. As things stood he was an executive for a couple of hours a day and spent the rest as a traditional Arab leader, doing weddings, funerals and visits. There was next to no co-ordination and ministers seemed to like it like that.

The minister for national assembly affairs, Dr Mohammed Al-Busairi, was the only one I met who really seemed to get it. Met Mohammed Al-Sanousi who was a businessman, ex-TV presenter, journo but had also been Minister for Comms and had tried to do the spokesman job which was one of the recommendations of the TB work. His problem has been lack of buy-in. He felt there would be obstructions to e.g. grid, and all the units we set up in No. 10, but felt we just had to do it. Some of them got it at an intellectual level but I was not sure it would happen. The Stefan and Dylan Pereira characters were really bright but the management consultancy speak grew wearing. They seemed to repeat the same conversations the whole time. Also odd to live away from home for so long. Not sure any had kids. Good bunch in many ways and they seemed to get something out of the discussions we had.

Good meeting with Sheikh Mohammad Abdullah al-Mubarak. Not in high formal position but apparently quite influential. The most Westernised of the ones I met. Old Etonian so we had a good laugh re that especially when he tried to tell me it was a progressive school. Chelsea fan. Modern kind of guy. He was not convinced we would make the progress we wanted to. He felt there was too much resistance though it was clear some of this was all inter-family strife. The day whizzed by OK though I was close to falling asleep a few times. Went out for a run then dinner with the Mubarak guy at a mall. Food OK. Chat OK. Got on very well with him. Really tired now though.

Monday 8 March

Slept OK. Breakfast with Dylan then interviewed one of the candidates for comms director. Bit of a blowhard. He had CB as a referee based on once involving her in a charity do. He was slightly better than the over-vivacious to the point of scatty South African we saw yesterday. But not A grade. Best one we saw later, a Kuwaiti woman who had spent nine years working for Arab groups in the States and was now in UAE. Really nice manner and also asked intelligent questions as well as giving thoughtful answers to ours. Wanted to do it for patriotic reasons but also wanted to be sure she would be central to the PM's operations. The impression I was gaining of the PM [Nasser Al-Sabah] was of someone who would not want these changes and even if he did would not know how to make them work.

To the Bayan Palace. Been there in 2003 with TB. OTT opulence and all that. Lots of men in full gear sitting around twiddling their beads. We were there to meet the son of the Emir [Al-Ahmad Al-Jaber Al-Sabah], Sheikh Nasser. I was told he was one of the keener ones. But the meeting was all about him letting off steam that we had not sent out copies of the Vision report and that we could not possibly have the bells and whistles launch planned for him and TB next week. He was a short dumpy guy and I reckon he shared my polyp problem. He had to leave the meeting for half an hour to go to a meeting with the Emir and the PM of Bahrain. When he came back I just told him 'We agree with you' and we then wrestled the thing back to a soft launch. This thing clearly mattered so much to the TB team but they were pushing uphill all the way. I said in the car there were three parts to this – TB's name, the team and the Kuwaitis. Without the last bit buying in nothing could really happen. Job ads had produced 3,000 responses. Nice Kiwi lady Heather Bowen managing that side and wanting me to see people in London.

I could not do this kind of consultancy stuff but I quite liked some of the team. I got the message – and later communicated it to TB – that he had to be less world leader and more project driver. Buzzed around for a few meetings, a debrief, a brief run, dinner at a beachside Indian, then off to the airport with Mohammed. Flew to Dubai. Airport there like a zoo. 2 a.m. and heaving. Shops bursting. Horrible. Odd to think Rory there tomorrow night en route to South Africa. Took another pill and slept more than six of the seven hours from Dubai to London. Not a bad trip but not really my thing.

Tuesday 9 March

Emirates beds not as good as BA, but a lovely stewardess who seemed to fuss over me more than the fat American Jewish guy next to me who whatever he got wanted more – drink, ice, food, help with this or that. Slept OK. To Bloomberg for the Sport Industry Awards. My third year. Not a bad crowd, supplemented by Trevor Beattie and also Kate Robertson of Euro RSCG [integrated advertising agency]. Some of the categories really poor. Others strong. The one I really fought for was Everton to get the community award for the work they did on mental health. Premier League in for Brand of the Year but their presentation was really poor. I did a Bloomberg interview mid-morning and had my third TV studio panic attack. My mind just went cloudy and mushy. Like asthma but not. I had a break but clearly there was something unhinging and unsettling me. Back to the judging and managed to stay for most of the day.

Several of the judges commenting that the political mood was changing. Left at half four and headed for Whitehall. I missed Peter's strategy group meeting which was apparently a bit tetchy. He wanted to change the manifesto launch date to make it 12th not 19th. I went through to see GB in the Cabinet Room. NI policing vote finally went through in Stormont, despite Tories fucking around with Ulster Unionists. Bush had got involved to try to push them in the right direction. GB felt Chilcot had gone OK albeit tarnished by Boyce having a pop. And today the coroner into the [Afghan bomb blast] deaths of four SAS reservists was pretty scathing on training and equipment. GB was a bit down about it, felt Cameron would do six questions on it, or maybe mix with crime and it would be very hard to get up Ashcroft. We had a few ideas for backbenchers but it would be tough.

Light relief came from watching the clip of DC sorting his hair by looking in the camera lens as a mirror. I didn't think I added much today, probably because I was keen to get away pretty quickly. In there for two hours. *Times* had done a piece on Charlie Whelan being Labour's Ashcroft. 'As in they are both deeply unpleasant people,' I said. GB grimaced a bit. Some of the candidates getting winnable seats was a disgrace. Trying to call Rory on his first day in South Africa at Street Child World Cup. Signed 112 books for next week's dinner.

Wednesday 10 March

Popped round to see Mash the newsagent who had been beaten up and robbed last night. Bastards, and probably part racist. Dentist, post, then Royal Free to chase date for operation. Did a note to TB re Kuwait. My sense is the buy-in from the Kuwaitis is limited and that the main task facing him next week was to get that buy-in, especially from the PM and his key people. Most didn't understand what we were proposing. I told them what Mohammed Al-Sanousi, who had tried the government spokesman role when Minister for Information, said – that the only way to co-opt the system (which he failed to do) was to 'just do' certain things which allowed you to show progress. I'd advised for example that from next week's event, the TB operation teams should start to do proactive one-off pieces of communications simply to show the kind of thing that could be done without changing the lifestyles of the ministers too much. They need to see some quick wins better to understand what is being proposed on the comms side.

The ministers and officials in support of the planned changes need to be given impetus by TB to persuade others. The whole project is dependent on three things – TB name and role and reputation. The quality of the TB team. And the approach of the Kuwaitis. I think the project team will get very frustrated quite quickly unless the mood around the project inside the government changes. JoP replied in greater depth than TB. He felt there were three aspects to it: 1, we are caught up in an internal fight which has recently got worse, which explains Nasser's nervousness about the event; 2, the PM himself doesn't want to change overly and fears this new operation is a threat; 3, the ingrained habits of the system which has stopped anything happening for decades combined with people like the Cabinet Secretary who are actively hostile to the project.

Watched PMQs. OK but Cameron more energy and GB not quick enough on his feet. As expected DC went on defence and got a bit hysterical. GB stayed very calm. Also got in a good spontaneous hit when DC claimed Tory credit for winning the Cold War and GB said he was still in school at the time. PG felt DC won it because he had verve and energy. I was not so sure, though energy was certainly a problem. GB did OK generally though the whack on Ashcroft was too forced. I was still trying to work out how to deal with the sheer volume of stuff coming to me via social media. Mark had delivered Vol. 2 and sent a sweet and rather moving email about how his personal and political lives were messed up and he needed and appreciated my support. I wrote a note to David Muir pointing out I never asked for anything but I did want to ask for help for Mark getting a [parliamentary] seat. He would be a lot better than some who were currently being selected by Whelan's machine. Set off for Greenwich early evening tweeting en route that I was mildly pissed off to be missing re-arranged Burnley v Stoke for a long-arranged fundraiser. It was Nick Raynsford's seat, not really under threat as others were, but David Prescott had talked me into it. Fine in so far as it went but a bit of a waste of my time. Also my voice was beginning to go and my nose closing up. The sooner I got this operation the better. Managed to avoid knowing the score so watched the game at half ten on Sky. One–all. Not great but still fighting.

Thursday 11 March

Spoke to Fergie about the Sport Industry Awards. He was fine with it provided that the date was OK. Convinced we were going to win, that the

Cameron posh-boy tag would stick. He did not get people. I did a blog on Greenwich – all the time now just talking up the change in mood, trying to use it to stir activism and undermine the Tories' confidence. Good response on both fronts. In to Victoria Street to see Chris Lennie and Joe Irvin to meet the former Tory who wanted to come over. Indian guy, lifelong Tory, Guards etc., but as he spoke I worried a combination of 'Who he?' and 'Did he get turned down for honours?' might make it a bit of a non-event. We asked him a few toughish questions, made some suggestions of change to his letter of resignation (though he seemed a bit confused as to whether he was still a member), then agreed to wait for the right moment. He was a nice and interesting enough guy but he was too keen to say we had changed to be more like them which was not really what we wanted. Also when he suddenly talked about someone being 'the nigger in the woodpile' and only half-correcting himself, I thought this could go badly wrong. Still some of his arguments were interesting. Really did not like Cameron because he felt he had had the chance to move to the centre but he hadn't and One Nation Toryism was dead. He also seemed to like GB's resilience and what he saw as courage in the difficult decisions of a year or so ago.

Late lunch with Natascha at Waterstones. Told her all about the panic attacks and she had some interesting ideas re how to cope better when they came. She felt it was all about feeling trapped and conflicted. She felt I had to tell GB about the book and felt it probably would not be as bad as I feared. She was really fired up about the way TB was being treated, felt that even though she marched against the war he did what he believed was right and should not be treated so badly. Said she found herself defending him all the time. Home to have another go at Volume 1 intro. Not right yet. Bill having a go. Phil Webster in Ed's office reading. Fascinating stuff he felt. Also felt it would be fine-ish if we lost, pretty damaging if in a hung parliament situation. That was about right and really starting to worry me. The news dominated by the expenses MPs in court.

Friday 12 March

Did a blog saying what Adonis announced on high-speed rail [London to Birmingham] was more important than the expenses. Andrew a real star at the moment. Also another way of showing we did policy and they didn't. He had apparently trounced Theresa Villiers [shadow Transport Secretary] in a debate recently. Spent the morning sorting medical problems. First experience of Park End surgery post-Bostock retirement. Dr Stewart, who was Michael Foot's GP so we had a nice chat about him. I had traipsed round the Royal Free yesterday trying to find out how to get a date for my polypectomy. Ended up being put through by phone to another hospital and told I was in the system. Lots of people saying I should go private. My other concern was recovery time. I was starting to feel a bit of mild-level panic and anxiety all the time. Didn't discuss that with Dr S but later, after a trip to the chemist to get a mass of nose-related drugs, including drops apparently so strong you could only take for five days, spoke to Sturgeon.

He felt Marr had been a panic attack inspired by anger and fear about what I might do. He thought the others fitted the pattern. Said it was all about being conflicted inside re big decisions being driven by others. I felt trapped by it all. So Natascha not far wrong. Good to talk to him. He felt I needed to decide what was right for me, and do it. That it was hugely flattering to be told they could not win without me and that fed the addict in me. But was it true and was it good for me? When we take our hand out of a bucket of water the water is still there without us… We are all dispensable. He could tell I was a bit worried. Got the pills and headed off to Sheffield party fundraiser. Feeling a big edgy all the way. Even getting occasional motorway sign and lorry lettering panic moments, as I had when I had my breakdown, seeing certain words and letters and them provoking weird reactions.

Checked in to the hotel. Feeling wired. Met by Dick Caborn and over to St Mary's centre for a Q&A. Graeme and Jamie [brother and nephew] arrived. I had a couple of bad moments but managed to hold it together. Did *Sheffield Star*. Book signing went really well. Felt good I had got through it and I think fired people up a bit. Two young women there doing their dissertations on me. No really tough questions but getting more edgy. Told Dick I had been getting panic attacks. Typical Dick, he said 'You were great kid, they love you up here.' And the dinner was indeed as friendly as could be but I had another bad one, right in the middle of my speech, so that my mind just went to jelly, I felt dry of mouth and empty chested. I stopped, said I had asthma and asked for water. They were all really understanding but I think some knew.

Phil Townsend and his brother were right in front of me, as was Graeme, and they looked worried. I felt like my lips were white. A few mini aftershocks after I got going again but I felt odd and probably spoke less than usual. Same old message – we can win. Them v us, social networking, record, policy, attack and it went down well. But I was getting more and more worried. Texted Sturgeon. He suggested diazepam before a speech until the new drug – which apparently upped anxiousness before calming it after five days – kicked in. Thankfully I had them with me because I had taken them in my washbag for Kuwait. It was a nice evening, full of nice people, half a dozen MPs including Blunkett and some of his family, loads of laughter, books raised four figures for them, great auction. But I was clearly panicking about panicking now and making it happen. Kept saying 'Not '86' to myself. But it was worrying. I could not possibly do a campaign-fronting job like this. Checked out and got to Mum's after 12. Up chatting till late which would not help the exhaustion.

Saturday 13 March

Felt a bit banjaxed after the shock of yesterday. I was becoming more worried about it. Dick called and felt it had all gone well. Breakfast with Mum, who was still in good nick despite needing a couple of operations on her foot, then off to Manchester. I was feeling wired the whole way and still was having too many little edgy moments for comfort. Calum and I went to Caffè Nero and had a good chat about stuff. He had asked to see me about something personal and it turned out it was about him seeing a thirty-year-old woman called Clare who ran a bar. I was rather pleased after all the things I thought it might be. Off to Burnley and had lunch with a very nervous Barry Kilby et al. Poor game and though we were not the worst team we lost 2–1 so all very disappointing at the end.

I had not really got into it. A combination of the nasal problems and the nervous stuff was making it all a bit grim. I was not really there a lot of the time, even when we scored. And when I did an interview pre-match with Trusupporter.com – again perfectly friendly – I was feeling on edge. Going into the boardroom at one point I also felt some bad breakdown déjà vu moments. Latched on to people like Barry and Fletch and felt OK after a bit. But not right. Calum came up for a drink while I did my AOL column. Didn't want to tell him I was feeling bad but I think he sensed. Not heard from Rory but at least I knew he had arrived in S Africa.

Off to Manchester and the fundraiser for Lucy Powell [Manchester Withington candidate]. Calum helped with the stall and it was another four figures out of the books. Taking a pill really helped and I was on good form. Fantastic reception at the end. Lucy was thinking she could win. Good atmosphere. Talia Akhtar, the student who had been at Burnley, was there and I did a big thing about her line on the need constantly to give her friends and family a reason to vote Labour. Stayed to about half ten and got back to watch us on *Match of the Day*. The general sense was growing that we were doomed to relegation.

Sunday 14 March

Got up at 6 and was home by before 10. The combination of the two drugs was making me a bit tired but I was at least not so edgy. The polls had widened again. I was sure the problems at the moment were all about the conflicts raging within between whether to help and whether not to, the feeling of service and duty v self. David S had been clear I should think of myself but it was not clear what that meant. Did a bit of work, then set out for PG's. He had agreed to give the house over for a longer than usual Peter M strategy group meeting. I sensed a bit of spikiness between Peter and DA in the way Peter talked of things that were not being done. Douglas was pointing out the lack of resources. I was pointing up lack of clarity in message about record, about us, about them, about the future. Things were not as fractious as the worst of '97 but there was too much talk and not enough committing to paper and to action.

There was a real need for energy and drive and it was a bit worrying this was the main group. I felt I was making a contribution but it was limited. Peter seemed to vary between disengagement and suppressed panic. He chaired it well though and at least by the end we had the outlines sorted though it needed to be fleshed out a lot more pretty soon. Our blessing was the sense that the Tories did not really appear to have their act together. There were all sorts of bad signs there. We pressed Ed M on the manifesto. To be fair the planned pledges were pretty good, both big-picture and detail. If anything there was too much to choose from within them. But at least they were detailed and substantial as well as big-message. The Tories were going for big picture. Ed M wanted to make 'national renewal' the key theme but it seemed a bit odd for a government that had been in power for so long. I tried to be upbeat and positive but I was neither there nor not. I was saying OK things and had some decent ideas. But I was not motoring as before. We were there three hours and a lot of it was detail I used to do and now felt these guys should have sorted ages ago.

After they had all left, and PG had gone to church, Peter M stayed back for a chat with me and Gail. He said so much depended on GB rising to the mark and Cameron falling away and he felt neither would happen. He was very down on Sarah, felt she was part of the Whelan–Balls side of things. Also that the candidates issue was going to become a big problem for us, as second-rate union people were put in there. The Tories were quite successfully promoting the idea of Whelan and Unite as our Ashcroft and with the British Airways strike looming it was going to be tough politically for GB. I wonder when the first time was I warned him about Whelan.

Told Gail about recent panic attacks and asked her if there was any option but immediate post-election publication. She was sympathetic but actually felt the problem was obvious. She said she did not know how I was able to keep all these balls in the air, and how I was able to help him so much when I knew so much about how he had tried to hinder us. Home for dinner then watched Cameron on *Tonight with Trevor McDonald*. It was a total blowjob on one level. But I felt it was not that good for him because it underlined his focus on process and presentation. He did come over OK in many ways but the posh-boy thing was pretty strong.

Monday 15 March

Blogged on the Street Child World Cup. Rory had done a terrific blog about the SA team. Sadly they got hammered in their first game. He was getting driven crazy by the bad organisation but seemed to be learning a lot. Out to Michael Foot's funeral. GB and Neil both spoke well. So did Peter Jones his mate from Plymouth Argyle and Tom Foot, Paul's son. Bruce Kent had a bit of a dig re nukes at GB which was out of place. Neil's was probably the best. He really got him and when I said so Neil said it meant a lot. He was pretty upset. Nice event though. Another pill to see me through. Nice chat with CB who came with Mary Wilson [widow of Harold, former PM]. She was a lot friendlier than usual and we chatted away a bit more like old times. Then when I mentioned I had been in Kuwait working on TB's project she looked strained again.

Not as many there as I expected, mainly I guess because it was ticket only. A screen outside and a few media. Lovely sunny day. Actually quite a celebratory event. Peter Hain and Ed M the only Cabinet ministers apart from GB. [Michael] Meacher [former Labour minister] I saw being sent to the overflow which was a bit embarrassing. Had a good chat with Dennis Skinner. 'Glad you're back, kid,' he said. 'I'm not as back as that,' I said. 'Owt's better than nowt,' he said. Lots of hanging about chatting. Bill Hagerty and I with the usual joke re why aren't you working on the book? Off to Keats House for the do, nice enough too, then home to do a bit of work. News did not even cover the funeral. Becks out of the World Cup. Kate Winslet marriage break-up.

Tuesday 16 March

A day late did a blog on why the Piers interview worked for GB but Trevor McD did not really work for DC. One challenged a perceived weakness – lack of humanity. The other underlined it – all about process and presentation. Polls moving back though. I had suggested to Ed and Gail a postponement of the first full volume. I was really worried now it would land as GB was still PM, possibly in a hung parliament. PG was adamant there was no way we were going to win and he was not remotely convinced there would be a hung parliament. Ed was clear too that in pure publishing terms it was a bit of a disaster. The GB dichotomy was pretty stark today. Two hours on proofs of Vol. 1, worrying what would be bad for him. Then in to see Peter M for another planning meeting – another spike up with DA who seemed to be getting quite pressured. David Muir had asked me to do debate prep on 28 March and I said it was the Blackburn game. He virtually begged me to do it. PG later told him to lay off it a bit. He came back with different dates.

I must be a bit of a nightmare for them at the moment. Peter M looking a bit tired and worrying lots of necessary preparation had not been done. Through to see GB. We were sure Cameron would do Unite and Whelan. GB was pretty defensive about it all. Kept saying 'Is this what politics has become?' Also that he did not want to answer directly when he last saw or spoke to him. I gave him a form of words but when he said 'I shouldn't have to answer when I last saw CW, when I last saw Alastair Campbell.' I did a mock table thump, said do not dare put us in the same bracket. I was there for two hours and we just went round in circles. I said to Bruce had it been TB we'd have wrapped it up in twenty minutes. I gave him one good line 'I am a member of Unite… The Bullingdon wouldn't have me.' We groped our way to a position of saying they were politicising while we were trying to resolve but it was not easy. All because he could not wean off people like Whelan. Alistair D also chasing me to see the Budget. Chatting to Alex re Sport Industry Awards to work out who would present the lifetime achievement award to him.

Wednesday 17 March

Working on proofs then into TB's office to interview a couple of candidates for the Kuwait comms director job. One strong, one less so. Chatted a bit to Matthew Doyle on what he might do in the campaign then home to wait for Syd and Chris Boffey. Nice to see them both. All the parts of the breakdown around though. Out with Syd to Dover Street wine bar for a PRs event I was doing. Verity Harding, Facebook friend who wanted books signed, came in. It turned out she was Vince Cable's press officer. Said she hoped we won because she hated the Tories. Another pill to get through the speech.

Mix of PR analysis and current politics. Colin Port, Avon chief constable, slagging off Yates of the Yard. Good crowd and got through fine. Chris Pharo of *The Sun* saying that the paper was worrying about their decision to back DC. Whelan did a one-on-one with Robinson. What a tit. Syd had a skinful but great to see him. He was strongly urging me to get out for good and let them get on with it. Phil Webster's view of the diaries – fascinating. Not sure how much *Times* would pay. My worry was more the hypocrisy of being in there by day and doing the book by night. Ed said my loyalty to Labour cost me a fortune.

Thursday 18 March

Media monitoring service had a good account of the *Times* story on [former Tory Cabinet minister Oliver] Letwin's meeting with candidates which appeared to leave them totally confused about what they were meant to be campaigning on. He talked of a policy pyramid with one slogan, three themes and six main promises. There were plenty of signs of confusion and I blogged on their failure to have sorted clarity, but there is no doubt the polls were closing again. Had a chat with PG who felt that the public had looked more closely at the Tories and not much liked them but were now looking at us and turning away again. We had not really built on the momentum. The Tories were still lacking in confidence but they had got GB at Questions yesterday to admit he had had to write to Chilcot to qualify his evidence on spending and that had hit his confidence a bit.

Catherine McLeod came up to the house with a copy of the Budget speech. It was not going to be a big announcements job so needed to be much more about argument and the sense of a realistic plan going forward. She was desperate for me to go in and work on it with Alistair. 'You're like a comfort blanket for them all,' she said. She said that she did not know how I ever managed to keep all the different balls in the air. Alistair wanted this to be a different sort of Budget speech but was not totally sure how to make that happen. GB not really engaging in it at this stage. In to see Margaret McDonagh and Alan Barnard [campaigns strategist] who wanted me to meet an ex-MTV guy and a girl called Jo who ran Sarah's charity. We were trying to get them to build networks to get a proper social media operation, in particular the edgy stuff.

Margaret was up for helping Labour of course but always reminded me I had helped keep GB in place when we could and should have got rid of him. Also was appalled at the candidates situation and all the useless old Labour lot being put in by the Whelan/Unite operation. She said it was shameful and all down to GB. Alistair's driver collected me and took me in for meeting with AD, Bradders, Mario and Steve, AD's spads, and Catherine. I hadn't really had time to read it properly but was able to give a few half-decent ideas e.g. maybe put announcements at top, also to have an argument that goes back to '97 and frame the whole thing around choices then, choices at time of crisis, choices now. AD his usual fairly relaxed self. Showed me a cutting of the North Korean Finance Minister who had been executed for missing his targets etc. Also re GB not really being interested 'nobody could accuse him of being overly interfering in this one'. He said he was not even aware that he had looked at the speech yet.

The structure was very same old, same old, and I suggested changing it if possible. Borrowing figures better than expected. Alistair seemed resigned to it being a tough speech to deliver. He did not want it to be too long. Equally it could not be shorter than forty to fifty minutes. He felt that there were some OK big stories to tell. He was resisting our efforts to persuade him that he could be more political than usual. He had to get down the sense of the choice. The Tories would go big on the deficit but we had to go on the sense of there being a realistic plan to take things forward. David Bradshaw and I had a chat. He said he sensed from some of the interviews I had done recently that I was not in great shape. He felt I really had to take care of myself. I know what you're like, he said. You will resist and resist but you'll be torn and eventually you'll go in and they will bleed you dry. He said he liked working with Alistair because he was straight and such a nice guy but he did not really want to get too involved. PG felt I had to start saying No more often so they knew I could not be there all the time and at their beck and call.

I missed the Peter M meeting because I wanted to get home and work through the proofs. Did some French with Grace then out to Chelsea for the LLR do at the temporary antiques fair set-up in 'Earl Cadogan's backyard' [vast estate]. [Charles] Cadogan was a classic old aristo. Nice enough to talk to and he and his wife full of praise for what I did for the charity. Introduced me to a couple, one of whom, though uber-posh, said she was 'a wog' because she was from Malta. Nice enough evening if you like that kind of thing. I spoke for ten, fifteen minutes on the charity and it went well. Jeffrey Archer did the auction which, considering how many rich people were there, ought to have raised more.

Friday 19 March

Mary Riddell was round first thing to do an interview for the Fabians' magazine. Not sure it was really worth the time as it was just the same old same old, but they had been very keen. She was pressing a fair bit on the role with GB and seemed to think he was a whole lot better since I had been in there. I pushed back in terms of taking any credit as the truth was I was not in there nearly as much as people thought and I was not really doing that much beyond PMQs and the debate rehearsals. And even on that I was not really doing the business. I did a blog on Hague following difficulties over Ashcroft and I was emphasising the differences between the two teams. They were so thin whereas we do have a fair few heavy-hitters. All another reason why the election ought not to be a foregone conclusion. PG felt it was all over whatever the recent polls were saying but part of that may have been because he was encouraging me to publish the book. I was still a bit edgy about that though the pills were kicking in a bit more.

I was due in at No. 10 from 1 till 4 for TV debate preparations. David

[Muir] and Justin said that GB was in a bit of a state because the BA strike appeared to be going ahead, added to which the RMT signalmen were voting for one too. He was in a rage when he came in, said there were people 'in our movement' determined to fuck us up, then raging at BA, saying they wanted the strike to cause us trouble and to break the union. These seemed to me to be conflicting points. It took him a while though to get into debate mode and gave an impression it was a bit of a waste of time. Bob Shrum was there to my surprise. Peter M had told me Bob was out of the equation but there he was and he was still clearly someone with access and maybe influence. GB seemed distracted and a bit disengaged though, especially at the start. He got a lot better a bit later on, but it was not brilliant. He also had this annoying habit of focusing on things he just could not affect. For example he was still complaining about the order of the debates. 'How have we allowed "Broken Britain" to be the first one?' I said it won't be broken Britain unless you let it be.

Theo had done a lot of work and was a good Clegg. I was kind of playing at it and was not terribly good as Cameron, other than in a getting on his nerves kind of way. We did health, education and crime, and he was OK on policy but his demeanour not great, especially when we did the post-mortem bit. Everyone – especially Bob – was trying to tell him he had done well, but he was just sitting with a face like thunder, occasionally erupting to have a pop at the union or the airline. He allowed stuff really to get to him and from then on he was distracted. Eventually said he could not spend any more time on it and had to sort out the strike. We hung around for half an hour or so but eventually David said I might as well go.

I took the chance to tell David both about the diaries and about the medical issue and the reason why I was not wanting to get drawn in even more. He was very nice about it, said maybe we could just treat the debates and PMQs as discreet projects and not get too drawn elsewhere. But of course Peter was desperate for me to do more, as were Marianna and Carol L. I was not sure how much we were getting from the debate rehearsals but David was really keen I do more. The diary proofs were waking me in the night.

Saturday 20 March

Calum in a bit of a state re an essay so he decided he couldn't go to the Wigan match. I wasn't that keen to go on my own but I had the tickets for the match and the train so set off. Peter had sent me overnight a Cameron speech on vested interests, on which I tweeted a couple of times but I decided to have a couple of days off the blog front. There was something about spending too much time with GB that drained me of political energy.

Sally [Morgan] had been on a couple of times in the last few days worried about some *Dispatches* collaboration with the *Sunday Times* about ministers offering to influence policy for cash. She was in a bit of a state but it sounded like she was not in deep whereas it later emerged Steve Byers might be. Pat H and Geoff Hoon also potentially in trouble. I was working my way through the proofs and getting there steadily. I just couldn't work out how much of a problem the diaries would be.

Got to Wigan and there was a lot of police around, partly because of the match but also because of an English Defence League march in Bolton which was expected to be trouble and there were cops at all nearby stations. The match was not at all bad for what till the ninety-second minute was 0–0. Then we lost in injury time. Gutting. I whacked out my AOL blog as I walked to the station. I'd met Scott Minto [former player turned Sky pundit] on the way to the game and met him again on the train back so spent most of the journey talking to him. Really nice guy. Knew his stuff. He reckoned we were going to lose the election and that Burnley were going down, so it could be a pretty grim week in May. I did a bit of work for Alistair on the Budget, trying to come up with decent phrases. Quite liked 'crisis would have been calamity' for the Tories, and 'calm after the storm' for us.

Sunday 21 March

I finally finished the proofs. Still conflicted about the whole thing but I arranged to deliver tomorrow. I did a piece for the Burnley v Rovers programme mainly on the Wigan fallout. Watched United beat Liverpool whilst revising Burnley info in advance of tonight's ESPN *Talk of the Terrace* show. Was due to be on with Richard Hughes [player] of Portsmouth and the lead singer of Reef. Learning loads of stuff I had known and forgotten many times. ESPN OK though I took a pill again to keep my nerves in check. The programme was pretty good. Whizzed by. I did pretty well in the quiz. Got nine in a minute. A couple wrong I should have got but there we go. Being uber competitive.

Monday 22 March

Yesterday had been dominated by the *Dispatches* programme about politicians being entrapped by a fake firm asking for politicians to help them. Byers, Hoon and Hewitt the hardest hit, which would be bad all round but also bad on the Blairite front too. Peter M said that GB had been in a state about it all weekend and he was worried the reaction would just make it worse. It was pretty ghastly stuff. In for Peter M meeting with the usual lot plus the Saatchis team who had quite an interesting idea, worked up with Ben WP, using a cartoon family for a ninety-second film version of what was in the manifesto, plus longer films that could be read online. Ed M very worried about the idea of not having a traditional written version. David and Douglas worried that GB would not be comfortable with it. We agreed that GB would have to do a fairly traditional manifesto event speech then Harriet present this. It would also need celebs to do the voices for it. I quite liked the Saatchi team taking us through the script.

Then they showed us a new branding idea for sets etc., which was a rising sun above a variety of backdrops with different versions for each policy area. Peter M and PG liked it. Philip was looking really tired and I was a bit worried about him. I popped into Vic Street on the way to Random House. Douglas and Ed M were working on the pledges for the launch. It felt busy in there but Greg Cook [pollster] said things had moved backwards. He said GB's post-Chilcot clarification was damaging. Basically people were looking at the Tories and not liking them but then looking at us and liking us even less. It was not a good scene. To Random House to hand over the proofs to Joanna. Brief chat with Gail who was really worried that PG was overdoing it all. She felt he was getting too sucked into the campaign – he was certainly calling me a lot and was at a lot of the meetings I was at. She felt we were both addicted to campaigns, and addicted to thinking we could solve the problems, even though we knew it was not good for us.

Earlier I'd tried to have a proper chat with Peter about my own situation but he called Ben in and it became a mix of him complaining re GB – still dysfunctional, Douglas and Ed M – constantly whispering to each other, said Peter, Ed Balls – always getting into GB's ear and upsetting the advice of others that GB might be taking. He said the good news was that come the campaign we – he meant him, me, PG, Patrick, Ben and one or two others – would pretty much be able to run it whilst the GB lot did whatever they did on the road. He was a bit panic-stricken-looking when I said I was planning to be away for a week. Out in the evening to the Strand Palace for a session with fifteen Dutch government and other public sector comms people who were here for a two-day course. Nice enough bunch. Did my usual spiel then a very long Q&A. Still feeling the need for the diazepam when I was doing stuff like this which was annoying, and I had to be careful on the addiction front.

Tuesday 23 March

The news was dominated by the fallout from Byers, Hoon, Hewitt who had now been suspended from the PLP, the programme having been seen last night. I didn't see it but by all accounts for once the reality was worse than the hype. I alluded to it at the top of my blog but focused on Obama getting his healthcare bill finally through and the importance of him being a success for politics as a whole. Sally M called in a bit of a state to say that Nick Brown and Ray Collins wanted to suspend her too. She said she could not cope with that on any level. She had not been in the same boat as Byers at all. She had said on air there was a ministerial code to adhere to. I sent an email to Sue, DM, Peter, PG and Chris Lennie to say if Sally was suspended I would not do anything more for the campaign. Sue came back straight away and said she was not being suspended and it was never contemplated. I bet it was. There was a fair bit of dumping on TB over the fact it was Byers, Hoon, Hewitt who were in the frame. Sally called very grateful later.

I went in for 5 for a PMQs meeting, largely about the sleaze stuff. GB seemed quite calm about it all but it was grim stuff. He had watched the programme himself, was shocked at Byers's stupidity but worse than anything perhaps was Hoon saying he could use the NATO position he had to make money. We did a bit on the economy then went up to the study to do debate prep. Theo getting better and better as Clegg. As Douglas pointed out I was just too general. Needed more detail and really tough questions. Douglas was feeding me some good lines but I felt I was not really in the zone. GB's tone getting better all the time though. We did a half-hour on the economy and then new politics, which Nick and I took to integrity, Chilcot, on/off election, 10p rate etc. He was unsure whether to engage or brush off. Also had a discussion about whether to say 'I know you don't like me' but it seemed quite odd. We were at it two hours or so and I think he was getting better but not sure by how much. The problem was a psychological one. He didn't really have the right mix of light and shade. Douglas was pretty frank with him. GB took some but not all of it. Douglas made a joke about racing to see whether my next book came before his.

Wednesday 24 March

Budget day and I was missing it. Did a blog re AD v DC and Osborne re credibility plus embedding Cameron's extraordinary interview with *Gay Times* when he was all over the shop, bumbling and stumbling. Finished acknowledgements then off to Euston. The driver was from Nigeria, been living here ten years. Said he really missed seeing me on the scene, thought I had been brilliant and would make a good strong PM. I said no, I could not do the top job, but he came back at me and was insistent I had made a lot of things happen and I had to get back in there. If you were there it would all change quickly, he said. Really warm guy and was confident we could still win but he said it needed me there now.

Peter M called re the meeting on Friday and who should be at it. We were looking to get some outsiders in for the story development side of the diary operation. GB called re PMQS. Wanted some new lines on Ashcroft. TB texted pissed off re Neil blaming him for the sleaze stuff. There was definitely an attempt to make this a Blair thing though as TB pointed out Hoon tried to get rid of him too, not just GB. The npower event [Climate Cops SOS] I was doing today, kids presenting ideas to save the world, was in its own way pretty inspiring. The kids were really into it and the DVD showing their journey was moving at times. They had all developed a lot as characters and on the issues too. I was always clear Selby [High School, Yorkshire] was the best, both their idea – books for primary schools to teach them about the environment – but also the execution. It was all a really nice event. Did a pretty good and hopefully quite uplifting speech about how they had all made a difference and urging them never to lose the idealism and the belief they could make a difference.

Made the 3 p.m. train and caught up with the Budget. AD seemed to have done OK. PG felt DC did OK too, full-on energy and brio. The general sense though seemed to be that Alistair played a tough hand well. Calum back, out for dinner for PG's birthday at Locatelli restaurant. Grace very excited to see Chris Martin and Gwyneth Paltrow [singer and actress, husband and wife] two tables away. PG going on and on about the election and I just could not get into it. He said Peter was really worried about me not being there, felt he could not do it unless I was. PG and Gail both felt I had to stay away for the week and not waver. PG was so two-minded about it. Always saying I should resist. But always wanting me more not less involved in practice. Gail was worried he was getting way too involved. The *Sun*/YouGov poll had the lead down to two. PG still felt the Tories were nearer ten ahead but it was surely there to fight for. But I could not get the fight in me going.

Thursday 25 March

AD did OK considering. He didn't do *Today* programme so Osborne got a bit of a free hit apparently but was also not that good. I did a blog on the need to see more of Alistair and Peter M in the campaign. Also Tories had taken on M and C Saatchi in addition to Euro RSCG so did a bit on that too. David Muir pressing me to do the Sunday debate with GB. Decided to hold firm. To Paddington to collect Rory, back from SA. PG convinced I should go for a TV show. Some pressing me re the FA. Not sure myself. I needed sense of project back. I think it had to be away from politics. Dinner at Broadway, where I was speaking to around twenty HR people, including next to me a very nice woman who ran Moto service stations.

Did a leadership speech which went down fine. Needed another pill to settle though. Had to watch I didn't get addicted to these damn things. Was on pretty good form though and there was no doubt the worries re Cameron were getting out there. Business people just didn't rate him.

Friday 26 March

To 70 Whitehall for a brainstorm on strategy and story development. Nobody really believed the polls. We all felt GB was still a problem. All felt AD an asset – GB was today virtually confirming him as post-election Chancellor. All felt that though online was important, TV still the most important outlet. All felt we were sharpening attack but it was still not good enough. Greg [Cook] stated the argument we had made to GB a while back – that this was the first post-crisis election not the Labour fourth-term election. Everything had to be posed as recovery v risk. They would pose it as time for change and five more years of Brown. Colin Byrne [public relations businessman] gave a very gloomy assessment. All felt apart from Peter we had few genuinely out-there communicators. Milibands not high-profile or political enough. DA too much politician. GB energy a real factor and we had to work at it the whole time.

Peter said he found the discussion priceless but that was really just because he was not used to this kind of frank and open dialogue from which at least some ideas flowed. He wanted to repeat. I was meanwhile busy trying to get e.g. Fergie, Denise Lewis, Clive Tyldesley, for Ben WP's 90-second manifesto animation idea. I asked Natascha and she said yes without hesitation. Chatted with Peter afterwards. He felt GB was capable of being better. Had amazing resilience. Out to St Albans with Rory for a school sports trip fundraiser. [Sir] Ian McGeechan [former rugby player, coach], then me, then Rory Bremner who was achingly funny. Said he was slightly dreading Tories in power because they had so few characters compared with us. Pretty Tory audience but again very little enthusiasm for Cameron. I played it pretty much totally for laughs with a bit of a sports message. Nice to see Ian again. Bremner quite serious re politics and engagement but totally hilarious on stage.

Saturday 27 March

Quite an important day with GB launching the pledges. Getting a fair bit of advance billing. Good *Guardian* interview. Did a blog on their significance and dealing with the idea of them being too vague. Also did a look back at some of the past pledges and speculated on the Tory problems in getting a pledge card together. Tweeted later re Cameron saying 'Forty days and forty nights to go.' Counting to forty is not an economic policy. Nice having all the family home. Rory out on the bike after regaling with some of Bremner's stories. I watched GB doing the pledges. He looked better than for ages and was confident. Young candidates looking good. Gloria De Piero alongside him. Alistair arrived and he, Maggie, son Calum, Catherine and three or four others piled in to the study where we did debate rehearsal with Michael Sheehan. AD got into it and improved as we went. We told Sheehan he could be pretty frank and he was. He said for example that from what he had seen he felt Osborne was better than Cameron. He had seen AD clips too and felt his best asset was that he seemed to think on his feet.

Once we got under way – I was Osborne and one of AD's advisors played a rather unconvincing Clegg – Sheehan made some very good observations about Alistair's style and body language. He tended to slump. His hands were out too wide. He backed away physically when I got aggressive. On content, he was strong, though I was pushing hard on the points I thought Osborne would go for – deficit, GB, deceit, lacking in energy. Catherine and Maggie were a bit like a double act with him. He needed a bit more content and rebuttal work but he did seem to appreciate the stuff Sheehan was telling him. We all assumed Osborne would soon do a reversal of the planned National Insurance contributions rise, and we had a bit of a discussion about how to deal with that. AD a mix of calm and nervy. Sheehan asked him if I had done content-wise what they would expect Osborne to do and he said it was pretty spot on. 'Even I was convinced at times,' he said. He said GB had told him he felt I sometimes enjoyed tearing into him too hard! Home for early night pre clocks going forward meaning I would have to be up at half five on the body clock to head off for the Burnley–Blackburn game tomorrow.

Sunday 28 March

Off just after half six. Got there fairly early. Helicopters hovering. Rovers fans being taken in convoys under police escort and all in two hours before kick-off. Crazy stuff. Sadly the game didn't live up to the hype. We were poor and even though their goal came from a dive that led to a penalty, we never really looked like scoring. Blackburn fans loving it. 'We're having a party when Burnley go down.' All a bit depressing. Just not good enough. Left on the whistle and so missed all the trouble that kicked off at the end.* Barry had said before the match that we might qualify for the Fair Play entry to Europe. Not going to happen. FA inquiry etc. Pretty

* Blackburn fans ripped out seats, and objects were thrown at the referee and some players as trouble flared between rival supporters.

grim day. Texted David to say maybe I should have stayed for the Sheehan session with GB. Dick Caborn and Adam Ingram both called having been stung a bit by the *Sunday Times–Dispatches* team. Not as bad as the others but Adam sounded worried about it and Dick wanted to go on the rampage in the House tomorrow.

Monday 29 March

Sue Macmillan [head of digital] asked me to do a blog on the idea members of the public could send in ad ideas that would go up on digital billboards in London and Manchester over Easter. Tories doing another one, this time pictures of GB with slogans on bad stuff followed by vote for me. E.g. 'I doubled the national debt – vote for me.' They bottled in that they used an OK picture of him. Sent a few last-minute lines through to Catherine pre the Chancellors' debate. AD really a lot more nervous about it but had definitely taken on some of the stuff from the weekend. Pissed off I was missing it for the Pudsey fundraiser but there you go. To Covent Garden for a meeting with Trevor Beattie, Andrew McGuinness [Beattie's business partner], Margaret McD and Alan Barnard. Trying to work out ways they could feed in thoughts and ideas, officially or unofficially. They too felt the Budget had gone OK for us and that the Tories were really vulnerable.

I was slightly worried about the determination to single out Osborne as the weak link as it suggested Cameron was strong. Osborne may not be popular but it was a general lack of strategy that was the problem and Cameron had not moved to the right place. He bounced around too much so there was no coherence. That was one of the themes of TB's speech for tomorrow. He had worked on it over the last few days and sent it to Peter and me to work on it. He did not want to go too heavy on DC personally but he had a good analysis on the vacuous nature of Time for a Change as a slogan, pointing out the totally different approach we took in opposition. Also on the way the Tories were pointing in so many different directions depending on what day or what policy it was. It would definitely make a bit of a splash. He was nervous about it. Really didn't like being in the UK and on our scene. He now felt it was winnable but we had to be more open and straightforward about plans, not hide away on the big questions. Also that if it was trad Tory v trad Labour there was only one winner. There would be the usual sneering tomorrow but the sheer volume of bids I was getting – and turning down – showed he still had the star quality.

I watched Osborne's press conference in which he announced a partial reversal of our planned national insurance rise. Done on debate day exactly as we predicted. He looked and sounded quite confident but he was certainly not getting a clean hit on it. AD and Cable were out with quite good attacks on it. I found it hard to think they wouldn't win but they were not where we were back in '97. Nowhere near, on any level. I asked David if we were going back in the polls and he confirmed we were. The Budget had gone down better with the commentariat than the public. We had improved for a while but strikes, Whelan, Unite, Hoon, Byers etc. had set us back and taken up too much of the oxygen. He seemed quite down again. I set off for Pudsey with Rayan. Reading up debate stuff. Cameron quite vulnerable on a lot of his lines. We needed to get GB into a more relaxed and reassured and reassuring place. He was definitely getting better tonally but the careworn snappy GB was never far away.

Jamie Hanley [Labour candidate] fundraiser at Oulton Hall [hotel]. He seemed a bright guy. Rachel Reeves from safer next-door seat. John Guthrie, owner of Conaglen estate, there to check me out. Nice chat, though he admitted he was out of his usual political zone. A woman called Patricia who had bought dinner with me in an auction thinking it was one-on-one! Mood OK. Fiona texted to say she thought Cable won the debate. AD did OK, Osborne poor. David felt it showed Sheehan was right – you needed good demeanour, one or two memorable lines, clarity, a clash but above all strategic points taken through. Cable played for humour and clearly won the audience. But AD was reckoned to have beaten GO. I did my usual speech with quite a lot on social networking. John Middleton from *Emmerdale* stayed on to do the auction which meant I could leave fairly early. Home by 1.

Tuesday 30 March

I did a few final comments on TB's speech at Trimdon [County Durham]. He wanted to say DC had moved on equality and gay rights so I got that taken out given his uncertainty on equality legislation in the Martin Popplewell interview for *Gay Times*, which had had a fair bit of play. It was a strong and well-crafted argument though. I did a blog trailing some of the themes and hitting my stuck button that the Tories have not done strategy. They have not done what we did. TB back in the fray was going to get a fair bit of attention. Amazing tan, even deeper than the last time I saw him. Good speech, went down well though the sneerers and commenters got in pretty quick. I chatted with Brendan Foster about various things. He felt we were back in the game. Felt too that TB back in the picture supportive of GB was a good thing.

In to No. 10 and up to the study for a session with GB, DA, David Muir and Stuart Hudson [advisor]. We did a bit of a post-mortem on the Chancellors' debate. The Lib Dems were going to be quite a problem. They could say what they liked without much pressure. They were also going to benefit just by being seen to be as significant as the other two. DA was trying to get GB to cut down on relying too heavily on instant rebuttal through facts. He had to use argument. Empathy, principle, policy, attack. GB's problem was that he always wanted to go straight to the factual rebuttal and the denial of any charge against him. Rather than stand at lecterns and do a debate, we fired questions at him more or less randomly. Sheehan had said to David whatever you do, do not let him learn any more facts. He was getting better but we needed more empathy and humour. He also needed to avoid the default position to a straight whack at Cameron or getting too grumpy and dour.

David said it was now all about building memory muscle. He felt we were improving. DA pretty down on GB though. *FT* had a story gunning for Ed M re the manifesto which clearly unsettled him.* They all still spent too much time worrying about positioning and the papers. General view on the debate was Cable, AD, Osborne. Interesting how GB and his team only really concentrated on him. He didn't even mention TB. Did not really talk about Alistair other than in relation to how it affected him. We went at it for an hour or so. We agreed he should call Cameron 'David'. Then GB went off on one again about Murdoch, Coulson, phone-hacking, Tory policy on their issues. He said there were now twenty people who had been told their phones had been hacked into. Gordon Taylor and Max Clifford settled. Others thinking about not settling, including David Davies.

Told GB re my texts from Rebekah this morning e.g. 'Nice to see you have TB campaigning for Old Labour.' I replied it must be worrying that Labour's rise followed the *Sun* switch against us. 'We have not even begun,' she said. Calm down for heaven's sake. GB felt there were three big scandals there waiting to be done. The *New York Times* were over working on it. Why could we not get British papers into it? He was raging about it now, saying he had had his own bank, building society, medical records broken into. There was systematic corruption. Coulson was at the heart of it. Murdoch's policy was driving the Tory policy and we could not get a debate about it going. Really steamed up about it. Also claimed to have evidence about four phone taps. Wanted me to get going on it. Not sure how.

I set off to Brentwood Resource Centre to open the new mental health facility there. Really nice set-up and good people. Did a little speech again with the help of a pill. Went down well. Book signing then off to the main Essex Book Festival event. Really good turnout. Did a few stories, talked about the novels then did a reading from both. Q&A really friendly. There

* The *Financial Times* reported that grassroots Labour Party members were urging the leadership to break its promise that there would be no uncosted pledges in the manifesto.

was a really nice atmosphere and the local books guy flogged a fair few books. Rayan said he loved both events, said he had never seen anyone who could attract warmth like I did and I really had to stand for Parliament. He never gives up, I'll give him that.

Wednesday 31 March

I went in for a meeting with Peter M, Douglas, David Muir, Ben, Justin, Sue, Marianna. It was a bit flat, certainly didn't feel like we were a few days from the campaign. All a bit bitty and without real clarity on message. Douglas seemed to get a bit defensive whenever I raised questions about what the main messages were – on us, them, the record, the future. Also I was worried looking at the grid that it would be overwhelmed by stronger firepower from the Tories. Sue Nye was trying to get sign-off on detail but it wasn't easy. I had a little chat with Peter at the end. He was disappointed I was going away and asked me to have a word with the family about coming back early. He said he worried GB just wouldn't be able to raise his game as he needed to. I pottered around for a bit then headed to LLR to see Kate White to discuss the 50th anniversary plans for 17 March. It meant missing the Sunderland game but we were probably going to be down anyway. I felt I was not doing enough for the charity at the moment. I was a bit flat all round. To Waterloo for a drink with Tim Kerr-Dineen and Keith Wenham [old university friends]. Nice to see them both and just reminisce a bit.

Thursday 1 April

The Tories had done a good job getting up a load of business names to support them on NICs. AD and Peter were due to do a press conference anyway but this really stole the march on them. They did OK but Peter should probably not have said the businessmen had fallen for a deception. I got the sense the Tories had loads of stuff like this lined up. It was a good hit though they were not getting a totally free ride on it. They had gone from deficit to tax cuts as the priority and we ought to be able to hurt them on that. Lunch with Moir Lockhead at the Camden Brasserie. Singing Andrew A's praises as ever. He seemed to think we were right back in it and that maybe a hung parliament was on or even a Labour win. We set off for Manchester in two cars – F and G, C and I – stopping off on the way to Scotland. It took more than six hours. Traffic jams, accidents, air ambulances, the lot. Dinner at some pub in Tatton [Cheshire] and then to the flat. Going into my usual fucking pre-holiday gloom, worsened by the conflict in myself about whether I should be going at all.

Friday 2 April

Off at half six to Scotland. F to Glasgow airport to collect Rory and his mates, so Calum and I got to Conaglen first. The scenery was more beautiful than ever on the last hour or so. Stopped at the Green Welly Stop [Crianlarich] where some guy came up and said I should get my pipes out to make some money. Small world – later he saw Charles Kennedy and told him the conversation we had verbatim – with a bit of anti-me thrown in. The first wave of visitors arriving – Peter Chittick and Carolyn Fairbairn [friends] plus three, Rory plus two, and all four Mills-Jowells. Plus Charles and Sarah K for dinner. The staff told Charles we were the nicest people who stayed there which was nice. He seemed on good form and so did she. Still no keener on Clegg. Even less keen on Cable who he felt talked a lot of nonsense a lot of the time and who was dreadfully right-wing on a lot of things. 'Ah but he is a saint,' said Sarah.

She was clearly desperate for us to win and she still felt it was doable. He was not so sure. He felt it would tip one way at the end and he felt it likeliest that it would tip to the Tories. Good laugh re – one year after I raised it with him – his efforts to get on to Twitter etc. He was on it but yet to send a tweet. Nice enough evening. Sarah felt I should be doing more to help GB. The NICs thing was really hurting us. The story was developed to Labour falling out with business which was not great. Charles a lot more relaxed, still off the booze, certainly not drinking to dangerous levels. He looked a lot healthier. We went for a walk so he could have a fag and I asked if it was under control. He said most of the time yes. Sometimes he would have one and then know from the first moment that he wouldn't stop till he fell asleep drunk. Other times like today he could go the whole day without even thinking about it. He asked when I knew I had a problem? I said when I asked people that kind of question. I said my golden rule question was do you think it is affecting your work, your health or your relationships? He nodded a bit knowingly at that one.

Saturday 3 April

Unbelievably cocky *Guardian* interview with Osborne. Blogged on it, suggesting a long way to go and NICs plan might not look too great later in the campaign. We went out for a long walk. Chatting to Tessa who in her gut felt we would lose, felt that ultimately people would not want GB back as PM. We all knew Cameron was not TB but he was not [Michael] Howard either. She felt there was real cruelty in the way TB was now portrayed. She felt her role should be to help younger MPs make sure New Labour survived and prospered. But it was hard to see how things would pan out well in the next parliament. David on great form, not least because he felt this time last year there a serious possibility he would end up in the clink.

Tristram Hunt [historian, broadcaster] selected from an imposed shortlist of three for Stoke-on-Trent Central. Local chair saying he might stand as an independent. All a bit messy. Tessa saying there will be more than that when people announce they are standing down next week. Big football day. United v Chelsea, bit of a disaster, losing 2–1. Then us v City. Total meltdown. 6–1. Three in the first seven minutes. I called Fletch who said he had tried to persuade Barry and Brendan a while back that they should admit they had made a mistake in appointing Laws and get him out and offer someone a million-quid bonus to keep us up.

I wasn't sleeping well. I was worrying about whether to go back. PG felt not. He said however the campaign was in poor shape and too much rested on Peter. The 'people's poster' idea had backfired because they chose such a bad one. Cameron as some popular TV character from a programme called *Ashes to Ashes*. Long chat with Peter who said GB had been in a rage about the business leaders but they did not have the capacity to fight back. They took ages to decide who went up and said what. Nice evening but still feeling very edgy and close to a big plunge if not careful. Nasty attack by Robert Harris in *The Guardian*. Did a blog on Osborne's cockiness. But they'd had a good week. News came later of a ten-point lead in the *Sunday Times*.

Sunday 4 April

Beautiful cold sunny day. Calum, Matthew and I went to church. Another bad night on the sleep front. PG saying on the one hand don't go back, on the other it was dire there. His view was we could only do so much because it wasn't our show. Greg and Karen [Nugent, friends] arrived yesterday when we were losing 5–0. Did a political blog based on PG and my notes to Peter re holding nerve and continuing to attack the economic incoherence of uncosted plans. Peter put out a very strong state-of-the-race memo. David Muir was not responding to my notes which was odd. The main thing was to show Cameron was making promises he could not fund and building that to economic risk. Talked to Tessa about the diaries. She felt it was OK provided context was clear. I was feeling anxious most of the time despite the medication. Went for a run but not motoring. Easter egg hunt earlier good laugh. Ditto swim in freezing river. Grace amazing the way she stayed in for ages.

Monday 5 April

Pouring with rain. Tess etc. off early, then the Chitticks, long walk in the wet afterwards. Cameron on marriage tax allowance saying 'the message matters more than the money'. PG texting to say it was all very flat. Peter Hyman had sent GB some words for Tuesday but it was not clear what GB was going to be saying yet. Peter M said he had some idea about announcing a major referendum on a whole set of issues after fifteen months and GB saying he would go if he lost. But it would look simply like he was saying have me for now and kick me out in a bit. It was about policy and direction. Peter said Ed M had looked really odd and ill at ease when he was out with David. They did not look close let alone a team. Douglas and David Muir were falling out a lot. All pretty crap. All reasons not to go back – and reasons to go back.

I spoke a couple of times to GB re PMQs. He had to get above Cameron somehow, not just go into rebuttal mode. He needed to start building the case at the despatch box about economic risk under the Tories. I suggested a first question from our side asking for a commitment not to take £6 billion out of the economy if re-elected. Use the answer to set up risk – 'Money out today, money at risk tomorrow. Money out today, jobs lost tomorrow. Money out today, growth at risk tomorrow.' Then to say of DC, 'To someone of his background – PR – I can see why he thinks message matters more than money. Let me tell him nothing matters more than the economy, nothing matters more than the jobs, living standards and public services people depend on and his plan to take 6bn out of the economy today would put those jobs, living standards and public services at risk tomorrow.' Even more though, GB needs energy and he needs to look like he really is up for a fight.

Nice enough day. Fiddled around with a piece *The Guardian* asked for, about what it is like when the campaign finally starts, which they liked and said would use on the front. I suppose that emphasised in a way I was half spectator half player. I was thinking back to pre-campaign launches before and how busy they were. If someone I had wanted in the campaign had gone away for a week, as I was, I would have been very pissed off, but Tessa said if I was there for the last three weeks that was a big commitment and more useful than the contribution of most. Peter was emailing a bit but she felt part of him would want to do it largely alone so he was clearly top dog. I was happy enough about that though had a lot of moments of feeling I ought to be doing more. Guilt kicking in.

PG was back from a week in Jordan, which he loved, and he was in the same position as me, feeling he had to help, rather than that he wanted to. Mind you Fiona felt Philip was still addicted whereas I had weaned myself off a bit. Talking of which I had done well staying right off the drink though I had got a bit worried re how much diazepam I was taking when feeling edgy. Aiming for a week of none. I was doing pretty well at controlling my addictions – drink broadly under control, work OK, politics kind of, though DS not so sure, erratic behaviour OK, but the one thing worrying me was the way these anxiety feelings were rising too often and I was just whacking a diazepam to calm me down. David Muir said GB was desperate to get some killer lines on DC, so I worked on that a bit. Exchanging notes and emails with PM and PG. Peter sounding OK but carrying a big part of the load himself. DM and Douglas not getting on great.

I spoke to Bruce G who was adamant I should not go back, that the short campaign was fine and also said not to worry about the book. But I did. Fiona felt just let it happen and don't do publicity. She felt the problems around *Maya*, when I got really agitato, were because I am never allowed to escape questions re all aspects of Labour politics. DS felt I sensed I was trapped and cornered into doing things I could happily do without.

Tuesday 6 April

Up to watch the election stuff kicking off. As I sat there, half watching the telly, half staring out at Ben Nevis, one of the reporters said I was in there somewhere helping plan it all. Lots of blather and then once GB went to the Palace and came back, DC jumped the gun to come out first and did a thing at County Hall with Parliament in the background. He looked to have lots of energy but he was quite negative in his message. GB came out after all the Cabinet lined up in the street. He was OK but a bit wooden. Emphasised the economy and the team. They all then set off to various places on the campaign trail and the media went into wall-to-wall mode. I did a blog on how Cameron was more negative than I expected, that it was all really about GB and five more years. He was starting to think about the last PMQs and later we had two long chats on the phone. He sounded down. He had definitely not got a psychological bounce by feeling the fight was now under way. Getting him up for the fight could be a problem. He was also far too quick to go into rebuttal fact mode when now was the time for big argument.

I said it was all about tone, getting our side fired up and showing he had a plan and all they could do was run Britain down. I said he also needed to keep emphasising the record and he needed to get going on them taking money out of the economy. But GB was sounding alarmingly defensive. I did a note saying he had to up energy and also the sense of this being all about the future. At one point he suddenly said 'Obama's on the line, I'll have to call you back,' which was quite a good big foot! GB was telling him he couldn't do the nukes conference [Washington nuclear security summit] next week. He called back later and said Obama had said 'Give them hell.'

PG called re groups. Not good. He said the dynamic was for the Tories.

They don't much like GB and the problem is they quite like DC, certainly more than we realise, and they can definitely see him in the job. They don't think the idea of Cameron as PM is ridiculous. David Muir was on saying there was no need for me to go back yet, that he would rather have me rested and short than grouchy and long. I was not getting that much of a rest though. The phone was steady rather than incessant. But I was thinking about it all the time and Tessa wanted to talk about it all the time.

Wednesday 7 April

Another GB call at breakfast re PMQs. Still defensive. None of us saw DC's first line of attack coming – not enough helicopters in Helmand. He was obviously trying to do trust again and avoid too much on the economy, even with NICs seeming to run in their favour. Also trying to present himself as capable and engaged on defence. Peter was doing quite a good job, if late, pulling together a response. Questions was not good though. GB was too defensive and once he got on to the economy the lines we had prepared sounded stagey and a bit out of context. I sent DM a note. He agreed GB had to get into a different mindset but said he was doing better on the road. Also GB had done a *GMTV* interview and had repeated 'deception' about the businesses but then didn't want to repeat it. I had sent a line through about the deception being not just on businessmen but all British people but he for some reason just got on the back foot and stayed there. Peter said it made him really fearful about the debates.

Greg [Nugent] had been working pretty hard on 2012 Olympics stuff and there was a real vitality to the stuff they were doing which we just lacked right now. Even the video for the mascots had a real creativity and imagination, the likes of which we were struggling to get. I did a bad run earlier. Real energy crash. I was wondering whether these drugs were having bad side effects, and fixed to call DS tomorrow. Peter M was pretty down judging by his texts. PG was saying Victoria Street was a bit of a shambles. He said Peter was doing his best but there were too many voices and not enough firepower. 'Fate beckons,' texted PM. A rather wet call from Ed M who said nobody seemed to like his topline for the manifesto, 'National renewal'. I didn't mind it and said if they had thought up others and kept coming back to this it was probably fine. The most important thing was being able to hang everything from it. I was blogging daily, walking a bit, agonising a lot about when to go back and feeling very stressed and tired. Fiona was getting pretty pissed off with me, saying she sometimes felt like a carer looking after my various mood turmoils. PG saying things not great with GB. He was getting down though better when serious people around him.

Thursday 8 April

Watched the GB–AD Peter M presser on NICs and eliminating government waste. They had taken their time to get there but it was an OK attack and the Tories were pushed on to the back foot. Then they came out with Michael Caine at a National Citizenship Service launch.* He looked a bit ridiculous and also seemed to be confused who was in government. Also I am not sure the celeb thing works much any more, as I would say to Eddie Izzard and others later, much as I welcomed him doing one of our broadcasts. PG was calling and sending notes. Thinking we were further behind than was being said. Lindsay said she was worried about me. I was agonising the whole time about whether to go back. At one point I just sat in the back office at Conaglen feeling tired and depressed. I had a chat with DS about whether to stay on pills. He said yes. I watched the news and tweeted that Nick Robinson's face and/or voice were on fifteen times in his Clegg package. Clegg was coming over well I thought.

Friday 9 April

I decided not to go to the Burnley game at Hull tomorrow and went for a long walk with Fiona who felt I really needed a long rest out of the public eye after this and that I needed to avoid all the things that stressed me out. She accepted I had got better in lots of ways but when it was bad, as now, it was very bad. She knew it was hard for me but sometimes she felt trapped by it, and the kids could sense it too. I had been very low-profile through the week yet some survey had me as the tenth most influential Twitterer. Tom Watson and JP at top. A few tweets through the day. Charlie K did one on his visit with Clegg to Glasgow and mentioned Donald being the university piper, which was nice. NICs still rolling on. AD was on with Osborne on the lunchtime news, and did OK. Sky were going massive on our candidate [Stuart MacLennan] in Moray – unwinnable – who was axed after sending offensive tweets. Cameron milking it for all it was worth, answering on that rather than economy.

All three leaders were in Scotland today. GB looking OK but still not energetic. The Tories were now moving towards married couples allowance plans [tax breaks]. Chat with PG. Things worse. No capacity. Money etc. All bad. Eddie Izzard call re his PEB. Mark Lucas and Gez Sagar, PG, Peter and DA. It all meandered a bit but Eddie seemed to get what he needed to do. Ditto Mark. I said we must not force it down people's throats. Less 'vote Labour' than 'why I am'. Also needs to show we are not perfect but

* Proposed voluntary service for all sixteen-year-olds to be able to join a two-month summer residential programme of outdoor activities and community work.

get a lot right. He sounded on form so should be OK. Peter went on a big one about how everyone apart from me hated Bush, thought he was useless and as he ran on compassionate Conservatism we should go at Cameron over that. Nobody went for it thank God. Eddie pretty good. Call went on for an hour or more. 'Peter Mandelson has left the building,' Eddie said at one point.

Ed M called re manifesto briefing. He said there was a lot of doubt, mainly from Peter, about national renewal. I sent him a note on how I felt renewal could work and then we did a conference call and he just read out my note and said it was terrific and let's go for that. I said hold on, I just tossed that off in five minutes without any knowledge of content. Laughter all round, PG and DA saying why change habit of a lifetime? PM's worry on 'National renewal' was that it was too lampoonable, as in 'Where have you been?' But I felt it was OK. TB didn't like it because he felt it was a typical distancing from the record. Another long walk trying to clear my head, and chase away the anxiety. F thinking I should have total rest and then get sorted after. It was a nice week really but I did feel stressed out.

Saturday 10 April

Another bad night, made worse by the pills clearly making me feel tired. We had breakfast then set off for Glasgow airport. Lovely sunny day. I had never seen Glencoe looking quite so fantastic. This time last year snow and fog. Now this. Peter M saying he was really looking forward to having me back. I warned him not to expect too much because of tiredness. He said he felt only five people would stand up to this campaign – me, him, PG, Ben WP and Patrick. He liked David and Justin but he was not sure they were strong enough. TB called. He said he felt 'National renewal' sounded ridiculous when GB had been part of the government from the off. I said all countries could go through different phases on change. I didn't hate it so much. He felt there should be a better way of signalling that he had the ideas for the future. He felt it should be heavy on new policy saying experience has taught us how to break new ground. In each area he should be taking the bold steps forward, building on what done so far. Big on reform, social exclusion and crime.

But he said none of it matters unless we deal with tax. 'And at present WE are saying tax credits i.e. state, and the Tories are saying tax breaks i.e. individual. So the combination of this, fairness and GB is to pit a traditional Labour case against a traditional Tory case – and it is a dangerous game.' He said the question tactically was whether there is an established dynamic to this campaign; or are we in a clawing-back situation? 'I think there's a dynamic established which is for the Tories. So we have to change that and break out. The only way I can think of, is to surprise with the manifesto.' He said nobody doubts GB will be 'fair'. But what else? Securing the recovery is too static. Where is the aspiration offer for the future? That is where Cameron is trying to get to.

PG reckoned the poll of polls showed the Tories ahead by 6 to 8. Recoverable, but PG felt momentum was with the Tories largely because of DC–GB. They got a hit on NICs though GB and AD pulled it back well if late. Now they are doing marriage and that too could be reframed in the context of the deficit and their opportunism. But we felt very weak on capacity. Also, as I said to TB, on strategy, if you think about it, he is not there, GB is not doing what he used to in terms of driving a campaign message, because he is the main message carrier; I'm not in the same place, PG is not as energetic for obvious reasons so a lot is falling on Peter. TB felt the debates would be key and so would, for once, the manifestos. The Tories just have to get through them 'good enough'. We have to do a lot better. A guy at the airport came up and said to tell GB he loved him and people couldn't stand Cameron.

We bumped into Mohni Bahra [Special Branch close protection] at the airport who was bound for Washington to advance DM's trip standing in for GB. He was interesting on the campaign. He said DM was doing a fair bit but he didn't really know what he was supposed to be doing. Everything was all a bit last-minute and he said there was no me or Anji types directing the traffic. So he felt they were slightly making it up as they went along. He also felt that GB and his team were a bit amateurish. But he felt people did not warm to the Tories and so were looking for reasons to come back if only we could provide them. Rayan collected us. Back home to sign books in front of Charlie Nicholas on Sky telling us the miracle news of our first away win of the season, against Hull. 4–1 and I bloody missed it.

Sunday 11 April

First day back, managed to avoid going in too early. Instead did a bit of work at home and watched the end of Marr. Paddy Ashdown was on with Neil and Michael Howard about the leaders' debates and he had a terrific line re the NICs and marriage tax allowance being like a Sarah Palin moment for the Tories, the point at which they dumped their strategy for a tactical gain. Good line which I tweeted out and later blogged on. The papers were fairly neutral but the media seemed to be running with a *Sunday Times* story that we had targeted cancer patients in a leaflet.*

* Leaflets saying the Tories would scrap a Labour guarantee on how quickly patients would see a cancer specialist had been sent to 250,000 women. Health Secretary Andy Burnham said allegations of targeting cancer sufferers were 'wholly wrong'.

Load of all bollocks but Peter was worried about GB retreating from it. He wanted to have an 'off-site' strategy meeting so we gathered at Philip's at half twelve. Gail was making tea and laying out food. PG looking a bit tired and had been telling me all morning that GB was not winning the dynamic. Douglas, Justin, DM, Pat, Ben, Matthew, Marianna. Good enough meeting. Peter basically took things around the table and we all said what we thought about where things were. He felt the Tories had had an OK week but we were still standing. They were not as far ahead as they probably wanted to be.

He was worried about clarity of strategy, and also about operational issues. Douglas complained when Peter was out of the room that he didn't have enough to do, that Peter was taking on too much and ministers were feeling excluded and unsure as to what they were supposed to be doing. PG felt Douglas had become a bit distant and whingy but he said to me he had been a courtier to GB twenty years ago and didn't want just to be a courtier to Peter twenty years later. Patrick L made a good point, that we worked best in the past campaigns when we had a series of major building blocks to the campaign and we developed everything around them. We needed positive cover to attack them more on the economy in particular. Peter was doing his usual thing of taking notes as people spoke and at the end we agreed that I should write a message note which PG would get tested later today.

I felt it was all about recovery plus future up against risk. Tories had to become a risk. I said we had too many different lines of attack on them. They had to be brought together to point forcefully in the same direction. That was risk. I also felt we needed Alistair D out there more, and we needed to identify people who were going to get out and chase the Tories. It was a good enough meeting though, even if there seemed to be a sense that the best we could do was hold them to not getting overall majority. There was also an acceptance that GB gave as many problems as he solved and that DC was doing pretty well. I still felt we could make more of Cameron not being as popular as he was cracked out to be. I felt he was as much problem as solution.

I sat down and wrote a long note about the recovery. How it was about the choices and changes we made now. Used that as a way to set our theirs and ours, and the impact on Britain's families and businesses, the impact on public services. We needed to admit we had not got everything right, but show GB and AD made the right calls when crisis struck. The Tories made the wrong calls. If we had heeded their advice, the recession would have been longer, more jobs lost, more businesses in trouble. They were wrong on the recession. They are wrong on the recovery. We needed to get over the contrast – experience and substance plus values plus judgement equals recovery and a future fair for all. Opportunism equals irresponsibility equals risk. Recession over, recovery under way. Recovery at risk with the Tories. Jobs and growth at risk, schools and hospitals at risk. PG took the note to groups, said the messages did well, the choice was the key. But he was worried about how credible people found DC.

Catherine McLeod called for a chat. She felt they were still not using AD enough on strategy. I went into Victoria Street, which was steaming hot. Unless I worked in a couple of the smaller offices, or on the bridge between the two sides, this could turn out to be impossible. It was fairly crowded too and would be more so through the week. I had forgotten how easy it was to get drawn into what effectively became rolling meetings. We would chat about the next day then go to a meeting on the next week which would go over the same ground. It all felt a bit thin and lacking in energy in there too. There was also a bit of criticism around the place of the GB tour but to be fair to Sue and co., they had nothing like the budget we were used to, even in '05 let alone in '97 when money seemed to be no object. It was all a bit grim really.

Douglas and I went downstairs to the media room to wait for GB who had been out on a visit. First had a chat with a red-haired guy who was watching the debate practice sessions of all three leaders, to make sure they understood the rules etc. I made a joke about the idea of bribing him and we had a chat about his non-disclosure agreements. He showed GB the clocks that would indicate when he was out of time (which he was going to have to watch) and then we went into a full ninety-minute rehearsal. He was much better than before. Better body language. More personal in his stories. Maybe too many easy quips that could be pushed back on. I felt it was a lot better though. We needed to push him to react, for example if Cameron pulled a stunt, like pulling out a letter, not just personal abuse or general attack. Afterwards he wanted to have more lines. Lines was always his answer. 'Where is the beef?' was the right area of attack on DC. But did it work?

Not sure. He was also agitating about the *Sunday Times* story on the cancer leaflet which was running on the news. Felt I had been able to help Peter a bit and that the strategy meeting had been useful, but it was going to be a long haul. Home for dinner, all the family plus Nina Parker [Grace's friend]. Grace very funny re wanting to be able to give GB some advice. Cameron was out walking with Ian Botham on his leukaemia walk which was a real pisser. Cathy was also pretty appalled by the extent to which he had hijacked it for a Tory visit. Looking good on the news though. Their pictures were terrific. GB sent his words through for tomorrow. I did a stack of rewriting, most of which they took in. I tried to make it fresher and less list-y. Also sent a note re demeanour etc.

Monday 12 April

Manifesto launch day. TB sent me an email with the message, 'Forward this to Peter if you like.' It was the same points he had been making to me – that we don't have a personal aspiration offer; and we aren't saying why the Tories are wrong other than saying they are 'unfair'. He felt GB's words on the manifesto had to show 'why we are good for you as an individual; why our policies are right and theirs are wrong'. It had to be about showing we could make people better off. He was convinced that if the fight was on 'values' we risk just underlining the difference the Tories want underlined.

The Cabinet all set off to Birmingham. Sunny in London. Cold up there. Mini controversy about doing the launch in a new-build hospital. It looked OK, but even on the big events though you could tell we lacked the big spend of the Tories. I did an advance blog on ours and theirs, really trying to drill down a few lines on Cameron. It was proving very hard to get up attack lines on him. We had too many and they did not all lead to an obvious place, e.g. risk. I argued through the day that we should be getting Alan J and DM, when back from the US, to co-do a series of attacks on Cameron. The launch seemed to go fine. GB spoke well, was very relaxed in the Q&A which was helped by a few hundred party supporters clapping and occasionally heckling the questioners. The media wouldn't like it. But he came over well. Brought in Alan J, AD and Andy B at various points, apparently to the annoyance of Ed Balls. Afterwards it was just a case of tracking the media and waiting for the trailers of the Tory manifesto to start. When it came, it was very much in the empowerment/Big Society area. Philip and I both pushing for one line on Cameron and the Tories. According to Marianna I was seemingly supposed to be doing attack but it was not clear to me in what way. Once the politicians all came back from Birmingham they went into a 'How did you think it went?' series of conversations which quickly became quite irritating. I told Ed M he should just get on to the next thing and move on. There was too much post-match analysis and not enough planning for the next one. Then news came through that the three Labour MPs who were up on expenses charges would get legal aid. Cameron leapt off his bus and did a rant about it. Top of ITV News. Opportunist crap but they loved it.

I asked DA and the press office to complain about it and try to get the ITV running order changed, which they did. Party HQ people felt quite buoyed that GB had done quite well. The mood in the campaign was getting a little fractious though, with a sense of the people off the road feeling they were whipping boys and the people on the road feeling that the Victoria Street politicians weren't really making decisions and also that they weren't understanding the huge pressures caused by the lower budgets.

The polls were pretty much still in the same place. Email exchange with TB about his mention at the press conference and GB's answer when GB said he was proud of the record under TB and the members applauded. He felt however it was all a bit too late on the policy front. Cameron was looking more opportunistic than ever when he got up on the legal aid story. Good meeting re a few stunt ideas including getting up an artwork made of 200k – inheritance tax cut for the rich.

Tuesday 13 April

In for the 7 a.m. meeting. Peter had just come off the 6.40 call and was pretty exasperated. He said he had listened to a meandering circular conversation. GB was getting too many strands of advice. He was never sure what to say. He was making too many mistakes. His big thing today was that we were excluding Ed Balls from the campaign. Apparently all because Ed had complained that GB called on Andy at the launch but not him. It was all getting a bit too factional for my liking. Harriet was there and later came over and said 'Alastair, I know we have not spoken properly for many years but I am so glad you're here.' We had a nice chat. She is resilient is Harriet, and she doesn't bear grudges. If she did, I'm not sure she would speak to me like that. I watched the Tory launch. They had very high production values. Battersea, images lasered on, big set. Lots of speakers. Cameron last with Big Society push, suggesting that was going to be his main message and his way of getting to the centre ground.

Probably a bit flash and too long an event but it would carry fairly well. Yet according to PG the groups later on didn't take to it much. They saw him as being too flash and the attack that it was all too gimmicky got through a bit.

I set off with Matthew and David Muir for Leeds. I did a bit of work on the train but [Sir] Nicholas Winterton [Tory MP] had a point about second class being harder to work in. Did a blog on their manifesto then started to think about the debate prep. We did a few hours of it in the presidential suite at the Radisson. GB was on quite good form but I was a bit worried he didn't yet have a clear enough opening minute. He was obsessed about the argument on risk and how to make people fear the Big Society was a risk. We worked on risk lines, also worked on a few arguments towards it. Michael Sheehan [debates advisor] was over and we had a real old-fashioned presentation from GB on how to build the argument year by year on the cuts they were taking out. He seemed energised by it but I felt it was still too reliant on assertion.

We were getting quite a good atmosphere going through. There were a couple of technical guys in there enjoying the laughs. I was relentlessly beating up GB. Theo as Clegg was really funny in how sanctimonious and irritating he became. David Muir was throwing out the questions, Douglas and Matthew watching. We did several goes round the block and when he got his energy levels up he was a lot better. He did look tired though. Had a long chat with Sarah who was holding up well. She said he was incredibly determined and also that they were getting a good reception out there. She felt the Tories had thrown most of the stuff they had and it had not really stuck against us. Had a chat with Sue Nye who seemed pretty strained.

I later chatted with Justin who said they were feeling got at. Working under massive strain and it was not easy. He felt he ought to be in Victoria Street but Peter M had felt he should be on the road. He said people in VS felt Peter was very cliquey and was surrounding himself with his own people rather than building a team. He wanted me to try to build the team and to lead on comms. I said I would do what I could subject to the limitations. He felt it was all getting scratchy. PG had gone to the US for a meeting but was checking in the whole time. He felt we were slipping back quite a lot. GB went from being up and energetic to suddenly at times looking like he was asleep. Sheehan was quite good with him. He kept saying the same things about staying loud and energetic, and with a smile. He had a good boxing analogy: don't go into a clinch… jab and move away.

We did two main sessions. One was very negative – just after we had been discussing risk – and we got to agreeing he should always try to be positive and be the man with the plan. It worked a lot better. He wanted me to go through for a one-on-one session, though Sarah was also there sitting on the bed on her computer. Should he use personal examples? Yes. Should he go for launching big attack? Yes then no. 'Should I say I would resign if we lost the constitutional referendum?' I said no. I asked Sarah what she thought. She agreed with me that it would be weakening. He said David M was keen. I always found it quite hard to talk to Sarah. She wasn't cold but she wasn't warm either. She was someone who never gave much away. GB was definitely having one of his phases of latching on to me. Douglas too seemed to address everything he said to me. He had a few good points but it could be meandering. Chatted with Rachel in the hotel bar. I think we were both driven as much by duty as anything. Both wishing it was over.

Wednesday 14 April

All day Leeds. Apart from a little asthmatic run I was stuck in the hotel all day. Around five hours' rehearsal in all. We did a lot of good work on the opening statement, cutting lines that were flabby, making it all hang together better. Bringing in the other leaders. Risk. He was obsessed with trying to get new lines on risk. Working away on that, and all the other lines. He came out with a good one himself about Cameron needing to phone a friend. Answer time. Meat in the pie. It was all a bit surreal but we did get into it as though the real thing. Theo was terrific as Clegg. Hilarious moment when GB referred to 'Strictly Come Ballroom'. Really going for a big hit on DC but struggling to get the language. Trish, who used to be Adam Boulton's producer, was running to get food etc. We did half a dozen sessions or so. Three good, three less good. Endless bananas. Sheehan had got his advice down to an acronym, SELL. Smile. Energy. Listen. Line. He was also saying 'no more facts'. He was worried GB would just go into rat-a-tat-tat factual stuff rather than message and argument.

I did a quick blog on Cameron complaining that the rules were going to make it too stultifying. His team had negotiated them for heaven's sake. Odd day really. Me, Theo and GB up there doing what we did. Douglas and Matthew watching. David moderating. Stuart Hudson doing facts. Sheehan chipping in with commands of energy, look up etc. It was mainly stuff TB would get instinctively. I did a whole load of tough Q&A. GB still agitating for the hard attack on the Tories and not getting it. Peter said Balls made a mess of the press conference because he allowed them to go to where the Tories wanted things. The Big Society. TB texting a few words of advice. Policy the key. He felt from the sound of it the DC launch was OK without being great. But he still thought trad Tory v trad Labour would see trad Tory win.

Thursday 15 April

Didn't sleep. Up for the morning conference call. It was usually GB, the Eds, Peter, Douglas and a few others. There was always someone dropping out from somewhere and lots of meandering conversations leading to very few decisions. GB was obsessing about the idea of a big attack on the Tories' spending weaknesses. He wanted to really get it up and had ideas for a big year-by-year thing. He had this habit of saying the same thing again and again. He was out on a visit and was not really motoring. Balls was constantly just going on about the need for a big cuts attack. I did a mood and lines note for GB on the train to Manchester. I was sure if he was at his best, could stay calm, authoritative, personable and energetic, he will beat him. It was all about how he felt going into the debate. I urged him not to overdo the preparation today, that rest was important, and getting the adrenaline to flow at the right time.

I said he should let his emotions rise during the day as a way of getting in the zone. I echoed Sheehan's point that he must not get sucked into sounding like a facts machine. When in doubt, leave it out. If they challenge on facts and you are unsure, move on. Cameron would try to drag him down into record and rebuttal mode. It was vital he stayed focused on the future and risk. It was important to be relaxed. I said the last thing he should say to himself before walking out is 'I am going to enjoy this. For years this guy has sought to belittle me and push me over and I am still standing, proud and tall. That is because I know who I am and what I believe. Tonight the people will see that. I will not be presented through the prism of a negative, hostile, cynical media. People can see me direct. They will see I have their interests and theirs alone at heart. I will focus relentlessly on the future. I will be upbeat and optimistic. But I will not miss an opportunity to put pressure on him, make him and the risk he poses the issue.'

He called as I was writing it and we went over some of the points. Humour key. Be serious when you have to be but do not be afraid to play with DC and NC. Listen to every word and where their words trigger humour and wit, go for it. Follow your instincts. Don't be over rehearsed and over prepared. Don't lean away from him when challenging him. Let him know you're there. I was also worried he would overdo the writing, like he did in meetings, constantly scribbling in his thick felt pen. He had to look like he was listening, and only react externally if he felt himself reacting internally. I also tried to persuade him it was entirely possible one of them would say something funny – so smile, or interesting – so look interested.

He knew the big points that have to come over. Recovery v risk. The future. Experience. Judgement. I felt despite being older he would have more stamina and we talked over some mental tricks to jab his mind if he felt himself tiring. He was probably dreading the whole thing but had to try to enjoy it. We went over some of the lines we had been working on.

- A riff on risk ended by 'David, you're a risk too far.'
- Big Society big cuts. And if we had listened to you there'd have been a Big Depression.
- This is not *Question Time*, David, it's Answer Time.
- You can airbrush your posters, you can't airbrush your policies.
- Thanks for putting my picture up around the country. At least I'm smiling.
- Do you want to phone a friend? Ask the audience?
- As the man in Bolton said to you David, where's the meat in the pie?
- Beneath the veneer there's more veneer.
- Cut through the generalities and what do you find – more generalities.
- I've learned from experience. You have a lot of experience to learn.
- A slogan is not a solution.

- You can beat me on posters and soundbites every day of the week, David. Let's talk policies and specifics.
- Get real, Nick.
- Presenting a case very well doesn't make it a good case.
- The Big Society may sound nicer than the old Tory Party. But money out of the economy, cuts and DIY services IS the old Tory Party.
- After four years I don't know what he stands for. I don't think HE knows what he stands for.
- Lots of us play Fantasy Football. This is fantasy economics, David.
- Four years? Long enough to build an Olympic stadium. Not long enough to find out how the Tories would pay for their promises.
- If he gets into power it's not a Cabinet he'll be leading but a school reunion.
- People might think he would do a better job running the country if he stopped running the country down.

Arrived and got a cab to the Radisson, and met him there. We worked several times on the opening script and by the end he quite liked it. It took a while to learn it though. The frame was set fine – economy, future, risk, values. We had several sessions of Q&A and he did OK. But the tiredness problem was real. At times he would just slump in a chair and put his hands over his eyes. Michael S was good with him. He would shout 'energy, pace, smile, stand up straight'. We worked on the riff on risk which was OK by the end. It was another lovely sunny day and I could see Calum's block from the balcony. We were in the same room as for his speech last time here. I got Alex to give him a call and just calm him down a bit. Fergie was of the view that GB's character wasn't maybe right for leadership. He didn't have the personality. He had strengths but the dourness and caution were problems. 'I want you to tell him what you said to [Gunnar] Solskjær and [Teddy] Sheringham [last-gasp Man Utd 1999 Champions League final victory, 2–1] at Barcelona. And tell him to calm down.'

They had a little chat and GB was jovial with him but then within minutes he was back to near despair at the lectern. He also had a disconcerting habit of walking away and doing toe-touching exercises (albeit with his knees bent). The camera guys looked on a bit bemused. I had been asking them their views the whole time and they were pretty clear he was very good when good and dreadful when bad. We had a major wobble in confidence halfway through. I went to Sarah and said please calm him down. She said it's OK, he always does this. I said fine but it is zapping too much energy. They went for a short walk and he was a bit better when he came back. The mad conflicts in my life were in sharp relief today. When I had a break I was snatching a few pages of TB's book which was superb. Very different for a political memoir. But I was also putting the final touches to my own. I even got the index through on my BlackBerry just as I was putting in a big attack on GB, as DC, over not being New Labour.

He was standing up to my attacks most of the time but when we did military stuff it was easy to get under his skin. I also trapped him twice into saying things that weren't true, on military spending and on higher education. David [Muir] and Stuart Hudson were worried he would get trapped on a factual thing. He was best in the last session when he did a good opening and then just asked us to pepper him with questions. There was energy there now. Peter M came over and said he liked the opening statement. He was a bit dubious about some of it in truth but we were too far gone now. The news was cranking up to it big-style but we also had a volcano pouring ash all over airspace from Iceland which meant airports shut. Chaos around the world. PG stuck in San Francisco. He had left but his flight had to go back after four hours. We were going to miss him. It was important we kept GB on one strand of opinion. Ed B was always pushing in a different direction. He was not really bound in. GB wanted him to be. Peter didn't really. Alistair D was not properly involved either. Nor was David M. I called him and Alan J and said we needed to see much more of them.

The clock ticked on and we had one last session before we headed over to the Hilton and GB went to the TV studios. People were really nervous. I said to him just before he left to relax, enjoy it and know Cameron felt worse. The word back was Cameron looked sick with worry. The Hilton was well set up for it. Massive media room where the spinning would happen afterwards. Osborne and Hague for the Tories. [Danny] Alexander [Inverness MP] and Cable for the Libs. Paddy there too. Douglas A and Peter, Alan J, Yvette and Ben. We all settled down to watch in a room on the second floor. Clegg went first and was pretty good. Nice manner. GB's mic didn't pick up the first few words but he did OK. Cameron poor. No mention of Big Society. I was tweeting every few minutes and getting bigger responses than anything before. People were really engaging. Clegg was doing well. GB was good especially after the first few questions got him warmed up and he was best by far on the economy.

DC was vague, too many stories, posing too much. He had the best makeup, smartest clothes but the phoney lightweight thing was coming through. He was also poor on policy. No Big Society. He said we were worse than Bulgaria on cancer, which people wouldn't like. Peter had his camera crew from a C4 doc with him which was a bit odd. I was staying out of it. He was texting and emailing lots of hacks. I was tweeting. Theo was linked to Vic Street rebutting and fact-checking. The general feeling was GB was beating Cameron. But Clegg was doing best according to the instant polls. He was certainly best at direct camera work and he was also saying the things people wanted to hear. And he was very clear on pushing back when GB wanted to draw him into a two v one attack. He was not playing.

As the thing closed I scribbled notes round the system with the topline that Clegg won on style, GB on substance. It was Cameron's to lose and he lost it. The lack of substance had been exposed. Not even to stick to his core arguments was so transparent. It was lines and slogans. My favourite tweet – Cameron has the look of a man about to be told by his team he did well because they need to cheer him up. I went down to the spin room and did a few interviews. The general sense seemed to be shared – Clegg excellent, GB better than expected, DC poor. Peter and I did the rounds. Alan J good on the lives. We did OK. A rise for Clegg would not be a disaster so long as it was not too big. David Muir and Justin sought me out for a 'couldn't have done it without you' moment. We were all very much pushing the line that DC losing was the big story. His anecdotes were starting to fall apart.

GB called from the car. He sounded a bit down. He felt he hadn't really done as well as he could have done. I said he did better than fine. Got some good lines in. Put Cameron under pressure. They were getting bogged down in trying to say GB was too aggressive or got facts wrong. But it was not working. Fiona texted to say Osborne looked sick about the whole thing. GB was worried about how well Clegg did. He said *The Guardian* would be a problem now though. People were going to think they could get a hung parliament by voting Lib Dem. TB texted to say we should be clear a hung parliament was a bad thing and Libs ultimately were not serious. I worried we needed to get a line worked out on them fairly soon. GB was beating himself up for being too aggressive, which he worried would have helped Clegg who was so reasonable. It is true people won't have liked the squabbling. But he needed to see the real picture. Cameron exposed. Tories would be worried. The polls and the papers were calling it for Clegg. It would mean a sense of a three-horse race opening up.

Friday 16 April

Gordon was still on the pre-debate landscape. We had a conference call first thing, sadly with Peter not on it, and it was almost as if the debate hadn't happened. Balls was agitating to get out with a big attack on the Tories on school cuts. GB wanted Alan J out as well on police numbers. I said till I was blue in the face that we needed a clear strategy and lines on the Libs, because they would be the focus today and, if we were not careful, for the next few days. Clegg had done well and there was no point pretending he hadn't. The media were still seeing it as all about the Tories. Up to a point it was but we had to move and welcome the new landscape. I said it needed a considered and measured speech saying what the landscape was. We were in anything goes mode. Cameron no longer a shoo-in. He was going to wobble.

The Libs were going to pick up and the talk would be Lib–Labbery etc. Even in our body language we would have to agree the pose to strike. I felt it was in the area of we agree on a lot but they have some silly policies and if they are going to be big players people need to know what they are. Hung parliament sounds nice. It's not. GB was convinced the Lib surge was all about expenses and rejecting the establishment and worst offenders. But a lot was about him I'm afraid. That was coming through. Even when he did well people did not want to give him credit.

On the Libs I called David Miliband and said he needed to get out there. We were also going to have to decide which to attack – child tax credits, child trust fund, winter fuel payments, amnesty for illegal asylum seekers. Clegg had pushed the crime immigration-type stuff, as had DC. So he was liberal where it suited him, anti-liberal where not. But actually getting agreement on how to play it was a nightmare. GB was out in Brighton with Eddie Izzard at a youth event during the day. He did an OK clip about how the debate energised everything and now the choice was clear etc. But the backdrop was awful. Clegg was really looking like the man of the moment. Milking it quite well.

Peter seemed a bit detached from it all. He said we should be studiously neutral. Fine. But what does that mean in terms of what we say? What do we say to our candidates? They will be shitting themselves in Lib / Lab marginals. They will be unsure of how to handle it. Do we go for them locally? Do we cuddle up? Do we go for the progressive majority? Do we say they are not credible or competent? The argument went on and off all day. We only finally resolved it when I forced a decision at the evening meeting. GB was there, ostensibly to discuss the economic attack for Monday. That was grim enough, with GB and Balls really pushing to get hard edge and hard figures and Alistair D on speakerphone warning that unless it was totally copper-bottomed it would backfire. Peter had said a couple of things in recent days which I now saw more clearly. GB's people hated each other more than they hated us. And there was near contempt for Alistair and DMil. I had seen it when I tried to get David into the foreign affairs preparation. They were not keen. Today they were all sighing as Alistair voiced his caution.

GB was in driller killer mode, wouldn't let go. Desperate to do a really big hit on them on figures. Torsten Bell [advisor, researcher] from AD's office seemed to be the figures man. He felt it was doable but not if we overstretched. I texted Peter in the meeting to say that this was like being on a radio show panel. We needed to decide. I kept banging on about the need for decision. One economic event or two. Which was the bigger? Positive or negative? What was weekend plan? Then on the Libs – what do we tell candidates? They need a note now, right now. It was not good enough to wait for the weekend. Douglas was like a commentator on this. Peter was fine on one level but a lot of it he was just letting wash over him. I was getting exasperated. I could see what needed to be done. But they didn't do it.

I was also alarmed how things I tossed off in five minutes became lines to take immediately or strategic positioning notes. E.g. my speech for Douglas today. I don't know if it was the right line or not but it became 'the line' very quickly. GB looked shattered. David said he was down about the debate 'so let's not have the post-mortem yet'. Peter said imagine how bad we would feel if it was Cameron who had walked it. Clegg had got the anti-political mood, that was all, added to which he was noticed in a big way on the kind of national event he rarely made it to. I said we now had to say openly there was a three-way race and so all parties had to be exposed to the same scrutiny. We had to talk up the Libs to get them talked down. Clegg was becoming a more attractive 'time for a change' candidate. Cameron was shown to be flaky. GB was GB. The media bandwagon was really going to roll for Clegg for a while though. It would help us for a bit but if it went too far we would lose a lot to them too. So we had to tread carefully.

Earlier meetings rolled into one. Big response to blog on how the debates now opened up the whole campaign. I nipped out to Random House to sort the Vol. 1 index. Also to see Susan and Caroline for chat re the TB book which I was really enjoying. Then back for more meetings and brainstorms. GB becoming needy again. He asked if I would look at his note for a speech tomorrow and improve it. It was a shambles. I worked on it while watching Burnley reserves [v Liverpool reserves] on LFC TV [Liverpool FC channel]. He called twice to go over the same ground. But he was hard to talk to. He fixated on certain things and it was impossible to move him off them. I saw the Libs situation as an opportunity, but he couldn't seem to get it. He kept saying sorry too for his performance yesterday. But it was important to remember in the polls a lot of people would mark him down whatever. Clegg was always going to win. First poll came in showing us in third place on the debate so we had to really watch for it now. The problem with the debate was people seeing it like *X Factor*. It was all about personality, not much on policy.

Saturday 17 April

Did a blog on the Libs, trying to think my way through it. It was good for us up to a point. Good because the Tories were the ones most hit by it. Also because the three-horse-race sense meant policy would or should come to the fore. I missed the conference call because they gave me the wrong number. TB and I exchanged a few views. He had such a better feel for this stuff than GB. His latest speech draft was so clunking as to be ridiculous. I had given him a few thoughts but they required subtlety. What came back was just the same old clunk-clunk. TB felt the Clegg surge was an opportunity but it meant going for them on policy and a hung parliament being a risk. The media were all majorly into Cleggmania. Quite ludicrous really, like the *Sunday Times* planning to splash on a poll that he had highest ratings since Churchill.

I talked to Peter and Ben about the event for Monday and the need for a proper positioning speech today. Then headed to Tower Bridge hotel for the LLR [Leukaemia and Lymphoma Research charity] 50th anniversary. I had been a bit pissed off to be missing the Burnley–Sunderland match but it was a really nice event. I did a poor man's Eamonn Andrews [late TV presenter] and did a This Is Your Life of the charity, interviewing key people in its history. It whizzed along and there was a lot of laughter as well as a lot of sadness along the way. Good interview at the end with a guy whose daughter had died. Really moving. Texts of our 2–1 defeat at Sunderland coming through. I did a book signing, then went to Victoria Street to see where we were. Lovely day. Polls showing Lib Dem surge. We were pushing on the idea of it showing a progressive majority for us.

GB conference call was still lacking in clarity about what the approach to the Libs really was. Volcanic ash causing more and more alarm. PG still stuck in the States. I did a couple of hours there just to show willing and also help Ben plan the broadcast we were planning to play for the start of Monday's press conference. We were doing spoof papers and radio reports for the day after the emergency Tory budget. Good idea. Home for dinner with all the kids there. Calum worried re his dissertation. Some of the polls had us in third. Chatted to Eddie Izzard on maybe doing some articles on the back of the broadcast. Agreed with GB we had to go for the Libs on policy and credibility. But we had to be more gentle than on the Tories. TB adamant we had to go for them harder. Not easy to get an agreed line. Douglas was complaining that he resented the way Peter was dominating the campaign.

Sunday 18 April

With GB on Marr, I knew he would be up early so got up very early myself and did him a note. It was vital we got the campaign back into a more sensible shape. Even the Lib Dems are not saying there can be any choice of PM apart from GB or DC. The ludicrous Churchill poll gives the opportunity to bring Clegg down with humour, then to be used as lever to get on to policy, and the choice of two futures. He needed to take both Cameron and Clegg apart on policy. I said he must be really relaxed, and not get trapped into Sunday paper rebuttal mode. Big picture. Big message. Humour. Energy. Future. TB was texting more and more furiously, stuck in the Middle East and feeling we were being too soft on the Libs. The Cleggmania thing was becoming totally ludicrous. GB kept saying it was an anti-politics thing. It was partly that. It was also however a feeling about him. They had rejected him. They didn't like Cameron. They didn't like politicians generally. But they had to take their feelings somewhere. Added to which it was the X-Factorisation of politics in a lot of ways. Clegg had had a good night, fact, and people were still talking about it.

GB just too cautious about everything. He had finally, finally decided not to go to Poland [for funeral of air crash victim Polish President Lech Kaczyński], after hearing Obama would not have time for a bilateral. He was saved in any event by the ash as a lot of the leaders couldn't go. The ash chaos was really not helping as a backdrop to the campaign, and it was not helping my mood and morale that Philip was still stuck in the US. There was a lot of talk around that Coulson was getting it from Cameron for agreeing to the debates, and [Steve] Hilton for pushing the Big Society. I stayed at home to watch GB on Marr. It was always interesting to watch with the kids. Calum thought we were too relaxed about Clegg – I was beginning to think so too. Rory felt GB was as good as he had seen him. He certainly seemed more relaxed and I think all the debate prep was making him sharper in his answers. He was pretty good, though as Peter said afterwards, we were judging the whole time against a low bar.

I went in for a rolling meeting on future events. GB came in and he and I sat at the lifts and talked over where we were. He felt it was all about dramatising the risk. The problem was that Clegg was where the media was at. From going from debate process now we were on to post-election process. There was never any focus on policy. Throw in the volcano news sponge and it was a problem. We were still being very gentle on the Libs – a few sideswipes at them over tax credits and child trust funds. But the reality was it was going to be tough. Tories in meltdown fine. But as Greg Cook kept telling me if it went too far it was bad for us. Meeting GB, PM, DA and AC. Agreed that the whole thing would be decided in a hundred Tory/Lab marginals. We had to watch the Libs did not take our votes there and let in the Tories. It was not going to be easy. The Tories still had a lot of advantages to press.

The volcanic ash was not really being gripped. There were thousands stranded abroad. Profiteering. Impact on economy. Yet apart from Andrew Adonis suspending his campaigning on high-speed rail and taking charge there was no sense of government urgency. I spooked GB into getting a grip by saying it felt to me like foot-and-mouth disease. Within an hour he had ordered a new ministerial group and Cobra set-up for the morning. But it was a bit alarming it had not happened already. Jeremy H was on holiday. James Bowler on the case. Andrew A doing well but this could be a nightmare all round. There was some discussion about cancelling the event tomorrow. I felt not. There was a risk that we kept cancelling and we lost any hope of momentum. Cameron was out at another lovely backdrop, mum and dad in attendance, doing pensioners and warning against a hung parliament. The media was still obsessing about Clegg and probably would now until Thursday.

The Tories were admitting we had outwitted them on imposing a narrative about the debate. But it was not easy to be sure how this Clegg thing would play out. GB was still pushing the same old, same old, and looking to us to inject some life and ideas. We went through all the stuff for tomorrow, which was pretty good. Impossible not to feel the tensions between GB and Alistair who was very cautious about how to frame this. GB also felt we could not push much beyond the 1,500 quid a year worse off after a parliament. The problem was the press felt we had done this already. But we had to keep going. And we had to be saying it was partly this that was getting the message through that the Tories were a risk. Clegg was doing fine. Calm. Measured. Warning he would come under attack. 'Vote Clegg get Brown' was the Tories' main line through the day.

Recorded the spoof bulletins in Soho. Home. Work on GB words for tomorrow. Back to the fundamentals. Out for dinner with Ian Kennedy and the boys. He seemed to think we would win because the Clegg surge would take out Cameron and we would come through at the end. Had to hope so. Peter M called me out, worried about the event tomorrow. Alistair was OK about the figures but worried about the ash. Douglas feeling squeezed in the campaign. Peter M was both central but also strangely detached. He said we were trying to win. If we could not win, we were trying to lose with dignity. And if we lost we wanted to show it was the Blairites who fought hardest to hold on and the Blairites who should rebuild afterwards. Ian felt I should watch myself health-wise. The week coming up was going to be pretty hellish so he was right.

Did a note on the debate post-mortem meeting. Sheehan's note on what went well and what didn't slightly damned GB with faint praise. GB kept saying he had not been light enough on his feet, which he hadn't. He had been too leaden. He hadn't talked directly to people. Not done big argument enough. Had a chat with GB and I said my worry was Clegg on Iraq and GB language on troops under attack from Cameron. It had to be about how he felt, soldiers died. It could be my son. We are all human beings.

Get it all focused on big argument and message. I said he needed to stop thinking about the others or the audience and speak directly to the people at home. They had to be imagined nodding along. That is what Clegg did.

Monday 19 April

Another nice day. Out early to take Calum to Euston then to Victoria Street. The volcano fallout was now even bigger as an issue. Morning meeting – Harriet had a good point about the Big Society being no good to you when something like this happened. Also again saying that there were not enough women in the campaign. Douglas also getting agitated that Peter was so much the public face of the campaign, on which he had a point. There was a brief discussion about whether we were right to be pressing ahead with the attack. Yes, we were but we had to be careful to separate out party and government. That's why I was not sure Peter should have been so prominent yesterday. 'Mandelson's Dunkirk' headline in one of the papers. The politics was still all Clegg and we were all still on Tory–Lab. We were right to be having another go and the overall presentation was strong. But the reality is the hacks were bored with us. We were old and tired and irrelevant to the story they were loving, namely Clegg–Cameron.

We went through the presentation with AD. He had a bad limp because of a trapped nerve and was worried how that would look. He was also a real trooper in many ways but very squeamish about anything that might land a real blow. I talked to him about energy and tried to pump him up a bit. Did a quick blog on the Dave–Nick blue–orange politics, Labour still on the economy, then set off to Bloomberg with Catherine, Pat and the rather impressive, and witty, Torsten who had put together the paper on the Tory plans. GB had been right though that it was not big enough for a big breakthrough. The press event was in the same room as the Sport Industry Awards. Looked good. Pre-meeting. I sat down with GB and wrote a few lines to put at the end of his opening statement. He was fairly calm. But I worried we were too Lab–Tory and not really adapting well enough. He said he was sure we just had to keep on this. I gave him a line on Clegg about how sometimes honeymoons were short, which he liked and used OK.

Alistair was taking lots of Nurofen for his trapped nerve. The hacks liked the humour of the spoof news report on Tory Britain. A fair few questions on the economic stuff. But actually they were only really interested in Libs and tactics of a hung parliament. GB was OK but I was getting more worried that we had no real vitality and we needed freshness to get to a different place. It was hard though to get the GB team to see what they needed and then do it. The whole thing was pretty amateur. Peter had to watch himself too. There was a feeling among ministers that he was excluding them. Douglas raised it at the first team meeting when we got back. Peter asked him to name names on who was complaining. DA said they could discuss it later. Peter said we're not girls so raise it here. 'Not girrrrls?' said DA.

It moved on and then I saw GB typing furiously – in both meanings – to Ed M. Balls was also getting at GB the whole time about not being involved properly. I pointed out we had lost the NHS as automatic vote winner. We had lost the pledge cards. We had lost renewal. Record. Future. Team. Energy. We did not give people positive reasons to vote. It was too negative. Peter said to me later that nothing happened in the campaign but for a small number of Blairites. He said I should help where I could but it was wise to have an element of detachment. They were already gearing up to play the blame game because that is what they did. They really did not get how to do this stuff. There was poor leadership, cliqueyness, bad management. They hated each other more than they hated us.

Clegg was still cruising. Tories not looking good. Hague poor in the foreign debate on the Beeb. D Miliband won it, though I thought he could have done better on Iraq. He looked commanding though. We needed him in the campaign more. He came in for a meeting on how to do more, maybe positioning speeches. I went for a tea and a moan with Sukie who said the GB operation was a shambles. Some of the Tory policy weaknesses were coming through which was good. But the campaign really did have a bit of the *X Factor* feel to it. Cameron was more Susan Boyle than Gladstone. But it was almost like nobody could say it.

Tuesday 20 April

Decided to work at home. Endlessly doing notes for Peter M etc. I did a pretty heavy number on the current state of the campaign and said if it did not move up gears on virtually every level we were fucked. Peter was calling for big speeches. I was calling for big positive events. I said the pledge card, renewal, team, future offer were all not there. Just launched then forgotten. Nothing we said had connected. We had to do something different now. This could not just carry on. Media still on Cleggmania and Tories in trouble which gave us opportunities but we were not exploiting them properly. David M called for a chat about a speech re *X Factor* politics. I said we had to keep the Tories down, recast views of the Libs and give a big forward offer. We were doing only one of those.

We were not adapting re Libs and we were therefore losing support to them along with the Tories. And we were also not doing the future. Getting any sense of urgency was a nightmare. David wanted to take apart

Clegg's line on sixty-five years of failure. It was nonsense. *Guardian* had a piece asking if Clegg was our Obama. What a lot of nonsense. Lovely sunny day. Glad not to have gone in. But I needed to decide whether I was really going to get involved and take it by the scruff of the neck. I sent through a different sort of script for the opening minute for Thursday's debate. David M sent through his draft but it needed to be more elevated. Peter M sent round a good note on the need to rethink the current format of GB campaign to allow him to make the big future statements about change / lessons from crisis / building on record in order to apply experience to big challenges. At the moment, the media were treating GB like an intrusion on the Cameron / Clegg race.

Peter felt he should do three major speeches – banks, financial regulation, re-balancing economy plus public service reform in new financially constrained times, and one on new politics? It certainly might help. And as he said, what was there to lose in him being more serious and seen to be so. The focus groups last night confirmed me in the view that there has to be a substantial change of gear on various levels. Unless we get traction on future / energy / team / forward offer, we will be stuck and the last five days will be too late. The truth is undecideds don't want us back. They don't like the Tories and are pleased the Cameron bubble has burst. I said Clegg looks different. They may think his success is a bubble too, but that is not yet certain. We have to give them a reason to stick with that view of the Tories, modify their view on the Libs (which should be rooted in policy and the danger of a hung parliament) and give them positive reasons for backing us. We were continuing to do the first of those only.

For obvious reasons, Thursday's debate was now more risky in many ways than the first. We had to start strategising for it in a different way. Peter M and I agreed there was a problem at the moment with GB / language. It lacks freshness and vitality. I had talked to him about it in relation to the debates but it is affecting all of his comms. The arguments don't need to change. The points of connection do. I also worried that we were still fighting the campaign we imagined we would be having – Lab–Tory – and had not accommodated properly the changed landscape post-debate / Clegg surge. The things we are saying about it are not interesting or arresting enough. It is almost as though we are becalmed. We keep saying it has energised the campaign but we don't seem energised by it.

I was also alarmed at the extent to which big moments have just come and gone. Pledge card – forgotten. National renewal – never mentioned since. Team – barely visible. Future offer – not clear. We needed a big event where talk of the Tories and the Libs was banned and we set out prosaically what we had done, why, what we would do next. On the team issue, my sense was that too many ministers have simply stopped thinking or acting politically. They wait to be told what to do. They should be champing at the bit with ideas, lines, arguments. Those deemed capable of that need to be brought into the centre. The only good news was that the Tories are in real trouble. The bad news was that we appear not to be benefiting from it. Only PG, still in the US, and Ben WP bothered to reply to the note on the need for a new kind of event. Ben said we could easily adapt the proposed event on Monday into what I had suggested. He did a good note on how we could take Health/Education/Home Affairs/Families and turn it into the kind of thing I wanted.

I also discussed with David a different way for GB to present himself, that would be high risk but fresh and arresting. On the lines of 'I know a lot of you don't like me. I may wish it wasn't so. But I live with it. You may not love me but I love this country and everything I do is about securing your future. And as you watch and choose, at least reflect that experience and judgement matter more than how you look or how you sound. Experience and judgement that led Britain and helped lead the world through the global crisis so we are now into recovery without the calamity predicted. Experience and judgement that meant no matter how difficult and unpopular, we did not bend in Iraq. Experience and judgement in Afghanistan. Difficult. Unpopular. But right. Our forces making your streets safer. (And we should be proud of them.) Experience and judgement in Europe, so that we are central not marginal as we work in alliances to tackle climate change, terrorism, nuclear proliferation, the Middle East. So we can build on the work we have done in Africa and alleviating poverty around the world. This is an island nation but an island with a big heart.

And this is not *X Factor* or *Pop Idol*. It is an election to choose your government at a time of uncertainty and danger. It is the fight for the most important and difficult job in this country. Back experience and judgement. Back me and my team. And I will not let you down.' DM worried it would unsettle him.

The Lib Dem bubble was not bursting. If it did it was not going to help us. The problem was that they had pretty much decided on GB and we were stuck. They had sent Cameron packing and asked him to rethink and come again and there was a truly ludicrous mood around Clegg – Dianafication was around. And we had not really agreed a strategy. We let the Tories attack them and we hung back. TB was sending me messages the whole time that it was a colossal error. It was tactical – GB could see that he might be able to stay as leader of a Lib–Lab coalition. But it was a disaster for the party. His emails started to get more and more apocalyptic. This is a blunder of epic proportions. It will destroy the party. Please persuade him to change his mind.

I managed to get a fair bit done at home and then set out with Rayan for the Merrill Lynch [financial services] dinner at the Grove [Hertfordshire hotel]. Numbers down because of flights grounded over volcanic ash. Very right-wing, very anti-GB. I was sitting next to a very right-wing business guru who had signed the *Telegraph* NICs letter. He and several others had nothing good to say about us. Nothing at all. One or two felt AD a good thing. But they really wanted us out. It was almost visceral. They were not keen on Cameron and thought the Clegg thing totally overblown. But they were really not keen on us. I played it mainly for laughs, did a bit of an election round-up and strategy stuff and then an OK Q&A. Books sold well too. OK event though not my kind of people. Then down to Cardiff in an Astra with a union driver sent by the party. St David's Hotel. Bed just after 1.

Wednesday 21 April

Lovely sunny day. Looked out from my room across Cardiff Bay, transformed under Labour. There was the Assembly, the opera house, the harbour looking great. And we were giving it away to DC and this ludicrous Cleggery. TB still urging me to get GB in a better place on the Libs. He said he was in despair watching it. 'Must be worse for you, having to be there.' Douglas had done some Cameron-ing rehearsal last night and said GB had been OK. But as we discovered through the day he got very antsy about the troops equipment stuff. We were also going to have to watch Clegg on Iraq and Trident. *The Sun* had a copy of [Lib Dem election team chair] John Sharkey's note to Clegg for the debate which had been left in a cab and had the line 'avoid unilateral nuclear disarmament implications'.

GB was out on a visit early on so I had breakfast with Theo, Justin and Douglas. The mood was not good. The Lib surge had not halted. When GB arrived I managed to stop us going straight for rehearsal and said we needed a proper discussion. We were stuck. Our campaign was lifeless. We had to get a lift and more of the same wouldn't do. Leaving it to the Tories hadn't worked. We looked like we were snuggling up for our own interest not the country's. We went round in circles, him raging at Cleggmania and the superficiality of the media, me saying we had not been clear enough about giving people reasons to vote Labour. He seemed very down, accepted we were stuck. We did four sessions through the day. Several times, on troops and on Iraq, he walked away saying it was hopeless, we couldn't win these arguments. When I pressed him on the military covenant [fairness promise to the armed forces] he went into a real rage.

I kept arguing that we needed to get on to bigger points – e.g. we are going to put future governments in a position where they can't take difficult decisions on war. Media and opposition make it impossible. Talk about the big strategic issues. I got him on to the script saying it was not a popularity contest and he knew people didn't like him, but he was really not keen. He went for it but I kind of felt he would move away from it. Theo was finding it harder to be Clegg. His positions were not strong. Cameron weak on Europe. But GB easy to take into rebuttal and PMQs mode which was hopeless for us. He had to get on to leadership, experience and judgement. He wanted to be man with a plan. Fine but it is too limited. The big story was still Clegg and hung parliament and where did it all go wrong for Cameron?

Conference call with Peter, DA and team and Peter said he was not coming to Bristol because there was so much briefing going against him and Harriet had decided she had to be there and to do her stuff. I felt we needed Peter there even if he was going to give us problems with the others. This next 48-hour period was vital for deciding forward strategy. We were in bad shape and it could easily get worse. GB not in as good a place as he was a week ago at this stage. Strangely becalmed apart from the odd eruption. I pushed back hard in lots of areas. We had to get him and the campaign to a better place. Peter wanted a press conference and a speech on Friday. I totally agreed. We had to get more policy up. I was keen to get home to see Calum. Same driver as yesterday with a bloody Astra and the fucking M4 was shut outside Cardiff. Home in the early hours.

Thursday 22 April

TB called, said I know what GB will be thinking, as ever tactically. He will think let the Tories attack them, then I can do a deal to stay in a hung parliament. That deprives him strategically of his one selling point, which is strength. Besides, he said, a hung parliament with the absurd Cleggery holding the balance of power would be a disaster for UK. 'This whole thing makes me weep.'

He felt the debates were doing what he always feared they would, sucking energy and ensuring there was even less focus on policy. I said GB had been doing a bit better but my God is it hard work. And we have lost so much ground. Getting changes of gear through the whole campaign so hard. Peter good but too prickly and too high-profile and now getting briefed against by the others. Douglas and Harriet, to a certain extent David and Ed M, commentators rather than players, Ed Balls on his own kick, Alan J invisible. He felt there was an epic failure in GB cosying up to the Libs, that it would end up destroying us if we were not careful.

I was tired, mainly because I was taking too much medication to stay calm. Out to the City for the Investec [asset management group] event with Portillo chaired by Kirsty Wark. Really nice taxi driver who said he thought we would come through at the end. He said his wife read the *Mail* cover to cover every day. Clegg came on the TV last night and she asked who was he? The breakfast do was fine. Kirsty chaired well and Michael and I sparred OK. He felt if the Tories had to give Clegg PR for a deal they would do it. TB sent me another email saying GB was too obviously tactical on this and we had to say that he was going for a majority government. Also that he was not interested in a deal because their policies were totally ridiculous. Portillo said he did not miss being involved at all. He said he was at a loss to know how the Tories should proceed now. They really had been stalled. We at least had a kind of 'keep on keeping on' message. I said that the markets response was less of a problem for the public who were less keen on the banks than they used to be. Did my usual whack at the media, said the debates were drowning out policy debate.

GB called and read me a new version of the opening statement. I said it was fine but in truth I was not that keen on it. It needed more of an admission that people did not like him so that he could do the contrast with their style v his substance. We redid the opening and the end. Then I worked out the best way to go for them was to have different attacks on them at the same time in different ways. We needed a prism that could give him a way of attacking both in different ways.

- 'Nick, your anti-Americanism is a problem. David, your anti-Europeanism is a problem.'
- 'Nick, you're a risk to our security because of a Trident. David, you're a risk to the economy.'
- 'Nick, you're as big a risk to our security as David is a risk to our economy.'
- 'David, you're not ready for this job. Nick, you never will be.'
- 'Nick, if you feel this is ganging up, I hate to think what Chancellor Merkel and President Sarkozy would do to you.'
- 'David, if you get this nervous at a TV debate, I dread to think how you'd react to a phone call in the middle of the night telling you a bomb's gone off.'

Stefan Stern [*Financial Times*] sent me a good line: 'Nick, David… Calm down now. This reminds me of bath time when my boys want to keep squabbling instead of going to bed.'

The statement really worked. The Sky hype machine was ludicrous. All interviewing each other the whole time. I tweeted why not remind people of what is in the manifestoes? They came straight back saying come on and talk about the manifesto. I wanted to get GB to a harder position re

Clegg and Cameron. He was getting there. I was sure DC would go hard on troops and in the domestic section put them together as Lib–Lab. GB really lost it when I raised the *Times* leader on the military covenant. He punched the lectern. 'Those fucking bastards. That fucker Murdoch, cunt.' I said 'That is not going to look good on telly,' and after everyone else laughed, so did he. We went through it again and again. We had to get to a place where he was making bigger points, like that in future nobody would be able to take the country to war. He needed to get a bit angry about things when they said they supported the war but didn't really. We did several hours of it.

The camera guys – Martin had given us the line about it not being a popularity contest – felt he was better as we went on. Martin said he would vote for me as Cameron over GB as GB. Bit worrying! There were some fairly big demos so we had to find a different way in. At one point the cops were saying he might have to go a different route – with the other two by boat. I did him another note with lines and prism. Had a chat with DMil who was down to do the media. He said if we finished third it was a total disaster and there was a danger we were finished. He was so angry that everywhere we went there was so much improvement but we never talked about it. The team had gone. Balls was at it the whole time. He was not sure about his brother. They were starting to brief against Peter who was clearly going to be blamed for the campaign. I said I would go all barrels if they did. The politicians were as weak as piss. They just did not fight as if their lives depended on it. Too many of them were like commentators. All GB-centric. The Eds were apparently starting to say that Peter and co. were only interested in setting up things for David M.

Over to the media centre. Did Sky and Beeb and a general chat. Kay Burley [Sky presenter] said it was all about body language. I took the mick mercilessly on that which she took in good nature. I was pushing substance. Had to be man v boys tonight. Had a little chat with Osborne downstairs. The guys with me said he was shaking when I went over to him. I quite liked Osborne actually. Yes a Tory toff but he was very political and he really knew what he thought whereas I'm not sure that Cameron did. Balls turned up uninvited and did some media. Whelan around too. Harriet. Bob Ainsworth. Douglas and DM plus the support team.

GB did pretty well [at second leaders' debate]. Halfway through we did the winning on substance line. Clegg OK again, if not as good as first time. Cameron a bit better but not that great even though the Tory papers would do comeback whatever happened. I felt GB was genuinely better. Got a lot of our best lines in. Plus the twin attack. It was more combative in general but the second half was too same old really. He did OK though and that was the general feeling without a doubt. Interesting to watch the politicians throughout as we watched. Balls feet up on his BlackBerry, saying nothing. Harriet cheerleading. Douglas always thinking about what he would say. I was getting massive Twitter response and I did sense GB doing fine. The *Sun* poll gave it to DC, surprise, surprise. There was a real danger in the Foxisation of Sky. Story doing the rounds of James Murdoch and Rebekah going into the *Indy* office and demanding to know 'What the fuck is going on?' with *The Indy*'s campaign on Murdoch. *Sun* would be hating this.

I scribbled a line to take on the debates analysis and then we swarmed the spin room. I did one with Osborne which was quite fun though far too short. They were trying to push Labour leaflets that DC had raised in which candidates were saying the Tories would take away a, b, c. I said that DC had changed the policy there and then. Also that this was meant to be the big fightback and all they could go on was a few leaflets. Not big enough. Chat with Paddy A. I asked him if he remembered that he said to me in Germany Clegg would not do a deal with anyone? He raised his eyebrows at that one. Did the rounds then back, got changed and headed home with some of the No. 10 team.

GB called. He had definitely done better. I said we now had to get on to policy. Had to have ideas and drive them hard. Had to make sure we made up for lack of campaign money with creativity and energy. We needed it on the economy and the debate plus tomorrow's GDP figures had to give us that. PG had finally made it back and was really worried about where the fire was coming from. Peter becalmed. DA weakened, he felt. No others apart from Alistair – in Washington – with a profile. Pretty hopeless. We went over what had worked and what had not. Everyone seemed to feel he had done better. But Clegg had done pretty well and Cameron didn't bomb. George was pushing it a bit when he said that it was a clear win for DC but there you go. We were all spinning away I guess. TB felt GB did better but 'the Tory boy' was not terrible. Home by 1.30. Tired. Too much on now. Plus GB really leaning on me the whole time.

Friday 23 April

I went into Victoria Street with Rory who was on his way to Chelsea Academy for the day. He felt last night was a bit of a draw, that Clegg did OK again. I went into the morning meeting which felt like a morgue. Peter was not himself. The briefings against him were getting to him, making him think he was being set up for a fall. Harriet, Balls, Ed M and Douglas were all reckoned to be briefing against him. But the problem was the general ideas-lessness. PG was back and though looking tired was fizzing with ideas. I was suggesting stuff the whole time. I was still pushing for my future event, maybe ten ministers announcing ten forward policy pledges each. But everything was meeting with inertia. Peter actually looked bad. Meanwhile I had to rewrite GB words for his press conference where we were trying to get the economy up again. Harriet was chairing it. Peter looked subdued.

GB did OK. Harriet had said on the way down to the press event 'Make sure I stay in control of this' and then annoyed the hacks by being schoolmarmish re one question at a time. It went OK though the Tories were getting a bit of traction with the leaflets smear story. GB and Peter dealt OK with it. Then GB asked me to go through and work on his speech for Coventry. It was the usual cut-and-paste melange which he then added to. He banged away at the computer, occasionally shouting for facts he had been asking for with Sue Nye popping in and out to say they needed to go. I ended up rewriting the whole thing from scratch, sending it on the train and then watching him deliver it word for word. It was all a bit of a shambles. Then I went into the planning meeting. More lethargy and lack of clarity. Peter looking a bit on edge.

At the end Marianna asked me if I could get a celeb for the weekend events and it was the straw that broke the back. I said it was pathetic – the Cabinet were meant to be the most important people in the country. They should know everyone. They should be building relationships all the time. And here we were in the middle of campaign and they were scrabbling. Douglas walked in and I let rip at him re JK Rowling, said who the fuck was supposed to be asking her to do a broadcast? We just talked and talked and people did nothing but moan about the campaign. Thought fuck it and went home. GB called after his speech, said thanks for doing the speech. I said the mood in Vic Street was bad. There were tensions inside and out. He said there were always only a few people who could do this stuff and it was mainly you.

I said he had to sort Balls out, get him properly engaged. If there was any nonsense I would go for it. He said he still believed we could pull something out of the fire but we had to rely on our instincts now. He said he was sorry so much was falling on me but I was the only one there really holding up. At the end of the day reckoned I had had four meetings with him and about ten calls. Definitely getting sucked in too much. I agreed with him though that we could still get up a bit. PG said on substance and economy we were doing OK. I was worried he was getting tired. Even though he had spent a few days holed up in a hotel, he wasn't rested and had been getting more and more stressed when he was out there. Gail was worried about him.

I was struggling to find the time to finish TB's book, which was really good. He clearly thought I was going crazy towards the end of my time with him but he was pretty warm about most of us. Very frank re GB. And all the things he said in the book he worried about vis-à-vis GB were now happening – not New Labour enough, lack of clarity, relying on bad advice etc. GB was desperate for me to go the strategy meeting on Sunday. I said I was desperate to go to Burnley. Home and chatted to Fiona who said she really thought once this was over I should decide that that was it, no more. If DM took over he would obviously want me to help him but she felt it would just mean five more years then five more and I would never be free of it.

Saturday 24 April

Balls was in the *Telegraph* on the post-election 'keep GB' scenario. Mad to be talking about possible defeat. *The Times* splashed on us changing strategy to up GB tempo, we think briefed by DA. Peter getting very fed up. He wanted a conference call with me and GB so we could read riot act but it never happened. GB called several times on the way to Corby. We were trying to get up the cancer guarantee attack. Cameron was out at a school saying there should be no more unelected PMs. Pretty cheap. Clegg day off with his boys back from having been stranded by the volcanic ash. I had a long chat with Peter who sounded really down. He said he could not get motivated by GB and he just felt that people were gunning for him. Balls had given up on GB a long time ago and seemed only interested in his own position. Ed M was also briefing against Peter and the campaign according to Gary Gibbon [*Channel 4 News*] via Ben. Ben said Peter was at the end of his tether.

He, David Muir and I had a good meeting and planned out the next few days. GB was calling the whole time. He was getting more involved in news planning. He wanted to get up on IHT more and on something he was calling an Ashcroft second home tax. He was motoring OK but I said he had to sort these central relationships or else we were fucked. He said Peter would come back in but basically we had to give him the strategy. He was in killer-driller mode, calling then calling back half-hour later to have the same conversation. TB texting asking how it was going. Morale low in HQ. Ben and David were solid citizens and we actually put together quite a good plan going forward. 11 p.m. conference call re the Sundays. A lot of briefing against Peter. A few bad Tory stories too. Earlier had the idea of getting a joint three-party letter to the broadcasters about covering policy. Spoke to Gove who was speaking to Osborne. David spoke to the Lib Dems and looked like we were on for it. West Ham beat Wigan so we were down tomorrow if we lost to Liverpool. Had to go to that.

Sunday 25 April

I didn't sleep well. Up before 6 and I worked on a speech for GB's youth event later in the day. He wanted to go big on fairness. Also seized on the story in *The Observer* that the Tories were planning top-up fees for nurseries. I did a thing on the five great fairness tests which I thought might carry. But again Clegg was going to dominate. He was on Marr effectively saying he would not prop up GB if we came third. Could become irritating to have all this post-election stuff coming at us when they had yet to win a single vote. I did the speech by 7 then long chat with GB. He was still banging on about hitting them on cuts and unfairness. It was fine but limited and the reality was the media were successfully putting us in a position of near irrelevance with Cameron and Clegg the main men.

Through the day our efforts to get the other two parties signed up to a 'more policy not process' letter to the broadcasters foundered. I had spoken to Gove yesterday and he sounded quite keen, as did the Lib Dem David spoke to. It wasn't clear who in both parties kyboshed it but it was briefed to Nick Robinson who did a blog on it. There was a terrible problem of cohesion at the centre. Peter and DA barely speaking. Papers today apparently full of briefing and counter-briefing on the campaign. I did a blog with a tail-end thing basically saying that it had to stop. Also took in a reference to the softness of the Lib Dem vote (around half saying could change mind) and Tories' silly briefings about us. The economy was still up there. GB's opening statement polled best in the groups. He was also winning as best PM. But it was constantly stated that he lost the debates.

Set off for Burnley with Rayan and Calum. A few calls. Missed the main strategy meeting in No. 10 which GB had wanted me to go to. PG said it was actually quite good. Peter said it was terrible and that we just went over the old ground and GB ended in a fairly Ballsian position, investment and cuts, the stuff the media were just not buying. GB calling and reading me the speech for later. Chatting to Barry Kilby during a really nice lunch. Everyone quizzing me on the election, especially the Liverpool chief executive [Christian Purslow] who seemed onside. He felt the Clegg bubble would burst. The match was odd. First half OK and we might have taken the lead. Second half they battered us. Final score 4–0. Relegated.

I did a blog and then kipped on the way back. I was getting a bit tired for all this. But got back reasonably early and went to Shawn Slovo's 60th. Bumped into Michael Palin on the way who seemed pretty onside, putting arguments as to why he thought it might come back to us. Mainly small talk and a bit of Cleggery at the do. TB texting saying that Cleggery was ridiculous and we had to stop it and warn people against the hung parliament being an easy option. Didn't feel as bad as I thought I would re going down because in a way it was expected, and also at least it would not now be the same week as an election we might easily now get hammered in.

Monday 26 April

For the first time, a policy story was heading up the news, Kent's Tory county council leader having warned of negative impacts for some schools of the Tory free schools plan. Balls was up and about on it, first of all jumpy because he was worried about being asked about *Sun* splash – fined for using mobile while driving – but then agreed to do it. It led to one of the longest sentences I had ever heard. It went on and on and on. Peter and I were watching on TV and he said we should send in the SAS to rescue the hacks. The clip on the news was OK though. Plus we had finally agreed a proper line on the Libs, focused on their arrogance in talking constantly about what was to follow the election rather than the issues. I kept banging on about the need to say policy not process but the morning meetings were pretty desultory. It was entirely possible to say something which fell entirely on deaf ears unless PG was there and he was trying too hard the other way.

Peter seemed a bit happier but not much more engaged. He was really fed up with it now. We had an OK meeting on the Libs and agreed Douglas A should poke them at the press conference. The Tories had somehow persuaded the media to run a story that our vote was collapsing and they had extended the list of Tory–Lab marginals. But then Cameron's visit was to a Lib–Tory marginal and Osborne did a press conference on the dangers of a hung parliament. So it was all a bit muddled. GB visits looking better today. Also got a standing ovation at the RCN [Royal College of Nursing] and a good Asda visit. Evening news best yet because we were on substance and they were on process and hung parliaments. Harriet trying to get us to reshape the campaign a bit. Wanting a bigger role for herself and other women. Also wanting us to understand this was all about emotional disconnect.

I worked on statements for Thursday. Various not very good meetings then got fed up and went home. Ben doing a good job but he too was getting dispirited a bit. Douglas said he was fed up of Peter and I shouting at him. Apart from once, when my target was GB, I hadn't. But he was pretty down. He had a lot of good points but he was not leading. I did an hour on the bike then GB called about his speech on families tomorrow. He was complaining that it was impossible to get traction for policy debate to run. The education story lasted one cycle then went. I said the news was good for us and we had to keep going in that vein. He said that he felt sure we could still win but it was all about getting on to the economy and staying there and getting to risk. We agreed he should let rip tomorrow and do a thing about how frustrating it was that we had people interested in tax credits, national minimum wage, Sure Start etc. and there was no focus in the media debate. We ended up writing a speech together over the phone which was always really annoying. Plonking hard on a computer, asking me basically to dictate and he would take it all down.

Tuesday 27 April

Worked on GB words early on. Bumped into Harriet on the way in and she made one or two insightful points on the nature of the campaign. It was an emotional disconnect problem. People knew the Libs were not serious but when we said it they seemed to reject it. They wanted to punish us and the Tories and this was the only way they knew. She said she didn't know how to get back to a more reasoned debate but it had to be better than this. The trouble was that she usually believed the solution was some kind of gender warfare. But she was right on one level. She was also right that we should be attacking the Libs on crime as they had said jail terms of less than six months should be replaced by community sentences. But the morning meetings were a series of disconnected points not driven by agreed strategy. Peter was strangely becalmed. I asked him if he was OK, and he said yes. But he wasn't. He basically felt that GB just couldn't do it, we had to face that and just go down with dignity. PG was tired but still trying to cheer people up.

Popped out, walked up to the Strand and back, just for a bit of escape then back for a bit before heading for lunch with Rebekah Brooks at Wapping. Friendly enough but sharp at times. She was coming from the position of basically feeling that she was there to help the Tories. David this and David that. [Trevor] Kavanagh popped in on his way to meet Gove for lunch. Rebekah telling me all the staff were voting Tory. She said Peter had been texting her abuse. She couldn't understand how he supported GB on any level. If TB was still there, he would have won and they would have supported us. She just felt we should all have moved to get rid of him. Miliband would have made a difference. James [Murdoch] not in but saw his waist-high desk set-up. She seemed OK but these were basically just right-wing puppets of RM. She got her driver to give me a lift to Euston.

Managed to get an early train and go up to Manchester alone. Did a bit of work and had a snooze. Conor Hanna at the *Mirror* phoned to say they were rushing in the Fergie piece tomorrow. Cab to hotel, Calum came over for a drink, then a walk to a Belgian beer bar before I came back to wait for GB. Seemed in OK mood. Did a few hours' debate prep at the end of which he took me and Douglas through to the bedroom and said he had an idea for the opening statement. It was a variation on the plan he had had at the start of the campaign to indicate that he would pull Labour candidates out of Lib Dem winnables and say he would resign if he lost the referendum on electoral reform. Now he had a different idea – say that he had done a deal with Obama etc. on the banks which gave us an extra £2 billion, say he had an economic plan for the year then the AV referendum and if he failed on either he would go. It was bold and ballsy but possibly fatal. The boldness attracted me. The only question was whether people – i.e. Clegg and Cameron – would immediately seize on it as lame duckery, a ploy to buy a bit more time.

However, it seemed to me that people were genuinely undecided about this election and that meant in a way the country didn't want to make up its mind. So this might be a way of saying this is a way of buying time for the country. The weakness of that is that the time for countries to decide is the election. We went round it for ages. We tried to write a version. Douglas was sceptical. So was I, apart from the fact it was a game changer. David was quite keen. He was also of the view we had to have a game changer and this was a game changer. I wanted to get the judgement of others but GB was adamant we discuss it with nobody. He felt Peter had rejected the last idea because he was not involved in the earlier discussions. He was not clear how he would go for this. I felt against.

I wanted to pick TB's mind on it. He was in Malaysia. I fixed for them to speak. When it came to it they had a general chat. But GB did not specifically mention this. Indeed, when I asked him if they had spoken – TB had already told me they had – he said no. The debate prep per se was OK. We had Joel Benenson [pollster] over from the US, who was good. Much more people-friendly than Michael but also good on message. I could see he felt a bit alarmed at times at GB's demeanour. He was also of the view that GB needed to go more on the 'same old Tories' line. We went through several versions of the intro, but not the one on the dramatic plan. He looked pretty grey and tired and was sitting down a lot when Theo and I were on our feet. He knew this had to be the big one and it was not going to be easy. Cameron could play safe. Clegg was looking more and more assured. Very good TV performer now.

Wednesday 28 April

Breakfast with Matthew [Doyle] talking about TB's book, which was clearly going to be big news. I did a quick blog on where we were campaign-wise then met Calum and Phil Townsend for lunch. GB was due back for 1, for another debate prep session. Just before I started to get a rash of texts etc. and calls asking for interviews on 'unguarded comments' the PM made re a voter in Rochdale. I could tell it was a moment based on the fact they were all calling at once. I ignored the calls, but the texts were all about 'How should he handle the fallout?' Then Jamie Redknapp called, and I answered – 'God, you've got your work cut out today, AC.' What's happened, I asked? 'You mean you don't know?' No, I'm having lunch with Calum and a pal, not been answering the phone. 'Oh my God, your man has fucked it big time.'

He described it. GB talking about immigration and other stuff, doing fine, nice manner, surrounded my media, listening to a woman go on about immigration, she seemed to like him then he gets in the car and his mic is still on and he calls her a bigot. He calls her a what? 'A bigot, Al, calls her a bigot.' Oh shit. At that moment GB's convoy came by. We settled up and I headed back. As I got to the fourteenth floor he was crossing the corridor from the debate prep room to his own suite. He asked me to see him. I have never seen him like it. 'I just lost us the election.' 'It can't have been that bad.' 'It was. It's a fucking disaster. I made a terrible mistake. I am so sorry I am so useless. I fucking hate myself.' He then tried to explain what had happened. 'I knew she was trouble. I couldn't understand why I was being pushed towards her. She had been heckling and Sue was pushing me towards her. She was coming out with stuff about immigrants and Rochdale being a third world country and then I get in the car and…'

He then went into a rage at the media. 'They have got all their dreams come true. Everything they have been working for – he's useless. He can't communicate. He's weird.' Then into a thing about the mic. 'The sound guy was happy not to use it because it was after I got in the car. But he was over-ruled. Fucking Sky. Fucking media. This is what our fucking politics has become. They can do anything and we let them. Would they have cameras and mics in the bath if they could? Yes. They are fucking evil.' I let him go on, interjected with a few 'We need to decide what to do'-type statements. He said he had done a clip. He had also been on Jeremy Vine and they had played the tape. I was getting texts that he had slumped and looked awful. On his own, being filmed. Dire. He wanted to do a press conference. Peter and I both felt that was the wrong thing to do. He had called her from the car. 'She is not going to be helpful. I tried to apologise but she was not really having it.'

At times his face would freeze then he would shake in anger. Kicked a chair. Said sorry again. Walked to the bedroom, came back out. He was like a wounded animal. I remember Donald Dewar [late Labour First Minister of Scotland] talking about his 'Heathcliff wounded animal look' and this was the animal. At one point he sat down and put his head back and I could see his eyes fill with tears and a look of abject pain creased his face. It was pretty horrible to watch. This is the end, he said. After everything else I now have this as an added stain on my character. It is the culmination of a concerted character assassination. 'You know what it's like,' he said. I said I do but they can only do to you what you let them. We have to move on. He said they will say it is the defining moment of the campaign. David [Muir], Douglas, Sue, Justin and Iain [Bundred, GB's political spokesman] came in at various points. I can't remember who first suggested he went to the house to see her but he seemed keen. He wanted to go straight away. He said he didn't think of people like that so why did he say it? People were shocked because it was a perfectly good conversation. All added to the sense he was a bit odd. Peter was in London and he and I had a couple of long conversations. Peter felt provided the woman would see him he should go now rather than have it drag on. I sensed GB needed to do this to get it out of his system. I called Rachel who was on her way with Anna Healy [party press officer] to the house and asked her to sus out whether the woman – she was called Gillian Duffy – would welcome a visit, and sus whether she felt she would use it against him. It was already a circus there. She spoke to the woman who agreed she could come in and then agreed that GB could come.

We talked about how he should handle it coming out. If she accepted the apology, just say he was mortified, that he had wanted to see her face to face because he felt so bad at the hurt he had caused her etc. He was very shamefaced now. There were a few, especially Matthew, still saying don't go, you have apologised and it will blow over. But it was obvious he was not going to be able to move on until he had. He went into another round of 'I hate myself'. Everyone who came in, he said sorry. He said at one point he was getting over it but he wasn't. Sarah was in London and he asked once or twice why she wasn't there. He had mentioned Sue as having organised it so there was a bit of the usual blame stuff going on. Rachel told us all was set and he put on a new shirt and suit, Sue did his hair and makeup and off they went. I sat down to do a blog, trying to say it was a human not political act to go, and we all gathered in the prep room to wait. It was now being covered in full circus mode.

The bizarre thing was that the initial chat had not been so bad. It really wasn't. So why did he think it had been? Peter was out doing a pretty good job both defending GB, and the handling, but it was a game changer for the worse. He texted me to say those who criticised us for not allowing him to meet members of the public might now reflect. I emailed TB, who was unaware. He said there has to be explanation as to why he is like that. But how do you explain? The worst thing was that it got immigration up in the context of us thinking it was bigoted to raise it as an issue, which was the worst possible context. The media blathered on for forty-five minutes and then eventually he emerged and said he had apologised and she had accepted that apology. He was looking a bit too smiley though. He looked a bit too much like a politician who had got away with it.

She was not coming out and then rumours started that she was doing deals with PR companies and papers. Needless to say Max Clifford's name was in the frame. We were getting into black humour mode but the two guys filming for the debate prep, whose judgement I had grown to appreciate, said to me they felt it was really bad. It was worse than JP and the punch [of an egg-throwing protester in 2001] because there was a policy read-across. And the policy was immigration. Hard to be worse really. Rachel was texting me during the GB/Mrs Duffy meeting to say it was all quite jolly. I said is she worried about the Lib Dems and their 'alternative' policy re Trident [nuclear missiles]! 'She hasn't raised it but I can see it is playing on her mind.' I loved having Rachel around at times like this. She was calm and funny.

GB came back and we had been hoping to find him feeling better. He wasn't. He said she had been not terribly helpful and was also not sure that she might not do a deal with a paper. He said she had sort of accepted his apology but she was not exactly friendly. She had come out with some pretty extreme views which she accepted she got from the telly. She liked the local police and thought schools and hospitals were OK. But she was really quite extreme in her views on immigration. I kept saying he had to try to move on. He had to get into the economic debate zone. But the reality was this was one of the moments of the campaign and the damage was real and lasting. Even though some people might have felt he was treated badly by Sky, given the understanding was if they were not on camera the mic was off, the reality was it showed him in a dreadful light.

We talked round and round and eventually he agreed we had to talk debate. Tim Allan suggested he write to party supporters apologising. Douglas and I wrote it and got that off. I suggested he go to meet Sarah at Piccadilly station and do a little walkabout so that he realised that the whole world was not obsessing with this. It was another day with policy wipeout. He came back feeling a bit better because people had been fine. We then had a chat – he, Douglas, Sarah and I – about his plan of signalling departure after a year if he failed to deliver as promised on the economy and to resign if he lost the electoral reform referendum. He felt today's events made it harder to do. In a way it was. In another way he was the issue, and this helped crank that up.

We worked out a formulation. I tried it on Peter who was against. He was now so down on him that he could see no good in him doing anything other than going. What? Now? Why not? The thing is lost, hopeless. He said he was going to be totally humiliated. It was the worst possible end. And all because he said something he didn't mean. It really was dire. I felt that the party risked going into meltdown now. As Fiona said we all knew he was not a leader. But we all helped him and convinced ourselves it would be different. He had a long chat with Peter – but it was odd how he resisted talking to people – then he said it was all about immigration now. He had given them an opening. Interesting how the Tories failed to latch on to that. Clegg's response was better.

We went through to rehearse without telling the others about the plan. He said he would 'put his job on the line' and I teased out what it meant. Theo got the point straight away and then we really went for him over it. It gave lift to his answers but everyone basically thought it wasn't working as a device. He was fighting back but this was not the device. To be fair, he saw that straight away after we stopped. He then tried a different one which was more about the banks and the economy. We were slightly going through the motions though. He was not really motoring or engaging. I kept trying to feed him openings but he wasn't taking them. He clearly couldn't get it out of his mind at all. He was just thinking it was dire and he was finished which in all probability he was.

As Theo and I spoke, as Clegg and Cameron, he would sit down and put his head in his hands. Sarah being there probably helped a bit. She was calming but I still found her strangely cold. He kept asking about what had happened and how it was all being seen and I kept saying let's try to focus on the economy. It was hard but he had to get to a better place or else we were into major meltdown. He went to bed about half ten. It felt like a long slow death we were witnessing. The fight had gone from him and his team. David said he had never felt so low. I was deliberately trying to stay a little bit detached. But I really hated the idea of the Tories winning. Deep down I had always thought they would. But this was it now.

Thursday 29 April

Grace called just after I got up and we had a lovely chat which cheered me up. She said she felt sorry for GB and Sky were shits. She thought a lot of people would be on his side. But the media would not let go with this. Michael Sheehan sent through an email saying he should tap the microphone tonight and say is this on? I drafted a new opening with a glance to it, saying there is a lot to the job and he may not always get it right, but he knew how to run the economy in good times and bad. David and Stuart H and Theo went on the train with GB and said it was a nightmare. He had gone back into sulk-rage mode and he was just not listening to their advice. He was convinced he had to have his Obama–Sarko–Merkel £2 billion banking plan and everyone was telling him it couldn't be done. He was really in a bit of a panic now. I had the feeling the debate was last-chance saloon and he had to seize it or we were dead, or at least had no chance of getting back. First place had pretty much gone but third would be a disaster. I got the train to Birmingham, had a nice chat with a young guy who was going to the debate. We agreed the debates had sucked a lot of the energy from the campaign. Cab to the Marriott while doing a blog making clear that whatever the polls said GB won the debate and it was all to play for. Yesterday got a big response in terms of hits and also in terms of comments. Today pretty big too.

I arrived at the hotel to work on the statements and chat to the guys. They wanted me to cut through any energy-wasting and any nonsense. GB came in and though he looked tired he got into it fairly quickly. He wanted us to fire questions at him then after an hour or so we started to work on the opening statement. It took us about an hour and a half. Then took my original opening and turned it into a new ending. He was on OK form but as Peter M said when he arrived he looked exhausted. Good note from Peter H which I used as part of blog. I showed it to GB, basically saying let rip. Unshackled and go for it. When Theo and I were going at him over immigration he clearly had moments where he was worrying about yesterday. We agreed the others were unlikely to mention it and he was not to let it into his mind. Sarah was next door with Janice Turner doing an interview for *Grazia*.

We did a few hours and DA and I both started to press him that we had prepared enough and the risk was he now became more exhausted. He went for a bath and then came back for a final quick-fire session which went pretty well. I said to him before we left he really had to get psyched up. Energy. Don't worry about papers which were bound to give it to DC. Just think about the public, the undecideds out there. Go for it. And don't hold back on the Tory risk. We headed for the university, through the rain to the venue past a few small demos of e.g. Fathers for Justice. OK set-up really. Liam Byrne and Yvette Cooper the main ministers with Peter and DA. Matthew Doyle doing a great job holding everything together.

The debate went OK I felt. Tweeted loads during it. I genuinely thought he did better, even if he looked tired. The Clegg act was beginning to grate. Cameron was doing much more direct into-camera stuff but I found it extraordinary the extent to which he didn't answer questions. The other two looked good though and GB did, especially towards the end, look tired. *The Times* had an instant poll that gave it to Cameron. There was clearly something pretty bent about these polls. GB was still smiling too much. We had done a line saying it was GB's to win and he won it and I felt he did well enough to go for that. Peter went to the spin room before it finished and I did the second wave. A security guy at the top of the stairs asked me about Burnley v Liverpool – 'We've had it,' I said. Some

Tory bright spark was straight out saying I had said GB had had it. So there was a mini frisson re that downstairs. Did ITV then got surrounded. Did maybe eight interviews then had a little chat with George Osborne and headed home with Rayan. Full circus panoply outside. Media going with the polls for DC. Ignoring the C4 and radio ones which gave it to GB. Home by half one.

Friday 30 April

TB called on his way to Harrow where he was doing a campaign visit. Looking really tanned and fit and was on good form. Sky carried it live, a bit surreal, him getting a blood pressure test. But he spoke well on how this was something we talked about all those years ago – polyclinics etc. – and now here they were. He was pretty on-message. We had talked earlier and suggested he go for the Libs but it didn't quite carry. He was planning to do *The Times*, though, and would go for Cleggery and the nonsense of a hung parliament. The mood in HQ was pretty low. The Tories were generating a sense of energy, that they had won the debate and were on the last stretch. Media totally up their backsides now. GB was joined by several ministers for a poster launch which, as Alistair was speaking, attracted some guy yelling, then someone bashed into his car, and we had a metaphor for the campaign.

Lots of black humour settling in at Vic Street. When Peter M and DA came back I told them that there was almost a demob-happy sense around the place. There was no real fight left there. People were starting to take pictures of each other and chat in little groups. At one point I shouted out that there was a fight on. We had a meeting with Alicia Kennedy who clearly thought the Lib Dem surge had now taken lots of votes from us in the Tory–Lab marginals and was hinting the Tories might have a majority. We had money for more direct mail. But they were scrabbling round e.g. for a helicopter for a few days. TB came in and got a fantastic reception on both sides of the building. Went round to say hello to everyone, then did a speech. Said that we could still turn it around. Talked of some of the things we had done because we won. Praised the party machine. Whacked the Tories as unchanged. Said that we had to stop this Lib Dem nonsense. 'If it is possible to be profoundly vacuous that is what they are.' Got a fabulous ovation.

I had suggested getting cameras in but Peter and Douglas were worried it would be bad for GB, morale and otherwise. Afterwards we had a little chat, first on the idea of framing the election as a series of Big Choices. Peter felt all GB would do was go for risk. It was all he wanted to talk about. We needed a positive in all this which currently wasn't there. I worked on a few message lines for PG to test. Also working on TB article. GB called a few times ahead of his Paxman interview. I suggested he say we were the only serious choice. Tories wrong values and policies. Lib Dems right values wrong policies. We were the only ones with a plan.

Gary Gibbon had done a blog on the way the pollsters weighted the debate instant polls. It made the audience more Tory for various reasons. I told GB and he went off on one re the media. He had written to Murdoch about the viciousness of their attacks on him over the troops. I said that was the kind of people they were. We had let them get away with too much for too long. He sounded fairly mellow. Called a couple of times. Same chat. General feeling growing that it was all over.

Out for Grace's birthday with Rory and Fiona to Camden Brasserie. Starting to feel tired. Later I chatted with Alistair. He felt it was going away from us. Even worried about his own seat. He was also feeling that GB had not really wanted to speak to him when we had been trying to get hold of him from Manchester. Catherine told the story of an old man they met who said 'He was fine, Labour was fine – but your leader's a cunt.' Chat with Peter. He felt that GB just wasn't a leader and even though we might have known it we could never have known it was like this. He said he knew there were people who felt Peter had the chance to pull the plug and he didn't do it, but it was not so simple.

Saturday 1 May

The Times splashed on TB's interview saying Clegg just wasn't serious. *The Times*, however, came out for the Tories – first time in years. And *The Guardian* came out for the Lib Dems, albeit with a flick towards us in Lab–Tory marginals. It was not exactly a morale-booster. Generally the media was moving even more towards Cameron. Sky was a disgrace but it was having an impact on the rest of them. PG had tested various messages and the best that came out was 'a fight for your future'. I went in for a 'last five days' meeting. Pretty desultory. DA called in and we worked up a plan for the next few days. I drafted a Peter state-of-the-race memo saying we were still in it and getting out the new line. A fight for your future. DA said it was a core vote strategy but nobody must say so. We had to get 3 per cent back from the Libs to prevent a meltdown.

I wondered if this could actually be an 'end of Labour'-type thing. The strange death of Labour Britain. I did an Irish interview for telly and as I did so was deploying lines that I thought if only we had got these up properly before – e.g. on the record, unchanged Tories, role of debates etc. – we would have done better. David was pretty down. I was not sure how bad things might be but I did know there had to be a sense of fighting to the end and doing so with real energy and drive. Home to watch Birmingham v Burnley [2–1], then had a kip before doing a stump speech for GB, built around 'Fight for your future'. It was strong and if only he would really go for it and stick to it, it might win back a few people.

He called later on and we had a long chat about it. He said he still felt that we could stop a majority, that the good news was people didn't want a Tory government. The bad news was that they didn't want him, but we never really articulated this directly. The Libs were trying to push us out of a two-horse race. Cameron with media help was trying to create unstoppable momentum for him. He was looking pretty good, though sounding posher than ever. He had the wind behind him, a bit like we did in '97. But he had not been tested at all, not to the same extent. GB called again after a bit and was still talking about maybe winning. I suppose he had to keep believing. But the troops were low. Marianna told me that the mood in the office on the day of Mrs Duffy was awful. People felt let down.

Sunday 2 May

GB call re stump speech. He liked it but wanted to mangle it a bit. He wanted to call it 'surge Sunday'. I said no, just go for 'Fight for your future'. He had ten visits around London through the day, with several stump speech opportunities. I said we should also go for this unstoppable momentum strategy. The real story of the campaign was that the public didn't want the Tories. He sounded OK but it was hard work getting him up for a real barnstormer. Cameron had a fantastic backdrop in Newquay, with the sea and rocks. All his visits looked really good. Ours looked a bit rushed and higgledy-piggledy but at least people noticed GB was still fighting. I caught the end of Cameron on Marr, in which he said we can read the body language – you're on a roll. Outrage. Blogged on it and about Murdoch setting an agenda for the Tories that the Beeb would regret.

Peter felt I should be on the road giving GB his words the whole time. He said he didn't listen to any of the people with him. Patrick said he would only listen to me, Peter or Ed Balls. I wasn't sure it would be a very good image for him to have me getting on and off a helicopter with him, telling him what to say. Slight feeling of people having given up. Not many in the office. Papers not as bad as they might have been but the Tories were definitely putting over a sense of unstoppable momentum. There was a bit of pick-up for my blog and the whack on Murdoch. I had a long chat with Peter on what to do on the night. Both Patrick and PG felt that we should, in defeat, frame the result from the word go. There had to be a focus on the centre ground. We were punished for leaving it.

The danger was Ed Miliband, Patrick thought, who would position himself between Ed Balls and David M. Neil had already seemingly come out for Balls, having backed Harman. It was clear that there would be a fair bit of blood-letting and that they would be trying to blame Peter and me. He said the line already being run was that since Peter came back he acted as a block on all the things that GB wanted to do. In other words he was prevented from being himself. It was nonsense but it would be run. There was some discussion about who was on the telly on Thursday. In addition to me on ITV they had Neil, John Reid and Geoff Hoon. Paying shedloads to try to compete with the Beeb. I said to Peter there was a becalmed feeling to the campaign and that there were things we were not doing that maybe we could be. Mark Lucas came in with the Ross Kemp PEB plus loads of outtakes. Excellent.

Called Paul O'Grady [comedian, TV presenter] to try to get him to do the Tuesday rally. He couldn't because of work but had a really nice chat. He was totally onside. Hated Murdoch and the Tories. Couldn't believe the way the Duffy story had gone. Felt it was bad to have used the secretly miked conversation. He thought the Beeb would really regret going along with the negativity. He came across as a really nice guy and said he was happy to support us in other ways but couldn't do this particular event. He sounded genuinely alarmed at the prospect of a Tory government. GB called later. He felt today had gone OK. Ten seats. He said they all seemed to think the Labour vote was holding up though you always had to be careful about candidates' wishful thinking coming through. The buzz we were getting locally was that Glenda Jackson [former actress, Labour MP] had had it though he said she spoke incredibly well. He said Fiona should have gone for that seat [Hampstead and Kilburn] and we might have held it. He said he had felt the message worked fine but he wanted to add a bit more bite, by doing the betrayal of the middle class.

He also wanted to inject a sense of what kind of Britain it would be – they would be cutting public services whilst doing the inheritance tax cut. He started to talk about the possibility of civil disorder if they did that. We had a long chat and he sounded OK. But he was always trying to inject new and different sub-messages. Meanwhile TB was reluctant to get involved in the event in Manchester on Tuesday because he felt it would look fin de siècle. In reality he was worried he was going to have to push too hard for GB. Polls still not great but Tories still only 33/34. Tweeted that the unstoppable momentum strategy was not really working. Clegg in Burnley – I really didn't want that to go Lib!

Monday 3 May

GB call at 7. He was still pressing for subtle and not so subtle changes of message and sub message. He wanted to say 'I am the most optimistic man in the country' and 'I am optimistic because I have a plan'. I said what about just sticking with fight for your future? He said it was fine but limited. I said it was a frame. I don't know who was getting at him about optimism but it did not work as a topline message. He was also going on about the idea of trouble in the streets if the Tories did IHT and child tax credits. We had half-hour or so and by the end I wasn't sure what to make of it. I gave PG a lift in and we agreed he just had to stick on the same message now. Also PG said tax credits were beginning to break through the groups as a real problem for the Tories.

We got the morning meeting to agree to a number of ideas to get it up, including a press conference with Yvette, also hard words to get into all of GB's speeches. First we had to try to get him on a conference call and make clear we thought that it did not make sense to shift gear on the language. That we had to stay on fight for future but with different areas. Laughably we were launching a seaside manifesto and a manifesto for older people. Laudable but they just were not going to connect or break through at this stage. Everything was polls- and process-driven. They were into stories about energy and all the rest of it. We were going to have to rethink how these elections were plotted out from now on in. The debates were a mistake, in terms of the impact on politics.

Harriet was extraordinary at these meetings, she kind of burbled away anecdotally with strategy. We met her in Starbucks and out came a torrent of this person said, that person said, and this is what we should say. It was the kind of stuff that should all have been folded into the campaign ages ago. Peter was pretty dismissive. He also knew that he would be getting whacked and briefed against left, right and centre. But he was very calm about that, said to me later he intended to say he took responsibility. He was of the view that it had to be David M who took over, but that the two Eds would be positioning away. Ed Balls was already probably trying to get out of the wreckage of the GB shadow. Ed Miliband would want to be between the two. David would want to be his own man but with a modernising tag. Whelan–Balls etc. were already doing stuff on how Peter was trying to get DM installed. It was all pretty schoolboy stuff. But I worried for the party post any defeat. I felt neither of the Eds would win an election against DC. DM did not have everything needed but he had more than the rest.

I worked on GB words for his stump speeches and then for his Citizens UK [community organising group] Westminster Hall event. I did a blog pre-press conference on the Tories stalling in early to mid-thirties, and how tax credits were a part of that. And then one later on GB's speech at Westminster Hall where he was terrific. Cameron did OK. Clegg good. Indeed, the response to Clegg was so good that I was worried GB would be overshadowed. But it was his best speech of the campaign. A lone heckler would get some coverage I guess but the speech would carry through. Really powerful. Values based. Passionate. Also he had shown some humanity when a young girl telling her story had a bit of a cry as she spoke. He sat there looking a bit embarrassed but he eventually went over and was very warm. He seemed to get a lot of inspiration from the audience. 2,500 people involved in doing good. Easily the best of the three. The only question would be who would see it and would it cut through? I left for home to start to work on more words for tomorrow. Also trying to get celebs for it. Out of the blue Konnie Huq called and she said she was so worried about the Tories that she wanted to do something for us. She said she had thought about things and she was sure we were right for the future and the Tories wrong.

Out for dinner with Catherine and George McL, Tess and Jessie, Sis etc. Tessa seemed a bit wired. I was pretty stressed out too. Getting grumpy. Fed up of anecdotal chat and people giving opinions the whole time without understanding we were where we were and all you get out of these closing days is the performance of the leaders. Getting tired too. And bizarrely putting on weight. That was a new one for a campaign. Maybe just not enough adrenaline. TB out campaigning again. Tamworth. Redditch. Said he found it all quite odd as to what was going on. He was not really sure himself. He felt that a lot of the don't knows were basically deserting us but didn't want to say. He felt that the party needed to be rebuilt from bottom up, that we had to get a new generation in and do the whole job all over again. He said weird things happened but he couldn't see this turning around.

Tuesday 4 May

The *FT* became the latest paper to switch to the Tories. The *Mirror* did a big number on tactical voting. Hain on TV and Balls in the *Statesman* were giving hints about supporting tactical voting. At the morning meeting Harriet was wondering whether she should get the word out that this was the wrong thing to say. She was quite steamed up about it, as were PG and I. PG had done some groups last night and said our problem was traditional Labour voters defecting to the Libs. If they thought we were giving them permission, it was a bit of a disaster. It could hit us in the Tory/Labour marginals. We were all trying to think of ways of pushing the GB speech of last night. Also trying to get Alistair to say something that would connect. Peter did a fairly half-hearted thanks to everyone at the end, said they had been a terrific team to work with etc. But it all still felt a bit flat. GB called pre his *GMTV* interview along with Sarah. He needed constant reassurance about staying on the same message. Sarah had a nice manner and they managed to get an OK mix of politics and personal. I then started to work on his words for the event in Manchester tonight and after a series of exchanges with Justin and David decided that I should go up for it.

Got Rayan to collect me and set off. I wrote a direct pitch to undecided workers which was really strong. Also trimmed down the rest of the speech and worked in some good new claplines and attack lines. Bit of a disaster when some candidate I had never heard of [Manish Sood] in a seat we couldn't win [Norfolk North West] came out with a local paper interview saying GB was the worst PM ever. Sky multiple orgasm time. Tom Baldwin saying he couldn't get any anti-Tory stories in *The Times*. I sent Fred Michel a few texts to the effect that Sky had become a disgrace. The speech was pretty good but he was on a train fiddling around with it, and running late so we were going to be looking at a real last-minute job to get it done. Arrived at Granada, settled in to do bits and bobs and waited for him. We had a run through it. Told him to let people applaud over the achievements and the forward stuff but really let the appeal to undecideds slow down and take its time. We were fiddling away to the end, even as he was getting dressed, shaving and putting in his lenses.

We got it done just in time. Gloria De Piero compering – she told me she was worried about her seat. Christ, if she was gone we had had it. Konnie had a good story to tell, a floater coming to us. Peter, Douglas, Ed B and Yvette around. GB, David and I got the speech done and out he went. Great performance for the second night running. Crowd loved it. Ought to cut through. He did the achievements well, and the attack and values stuff. It was values that gave him a lift. Really good reception. Got Calum to come and say hello. GB was pretty pumped up. He knew he had done well. Actually gave me a kind of hug, and said he would always be grateful for the help I had given him. He had certainly found his voice. I think the debates had just hung over him and he had only felt liberated since the third. He had endured a lot of ups and downs and felt a bit of momentum coming back to him. Our troops certainly felt a lot better for the last couple of days.

He wanted to sit and work out how to do the speech in Dumfries tomorrow which now had to be another humdinger. He pulled out a sheaf of papers and scribbled away. I said what about imagining a Britain that had not had Labour governments. All the things that would never have happened. I ran through the kind of thing that might work. That's genius, he said. Calum was listening and I could see him smile. GB was now rat-a-tatting away with his thick felt pen, writing out lines of attack on the lines of we did this, now this, and here is the risk. He was definitely fired up.

YouGov had us back in second and closing the gap. Peter and Douglas briefed the travelling press and the mood was pretty up. Sarah was telling me very intensely that she felt the Tories had been shocked they had not been able to pull away. Also that she felt we had had virtually every arm of the establishment against us and for him. DC had certainly had an easy ride. Nice atmosphere though and both of them were very nice to Calum.

We left about 9 and were home before midnight. I was stepping up the tweeting on the amazing news bias against GB. TB had done *The Guardian* and said he was totally opposed to tactical voting. You have to vote on policy and think it through. Earlier I had asked Balls what on earth he was doing. He denied having said what he was quoted as saying. So did Tessa, who was being folded into the same story. PG felt we were in a lot of trouble. Said Alicia had told him we had said goodbye to the first three tranches of marginals. Cameron was off doing 24-hour non-stop through-the-night campaigning. Like we tried to get TB to do. The crazy anti-GB candidate was a bit of a nightmare for a few hours but I worked out a line with DA and Roger Baker and Ray Collins, not too agitated. He was clearly bonkers most people would think. It had gone by later on though the Tory papers would love it. Wrote a few passages for GB's tomorrow speeches on the way back. Just trying to find new ways of doing good values and delivery.

Wednesday 5 May

Long blog on GB depth and resilience v the shallowness and process-obsession of the other two. Really good blog though I say so myself. It was odd how much I had warmed to GB in the last few days. He was a strong character in lots of ways but also very vulnerable in his own way, and insecure. But I did admire the way he kept going, even if I could see so many weaknesses. He was not a modern politician. He was better suited to a different era, but he was who we had and that was that. TB felt, and was probably right, that we could have won with a different leader. But GB had seen them all off and we were where we were. The feedback coming in from round the country was very mixed. The Tories had slipped a bit during the campaign, but they had been ahead for ages and there was nobody really saying, or at least thinking, that we were going to win. But the polls had been steadily pointing towards a hung parliament. There was also a bit of anti-Cameron, Anyone But Cameron, coming through. Maybe too late. A bit like GB momentum. I was pottering a lot, watching the news – mix of protests against the austerity measures in Athens and the election – while working on GB's various speeches.

He had two big ones and a few little ones. The first big one was at

Bradford Uni, which went well. We then spent a fair bit of time working on his answers for the Beeb six o'clock news, which was carrying the three leaders live. We reckoned DC would do sleeves rolled up while Clegg would do 'Don't let anyone tell you your vote can't make a difference.' They were really sticking to those process messages. DC getting lots of coverage for his through-the-night campaigning. It said energy but he had nothing to say on policy. Clegg was all process too. I tweeted loads, with a few on the rolled-up sleeves bollocks and also how Miriam [wife] looked bored with 'Don't let anyone tell you' – I agree with Miriam. GB must have called ten times from the train to Carlisle re the clips for the Beeb. We agreed the words, then he came back again and again to rehearse and fiddle. Did OK though.

GB then calling about his rally in Dumfries. I wanted to get another direct pitch to the undecided voter. We worked out a few good lines. He and I wanted to bring it forward. But the media team had agreed the broadcasters would do their final two-ways with GB and the crowd in background. I stupidly went along with it. In the end we had the usual overdose of Robinson, so the final clip was from a rather sad event in Blackpool. The fucking broadcasters had been a disgrace in this election. *Newsnight* the usual cynical crap as well. Feeling quite down as I went to bed.

Thursday 6 May

Fiona's first words of the day 'I just feel so sad.' As I left the house, Grace said 'Don't be too sad if we lose.' In a way I felt OK. I didn't sense the Tories were going to wipe us out, even if they won. Also there was an OK mood around the place. Rayan drove me to the Kuwaiti Embassy. Needless to say he was convinced we were going to win. He was full of it. I warned him not to get too excited. Trust me, he said. I feel a good spirit in the air. It was a bit surreal doing a session with the TBO Kuwait team. Nice enough bunch. Did my usual spiel on crisis management, plus a fair bit on the current scene. Ben after me, saying he felt the Tories were doing better than we expected. Messages from Fiona who was reporting really big turnout in our area. No sign of Tories so maybe a Lib surge.

From the Embassy to the Marriott Chancery Lane for a paid gig, Invista estate agents. Did my ten points of leadership then a very friendly Q&A. They were not, to my surprise, very Tory. Really warm and friendly. Duncan Owen, the boss, said they had voted all ways. He reckoned if TB had still been there we would have walked it. No real desire for Cameron and Osborne. I was on form and managed without a pill. It was the rest of the day that was going to be tricky. Home to blog on last-minute stuff before working on all the various different scenarios ahead. For straight defeat

GB had already sent through a draft which had him resigning immediately. For hung he wanted to offer the Libs a deal on PR referendum and working together on the economy. For win it was unalloyed triumph over expectation. Nobody was really thinking we could win at this stage. But what we could do was stop them winning an overall majority. We had to really go for it. It would be hard though now. Rachel was keeping me in touch with the mood up in Scotland. She said they feared the worst. The feeling was high Tory turnout and no collapse of Lib Dems.

This was the first election in ages I had not been in Sedgefield. The day passed slowly. Up and down the stairs to see how things were locally – Fiona and the boys busy with it. GB called once or twice but it was time-passing. Nothing really to say at this stage. I left just after 9 for County Hall, doing ITV Live. I was rude to anyone who had switched to the Lib Dems. Jonathan was there and he said – half in jest – well done on the campaign. He said GB going would have swung it. He had to go now. I said I was not sure I should say that tonight. PG called with flavour of exit poll. Tories just over 300. Us around 250 or a bit more. Lib Dems 55-ish. 37–28–23-ish. Could have been a lot worse. He said we had performed a fucking miracle. Real exit poll not far off that. No real excitement around the place. So not like '97.

Archie Norman [chairman ITV, former Tory MP] – on his way to central office – said if they got more than 300 they would get Lib Dem support for a Budget and Queen's Speech and go for it. But I was not sure that Clegg could do a deal with the Tories at all. We had to start agitating on this straight away. My line was we had stopped a Tory majority government and we had shown this is a progressive country. Did first slot solo then another with Piers. We followed David M and Osborne. George looked really down. Yet he was claiming victory. Piers and I were both on the idea of the Tories being the losers and of Clegg having had a hard time and now weakened. I was quite keen to get away. Couldn't stand the hanging round, people drinking and chatting. This needed focus.

Fiona, Rory and Grace joined me for the Beeb bash on a boat. Al Murray. Good atmosphere in part I hoped because it was clear the Tories hadn't won. I did a fairly feisty slot with Andrew Neil. Paddy [Ashdown] and I were developing the same line – that the Tories were trying to give a sense of inevitability but if they did not have the numbers, they could not do it. So we were definitely in hung parliament territory. We were also able to stave off for now the GB question, though it would come. We had worried as early as yesterday we would be third and we were avoiding that pretty well. Chat with Mark Thompson and one or two others wondering if Tory minority government might be best. We were certainly in slightly better shape. Off to Vic Street, where there was a sudden rash of really good saved seats prompting huge cheers around the TVs. I did a round of interviews downstairs, including Boulton and I said the TV had been biased. He went off on one, so I did a bit of get off your high horse, you can give not take. The media has been biased etc. Got loads of tweets in support. Sky really had been an outrage.

Peter, PG and I were then in the Hamlyn Room at HQ just assessing and watching. Great the kids were there, only Georgia and Calum missing. Real up and down night. Looked at one stage that Balls might lose. He survived. Peter did one of his 'never mind' looks. Had seen Whelan at the ITV do but I found it hard to be civil to him. I just couldn't be bothered. That politics had to die whatever happened. GB spoke pretty well at his count. Slight air of resignation but that might be tiredness. Cameron and Clegg didn't look too great either. Harriet popped in. 'Ah, your girlfriend,' said Peter. Fiona and Grace went home about 3. GB arrived closer to 5. GB came in, all the staff lined up, he shook hands, said nice things re Harriet and Peter, made a good speech about how proud he was of what we had done – the campaign had been up against it but here we were, not out of it, difficult decisions to face but let us be proud of the past thirteen years and of the campaign we have fought. Spoke well. I still felt it would end with him gone and Cameron in there. But there was still fight in him.

Bacon sandwiches in the Hamlyn Room. A bit of salmon and cheese. GB, Peter, me, Sue, David, one or two others popping in. Greg Cook gave us the score of where we were now. Told us of some of the possibles ahead. Looked like the Tories were a fair few short of a majority. Our only hope was alliance. He was scribbling away with his mad felt pen. Totting up numbers. Asking if we could get Unionists on the phone. Adonis on the phone. Then we discovered he was in a TV studio. Got him out to come back to us. GB had spoken to the hacks on the plane and had made clear we had to see all the results in and we had to be clear that we would manage the situation through. I asked if there had been any contact with Clegg. Peter M was rolling his eyebrows a bit at GB. He was saying that there was no way Clegg would speak to us first. He had been clear in the campaign that he would speak to the largest party first. That was the Tories. He had not been good about us during the campaign. Equally there were so many areas of major difference between them and the Tories. I was pretty sure that GB could not cling on, but we kept getting other results in and it was still in flux.

He just kept saying that nobody was going to be able to get a majority and therefore we had to look at all the options. I was in email exchange with Jeremy Heywood who felt that Lib–Lab was just as viable as minority Tory government. Greg felt it would be close to the exit poll. We did well in Wales and Scotland. We were doing badly in the Midlands. Immigration definitely hit us though we won in Rochdale. Lost Burnley to the Libs which was annoying. GB was gulping down bacon sandwiches as he wrote all the numbers out. More losses coming in. He wondered if he should say something tonight. I said he should go back to No. 10, we put out a line that says that he was going back to No. 10 to get some rest and take stock. I said we should say he was going to consult colleagues and civil servants so that people realised he was not there having somehow thought he had won. It was light when he left.

Still good news and bad coming in. I really felt the Tories would not be delirious with this. The word was Clegg was deflated too, and not really sure what to do. Neil K doing lots of telly and sending me messages saying we were saying same things. Had to watch the PR front though. Not sure we would want to promise PR as the price of keeping GB a bit longer. Charles Clarke lost his seat. I send him a message saying sorry. He sent one back to the effect that if we had done what we should have done a while back instead of letting one man's vanity take us down, we would not be in this mess. He said don't let anyone tell you the result is anything other than a disaster.

Margaret Hodge easily saw off the BNP which was great news and delivered a really hard message to Nick Griffin too. In some seats we were doing really well. In the council elections we seemed to be doing well. In some areas we were doing badly. But Tories nowhere in Scotland or Wales, poor in the north, London. I was tinkering with some of the draft scenarios. But what was clear was that we would definitely be in hung parliament territory. I went home around 7 to get a bit of sleep. The phone going the whole time but got a couple of hours and was refreshed afterwards. Felt actually that we had done a pretty good job to stop the Tories from doing better.

Friday 7 May

Neil felt that the Lib–Lab approach was the right way. He thought that GB had to get Cabinet signed up to that kind of approach straight away. I spoke to Peter a couple of times who was at the Cabinet Office. He seemed to have moved from the idea that a deal with the Libs could not be done to the idea that it could. Clegg was the main event first thing, saying outside Cowley Street that he would talk to the Tories first. He looked and sounded pretty deflated. GB called and asked me to go into No. 10. He was still very much on a survival strategy. He said he felt Clegg was probably not that keen on the idea of a deal with the Tories though he had got caught by saying he would speak to the largest party first. He might be worried about whether we had the numbers between us which we didn't.

But GB was already making calculations about the Speaker, Sinn Féin etc. The one thing he was clear on was that the Tories could not offer much in the way of electoral reform whereas perhaps we could. GB was round in my old office in No. 12, with Peter, Andrew Adonis and one or two others. He had drafted a statement. It was a bit clunky, too obvious what he was up to – trying to stay on the back of electoral reform. I said he should make it much more process-y and in so doing it would be more statesmanlike. He had to be steering the country, devoid of party interest, through this odd outcome. He should not be making claims but he should say something on the economy and he should also be clear he accepted what Clegg and Cameron intended. Clegg was clearly the man of the moment despite the disappointing results for him. We had also heard Cameron was planning to make a statement at 2.30. GB felt he had to say something before that.

I rewrote the draft with Andrew Adonis at my shoulder. I said the purpose had to be to act as PM not Labour leader, to set out something of the process ahead, to make clear Clegg was right to talk to Cameron but make clear that if that came to nothing, then we could do the economy together and 'immediate legislation on electoral reform with a referendum'. We improved the statement hugely, also put in stuff re the economy. I asked Andrew where he felt the Libs were. He said he now agreed with my lifelong view that they just were not serious people. However, he felt there was a chance Clegg could bring his party to us. He was clearly not really for budging. Balls and Woodward came in. Balls not really clear where he was on it all. Seemed to be saying GB should be explicit that he expected that he had to go if this all came to nothing. Shaun not saying much. Andrew in and out giving his assessment of where the Libs might be. Did several rewrites.

Gus O'D said via Jeremy it could be done in the street but not the building. A bit odd. GB was worried about doing it in the street because he felt that the street was for either coming or going. I thought it was fine. So did the others. He went out. Good tone. Delivered it well. No questions. OK response. Managed to avoid too much of the 'clinging on'. He and Balls were now in conflab. I said we needed voices out there on the back of Cameron. GB said why don't you and Ed do it? I said Ed M might be better because this needed a bit of the Liberal touch. I went out to College Green and did a stack of interviews on the back of Cameron's statement. He talked about launching a process of discussion with Clegg. I was watching with Andrew Neil who said 'He's giving nothing on the things that matter to the Libs – PR or Europe.' I was mainly pushing the obvious lines – nobody won, tough for Clegg, Tories first right, but there may be the prospect of Lib–Lab-plus and they all had a duty to explore this.

I slipped off after about eight interviews and headed home to potter pre Channel 4, which was fine. Then out with Fiona to the Richard Steel pub to celebrate with the Labour team in Camden, especially Georgia who looked really happy, as did the boys. PG tired. He and I chatted about the situation. He felt I had to be careful. I had done what I did to help stave off a dreadful defeat. But I should not now become the person who shored him up. Let it take its course. Good atmosphere in the pub and some nice people, not all Tories, wanting a chat and photos and stuff. One guy said 'I thought you were a cunt but you seem OK.' PG said 'Maybe you're the cunt for thinking he was a cunt.' Peter H at *Newsnight*. He felt we had done a miracle but whatever happened GB had to go.

David M texted then called, said he was not sure what I was up to with the Libs. I said we had to let GB explore this stuff. We were almost certainly going to end with a Tory–Lib alliance or a minority government. Along the way we had to weaken both other parties. GB could not be seen to leg it now. He sounded like Ed M was also going to stand. 'He is not ready but he has inhaled all the propaganda from the Guardianistas. Truth is Ed would make a good leader of the Lib Dems.' Did OK on *Newsnight* despite tiredness and medication. Danny Finkelstein looking pretty down. Best thing of the result is the Tories really did not get what they wanted.

Saturday 8 May

I was still tired. Cellular tired. We went out for breakfast at Kalendar. Pushy mums' training group out there. Quite a laugh with them. Did some pictures which they put on Twitter. Then ran into Tony Woodcock [ex-footballer]. Nice atmosphere out there. People very friendly. Maybe thinking that they had done the right thing. Rejected us but not too hard, and not given the Tories a mandate. I did a blog on the campaign, saying that all things considered we did a pretty amazing job. Bruce called, said it was humiliating to see us offering the Libs what they wanted. He felt a minority Tory government was the right outcome now. Sally the same. Anji felt we had done a great job. But now we had to sort out the future generation. Lovely text from David Muir who said 'The real hero of the campaign was you.' Patrick said 'You need a really long diary entry tonight.'

TB called early on. What are you up to, he said? I said what do you mean? You do realise he has to go, he said. For once the party interest and the national interest are aligned. He lost. He did not win. He has been rejected. He did fine yesterday but if he clings on in some rag-bag rainbow coalition it will be awful. Added to which if the price is PR we will never win again. He said the definition of a Lib Dem is someone who is not serious and cannot make a decision. They will run a mile at the first hint of trouble. They cannot do it. They cannot govern. I said I agreed the likeliest outcome was a minority Tory government but getting there GB had to be allowed to explore and he had to be able to plan with dignity. TB said fine, but we both know all he is thinking about is how does he survive? He was pretty clear about it. I said so what is my best advice? He said you have to be supportive but you do need to try to have an honest conversation.

GB had called me earlier and asked me to go in at 2. He said he was sure Clegg could not do a deal with the Tories because of PR. Brendan Cox and others had been organising thousands of emails to top Liberals. GB's whole tone though was one of survival as leader of a coalition. He felt yesterday went fine and he was in a much better place. TB said he would be seeing the result as inconvenient but not deadly. He said you guys did an incredible job. I had feared the worst. I mean really bad, and it didn't happen. That surge of votes we had p.m. Thursday were anti-Tories coming out. I was now pushing the line that the Lib Dems got a lot of votes from people who voted tactically to stop Cameron. Clegg did not have the mandate for a deal with Tories based on that. At least we had similar values and positions on a lot of areas.

TB's last words 'Be careful. You know what he is like. It will be a disaster if we limp on with the Libs. At the end the Tories will wipe us out. And if we give them PR it is a disaster of a different sort.' I said I was aware of all that but this had to be managed. I went in by cab. Through the Cabinet Office. GB was in my old office with Peter, Andrew, Jeremy, Sue, David, Gavin Kelly [deputy chief of staff], Stewart Wood, Iain Bundred. Not a good sign. He liked big meetings when he was trying to avoid honest discussion. They were discussing a statement in which he set a deadline for discussions – Tuesday – and made clear that if nothing was sorted by then, or if it was clear there could be no Lib–Lab, he would go. Peter – who was very scratchy and whose actual position I could not establish – wanted to take out reference to GB going. Andrew felt there had to be pressure on Clegg to decide. Jeremy came back with Gus O'D's view that it was a mistake. That it would contradict yesterday's line that they should take as long as they needed. Also that it was not a sensible thing to do. Clegg would feel manipulated. I said it would only work if all three agreed to it.

There was very little contact with Cameron's team. Earlier GB, Cameron and Clegg had all walked out together for a VE [Victory in Europe] Day ceremony. Great pictures. One of those moments. It meant GB had a black tie. 'Please take your tie off, Gordon,' I said. He laughed and tore it off. Sue in and out trying to get him on the 2.30 flight to Edinburgh. They felt it was better he was out of the bunker avoiding allegations of squatting. He clearly didn't really want to go. He asked me to have a private chat. We sat at his desk and he said I still think I can do this. Clegg is not ruling it out. We let them run the course with the Tories and then see. I said fine but you need to think through if it is sustainable. I worried he would hang on and on and we would all be weakened. He said this cannot go beyond Tuesday. He accepted that if things were not resolved it meant we were looking at minority Tory government and DC was in. I was moving to the position that a legacy of best ever Chex [Chancellor of the Exchequer], steer country through recession, troops home from Iraq, cement deal in Ireland, and stop a Tory majority, was good.

After he had gone I said that to Peter and Sue. Sue and Justin seemed to be in that place too but had not said it to him. Peter was due to meet the Libs' team at 4 with Andrew A and Ed M. Harriet, however, had installed herself in my other old office, apparently at GB's agreement, and he went to see her and she insisted she had to be part of the agreement. So Ed M – who Peter blamed for telling her it was happening – was going to be dropped. Peter said to me this was Keystone Cops time. Also Harriet had got herself on to Marr. Peter said to GB you have to tell her she can't do that. I said why does it take the PM – a press officer should do it. Hain and Bradshaw were out on the Lib–Lab line and that made her want to do it more. GB was meanwhile off now. Peter and I watched him go from the window in my old office. There is an elephant in the room, I said. I know, he said. But we can't get him to see it yet. I decided to do just that though. I wrote a note to Sue, Justin, David, which I asked them to read and discuss and decide whether they felt GB should also see. I did.

I said I was worried that he was not thinking things through, and was going for short-term tactical stuff that buys time rather than working out where it was likely to end. If he really believed a Lib–Lab-plus deal was possible, fine. It is a big if but let's say it can be done. Does he then really believe that would provide strong and stable government? The Lib Dems by nature do not make difficult decisions. It is why they know what they are against but don't know how to make happen what they are for. So we could end up with a weak and unworkable government. Added to which the price – if a PR system that means no majority government ever again, and every election followed by this kind of horse trading – would be too high. I said if, in his gut, he feels this is going to end in a DC premiership some day soon, he should start planning as to how that happens, with maximum reputational protection for himself, and optimum positioning for the party.

Yesterday went fine, and though some of the media were hostile, reasonable people understand his position. He acted and spoke properly and well. But the numbers are clear – the Tories did better than us, we did not win, and we do not have the numbers with the Libs. Added to which the mood music from Clegg is not warm, and the price might be too high. Clearly we have to let events take their course, I said. But the moment he senses it is all over for him, he needs to have a resignation statement on these lines:

> Election unclear. Gave space for discussions. We helped facilitate.
>
> Only three options. Minority Tory. Tory–Lib. Lib–Lab-plus.
>
> I have reached the conclusion the last two of these are unlikely. Differences between Tories and Libs obvious. Some areas of agreement between us and Libs but clear differences on a, b, c and the process of negotiations could damage the UK if prolonged. Of course discussions can continue but I think minority Tory govt likeliest outcome.
>
> Not ideal for anyone but then again none of the parties got the result they wanted. We have to accept the verdict.
>
> But I think it is in the national interest that I make clear that unless a Tory–Lib or Lib–Lab-plus deal can be agreed in outline within xx, I should tender my resignation to the Queen and suggest that she ask DC to form minority govt.
>
> (If resigns) It has been great privilege etc. Look back on a, b, c:
>
> - I was longest-serving Chancellor.
> - I steered Britain through econ crisis.
> - Brought the troops home from Iraq.
> - Cemented the final deal in NI.
> - Led our mission in Afghanistan.
>
> And against the odds led Labour in an election campaign in which we managed to stop what seemed at one point inevitable – a majority and even landslide Tory government.
>
> I now think it is clear Britain is looking to a new generation of political leadership and whilst I will always be around to offer support and advice I think I should make way not just as PM but leader of the Labour Party.

I said I really believed if he did this he would cement a good place in popular and political judgement. If he hangs on when in his heart he knows he shouldn't I think it will damage him and the party. On the other hand, if he stays above it, is genuinely seen to be putting national interest above self, he ends in a good place. He also leaves the party able to regroup, refresh and be in good shape for the next one whenever that comes. I said it was up to them whether to show him the note. But I felt there was an elephant in the room today and it needs to be addressed openly.

Sue texted me to say she had sent it on to him. I never heard from him for the rest of the day. I assumed they were going into 'for us or against us' mode but Jeremy, to whom I sent a blind copy, said they were in broad agreement with it. Sent to TB who said it was sound advice for him, party and country. Sent to Peter who did not get back to me. He was playing a very odd game. TB felt he was probably thinking he could stay in government. Andrew was probably getting a bit too excited by the process, as the Libs would be. Sue and Justin seemed to think he should go with dignity. Not there yet. Then Peter said much the same, less clearly. I left for home and a kip. GB arrived in Scotland. Clegg was meeting his various groupings then later seeing Cameron. Tory–Lib deal looking quite likely according to the media. Wall-to-wall stuff. GB must go – *ST* poll. Blatherology in overdrive.

Nothing much to do unless he asked me to. Hysterical calls and emails from Gez Sagar on how to sort it. Brendan Cox had done well working on Lib Dems to come out against a Tory deal. Big demo earlier re Fair Votes – Tories already making clear PR just not the thing. GB had prepared a note on the areas we could co-operate with Libs. Long list. I spoke to TB again. We agreed if Clegg said GB going was a part of deal GB was entitled to say no. But there was a feeling that would have to happen. Fiona was clear GB had to accept he had been rejected and could not just cling on and on. Home for dinner. Really knackered now.

Sunday 9 May

TB sent an email early on saying he had had a 'scary and eerie' chat with GB who was clearly hell-bent on staying. The election was but a minor inconvenience in his plans to stay in power. TB was also talking to Paddy who was clearly briefing and to some extent guiding and mentoring Clegg. Paddy was of the view that GB had to go as part of any deal. Also that though they would let the talks with the Tories go on, the Libs would prefer to be with us than with the Tories. TB and I chatted a few times and said we had to see that though there may be short-term interest in keeping GB, long term it was a disaster. He felt in his gut that a minority Tory government was probably the outcome. But we were right to explore other options. Justin Forsyth sent me an email after Paddy on Marr was dropping hints GB was not the right kind of guy to lead a coalition. Also pointing out that we did not have the numbers.

Following their call yesterday, GB had got Clegg to agree to a meeting later which was fixed for the FCO. I was getting a lot of conflicting noises around – the Bruce Gs saying never do a deal with the Libs (which is where Jack S was, who was also getting agitated at the lack of a Cabinet discussion on this). Harriet was squatting in No. 10 again, clearly hoping for the caretaker role she thought of. Jeremy totally agreed with my analysis, that there was a major problem with legitimacy, also that there might be a way of replacing him whilst not having an election but didn't feel GB was there yet. He said a lot of GB's team felt the same but didn't want to say so. Fiona was going on about how awful it would be if he limped on as leader of a traffic lights coalition and then we collapsed and Cameron killed us in a future election. Papers not great. He really had to get to a moral high ground position and stay there. Markets meltdown tomorrow if we weren't careful. Alistair D needed to be out and about. I sent a note round saying that he needed to settle things and should also make clear he was talking to Osborne and Cable.

GB was also talking to Cable who was making clear that he did not support a Tory deal on any terms. PG called, said the public would probably be OK with a Cameron–Clegg deal. Cameron tempered by someone else was OK. GB was not. Peter M texted to say Blunkett was going up on Sky. I got hold of him and moved him from 'GB will do the right thing' i.e. resign, to a more nuanced position. Then a mad rant from Gez Sagar saying he would 'blow open the true story of the campaign and how you guys fucked it up' if we let Cameron through the door. Blunkett did feel though that we should let the Tories get on with it. That they could screw up with or without the Libs then we win next time. Gus apparently furious at *Observer* story on Hague draft letter to DC as PM.*

TB on several times. Kept saying he could not really believe the conversation with GB. It was pretty hopeless. GB was totally gung-ho. In denial. I was not so sure. I think there was just a process to go through. TB said no, he sees the election as but an inconvenience. He will damage himself and all of us if he stays too long. He was also talking to Paddy. Paddy felt that it was possible for a Lib–Lab deal, but not with GB there. He had been rejected. They were wondering whether it might be possible to put together a deal that was PR plus coalition under a new leader. Was it doable, politically, publicly? I said it might be, but there was still a problem with the numbers. Also there was also the issue of whether either party would wear it. And how can we be sure re GB and his position? He was not exactly one to throw in the towel. Alistair D was excellent on the news, good tone on the economic and political situations.

TB said he and Paddy were speaking to DM and Clegg as kind of mentors. Neither of us was sure who would win the Labour leadership but I had a sense DM might not, even though he was such a favourite. TB felt it would be DM but Ed was slight flavour of the month. TB said he had a

* The document, a draft letter 'from the Foreign Secretary to the Prime Minister', outlined a hardline Eurosceptic stance to be adopted by a Cameron government.

rough chat with GB. 'But you were in favour of this rapprochement with the Liberals.' Yes, but we won, said TB. Chat with Neil and he agreed we needed twin track – GB planning the coalition to stay whilst we worked a soft landing for him going in case. Long chat with Charles K. He felt that though there was a lot of pressure re PR Libs felt a referendum might be lost, so it was not a total red line. On us, however, he thought they would be up for helping with GB going with dignity. But there was no way they would have GB stay as PM – it was not even raised at their meetings yesterday. Total non-starter. Paddy came close to saying as much on Marr. Charlie said Clegg and cohorts were close to a deal and if we wanted to get in there it had to be soon. His hunch was they wanted something but short of coalition. There were others pushing towards us, but he felt it was unlikely. Peter M felt GB was still determined to stay. PG felt he had to go and that another unelected leader was not an option.

I got in for 3 p.m. Then into long rolling meetings. I couldn't believe the Harriet situation. She hung around the building but they didn't want her in the main meetings and so GB would wander off every now and then to talk to her. Peter said she was obsessed with the idea of being the acting leader for a while. I found GB's office management style odd. People just wandered in and out. He didn't have a gatekeeper. Sue did it, but she was often in the room. I found Ed M's wanderings odd. He would wander in, ask a few questions of us, then wander out again. We were just getting to it when the two Eds walked in again. Ed Balls's position was quite hard to work out. He said that the MPs he was talking to were worried that their majorities were smaller and maybe the best way to avoid defeat was for the Tories to fuck it up. GB said if they got in he did not believe it would be easy to get them out. Ed M just asked questions. He never seemed to come to a view. Added to which according to Peter Ed M was off the whole time briefing Harriet.

GB went through what he intended to propose to Clegg. He was meeting him at the FCO at 4. He felt that Clegg would have to be Deputy Prime Minister. We would emphasise the Tories could do nothing for him on Europe, industrial strategy. Electoral reform – they would never fight for a yes vote. We went through the areas where we would need lots of policy work done. We kept pushing him on the question of his own position. It has been obvious from all our contacts that he would have to go, but he wouldn't say anything clear, didn't want to get drawn. Sue and Justin felt he was there but couldn't articulate it yet. There were masses of media in the street but most missed him going through to the FCO. Someone spotted Clegg's car though and after a while they put two and two together. He came back and was not really clear what was said. In particular he wasn't totally clear what he said about his own position. Meanwhile the Tories and Lib Dems met for hours. There was still no agreement.

GB was clearly for hanging in until it became clear. Cabinet starting to get a bit jumpy. GB calling round them. He was also talking to Cable who seemed pretty clear he wouldn't go in with the Tories. Also Ming Campbell. Then a rather spiky conversation with Mervyn King. GB was convinced the Tories were trying to provoke some kind of economic crisis, and King was definitely on that end of the market, trying to get him to go. Peter, AA and I went over to Peter's office in the Cabinet Office to take stock. Peter was sure GB would be gone soon. AA still felt the Libs might do something. We were effectively hanging around waiting to be told by Danny Alexander whether they would be meeting on policy or not. Then came a call that Clegg would like to see GB, with Danny and Peter, at half nine.

We went back to see GB and Peter and I pinned him down on his own position. We said it was clear from all sources that his own position made things difficult. I do know that, he said. I said there were lots of ways of reading the election, but we lost and he was rejected and it was difficult for the Libs to sell any kind of deal as a coalition of the losers. He said he understood that. He would not be staying longer than he had to but there was a constitutional position to resolve and he had to do that. He would see what Clegg had to say. 'Alastair, what do you want to happen?' he said at one point. I said it would be great to keep the Tories out but that was not enough at the moment – he genuinely had to be guided by the national interest which I agreed was not clear-cut following the result. I also said I wanted to avoid unnecessary reputational damage to him and the party. In my heart, I said, I felt him going was almost inevitable but it was still worth exploring what might come from Clegg.

They went off to see Clegg. We had not told anyone else in the office it was happening, apart from Sue, so most of them had gone to the pub, leaving Sue and I to have a chat about things. When they got back, Peter and I had an honest conversation with him. It was clear that what GB had told us about the earlier meeting with Clegg – which Clegg had taken to mean he would go soon – was not how GB had presented it to us. So GB was seeming to backtrack, said it would depend on the referendum. Danny made clear they felt GB's position made it very difficult to have GB as leader of that campaign. Anyway, pre-meeting GB was clear that his main pitch had been on policy. Can the Tories deliver electoral reform? A proper position on Europe? An agreed plan on the economy? He felt Clegg bought all that, that he realised he wanted to be in a position to make sure he was part of a change government. They wanted to know what they could do to make this a change government. Clearly it was code for saying a government without you.

I said it was partly about numbers and legitimacy. It was also about ideas. And it was about the leadership personnel. I understand that, he said. He said he was grateful for my note of yesterday which set everything out so frankly. I said I wanted him to understand I was not proposing this as a thought-through position but I wanted him genuinely to be guided by the national interest and also I wanted him to think of how the party could best emerge from this, and how it could affect him reputationally. The election had in a way rejected all three leaders. But him maybe more than the other two. He had to be honest about that. They did not want him or DC as leader but they could maybe live with Labour in coalition with someone else in charge. He said there was no constitutional position for that. I said Jeremy had said there was, that he could signal his departure and we could have a leadership election.

He said if he resigned to the Queen the Tories were in. He said Cameron had made a big mistake in saying that he would do all this dealing. He should have done a Harold Wilson, stopped the Libs from effectively being handed the balance of power, then formed a minority government if they could and get on with it. He should have done that on Friday. They could have got in, blamed us for everything, said it was worse than feared etc. and so on, then called an election in six months or so. But they were locked in to these talks and Clegg was going to have to decide one way or the other. I said yes but they basically felt you were a problem. He had to see that. Yes, I do, he said. I know that. I said I think if you just give some kind of vague pledge it won't be enough. They don't feel a referendum campaign can be won with you at the helm. I understand that, he said.

Where it seemed to me to be heading was a Lib–Lab deal where the Tories were kept out, we had a deal on electoral reform but GB had to signal his departure. Peter M said he agreed but GB was not there yet. He kind of knew he had to go. Equally he saw himself as a titanic figure and only he could deliver these twin projects of electoral reform and economic recovery. The word from the Tory talks in the Cabinet Office was that they were not going that well. The Tories seemed to be offering them pretty much anything they wanted. Maybe even PR. Cameron had clearly decided power at all costs. I couldn't work out where Balls was in all this. David M sent me a text saying he didn't believe a second unelected PM was possible. He was worried that it could be a poisoned chalice. He did not think that it would work. But equally he was not saying stop doing what we were doing. Also TB was still pushing in this direction too.

Peter said he had basically been at the second Clegg meeting as a note-taker. We were winding him up about being the next PPS to Danny [Alexander] boy. When Sue and I had been waiting around I said it was odd the extent to which all these interweaving histories played out. She asked what Fiona thought. I said probably that it was hopeless but we had to do what we could to make it happen and keeping the Tories out was an enormous prize. GB and Peter came back as Burnley Spurs was coming on *Match of the Day*. So as well as missing it live I now missed the goals. He did seem to end the day a bit more down. Pen out again. Went through all the points he made. Europe. Economy. Voting reform etc. However, Danny had quite explicitly raised the idea of GB's position and Peter and I pressed him to be clear what his feeling was on this. GB said that did not need to be an issue. Clegg was seeing his MPs tomorrow.

I said we needed at least get on the pitch. We had to be in the talks in the same way as the Tories. He said he was happy to throw his own position into the mix. Peter was really tired. He said there is nothing more to do. We should sleep on it and see where we are. GB looked pretty exhausted. He looked at Sue and shrugged. There was a chance this would be all over soon. If the Tories did a deal with the Libs it was all over. If they did a deal with nobody it was all over. There was another GB / Clegg meeting for tomorrow. Lots still to play for but I think most people felt it was coming to an end. Had to really admire GB's resilience though in just keeping going. Peter gave me a lift home and on the way we chatted re this and also future leadership etc. Peter had become totally addicted to his BlackBerry. He was never off it. His driver took me on home and Peter's last words were 'See you tomorrow. I think it could be the end.'

Monday 10 May

GB debrief on his meetings with Clegg. They had talked a lot about a shared constitutional agenda. Cut the Commons. Elected Lords. A ban on MPs taking second jobs. AV – but they wanted without referendum because they feared they would lose it. Joint work on economic council. Plans for localism. ID cards shelved for a parliament. National ID cards for foreign nationals stay. Biometrics Scottish system. Civil liberties. Press laws / monopoly. Freedoms e.g. protest, trespass, whistleblowers, a Freedom Bill. Extradition treaty with US. Euro crisis joint plan. He said to him we can get a pro-Europe, pro-Keynesian majority. Go for Living Wage. Discuss minority parties... Tessa and Jack both agitating. I called Tessa to calm her down. TB called first thing. He said he felt strongly now that the only way we might get to stay in power was in a coalition of which GB was not the head. He felt there would be a legitimacy problem because of the numbers and also the idea of a second unelected leader, but it was worth exploring. Did I think it was a runner? I felt it might be. Tough but maybe.

We came to a view – as was Peter and as was GB, though not quite in the same way, that he could announce he was going to stay to stitch together the coalition, leave if he failed and leave anyway at conference if he could pull it off. He said I should speak to Paddy, which I then did. He said Clegg and Cameron got on personally very well. But the party would much prefer to deal with us. He felt the opportunities were immense. He said Clegg had felt a bit bullied by GB, which is not how Peter had seen it. He said there was not a single Lib Dem who felt this could be done with GB. There was an understanding he had to go with dignity, but he did have to go. Paddy said we had to persuade GB this was his final gift – keeping the Tories out and putting together a deal that led to major electoral reform. As we spoke, it felt more doable than it did yesterday. GB says he will go into talks with Libs. We set out the areas. We try to settle the markets. He sets out timetable for his own departure. He felt too this was the only way.

Peter called me and said when I came in could I please see him first and not get kidnapped and drawn into what GB was doing. GB was seeing Andrew to try to fix any policy situations. Peter was talking to Sue when I arrived. He said it was all pretty hopeless really. Nobody on the Lib side really felt GB could stay. GB didn't see it. He also didn't see that the Tories probably would decide to go into bed with the Liberal Democrats. Andrew joined us and we chatted over the options. They all seemed to point in one direction. I started to work on the statement he would deliver if we managed to get to a position where the talks with the Libs could formally be started. Focus on economy, electoral reform, and then his own position. I did a good draft which we fiddled with. Paddy was pushing Clegg towards getting us in the right position. Namely that we said Clegg has asked to talk to us too.

There were meetings going on all over the place. Also the odd spectacle of the cameras following the Tories and Lib Dems up and down Whitehall. They came over as a real rabble. However, the media seemed to think they were going somewhere. Then finally we got Clegg on the phone, GB read him the relevant passages about the talks between us, and he said fine. I still felt it was unlikely to lead anywhere but he was not ruling it out. We got the lectern in the street set up. GB was clear he wanted to be out there with it first so we did it fairly quickly. He read it well and the press were totally taken aback by it. Two genuine big elements they had not seen coming – the talks with the Liberals and GB was definitely going, by conference latest. At least we were back in the game. There was a Cabinet meeting at 6. We had an hour to fill the airwaves.

Andrew, Douglas and I went over to College Green and blitzed the place. The media liked it. I did a long session with Peter Allen [Radio 5 Live], then Andrew and I with Huw Edwards [BBC News presenter] and a beaming David Steel – all the former leaders wanted to go with us not the Tories. Robinson was straight on to the numbers and the unelected point.

Andrew and I did OK though. Then to Sky and what instantly became one of the moments of the entire campaign. Jeremy Thompson, Boulton and I. Before we were on air I said 'What do you think?' Adam said 'It doesn't make me feel any better about you.' 'Oh God, are we going to have one of your pompous modes?' He was clearly a bit on the edge. Starting to get agitato, clearly and then when I said on air he was clearly disappointed Cameron was not PM he went off on one. It's true I was provoking him a bit, but he was way OTT and out of order. I thought at one point he was going to headbutt me. He was raging and his face getting more and more purple. Dignity, I said, show some dignity. Years of pent-up rage were pouring out of him. I wound him up a bit more as I left, to do another round. All fine. Clearly though the Boulton thing was going to become a cause célèbre. Up on YouTube immediately.

I got applauded back into the office when I arrived. Leanne saying that the whole of the office had been watching it on the rewind, including half the Cabinet. Went round to see them coming out of the Cabinet. Seemed to have gone well. People worried about it but not so that they would rebel. Jack S definitely the one he worried about most. John Reid out and about attacking it. Over to Channel 4. Jon Snow was clearly quite excited by it. Back to the office again and then see GB again. The first meeting of the policy teams – Peter, AA, the Eds and Harriet – tonight. Douglas gave me a lift home. He wasn't convinced Balls would stand in a leadership election. Ed M and David would oppose each other. Not sure who else. He felt both DM and EM felt a very strong sense of entitlement that they should be doing really big jobs. E.g. they wouldn't say they would lecture but they would run the LSE.

Douglas was clearly of the view it was all over and that now he had to back David. He did not seem that keen on Ed or Harriet. Home to potter a bit and try to keep up with everything else. Pretty sure it was coming to a close. Who knows? Paddy sent me a message saying it wasn't going well, that Peter and AA were fine but the others were churlish and rude. They were clearly texting out as it happened and everyone seemed to know what they were doing in there. I told Andrew he now had to accept they were not serious people. He said he accepted that. David M called. Not sure what I was up to, he said. I did my best to explain. It was probably going to end in GB going, and soon, but we had to see if this could work.

Tuesday 11 May

Peter M texted me early. 'Blunkett alert'. He was about to do the *Today* programme and I assumed he was going to echo John Reid of last night, who had said it was mutually assured destruction. Blunkett said he would be calm and careful but he believed we were doing the wrong thing and intended to say so. We could not go on pretending we hadn't lost. I said nor did the Tories win, and we had to see if this could work. GB felt Blunkett [a *Sun* columnist] was probably doing News International's bidding. Peter was adamant that the talks were going better than the Liberals were pretending. He was also sure that GB had the chance to move it in a different direction. I had woken up pretty sure this would be the end. It just felt that way. Paddy and Charles K both sent me messages saying that it was slipping away unless we offered them more. Paddy said the word from the talks was that the Eds and Harriet had been really rude to their team, Alexander, Huhne, [David] Laws [Treasury spokesman] etc. I checked with Peter who said that on the contrary Ed had been rather polite and charming for him, whilst all they had done was try to engage properly. Peter did not feel they were that serious. They were due to see them again.

The response to the Boulton incident was astonishing. Hundreds of thousands on YouTube. Masses of comment online. Everywhere I went people asking me about it. Nice driver – again – yesterday Sierra Leonean who loved us for saving his country. Today Ghanaian who wanted to make sure we got back. He asked me to get a seat and stand to get in. I thought I ought to go in to No. 10, but I had made a commitment to Cystic Fibrosis trust that I would play in their match at Stamford Bridge. Nice crowd. Ed Owen, who had organised it, was really on the Jack Straw end of the argument. He couldn't see why we were doing it. I said I was sure it would not work because we did not have the numbers and both main parties were against in fairly large numbers. I was warming up on the pitch when I got a message to call GB urgent. Could I speak to Paddy? And if needed so would he. What did they need? I called Paddy from pitchside. He said the problem was the would-be next leaders seemed to be lukewarm. He said I can feel this slipping through our hands.

I said I would do what I could. I got GB and Paddy to speak. GB told him that he could get the Eds, Harriet and Alan J to put out statements. Alistair D would get David. After the match – we won 3–1 and I played pretty well – I called Paddy again and he felt DM was the one they needed to hear. I texted and called and after a while David came back to me. He was very unsure of the whole thing, as he had been yesterday. I said this may well come to nothing. In fact, it almost certainly will. But what is the harm in saying, as Alistair did last night, that he was a progressive and if we could make this work, we would and that he would support it. Alan and Ed were out there. David was clearly not going to. I detected a certain evasiveness in the way he spoke. Same with Burnham who was also at the football. He was clearly sitting it out. Never told me but shortly afterwards he became the first minister to criticise the idea publicly.

David said it was all very unpopular and nobody felt it would work. I said if there was the slightest chance of stopping those Tories going in, we had to try it. We had to weaken them both if they went ahead with it. I understand, he said, but that is not why I feel this is not going to work. It just isn't. Look at the state of the parties we will have. I said that is all evident but there is a case for you saying something, as the others are. I felt he lacked subtlety and guile. As I said to TB later, TB was always looking after No. 1 but it was not always so obvious. TB was saying I really had to help David. I said I would. But I did not want to get sucked in. And I had big doubts about whether he would win. Paddy getting more and more desperate. GB ditto.

We had three calls during the game. He said people would hold it against David if he did not show leadership and make decisions. I thought about saying how he used to go AWOL at times. I didn't though, and instead just smiled. I said I would try David again. I went to the ceremony afterwards. Mark Bright effusive re the Boulton thing. So was everyone. It was amazing how big it had connected. Later Trevor Beattie told me that it was the Moment of zen on *The Daily Show* [US satirical news show]. It had gone a bit mental. Got a car to No. 10. GB was over seeing Clegg. There was a lot of hanging around. Checked the website. It had had record visits yesterday even without a blog. Even more today after I did a big piece on the idea behind the Lib–Lab stuff.

No. 10 was in limbo waiting for GB to come back. The talks with our teams had gone nowhere it seemed. I went through to Peter's office. He was with Justin and Iain B and Patrick. He was writing a note. I could tell it was one of his background briefings which would be explaining why the talks were failing. I looked over his shoulder and he was writing e.g. about energy, i.e. no nuclear, also re defence, crime and terror, not being serious. I said can't we throw in that they want free condoms for thirteen-year-olds and a new human rights act for paedophiles to be allowed in schools? He said it was nonsense our team had been rude or excessively demanding. He was of the view they were going through the motions, that they had already decided on the Tories.

Word came back that GB was on his way back. We all trooped down to his office. He was still of the view Clegg was genuinely torn. We said we doubted it. They were getting pretty much everything they wanted from the Tories and now they knew it so could use us to get a bit more time with their own side and also get more out of the Tories. GB still felt that if we could get more leadership contenders out there we could turn it. Charles and Paddy texting how depressed they were. TB that he felt it was hopeless. GB said Clegg had said there were no major policy issues to resolve and if there were they could solve them. He said the problem was workability. Could it work? We did not have the numbers. Also we did not have a PLP we could keep on board for it. The Campaign Group [of Labour MPs] would be disproportionately large and the Libs would also have their rebels.

GB said Reid was no longer an MP. Blunkett was in the pay of the Murdoch lot. He warned DB Murdoch would do everything they could to get them out and force an early election without them. The country had voted to keep the Tories out and he put them in. He said he had told him – and he repeated this in later conversations – that this was a historic opportunity for a progressive moment and they were blowing it. Why? These Tories would not give you what you wanted or needed, you know that. He said Clegg realised it could not drag on and we had to decide today or else it was finished. Clegg was going to mull and decide later. He would meet his MPs or one of his other groupings and take it from there. He wanted to be clear that he was acting in good faith but we didn't believe it. Added to which he had been whacked by the press today over so-called two-timing and he would be getting jittery. He was terrified of the press.

I said to GB he should suggest a media reform bill. He liked that if only for mischief. Peter and Andrew were even more sure than I was that this was not happening. We were going to have a long afternoon waiting for it all to come to an end. GB kept clutching at a few straws. A few 'Where is David?' calls. David behaving more like GB than TB here. The mood in the office veered from light and jocular to sad and heavy. GB was pretty relaxed except when he had his moments of sudden maybes – maybe we can keep it alive. Peter was already briefing Phil Webster why the talks failed. We were texting friends that it was coming to an end. I was working on his statement. Clegg was planning to call around 5.

Then an issue with the Palace. The Queen's private secretary, a big bald man – Sir Christopher Geidt – had said to Jeremy that she didn't want to see GB and accept his resignation until she knew Cameron could form a government. I said that was ridiculous. It was also humiliating. The media were already starting to say that he was going. Was he supposed to hang around to give Clegg a bit more time to square his MPs or buy time and concessions from the fucking Tories? Others felt even more strongly. Fine, said Jeremy when everyone but GB, Peter and I had left the room, but he said I don't want your last day to see a big row with the Queen. At least he had a joke or two left in him. GB said 'Why should I worry – I'll never see her again.' I laughed. I said 'Gordon, I think you will.' In any event let's try again. Jeremy did and they accepted it was not necessary. If GB could not form a government he resigned. If he resigned she called Cameron. If he could not form a government that was his lookout.

Quite a bit of joking around. We were just waiting for a call. Clegg called and asked for more time, then again, but finally GB said time for what? Unless you can tell me you have broken off talks with the Tories in favour of discussion with us, I will assume you are going with the Tories. He said he had had five days. This could not go on indefinitely. He said Clegg had made clear there were no policy issues outstanding, at least none we could not resolve, but the issue was workability. So why not work on that? I was only hearing GB but from the sound of it Clegg was getting desperate. Nick, Nick, listen to me, just listen to me… He said the Queen was waiting and this was getting discourteous. The country needed clarity. You keep asking for more time but time for what? We were now of the view Clegg wanted more time to sort his party to go with the Tories and also to screw more concessions. But GB had decided he was resigning because he could not form a government and so he had to go. He gave him a final five minutes.

He was clearly going back to get more out of the Tories, maybe on Europe. But GB was clear unless they broke off with the Tories he would have to go to the Palace. He said Nick, I respect you, you're clearly a good guy and you are going to be a big figure. But I really thought this could be the progressive moment. I sacrificed myself and my position for it, because I thought it was worth it. Clegg said he was worried about all these hostile voices. GB said we can manage that. Clegg said he was not sure it could be stable. Eventually GB said 'Nick, I think you have made your choice. It is a mistake. The Tories will use the Murdoch press to kill you, they will say things are worse than they thought and they will go for another election to get their own mandate. I was hoping for a pact but it can't happen. I am now in an impossible position. I have to go to the Palace. Nick, Nick, Nick… I have to do this now. I can't stay on. I have tried everything but now all that is happening is you are using me for a bit more negotiation with the Tories.'

Douglas and Ed Balls mouthed to me that it was demeaning – and also that there was nobody in the party who felt this could work. GB said I think you are giving up a historic opportunity. Paddy had called a bit before and said just maybe if we gave them more to play with we could still salvage something from this. But GB said to Clegg he felt the country would not wait another day. 'It is a choice one way or the other and you have made the choice. I'm not going to hold on.' The final words were 'OK, thanks, Nick, goodbye.' Then he turned to us and said 'OK, let's do it.'

We had a last look at the speech, which he had improved with the references to his family and the troops. Also he wrote a lovely little note to Grace who had chosen the red tie I had with me and when GB said I want a red tie I gave it to him. We got the words done, then Sue and Jeremy got the staff lined up. He went round talking to people. He said to me – you are a total genius you know. You can be totally central to the reshaping of the party. Whoever wins cannot do it without you. I know we have had our differences but I knew I had to get you back. I wish you had come back when I asked but I do understand why you didn't want to. I am very grateful you did... I finally told him about the diaries coming out on 3 June. He said listen, you came back and helped me when you didn't have to. You made a massive difference. You helped save me from humiliation in many ways. You have helped me more than I can say in these past few days. So I can hardly complain about a book or two.

He seemed mellow, almost liberated. There were quite a lot of tears among the staff. His own team had perhaps felt usurped by Peter and me, but they were grateful too I think. The mood was nice. The news was saying it was about to happen. One of the most poignant moments was earlier when TB called and spoke to GB, and Peter and I were the only two in the room. I looked at Peter and said 'Start to finish.' GB said to TB he had decided he had to go. He had tried to give it a go but it wasn't to be. 'Thanks for what you did in the campaign ... No, it was important ... And I know it has not always been easy but you know it has been amazing what we have done.' Ed Balls came in and we had a chat about things but there was still always a mutual wariness there, even if he and Peter seemed to get on better now. Once everyone was lined up Sarah and the boys came in and GB gathered everyone round as he made a speech. 'Come on, Daddy, we're going.' He thanked everyone, said they had been a great team and what we had achieved we had done together. There were lots of people crying now.

He really did the values stuff too but had told me earlier of the three speeches he would make the one he really cared about was the one to the party. He wanted to do it with full autocue etc. When he had finished there was long applause. I was standing with Peter. I said 'Why couldn't we get this out of him till the end?' He shrugged. Most people still felt we might have done it with a different leader but he had shown a great nobility and courage in the last bit. Only once, in a rage at Murdoch, did he say it wasn't fair. Maybe it wasn't but the truth is he was going and we had to make the most of it. Once he had spoken it was very quiet after the applause. Please speak, he said. The lectern was being put out and the media were going into final throes stage. He went off and we watched on the TV in No. 12.

He was quite emotional at the end. Then went in to get the boys and they walked off together down the street, into the cars and gone. He did it well, even those against him were saying. I got a lift from Douglas down to Victoria Street. The staff were lined up inside and outside. Nice welcome from Carol L and team as we arrived. I did a couple of interviews as we waited for GB to come back from the Palace. He got a great reception when he did, then into the media centre. Rachel had got it all set up and the mood was good if, again, lots of tears. He spoke well, a real Labour speech, about values, what we stood for, what we had achieved, how we would fight on. Then off he went. Great reception. Peter, Pat and I stood around chatting then first Peter, then I did doorsteps outside. Talked about how proud I was of what we had done, said GB behaved with real dignity and the party was fantastic.

Catherine McLeod arrived and was in tears standing listening. She and I went round to the Old Star pub where all the party were gathering. Nice atmosphere considering. Catherine said Alistair was thinking about standing. He probably wouldn't but lots of people were saying he should. I had seen him yesterday and he was very much of the view it was all over, but he had been a team player to the end. Catherine said she felt sorry for Labour, and for the country, but not for GB, as he had frankly been awful to TB and awful to Alistair, and awful to a lot of other people. Yes maybe, I said, but you'd rather have him than DC.

I stayed for a bit then home briefly, gave Grace her letter, which she loved, then out to *Newsnight* with Calum. Polly Toynbee saying she had tried to keep the paper Labour. Also that Peter and I could have got rid of him and we didn't and that was why we lost. Maybe. Who knows? I did a piece with Kirsty Wark, interviewed with Evan Harris ex Lib Dem MP. I was starting to crank up the idea of pressure on the Lib Dems because their voters and activists would feel betrayed. Also talking up GB. I missed the final montage at the end which Catherine Rimmer said had her in tears because we all looked so young back then!

Index